AF870481

Financial Information Management and Control Systems in Digital Enterprises

Afef Amdouni
https://orcid.org/0000-0001-9625-300X
Taibah University, Saudi Arabia

IGI Global
Scientific Publishing
Publishing Tomorrow's Research Today

VP of Publishing Ethics & Research Integrity	Melissa Wagner
Director of Acquisitions	Mikaela Felty
Director of Book Development	Jocelynn Hessler
Production Manager	Mike Brehm
Cover Design	Jose Rosado

Published in the United States of America by
IGI Global Scientific Publishing
701 East Chocolate Avenue
Hershey, PA, 17033, USA
Tel: 717-533-8845 | Fax: 717-533-7115
Website: https://www.igi-global.com E-mail: cust@igi-global.com

Copyright © 2027 by IGI Global Scientific Publishing. All rights reserved. No part of this publication may be reproduced, stored or distributed in any form or by any means, electronic or mechanical, including photocopying, without written permission from the publisher. Use of this publication to train generative artificial intelligence (AI) technologies is expressly prohibited. The publisher reserves all rights to license its use for generative AI training and machine learning model development.

Product or company names used in this set are for identification purposes only. Inclusion of the names of the products or companies does not indicate a claim of ownership by IGI Global Scientific Publishing of the trademark or registered trademark.

Library of Congress Cataloging-in-Publication Data

Names: Amdouni, Afef, 1983- editor
Title: Financial information management and control systems in digital enterprises / [edited by] Afef Amdouni.
Description: Hershey, PA : IGI Global Scientific Publishing, [2027] | Includes bibliographical references and index. | Summary: "This book presents relevant theoretical perspectives and recent empirical research related to financial information management and control systems in digital enterprises"-- Provided by publisher.
Identifiers: LCCN 2026012002 (print) | LCCN 2026012003 (ebook) | ISBN 9798337392301 hardcover | ISBN 9798337392318 paperback | ISBN 9798337392325 ebook
Subjects: LCSH: Finance--Management | Management information systems
Classification: LCC HG173 .F4926 2027 (print) | LCC HG173 (ebook) | DDC 332.0285--dc23/eng/20260626
LC record available at https://lccn.loc.gov/2026012002
LC ebook record available at https://lccn.loc.gov/2026012003

British Cataloguing in Publication Data
A Cataloguing in Publication record for this book is available from the British Library.

All work contributed to this book is new, previously-unpublished material.
The views expressed in this book are those of the authors, but not necessarily of the publisher.
This book contains information sourced from authentic and highly regarded references, with reasonable efforts made to ensure the reliability of the data and information presented. The authors, editors, and publisher believe the information in this book to be accurate and true as of the date of publication. Every effort has been made to trace and credit the copyright holders of all materials included. However, the authors, editors, and publisher cannot assume responsibility for the validity of all materials or the consequences of their use. Should any copyright material be found unacknowledged, please inform the publisher so that corrections may be made in future reprints.

Table of Contents

Detailed Table of Contents

integrated systems enhance the reliability of reporting, efficiency of operations and risk management. The results emphasize that integrated governance and control processes are needed to convert financial information into credible, practical knowledge to drive strategic decisions and sustainable business performance.

Accounting models, consolidation techniques, internal controls, compliance systems, and sophisticated financial analytics are all part of the financial reporting procedures that this chapter examines in complex business contexts. Integrated reporting frameworks, digital financial governance systems, generally accepted accounting principles (GAAP), and international financial reporting standards (IFRS) are all put to the test. Topics covered in this chapter include financial management systems hosted on the cloud, fraud detection, automated reconciliation, and forecasting powered by AI. We take a close look at the difficulties associated with data integration, complicated regulations, cybersecurity, financial crime, and lack of transparency in reporting. New topics covered include intelligent financial ecosystems, ESG reporting, blockchain-based accounting, and real-time reporting. Organisations benefit from improved operational efficiency, compliance with regulations, transparency, and strategic financial management when their financial reporting systems are efficient.

Digitalization has made the making of financial plans more constant and driven by data. This chapter studies how the strategic financial planning of digital enterprises increases when big data analytics, real-time dashboards, and AI are integrated. By analysing large amounts of financial and behavioural data, big data enhances the accuracy of forecasts, risk analysis, and the allocation of resources. Interactive dashboards put complicated metrics into actionable visualizations, speeding up managerial decisions. Predictive and prescriptive models are powered by AI to generate future scenarios, suggest the best changes, and are continually updated with live and historical data. The chapter introduces a unified mechanism between

investment, and financial decisions. It develops and empirically tests a conceptual framework linking explainable ML, managerial interpretability, governance, and risk management effectiveness. The findings demonstrate that XML enhances decision transparency, strengthens internal control systems, and supports trust in AI-driven financial environments. The chapter contributes to the literature on explainable AI in financial analytics and offers practical insights for its responsible implementation.

The development of digital technology has changed the way the banking industry operates, particularly through the implementation of the Open Banking concept. In this study, banks no longer stand as closed entities but become part of a financial ecosystem interconnected through Application Programming Interfaces (APIs). This structured data exchange opens opportunities for increased operational efficiency, more responsive financial services, and expanded access to banking services. This study discusses financial data governance in the context of Open Banking by integrating perspectives from information systems, internal control, and banking regulations. The discussion focuses on how the role of internal control needs to be adjusted to effectively manage cross-system data flows, and on its implications for the stability and resilience of the banking system in the digital era.

This chapter examines the growing importance of digital risk management and financial control systems in the context of digital transformation in the public sector. As governments increasingly adopt digital financial management systems to support budgeting, accounting, and financial reporting processes, new risks related to cybersecurity, data integrity, system integration, and governance emerge.

Foreword

We are living in an era where technological innovation has fundamentally redefining how organizations generate, process, analyze, and govern financial information. The rapid adoption of artificial intelligence (AI), machine learning, big data analytics, block-chain technologies, and digital platforms has transformed traditional financial management practices into highly interconnected, data-driven, and intelligent ecosystems. In this dynamic environment, organizations face unprecedented opportunities to enhance transparency, efficiency, accountability, and strategic decision-making. At the same time, numerous challenges should be addressed regarding data privacy, cybersecurity, governance, risk management, regulatory compliance, and organizational control. These developments make the study of financial information management and control systems more important today than ever before. The edited book, *Financial Information Management and Control Systems in Digital Enterprises*, appears at a crucial moment. Under the excellent editorial leadership of Dr. Afef Amdouni, this book offers a timely and comprehensive examination on how digitalization and AI-driven models are reshaping financial information systems and control mechanisms across organizations and societies. It consolidates contributions from an international group of eminent scholars and practitioners who collectively explore the evolving linkage between technology, financial management, governance, organizational performance, and strategic control. The book's scope and intellectual wideness provide readers with a rich understanding of both the theoretical foundations and practical implications of digital transformation and AI-driven processes in financial management.

One of the major strengths of this book lies in its *multidisciplinary* perspective. The chapters go beyond traditional accounting and finance concepts to integrate insights from information systems, management control, data governance, artificial intelligence, risk management, and digital transformation. The opening chapter establishes a strong conceptual foundation by re-conceptualizing financial information management and control systems through a socio-technical and control-oriented lens. This framework provides an essential platform for understanding the broader transformations discussed throughout the book. The subsequent chapters examine critical dimensions of digital transformation, financial data quality, reliability of information, governance structures, and strategic decision support. Readers are provided with valuable insights into how organizations can leverage modern technologies to improve the accuracy, timeliness, and usefulness of financial information while simultaneously strengthening internal controls and organizational oversight.

A particularly notable contribution of this book is its extensive treatment of artificial intelligence and machine learning in financial management. Several chapters investigate the integration of AI-driven analytics, intelligent dashboards, automated accounting systems, machine learning-enabled accounting information systems, and explainable artificial intelligence in financial decision-making. Importantly, the book does not merely celebrate technological innovation; it critically examines issues of transparency, interpretability, reliability, and accountability that accompany the growing use of intelligent systems in financial environments. Risk management and governance also receive significant attention throughout the book. As digital enterprises become more interconnected, vulnerabilities associated with cyber threats, data breaches, regulatory complexity, and algorithmic decision-making continue to increase. The contributors address these concerns by exploring innovative approaches to digital risk management, enterprise risk frameworks, open banking governance, public-sector digital financial systems, and explainable machine learning for financial risk analysis. Another distinguishing feature of this volume is its international and cross-sectoral perspective. The chapters draw examples and evidence from diverse settings, including private enterprises, banking institutions, e-business environments, public-sector organizations, emerging economies, and developing countries. By examining the role of digital transformation maturity and sustainability-oriented financial accounting practices, the book highlights how financial information systems can support not only organizational efficiency but also long-term value creation and sustainable development. As organizations increasingly strive to balance financial performance with environmental, social and governance (ESG) responsibilities, the integration of green digital accounting and financial sustainability considerations become essential. This broad perspective enhances the book's value for readers across geographical regions and professional contexts.

As readers engage with the chapters that follow, they will realize a thoughtful and forward-looking exploration of one of the most important developments shaping modern enterprises. This book makes a significant contribution to the evolving debate on digital finance, information governance, organizational control, and intelligent decision-making. It stands as a timely reminder that the future of financial management will be defined not only by technological innovation but also by the institutions, governance mechanisms, and human capabilities that ensure technology serves organizational and societal objectives effectively. Its rigorous conceptual frameworks and foundations, empirical evidence, managerial implications, and future research directions make it an indispensable reference for anyone seeking to understand the future of financial information management in the digital era. I am confident that *Financial Information Management and Control Systems in Digital Enterprises* book will become an important reference in the fields of accounting, finance, information systems, and governance, inspiring scholars, practitioners and policymakers for years to come.

Mohamed Chakib Kolsi
The University of Dubai, UAE

Preface

INTRODUCTION

Digital transformation is changing not only the technologies used to manage financial information, but also the organizational logic through which that information is produced, controlled, interpreted, and used. Enterprise resource planning systems, cloud platforms, advanced analytics, artificial intelligence, machine learning, digital payment infrastructures, and automated reporting environments increasingly connect activities that were once separated across accounting, finance, risk, and control functions. Financial information management is therefore moving away from predominantly periodic and transaction-oriented processes toward more integrated, real-time, and analytically intensive environments.

The implications of this shift are not straightforward. Faster processing, wider connectivity, and greater analytical capacity can improve the timeliness and visibility of financial information, yet these capabilities do not in themselves ensure reliability, effective control, or better decisions. The same infrastructures that reduce fragmentation can introduce new dependencies; automation can strengthen consistency while making processes less transparent; and increasingly sophisticated models can support judgment while also making it more difficult to understand how particular outputs were produced. Data quality, cybersecurity, accountability, algorithmic opacity, and regulatory complexity consequently become part of the financial-control problem rather than separate technical concerns.

This tension between digital integration and financial control provides the organizing logic of the volume. Financial Information Management and Control Systems (FIMCS) are treated here as socio-technical arrangements in which technology, data, organizational processes, governance mechanisms, internal controls, and managerial judgment interact. From this perspective, the relevant question is not simply whether digital technologies improve financial management. More important is whether organizations possess the complementary capabilities required to convert technological capacity into financial information that is sufficiently reliable, interpretable, and controllable to support sound decisions.

The chapters approach this question from different but connected directions. They examine the quality and governance of financial data, the changing architecture of reporting and decision support, the use of AI and machine learning in accounting and management information systems, and the implications of digitalization for risk, explainability, customer protection, public accountability, and sustainability. Across these settings, a common pattern emerges technological sophistication is most useful when it is matched by governance and organizational capability. More information is not necessarily more useful information; real-time access does not by itself improve judgment; and predictive or automated systems remain dependent on the quality of the data, controls, and human oversight surrounding them.

The volume deliberately brings together conceptual, analytical, documentary, and empirical contributions. This methodological diversity reflects the breadth of the underlying problem. Some chapters develop frameworks and propositions that clarify relationships requiring further empirical testing; others examine documented practices and institutional settings; and the empirical studies provide evidence on managerial and organizational conditions associated with intelligent AIS/MIS performance and on the relationship between green digital accounting and financial sustainability. The aim is not to impose a single explanatory model across these settings, but to show how a common set of financial-information and control questions takes different forms as technologies, institutions, and organizational contexts change.

Viewed as a whole, the book traces a progression from the foundations of digital financial information and control to more specialized questions of intelligent decision support, digital risk, institutional governance, and sustainability. In doing so, it maintains a critical distinction that runs throughout the volume: digital capability creates possibilities, whereas reliable financial value depends on how those capabilities are governed, interpreted, and embedded within organizational control systems.

CHAPTER OVERVIEW

The chapters are arranged as a cumulative discussion rather than as a collection of isolated applications. The opening contributions establish the conceptual and informational foundations of FIMCS; subsequent chapters move into reporting, planning, and intelligent accounting systems; the discussion then turns to risk, explainability, and governance across organizational boundaries before concluding with public-sector, country-specific, and sustainability perspectives.

Chapter 1: Reconceptualizing Financial Information Management and Control Systems in Digital Enterprises: A Socio-Technical and Control-Based Framework

The opening chapter provides the conceptual anchor for the volume by re-framing Financial Information Management and Control Systems as integrated socio-technical arrangements rather than stand-alone technical systems. Through a selective conceptual synthesis, it develops five propositions connecting financial data quality, information-processing capability, control-system effectiveness, and decision-making quality. Digitalization is treated as a conditional influence: integration and automation may reinforce control, but opacity and complexity may weaken it when organizational oversight fails to develop at the same pace. By setting out boundary conditions, candidate measures, alternative explanations, and directions for testing, the chapter establishes a framework that the later contributions can extend into more specific settings.

Chapter 2: Digital Transformation of Financial Information Management in Modern Enterprises

Attention then shifts from conceptual architecture to the broader transformation of financial information management in modern enterprises. The chapter traces the movement from periodic, transaction-based systems toward integrated, real-time, and analytics-driven environments, drawing on contemporary literature, professional accounts, and documented organizational practices. ERP platforms, cloud systems, automation, and analytics are considered alongside the organizational requirements that condition their use. The resulting account is deliberately non-deterministic: improved visibility and coordination remain dependent on data governance, cyber-security, skills, accountability, and alignment between technological change and organizational processes.

Chapter 3: Financial Data Quality, Reliability, and Decision Support in Digital Enterprises

The third chapter isolates a prerequisite that can easily be obscured by enthusiasm for advanced technology: the quality of the underlying financial data. Accuracy, completeness, consistency, and timeliness are examined in relation to decision support, budgeting, management control, performance measurement, and strategic decision-making. The discussion also considers how ERP systems, cloud accounting, analytics, and automated controls affect data integrity. Its central contribution is to make explicit that analytical sophistication cannot compensate for weak or poorly governed inputs; the reliability of digital financial decision support begins with the reliability of the data on which it depends.

Chapter 4: Data Governance and Financial Control Systems in Digital Enterprises: Managing Financial Information Flows for Strategic Decision-Making

From data quality, the volume moves naturally to data governance. Chapter 4 develops a conceptual model that connects governance structures, financial-information flows, and financial-control mechanisms across interconnected digital platforms. Drawing on interdisciplinary literature, industry evidence, and illustrative cases, it considers data ownership and stewardship, standards, validation, access controls, audit trails, and real-time monitoring as parts of an integrated control environment. The chapter is especially useful in distinguishing the availability of real-time information from the organizational capacity to govern and use it effectively: integration enables stronger decision support but does not guarantee it.

Chapter 5: Financial Reporting Processes in Complex Enterprise Environments

Financial reporting provides the next setting in which these issues converge. Chapter 5 treats reporting as a socio-technical process shaped simultaneously by accounting requirements, enterprise systems, AI, organizational governance, and internal control. Its scope ranges from consolidation and IFRS/GAAP requirements to automated reconciliation, fraud detection, forecasting, ESG reporting, blockchain-based accounting, and real-time reporting. Rather than presenting ERP and AI as substitutes for established controls, the chapter shows how their value depends on data quality, cybersecurity, employee competence, management support, regulatory knowledge, and organizational readiness.

Chapter 6: Integrating AI-Driven Insights into Financial Dashboards for Real-Time Decision Making in Digital Enterprises

Chapter 6 turns toward forward-looking financial planning and asks how big-data analytics, interactive dashboards, and AI can be combined to support real-time managerial decisions. The proposed mechanism begins with governed data infrastructure, moves through predictive and prescriptive analytics, and culminates in dashboards that translate analytical outputs into information managers can act upon. Documented industry cases provide practical illustrations in credit, risk, forecasting, and planning, while the chapter appropriately avoids treating reported organizational outcomes as independent causal evidence. The emphasis is therefore on architecture and plausibility: how analytics, visualization, and AI can support more continuous planning without displacing governance or human interpretation.

Chapter 7: Managerial and Organizational Determinants of Machine Learning–Enabled Accounting and Management Information Systems Performance

The seventh chapter provides an empirical counterpoint to the preceding conceptual discussions by examining the managerial and organizational conditions surrounding machine-learning-enabled AIS/MIS. Survey evidence from 524 professionals in manufacturing, banking, and service organizations is analyzed using structural equation modeling. The reported results associate organizational control and ML adoption with stronger system performance, while managerial challenges constrain adoption and effectiveness. Decision-support effectiveness operates as a partial mediator, and supportive organizational culture moderates the effects of managerial challenges. These findings reinforce a theme developed earlier in the volume: intelligent systems perform within organizational settings, not outside them.

Chapter 8: Harnessing AI-Driven Accounting Information Systems for Enhancing Authenticity, Transparency, and Automation in E-Business Accounting and Auditing

Chapter 8 brings the discussion into e-business accounting and auditing, where transaction volume, speed, and complexity place particular demands on Accounting Information Systems. It considers automated processing and validation, anomaly detection, predictive analytics, real-time reporting, continuous monitoring, and automated assurance as mechanisms through which AI may support authenticity, accuracy, reliability, and transparency. The chapter also recognizes the changing role of accounting professionals as routine processing becomes more automated. Crucially, this transition is not framed as a simple substitution of machines for professional judgment; data governance, algorithmic accountability, regulatory adaptation, ethical safeguards, and human oversight remain integral to credible AI-enabled accounting and auditing.

Chapter 9: Risk Management and Control Systems in Digital Organizations

Chapter 9 broadens the discussion from financial-information processes to enterprise-wide digital risk and control. It brings cybersecurity, enterprise risk management, fraud detection, digital compliance, predictive risk analytics, cloud-based monitoring, blockchain, zero-trust architectures, and explainable AI into a common governance perspective. The chapter proposes an integrated digital risk management framework linking risk identification and assessment with organizational control systems, AI and machine learning, cloud infrastructure, blockchain, and organizational resilience. Its main contribution is to show that risk management in digitally dependent organizations cannot remain a periodic assessment exercise: identified risks must be translated into preventive, detective, corrective, and monitoring controls that can adapt as technologies and threat environments change.

Chapter 10: Explainable Machine Learning–Driven Risk Management and Control Systems in Digital Organizations: Interpreting Credit, Investment, and Financial Decisions

The following chapter narrows the risk discussion to a problem that becomes increasingly consequential as machine learning enters credit, investment, and other financial decisions: the opacity of algorithmic outputs. Chapter 10 links explainable machine learning with managerial interpretability, governance, and risk-management effectiveness. Its empirical analysis indicates that explainability is associated with greater decision transparency, stronger internal control, and greater trust in AI-supported financial environments. The chapter moves beyond explanation techniques themselves to consider data quality, model drift, explanation stability, documentation, governance, and human oversight, thereby positioning explainability as part of the control architecture surrounding algorithmic decisions.

Chapter 11: Financial Data Governance Mechanisms in Open Banking: Balancing Digital Innovation with Customer Protection

Open Banking extends the governance problem beyond the boundaries of a single organization. Chapter 11 examines how API-based financial-data exchange creates an ecosystem involving banks, customers, and third-party providers, and how this alters conventional assumptions about ownership, access, control, and accountability. By bringing together information-systems, internal-control, data-protection, cybersecurity, and banking-regulation perspectives, the chapter addresses consent, privacy, authorization, third-party risk, data leakage, and regulatory coordination. Innovation and customer protection are therefore treated as interdependent design requirements rather than competing endpoints.

Chapter 12: Digital Risk Management and Financial Control Systems in Public Sector Organizations: Evidence from Indonesia's E-Government Transformation

A public-sector perspective follows in Chapter 12 through a documentary case analysis of Indonesia's e-government transformation. Digital budgeting, accounting, reporting, and public-finance systems are examined alongside cybersecurity, data integrity, interoperability, governance, and institutional capacity. Drawing on documentary and secondary empirical evidence, the chapter develops a framework and risk-management cycle linking internal control, IT governance, and public accountability. The Indonesian case is particularly instructive because it separates technological implementation from control maturity: expanding digital infrastructure may increase control capacity, but effective outcomes still depend on accountability, user capability, institutional coordination, data integrity, and assurance.

Chapter 13: From Green Digital Accounting to Financial Sustainability in Developing Economies: The Role of Green Cumulative Advantage and Digital Transformation Maturity

The volume concludes by extending digital financial information management into the sustainability domain. Drawing on the resource-based view, Chapter 13 examines green digital accounting as an organizational capability and tests its relationship with financial sustainability through digital transformation maturity and green cumulative advantage. Using survey data from 637 firms in Pakistan and PLS-SEM analysis, the study reports a positive association between green digital accounting and financial sustainability, identifies digital transformation maturity as a significant mediating mechanism, and finds support for the moderating role of green cumulative advantage in the relationship between digital transformation maturity and financial sustainability. The chapter closes the volume by showing how digital accounting capabilities may contribute to longer-term financial outcomes when they are reinforced by complementary organizational and environmental resources.

CONCLUSION

Across the thirteen chapters, a consistent conclusion emerges: the digital transformation of financial information management and control is not reducible to technology adoption. Digital infrastructures can expand the capacity to collect, integrate, analyze, visualize, and act upon financial information, but the consequences of that capacity depend on the quality of the information and on the organizational arrangements surrounding its use. Data quality, governance, internal control, managerial competence, technological maturity, and institutional context repeatedly appear not as secondary implementation issues, but as constitutive elements of effective FIMCS.

This is particularly evident in the relationship between integration and control. ERP systems, cloud platforms, dashboards, AI, machine learning, APIs, and automated controls can reduce fragmentation and make financial processes more responsive. Yet greater connectivity also increases interdependence, cyber exposure, accountability challenges, and the difficulty of tracing or explaining automated decisions. The managerial problem is therefore not to maximize automation, but to determine where automation adds value and where visibility, challenge, and human judgment must be preserved.

The volume also cautions against equating information abundance with decision quality. Timeliness and processing speed matter, but they are only part of the information problem. Financial data must be credible; analytical outputs must be interpretable; and controls must remain capable of identifying errors, drift, inappropriate access, or unjustified automated conclusions. As AI becomes more deeply embedded in accounting, auditing, risk assessment, credit, investment analysis, and planning, explainability and human oversight become increasingly inseparable from the design of financial control itself.

Context further limits the usefulness of universal prescriptions. Open Banking redistributes governance across organizational boundaries, public-sector digitalization places financial control within structures of public accountability and institutional capacity, and the sustainability chapter connects digital accounting with organizational and environmental capabilities in a developing-economy setting. These differences matter because the same technology may produce different control demands and different organizational outcomes across institutional environments.

The research agenda is correspondingly broad. Several conceptual relationships developed in the volume require testing across industries, jurisdictions, firm sizes, and levels of digital maturity. Cross-sectional evidence would benefit from longitudinal and mixed-method extensions, and future studies should place greater emphasis on objective performance indicators alongside managerial perceptions. Further work is also needed on explainable AI, continuous auditing, automated controls, cybersecurity governance, model monitoring, and the evolving division of responsibility between human decisionmakers and intelligent systems.

The broader implication is that the future of Financial Information Management and Control Systems will depend less on the amount of technology organizations acquire than on how effectively digital capabilities are embedded within reliable data structures, accountable governance, effective controls, and informed managerial judgment. The enduring challenge is therefore one of alignment: converting digital capacity into financial information and control arrangements that remain credible, interpretable, resilient, and sufficiently governable to support decisions in increasingly complex enterprise environments.

Afef Amdouni
Taibah University, Saudi Arabia

Acknowledgment

I would like to express my sincere appreciation to all the contributing authors whose scholarly expertise, commitment, and thoughtful revisions made this edited volume possible. Their diverse perspectives and contributions have been instrumental in shaping the scope and intellectual coherence of Financial Information Management and Control Systems in Digital Enterprises.

I am particularly grateful to Dr. Mohamed Chakib Kolsi for accepting my invitation to contribute the Foreword to this volume and for generously offering his time and scholarly perspective to the project.

I also extend my sincere appreciation to the reviewers for their careful evaluations, constructive comments, and valuable recommendations, which contributed to strengthening the quality of the chapters included in this volume.

Finally, I would like to thank the editorial and production team at IGI Global for their guidance and support throughout the development of this book.

Afef Amdouni
Taibah University, Saudi Arabia

Chapter 1

Reconceptualizing Financial Information Management and Control Systems in Digital Enterprises: A Socio-Technical and Control-Based Framework

Afef Amdouni
http://orcid.org/0000-0001-9625-300X
Taibah University, Saudi Arabia

ABSTRACT

This chapter reconceptualizes financial information management and control systems (FIMCS) in digital enterprises through an integrative socio-technical framework. Drawing on information systems, information processing, management control, and digital transformation literature, it develops five propositions linking financial data quality, information processing capability, control effectiveness, and decision-making quality. Digitalization is treated as a conditional moderator: integration and automation can strengthen control, while complexity and algorithmic opacity can weaken it when oversight capability lags. The framework specifies boundary conditions, candidate measures, and alternative explanations for empirical testing. Published studies and a hypothetical financial workflow illustrate its application without claiming validation. The chapter contributes a testable synthesis of techno-

DOI: 10.4018/979-8-3373-9230-1.ch001

) 2027, IGI Global Scientific Publishing. Copying or distributing in print or electronic forms without written permission of IGI Global Scientific Publishing is prohibited. Use of this chapter to rative artificial intelligence (AI) technologies is expressly prohibited. The publisher reserves all rights to license its use for generative AI training and machine learning model development.

logical, organizational, and control dimensions, distinguishing the enabling role of digitalization from risks arising when digital capabilities outpace organizational oversight.

1 INTRODUCTION

Digital transformation changes how enterprises generate, combine, interpret, and act on financial information. Yet technical improvements in data processing do not by themselves explain whether managers detect relevant exceptions, assign responsibility, or make defensible decisions. This chapter examines those connections through financial information management and control systems (FIMCS), defined here as the combined arrangements through which financial data is converted into information, subjected to organizational controls, and used in decisions.

Information systems research offers established approaches for evaluating information quality, system quality, use, and benefits (DeLone & McLean, 2003). These provide useful foundations, but their general system-success focus does not supply a detailed account of the financial control activities examined here. The proposed framework therefore draws on these concepts without characterizing the existing literature as uniformly linear or technically deterministic.

Management control research addresses strategic direction, performance evaluation, accountability, and feedback (Simons, 1995; Otley, 1999). These approaches already recognize organizational tensions and adaptation. The issue for this chapter is how their control functions are implemented when financial information passes through interconnected applications, analytical models, and automated workflows.

Digital transformation research provides a broader account of organizational change and technological disruption (Vial, 2019). The automation–augmentation paradox further explains why automation and human judgment can be interdependent rather than separable alternatives (Raisch & Krakowski, 2021). Neither perspective alone specifies the financial data-to-control relationships developed below.

The research question is: through which processing and control mechanisms can financial data quality support decision-making quality, and under what conditions does digitalization strengthen or weaken these mechanisms? The contribution is a focused integration of existing ideas, not a claim that no prior work connects accounting, information systems, and control. Granlund (2011), for example, explicitly examines this interface.

The chapter takes a socio-technical perspective in which technologies, human interpretation, and organizational arrangements interact. Orlikowski's (1992) account of technology and organizational practice informs this perspective; it is not treated as the sole origin of socio-technical systems theory.

The intended audience comprises accounting information systems and management control researchers, advanced students, finance leaders, controllers, and digital transformation professionals. The analysis concerns enterprise-level financial workflows. It does not evaluate a particular software product or offer empirical estimates of the proposed effects.

The framework places information processing capability between data quality and control effectiveness, drawing on the fit between task uncertainty and organizational information processing arrangements (Galbraith, 1974). It distinguishes the production of usable information from the authority and routines required to act on it.

Five propositions specify the core relationships. Three concern data quality, processing capability, control effectiveness, and decision quality; two address the enabling and constraining conditions of digitalization. Feedback and contextual conditions are treated explicitly so that the sequential representation is not mistaken for an empirically established causal chain.

The chapter proceeds from theoretical foundations to model development, practical implications, critical discussion, and a research agenda. Published studies provide empirical context, while a worked illustration shows how the proposed mechanisms could be examined in a financial workflow.

1.1 Conceptual Approach and Scope

This is a conceptual chapter based on a selective narrative synthesis, not a systematic literature review, meta-analysis, or primary empirical study. The synthesis groups the cited literature by its contribution to information quality, processing capability, management control, and digital change. Foundational theories supply constructs and mechanisms; selected empirical studies illustrate relevant relationships and their limits; governance publications inform practical design considerations. No exhaustive database coverage, formal screening protocol, new interviews, or original dataset is claimed.

The propositions are analytical deductions from this synthesis. Published evidence is used to assess plausibility and relevance, not to establish that the complete model has been validated. This approach permits theoretical integration but remains vulnerable to selective source inclusion and alternative explanations. These limits are addressed through thematic comparison, explicit boundary conditions, and a research agenda specifying how the model could be challenged.

2 THEORETICAL FOUNDATIONS

2.1 From Fragmentation to Integration: A Socio-Technical Reframing

An integrative account requires distinguishing what each literature explains. Information systems research addresses information and system success; management control research addresses how objectives, behavior, and feedback are coordinated; digital transformation research considers technological and organizational change. Their analytical boundaries overlap, but their focal outcomes differ.

A socio-technical interpretation makes the relationship between technology and organizational practice central. The same application can be associated with different control arrangements when access rights, responsibilities, incentives, and user interpretations differ. This is a premise of the present model, informed by Orlikowski (1992), rather than a finding from a new field study.

Consequently, the chapter treats FIMCS as an organizational configuration rather than a stand-alone technical artifact. Processing infrastructure, employees' interpretive skills, and control responsibilities must be considered together when evaluating the proposed relationships.

2.2 Financial Information as a Dynamic and Constructed Resource

Financial data and financial information are distinguished by their role in a particular workflow. Transaction amounts, dates, and account codes are data inputs; reconciled balances, variance explanations, and forecasts are information produced by organizing and interpreting those inputs. Interpretation does not make accounting records arbitrary: it makes source traceability, accounting definitions, and validation procedures essential.

Research on digital capabilities suggests that the effectiveness of data-driven systems depends not only on data availability but also on the organization's ability to integrate and process heterogeneous data sources (Annarelli et al., 2021). In digital environments, financial information is increasingly generated across multiple platforms, systems, and organizational units, leading to challenges related to consistency, reliability, and contextual interpretation.

The framework therefore separates data quality from the capability to use data. Increasing the number of available records may increase analytical options while also increasing reconciliation requirements. Whether the additional records improve a decision depends on their relevance, their integration, and the controls applied to their use.

2.3 Rethinking Control Systems in Digital Contexts

Management control systems have traditionally been conceptualized as formal mechanisms designed to ensure alignment between organizational objectives and employee behavior. Within this tradition, frameworks such as Simons' Levers of Control emphasize the role of diagnostic and interactive controls in guiding organizational performance (Simons, 1995).

Digital infrastructures change the implementation of these mechanisms. For example, a budget threshold can be enforced through a workflow rule, while an interactive review can use a dashboard to question assumptions. Automation can change when and by whom a control is exercised without eliminating its organizational purpose.

Quattrone (2016) provides a basis for questioning whether greater digital precision necessarily produces wiser management accounting. This chapter develops that concern into a conditional argument: control effectiveness depends on whether users can interpret outputs and contest decisions, not simply on whether processing is automated.

These developments suggest that control systems should be reconceptualized as dynamic processes embedded within socio-technical infrastructures, rather than as static sets of formal procedures.

2.4 Digitalization as a Transformative and Contingent Force

Digitalization is defined here as the use and integration of digital technologies in financial workflows. Digital transformation denotes broader changes in organizational arrangements and value creation associated with those technologies, consistent with the scope discussed by Vial (2019). The terms are related but not interchangeable.

A negative effect of digitalization is not assumed to occur at a universal level of technology adoption. Instead, the framework proposes that problems arise when the complexity or opacity of automated processing exceeds the organization's ability to supervise it. This mismatch is a theoretical boundary condition to be tested.

Accordingly, the model distinguishes integration and automation from oversight and interpretability. An enterprise can have high digitalization and strong oversight, or high digitalization and weak oversight. These configurations should not be assigned the same expected control outcome.

This distinction prevents the enabling proposition and the constraining proposition from contradicting each other: each applies under explicitly different organizational conditions.

2.5 Toward an Integrative Theoretical Framework

Building on the preceding discussions, this chapter argues that financial information management and control systems in digital enterprises can only be understood through an integrative perspective that captures the interactions between:

- financial data as a dynamic resource,
- information systems as processing and integration mechanisms,
- control systems as adaptive governance processes, and
- digital technologies as transformative and contingent forces.

This perspective shifts the focus from isolated components to interdependent relationships, emphasizing the processes through which financial information is transformed into organizational decisions.

Accordingly, the next section develops a conceptual model that formalizes these relationships and provides a foundation for the formulation of theoretical propositions.

2.6 Comparison of the theoretical streams

Table 1 compares the analytical roles assigned to the literature in this chapter. The limitations concern what each perspective leaves outside the present research question; they are not claims that entire fields ignore those issues.

Table 1. Thematic synthesis and the integration proposed in this chapter

Stream and sources	Primary contribution	Question carried into FIMCS
Information systems success DeLone and McLean (2003)	Quality and use of information systems and their benefits.	How does usable financial information become an accountable control response?
Information processing Galbraith (1974)	Fit between uncertainty and information processing arrangements.	Which integration and interpretation routines enable financial exception handling?
Management control Simons (1995); Otley (1999); Granlund (2011)	Objectives, accountability, performance feedback and the accounting–IT interface.	How are control responsibilities enacted through automated workflows?

continued on following page

Table 1. Continued

Stream and sources	Primary contribution	Question carried into FIMCS
Socio-technical and digital change Orlikowski (1992); Vial (2019); Annarelli et al. (2021)	Interaction of technology, organizational practice and digital capabilities.	When do infrastructure and skills complement each other in financial control?
Digital accounting and AI tensions Quattrone (2016); Raisch and Krakowski (2021)	Interpretation and the interdependence of automation and human judgment.	When does digitalization outpace the ability to explain and supervise decisions?

3 CONCEPTUAL MODEL DEVELOPMENT

3.1 Definitions and Analytical Boundaries

The unit of analysis is an enterprise financial workflow, such as expenditure approval, reconciliation, forecasting, or management reporting. Financial data are recorded inputs; financial information is their contextualized output. Information systems comprise applications, infrastructure, procedures, and users that process those inputs. Control systems comprise the rules, responsibilities, monitoring, escalation, and corrective action governing their use. Software may implement a control, but software and control are not identical.

Data quality concerns the fitness of input records for a specified financial task. Information processing capability concerns organizational integration, analysis, and interpretation. Control effectiveness concerns whether controls identify and address relevant deviations. Decision-making quality concerns the defensibility, timeliness, and objective alignment of a decision, rather than its financial outcome alone. A justified decision may still produce an unfavorable outcome under uncertainty.

These working definitions prevent circular measurement: data quality is not defined by decision success, and control effectiveness is not measured solely by decision quality. Digitalization refers to technology use and integration; oversight capability concerns the ability to inspect, challenge, and correct that use.

3.2 Financial Data Quality and Information Processing Capability

Financial data constitute the foundational input of financial information systems; however, their contribution to organizational outcomes is contingent upon their quality. Data quality—typically defined in terms of accuracy, completeness, consistency, and timeliness—determines the extent to which information can be effectively processed and utilized.

Within the information systems literature, the DeLone and McLean IS Success Model identifies information quality as a central dimension of information-system success and its associated use and benefits (DeLone & McLean, 2003). Building on this role of information quality, the present framework distinguishes the quality of financial data inputs from the organizational capability required to integrate, analyze, and interpret them.

In digital enterprise environments, where financial data are generated across multiple heterogeneous platforms, integration capabilities become particularly important. Research on digitalization capabilities highlights the organizational importance of integrating and processing heterogeneous digital resources (Annarelli et al., 2021). On this basis, the chapter proposes that higher-quality financial data should facilitate information processing capability.

Proposition 1 (P1)

Financial data quality is expected to positively influence information processing capability in digital enterprises.

3.3 Information Processing Capability and Control System Effectiveness

Information processing capability refers to the organization's ability to transform raw data into meaningful, actionable insights through processes of integration, analysis, and interpretation. This capability is central to managing uncertainty and complexity in organizational environments.

Drawing on Galbraith's (1974) information-processing perspective, organizational arrangements can be understood in relation to the information demands created by uncertainty. The present framework extends this logic to financial control. Here, processing capability means the repeatable ability to integrate, analyze, and interpret relevant financial data. Processing capacity refers more narrowly to the volume or speed that infrastructure can handle. Greater capacity is not equivalent to better interpretation.

In digital enterprises, enhanced processing capabilities—enabled by analytics, artificial intelligence, and real-time systems—allow organizations to monitor activities, detect deviations, and respond to risks more effectively. However, the effectiveness of control systems depends not only on data availability but also on the organization's ability to interpret and utilize information within decision contexts.

Processing capability is thus proposed as an enabling condition for effective control. It is insufficient when managers lack authority to investigate exceptions or when incentives discourage escalation. These social conditions limit the expected positive relationship.

Proposition 2 (P2)

Information processing capability is expected to positively influence control system effectiveness.

3.4 Control System Effectiveness and Decision-Making Quality

Control systems play a central role in guiding organizational behavior and ensuring alignment with strategic objectives. Effective control systems provide reliable feedback, enforce accountability, and support informed decision-making.

Management control research links information with objectives, accountability, performance evaluation, and feedback (Otley, 1999; Simons, 1995). Extending this logic, the present model treats an effective control as one that identifies a meaningful deviation and enables a proportionate response by an accountable decision-maker. This mechanism is distinct from simply generating more reports.

In digital environments, control systems increasingly incorporate automated and algorithmic elements, enabling real-time decision support. However, their effectiveness depends on their ability to balance flexibility and governance, as well as transparency and automation.

The relationship is therefore formulated as a theoretical expectation that effective controls contribute to decision quality, subject to incentive alignment and the avoidance of excessive approval delays. Decision-making quality, as defined in this chapter, is not treated as an outcome directly tested by Otley (1999) or Simons (1995), nor is it inferred from evidence about firm resilience.

Proposition 3 (P3)

Control system effectiveness is expected to positively influence decision-making quality.

3.5 The Moderating Role of Digitalization

Digitalization fundamentally reshapes the relationships between data, information processing, and control systems. On the one hand, digital technologies enhance information processing capability by enabling automation, real-time integration, and advanced analytics. This strengthens the link between processing capability and control effectiveness.

On the other hand, digitalization introduces new forms of complexity, including algorithmic opacity, system interdependencies, and reduced interpretability. Research on artificial intelligence highlights that technological systems may simultaneously enhance and constrain organizational capabilities, giving rise to an automation–augmentation paradox (Raisch & Krakowski, 2021). Finance-specific analyses identify data quality, model accuracy, system transparency, data privacy, and ethical considerations among the challenges associated with AI-enabled financial applications (Amdouni, 2025a, 2025b).

The enabling mechanism concerns access to timely, integrated information; the constraining mechanism concerns whether the resulting outputs and dependencies remain governable. Their balance is expected to depend on data integration, employee expertise, decision criticality, and the ability to investigate and override an automated output.

Proposition 4 (P4)

Digitalization strengthens the positive relationship between information processing capability and control system effectiveness when financial systems are interoperable and users have adequate interpretive skills and oversight arrangements.

This is a conditional proposition developed in this chapter, informed by the digital transformation and information processing perspectives.

Proposition 5 (P5): Conditional Adverse Effect

When digitalization increases processing complexity or algorithmic opacity faster than oversight capability develops, control system effectiveness is expected to decline, other conditions held constant.

This proposition extends the automation–augmentation argument of Raisch and Krakowski (2021). It does not establish a universal inverted-U relationship or an empirically estimated threshold.

3.6 Dynamic Feedback and Systemic Reinforcement

Although the proposed relationships are presented sequentially, they operate within a dynamic and iterative system. Decision-making outcomes influence subsequent data generation, system configurations, and control mechanisms, creating feedback loops within the system.

This dynamic interaction is consistent with Orlikowski's (1992) structurational account of the reciprocal relationship between technology and organizational practice. It also reinforces the view that financial information management and control systems should be understood as ongoing and adaptive processes rather than static structures.

3.7 Summary of the Model

The proposed framework advances a systemic understanding of FIMCS by:

- Linking data, systems, control, and decision-making in a unified model
- Introducing digitalization as a contingent and transformative factor
- Specifying conditional effects and feedback mechanisms for future testing

Figure 1 distinguishes the three proposed positive paths from conditional digitalization effects. P4 concerns moderation of the capability-to-control path; P5 concerns an adverse effect on control effectiveness when oversight lags. The dotted feedback route represents a learning mechanism rather than an additional tested proposition.

Figure 1. A Socio-Technical and Control-Based Framework of Financial Information Management and Control Systems in Digital Enterprises

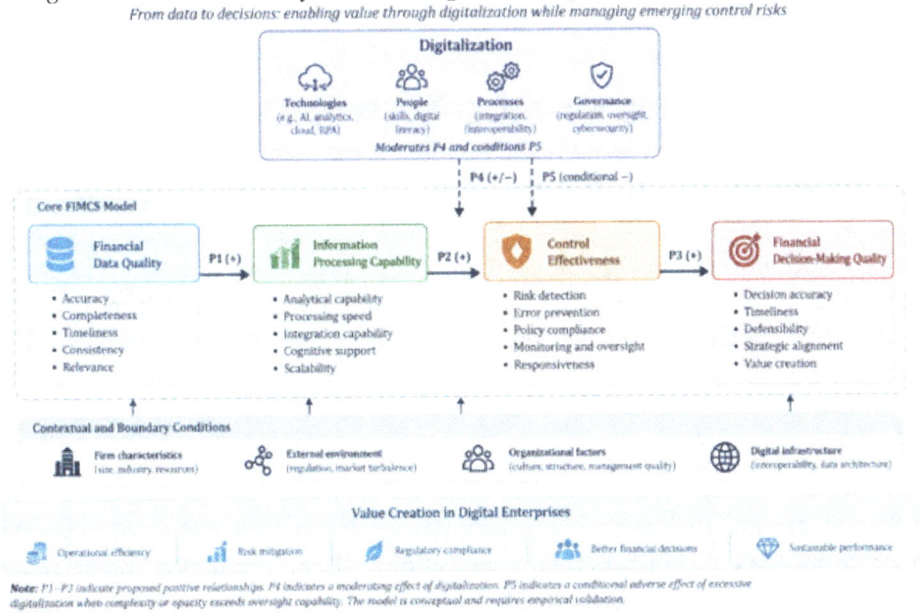

The arrows summarize theoretical expectations, not estimated coefficients. Decision outcomes may prompt revised data definitions, new analytical routines, or changes in approval rules. Such feedback can alter the relationships over time and should be distinguished from their initial direction in empirical designs.

The framework's value is therefore assessed by whether it helps distinguish observable mechanisms and competing explanations, rather than by the visual simplicity of the sequence.

3.8 Boundary Conditions and Governance

Four contextual conditions delimit the model. First, task uncertainty and transaction diversity affect the information required: a routine reconciliation differs from a novel investment judgment. Second, system fragmentation and dependence on third-party services affect whether relevant records can be combined and traced. Third, interpretive skills, escalation authority, and incentive alignment determine whether information can trigger corrective action. Fourth, decision criticality and applicable reporting or regulatory obligations determine the evidence and oversight needed.

These conditions are expected to vary by firm size, industry, and digital maturity. A small enterprise with simple processes may achieve adequate control without extensive automation; a highly automated enterprise may sustain strong control through disciplined oversight. Neither configuration is inherently superior. Cybersecurity, traceability, and accountability are incorporated as governance conditions affecting the reliability and actionability of the information flow, rather than deferred entirely to future research.

4 THEORETICAL AND MANAGERIAL IMPLICATIONS

4.1 Theoretical Implications

The contribution is an explicit account of how processing and control connect financial data with decisions. The framework combines constructs that are often investigated at different levels and specifies what remains to be demonstrated empirically.

Integrating Information Systems and Management Control

The integration does not replace information systems success or management control frameworks. It narrows their intersection to the conversion of financial data into accountable action. Granlund (2011) supplies a direct precedent for studying that intersection, while the present model specifies five propositions and their boundary conditions.

A proposed distinction is between producing an interpretable exception and ensuring that the exception triggers an authorized response. These are analytically separable processes and require different measures in future research.

Reframing Information Processing as a Control Mechanism

Information processing capability is positioned as a potential mediator, not as a synonym for control effectiveness. A finance team may reconcile data and generate accurate forecasts while lacking the authority to correct transactions or challenge assumptions. This separation makes the model falsifiable.

The sequential model is deliberately parsimonious. Direct effects of data quality on decisions and reciprocal effects of control on data quality remain plausible and are considered in the research agenda.

Extending Management Control Theory into Digital Contexts

Digital controls are examined through the distribution of responsibilities between people and systems. The model therefore complements existing work on control and strategic renewal rather than assuming that earlier theories require stable environments.

Accountability and the ability to challenge an output are incorporated into the conditions under which processing can improve control. This makes the social component of the framework operationally consequential.

Specifying the Digital Control Paradox

The term digital control paradox describes the proposed coexistence of improved processing and weakened oversight within the same workflow. These outcomes can occur on different dimensions and should be measured separately.

The model does not claim that adoption intensity alone predicts this tension. It locates the potential adverse effect in a mismatch between automation and oversight, leaving the functional form and threshold to empirical investigation.

4.2 Managerial Implications

Beyond its theoretical contributions, the proposed framework offers important implications for managers operating in digital enterprise environments.

Treating Data Quality as a Strategic Capability

A finance leader can translate the data-quality construct into named ownership of critical fields, documented validation rules, and a log of unresolved reconciliation exceptions. The relevant question is whether a financial output can be traced to its source and whether material discrepancies are resolved before use.

Developing Information Processing Capabilities

Information processing capability can be developed through common data definitions, documented transformations, and staff able to explain analytical outputs. Managers should examine the time and effort needed to reconcile records and investigate anomalies, alongside infrastructure speed.

Redesigning Control Systems for Digital Environments

Control redesign requires specifying which decisions may be automated, which exceptions require escalation, who can override a rule, and how overrides are reviewed. These are proposed applications of the framework; their effectiveness must be evaluated in the organization's context.

Managing the Digitalization Paradox

Digitalization should be evaluated using both processing and oversight indicators. A reduction in processing time should be examined alongside unresolved exceptions, missing evidence, and the ability to explain decisions. Improvements on one dimension do not establish improvements on the others.

The following evidence and illustration make these managerial implications concrete while maintaining the distinction between published observations and the chapter's own proposals.

4.3 Published Empirical Evidence and its Limits

Earlier evidence from US manufacturing documents differences in the adoption of data-driven decision-making associated with firm size, IT, educated workers, and learning (Brynjolfsson & McElheran, 2016). It motivates attention to complementary organizational resources rather than using technology presence alone as the measure of capability.

Three studies illustrate different parts of the argument. They use different settings and outcomes, so they cannot be combined as direct validation of P1–P5.

Their findings also caution against treating technology adoption as equivalent to capability or decision quality.

Roffia and Dabić (2024) analyze 143 questionnaires from SMEs in two Italian provinces during the COVID-19 context. Budgeting, continuity tools, supplementary financial resources, and entrepreneurial resilience were positively associated with resilience. Higher intention to use ERP systems was also associated with higher resilience, whereas ICT use for smart working was not statistically significant. For FIMCS, the study supports examining management arrangements alongside information systems. Its ERP measure concerns intention, and its outcome is resilience rather than decision quality; it therefore does not directly establish the proposed capability-to-control-to-decision pathway.

Fedyk et al. (2022) examine AI employment using more than 310,000 resumes across the 36 largest US audit firms and supplement the analysis with 17 audit-partner interviews. They report associations between AI investment and improved audit quality, reduced fees, and subsequent workforce changes. This provides a documented application of analytics to financial assurance. The setting is external audit, the adoption measure is AI human capital, and the study predates widespread generative AI use. Its results cannot be assumed to apply unchanged to internal enterprise controls or to establish the adverse effect proposed in P5.

Rieg (2026), published online in 2025, studies digital dashboards using data from German management accountants. The framework connects information quality and decision quality with technology acceptance and dashboard use. This is particularly relevant to the interpretation of financial information in control routines. However, decision quality is positioned as an antecedent in that study, whereas it is primarily an outcome here. This difference provides a substantive reason to test competing directions and feedback, rather than assuming that the proposed sequence is the only valid explanation.

The evidence supports the relevance of the chapter's constructs but leaves the full mediation chain and oversight mismatch untested. A practical implication is to evaluate an implementation with measures of data, processing, control, and decisions separately instead of relying on a single adoption or financial-performance indicator.

4.4 Worked Illustration of an Expenditure Approval Workflow

The following scenario is hypothetical and is not an observed case study. Consider an enterprise combining purchase orders, supplier invoices, goods-receipt records, and payment data in an ERP-linked dashboard. The scenario shows where the proposed constructs enter the workflow and what evidence could be collected; it claims no realized performance improvement.

At the data stage, duplicate supplier identifiers and inconsistent receipt dates can prevent reliable matching. The finance team assigns responsibility for master data and reconciles the fields before payment. At the processing stage, the dashboard brings together the records, identifies mismatches, and allows staff to inspect the underlying transactions. These activities illustrate P1 without assuming that software corrects missing or inaccurate inputs automatically.

At the control stage, an exception is routed to a named owner, payment is held where appropriate, and the resolution is documented. This illustrates the distinction underlying P2: an accurate alert alone is insufficient if nobody can investigate it or stop payment. For P3, decision quality can be assessed by whether the release or hold decision is justified by available evidence and made within the required time, rather than by the count of alerts displayed.

For P4, interoperable records and trained users could allow automated matching to improve exception handling. For P5, an opaque scoring rule could recommend release without a traceable explanation, while staff lack authority to challenge it. The managerial response is to define escalation and override rights and retain the records needed to reconstruct the decision. These are proposed design choices, not proven effects. Repeated exceptions should feed back into data definitions and rule design instead of being treated as isolated errors.

4.5 Cybersecurity, Accountability, and Regulatory Mapping

Cybersecurity matters to FIMCS because access compromise, unauthorized data changes, and service disruption can affect financial records and the controls that depend on them. The NIST Cybersecurity Framework 2.0 provides a non-prescriptive structure for organizing cybersecurity outcomes across organizations (Pascoe et al., 2024). The AI Risk Management Framework offers voluntary guidance for managing risks associated with AI systems (Tabassi, 2023). These publications inform governance design; neither provides empirical proof of this chapter's propositions. Related finance-focused work also highlights data quality and system transparency as material challenges in AI-supported fraud detection (Amdouni, 2025a).

Applied to the model, managers should identify who may change financial data, analytical models, and control rules; separate incompatible responsibilities; retain suitable logs; and test recovery and manual fallback procedures. For AI-assisted decisions, proposed safeguards include documented model purpose, input lineage, exception review, and responsibility for overrides. Bias or unexplained differential treatment should be investigated where the decision affects customers, employees, or counterparties. These controls link ethical concerns directly to P2, P3, and the oversight condition in P5.

Regulatory mapping is jurisdiction- and activity-specific. An enterprise should identify its applicable accounting, privacy, record-retention, and sector requirements and connect each obligation to a control owner and evidence requirement. This chapter makes no claim that using a general framework establishes legal compliance. A documented mapping of obligations to financial workflows is the proposed management practice; determining the obligations themselves requires the relevant authoritative rules.

4.6 Implementation Priorities and Evidence

Table 2 translates the framework into an illustrative implementation sequence. Owners and indicators should be adapted to the enterprise's material risks and decision cycles. The indicators are proposed management aids, not validated thresholds or required universal standards.

Table 2. Proposed implementation sequence

Stage	Accountable role and action	Evidence to retain
1 Define the decision	Finance process owner specifies the financial decision, objectives and relevant records.	Workflow map and decision criteria.
2 Establish data ownership	Data owner defines critical fields and reconciliation rules.	Source lineage and unresolved discrepancy log.
3 Evaluate processing	Finance and IT document transformations and test outputs against source records.	Reconciliation results and explanation of exceptions.
4 Assign control authority	Control owner defines escalation, approval and override responsibilities.	Exception resolution and override records.
5 Assess digital oversight	IT security and model owners review access, changes, interpretability and recovery.	Access review, model-change record and recovery test.
6 Review outcomes	Decision owner compares timeliness and documented rationale with agreed objectives.	Decision review and updates to data or control rules.

5 DISCUSSION AND LIMITATIONS

The framework makes a conditional argument: high-quality data can support decisions through processing and control, but these mechanisms are neither sufficient nor necessarily exclusive. Its contribution depends on maintaining distinctions between constructs and testing where the sequence breaks down. It should not be interpreted as evidence that a technically advanced enterprise necessarily has effective governance.

5.1 Three Ways the Proposed Explanation Could Fail

First, the sequential chain may be incomplete. Managers may use high-quality financial information directly, without the particular controls represented in the model. If direct effects dominate, the proposed mediation would explain only a small share of decision quality. Second, technical capability may be decoupled from action: even accurate analysis will not improve control where authority is unclear or incentives favor ignoring exceptions. Third, apparent nonlinear effects may reflect implementation disruption, industry differences, or poor measurement rather than an adverse effect of digitalization. A pooled inverted-U pattern would not establish the oversight mechanism in P5.

5.2 Assumptions and a Competing Explanation

Two assumptions require evidence. The model assumes that improved information is available to decision-makers with both authority and motivation to use it. It also assumes that the benefits of better control are not offset by delays, excessive restrictions, or the cost of investigating false alerts. These assumptions should be examined rather than embedded in the definition of effectiveness.

A competing explanation is that underlying management quality causes better data practices, stronger controls, greater digital investment, and better decisions simultaneously. Reverse causality is also plausible: effective managers may improve data governance after successful decisions, and existing controls may determine which data are recorded accurately. Cross-sectional associations among the constructs cannot resolve these alternatives.

5.3 Limits of the Conceptual Synthesis

The chapter uses a selective narrative synthesis and does not establish the completeness of the literature. The empirical illustrations concern particular countries, firm types, technologies, and periods. They provide context rather than a unified dataset. The proposed indicators require validation, and no digitalization threshold, causal coefficient, or universal effect size is estimated. The framework's generality therefore remains a research question, particularly across regulated and less regulated sectors and across firms with different resource constraints.

6 RESEARCH AGENDA AND EMPIRICAL OPERATIONALIZATION

6.1 Candidate Constructs and Measures

Table 3 offers candidate indicators for operationalizing the model. They are newly proposed measurement directions, not scales adopted from the cited studies. Researchers should assess content validity, reliability, dimensionality, and discriminant validity before testing the structural paths. Workflow-level measures should not be combined with enterprise-level outcomes without an explicit aggregation rationale.

Table 3. Candidate measures for future testing

Construct	Candidate indicators	Measurement caution
Financial data quality	Verified discrepancy rate; completeness of critical fields; timeliness against the decision cycle.	Assess input quality independently of the decision outcome.
Information processing capability	Ability to reconcile heterogeneous records; explain transformations; investigate anomalies.	Separate skills and routines from computing speed or capacity.
Control effectiveness	Resolution of material exceptions; authorized approvals; operation of escalation and corrective action.	Do not use report volume or decision success as sole proxies.
Decision-making quality	Documented rationale; timely action; consistency with objectives and available evidence.	Separate ex ante decision quality from ex post financial returns.
Digitalization	Workflow integration; extent of automation; use of analytical systems.	Do not equate adoption intensity with organizational maturity.
Oversight capability and context	Traceability; ability to contest outputs; override review; skills; task uncertainty.	Measure oversight separately from control outcomes; test contextual differences.

6.2 Testing Pathways and Rival Explanations

A longitudinal design could measure data quality before processing capability, followed by control operation and independently assessed decisions. Combining transaction logs, control records, and multiple respondents would reduce reliance on a single self-report source. The proposed sequence should be compared with models allowing direct data-to-decision effects, reciprocal control-to-data effects, and common antecedents such as management quality, firm resources, and prior performance. Temporal ordering improves interpretation but does not by itself establish causality.

P4 requires an interaction test showing whether digitalization changes the capability-to-control relationship under the specified skills and integration conditions. P5 requires separate measures of opacity or complexity and oversight capability. Researchers could compare a mismatch interaction with nonlinear specifications, rather than assuming a quadratic relationship in advance. A threshold claim would require observations on both sides of an estimated turning point and evidence that the result is not driven by sample composition.

6.3 Context, Learning, and Ethical Outcomes

Comparative studies could examine firms of different sizes, industries, and digital maturity, including settings where manual controls remain effective. Process studies could trace whether repeated exceptions change data definitions and control rules over time. Experiments could examine how explanation quality and override authority influence judgment while keeping the financial task constant. Outcomes should include accountability and unjustified differential treatment where relevant, alongside decision timeliness and accuracy. No such data collection or testing is reported in this chapter.

7 CONCLUSION

This chapter proposes an integrated account of financial information management and control systems in which data quality, processing capability, and control effectiveness connect financial records with organizational decisions. Its five propositions distinguish the potential enabling role of digitalization from the adverse conditions that may arise when complexity and opacity outpace oversight.

The contribution is a conceptual synthesis with explicit definitions, boundary conditions, practical applications, and candidate measures. Published studies illustrate the relevance of the constructs, while the hypothetical expenditure workflow demonstrates how they could be examined in practice. Neither constitutes validation of the full model. For managers, the principal implication is to evaluate data, processing, control, and decisions separately and assign responsibility for the transitions between them. For researchers, the priority is to test the proposed relationships against direct, reciprocal, and common-cause alternatives.

REFERENCES

Amdouni, A. (2025a). Artificial intelligence and financial fraud detection: Applications and challenges. In Derbali, A. (Ed.), *Artificial intelligence for financial risk management and analysis* (pp. 271–280). IGI Global Scientific Publishing., DOI: 10.4018/979-8-3373-1200-2.ch013

Amdouni, A. (2025b). Artificial intelligence and financial market forecasting: Applications and challenges. In Derbali, A. (Ed.), *Artificial intelligence for financial risk management and analysis* (pp. 111–122). IGI Global Scientific Publishing., DOI: 10.4018/979-8-3373-1200-2.ch005

Annarelli, A., Battistella, C., Nonino, F., Parida, V., & Pessot, E. (2021). Literature review on digitalization capabilities: Co-citation analysis of antecedents, conceptualization and consequences. *Technological Forecasting and Social Change*, *166*, 120635. DOI: 10.1016/j.techfore.2021.120635

Brynjolfsson, E., & McElheran, K. (2016). The rapid adoption of data-driven decision-making. *The American Economic Review*, *106*(5), 133–139. DOI: 10.1257/aer.p20161016

DeLone, W. H., & McLean, E. R. (2003). The DeLone and McLean model of information systems success: A ten-year update. *Journal of Management Information Systems*, *19*(4), 9–30. DOI: 10.1080/07421222.2003.11045748

Fedyk, A., Hodson, J., Khimich, N., & Fedyk, T. (2022). Is artificial intelligence improving the audit process? *Review of Accounting Studies*, *27*(3), 938–985. DOI: 10.1007/s11142-022-09697-x

Galbraith, J. R. (1974). Organization design: An information processing view. *Interfaces*, *4*(3), 28–36. DOI: 10.1287/inte.4.3.28

Granlund, M. (2011). Extending AIS research to management accounting and control issues: A research note. *International Journal of Accounting Information Systems*, *12*(1), 3–19. DOI: 10.1016/j.accinf.2010.11.001

Orlikowski, W. J. (1992). The duality of technology: Rethinking the concept of technology in organizations. *Organization Science*, *3*(3), 398–427. DOI: 10.1287/orsc.3.3.398

Otley, D. (1999). Performance management: A framework for management control systems research. *Management Accounting Research*, *10*(4), 363–382. DOI: 10.1006/mare.1999.0115

Pascoe, C., Quinn, S., & Scarfone, K. (2024). *The NIST cybersecurity framework (CSF) 2.0* (NIST CSWP 29). National Institute of Standards and Technology. DOI: 10.6028/NIST.CSWP.29

Quattrone, P. (2016). Management accounting goes digital: Will the move make it wiser? *Management Accounting Research*, *31*, 118–122. DOI: 10.1016/j.mar.2016.01.003

Raisch, S., & Krakowski, S. (2021). Artificial intelligence and management: The automation–augmentation paradox. *Academy of Management Review*, *46*(1), 192–210. DOI: 10.5465/amr.2018.0072

Rieg, R. (2026). Exploring the determinants and performance effects of digital dashboard use by management accountants. *Journal of Management Control*, *37*(1), 75–110. DOI: 10.1007/s00187-025-00400-0

Roffia, P., & Dabić, M. (2024). The role of management control and integrated information systems for the resilience of SMEs. *Review of Managerial Science*, *18*(5), 1353–1375. DOI: 10.1007/s11846-023-00657-6

Simons, R. (1995). *Levers of control: How managers use innovative control systems to drive strategic renewal.* Harvard Business School Press.

Tabassi, E. (2023). *Artificial intelligence risk management framework (AI RMF 1.0)* (NIST AI 100-1). National Institute of Standards and Technology. DOI: 10.6028/NIST.AI.100-1

Vial, G. (2019). Understanding digital transformation: A review and a research agenda. *The Journal of Strategic Information Systems*, *28*(2), 118–144. DOI: 10.1016/j.jsis.2019.01.003

KEY TERMS AND DEFINITIONS

Algorithmic Opacity: A condition in which the logic, transformations, or basis of an algorithmic output is difficult for relevant users or control owners to inspect, explain, or challenge.

Control System Effectiveness: The extent to which control arrangements identify relevant deviations and enable accountable, proportionate responses through monitoring, escalation, authorization, and corrective action.

Decision-Making Quality: The defensibility, timeliness, and alignment of a financial decision with organizational objectives and the evidence available at the time; it is distinct from the decision's ex post financial outcome.

Digital Control Paradox: The proposed coexistence of enhanced information-processing capability and weakened control when digital complexity or algorithmic opacity develops faster than the organization's oversight capability.

Digitalization: The use and integration of digital technologies, automation, analytics, and interconnected information systems within financial workflows.

Financial Data Quality: The fitness of financial input records for a specified task, reflected in attributes such as accuracy, completeness, consistency, and timeliness.

Financial Information Management and Control Systems (FIMCS): The integrated socio-technical arrangement through which financial data are processed, interpreted, governed, and connected to organizational control and decision-making.

Information Processing Capability: The organizational ability to integrate, analyze, reconcile, and interpret relevant financial data so that it can support control and decision processes; it is distinct from computing speed or processing capacity alone.

Oversight Capability: The organizational capacity to inspect, understand, challenge, override, and correct technology-mediated outputs and decisions, supported by appropriate authority, skills, traceability, and accountability.

Socio-Technical Perspective: An analytical perspective that treats technologies, human interpretation, organizational roles, routines, and governance arrangements as interdependent elements of financial information and control.

Chapter 2
Digital Transformation of Financial Information Management in Modern Enterprises

Razia Nagina
http://orcid.org/0000-0002-0305-8393
Lovely Professional University, India

ABSTRACT

The chapter aims to analyze how digital transformation is transforming financial information management in the contemporary businesses. Its importance lies in explaining the shift from periodic, transaction-based accounting toward integrated, real-time, and analytics-driven financial systems that support strategic decision-making and organizational control. Using the extensive study of modern literature, the chapter concludes that digital technologies increase the timeliness, visibility and strategic relevance of financial information and improve the coordination and transparency of the functions. Nonetheless, these advantages are supplemented by organizational, technological, and managerial issues of skills, governance, cybersecurity, and accountability. The chapter suggests that to manage the financial information in digital businesses, an excellent data governance, building capacity, and ensuring that technology, administrative discretion, and control systems are coherent should be considered.

DOI: 10.4018/979-8-3373-9230-1.ch002

2027, IGI Global Scientific Publishing. Copying or distributing in print or electronic forms without written permission of IGI Global Scientific Publishing is prohibited. Use of this chapter to
rative artificial intelligence (AI) technologies is expressly prohibited. The publisher reserves all rights to license its use for generative AI training and machine learning model development.

INTRODUCTION

The digitalization of financial information management is the defining feature of modern companies that have been forced to operate in the environment of growing complexity, increasing information volumes, and the use of technology (Zong and Guan, 2025). Unlike in the past, when financial data was created and processed in a largely manual, functionally separate system, it is now integrated into digital systems that enable continuous data collection, real-time processing, and advanced analytics (Ionescu et al., 2025). This metamorphosis is indicative of wider change in the organizational design, competition, and regulation in which the availability of timely, reliable, and transparent financial information is becoming essential to the operational effectiveness and strategic decision-making. As a result, financial information management has outgrown the boundaries of accounting departments, becoming an enterprise-wide capability that underpins coordination, control, and value creation across digital business models (Hossen, 2025).

The development of digital technologies has significantly changed the essence and extent of financial information systems. Cloud-based systems, enterprise-wide platforms, automation tools, and data analytics have been increasing the amount, speed, and types of financial data accessible to organizations (Prasetianingrum & Sonjaya, 2024). Financial information is not generated solely from traditional accounting transactions but also from digitally enabled activities such as online sales, platform-based transactions, integrated supply chains, and digitally mediated customer interactions. Subsequently, financial information management is becoming increasingly complex with big, networked data sets rather than individual accounting records (Theodorakopoulos et al., 2024). Modern studies show that this has increased the strategic importance of financial information by improving forecast accuracy, enabling scenario analysis, and facilitating more dynamic performance management in a volatile business environment.

The digital transformation has also altered the ways in which data is stored and distributed in enterprises in the form of financial data. The shift of on-premise, department-related databases to centralized or distributed digital systems has enhanced accessibility and uniformity of data in any organizational unit (Mahmud & Ikbal, 2024). Standardized data definitions, automated consolidation, and real-time reporting are only possible through integrated systems, which minimize delays and reconciliation errors that used to limit financial visibility (Alao et al., 2024). Managerially, this integration facilitates cross-functional coordination as the teams in finance, operations and strategy can use the same information base. Scholarly and workplace sources are also becoming more insistent that this type of integration leads to improved transparency and accountability, especially in large, geographically decentralized, or online networked businesses (Agostino et al., 2022).

At the same time, the online nature of financial information management creates new organizational and managerial implications. Real-time financial data is changing the way decisions are made by shifting the focus from backwards-looking performance measurements to prospective analysis and ongoing performance monitoring (Kashchena & Nesterenko, 2022). Managers are currently expected to interpret complex dashboards, analytics outputs, and predictive insights rather than just reviewing financial statements. This change requires new data literacy, systems thinking and digital governance competencies, and places financial managers in the middle between technological potential and organizational goals. According to the research in the fields of management accounting and information systems, the usefulness of digital financial information depends not only on the level of technology but also on organizational coordination, user capacity, and control systems (Sonjaya & Prasetianingrum, 2024).

Although digital transformation offers advantages, it also poses significant challenges for the management of financial information. More system integration increases reliance on digital platforms, which makes organizations more susceptible to system failures, cyber risks, and data integrity problems (Avira et al., 2023). The increase in data sources may contribute to information overload, making assurance, validation, and control processes more difficult. Also, the combination of the old systems and new digital systems may bring technical and organizational challenges, especially within companies that have deeply-rooted organizational structures and habits. Modern research indicates that, in the absence of sound governance structures, digital financial systems can lead to a decline rather than an increase in the credibility and confidence in financial data (Al-Ansi et al., 2024).

In the control and compliance dimension, digitally transformed financial information systems also raise questions about accountability, transparency, and regulatory alignment (Gunasilan, 2024). Unless well-designed and documented, automated processes and algorithm-based reporting can hide the logic of decisions and the responsibility for control. The key point that regulators and standard-setting organizations are stressing more and more is the necessity to have robust internal controls, data governance policies, and auditability in the digital financial contexts (Šuvakov & Sekicki, 2025). Therefore, financial information management in digital businesses should achieve a balance between efficiency and innovation, control, assurance, and ethical concerns. This equilibrium lies at the centre of the larger topic of monetary information handling and control systems in online companies.

In the academic literature, there is an increasing interest in the intersection between the digital transformation, the financial information systems, and the organizational control (Singh et al., 2024). Nonetheless, studies remain disjointed across fields such as accounting, information systems, and strategic management. Integrative analyses bridging the gap between technological advances and the transformation of the financial practices, information flow and managerial functions are needed. These analyses are especially applicable at a time when enterprises remain engaged in digital infrastructures as they face uncertainty, competition, and changing stakeholder demands (Garad et al., 2024).

In this regard, the current chapter is intended to make contributions to both theory and practice by providing a systematic and critical analysis of the digital revolution in financial information management in contemporary businesses. In line with the chapter's goals and the book's general theme, it has integrated current research and professional experience to clarify how digital technologies are transforming the creation, storage, distribution, and application of financial data. Drawing on the significance of combined online platforms and emerging organizational, technological, and management issues, the chapter offers a logical basis for the perception of digital financial information systems. It lies in the gap between conceptual approaches and the practical implications of effective financial information management and control in the digital business world.

REVIEW OF LITERATURE

There is no doubt that the digital transformation of financial information management has been widely discussed in the intersecting fields of financial accounting, information systems, and management studies. Modern literature has always recognized the fact that digital technologies have radically changed the way financial information is generated, processed, and used in modern businesses (Schiavi et al., 2024). Preliminary studies of financial information systems prioritized the efficiency and accuracy of transaction-processing; more recent studies go beyond this to include strategic integration, real-time visibility, and decision support on the basis of digital platforms (Akula et al., 2025). Researchers argue that financial information management has ceased to be a back-office, compliance-based activity and has become one of the core aspects of organizational value generation in the digital business world.

There is considerable literature on how digital technologies, including enterprise-wide systems, cloud computing, automation, and data analytics, transform financial information practices (Huang & Yin, 2023). Research emphasizes that built-in digital platforms enable smooth transfer of information throughout organizational activities, hence creating a decrease in informational silos and improving consistency in financial reporting. Management accounting studies indicate that this kind of integration enhances the timeliness and relevance of financial data, thereby contributing to ongoing performance measurement rather than ad hoc, backward analysis. The literature also points out that real-time financial information enables more flexible planning, budgeting, and forecasting, especially during dynamic, uncertain business cycles (Jain & Kulkarni, 2023).

The other theme that stands out concerns the transformation in the production and storage of financial information. Digital business models generate large amounts of granular data from various sources, such as digital transactions, platform interactions, and automated processes (Remané et al., 2022). According to researchers, this increase in data scope disrupts conventional accounting categories and measurement procedures. There is an increasing trend toward financial information systems supporting both structured accounting data and semi-structured or unstructured data, which requires new data architectures and governance structures (Faccia et al., 2022). Research into cloud-based financial systems also offers benefits such as scalability, cost-effectiveness, and remote accessibility, but raises concerns about data safety, privacy, and regulatory compliance (Subramanyam, 2025).

There is also a great deal of scholarly interest in the dissemination and utilization of financial information in digitally transformed businesses (Gao, 2023). The literature on integrated reporting and enterprise information systems suggests that digital platforms increase transparency by enabling managers to access a single dashboard and analytics tools (Solano & Cruz, 2024). These tools facilitate the coordination of various functions by aligning financial performance and non-financial indicators. According to researchers the enhanced visibility of information enhances organizational control as it makes it more accurate to detect deviations and take corrective measures (Putra et al., 2025). Simultaneously, some researchers warn that overreliance on automated reporting can undermine critical judgment when users lack sufficient knowledge of the underlying data and system logic.

Another area of focus is the role of digital transformation in redefining financial control and governance. Researchers note that automation and integration of the system transform manually operated control mechanisms into embedded, system-based controls (Wijesooriya & Basnayake, 2024). Although these controls are useful for increasing consistency and reducing human error, the literature also notes risks associated with system dependence and decreased transparency of control processes. Auditing and governance studies emphasize the need to have solid internal control systems, data governance policies, and audit trails to ascertain reliability and accountability in digital financial information systems (Udoh, 2024).

Digital financial information management is an aspect that has widespread organizational and managerial implications, which are widely discussed in recent studies. As it is mentioned in literature, digital transformation requires a radical rethink of the skills, positions, and organizational frameworks (Chen et al., 2022). Financial managers are increasingly required to have skills in information analytics, digital information, and strategic analysis. Resistance to change, skills gaps, and cultural obstacles have been identified as major hurdles to effectively embracing digital financial systems. Successful digital transformation, therefore, is considered to be a socio-technical process that relies upon the correspondence between technology, organizational design, and human capacity (Thomas, 2024).

Although there has been extensive research on this topic, the literature also presents gaps and open debates. Though numerous studies report data on the positive impacts of digitalization, fewer of them are integrative and thus can be used to connect the adoption of technology with financial information quality, managerial decision-making, and the effectiveness of control. Also, a lot of the empirical data is situation-specific, i.e., it considers specific industries or technologies and, thus, does not allow one to generalize the results. There is also a growing need among scholars to adopt comprehensive models that reflect the interdependent quality of digital technologies, financial information flows, and organizational control mechanisms.

All in all, the current literature offers a solid basis for understanding the digital transformation of financial information management and also identifies unexplored challenges and research opportunities. This chapter is based on the previous research but adds a new approach to the analysis, synthesizing the results of academic studies in accounting, information systems, and management to provide a broad perspective of how digital technologies transform financial information practice in contemporary businesses. By doing so, it will help promote the development of conceptual clarity and practical understanding in the field of financial information management and control systems in digital enterprises on a larger scale.

Critical Evaluation and Practical Challenges

Although the current literature offers substantial evidence of the positive impact of digital transformation on financial information management, a more critical analysis reveals that some practical issues remain unresolved and have not been sufficiently explored. First, much of the literature focuses on technological capabilities and underestimates the complexity of implementation. Empirical research indicates that digital transformation programs often go beyond budget, timeframes, or anticipated performance results because of a mismatch between technological conception and organizational procedures. This indicates that digital transformation should be perceived as a socio-technical process instead of technological upgrade.

Second, data quality and data governance become serious limitations. Even though integrated systems enable real-time financial reporting, discrepancies in master data, inadequate data definitions, and poor governance frameworks may undermine the reliability of financial deliverables. Increasingly, the literature indicates the so-called garbage-in, garbage-out challenge in more advanced analytics settings, where poor input data can distort predictive insights and management actions.

Third, system vulnerability and cybersecurity are emerging issues of digitally transformed financial ecosystems. With the financial systems moving to cloud-based and networked systems, they are now susceptible to the risk of data breaches, unauthorized access, and disruption of the system. Although these risks are acknowledged, the literature does not provide adequate convergence between financial information management and cybersecurity governance models.

Fourth, human and organizational aspects are also a thorny problem. Research reveals that change resistance, skills shortages, and poor data literacy are obstacles to the effective use of the system. Even sophisticated digital solutions cannot deliver value when users cannot interpret analytics outputs or challenge automated responses.

Lastly, automation accountability and auditability are conceptually and practically challenging areas. The use of algorithms may result in a loss of clarity in decision-making processes, and it may be hard to identify who was responsible in the event of inaccuracies or falsehoods. This places strong demands on explicit system design, explainable analytics, and unrelenting audit systems.

OBJECTIVES

1. To examine how digital technologies have reshaped financial information management practices in modern enterprises.
2. To analyze changes in financial data generation, storage, and dissemination in digital business environments.
3. To assess the role of integrated digital platforms in improving financial visibility, coordination, and transparency.
4. To identify emerging organizational, technological, and managerial challenges in digitally transformed financial information systems.

METHODOLOGY

This chapter takes a qualitative and conceptual approach with its methodology based on an expansive review and synthesis of the available scholarly literature, professional accounts, and recorded organizational practices when it comes to digital financial information management.

Objective 1: Examining How Digital Technologies Have Reshaped Financial Information Management Practices in Modern Enterprises

Digital technologies have reconfigured the dogma of financial information management by altering the practices of capturing, processing, integrating, and using financial data in decision-making in modern business. Traditional financial information systems were largely transaction-driven, infrequent, and functionally separate, and were designed to support a primary goal of bookkeeping, statutory accounting, and internal control (Ionescu & Diaconita, 2023). Conversely, the new digital financial systems are characterized by integration, real-time processing and analytics-driven functions, which can provide the functions of finance with a more strategic and value-focused role in organizations.

The application of enterprise-wide digital systems, especially enterprise resource planning (ERP) systems, has been one of the most important developments. ERP adjoins finance and operations, procurement, supply chain, and human resources and makes one source of financial reality throughout the organization (Katuri, 2025). This has changed the face of financial information management through automation of recording of transactions, standardization of data definitions and real-time consolidation and reporting (Nofel et al., 2024). Indicatively, multinational organizations that have implemented ERP software by vendors like SAP have substituted the disjointed legacy systems with coherent financial structures that have increased information consistency, quickness of reporting, and managers of the managers (Maddipudi, 2025). Scholarly and practical research show that ERP-based integration leads to fewer reconciliation processes and an increased level of reliability in the financial information used by managers and other external stakeholders.

Cloud computing has also changed the nature of financial information management by reinventing how it is stored, accessed, and maintained. Clouded financial systems enable businesses to expand their financial operations without necessarily investing heavily in infrastructure development to enable businesses to access financial information anywhere, anywhere. This has notably affected multinational, digitally dispersed businesses in which financial departments operate across geographies and time zones (Nutalapati, 2024). Cloud solutions can also facilitate ongoing system upgrades and regulatory compliance efforts, thereby reducing the burden on internal IT services (Ajayi, 2025). Major technology-based companies, including Microsoft, have publicly described how cloud-based financial systems have allowed real-time financial visibility and accelerated close cycles and how cloud use is transforming finance as a periodic reporting service to a continuing information service.

Robotic process automation (RPA) and other automation technologies have transformed the landscape of financial management information management by removing manual and rule-based processes, such as invoice processing, account reconciliations, and journal entries. Automation enhances precision, accelerates processing speed, and gives finance professionals the freedom to focus on analysis and interpretation rather than data entry (Zareen et al., 2024). According to research on accounting information systems, automation reduces operational risk from human error and improves the timeliness of financial information. Many major organizations in the banking, manufacturing, and retailing industries have been embracing RPA to simplify the finance processes which are more transaction-intensive and create quicker period ends and more dependable financial information to utilize by the managers (Noviyanti, 2025).

The use of advanced data analytics and artificial intelligence (AI) has only widened the scope of financial information management and its strategic importance. The old system of finances was mostly favorable to descriptive reporting, which describes what and why it happened, whereas the latest digital technologies became prescriptive analytics, which enables the functions of finance to anticipate trends, evaluate risks and simulate other outcomes (Ionescu & Diaconita, 2023). For example, e-commerce and platform-based businesses worldwide, including Amazon, use sophisticated analytics to combine financial, operational, and customer data, which helps them set dynamic prices, make demand predictions, and make investments. Even though proprietary system information is not shared by such organizations, the available literature and professional analysis support the fact that an analytics-based financial information system is the core of scale, complexity, and thin margin management in digital business models (Paul, 2023).

Financial information management has also been transformed by digital technologies since it has blurred the lines between financial and non-financial data. The use of operational, environmental, and customer-related data in the same dashboards is becoming more common among modern enterprises (Ombai et al., 2024). This integration assists in performance management systems, which synchronize financial results and operational drivers, with the strategic objectives. Management accounting studies indicate that performance measurement systems that are digitally enabled enhance the quality of decisions since they supply a contextualized financial information as opposed to accounting numbers in isolation. This leads to the fact that finance functions are becoming more business partners, helping with strategic planning and performance management throughout the organization (Gholami et al., 2025).

The other significant change concerns the speed and frequency of financial reporting. Digital technologies enable the continued operation of accounting and provide near real-time reporting, reducing the reliance on periodic financial statements (Ajibade, 2025). This change is especially notable in the case of digitally native businesses, where transaction data is sent directly into financial systems in real time. Greater access to financial data will make organizations agile so that managers can react quickly to changes in the marketplace, fluctuations in costs, and disruptions in operations. The current literature stresses that this responsiveness is a competitive edge of the utmost importance in a changing (digitally powered) market (Ahmad, 2025).

But it is also a case of the new complexities as financial information management is redesigned using digital technologies. Greater system integration increases reliance on digital infrastructure, and system reliability and cybersecurity become critical issues to the operations of the finance functions. Besides, the volume and sophistication of information produced by digital systems may put pressure on traditional control systems and require innovative governance structures. It has always been emphasized in research that the advantages of digital financial technologies can only be guaranteed by the competencies of users, strong internal controls, and data governance (Ajayi et al., 2025).

Overall, digital technologies have shifted financial information management practices, transforming finance into an integrated, real-time, and strategically directed capacity. Cloud computing, automation, and analytics have helped modern enterprises improve the accuracy, timeliness, and relevance of financial information and increase their involvement in decision-making and control through ERP systems. These changes are the basis of interpreting the modern financial information management and a critical background to studying the integration, transparency, and new challenges in digital businesses.

Objective 2: Analyzing Changes in Financial Data Generation, Storage, and Dissemination in Digital Business Environments

The nature of financial data creation, storage, and sharing has changed significantly in the modern business setting due to digital business environments (Jiang, 2024). These changes can be traced to the widespread adoption of digital technologies across the business's fundamental operations, in which transactions, customer services, and business operations take place online. As a result, management of financial information is no longer a periodic, internally focused accounting process, but rather a continuous, enterprise-wide information flow that underpins real-time decision-making, transparency, and control (Hossen, 2025).

These changes in the production of financial data are most evident in businesses that embrace a digital, platform-based business model. Conventionally, financial records were mostly created from internally documented accounting transactions, such as sales invoices, purchase orders, and payroll documents (Yuniarto & Siregar, 2025). On the contrary, online businesses generate financial information consistently through online transactions, subscription plans, online payments, and automated business systems (Minarni, 2025). Amazon, for example, generates huge amounts of financial data in the form of millions of transactions between customers every day, sales from the third-party marketplace, logistics, and digital services. Every transaction will at the same time provide a number of financial data concerning the recognition of the revenues, commissions, the cost of fulfillment, and the tax. According to the empirical and professional literature, this type of event-based data generation enables near-real-time accounting, but it also complicates data validation and financial controls.

On the same note, digital service providers that use subscription-based strategies generate recurring financial information tied to usage patterns rather than a single sales transaction (Lindström et al., 2024). Businesses like Netflix use automated systems to generate revenue information based on subscription billing systems, customer retention data, and area-based cost frameworks. This has reorganized the management of financial information to bring it closer to the customer behavior and service delivery metrics (Lindström et al., 2024). Management accounting studies indicate that such integration enhances revenue forecasting and lifetime value analysis but requires complex systems to ensure accurate forecasts and compliance with accounting standards.

There has also been a significant change in financial data storage practices in the digital business environment. On-premises accounting systems have been gradually replaced or augmented by cloud- and hybrid-based storage architectures. These systems allow businesses to archive and process large amounts of financial and operational data as well as facilitate worldwide access and system expansion (Pillai, 2025). In such a case, Microsoft has publicly stated that it will move to cloud-based financial systems to enable global operations and achieve real-time financial visibility across all business units. Consolidations, standardized reporting, and constant updates of the system are also highly beneficial to multinational businesses in the active market and are easier to achieve through cloud storage (Prokopenko et al., 2024).

In addition to cloud-based databases, modern enterprises are increasingly using data warehouses and data lakes to store financial, operational, and customer data. This combined storage system augments superior analytics, scenario assessments, and risk evaluations. Examples of this change include global manufacturing and technology companies that have implemented enterprise-wide systems by SAP because they store their financial data in centralized systems, which combine procurement, production, sales, and finance (Al Maruf, 2025). Literature sources have argued that such cohesive storage enhances data consistency and analytical potential; however, it also requires robust master data management and governance to ensure data integrity and auditability.

Digitalization has also changed the distribution of financial information. In conventional companies, communication was done through periodic financial statements and reports to management. Enterprises are now digitally dependent on real-time dashboards, automatic notifications, and built-in analytics to disseminate financial data in real time (Yuliantini et al., 2024). The global automotive industry, including Tesla, uses digitally integrated systems to provide managers with real-time data on production costs, inventory levels, and financial performance. This will enable faster operational and strategic decision-making, particularly in a rapidly evolving, volatile market.

On the internal front, the digital dissemination will reduce information asymmetry by enabling common access to financial information across departments and managerial levels. A live financial dashboard will enable operational managers to understand the financial impact of their decisions, thereby enhancing coordination among finance and other functions. On the outside, digital dissemination can increase transparency and accountability by improving the quality and timeliness of information transmitted to auditors, regulators, and investors. Automated reporting systems provide transparency in the audit trail and consistency in disclosure, which are crucial in a digitally intricate business (Solihah, 2026).

However, the topic of digitally enabled dissemination also poses challenges, as research highlights. The user can be overwhelmed with the speed and volume of financial information, and over-dependence on automated outputs can diminish the critical analysis. As a result, researchers underline that digital distribution should be facilitated by a strong analytical ability, professional judgment, and unbiased reporting systems to support the efficient utilization of financial data.

Overall, digital business contexts have created continuous, event-driven financial data generation processes, storage configured for scalable, integrated digital architectures, and real-time dissemination through advanced analytics and dashboards. These changes increase transparency and decision support, but they also increase complexity and governance requirements. These changes cannot be successfully managed without a deep understanding of financial management and control within the digital enterprise.

Objective 3: Assessing the Role of Integrated Digital Platforms in Improving Financial Visibility, Coordination, and Transparency

Integrated digital platforms are considered one of the elements of financial information management in modern enterprises, particularly when the company operates in a complex value chain, a global market, and digitally facilitated business models (Basiru et al., 2023). Financial systems have traditionally been fragmented, with separate applications used for accounting, procurement, sales, inventory, and human resources. This disintegration has led to limited financial transparency and performance, poor inter-functional coordination, and reduced transparency due to inconsistent information and late reporting. These limitations have been alleviated with integrated digital systems, especially enterprise resource planning (ERP) systems, cloud-based financial suites, and enterprise analytics platforms, which have brought financial and operational data together into a single digital system (Ger, 2025).

One key role of integrated digital platforms is increased financial visibility. Financial visibility refers to the extent of accessibility of managers and decision-makers to accurate, timely, and complete financial data across organizational functions and processes (Genotiva, 2025). These platforms bring together the transactional data of various functions and keep updating financial records on a continuous basis, thus giving real-time or near-real-time information about revenues, costs, margins, and cash flows. This ability is a significant break to the traditional periodic reporting cycles, where the performance of the financial level was analyzed in the past. In the case of a large multinational enterprise, increased visibility is especially essential, as geographically dispersed operations and diverse product lines contribute to greater financial complexity. By using integrated platforms, the firms enable the tracking of performance more efficiently along the granular dimensions of product, customer, or regional dimensions without losing the overall enterprise-wide financial view (Alonge et al., 2024).

The advantages are demonstrated by global consumer goods firms. Firms like Unilever have shifted to a globally integrated ERP system that consolidates financial information across subsidiaries and business units. Through this integration, consolidation is expedited, margins and costs are more easily monitored across markets, and more standardized corporate-level financial reporting is obtained. Reduced dependency on several legacy systems will increase management's ability to identify performance trends, enabling the quickest possible response to changes in operations or the market (Khojasteh et al., 2026).

In addition to increasing visibility, the integrated digital platforms play a critical role in improving the organizational coordination. The problem of coordination often arises due to the fact that the work of the departments is characterized by disjointed information systems, which create inconsistent data and duplicate efforts, negatively affecting decision-making. Integrated platforms help to overcome these problems by integrating standardized processes, common definitions of data, and automated processes across functional boundaries. The financial information generated across operational activities, including procurement, production, and sales, is transparently updated in the finance modules and instantly accessible to other functions. This harmonious flow of information improves communication between the managers in charge of finance and operations and aligns financial planning with the execution of operations (Wulandari & Maulana, 2023).

Integrated platforms provide critical coordination, particularly in manufacturing- and supply-chain-intensive industries. A case in point is automotive and industrial companies, such as Toyota, relying on centralized systems to coordinate procurement, production workload, inventory, and cost accounting in the complex web of supply chains. These platforms provide a direct connection between operational decisions related to production volume or sourcing approach and financial performance, thereby enabling stricter control of costs and greater forecasting accuracy (Vummadi & Hajarath, 2025). It is always shown in the scholarly literature that such integration minimizes working-capital requirements, enhances inventory turnover, and enhances organizational efficiency in general.

Integrated digital platforms also have significant advantages for service-oriented and project-based organizations. The global professional services firms, like Accenture, use combined financial and project management platforms to align revenue recognition, resource allocation, and cost tracking for client engagements. These tools allow finance departments to track the project's profitability in real time while facilitating decentralized project implementation (Pourkhodabakhsh & Khajeh, 2026). This, in turn, improves coordination among finance, project managers, and operational teams by ensuring that strategic objectives are supported by accurate, timely financial information.

Combined digital platforms also promote financial transparency at the internal and external levels. On the inside, transparency is improved with standardized data formats, on-board controls and calculable audit trails to link financial results with the underlying transactions and processes (Gao, 2023). The managers stand to gain a better understanding of the determinants of financial performance, thereby strengthening accountability and performance measurement. Integrated platforms reduce ambiguity and limit disagreements over figures and interpretations by ensuring that all users refer to the same data and the same logic behind reporting.

On the outside, transparency has become increasingly significant due to the rise in regulatory oversight and the escalating demands on stakeholders. Digital platforms that are integrated allow consolidation and standardized reporting to be performed in an automated manner, thus reducing the risk of both manual errors and discrepancies in financial reporting (Ajibade, 2025). Multinational firms in industries such as food and drinks, energy, and pharmaceuticals have adopted integrated platforms to ensure consistency in cross-jurisdictional financial reporting. Other companies, such as Nestle, have highlighted how standardized and integrated financial systems can improve the comparability and reliability of the information reported to investors and regulators (Magli & Amaduzzi, 2025).

Cloud-based integrated platforms also promote transparency by allowing auditors and regulatory bodies to access financial information through controlled, secure access. This feature assist audit with greater efficiency and has a positive impact on the trust in the reported financial data through enhanced system traceability and automatically generated audit trails (Oluoha et al., 2025). Companies implementing cloud-based financial systems from providers such as Oracle have reported improvements in audit coordination and the timeliness of reporting, which they attribute to a centralized data management system and built-in control mechanisms (Limba et al., 2025). Such platforms are a sign of a larger shift to digitally enabled assurance and continuous surveillance.

Despite these advantages, the literature warns against the fact that the usefulness of integrated digital platforms depends on organizational and governance considerations. Lack of data governance, poor process redesign, or inadequate user training may hinder visibility, coordination, and transparency. Additionally, unified platforms can increase reliance on technology and, in turn, the risks of system dependency, cybersecurity, and the privacy of information. To this end, effective implementation will require effective governance structures, strong internal controls and long-term capability building in finance functions.

On the whole, digital platforms have radically transformed financial information management in the modern business. These platforms enable the finance functions to go beyond the traditional reporting duties and to play a more decisive role in strategic decision-making and organizational governance by increasing their financial visibility, improving cross-functional coordination, and increasing transparency. Their input, therefore, is central to understanding how digital enterprises manage financial information in the ever-evolving, multifaceted business context.

Objective 4: Identifying Emerging Organizational, Technological, and Managerial Challenges in Digitally Transformed Financial Information Systems

As much as the digital transformation has resulted in better efficiency, scope, and strategic usefulness of financial information systems, it has also presented novel organizational, technological, and management issues to contemporary businesses (Pazouki et al., 2025). Financial information systems redesigned digitally are more integrated, data-driven, and automated, which makes them potentially more valuable and complex. The description of these new challenges is crucial in developing robust financial information management and control systems in online businesses (Odunaike, 2025).

As an organizational issue, a highly visible challenge is associated with structural and cultural change. Digital financial systems tend to force enterprises to abandon functionally siloed structures and adopt a process-based, cross-functional approach (Schrader et al., 2025). The functions of finance are likely to work closely with the operations, information technology, data analytics, and strategy divisions. Nonetheless, organizations that experience resistance to change do so more often, especially when the digital transformation threatens the hierarchy, routine, and roles (Garad et al. 2024). Employees who are used to the old way of doing things in accounting might feel threatened by automation and systems that rely on analytics, which could take away their jobs or professional identity. Consequently, the successful utilization of digitally transformed financial systems is potentially constrained by organizational inertia and cultural misfit.

The other organizational issue is that of skills and capability gaps. Digital financial information systems require competencies beyond traditional accounting and financial reporting skills. There is a growing expectation among finance professionals to read real-time dashboards, operate with sophisticated analytics, and be familiar with the logic of automated systems (Prasetianingrum & Sonjaya, 2024). Numerous businesses suffer from a skills shortage of hybrid professionals with accounting, data literacy, and technological knowledge. Organizations can effectively use digital systems without specific training and building digital capability, or overuse the technical expertise of the role, undermining the strategic position of the finance function (Issah et al., 2025).

System complexity and integration pose significant challenges on the technological front. Financial information systems that have been digitally transformed usually comprise connected platforms, such as enterprise resource planning systems, cloud-based financial systems, analytics, and external data interfaces (Nutalapati et al., 2024). The technical nature of integrating these parts, particularly when the old systems are still in service, may be expensive. During and after system deployment, companies often face data errors, interface crashes, and process incompatibility. For example, global enterprises deploying enterprise-wide systems from vendors such as SAP or Oracle must manage multifaceted integration initiatives across regions, business units, and jurisdictions. Lack of integration may compromise data quality and erode trust in financial data (Pasumarthi & Joyce, 2025).

Another technological issue that has become popular in online finance is data governance and cybersecurity. Systems that are digitally transformed produce and retain large volumes of sensitive financial and operational information, which may be stored in a cloud-based or hybrid infrastructure. This increases vulnerability to cyber threats, data breaches, and unauthorized access (Brahmandam, 2025). The integrity of financial data is essential to the managerial decision-making process, regulatory compliance, and stakeholder confidence. Having strong access control, encryption, data provenance, and audit trails has thus become a fundamental need of digital financial information management. Companies that do not properly address cybersecurity threats can lose their finances and reputation and face fines (Zamil & Faruq, 2022).

The other technological issue concerns dependence and automation risks in systems. With the increased automation of financial processes in terms of embedded rules, workflows, and algorithms, organizations can become so dependent on system outputs (Debbadi & Boateng, 2025). Mistakes in system configuration, defective algorithms, or poor-quality input data can easily spread across integrated platforms, influence financial reports, and affect large-scale decision-making. Automated errors can also be systemic and may not be realized without proper monitoring systems, unlike their localized counterparts, which are easy to detect. The difficulty of this issue highlights the significance of sustained controls, authentication controls and human supervision in digitally revolutionized financial systems.

Complexity in decision making is a major challenge in the managerial front. The financial systems that have been digitally transformed will offer managers unparalleled access to real-time and multidimensional data. This will enrich information, but may also cause information overload (Aro, 2024). This can be because managers are not always able to differentiate between critical insights and excessive detail, especially when dashboards and analytics tools are not designed appropriately or are not aligned with decision-making needs (Rahman et al., 2025). According to management control research, increased information does not necessarily lead to improved decision-making; rather, the significance, understandability, and interpretability of financial information are the key factors.

The evolving role of finance leaders is also a challenge to management. CFOs and top-level financial managers are increasingly taking on the role of strategic partners, leading to the implementation of digital transformation efforts and ensuring financial integrity and control. The innovation and risk management may conflict with this dual responsibility. For example, the implementation of high-tech analytics or artificial intelligence can be beneficial in terms of strategic value, yet it will introduce issues of explainability, accountability, and compliance. Such conflicting demands require effective leadership, well-defined governance systems, and cooperation among finance, IT, and risk management functions to achieve balance.

Governance and accountability structures also have managerial issues. Financial information systems have been digitally transformed, eroding historical lines of responsibility, with financial data flowing across functions and being affected by automated processes. In highly integrated environments, it may be hard to determine who is responsible for data quality, system configuration errors, and control failures. Businesses have then been forced to redefine functions, roles, and escalation processes to ensure accountability is clearly assigned and understood. In the absence of such transparency, digital systems might hide control and transparency rather than improve them.

The challenges are depicted in real-life experiences of international businesses. Megafirms that are technologically advanced, like Microsoft, have stressed the need to continuously upgrade skills and governance systems to handle complex, cloud-based financial systems. Equally, multinationals operating across various regulatory environments constantly struggle to harmonize global online platforms with local regulatory obligations. These illustrations show that digital transformation is not a single venture but a continuous process that requires ongoing adjustment.

In short, the digitally transformed financial information systems have a spectrum of emerging organizational, technological, and managerial challenges. Organizational resistance, lack of skills, complexity of the system and cybersecurity, reliance on automation, overload of information and uncertainty about governance are all problematic issues in contemporary enterprises. To overcome these hurdles, they need to be approached in a holistic manner which incorporates the capacity of the organization and technology, managerial skills and effective governance structures. It is important to identify and address these challenges to ensure that, rather than weakening financial information management and control, digital transformation empowers contemporary businesses.

ILLUSTRATIVE PRACTICAL CASES

The practical examples will shed more light on how the digital transformation realizes the redesign of financial information management in the real world. A successful project that took place is Unilever, which embarked on a massive change by adopting a globally standardized enterprise resource planning (ERP) system. This project helped the company align financial information across subsidiaries and geographic locations. This saw Unilever save a lot on its financial closing cycle and enhance consistency in reporting and compliance. Nevertheless, the shift demanded significant data standardization, process reengineering, and alignment of local practices with international financial procedures, underscoring the complexity of such changes within the organization.

The other high-profile case is that of Microsoft, which shifted its financial systems to a cloud-based platform. This change facilitated continuous accounting operations and real-time access to financial information in the global operations. Microsoft said that the financial visibility had been improved, faster consolidation had been achieved, and collaboration between finance and operational departments. Meanwhile, the company also focused on enhancing cybersecurity, identity and access controls, and governance structures to address risks related to cloud-based financial information.

Amazon is one company that has integrated financial information and sophisticated analytics in the digital commerce industry. Its financial management platforms serve large volumes of real-time transactional information generated by online sales, logistics, and third-party marketplaces. Such systems assist in dynamic pricing, demand forecasting and cost optimization. But these data-intensive environments require advanced validation systems and pose risks to transparency in algorithms and regulatory compliance.

In the same way, Tesla has digitally integrated dashboards that track the financial and operational performance in real time. At the same time, managers can monitor production costs, inventory, and revenue streams, enabling quick decision-making in a highly dynamic industry. However, the use of automated reporting systems would require effective internal controls to maintain data accuracy and prevent misinterpretation of real-time metrics.

Such examples indicate that, though digital transformation can improve efficiency, transparency and strategic decisions, its implementation requires strong governance, data quality management and organization preparedness.

FINDINGS

The analysis shows that digital transformation has fundamentally reshaped the management of financial information in contemporary business by altering how it is produced, processed, assembled, and applied in decision-making and control. Among the key findings is that financial information management has evolved into a discontinuous, strategic capability within an enterprise, no longer periodic or transaction-driven but a continuous, enterprise-wide support function. The adoption of digital technologies, especially enterprise-wide solutions, cloud solutions, automation solutions, and analytics has increased the breadth, accelerated, and strategic value of financial information at the organization levels.

One of the most important findings is that digital technologies have significantly enhanced the timeliness and granularity of financial information. Finance Data has ceased to be confined to conventional accounting engagements and is now created through digitally enabled business operations such as platform-based services, automated supply chains, and real-time customer interactions. This has enhanced the organizational capabilities of performing futuristic analysis, scenario mapping, and continuous performance tracking, particularly in a highly unstable and competitive business landscape.

The chapter also finds that integrated digital platforms are crucial for improving financial visibility, coordination, and transparency. Through the integration of financial and operational information in single systems, organizations will be in a better position to attain uniformity in reporting, minimize reconciliation mistakes and enhance cross-functional congruency. Not just the aggregate organizational level but also the granular levels of product lines, customer groups, and geographic areas have become more financially visible. This increased visibility helps make responses to managerial decisions quicker and more informed strategic decisions.

The other significant discovery concerns the role of finance professionals and managers. Digital transformation has changed the focus of managers who are less interested in retrospective reporting, and more in constant monitoring and predictive analysis. Finance experts are also increasingly asked to read and understand complex dashboards and analytics reports, which makes them strategic partners rather than technical specialists. The chapter, however, emphasizes that the worth of digital financial systems is largely based on its organizational alignment, data governance, and user capabilities and not on technology.

Meanwhile, the results highlight the fact that digital transformation brings with it major organizational, technological, and managerial challenges. More system integration leads to a high reliance on digital infrastructure, which raises issues in cybersecurity, data integrity, and system reliability. Increasing the number of information sources may also lead to information overload, complicating control and assurance activities. Additionally, poorly defined governance structures may blur accountability due to automation and algorithm-driven reporting.

In general, the chapter concludes that despite the beneficial impact of digital transformation on efficiency, transparency, and strategic insights in financial information management, these advantages depend on good governance, skills development, and alignment of technology and organizational processes. Digital transformation, then, is more of a socio-technical change than a mere technological upgrade.

IMPLICATIONS

The implications of the findings described in this chapter are significant to managers, organizations, and policy makers who are interested in the stewardship of financial information in digital companies. One implication for managers is the need to redefine the role of finance. With the shift to more real-time, integrated and analytics-driven financial information, finance leaders no longer have to be satisfied with the traditional reporting responsibilities and they, in fact, must actively participate in the strategic planning, risk management, and optimization of performance. Such a change requires developing the ability to interpret data, manage digital governance, and work across functions.

At the organizational level, the findings denote that successful digital transformation of the financial information systems needs structural and cultural adjustment. Business organizations are supposed to increase the level of integration between finance and operations, information technology, and analytics functions. The benefits posed by digital platforms can be undermined by siloed organizational structures and strict role definitions. This means that organizations have to invest in change management, training and development of capabilities to make sure that the personnel are prepared to use digital financial systems properly.

On a control and governance basis, the chapter highlights the necessity to enhance data governance structures. With increasingly automated and interconnected financial information systems, organizations should ensure they have strong internal controls, clear accountability structures, and unambiguous audit trails. Automated reporting and embedded controls make things more efficient, but without effective supervision, they can lead to systemic risks. Managers should thus balance the need for innovation and efficiency with that for assurance, compliance, and ethics.

The implications of the results for policymakers and regulators are that traditional regulatory and assurance frameworks may need to change to address digitally transformed financial systems. Real-time reporting, automation, and analytics that employ algorithms disrupt traditional ideas of disclosure and periodic checks. Regulators might thus have to focus more on system governance, data integrity, and ongoing assurance systems rather than only on end-of-period financial statements.

Lastly, the chapter suggests that digital transformation is a process rather than a one-time project. Organizations are required to constantly change their financial information management practices with the advancements in technologies, business models, and regulatory expectations. The creation of long-term values depends on the possibility to align digital capabilities with organizational strategy, managerial judgment and efficient control systems.

CONCLUSION

In this chapter, the digital transformation is discussed as it is transforming financial information management in modern businesses, with changes in financial practices, data flows, and control processes. The analysis proves that the area of digital technologies has transformed monthly, hindsight-based financial information into an ongoing, integrated, and strategically valuable asset. Organizations have enhanced timeliness, visibility, and relevancy of financial information through cloud infrastructures, enterprise-wide platforms, automation and analytics.

At the same time, the chapter also reminds us of the fact that these developments also come with great organizational, technological and managerial challenges. Increased system integration, automation, and data complexity raise issues of governance, accountability, cybersecurity, and managers' interpretation of the data. These difficulties highlight the fact that digital transformation is not just a technical update but a holistic organizational change process that rearranges and reallocates roles, duties and control systems.

The chapter strengthens the perception that the management of financial information in digital businesses should be based on coordinated technology and organizational design, managerial skills and governance models. Online applications can only increase transparency and decision support when supported by relevant controls and human insight. The chapter synthesizes the perspectives of accounting, information systems and management to contribute to the further insight into financial information management and control systems in the digital age to form a premise of future research and practice.

FUTURE SCOPE OF THE CHAPTER

Future studies can build on the research by conducting empirical studies on the impact of disparate industries and organizational settings on the results of digital transformation in the financial field. Inter-industry and inter-regional comparative investigations would also provide more information about the best practices and contextual issues. It is also possible to research emerging technologies such as artificial intelligence, continuous auditing, and real-time regulatory reporting, and their effects on financial governance and assurance. The longitudinal studies might also investigate changes in digital financial information systems over time and how they influence managerial decision-making and organizational control.

REFERENCES

Agostino, D., Saliterer, I., & Steccolini, I. (2022). Digitalization, accounting and accountability: A literature review and reflections on future research in public services. *Financial Accountability & Management, 38*(2), 152–176. DOI: 10.1111/faam.12301

Ahmad, N. R. (2025). Strategic Agility in Crisis: How Pakistani Businesses Adapt Financially to Global Disruptions and Market Shocks. *Center for Management Science Research, 3*(3), 31–39.

Ajayi, O. O., Alozie, C. E., & Abieba, O. A. (2025). Enhancing cybersecurity in energy infrastructure: Strategies for safeguarding critical systems in the digital age. *Trends in Renewable Energy, 11*(2), 201–212. DOI: 10.17737/tre.2025.11.2.00192

Ajayi, R. (2025). Integrating IoT and cloud computing for continuous process optimization in real-time systems. *Int J Res Publ Rev, 6*(1), 2540–2558. DOI: 10.55248/gengpi.6.0125.0441

Ajibade, O. A. (2025). Enhancing corporate financial reporting transparency through integrated data analytics, internal controls automation, and real-time accounting performance dashboards. *Int J Comput Appl Technol Res, 14*(4), 148–166.

Akula, D. K., Mohammed, Y. S., Syed, A., Haque, G. M. M., & Arafat, Y. (2025). The Role of Information Systems in Enhancing Strategic Decision Making: A Review and Future Directions. *Emerging Frontiers Library for The American Journal of Management and Economics Innovations, 7*(8), 80–105. DOI: 10.37547/tajmei/Volume07Issue08-07

Al-Ansi, A. M., Garad, A., & Jaboob, M. (2024). Unraveling the complexities of financial innovation and digital transformation within banking systems. *Multidisciplinary Reviews, 7*(11), 2024265–2024265. DOI: 10.31893/multirev.2024265

Al Maruf, A. (2025). A systematic review of ERP-integrated decision support systems for financial and operational optimization in global retails business. *American Journal of Interdisciplinary Studies, 6*(1), 236–262. DOI: 10.63125/qgbrmf24

Alao, O. B., Dudu, O. F., Alonge, E. O., & Eze, C. E. (2024). Automation in financial reporting: A conceptual framework for efficiency and accuracy in US corporations. *Global Journal of Advanced Research and Reviews, 2*(02), 040-050.

Alonge, E. O., Dudu, O. F., & Alao, O. B. (2024). The impact of digital transformation on financial reporting and accountability in emerging markets. *International Journal of Science and Technology Research Archive, 7*(2), 025-049.

Aro, O. E.Opeyemi E Aro. (2024). Data analytics as a driver of digital transformation in financial institutions. *World J. Adv. Res. Rev.*, *24*(1), 1054–1072. DOI: 10.30574/wjarr.2024.24.1.3124

Avira, S., Setyaningsih, E., & Utami, S. S. (2023). Digital transformation in financial management: Harnessing technology for business success. *Influence: International Journal of Science Review*, *5*(2), 336–345. DOI: 10.54783/influencejournal.v5i2.161

Basiru, J. O., Ejiofor, C. L., Onukwulu, E. C., & Attah, R. (2023). Enhancing financial reporting systems: A conceptual framework for integrating data analytics in business decision-making. *IRE Journals,[online]*, *7*(4), 587-606.

Brahmandam, B. A. (2025). Cloud Migration and Hybrid Infrastructure in Financial Institutions. *International Journal of Computer Science and Engineering Technology*, *9*(1), 42–46.

Chen, Y., Hao, S., & Li, A. (2022). Do governmental, technological and organizational factors influence the performance of financial management systems? *Kybernetes*, *51*(3), 1127–1150. DOI: 10.1108/K-11-2020-0808

Debbadi, R. K., & Boateng, O. (2025). Developing intelligent automation workflows in Microsoft Power Automate by embedding deep learning algorithms for real-time process adaptation. *Int J Sci Res Arch*, *14*(2), 802–820. DOI: 10.30574/ijsra.2025.14.2.0449

Faccia, A., Cavaliere, L. P. L., Petratos, P., & Mosteanu, N. R. (2022, August). Unstructured over structured, big data analytics and applications in accounting and management. In *Proceedings of the 2022 6th International Conference on Cloud and Big Data Computing* (pp. 37-41). DOI: 10.1145/3555962.3555969

Gao, X. (2023). Digital transformation in finance and its role in promoting financial transparency. *Global Finance Journal*, *58*, 100903. DOI: 10.1016/j.gfj.2023.100903

Garad, A., Riyadh, H. A., Al-Ansi, A. M., & Beshr, B. A. H. (2024). Unlocking financial innovation through strategic investments in information management: A systematic review. *Discover Sustainability*, *5*(1), 381. DOI: 10.1007/s43621-024-00542-6

Genotiva, K. (2025). Enhancing Financial Visibility: A Proposal to Implement Power BI for Group Accounting Analysis and Reporting.

Ger, P. P. (2025). Enabling Agile Finance Through ERP Modernization: A Comprehensive Analysis of Cloud-Based Enterprise Resource Planning Transformation. *Journal of Computer Science and Technology Studies*, *7*(6), 430–435.

Gholami, A., Khanmohamadi, M. H., Vakilifard, H., & Ranjbar, M. (2025). Presenting the Management Accounting Model in the Digital Era. *Management Strategies and Engineering Sciences*, *7*(4), 71–80. DOI: 10.61838/msesj.7.4.8

Gunasilan, U. (2024). Digital transformation technologies reshaping financial reporting, transparency, and accountability in public sector organizations. *Accountancy Business and the Public Interest*, *40*, 106–113.

Hossen, M. (2025). Integrating Accounting Information Systems and Enterprise Risk Management for Real-Time Financial Risk Monitoring. *International Journal of Accounting Innovation*, *1*(3), 241–254.

Huang, C., & Yin, X. (2023). The Impact of Digital Transformation on Enterprise Accounting. *European Online Journal of Natural and Social Sciences*, *12*(4), pp-418.

Ionescu, S. A., & Diaconita, V. (2023). Transforming financial decision-making: The interplay of AI, cloud computing and advanced data management technologies. *International Journal of Computers, Communications & Control*, *18*(6). Advance online publication. DOI: 10.15837/ijccc.2023.6.5735

Ionescu, S. A., Diaconita, V., & Radu, A. O. (2025). Engineering Sustainable Data Architectures for Modern Financial Institutions. *Electronics (Basel)*, *14*(8), 1650. DOI: 10.3390/electronics14081650

Issah, O., Baah, S. A., & Asare, C. A. (2025). Digital Technology and Financial Institutions' Sustainability: The Mediating and Moderating Effect of Staff Competency and Training Programs. *African Journal of Procurement, Logistics &. Supply Chain Management*, *8*(3), 65–89.

Jain, V., & Kulkarni, P. A. (2023). Integrating AI techniques for enhanced financial forecasting and budgeting strategies. *International Journal of Economics and Management Studies*, *10*(09), 9–15. DOI: 10.14445/23939125/IJEMS-V10I9P102

Jiang, J. (2024). A study on the digital transformation trends in financial management for small and micro enterprises. *International Journal of Global Economics and Management*, *3*(1), 355–363. DOI: 10.62051/IJGEM.v3n1.42

Kashchena, N., & Nesterenko, I. (2022). *Digitalization of the innovative development management information service of the enterprise. Mechanisms for ensuring innovative development of entrepreneurship. Monograph*. Teadmus OÜ.

Katuri, D. R. K. (2025). Streamlining Procure-to-Pay Processes in Large-Scale Companies with ERP Finance Systems. *European Journal of Computer Science and Information Technology*, *13*(38), 174–190. DOI: 10.37745/ejcsit.2013/vol13n38174190

Khojasteh, Y., Mousavi Jahan Abadi, S. M., & Ng, C. (2026). Enabling supply chain transformation with cutting-edge digital tools. In *Emerging Technologies in Supply Chains: Towards Digital Transformation* (pp. 3–47). Springer Nature Switzerland. DOI: 10.1007/978-3-032-01218-0_1

Limba, F. B., Sapulette, S. G., & Talla, A. (2025). The Role Of Cloud-Based Accounting Systems In Enhancing Financial Information Quality. *International Journal of Finance & Economics*, *2*(3), 895–913.

Lindström, C. W. J., Maleki Vishkaei, B., & De Giovanni, P. (2024). Subscription-based business models in the context of tech firms: Theory and applications. *International Journal of Industrial Engineering and Operations Management*, *6*(3), 256–274. DOI: 10.1108/IJIEOM-06-2023-0054

Maddipudi, S. (2025). RISE with SAP: Modernize Your Legacy ERP with an AI-Enabled Cloud ERP to Thrive in the Cloud. *IJSAT-International Journal on Science and Technology, 16*(1).

Magli, F., & Amaduzzi, A. (2025). News in Financial Measures. In *Innovations in Corporate Reporting: The Effects of Digital Innovation, Sustainability, and AI* (pp. 45–127). Springer Nature Switzerland. DOI: 10.1007/978-3-031-80404-5_5

Mahmud, D., & Ikbal, M. Z. (2024). Power BI and data analytics in financial reporting: A review of real-time dashboarding and predictive business intelligence tools. *International Journal of Scientific Interdisciplinary Research*, *5*(2), 125–157. DOI: 10.63125/yg9zxt61

Minarni, E. (2025). Impact of Digital Payment Systems on Financial Inclusion and Small Business Growth in Developing Economies. *International Journal of Innovation and Thinking*, *2*(1), 1–12. DOI: 10.71364/ijit.v2i1.6

Nofel, M., Marzouk, M., Elbardan, H., Saleh, R., & Mogahed, A. (2024). From sensors to standardized financial reports: A proposed automated accounting system integrating IoT, Blockchain, and XBRL. *Journal of Risk and Financial Management*, *17*(10), 445. DOI: 10.3390/jrfm17100445

Noviyanti, A. P. (2025). The Evolution of Accounting Information Systems: Recent Trends and Future Directions. *Accounting Research Journal*, *1*(1), 24–38.

Nutalapati, P. (2024). A Review on Cloud Computing in Finance-Transforming Financial Services in the Digital Age. *International Research Journal of Engineering & Applied Sciences| Irjeas. org, 12*(3), 35-45.

Odunaike, A. (2025). Integrating real-time financial data streams to enhance dynamic risk modeling and portfolio decision accuracy. *Int J Comput Appl Technol Res, 14*(08), 1–16.

Oluoha, O. M., Odeshina, A., Reis, O., Okpeke, F., Attipoe, V., & Orieno, O. H. (2025). Designing advanced digital solutions for privileged access management and continuous compliance monitoring. *World Scientific News, 203*, 256–301.

Ombai, P., Kiflemariam, A., & Odollo, L. (2024). Financial and Non-Financial Information on Strategy Management Process; A Systematic Literature Review. *Journal of Strategy and Management, 8*(1), 33–64.

Pasumarthi, A., & Joyce, S. (2025). Leveraging SAP's Business Technology Platform (BTP) for Enterprise Digital Transformation: Innovations, Impacts, and Strategic Outcomes. *International Journal of Computer Technology and Electronics Communication, 8*(3), 10720–10732. DOI: 10.15680/IJCTECE.2025.0803008

Paul, R. (2023). AI integration in e-commerce business models: Case studies on Amazon FBA, Airbnb, and Turo operations. *AIRBNB, AND TURO OPERATIONS (May 05, 2023)*.

Pazouki, S., Jamshidi, M. B., Jalali, M., & Tafreshi, A. (2025). The integration of big data in Fintech: review of enhancing financial services through advanced technologies. *World Journal of Advanced Research and Reviews, 25*(1).

Pillai, P. (2025). Cloud vs. On-Premise Data Warehousing: A Strategic Analysis for Financial Institutions. *Journal of Computer Science and Technology Studies, 7*(3), 503–513. DOI: 10.32996/jcsts.2025.7.3.57

Pourkhodabakhsh, N., & Khajeh, E. (2026). Strategic Management Consultancy in the Age of Industry 5.0: Leveraging the Gig Economy for Business Transformation. In *Smart and Sustainable Gig Economy in the Industrial 5.0 Era* (pp. 303-335). CRC Press.

Prasetianingrum, S., & Sonjaya, Y. (2024). The evolution of digital accounting and accounting information systems in the modern business landscape. *Advances in Applied Accounting Research, 2*(1), 39–53. DOI: 10.60079/aaar.v2i1.165

Prokopenko, O., Koldovskiy, A., Khalilova, M., Orazbayeva, A., & Machado, J. (2024). Development of blockchain technology in financial accounting. *Computation (Basel, Switzerland), 12*(12), 250. DOI: 10.3390/computation12120250

Putra, H., Qatrunnada, R., Rahmadoni, J., & Khairati, F. (2025). Enhancing Organizational Control Through Business Intelligence: Monitoring and Automated Alerts. *Electronic Journal of Education. Social Economics and Technology, 6*(1), 112–120.

Rahman, M. A., Alam, M. S., & Mrida, M. S. H. (2025). How interactive dashboards improve managerial decision-making in operations management. *American Journal of Advanced Technology and Engineering Solutions*, *1*(01), 122–146. DOI: 10.63125/cqm5jk84

Remané, G., Schneider, S., & Hanelt, A. (2022). Digital business model types: Understanding their mechanisms as recipes to commercialise digital technologies. *International Journal of Innovation Management*, *26*(03), 2240019. DOI: 10.1142/S1363919622400199

Schiavi, G. S., Behr, A., & Marcolin, C. B. (2024). Institutional theory in accounting information systems research: Shedding light on digital transformation and institutional change. *International Journal of Accounting Information Systems*, *52*, 100662. DOI: 10.1016/j.accinf.2023.100662

Schrader, P., Heidelbach, J., Ungern-Sternberg, R., Groß, E., & Bauernhansl, T. (2025). Organizing Digital Innovations. *Journal of Open Innovation*, *11*(3), 100615. DOI: 10.1016/j.joitmc.2025.100615

Singh, N., Vishnani, S., Khandelwal, V., Sahoo, S., & Kumar, S. (2024). A systematic review of paradoxes linked with digital transformation of business. *Journal of Enterprise Information Management*, *37*(4), 1348–1373. DOI: 10.1108/JEIM-07-2023-0397

Solano, M. C., & Cruz, J. C. (2024). Integrating analytics in enterprise systems: A systematic literature review of impacts and innovations. *Administrative Sciences*, *14*(7), 138. DOI: 10.3390/admsci14070138

Solihah, R. (2026). The Dynamics of Information Asymmetry in Corporate Financial Decision-Making in the Digital Era. *Riwayat: Educational Journal of History and Humanities*, *9*(1), 86–96. DOI: 10.24815/riwayat.v9i1.112

Sonjaya, Y., & Prasetianingrum, S. (2024). Harnessing the Power of Digitalization and Accounting Information Systems for Enhanced Efficiency and Accuracy. *Advances: Jurnal Ekonomi & Bisnis*, *2*(3), 121–135.

Subramanyam, S. V. (2025). Cloud-based enterprise systems: Bridging scalability and security in healthcare and finance. *IJSAT-International Journal on Science and Technology*, *16*(1).

Šuvakov, P., & Sekicki, V. (2025). Contemporary Trends in the Standardization of Accounting and Auditing at the International Level. *Journal of Agronomy, Technology and Engineering Management*, *8*(1), 1411–1428. DOI: 10.55817/YNPH2883

Theodorakopoulos, L., Thanasas, G., & Halkiopoulos, C. (2024). Implications of big data in accounting: Challenges and opportunities. *Emerging Science Journal, 8*(3), 1201–1214. DOI: 10.28991/ESJ-2024-08-03-024

Thomas, A. (2024). Digitally transforming the organization through knowledge management: A socio-technical system (STS) perspective. *European Journal of Innovation Management, 27*(9), 437–460. DOI: 10.1108/EJIM-02-2024-0114

Udoh, O. R. (2024). Enhancing Internal Audit Efficiency For Effective Risk Management and Corporate Governance Frameworks. *International Journal of Research Publication and Reviews, 5*(12), 3646–3659. DOI: 10.55248/gengpi.5.1224.250122

Vummadi, J. R., & Hajarath, K. C. (2025). *Resilient Horizons: Strategic Planning for Advanced Supply Chain and Logistics Management.* IPR Journals and Book Publishers.

Wijesooriya, C., & Basnayake, R. (2024). Digital transformation in redefining the role of the finance and audit professional of the future. In *Digital Transformation in Accounting and Auditing: Navigating Technological Advances for the Future* (pp. 61–104). Springer International Publishing. DOI: 10.1007/978-3-031-46209-2_3

Wulandari, S. S., & Maulana, K. (2023). Enhancing operational efficiency and financial reporting through Oracle NetSuite ERP implementation: A case study in a logistics company. *International Research Journal of Science, Technology, Education, and Management, 3*(3), 103–121.

Yuliantini, Y., Saribanon, E., Olfebri, O., Rahmawati, A., & Yulihapsari, I. U. (2024). Digital Marketing and the Presentation of Corporate Financial Statements: An Analysis of the Literature on Transformation and Impact. *Atestasi: Jurnal Ilmiah Akuntansi, 7*(2), 1072–1090. DOI: 10.57178/atestasi.v7i2.912

Yuniarto, A. A., & Siregar, I. W. (2025). From Manual to Digital: Modernizing the Sales Recording System for Growth at MSME Rumah Abon. *Journal of Scientific Insights, 2*(5), 510–525. DOI: 10.69930/jsi.v2i5.537

Zamil, M. H., & Faruq, M. O. (2022). Cybersecurity And Data Integrity in Financial Systems: A Review of Risk Mitigation and Compliance Models. *International Journal of Scientific Interdisciplinary Research, 1*(01), 27–61. DOI: 10.63125/azwznv07

Zareen, M., Hamdan, A., & Binsaddig, R. (2024). The Impact of Robotic Process Automation (RPA) on Accounting Profession. In *Business Development via AI and Digitalization* (Vol. 1, pp. 191–199). Springer Nature Switzerland. DOI: 10.1007/978-3-031-62102-4_16

Zong, Z., & Guan, Y. (2025). AI-driven intelligent data analytics and predictive analysis in Industry 4.0: Transforming knowledge, innovation, and efficiency. *Journal of the Knowledge Economy*, *16*(1), 864–903. DOI: 10.1007/s13132-024-02001-z

Chapter 3
Financial Data Quality, Reliability, and Decision Support in Digital Enterprises

Smitha Pillai
http://orcid.org/0009-0007-7049-2871
Bhopal School of Social Sciences (BSSS), India

ABSTRACT

In digital enterprises, financial decision-making increasingly depends on the quality, reliability, and timeliness of financial data generated by integrated information systems. As organizations adopt enterprise resource planning (ERP), cloud-based accounting platforms, and advanced analytics, ensuring the integrity and usability of financial data has become a central managerial and governance concern. This chapter examines financial data quality and reliability as foundational elements of effective financial information management and control systems in digital enterprises. It explores how high-quality financial data supports managerial decision-making, organizational control, and strategic planning, while poor data quality can undermine accountability and performance outcomes.

1. INTRODUCTION FINANCIAL DATA QUALITY IN DIGITAL ENTERPRISES

Building on this shift, the remainder of the chapter traces how financial information management has evolved, examines the digital ecosystems in which today's

DOI: 10.4018/979-8-3373-9230-1.ch003

2027, IGI Global Scientific Publishing. Copying or distributing in print or electronic forms without written permission of IGI Global Scientific Publishing is prohibited. Use of this chapter to rative artificial intelligence (AI) technologies is expressly prohibited. The publisher reserves all rights to license its use for generative AI training and machine learning model development.

financial data is generated, and sets out why sustaining accuracy, completeness, consistency, and timeliness has become an organizational priority in its own right.

1.1 Financial Information Management Evolution

The emergence of computerized accounting systems in the late twentieth century was the first significant change in technology in the management of financial information. The accounting programs that were based on computers allowed organizations to capture the financial transactions electronically and automate the simple accounting tasks like journal entries, update of ledgers, and preparation of financial statements. Such systems enhanced efficiency in reporting and minimized chances of making errors in calculations manually. The accounting systems however that were initially implemented with computerization were usually undertaken in a standalone mode and could run without connection to any other operational system in the organization.

Most of the latest technological advancements have also revolutionized the financial information management by integrating artificial intelligence, cloud computing, and advanced analytics to financial systems. There is rising use of artificial intelligence technologies to study financial data patterns, anomalies and aid in predictive financial analysis. Challoumis (2024) argues that artificial intelligence is transforming the manner in which financial management is conducted as it has the capacity to analyze intricate financial data automatically, and enhances the predictive accuracy of financial forecasting models.

SAP enterprise software platforms have also contributed greatly towards the modernization of financial controlling systems. As Sharma and Sharma (2025) describe, intelligent enterprise systems drive operational data analytics with financial reporting and, thus, enhance financial transparency and managerial control. Financial systems using SAP will offer financial dashboards that enable managers to monitor revenue output, cost structure and financial performance indicators of various organizational units.

The technological development has also had an impact on the wider organizational setting within which financial information is exercised. Digital transformation has enhanced access to organizational data and raised the level of analysis that can be used by managers. Lim et al. (2023) emphasize that digital information environment makes organizations analyzing consumer behavior, operational performance, and financial results at the same time possible. Financial information systems in these situations play the role of central databases that integrate financial and operational information to facilitate a thorough analysis of the organization.

Figure 1. History of Financial Information System in Organizations.

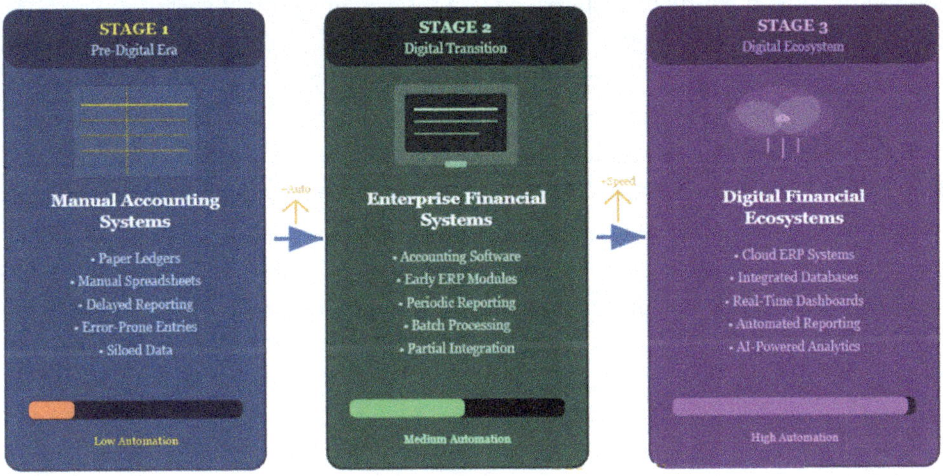

Figure 1 traces financial information systems through three stages: manual, paper-based ledgers; computerized accounting and early ERP systems; and digitally cohesive ecosystems, where cloud-based ERP, AI analytics, and financial dashboards enable real-time surveillance and automated reporting.

1.2 Digital Enterprises and Financial Data Ecosystems

Digital businesses are based on a network of technological infrastructure in which financial information circulates among various operational and analysis systems. Operational activities include the source of financial transactions through buying raw materials, sales of products or services, payment of employees, and inventories; in short they are the activities of operational activities. Each of them produces financial information that has to be captured, processed and analyzed in financial information systems. In online businesses, operational transactions are automatically recorded on inbuilt digital platforms that bridge operations and accounting systems.

According to Shinkevich, Kudryavtseva, and Samarina (2023), digital financial ecosystems are systems of interconnected technological systems that help organizations to organize financial operations more effectively.

Digital business ecosystems support the cooperation of organizations with external partners as well. According to Götz, Buck, Rosemann, and Meckl (2022), the digital ecosystems imply the relationship between the enterprises, service providers, and technological platforms via common information infrastructures. Financial information produced in a single organization can interface with other systems, like banking networks, payment systems, and supplier management systems.

According to Osiyevskyy, Umantsiv, and Biliavska (2023), digital ecosystems are a novel organization of the economy when businesses conduct their operations via digital networks that organize the information flows and the economic processes. The main element of such network is financial data ecosystems since financial information is the quantitative basis of assessing economic activities and organizational performance.

Regulation is a further significant factor: Rhodes and Zhou (2026) note that organizations in digital ecosystems must respect regulatory systems governing data privacy, financial transparency, and reporting standards, which requires financial information systems capable of generating reliable reports and safeguarding financial data.

Figure 2. Digital Financial Data Ecosystem among Enterprises.

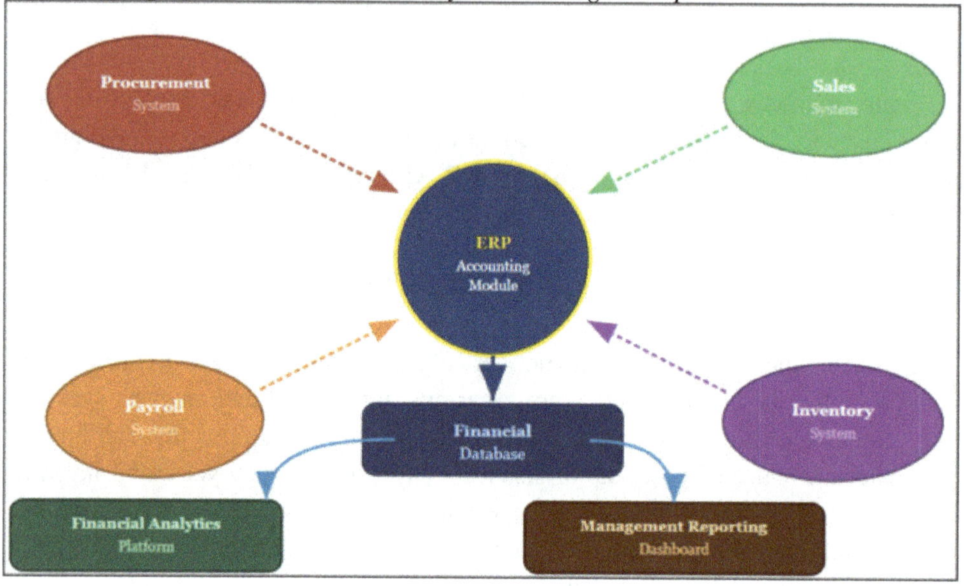

Figure 2 shows the flow of financial information in a digital enterprise ecosystem.

1.3 Significance of Financial Data Quality to Organization

The quality of financial data is a major determinant of the success of financial information management systems. Financial information is important because organizations use it to measure financial performance, plan resources, analyze investment opportunities and achieve regulatory reporting obligations.

According to Al-Farsi and Lee, the financial big data environments demand powerful governance systems in order to maintain a state of statistical integrity of the financial information (2025).

Empirical research also demonstrates that the quality of data has a considerable effect on the managerial decision-making process. According to Khong et al. (2023), the organizations that function in the information-rich industries tend to have better decision-making abilities when their data management systems possess high data accuracy and reliability rates.

Serra et al. (2024) also emphasize the role of contextual factors that have an impact on the way organizations handle data quality. Financial information has to be framed in organizational settings which encompass operational procedures, regulatory provisions and technological systems.

1.4 Motivation for the Study

Due to the rapid digitalization of the financial management systems, new issues connected with the financial data governance and financial reporting reliability have arisen. Companies become more dependent on complicated technological infrastructures with financial information being created by various systems that are interconnected. To handle financial information in these settings, financial systems need superior governance systems that have the ability to make financial information precise and coherent over various platforms.

Yahaya (2026) emphasizes the fact that governance frameworks in organizations are closely related to the quality of financial reporting. The presence of good governing mechanisms makes financial information liable to monitoring, validation, and verification procedures that minimise the chances of reporting mistakes or manipulation.

The other reason to study the data quality of financial data comes about due to the growing application of artificial intelligence and automated decision-support systems in financial management. According to Bondac et al. (2026), decision-support systems related to AI depend vastly on quality data.

2. THEORETICAL BASICS OF FINANCIAL DATA QUALITY AND RELIABILITY

Perceiving financial quality and reliability cannot be made without a conceptual background, which elucidates the generation, assessment, and application of financial information in contemporary digital companies. The quality of financial data has emerged as a primary concern in the management of financial information since organizations are more and more depending on the digital system to handle high amounts of financial transactions and generate analytical reports that managers use in their decision making. Financial information in these environments do not exist as standalone accounting records but as data streams that run through various organizational systems such as enterprise resource planning systems, financial analytics systems and cloud-based accounting systems.

Financial data reliability is another supplementary notion that dwells on the reliability and credibility of financial information systems. Quality financial information is one that would provide financial reports and other financial indicators to reflect the organizational operations and the financial data can be utilized by the managers, auditors and other external parties with confidence. Reliability is a concern in digital financial settings where financial data is automatically generated by integrated systems with technological infrastructure and data governance practices being essential. Organizational processes should be in place to guarantee that financial information is recorded properly, processed uniformly and avoid manipulation or computer breakdowns.

2.1 Financial Data Quality Definition

Financial data quality is the extent to which financial information provides an accurate portrayal of the economic transactions and can be utilized effectively to make decisions and determination of financial reporting. Financial data quality in digital financial systems is defined by a combination of various attributes such as accuracy, completeness, consistency, and timeliness being the main ones. All these attributes will define whether financial data can be used to conduct a credible financial analysis and managerial decisions. Failures to comply with these quality standards in financial data can lead to inaccurate financial reporting in an organization, timeliness in financial information, and decreased trust in financial information systems.

One of the most basic dimensions of the financial data quality is accuracy. The accuracy of financial data means how well financial transactions reported in different accounting periods are accurate and reliable in the underlying economic events recorded. E.g. in the case where a procurement transaction is registered in an enterprise resource planning system, the sum that is entered in the accounting module should be exactly the same amount that was being paid to the supplier. In case the recorded value is not accurate to the real transaction value as a result of input errors or system inconsistencies, the financial data will not be accurate and can result in wrong financial reporting.

The increased significance of financial data quality has contributed to the invention of dedicated tools and strategies to help monitor and assess data quality in information systems. Ehrlinger and Wöß (2022) point out that the use of data quality measurement and monitoring tools by organizations has become more and more popular because of the need to assess the reliability and completeness of organizational datasets.

Even the quality of data has emerged as a valuable methodological issue in digital data collection settings. As stated by Roehl and Harland (2022), to ensure high data quality, methodological rigor should be balanced with the privacy and ethical concerns of data collection concerning organizational or participant data.

The studies on comparisons of various data collection platforms also emphasize the significance of high standards of data quality. Douglas, Ewell, and Brauer (2023) explain that variation in data collection systems may affect the trustworthiness of data collected. Even though their study is about the data collection platforms that involve human subjects, the results depict a general principle in respect to financial information systems, i.e. quality of data collected and its management hinges on the quality and dependability of systems applied to collect and process the information.

The definition of data quality is also changing with the emerging technology like artificial intelligence and analytics of big data. According to Wang and Leem (2026), new data environments demand the use of broader data quality frameworks that can support unstructured data and other more complicated analysis situations.

2.2 Financial Data Reliability Concept

Reinhardt (2026) points out the significance of operational resilience in financial information systems, noting that reliability engineering activities like error budgeting and system monitoring cannot ensure organizations with resilient financial information processing environments.

Machine learning is also increasingly applied to financial data monitoring to detect anomalous transaction patterns indicative of fraud, and financial large language models are emerging as tools for analyzing complex financial data; both applications depend fundamentally on the reliability of the underlying data, a relationship examined in detail in Section 2.6.

2.3 Financial Data Quality Dimensions

Measuring financial data quality is generally performed by using a variety of measurement dimensions that reflect various data reliability and usability dimensions. Four main measurement constructs are of specific interest in digital financial systems and they comprise financial data precision, reporting promptness, system integration consistency, and decision-support efficiency. The constructs offer a systematic guideline on assessing the presence of financial data that underpin the successful financial management process.

Table 1. Measurement Variables and Indicators of Financial Data Quality

Construct	Measurement Indicator	Description
Financial Data Accuracy	Transaction Error Rate	Degree to which recorded financial transactions correctly represent actual business activities
Financial Data Accuracy	Data Verification Consistency	Frequency of successful validation of financial records during system checks
Reporting Timeliness	Financial Report Generation Time	Speed at which financial reports are produced after transaction recording
Reporting Timeliness	Real-Time Reporting Availability	Ability of financial systems to provide up-to-date financial information
System Integration Reliability	ERP Module Data Synchronization	Consistency of financial data across integrated ERP modules
System Integration Reliability	Cross-System Data Consistency	Alignment of financial data between operational systems and financial databases
Decision-Support Effectiveness	Financial Dashboard Usability	Extent to which financial reports support managerial decision-making
Decision-Support Effectiveness	Decision Response Time	Speed of managerial decisions based on available financial information

The table illustrates the four constructs of measurement that determine financial data quality in the digital financial systems.

Table 2. Data Sources and Sample Characteristics

Dataset	Data Source Description	System / Platform	Observations
Dataset 1 – ERP Financial Transaction Records	Financial transaction records including accounts payable, accounts receivable, payroll entries, and inventory-related financial postings extracted from enterprise accounting systems	SAP S/4HANA Financial Accounting modules	24,860 financial transactions from 18 organizations
Dataset 2 – Cloud Accounting Financial Reports	Consolidated financial reports including income statements, balance sheets, and cash flow statements generated through cloud accounting platforms	Oracle NetSuite ERP, QuickBooks Online, Zoho Books	1,240 financial reporting records from 18 organizations
Dataset 3 – Finance Professional Survey Responses	Structured survey responses from finance managers, financial analysts, and accounting supervisors responsible for financial reporting and decision-support activities	Online structured questionnaire	124 respondents
Industry Distribution	Manufacturing sector	—	46 respondents (37%)
	Retail and E-commerce sector	—	38 respondents (31%)
	Technology and Digital Services sector	—	40 respondents (32%)
Organizational Size	Medium enterprises (100–500 employees)	—	52 organizations
	Large enterprises (more than 500 employees)	—	72 organizations
Data Analysis Tools	Statistical and data processing tools used for empirical analysis	IBM SPSS Statistics Version 28; Microsoft Excel 365	Used for correlation and regression analysis

The table summarizes the same empirical datasets described in Section 3.4: 24,860 ERP transaction records from SAP S/4HANA, 1,240 financial reporting records from cloud accounting systems, and survey responses from 124 finance professionals.

According to Ridzuan and Zainon (2024), there are several data quality dimensions that are associated with big data settings: accuracy, completeness, consistency, and timeliness. Likewise, Wang et al. (2024) state that data quality frameworks should take into account technical and organizational units that have an impact on the creation and interpretation of data.

Carvalho et al. (2025) believe that the dynamic nature of the digital setting demands the new data quality models that have the potential to accommodate the emerging types of data complexity. This complexity in financial information systems is due to the combination of various operational data sources with analysis tools. Hosseinzadeh et al. (2025) also note that there is a need to have systematic data quality assessment approaches in order to have reliable data management practices in the complicated information environments.

2.4 Hypothetical Approaches to Information Quality

The idea of financial data quality can be realized through a review of theoretical views of information quality in the organizational information systems. The information quality theory describes the relationships that exist between data elements and the utility of the information to make a decision. The quality of information in the financial management situations dictates whether the financial reports can offer the right information about the financial performance of the organization.

According to Abu Afifa, Saleh and Vo Van (2025), the introduction of an enterprise resource planning system considerably increases the quality of accounting information because it consolidates the financing information throughout the business procedures. ERP systems will minimize the issue of data fragmentation and the generation of financial information will be done in a uniform manner across various units of an organization.

The effectiveness of management control systems is also dependent on the quality of information systems. As Papiorek and Hiebl (2024) show, quality information systems enhance management accounting practices because they present relevant financial indicators that can be used in the process of performance monitoring and strategic decisions.

More information about the effects of digital transformation on accounting information quality is also offered by the resource dependence theory. According to Song, Lu, and Yang (2025), digital transformation allows organizations to have access to more available information resources, hence enhancing the quality of accessible accounting information to managers.

2.5 Financial Information Quality of Digital Organizational Structures

Digital organizational models become largely dependent on the integrated financial information systems to process financial information concerning various operational processes. To ensure the financial data quality in such constructs, the type of data governance and standard data architectures is mandatory.

Figure 3. Financial Data Quality and Organization Control Conceptual Framework.

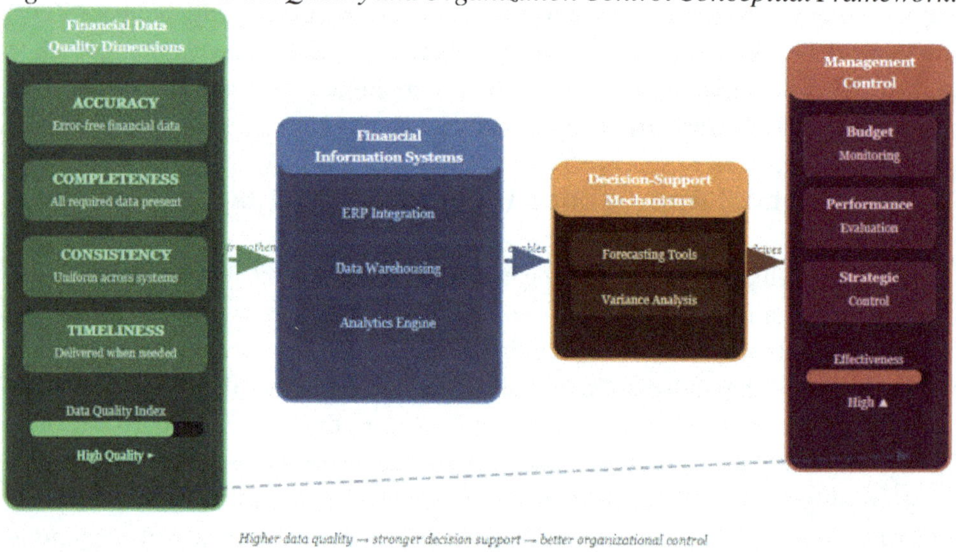

The figure 3 shows the conceptual linksage of financial data quality dimensions, financial information systems, decision-support mechanisms, and management control effectiveness.

Data governance is important in ensuring that financial data of digital organizations have the right quality. According to Karkošková (2023), it is necessary to introduce data governance model in financial institutions that would facilitate uniform data management practices within organizational systems.

Further, the authors state that financial big data ecosystems must be well governed to ensure statistical integrity and institutional accountability in financial reporting (Al-Farsi and Lee 2025). Equally, Odunayo et al. (2023) show that digital disruption of accounting information systems is a major factor that affects the quality of financial reporting; by enhancing the data integration and transparency in reporting.

The results of this research point to the fact that the quality of financial data in digital businesses is solely determined by the technological systems as well as the governance frameworks, which imply the presence of effective financial information management procedures.

2.6 Artificial Intelligence and Machine Learning in Financial Data Validation

Artificial intelligence and machine learning are increasingly embedded in the validation layer of financial information systems, extending traditional rule-based checks with adaptive, pattern-based detection. Bello, Ige, and Ameyaw (2024) show that adaptive machine learning models can analyze real-time financial transactions to flag suspicious or anomalous activity, improving both the speed and reliability of fraud detection compared with manual review. Mhaskey (2024) similarly notes that AI-enabled ERP systems can process large volumes of transactional data to identify anomalies, assess fraud risk, and generate predictive analytics that support proactive rather than reactive data governance.

Beyond transaction-level anomaly detection, AI is reshaping how financial data is interpreted and validated for downstream analysis. Yang, Liu, and Wang (2023) describe the emergence of financial large language models that can analyze complex financial data; because these models are trained and operated on the underlying data, any inaccuracies or inconsistencies in that data propagate directly into unreliable analytical outputs. Zhang, Xue, and Li (2024) reach a related conclusion, showing that AI-enabled financial decision-support systems raise specific governance and control challenges, since automated validation and analysis functions must remain auditable to satisfy both managerial and regulatory expectations.

Realizing these benefits depends on trust and transparency. Bondac et al. (2026) find that the effectiveness of AI-based decision support is conditioned on data quality as well as the transparency of a model's reasoning, since managers are unlikely to act on AI-generated flags they cannot interpret or verify. Organizations therefore need validation workflows that pair automated detection with human review, clear audit trails for AI-flagged transactions, and governance policies of the kind Papagiannidis et al. (2023) call for, so that AI-driven analytics remain accountable and explainable rather than opaque.

3. FINANCIAL INFORMATION SYSTEMS AND DECISION SUPPORT MECHANISMS

In digital-based enterprises, financial management is mainly centralized on financial information system (FIS) as it allows organizations to record financial transactions, manipulate financial information and generate analytical insights, which is used by managers to make managerial decisions. In the modern day organizations, the management of finance relies so much on the integrated technological frameworks whereby the transactions of activities in the organizations automatically create financial records.

The growing sophistication of online businesses has broadened the scope of financial information systems to time-honored accounting tasks. By combining accounting data and operational information that is produced within the organizational units, these systems have become helpful in financial forecasting, performance monitoring as well as strategic planning. Halimuzzaman et al. (2024) underline that the accounting information system provided through ERP drastically enhances financial control in the organization, as it combines the financial data with the operations. These systems minimize accounting errors and distortions in financial reporting because of automated recording of transactions and central storage of data where information is stored in a central location and is therefore accurate representation of current activities in the operations.

Also, the digital transformation has enhanced the speed and accessibility of financial reporting. According to Greg (2026), the use of ERP in real time financial reporting enables the organizations to create financial indicators of performance immediately transactions are made. Real-time reporting will help managers to keep track of financial performance and act faster on financial risks or operational inefficiencies. Likewise, Miaoquan et al. (2023) state that digital financial systems also improve the financial analysis power because they can help organizations analyze big financial data with specialized analytical software. Such advances reveal that the financial information systems have become important decision-support systems which aid managerial decision-making in electronic businesses.

3.1 Financial Information Systems of Digital Enterprises

ERP accounting modules are the main tool of recording the financial transactions. As people conduct business transactions among organizational systems, the ERP platform automatically creates respective accounting records. An example would be a procurement entry would result in accounts payable entries whereas a sales entry would result in revenue and revenue accounts receivable entries. This automated recording of the transaction makes the financial records to be in tandem with the operational activities.

The transaction records produced by ERP systems are kept in financial databases, which keep structured financial data made of financial reporting and analysis. These databases are linked to analytics platforms where financial data is processed to form performance indicators in the form of revenue trends, cost structures, and profitability measures. Managers can get these insights in the form of financial dashboards that indicate important financial indicators on which they use to make decisions.

Figure 4. The architecture of Integrated Financial information Systems.

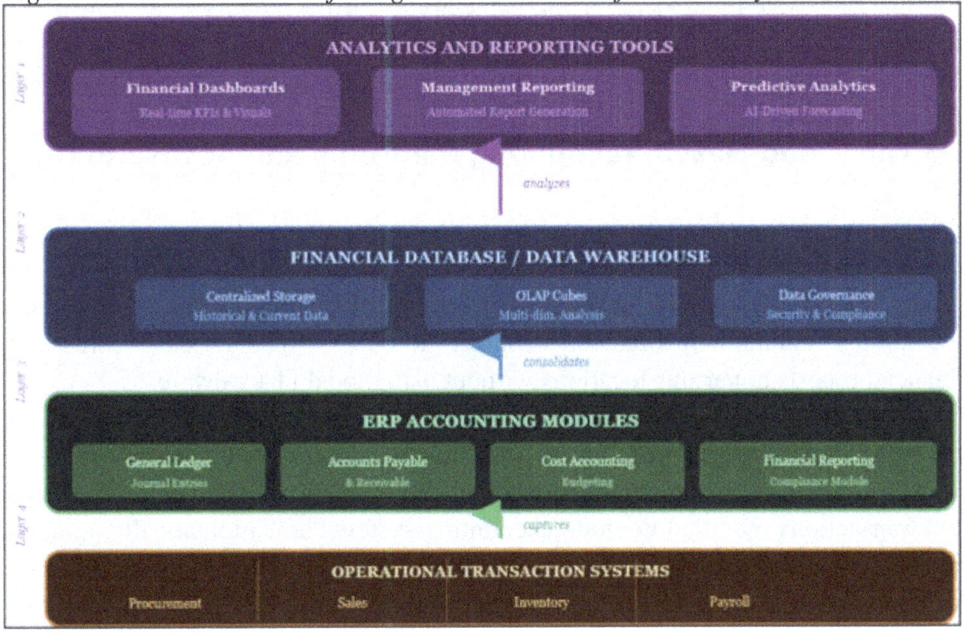

The figure 4 illustrates the structure of the financial information systems owned by digital enterprises.

3.2 Financial Data Integration and Enterprise Resource Planning Systems

Enterprise resource planning systems have a significant role to play with regard to integrating financial data in organizational processes. ERP solutions interlink business modules like procurement management, sales management, inventory management and human resource management to financial accounting modules.

This integration will provide that financial information produced by the way of the operative activities is automatically entered into accounting systems.

As Hasanudin (2024) describes, ERP implementation can be used to greatly enhance financial management efficiency due to the fact that financial data concerning various organizational units are consolidated into centralized databases. Integrated financial reports are also able to provide managers with a full picture of financial performance. Also, the ERP systems ensure standardization of accounting processes and ensure that discrepancies in accounting records are minimized.

ERP systems are also incorporating artificial intelligence to enhance financial analysis capabilities, as discussed further in Section 2.6. Halimuzzaman et al. (2024) note that ERP systems also strengthen financial control by keeping records consistent across departments and maintaining audit trails that allow transactions to be traced through organizational processes.

3.3 The Cloud-Based Accounting Platforms and Access to Data

The other major development in financial information systems is cloud-based accounting platforms. Using these platforms, financial data are stored on distant servers and the user has secure access to online financial reporting tools. Cloud accounting systems help financial managers to access financial dashboards and financial reports at various locations without using local IT hardware.

According to Limba, Sapulette, and Talla (2025), cloud-based accounting systems can be used to improve the quality of financial information by maintaining that the financial data is automatically updated by different organizational systems. Financial transactions recorded in cloud accounting systems are automatically updated and, therefore, the availability of updated financial information is made available to the authorized users. This will enhance timeliness of financial reporting and will facilitate quicker decision making.

Cloud accounting systems also enhance the accuracy of financial reporting as there is less data entry error. Oyewobi (2024) discovered that the quality of financial reporting is greater when companies introduce cloud-computing accounting systems since the potential differences between operational and accounting records are minimized through automated synchronization. Moreover, the cloud accounting solutions decrease the infrastructure expenses of smaller companies, and they enhance the effectiveness of financial reporting (Osah, 2025). According to comparative studies conducted by Gaurav and Ambar (2025), companies that operate on accounting systems that run on clouds will create financial reports faster since data processing and report generation will be done automatically in clouds.

3.4 Research Design and Data Sources

Various datasets that reflect financial transactions, financial reporting records, and managerial perceptions of the quality of financial data are the empirical analysis in this chapter. Data on financial transactions were retrieved at the ERP accounting modules deployed by the participating organizations on the SAP S/4HANA systems. These systems produced 24,860 records on financial transactions that were in form of procurement payment, sales revenue records, payroll expenses and inventory records.

The data on financial reporting was accessed on cloud accounting systems such as Oracle NetSuite, QuickBooks Online, and Zoho Books. These systems generated 1240 financial reporting records such as cash flow, balance sheets and income statements utilized by managers to undertake financial analysis. A formal survey was also implemented among 124 finance professionals working in the manufacturing, retail and technology businesses in addition to transactional and reporting data. The survey gathered managerial ratings on the quality of financial data, system integration effectiveness, and whether the financial information systems were useful in supporting decision-making activities.

3.5 Data Evaluation Instrument and Method

IBM SPSS Statistics (version 28) and Microsoft Excel 365 were used to analyze the datasets, with correlation analysis in SPSS examining the relationships between financial data accuracy, reporting timeliness, and decision-support effectiveness.

3.6 Financial Data Quality and Decision Support Variables Measurement

The empirical model assesses the quality of financial data and decision-support effectiveness through four constructs, such as the financial data accuracy, reporting timeliness, system integration reliability, and managerial decision-support effectiveness. Financial data accuracy quantifies the accuracy of the registered financial transactions as compared to the records of operational transactions. Timeliness measures how fast finances will be available to the managers after the operation transactions have been made.

Reliability in system integration is used to determine the consistency of financial data in the ERP systems and cloud accounting systems. Decision-support effectiveness is a test of the usefulness of financial information systems in supporting the managerial decision-making process.

Figure 5. Financial Data Quality and Decision Support Empirical Research Model.

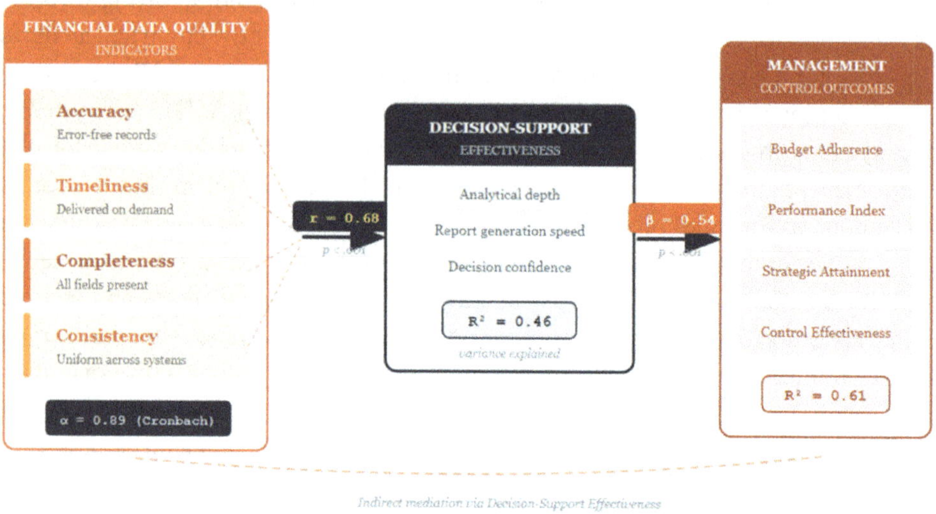

Figure 5 shows the analytical relations that are considered in the empirical model.

3.7 Industry Case Illustrations

Several documented cases illustrate how the issues discussed above play out in practice. Kusumaningtyas and Santoso's (2025) case study of DEF Limited Company shows how inconsistent data entry practices across departments slowed financial reconciliation and forced accounting staff to manually trace discrepancies between operational and financial records, an outcome the company addressed by standardizing entry procedures and introducing automated validation checks.

Cybersecurity incidents provide a further illustration. Kafi and Akter (2023) document several cases in which ransomware attacks on accounting systems disrupted financial reporting processes and compromised the integrity of financial records, in some instances forcing affected organizations to rebuild transaction histories from secondary sources before financial statements could be certified.

The dataset used in this chapter's empirical analysis (Section 3.4) offers a complementary, contemporaneous example. Organizations running SAP S/4HANA alongside cloud platforms such as Oracle NetSuite, QuickBooks Online, and Zoho Books reported markedly fewer reconciliation delays than organizations relying on standalone systems, consistent with Rachmad et al.'s (2024) finding that integrated financial information systems produce more reliable reporting than fragmented ones.

4. FINANCIAL DATA QUALITY AND MANAGEMENT CONTROL SYSTEMS

Financial information is managed to measure performance of the organization, to determine the budgetary implementation, and to secure observable alignment of operational activity with strategies of an organization by the management control systems. The financial information systems are critical in creating financial data in digital enterprises which are used in these control mechanisms. Qualitative financial information enables managers to assess financial performance indicators, determine how operations are inefficient, and track variances between projected and actual financial performance.

The quality of financial data will thus have a direct impact on the quality of management control systems. With the accuracy and promptness of financial information, managers can be confident in the financial indicators to assess performance and make corrective decisions. Nevertheless, when there are errors in financial information or a failure to report, management control systems can foster misrepresentative financial signs that undermine organizational control.

4.1 Digital Organization Management Control Systems

The management control systems of the digital organizations combine the performance monitoring processes with the financial information systems. Such systems process financial information created by ERP accounting modules and cloud accounting systems to create indicators consumed in budgeting, cost management, and profit analysis.

Figure 6. Financial Data flow within the Management Control Systems.

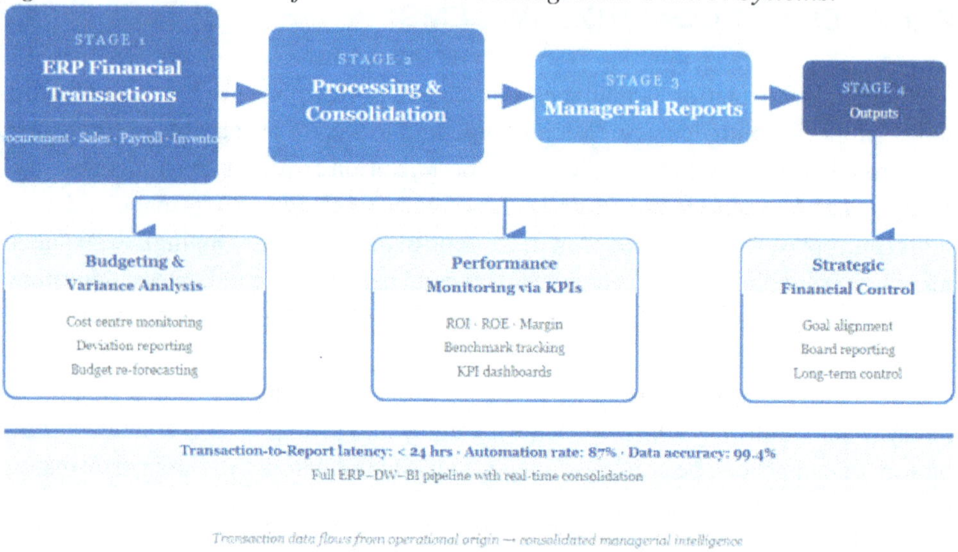

The figure 6 shows how data on financial transactions created by working systems are input into accounting modules of ERP and the transformation into financial performance indicators to be controlled by managers.

4.2 Quality of Financial Data and Decision Support Results

The quality of financial data is an important factor in the performance of the decision-support systems applied by the managers in assessing the organizational performance.

Table 3. Correlation Between Financial Data Quality Indicators and Decision Support

Variable	Financial Data Accuracy	Reporting Timeliness	Decision-Support Effectiveness
Financial Data Accuracy	1.00	0.57	0.68
Reporting Timeliness	0.57	1.00	0.61
Decision-Support Effectiveness	0.68	0.61	1.00

The correlation results show a high positive relationship between financial data accuracy and decision-support effectiveness ($r = 0.68$), and a similarly positive relationship for reporting timeliness ($r = 0.61$), indicating that accuracy and timeliness are the data-quality dimensions most closely tied to managers' use of financial information in decision-making.

4.3 Financial Quality and Budgetary Control

Budgetary control systems primarily rely on sound financial information to draw realistic financial projection and deviation between scheduled and real spending. When the organizations are using the integrated financial information systems, the financial data on which they are using in budgeting records the actual operational transactions and not the old accounting reports. This enhances better preparation of the budget and minimizes forecasting mistakes. Good financial data will enable the managers to spot the variances in the expenditures at an early stage and make changes in the operations. Financial systems based on integrated ERP thus show enhanced reliability of budgeting and better cost management practices in organizations.

4.4 Financial Data Quality and Performance Measurement

The financial indicators on which financial performance measurement systems are based include operating margins, revenue growth rates, cost efficiency ratios and return on assets in measuring the performance of the organization. The accuracy and completeness of the financial data produced by the financial information systems is the determinant of the reliability of these indicators. Performance indicators help in giving valid information about organization efficiency and profitability when the financial data is factual and consistent between systems. On the other hand, poor financial records can falsify performance indicators of the financial performance and mislead managers in interpreting financial results. Good quality financial information is thus able to consolidate better performance control systems and help managers make strategic decisions based on evidence.

4.5 Internal Controls and Financial Data Integrity

Internal control measures are very crucial in the integrity of financial data in digital businesses. These controls also make sure that the financial transactions which are registered in the enterprise system is correct, approved and documented. ERP systems have automated validation procedures that identify financial transactions upon entry into the system and reconciliation procedures that compare the records of financial transactions between operational and accounting systems. The internal audit functions also analyze financial datasets with the view to detecting inconsistencies or irregularities that could be an indication of errors or fraud.

Figure 7. Internal Control Processes that Facilitate Financial Data Integrity.

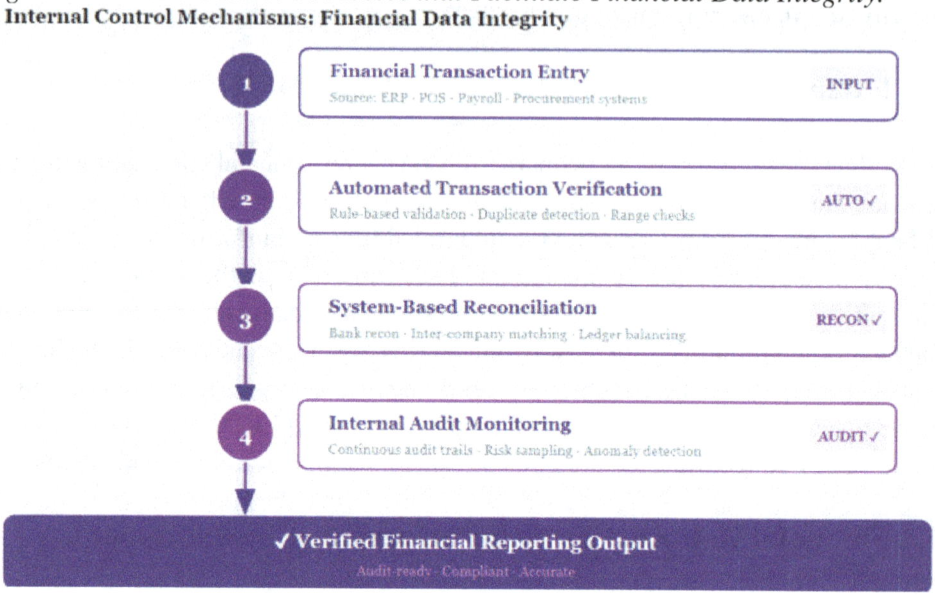

The figure 7 shows the layered control checkpoints applied to financial data: automated transaction verification at entry, cross-system reconciliation to check consistency, and internal audit monitoring to identify abnormalities and verify adherence to reporting requirements.

4.6 Financial Data Quality and Strategic Control

Strategic control mechanisms provide the test on whether the organization activities are meeting the long term financial goals. Quality financial information is fundamental to strategic control as the managers use financial performance indicators to analyze investment results, growth

Table 4. Regression Results: Financial Data Quality and Management Control Outcomes

Predictor Variable	Dependent Variable	Standardized Coefficient (β)	Significance Level
Financial Data Accuracy	Management Control Effectiveness	0.54	$p < 0.01$
Reporting Timeliness	Budgeting Reliability	0.42	$p < 0.05$
System Integration Reliability	Management Control Effectiveness	0.37	$p < 0.05$

The regression results show that management control effectiveness is strongly predicted by financial data accuracy ($\beta = 0.54$, $p < 0.01$), with reporting timeliness also positively associated with budgeting reliability ($\beta = 0.42$, $p < 0.05$).

5. CHALLENGES IN ENSURING RELIABLE FINANCIAL DATA

Digital businesses are based on the integrated financial information system to create the valid financial reports and assist with the managerial decision-making. Nevertheless, to guarantee the integrity of financial information in such systems, there are various operational and technological challenges. Financial information is created in various interlinked systems which include ERP system, procurement system, customer relationship management system and cloud accounting system. These systems should work in unison to have financial records to be in sync and all the records be futile throughout organizational processes.

5.1 Data Integration and Interoperability Problems of the System

Tomar and Periyasamy (2023) note that inconsistencies in reference data can be one of the significant hindrances of financial data analysis as various systems can classify financial transactions based on data structures that cannot be matched. As an illustration, payments to suppliers made on procurement systems can not conform to accounting categories made in ERP modules resulting to differences between financial reporting. These inconsistencies would need further reconciliation tools to make sure that financial records depicted the organizational transactions.

Empirical studies also show that the quality of financial reports is greatly influenced by the connection between the financial information systems and internal control systems as well as information technology infrastructure. Rachmad et al. (2024) discovered that organizations having well-integrated financial information systems generate financially reliable financial reports, as the integrated systems help organizations to maintain financial data consistency across the platforms of operations and accounting. On the other hand, the delay in the financial reporting of organizations in which information systems are fragmented is characterized by the issues of data synchronization.

The problem of interoperability is especially apparent in the context of the financial management systems of the public sector where various agencies are operating on different financial reporting systems. According to Pasape and Godson (2022), local government administrators deploying financial management information systems usually face integration issues since various departments have their own data systems, all of which are not fully compatible with centralized financial reporting systems. These interoperability challenges not only take long in reporting financial performance, but also in monitoring financial performance.

Azevedo et al. (2025) similarly note that improving interoperability is itself a key milestone in digital transformation, since standardizing financial data formats and data-exchange protocols helps organizations improve reporting efficiency and reduce discrepancies between operational and financial data systems.

5.2 Data Entry Errors and Process Inefficiency

As Kusumaningtyas and Santoso (2025) show, data entry procedures have a major impact on the Corporate administrative processes. Any missing or inaccurate transaction records may slow down the financial reconciliation activity as the accounting departments need to search the reasons behind operational records and financial statements differences. Even minor errors in data entry can be combined and create serious discrepancies in financial data when organizations take large amounts of financial transactions a day.

Financial data quality problems are also caused by business process inefficiencies. According to Ekasari et al. (2022), the poorly developed business processes frequently lead to duplications of the financial data management system. To illustrate, when various departments record, but in a non-standardized manner, the same financial transactions, duplicate records in financial databases could be found. These irregularities make financial reporting difficult and involve more verification procedures.

Financial automation is one of the practical approaches to minimizing the error of data entry and enhancing the level of accounting accuracy. According to Hashin and Wan Fauzi (2025), automated financial systems decrease the operational risks through lessening manual data input and system-based verification processes.

5.3 Data Security and Cyber Risks

According to Shafa and Islam (2025), data privacy and cybersecurity have become a major constituent of the contemporary accounting information systems. The information stored in the enterprise systems in financial data is sensitive in nature and is associated with the organizational transactions, financial performance and strategic investments. To prevent the use of this information by unauthorized individuals, it is imperative to have effective cybersecurity systems which would comprise of encryption systems, access controls and monitoring systems.

Accounting databases are among the primary targets of cyberattack; the ransomware cases documented by Kafi and Akter (2023) and discussed in Section 3.7

illustrate how such attacks can cause organizations to lose access to financial records or suffer losses through data manipulation.

The role of cyber risk management is thus becoming very critical in financial data governance. As Livanis, Doumpos, and Zopounidis (2023) emphasize, financial institutions should establish frameworks of cybersecurity risk management that assess the possible vulnerabilities of financial information systems and create ways to address the vulnerability.

This shift is increasingly reflected in regulatory expectations as well: financial regulators are extending reporting and internal-control obligations to explicitly cover data security, meaning that cybersecurity failures now carry compliance as well as operational consequences and reinforcing the governance frameworks discussed in Section 6.

Figure 8. The Risk Factors which influence the Financial Data Reliability.

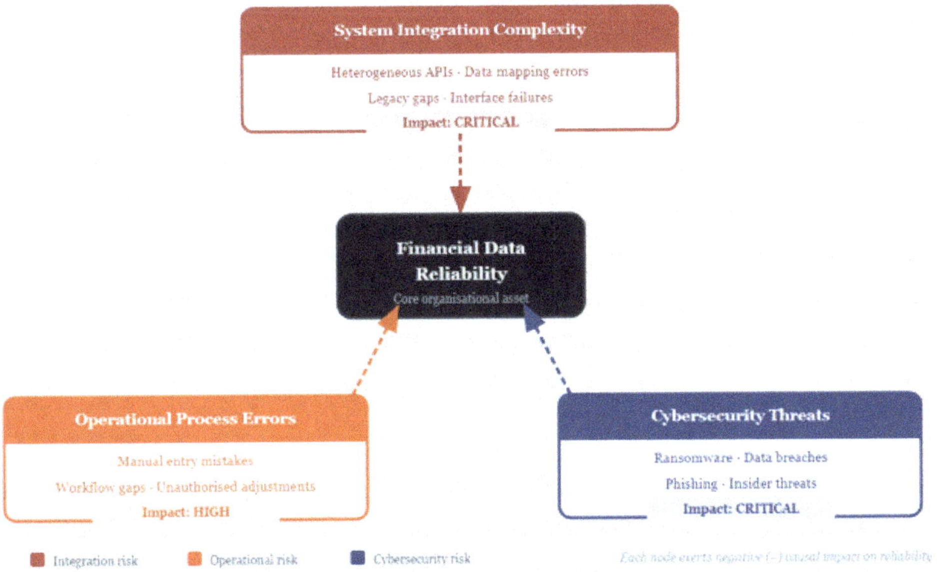

The figure 8 groups the risks affecting financial data reliability into three categories: system integration complexity, operational process errors from manual data entry, and cybersecurity threats such as unauthorized access, data breaches, and ransomware attacks.

5.4 Data Governance Problems and System Complexity

Kothandapani (2022) points out that the financial data governance models are necessary to manage financial data stored in a large-scale data repository like enterprise data lakes. The policies are outlined in these structures to determine how data is accessed, what data is validated, and what data undergoes the regulatory reports. Organizations can instill appropriate governance rules that will make sure that financial data is accurate and consistent used in reporting and analysis.

The problem of managing financial data in multi-clouds poses more governance issues. According to Katari and Ankam (2022), the future of financial services involves the storing of financial data by financial services organizations on various cloud systems to enhance the scalability and performance of the systems. Nonetheless, system administration in distributed cloud environments demands robust governance frameworks that guarantee consistency and security of data in all platforms.

5.5 Reporting and Regulatory Compliance

There are various financial reporting regulations that digital enterprises are obligated to adhere to with the aim of ensuring accountability and transparency, in financial reporting. Global accounting principles have been put in place by the International Financial Reporting Standards (IFRS) with references to the preparation of financial statements. The Sarbanes Oxley Act (SOX) demands organizations to have internal control systems that are used to verify the reliability of financial reporting. Moreover, companies have to have internal audit mechanisms that ensure that financial information relied upon to make decisions and report erroneously is accurate.

Rachmad et al. (2024) note that the organizations with integrated financial information systems have a higher level of adherence to financial reporting regulations due to the availability of automated accounting systems that impose standardization of financial reporting practices. Audit trails are also maintained in integrated financial systems that enable auditors to follow or trace financial transactions to their source of operations, to financial statements.

Olajide et al. (2024) also emphasize that global supply chains pose more regulatory challenges since organizations based in various areas of operation are required to abide by various financial reporting standards and regulatory framework. Regulatory compliance thus involves having financial information systems that can keep proper records of financial information whilst supporting reporting needs in a wide range of a regulatory environment.

Data-privacy regulation adds a further layer of compliance risk that intersects directly with the cybersecurity concerns discussed in Section 5.3. As financial systems capture and store increasing volumes of personal and transactional data, frameworks such as the EU's General Data Protection Regulation (GDPR) impose obligations around data access, retention, and breach notification that financial information systems must be designed to satisfy.

6. GOVERNANCE AND BEST PRACTICES

Organizations practicing good financial data governance are in a better position to deal with the complexity of digital financial ecosystem. Governance mechanisms specify financial data management responsibilities, data structure standardization, as well as the implementation of monitoring mechanism that identifies the data anomalies or security threats. Through the integration of governance and the use of advanced technological solutions, it is possible to enhance the reliability of financial data and enhance the process of making financial decisions within an organization.

6.1 Financial Data Governance Frameworks

Financial data governance schemes establish rules that control the ownership, accountability, and reporting principles of financial data in the organizations. These structures define the roles and duties of financial data management and ascertained that financial information systems are run under standardized processes.

Papagiannidis et al. (2023) emphasize that there is a need to have good governance frameworks in place to handle advanced technologies like the artificial intelligence and digital analytics systems. Governance policies help in ensuring the existence of data-driven technologies that run in a transparent way and give sufficient analytical results.

Because digital financial ecosystems evolve quickly, static governance rules can become outdated. Nookala (2024) makes the case for adaptive data governance frameworks that can adjust as organizational data environments and technologies change, rather than treating governance as a fixed, one-time policy exercise, an approach particularly relevant to institutions integrating the AI-based analytics and validation tools discussed in Section 2.6.

6.2 Data Quality Management Strategies

Companies have to adopt systematic methods of ensuring data quality in financial systems throughout the enterprise information systems. Data validation processes are the means to make sure that the financial transactions in accounting systems are accurate to the predetermined criteria. Reconciliation procedures are processes that compare financial documents in operational and accounting systems in order to identify differences.

Adepoju et al. (2023) note that big data governance programs should also entail the mechanisms of minimizing the data redundancy and enhancing the process of data validation. Constant monitoring of financial data will enable organizations to detect anomalies in their data and rectify errors prior to the production of financial reports.

Miller et al. (2025) also emphasize the significance of structured data quality frameworks specifying standardized ways of quantifying and enhancing data quality within the organization systems.

6.3 Financial Data Processes Standardization

The interoperability between enterprise financial systems is greatly enhanced by standardizing financial data structure and reporting formats. Standard financial data models make sure that financial transactions that are registered in various systems are classified in a similar manner.

6.4 Technology-Based Solutions on the Reliability of Data

There is also the use of technological solutions to enhance the reliability of financial data. Automated reconciliation systems analyze financial records in systems and identify anomalies in financial data sets. Financial analytics applications process financial data to determine anomalies or other patterns of transactions.

Biagi and Russo (2022) note that information systems in enterprises can be effectively monitored with the help of data-driven governance technologies. In the same vein, McNulty, Miglionico, and Milne (2023) elaborate that contemporary financial regulations are becoming more and more based on digital technologies of accessing data that assist the regulators to oversee the financial activity with greater efficacy.

6.5 Organizational Roles and Responsibilities

Naguib, Kassem, and Naem (2024) point out that IT governance and data governance that are well coordinated helps enhance organizational performance greatly. Marcucci et al. (2023) also emphasize that the presence of clear governance roles will ensure that organizations have clear and responsible data management practices.

7. MANAGER IMPLICATION

Sharairi et al. (2024) also highlight that proper financial decision-making in contemporary organizations should be based on appropriate data governance systems that regulate the collection, processing, and analysis of financial data. Financial managers should thus adopt data validation processes and data reconciliation systems that would help to keep financial records to be correct and should reflect transactions conducted in the operations. Moreover, the financial managers should work with information technology teams to guarantee that the enterprise financial systems run as per the standard data management policies.

Compliance with regulations and financial transparency is also facilitated by financial data governance. Arner, Castellano, and Selga (2022) emphasize that the governance structures present in the roles of financial data management are the keys to the reliable financial reporting mechanisms. Financial managers can enhance the financial monitoring systems and enhance financial planning procedures in the organizations by concentrating on the accuracy of financial data and ensuring timelines of reporting the data.

Choowan and Daovisan (2025) find that governance frameworks supported by advanced analytics improve financial decision-making because the underlying datasets can be treated as reliable and well-organized, while Elugbaju, Okeke, and Alabi (2024) show that data-driven governance empowers decision-making by giving managers organized financial data to assess performance and plan future initiatives. Governance capacity also supports digital transformation: Yu, Chen, and Xu (2025) find that robust data governance helps organizations adopt digital technologies in financial management, and Aro (2024) adds that analytics tools support this by helping organizations track performance trends and evaluate digital innovation.

8. CONCLUSION

8.1 Summary of Key Insights

This chapter examined the importance of financial data quality and reliability for financial information management and management control in digital enterprises, showing that financial information systems are critical infrastructure for producing the financial facts organizations rely on for decision-making, as transactions generated by operational processes are captured in integrated ERP and cloud-based accounting systems and transformed into structured data for reporting and analysis.

The chapter has brought out the fact that financial data quality, which is accurate, complete, consistent and timely, can greatly affect the efficacy of financial decision-support mechanisms. Empirical data indicated that financial data quality indicators were strongly related to decision-support effectiveness, indicating that organizations that have the right and timely financial data have a better financial surveillance and managerial decision outcomes. Quality financial information also enhances the management control systems through enhancement of budgetary systems, performance monitoring systems and strategic planning ability.

8.2 Research Future Direction

Future studies can build on this chapter by examining how advanced technologies, particularly machine learning and artificial intelligence, can further support financial data management, and how these technologies affect financial data governance and reporting accuracy over time.

A related opportunity lies in strategic decision-making supported by advanced financial analytics: research is needed on how analytics tools capable of processing large financial datasets can be integrated into financial information systems to strengthen decision-support mechanisms.

REFERENCES

Abu Afifa, M., Saleh, I., & Vo Van, H. (2025). Accounting information quality in the digital era–a perspective from ERP system adoption? *Global Knowledge, Memory and Communication, 74*(5-6), 2022–2046. DOI: 10.1108/GKMC-03-2023-0101

Adepoju, A. H., Austin-Gabriel, B., Eweje, A., & Hamza, O. (2023). A data governance framework for high-impact programs: Reducing redundancy and enhancing data quality at scale. *International Journal of Multidisciplinary Research and Growth Evaluation, 4*(6), 1141–1154. DOI: 10.54660/.IJMRGE.2023.4.6.1141-1154

Al-Farsi, N., & Lee, B. (2025). Governing Financial Big Data Ecosystems: Data Quality, Statistical Integrity, and Institutional Accountability in Monetary and Financial Statistics. *European Journal of Emerging Data Science and Machine Learning, 2*(02), 1–6.

Arner, D. W., Castellano, G. G., & Selga, E. K. (2022). Financial Data Governance. *The Hastings Law Journal, 74*, 235.

Aro, O. E.Opeyemi E Aro. (2024). Data analytics as a driver of digital transformation in financial institutions. *World Journal of Advanced Research and Reviews, 24*(1), 1054–1072. DOI: 10.30574/wjarr.2024.24.1.3124

Azevedo, R. R. D., Lino, A. F., Carrara, L. G. C., Aquino, A. C. B. D., & Cardoso, R. L. (2025). Interoperability of financial management systems in local governments and opportunities for digital transformation. *Revista de Administração Pública, 59*(2), e2024–e0249. DOI: 10.1590/0034-761220240249x

. Bello, H. O., Ige, A. B., & Ameyaw, M. N. (2024). Adaptive machine learning models: concepts for real-time financial fraud prevention in dynamic environments. *World Journal of Advanced Engineering Technology and Sciences, 12*(02), 021-034.

Biagi, V., & Russo, A. (2022). Data model design to support data-driven IT governance implementation. *Technologies, 10*(5), 106. DOI: 10.3390/technologies10050106

Bondac, G. T., Stanescu, S. G., Ionescu, C. A., Duica, A., & Uzlău, M. C. (2026). Decision-Making in Complex Systems Using AI-Based Decision Support: The Role of Trust, Transparency, and Data Quality. *Electronics (Basel), 15*(2), 372. DOI: 10.3390/electronics15020372

Carvalho, A. M., Soares, S., Montenegro, J., & Conceição, L. (2025). Data Quality: Revisiting dimensions towards new framework development. *Procedia Computer Science, 253*, 247–256. DOI: 10.1016/j.procs.2025.01.088

Challoumis, C. (2024, October). The evolution of financial systems-AI'S role in reshaping money management. In *XVI International Scientific Conference* (pp. 128-151).

Choowan, P., & Daovisan, H. (2025). Artificial Intelligence in Data Governance for Financial Decision-Making: A Systematic Review. *Big Data and Cognitive Computing, 10*(1), 8. DOI: 10.3390/bdcc10010008

Douglas, B. D., Ewell, P. J., & Brauer, M. (2023). Data quality in online human-subjects research: Comparisons between MTurk, Prolific, CloudResearch, Qualtrics, and SONA. *PLoS One, 18*(3), e0279720. DOI: 10.1371/journal.pone.0279720

Ehrlinger, L., & Wöß, W. (2022). A survey of data quality measurement and monitoring tools. *Frontiers in Big Data, 5*, 850611. DOI: 10.3389/fdata.2022.850611

Ekasari, K., Eltivia, N., Pratama, B. B., & Azizah, N. (2022). Improving the quality of business processes with Financial information systems. *International Journal of Informatics, Economics. Management Science, 1*(2), 125–135.

. Elugbaju, W. K., Okeke, N. I., & Alabi, O. A. (2024). Conceptual framework for enhancing decision-making in higher education through data-driven governance. *Global Journal of Advanced Research and Reviews, 2*(02), 016-030.

Gaurav, A., & Ambar, M. T. (2025). Cloud-Based Accounting Systems and Financial Reporting Efficiency: A Comparative Review. [IJARMT]. *International Journal of Advanced Research and Multidisciplinary Trends, 2*(1), 882–893.

Götz, F., Buck, C., Rosemann, M., & Meckl, R. (2022). Digital business ecosystems: a comparison of different industries. In *Handbook on digital business ecosystems* (pp. 530–548). Edward Elgar Publishing. DOI: 10.4337/9781839107191.00043

. Greg, J. (2026). ERP-enabled real-time financial reporting.

Halimuzzaman, M., Sharma, J., Karim, M. R., Hossain, M. R., Azad, M. A. K., & Alam, M. M. (2024). Enhancement of Organizational Accounting Information Systems and Financial Control through Enterprise Resource Planning. In *Synergy of AI and Fintech in the Digital Gig Economy* (pp. 315–331). CRC Press. DOI: 10.1201/9781032720104-20

. Hasanudin, H. (2024). Optimizing the implementation of enterprise resource planning (ERP) in company financial management. *Jurnal Ekonomi, Akuntasi dan manajemen Indonesia (JEAMI), 2*(02), 104-114.

. Hashin, N. Q., & Wan Fauzi, W. N. A. (2025). Enhancing accounting accuracy and efficiency by automating financial processes to mitigate risks. *Accounting Insights Compilation books: A Compilation of Students Practical Papers, 1*, 112-115.

Hosseinzadeh, E., Afkanpour, M., Momeni, M., & Tabesh, H. (2025). Data quality assessment in healthcare, dimensions, methods and tools: A systematic review. *BMC Medical Informatics and Decision Making, 25*(1), 296. DOI: 10.1186/s12911-025-03136-y

Kafi, M. A., & Akter, N. (2023). Securing financial information in the digital realm: Case studies in cybersecurity for accounting data protection. *American Journal of Trade and Policy, 10*(1), 15–26. DOI: 10.18034/ajtp.v10i1.659

Karkošková, S. (2023). Data governance model to enhance data quality in financial institutions. *Information Systems Management, 40*(1), 90–110. DOI: 10.1080/10580530.2022.2042628

Katari, A., & Ankam, M. (2022). Data governance in multi-cloud environments for financial services: Challenges and solutions. [IJMCER]. *Educational Research, 4*(1), 339–353.

Khong, I., Yusuf, N. A., Nuriman, A., & Yadila, A. B. (2023). Exploring the impact of data quality on decision-making processes in information intensive organizations. *APTISI Transactions on Management, 7*(3), 253–260. DOI: 10.33050/atm.v7i3.2138

Kothandapani, H. P. (2022). Optimizing financial data governance for improved risk management and regulatory reporting in data lakes. *International Journal of Applied Machine Learning and Computational Intelligence, 12*(4), 41–63.

Kusumaningtyas, F., & Santoso, B. (2025). Data Entry Contribution to Efficient Corporate Administration-A Case Study of DEF Limited Company. [IJEEFA]. *International Journals of Energy Economics and Financial Analysis, 1*(2), 20–26.

Lim, W. M., Kumar, S., Pandey, N., Verma, D., & Kumar, D. (2023). Evolution and trends in consumer behaviour: Insights from Journal of Consumer Behaviour. *Journal of Consumer Behaviour, 22*(1), 217–232. DOI: 10.1002/cb.2118

Limba, F. B., Sapulette, S. G., & Talla, A. (2025). The Role Of Cloud-Based Accounting Systems In Enhancing Financial Information Quality. *International Journal of Finance & Economics, 2*(3), 895–913.

Livanis, E., Doumpos, M., & Zopounidis, C. (2023). Financial analysis and management of cyber risk. In *Handbook of Research on Artificial Intelligence, Innovation and Entrepreneurship* (pp. 255-271). Edward Elgar Publishing. DOI: 10.4337/9781839106750.00027

Marcucci, S., Alarcón, N. G., Verhulst, S. G., & Wüllhorst, E. (2023). Informing the global data future: Benchmarking data governance frameworks. *Data & Policy*, *5*, e30. DOI: 10.1017/dap.2023.24

McNulty, D., Miglionico, A., & Milne, A. (2023). Data access technologies and the 'New Governance'techniques of financial regulation. *Journal of Financial Regulation*, *9*(2), 225–248. DOI: 10.1093/jfr/fjad008

Mhaskey, S. V. (2024). Integration of artificial intelligence (AI) in enterprise resource planning (ERP) systems: Opportunities, challenges, and implications. *International Journal of Computer Engineering in Research Trends*, *11*(12), 1–9. DOI: 10.22362/ijcert/2024/v11/i12/v11i1201

Miaoquan, X., Yu, K. W., Xuewen, L., Yi, W., Jun, Y., & Loang, O. K. (2023). The impact of digital transformation on financial reporting and analysis in the accounting industry. *The International Journal of Accounting*, *8*(50), 324–336.

Miller, R., Chan, S. H. M., Whelan, H., & Gregório, J. (2025). A comparison of data quality frameworks: A review. *Big Data and Cognitive Computing*, *9*(4), 93. DOI: 10.3390/bdcc9040093

Naguib, H. M., Kassem, H. M., & Naem, A. E. H. M. A. (2024). The impact of IT governance and data governance on financial and non-financial performance. *Future Business Journal*, *10*(1), 15. DOI: 10.1186/s43093-024-00300-0

Nookala, G. (2024). Adaptive data governance frameworks for data-driven digital transformations. *Journal of Computational Innovation*, *4*(1).

Odunayo, J., Akintoye, R. I., Aguguom, T. A., Sanyaolu, A. W., Omobowale, A., & Osunusi, K. A. (2023). Digital disruption of accounting information and quality of financial reporting of listed money deposit banks in Nigeria. *International Journal of Applied Economics. Finance and Accounting*, *17*(2), 337–352.

Olajide, J. O., Otokiti, B. O., Nwani, S., Ogunmokun, A. S., Adekunle, B. I., & Fiemotongha, J. E. (2024). A regulatory compliance model for financial reporting across global supply chain functions. *International Journal of Scientific Research in Science and Technology*, *11*(4), 619–635. DOI: 10.32628/IJSRST241151217

. OSAH, A. A. (2025). Impact of cloud-based accounting software on financial management efficiency in small firm businesses in port harcourt. *INTERNATIONAL JOURNAL OF ECONOMICS, FINANCE, ACCOUNTING AND MANAGEMENT*, *1*(2), 67-77.

. Osiyevskyy, O., Umantsiv, Y., & Biliavska, Y. (2023). Digital ecosystem: A mechanism of economic organization of enterprises of the future.

. Oyewobi, I. A. (2024). Cloud-based accounting information systems and financial reporting quality of listed information and communication technology firms in Nigeria.

Papagiannidis, E., Enholm, I. M., Dremel, C., Mikalef, P., & Krogstie, J. (2023). Toward AI governance: Identifying best practices and potential barriers and outcomes. *Information Systems Frontiers*, *25*(1), 123–141. DOI: 10.1007/s10796-022-10251-y

Papiorek, K. L., & Hiebl, M. R. (2024). Information systems quality in management accounting and management control effectiveness. *Journal of Accounting & Organizational Change*, *20*(3), 433–458. DOI: 10.1108/JAOC-09-2022-0148

. Pasape, L., & Godson, E. (2022). Challenges affecting effective implementation of financial management information systems in local government authorities in Tanzania as part of the digital ecosystem.

Rachmad, Y. E., Bakri, A. A., Irdiana, S., Waromi, J., & Sinlae, A. A. J. (2024). Analysis of the influence of financial information systems, internal control systems, and information technology on quality of financial reports. *Jurnal Informasi Dan Teknologi*, *6*(1), 266–271. DOI: 10.60083/jidt.v6i1.513

Reinhardt, L. (2026). A Holistic Framework for Operational Resilience: Error Budgeting Strategies in Financial Site Reliability Engineering. *Academic Reseach Library for International Journal of Economics Finance & Management Science*, *11*(01), 61–66.

. Rhodes, A., Zhou, J., & Zhou, J. (2026). Digital ecosystems and data regulation.

Ridzuan, F., & Zainon, W. M. N. W. (2024). A review on data quality dimensions for big data. *Procedia Computer Science*, *234*, 341–348. DOI: 10.1016/j.procs.2024.03.008

Roehl, J. M., & Harland, D. J. (2022). Imposter participants: Overcoming methodological challenges related to balancing participant privacy with data quality when using online recruitment and data collection. *The Qualitative Report*, *27*(11), 2469–2485. DOI: 10.46743/2160-3715/2022.5475

Serra, F., Peralta, V., Marotta, A., & Marcel, P. (2024). Use of context in data quality management: A systematic literature review. *ACM Journal of Data and Information Quality*, *16*(3), 1–41. DOI: 10.1145/3672082

Shafa, H., & Islam, A. (2025). Impact of data privacy and cybersecurity in accounting information systems on financial transparency. *International Journal of Scientific Interdisciplinary Research*, *6*(1), 254–292. DOI: 10.63125/xs0xt970

Sharairi, J. A., Saatchi, S. G., Rahahle, M. Y., Maabreh, H. M. A., Sarram, M., Anagreh, S., & Al-Hawary, S. I. S. (2024). How big data governance meets financial decision-making: evidence from banking sector in emerging economies. In *Artificial Intelligence and Economic Sustainability in the Era of Industrial Revolution 5.0* (pp. 1295–1311). Springer Nature Switzerland. DOI: 10.1007/978-3-031-56586-1_94

Sharma, R., & Sharma, C. (2025). *The evolution of finance and controlling: SAP and intelligent systems*. World Journal of Advanced Research and Reviews.

Shinkevich, A. I., Kudryavtseva, S. S., & Samarina, V. P. (2023). Ecosystems as an Innovative Tool for the Development of the Financial Sector in the Digital Economy. *Journal of Risk and Financial Management, 16*(2), 72. DOI: 10.3390/jrfm16020072

Song, H., Lu, Y., & Yang, Z. (2025). Digital Transformation of Enterprises and Accounting Information Quality: A Resource Dependence Theory Perspective. *Emerging Markets Finance & Trade*, •••, 1–17.

Tomar, M., & Periyasamy, V. (2023). The role of reference data in financial data analysis: Challenges and opportunities. *Journal of Knowledge Learning and Science Technology ISSN: 2959-6386 (online), 1*(1), 90-99.

Wang, J., Liu, Y., Li, P., Lin, Z., Sindakis, S., & Aggarwal, S. (2024). Overview ofdata quality: Examining the dimensions, antecedents, and impacts of data quality. *Journal of the Knowledge Economy, 15*(1), 1159–1178. DOI: 10.1007/s13132-022-01096-6

Wang, N., & Leem, S. G. (2026). *Modernizing Data Quality: Evolving Dimensions for Unstructured Text Data in Big Data*. AI and Ethical Contexts.

Yahaya, O. A. (2026). Does board gender diversity affect financial reporting quality in Nigeria. *Journal of Accounting and Finance Research, 21*(1), 716–769.

Yang, H., Liu, X. Y., & Wang, C. D. (2023). Fingpt: Open-source financial large language models. *arXiv preprint arXiv:2306.06031*. DOI: 10.2139/ssrn.4489826

Yu, Y., Chen, H., & Xu, N. (2025). Data governance, financial environmental regulation, and enterprise digital transformation. *Finance Research Letters*, 109274.

Zhang, J., Xue, R., & Li, H. (2024). Artificial intelligence–enabled financial decision support systems: Implications for governance and control. *Journal of Information Systems, 38*(1), 35–52.

Chapter 4
Data Governance and Financial Control Systems in Digital Enterprises:
Managing Financial Information Flows for Strategic Decision-Making

Annaev Umidjon
Termez University of Economics and Service, Termez, Uzbekistan

Ravikumar R. N.
http://orcid.org/0009-0009-3705-1681
Jain (Deemed to be) University, Bangalore, India

S. Aarthi
http://orcid.org/0009-0006-9064-2091
Marwadi University, Rajkot, India

Ismailov Azizbek
Alfraganus University, Tashkent, Uzbekistan

Dadaboev Umidjon
Tashkent State University of Economics, Tashkent, Uzbekistan

Akmal Allakuliev
Kimyo International University in Tashkent, Tashkent, Uzbekistan

ABSTRACT

Digital businesses are becoming more and more dependent on interconnected systems to create, process and analyze financial information, which allows them to gain real-time information but presents a set of challenges regarding data quality, governance and control. This chapter discusses the combination of data governance structures and financial control systems to control financial information flows. An abstract model is offered which connects the governance structure, data flow processes and control mechanisms to guarantee accuracy, transparency and regulatory compliance.

DOI: 10.4018/979-8-3373-9230-1.ch004

© 2027, IGI Global Scientific Publishing. Copying or distributing in print or electronic forms without written permission of IGI Global Scientific Publishing is prohibited. Use of this chapter to train generative artificial intelligence (AI) technologies is expressly prohibited. The publisher reserves all rights to license its use for generative AI training and machine learning model development.

Using the new ERP and cloud-based finance cases evidence, the chapter shows how integrated systems enhance the reliability of reporting, efficiency of operations and risk management. The results emphasize that integrated governance and control processes are needed to convert financial information into credible, practical knowledge to drive strategic decisions and sustainable business performance.

1. INTRODUCTION

Organizations are in a rapid transformation period as they evolve into a digitally facilitated business, thus, changing the ways financial data is produced, processed and used. Finance data is no longer limited to the conventional accounting system, but is dynamically moved between the integrated systems, including Enterprise Resource Planning (ERP) systems, financial applications in the cloud and the existing analytics environment. This change has accelerated financial reporting speed, accuracy and accessibility and provided the real-time decision-making possibilities. But it has brought about complexities that involve data consistency, governance and control as well (Majstorovic et al., 2020). Organizations presently need to make sure that distributed systems have reliable, secure and compliant financial information. In this regard, the data governance and financial control systems have been critical mechanisms in controlling financial flows of information. They offer frameworks to guarantee data integrity, accountability, and facilitate strategic decision-making across the digital ecosystems which are becoming more complex.

1.1 Digital Finance Context

Digital finance Digital finance is the incorporation of the latest technologies in financial management systems that allow automation and real-time reporting, as well as making decisions based on data. The contemporary businesses operate with interrelated systems like ERP, cloud accounting software, and data warehouses to handle financial transactions and reporting processes. With the help of these systems, financial data can be produced and processed in real-time, which helps to make timely conclusions about the performance of the organization. The integration of digital finance tools has led to increased efficiency in operations by eliminating manual operations and improving data quality (Singhania et al., 2025). Besides, analytics and Artificial Intelligence can be used to conduct predictive financial planning and risk assessment. However, increased amount and speed of financial information must have powerful systems in place to ensure uniformity and dependability (Bisht et al., 2022). Without a proper management, digital finance environments may pose fragmented information, disparities, and increased vulnerability to mistakes and risk, which highlights the necessity to embrace organized data management culture.

1.2 Data Governance Need

Increasing complexity of digital financial landscapes has introduced data governance as an important organizational need. Data governance refers to policies, standards, roles, and processes that provide the data with a proper management throughout its lifecycle. Governance in the financial aspect makes sure that the data is accurate, consistent, secure and meets regulatory requirements (Roth et al., 2016). Organizations are challenged by multiple systems and departments with a flow of financial data and the need to ensure quality and avoid duplication or inconsistency of data. The best way to mitigate these issues is to have a good data governance structure that defines roles of data ownership and data stewardship and has a uniform method of data validation and integration. Moreover, the governance practices allow transparency and accountability, and thus, organizations are able to trace the sources of data, and make them auditable (Harvey, 2003). Through effective data governance, businesses can increase the accuracy of financial data, mitigate risks of data misstatements and assist in making decisions.

1.3 Control System Role

Financial control systems are crucial in maintaining integrity and reliability of financial information in the digital businesses. These systems are made up of policies, procedures and technological mechanisms, which are used to check and control financial activities. Control systems in digital environments are becoming more automated and have the capability of real-time validation, audit trail, and access controls (Kitsantas, 2022). The mechanisms can be used to avoid any errors, identify anomalies and also to uphold internal policies and external regulations. Accountability is also promoted since control systems help to trace the financial transactions and detect anomalies. Combined with data governance systems, financial control systems offer a holistic method of controlling financial information flows (Mrima & Ronald, 2022). They make sure that information is not only precise and consistent but also safe and can be utilized in making decisions. Control systems are critical in ensuring trust in the financial reporting and supporting the strategic objectives as organizations increasingly turn to digital platforms.

2. BACKGROUND TO THE STUDY

Technological changes and organizational changes have been intertwined with the evolution of the financial information management. Financial systems that were traditionally in use were very manual and isolated and restricted the speed and extent of financial reporting. With time the computerized accounting systems and enterprise applications have enhanced efficiency and accessibility of the data. Over the past few years, the digital transformation has widened the area of financial information management and involved financial data into the broader organizational data ecosystems. This integration has brought about new opportunities of making decisions that are data-driven and has also brought about challenges in regards to data governance and control (Elragal & Hassanien, 2019). To analyze the processes of controlling financial flows of modern enterprises, it is crucial to understand the background of these developments. It gives an idea of how the traditional systems can be changed to digitally integrated settings and the role of governance and control mechanisms in promoting reliability and strategic value of data.

2.1 Evolution of Financial Systems

The financial systems have expanded so much as the manual bookkeeping system has advanced to the highly automated digital system. Recording in paper and manual computations was the basis of financial management in the early days, and this was very time consuming and prone to error. When introduced, computerized accounting systems made a big difference in that they could handle more and faster with accuracy (Carlsson-Wall et al., 2022). With the development of Enterprise Resource Planning systems, the financial data became related to other processes in the organization, such as supply chain and human resources. This integration increased the data consistency and gave a bigger picture of organizational performance. Over the past few years, financial systems have been further revolutionized through cloud computing and digital technologies, which enable real-time processing of data and access to financial data remotely. The developments have enhanced efficiency and scalability, though have added complexity to the management of financial information (Guo & Polak, 2024). This has led to organizations implementing sound governance and control systems in order to have integrity and reliability of data. Table 1 Comparisons of the traditional, ERP-based and cloud-based financial systems in terms of major features.

Table 1. Evolution of Financial Systems

Aspect	Traditional Systems	ERP Systems	Cloud Finance Systems
Data Processing	Manual / Batch	Integrated	Real-time
Data Storage	Local / Paper	Centralized Database	Cloud-based
Accessibility	Limited	Department-wide	Anywhere, anytime
Integration	Low	High (internal)	Very high (cross-platform)
Reporting	Periodic	Faster	Real-time dashboards

2.2 Digital Enterprise Ecosystems

Digital enterprise ecosystems are defined as networks of systems, platforms and stakeholders that are interconnected and enable the exchange of information between organizations. These ecosystems in the financial context are ERP systems, cloud-based applications, data warehouses and analytics platforms. These systems generate and share financial data which allows organizations to have detailed insights on their operations. The combination of non-financial and financial data helps to make decisions in a more informed way and improve coordination of the organization (Andelina & Santoso, 2021). Nevertheless, the intricacy of digital ecosystems also brings about the issues of data consistency, security, and governance (Li & Guo, 2024). The data can come of various sources and be handled on various platforms, which enhances the possibility of inconsistencies and errors. Ecosystems of digital enterprises have to be managed with effective governance arrangements and unified data practices. Organizations can enhance efficiency, transparency and strategic decision-making abilities by ensuring the flow of financial information across the systems is seamless (Liu, 2024). Figure 1 Shows the movement of financial data between the ERP, cloud applications, data warehouse and analytics platforms under integrated data governance and financial control systems to assist in strategic decision-making.

Figure 1. Digital Enterprise Ecosystem for Financial Information Flow

2.3 Governance and Control Foundations

The principles of risk management, accountability and transparency are the basis of data governance and financial control systems. Data governance frameworks determine the policies and standards that govern the way data is handled, and financial control systems are in place to ensure that the policies are well enforced and monitored. They can be collectively applied to the management of financial information in organizations. Governance frameworks ensure that there are roles like data owners and data stewards whose responsibility is to maintain data quality and compliance with organizational standards. Financial control systems on the other hand are aimed at monitoring of transactions, detecting anomalies and ensuring compliance to policies (Cosmulese, 2021). These foundations are facilitated in digital worlds through sophisticated technologies, including automated validation systems and live-monitoring systems. The reliability of financial information, reduction of risks, as well as strategic decision-making processes could be enhanced with the integration of governance and control systems.

2.4 Theoretical Foundations

The integration of data governance and financial control systems is based on Agency Theory (Jensen & Meckling, 1976), the COSO Internal Control Framework (COSO, 2013) and the Data Governance view (Khatri & Brown, 2010; Abraham et al., 2019). The Agency Theory emphasizes the importance of accountability, transparency and monitoring in minimizing information asymmetry between agency owners and managers, employees and agency owners and managers, and gainers and losers. The COSO Internal Control Framework provides a framework for conducting a risk assessment in a digital financial environment, including control activities, communication and information and ongoing monitoring (Jim & Chang, 2018). The Data Governance perspective takes these concepts further and introduces the concepts of data quality, standards, data stewardship, data ownership, metadata and data lifecycle control. These perspectives work in unison to support the conceptual model and provide a basis for how governance policies can be converted to practices and operational controls like validation rules, access restrictions, audit trails and real-time monitoring controls. Together, they increase the trustworthiness, security, transparency, and consistency of financial information and help achieve a regulatory compliance and strategic decision making in interconnected digital enterprise systems.

3. RESEARCH OBJECTIVES

The increasing sophistication of the financial flows of data of digital business requires clear research aims that would bring the data governance practice in consonance with the financial control system. These objectives are geared towards improving the reliability of data, efficient control procedures and strategic value of financial information. The study will offer a systematic basis to optimal management of financial information in digitally integrated settings by covering both the technological and management aspects.

- To examine the integration of data governance frameworks with financial control systems for managing financial information flows effectively.
- To analyze how governance mechanisms improve financial data quality, consistency, and regulatory compliance across digital platforms.
- To evaluate the role of automated and real-time financial control systems in enhancing transparency, accountability, and risk management.
- To investigate how integrated financial information systems support strategic decision-making through accurate and timely insights.

- To propose a conceptual approach for aligning data governance and financial control practices with organizational strategic objectives in digital enterprises.

These objectives provide the analytical basis for developing the conceptual model presented in the following section, which integrates governance structures, financial information flows, and control mechanisms within a unified digital-enterprise framework.

4. CONCEPTUAL MODEL

The conceptual model offers an organised illustration of the interaction of data governance and financial control systems in digital enterprises to control the flows of financial information in a functional manner. Multiple sources create financial data in highly-integrated environments that is exchanged across interrelated platforms and requires coordinated governance and control procedures (Arisandi & Khudri, 2021). The model concentrates on three core dimensions, which include: the design of the governance framework, financial data flow structure, and a mix of control systems and governance practices. All these dimensions ensure that the financial information is precise, uniform, safe and conforming to the organizational goals. The conceptual model allows the data complexity to be managed by establishing transparent roles, standard processes and technological support systems to promote transparency and accountability (Jayeola et al., 2020). It also puts emphasis on the need to harmonize the policies governing governance with the operational control mechanisms to facilitate real time monitoring and decision making. Finally, the model provides a basis of converting financial information into valid and actionable information to be used in strategic planning. Figure 2 shows how the governance frameworks, financial data flows and control mechanisms are integrated to provide data accuracy, transparency and facilitate strategic decision-making.

Figure 2. Data Governance–Financial Control Integration Model

4.1 Governance Framework Design

Design of governance structure is aimed at setting up of structured policies, roles and standards to govern financial information in digital firms. It involves establishing data ownership, data stewardship roles and the development of standardized data collection, validation and integration processes(Wulandari, 2020). An effective structure makes sure that financial data is processed in a similar manner throughout the departments and systems, eliminating repetition and errors. It also involves regulatory compliance requirements, making sure that the financial data complies with legal and organizational requirements. Governance Systems are based on well documented policies and guidelines that promote transparency and accountability in data management procedures (Chang et al., 2020). Metadata management systems and data quality monitoring platforms are technology-enabled tools that help in governance design in digital environments. These tools assist in enforcing governance rules and have visibility of data use and performance. Through creating a strong governance framework, organisations are able to enhance the reliability of the data, better the coordination among systems and facilitate efficient financial decision-making. Table 2 Highlight of the governance aspects like policies, data owners, and data stewards.

Table 2. Data Governance Components and Roles

Component	Description	Role
Data Policies	Rules for data handling	Ensure compliance
Data Ownership	Assigned accountability	Responsible for data
Data Stewardship	Data quality management	Maintain accuracy
Metadata Management	Data description	Improve understanding
Data Standards	Uniform formats	Ensure consistency

4.2 Financial Data Flow Model

The financial data flow model is a model that reflects the flow of financial information across systems, processes and levels of organization within digital enterprises. It records the lifecycle of financial data, including its creation by transaction processing systems, and its consolidation, storage and analysis in data warehouses and analytics platforms. The model focuses on the combination of financial data and operational and external data sources, which allow gaining in-depth understanding of organizational performance (Calzada, 2024). It also emphasizes the need of standard data format and interface to have seamless data exchange among systems. Good data flow models have data validation checkpoints, data transformation procedures and integration tools to ensure the accuracy and consistency of data. Real-time data streams in digital businesses allow reporting and decision-making in real time, yet they demand effective monitoring to avoid mistakes and discrepancies (Mohd Zain et al., 2024). Organizational financial data flows can be effectively structured by managing them to increase the availability of financial data, enhance the accuracy of reporting, and assist with strategic planning. Table 3 Illustration of how financial data moves across ERP, cloud systems, and analytics platforms.

Table 3. Financial Data Flow Across Digital Platforms

Stage	System	Process	Output
Data Generation	ERP / Transactions	Entry & Capture	Raw Financial Data
Data Processing	ERP Modules	Validation & Posting	Processed Data
Data Integration	Data Warehouse	Consolidation	Unified Data
Data Analysis	Analytics Tools	Reporting & Insights	Decision Reports

4.3 Control–Governance Integration

Control-governance integration is concerned with integrating the financial control systems with data governance systems to promote effective monitoring and management of financial information. This integration allows organizations to implement governance policies via automated control mechanisms like validation rules, audit trails and access controls. Financial control systems offer a round-the-clock monitoring of the data flows, identifying the presence of anomalies and making sure that the standards are followed. These systems are used to increase accountability when they are combined with governance structures; data management duties are connected with control processes (Imane et al., 2023). Advanced technologies like real-time monitoring tools and automated reporting systems, which offer real-time insights on the financial activities, support integration in digital environments. This alignment is to make sure that the policies of governance will not just be defined but also implemented between systems (Zhang, 2025). Combining control and governance systems, organizations may enhance the quality of data, minimize risks, and guarantee that financial information will be reliable and secure, which will eventually help to make informed and strategic decisions. Having established the conceptual relationships among governance, financial data flows and control mechanisms, the following section explains the methodological approach used to synthesize the relevant literature and case evidence.

5. RESEARCH METHODOLOGY

The methodology of the research provides a rational framework of analyzing the ways the data governance and financial control systems can be merged in the digital enterprises. The study is conceptual and interdisciplinary in nature and therefore, the systematic approach to qualitative approach is adopted to comprehend the theoretical premises of the study, industry practices and emerging trends (Arzberger et al., 2004). The methodology is a combination of the expertise of accounting, information systems, and management courses in the development of an overall perspective of the flows of financial information in digital environments. The primary source of analysis is the primary sources of secondary data including academic articles, industry reports and regulatory guidance. The study is based more on analytical synthesis rather than on the empirical testing, therefore, enabling the derivation of a conceptual model which can be implemented in the real practices. Moreover, the approach also includes the evidence of illustrative cases as a way of contextualizing theoretical knowledge (Faboyede et al., 2022). The study is rigorous and consistent and relevant by utilizing a well-organized and clear research process.

It is the methodological approach that facilitates the identification of the main governance mechanisms and the control practices and their influence on strategic decision making in digital enterprises.

5.1 Research Design

The research design is qualitative and exploratory with the aim of understanding the multifaceted relationship between the data governance and financial control systems. It is mostly theoretical, and puts emphasis on development of theories and the building of frameworks as opposed to testing of hypothesis. The design incorporates the knowledge of various fields such as financial management, information system and organizational governance which offers a comprehensive view (Jiang, 2021). A methodological literature-based strategy is embraced in order to be able to determine some of the major themes, trends and gaps in the current studies. There is also a comparative approach in the study as practices are studied in the context of various digital enterprises. This will allow the recognition of generalized governance and control mechanisms that can be generalized across organizations. The research design focuses on logical coherence, clarity of concepts, and relevance (Georgiou et al., 2024). The design will be effective as it organizes the study in terms of goals and thematic areas that ensure the study is focused and consistent with the purpose of the whole research of enhancing financial information management in digital enterprises.

5.2 Data Sources and Tools

The study uses primarily secondary sources of data to come up with an in-depth understanding regarding data governance and financial control systems. Some of the most important sources of information are academic journals, conference proceedings, industry white papers and regulatory documents. These publications give an understanding of the present practices, technological advancements and governance issues in digital businesses (Mokrani & Abaoub, 2024)Moreover, case studies and organizational reports publicly available are utilized in order to demonstrate the practical implementation of governance and control mechanisms in the real world. The data that are gathered is organized, and analytical tools, such as thematic analysis and content synthesis, are used to analyze the data. The systematic arrangement of data and the identification of patterns in the sources are aided by the digital tools, such as the reference manager software and data visualization tools (Smith, 2024). The credibility and validity of the study is increased by the use of different and reliable sources of data. The synergy of different perspectives enables the study to possess a close-up image of the financial information management practices in digitally empowered environment.

5.3 Analysis Approach

The analysis approach is based on a qualitative literature and case-based synthesis to develop a synthesized understanding of the study problem. The authors use thematic analysis to determine the recurrent patterns concerning the data governance practices, financial control mechanisms and how they are integrated in digital enterprises (Rachmat et al., 2024). The most significant ideas and findings of the literature are categorized into the themed areas which overlap research objectives. Comparative analysis is also used to analyze the differences and similarities between the organizational practices and the best practices and common challenges are identified. The methodology is centered around the meaning of the connections between the governance structures, control systems, and flow of financial information (Rachmat et al., 2024). Besides, a conceptual mapping process is also part of the analysis to relate theoretical knowledge and practical applications. This systematic methodology will make sure that the results are logically arranged and that they are directly pertinent to the research aims. The information synthesis of different sources of information facilitates the analysis to provide a comprehensive and realistic perspective of how financial information management may be improved in digital businesses.

6. LITERATURE REVIEW

The literature in data governance and financial control system focuses on the greater importance of financial flows management in digitally empowered business. With integrated platforms and real-time data processing, the traditional method of managing finance is re-invented in organizations. In the existing body of literature, it has been emphasized that the financial information is no longer confined to the accounting systems but it is spread across the enterprise-wide digital ecosystems (Group, 2022). The change necessitates the introduction of formal systems of governance and advanced control systems to ensure the data reliability, transparency and alignment. It is also indicated in the literature that organizations are increasingly resorting to data-driven decision-making and it requires quality and timely financial information (Group, 2022). As a result, the consistency between the system of governance and control has become one of the key themes of the modern-day research. Researchers have always believed that a successful incorporation of these factors improves the performance of the organization, minimizes risks, and promotes strategic decision-making in complicated digital surroundings.

6.1 Data Governance Practices

Data governance practices research is concerned with policies, standards, and roles to govern data throughout its lifecycle. Research indicates that clear data ownership and stewardship roles are necessary to promote accountability and quality of the data. Consistency, transparency, and compliance are some of the principles in governance structures that are necessary in ensuring reliable financial information (Chauke & Ngoepe, 2025). The role of standardized data model and metadata management in enhancing data integration across systems is also highlighted in the literature. Technological tools facilitate data validation, monitoring and reporting in the governance practices of digital enterprises (Mushtaq et al., 2025). According to scholars, organizations that have developed governance structures have less data discrepancy and enhanced regulatory adherence. Nevertheless, there are still difficulties in applying the practice of governance in distributed systems and balancing the technical and managerial viewpoints. In general, the literature highlights that effective financial information management is based on the strong data governance.

6.2 Financial Control Mechanisms

Financial control mechanisms are a common topic in literature as a significant tool to guarantee the accuracy, integrity and security of financial information. Conventional control mechanisms, including internal audits and manual verification mechanisms have been transformed into automated and real-time tracking mechanisms in electronic settings. The research points out the significance of controls like validation rules, access management, and audit trails in error prevention and anomaly detection (Ravikumar et al., 2025). The incorporation of these controls in the digital platforms promotes efficiency and minimizes the chances of fraud and data manipulation. Researchers also highlight the importance of continuous monitoring and analytics in enhancing effectiveness of control (Mohammed & Trzcielinski, 2022). Although such developments have been made, the literature points to issues of complexity of the system and the constant requirement of updating systems control mechanisms to address emerging risks (Mohd Fariz et al., 2020). Financial control systems, in general, are considered to be important components that supplement the frameworks of governance by providing the assurance that the policies can be implemented and enforced. Table 4 Overview of major control mechanisms like audit trails, validation rules and access controls.

Table 4. Financial Control Mechanisms in Digital Enterprises

Control Type	Description	Benefit
Access Control	Restrict user access	Data security
Audit Trail	Track changes	Accountability
Validation Rules	Automated checks	Error reduction
Approval Workflow	Multi-level approvals	Compliance
Real-time Monitoring	Continuous tracking	Risk detection

6.3 Digital Integration Insights

Recent research has given much attention to integrating digital technologies in financial information systems. Research on the use of technologies like cloud computing, data integration platforms, and advanced analytics in consolidating financial data across various sources is emphasized (Saeed et al., 2023). This integration helps in real time reporting and increase the capacity of organizations to create strategic insights. Another point of focus of the literature is that cross-functional collaboration is easy when integrating digital information as it enables the connection of financial data to the operation and external information. Nevertheless, it presents the issues of data fragmentation, data security and governance (Manion & Porth, 2025). According to researchers, the absence of an adequate integration framework can lead to inconsistencies within organizations, as well as low data reliability. Developing an effective integration needs to have standard data architectures, and coordinated governance practices. The literature findings are that with good governance and control systems, digital integration can greatly increase the value of financial information and help organizations make more informed and strategic decisions.

6.4 Research Gap and Analytical Synthesis

The existing studies offer good insights into data governance, financial control mechanisms, ERP systems, cloud finance platforms and digital transformation. These lines of research are, however, rather isolated. While data governance studies most often focus on data ownership, stewardship, standards, and data quality, financial control studies focus on audit trails, validation, authorization and compliance. In the same way, studies on digital finance tend to focus on technology adoption and efficiency of processes while neglecting to consider the joint role of governance and control mechanisms in influencing the flow of financial information through the interconnected financial enterprise platforms. Finally, there is a lack of integration of the technological, managerial and strategic points of view in a single framework.

The current literature also lacks attention to new risks related to AI-fueled analytics, cloud reliance, cybersecurity, lack of algorithmic transparency, international data management, and automated decision-making. To fill these gaps, this study is dedicated to developing a novel perspective on governance, control, financial-data-flow, and strategic-decision aspects in an integrated conceptual framework for a digital enterprise. The gaps in the theory and practice, identified above, are used to discuss ERP and cloud-finance as cases of governance-control integration.

7. CASE STUDY

The case study area provides examples of how the data governance and financial control systems have been applied in real organizations in the modern digital enterprises. Recent studies show that companies have become more and more convinced of the value of integrated systems, such as ERP, cloud-based financial systems, to manage financial information flows effectively. These systems make it possible to have centralized data management, real-time analytics, and enhanced compliance with regulatory requirements. They should, however, be implemented with great governance structures and control measures to guarantee data accuracy, consistency and security. The case studies that have been chosen are based on the ERP integration and cloud finance systems, both of them being the important technological advances in the sphere of financial information management (Arzberger et al., 2004). The section will demonstrate through these case studies how companies deal with problems related to data fragmentation, system interoperability and effectiveness of control. This body of knowledge based on these examples gives empirical data on the benefits of integrated governance and control systems to financial transparency, efficiency, and strategic decision-making in digital enterprises.

7.1 Case Study I: ERP Integration

The most recent case study of an ERP-based financial integration demonstrates how businesses can enable financial governance and control through the use of enterprise systems. ERP implementation was used in a financial services organization to integrate accounting, risk management and operations into a single platform. The system consolidated the financial information which allowed a single source of truth and minimized interdepartmental inconsistencies. The accuracy and timeliness of financial reporting was enhanced with automated workflows such as approval mechanisms and validation checks (Mohasseb, 2024). In addition, analytical opportunities in real-time also allowed letting the management to monitor the financial performance and identify the potential risks beforehand. Internal control mechanisms were also reinforced as part of the implementation process, through the inclusion of audit trails and access controls, which also guaranteed transparency and accountability. Organizations claimed to have improved their regulatory compliance and endured audit preparedness (Mohasseb, 2024). The integration process of ERP removed manual reconciliation processes and minimized operational inefficiencies through automation of data flows between systems. Research has shown that the integrated ERP environments dramatically enhance the accuracy of financial reporting and facilitate decision making based on data (Alsharari, 2022). All in all, the case shows that ERP integration is a key aspect in aligning the financial data governance with control systems to help organizations realize higher efficiency, transparency, and strategic financial management.

7.2 Case Study II: Cloud Finance Systems

The new case study of cloud-based financial systems shows how digital organizations can use cloud-based solutions to facilitate financial information flows in a distributed environment. Using cloud finance solutions, organizations are able to consolidate various financial functions such as accounting, procurement and reporting into a scalable, yet centralized, digital system. Cloud services make it possible to access the data in real time and in this way, managers can track the financial performance and make the necessary decisions (Hustad et al., 2021). One implementation of the enterprise finance system saw the introduction of cloud finance systems, which interacted with enterprise applications via APIs and middleware, and allowed the flow of data between departments. This integration minimized data silos and enhanced consistency when reporting financial data. Also automated controls like real-time validation, anomaly detection and role-based access enhanced the security of data and reduced the chances of errors and fraud (Badgujar, 2023). Research points out that the use of financial systems that are enabled by clouds makes them to be more scalable and flexible in their operations as well as lowering the costs of infrastructure. In addition, enhanced reporting cycle, increased speed in the financial close process, and improved decision-making processes have been linked to the use of integrated cloud platform (Dagar et al., 2024). Companies claimed to have had increased transparency of financial activities and enhancements of cross-functional cooperation. In this case, it can be seen that cloud finance systems, reinforced with the governance and control systems, can be successful in enhancing financial information management in electronic businesses.

7.3 Cross-Case Insights

The comparative analysis of the ERP integration and cloud finance system has yielded some valuable information on how financial information in online enterprises is managed. The two cases emphasize the importance of centralized data and real-time data processing in improving financial transparency and decision making. Compared to ERP systems, cloud finance systems are scalable and flexible, but the latter has good integration and control capabilities. Among the similarities in the two instances is that data governance is a key element that must be ensured to ensure data quality, data consistency and data compliance. Moreover, both strategies emphasize the use of automated control measures, including validation rules and audit trail, to ensure the integrity of data (Stoica & Stefan, 2018). The ERP systems are usually suitable in large scale, structured environments but cloud systems are more flexible towards dynamic and distributed operations. These cases, combined, show that it is imperative to combine governance structures with financial controlling systems to address multifaceted financial data flows and be able to support strategic organizational goals. Table 5 Comparative analysis of ERP integration and cloud-based finance system on performance measures.

Table 5. Case Study Comparison – ERP vs Cloud Finance Systems

Criteria	ERP Integration	Cloud Finance Systems
Deployment	On-premise / Hybrid	Fully Cloud
Data Integration	Internal systems	Cross-platform
Scalability	Moderate	High
Cost	High initial cost	Subscription-based
Flexibility	Limited	High
Real-time Capability	Moderate	High

The cross-case comparison provides the empirical and conceptual observations that are synthesized in the following discussion.

8. RESULTS/DISCUSSION

The results show that the implementation of data governance frameworks into financial control systems enhances data governance of financial information in ERP and cloud-based environments. This is not just about technology but about aligning the governance aspects with the operational aspects. ERP systems offer a structured and centralized control environment, and cloud-based platforms offer increased flexibility, scalability, and real-time access to financial information (Henninger & Mashatan, 2021). There are also some key trade-offs to consider, however, with greater technology integration, such as implementation complexity, reliance on vendors, interoperability issues, cybersecurity risk, and ongoing control re-assessment. It is important to note that technological integration does not necessarily imply better governance or better control effectiveness. It requires proper governance design, due accountability, institutional capacity, monitoring and flexibility of governance in response to the evolving technological and regulatory landscape. The results of these are the basis for a detailed discussion of the data quality, the effectiveness of data control, and the outcome of the decisions in the following subsections.

8.1 Data Quality Outcomes

The comparative analysis shows that the two solutions offer different approaches to improving data quality, ERP and cloud-based financial systems. For ERP environments, the biggest benefits of consistency are a single source of financial data and the uniformity of transaction processing, while for cloud platforms it is the ability to synchronize between distributed applications (Yang et al., 2019). But technological integration alone is not responsible for the improved data quality. It relies on data ownership, data validation procedures, and monitoring (Ravikumar et al., 2026). So, the findings indicate that governance mechanisms are an organizing layer that help to shape the link between technological integration and reliable financial information.

8.2 Control Effectiveness

The results show that automated controls enhance financial monitoring because they are built into the digital process itself and encompass validation, authorization, audit trails, and anomaly detection. But any such controls have to be continually modified to meet evolving business processes and technological risks. The ERP system has comparatively structured control environments, while the Cloud-based system has more flexibility but can create extra dependencies due to distributed systems and external service providers. So, a proper degree of automation, governance supervision and re-evaluating controls at regular intervals is needed to ensure effective financial control (Stepanovic et al., 2025).

8.3 Decision-Making Impact

Integrated governance and financial control systems are not only about faster reporting but the quality and credibility of managerial decision making. Financial information is reliable and timely, which helps to minimize uncertainty and allows managers to tie operational performance to strategic priorities. Yet with real-time information does not equal better decision. It relies on the analytical skills of the manager, interpretation of financial indicators, and the confidence in the control processes and data. The findings thus offer a new perspective on governance and control integration: it is a necessary but not sufficient condition to ensure effective and informed decision making, not an indicator of better organizational performance (Bao et al., 2022). Table 6 Major results with the improvements in the quality of data, effectiveness of control, and strategic decisions.

Table 6. Impact of Governance and Control on Decision-Making

Factor	Without Integration	With Integration
Data Quality	Inconsistent	High accuracy
Reporting Speed	Delayed	Real-time
Risk Level	High	Reduced
Transparency	Low	High
Decision Quality	Reactive	Proactive

9. FUTURE RESEARCH

The field of data governance and financial control systems is likely to continue growing in future studies in reaction to the growing complexity of digital enterprise settings. With organizations still embracing the latest technologies and integrated platforms, there will be emergence of new challenges and opportunities in the management of the financial flows of information. Current literature has served as a baseline, although there is an increasing demand of empirical support of governance systems and control mechanisms in various organizational settings. More studies should be conducted to study the interaction of technology, governance systems and managerial practices in dynamic way. In addition, the dynamism of digital ecosystems presents an issue of continuous changes in the forms of governance to ensure stability and safety of information and compliance with laws (Saxena et al., 2023). The scales and compatibility of governance systems in international business can also be explored. By tackling these aspects, future research can help to come up with more dynamic and resilient financial information management systems that can be used in making strategic decisions in more data-intensive contexts.

9.1 Emerging Governance, Technology, and Control Risks

The use of AI, cloud computing platforms, blockchain, automated controls and financial systems that are interconnected have created new governance and control challenges. The outputs of AI/machine-learning applications can be biased or inaccurate, models can drift, and there may be concerns of explainability and automation-bias when managers over-rely on algorithmic recommendations (Alles et al., 2021). Risks in cyber security are growing as well with ransomware, compromised credentials, API attacks, and manipulation of financial data pipelines. Cloud-based financial systems involve other worries, including vendor lock-in, service disruptions, concentration risk, and dependency on particular jurisdictions (Dolhopolov et al., 2024). The issues with data governance are not clear ownership, not strong data lineage, not consistent metadata, and not allowing cross-border data flows. An automated anomaly-detection system also can generate false positives or false negatives, reducing the effectiveness of control where human control is limited. Organizations' control boundaries are further extended due to third-party SaaS providers, APIs, and external datasets (Makhmudov et al., 2026). There are tensions between immutability and correcting erroneous financial records with blockchain-based systems, and privacy and who is responsible for governing the system are salient issues. These risk factors need adaptive governance, regular control evaluation, and enhanced human control.

9.2 Governance Challenges

Even with the development of digital technologies, there are still a number of governance challenges related to the management of financial flows of information. The main problem that can be highlighted is maintaining data consistency between distributed and heterogeneous systems. With the implementation of various platforms, it becomes more challenging to have consistency in data standards across organizations. The other issue concerns the security and privacy of data, especially on cloud-based and cross-border data environments. There are also complexities in regulatory compliance whereby organizations have to comply with the changing legal requirements in various jurisdictions (Marfuah et al., 2023). Also, the correspondence of technical governance mechanisms with managerial practices is usually minimal, which results in implementation gaps. There is also organizational resistance to change and shortage of skilled personnel which also complicates governance efforts.

Research to be conducted in the future should center on finding solutions to counter these obstacles and come up with flexible governance models. These concerns will be critical when it comes to making sure that financial information is reliable, secure and in line with organizational goals in digital businesses.

9.3 Research Directions

The direction of the future research should be based on the creation of systems of data governance, financial control systems, and digital technologies that are organized into a single framework. Conceptual modeling ought to be empirically tested and its effectiveness in real organizational setting can be established. The inter-industry comparative research can offer an insight on the best practices and challenges of context. Also, the financial information management can be improved with the help of interdisciplinary methods that help to combine the views of accounting, information systems, and management (Charles et al., 2023). The role of organizational culture and leadership in successful implementation of the governance and control systems should also be researched. The next significant direction is the creation of performance measures that would help to assess the efficiency of governance structures and control systems. By addressing these aspects, the future research will help to enhance the knowledge base and offer practical recommendations to organisations interested in enhancing the management of financial information within digital settings.

10. MANAGERIAL IMPLICATIONS

Combining data governance and financial control systems has profound effects on the managerial practice in the digital enterprises. The managers need to become more strategic and data-driven in financial information management, and the governance policies and control mechanisms should be put in place. The results reveal the need to have defined roles and responsibilities regarding data management and investing in technologies that can help in real-time monitoring and analysis. The managers also have to make sure that the financial information is in line with organizational goals and is used to make decisions. Moreover, there is the growing complexity of digital systems, which needs a constant learning and adaptation to new technologies and governance practices (Kwon et al., 2023). Through integrated strategies, managers are able to increase transparency, optimize operations and boost organizational performance. The implications highlight that the management of financial information flows is more than a technical issue but a strategic ability that is important.

10.1 Governance Implementation

Good governance requires that organizations possess clear policies, roles and processes as far as financial data management is concerned. To establish accountability and consistency, managers need to establish data ownership and allocate data stewardship responsibilities. All systems should have generalized data validation, integration and reporting processes that should be developed and put into place. Technology-enabled tools such as data quality monitoring systems, metadata management platforms, etc., can be used to implement governance structures. There is also a need to have training and awareness programs to make sure that employees are aware and compliant to governance policies (McKeen & Smith, 2007). Moreover, the implementation of governance should be done in accordance with regulatory requirements to minimize risks and guarantee compliance. The managers need to keep on observing and assessing the practices of governance in order to determine areas where they can improve. Through the implementation of a systematic governance, organizations may improve the quality of data, increase transparency, and aid in making effective financial decisions.

10.2 Control System Adoption

Implementation of financial control systems is pivotal towards integrity and security of financial information of digital enterprises. Financial activities should be monitored by the managers who should put in place control mechanisms like access controls, audit trails and automated validation procedures. The combination of these controls into digital platforms makes them efficient and minimizes the probability of errors and fraud. It is also recommended that companies should adopt the use of real-time monitoring systems that will enable them to track the financial activities and data flows (Carlsson-Wall et al., 2022). Adoption should be undertaken in a well-planned manner, and aligned with organizational objectives to achieve effective and scalable control systems. Change management programs and training are needed to support successful implementation of control systems. Moreover, the managers should often review and update control mechanisms to address the new risks as well as changes in technologies. Strong control systems will help organizations to improve accountability, compliance and reliability of financial information.

10.3 Strategic Alignment

Strategic alignment is the process of making sure that the overall goals of the organization are supported by data governance and financial control systems. In order to streamline decision making using data, managers must integrate financial information management practices and processes with strategic planning (Mamadiyarov et al., 2026). This requires that the governance policies and control mechanisms should be aligned to organizational goals, performance indicators and risk management strategies. Online systems can be used to enable organizations to bridge the gap between financial data and operating and strategic data to provide the entire performance picture. Managers also should strive to acquire analytical skills that would help them analyze financial data and make actionable conclusions (Zhang, 2025). Interdepartmental communication and cooperation play a vital role in achieving alignment and making sure that financial information is aligned to organizational priorities. The benefits of aligning the systems of governance and control with the strategic goals of organizations in the digital environments to enhance decision-making, performance and achieve long-term sustainability are many.

11. CONCLUSION

The chapter gives a detailed insight as to how data governance and financial control systems work together in facilitating effective financial information flows in digital enterprises. The main conclusions are that the combination of the governance structures with the modernized control systems will greatly enhance the quality, consistency, and transparency of data that will be exchanged between the interconnected systems. As the discussion reveals, ERP integration and cloud-based financial systems are paramount in the creation of centralized yet elastic data environment that will see organizations achieve real-time reporting and amplified operational effectiveness. The paper also highlights that tools like automated control, including validation rule, audit trail, and access control are vital in ensuring accountability and minimizing risks associated with errors and fraud. The chapter is strategic in that it provides a conceptual model that assists organizations to transform complex financial information into clear and credible actionable information, through aligning the governance practices with financial control systems. This alignment helps in informed decision making, improved compliance as well as improved performance of the organization. Moreover, the discussion highlights the fact that management of financial information cannot solely rely on technology but rather, it will need well-coordinated policies, well defined roles and constant monitoring. The results indicate that organizations need to implement a holistic strategy that incorporates governance, control, and digital technologies to deal with the issues of data fragmentation and complexity in systems. The final lesson is that the ability to secure the successful circulation of financial information will become one of the major criteria of strategies success, organizational transparency, and sustainability of the data-oriented business environment as digital companies develop and change continuously.

REFERENCES

Abraham, R., Schneider, J., & vom Brocke, J. (2019). Data governance: A conceptual framework, structured review, and research agenda. *International Journal of Information Management, 49*, 424–438. DOI: 10.1016/j.ijinfomgt.2019.07.008

Alles, M. G., Dai, J., & Vasarhelyi, M. A. (2021). Reporting 4.0: Business reporting for the age of mass customization. *Journal of Emerging Technologies in Accounting, 18*(1), 1–15. DOI: 10.2308/jeta-10764

Alsharari, N. M. (2022). Cloud computing and ERP assimilation in the public sector: Institutional perspectives. *Transforming Government, 16*(1), 97–109. DOI: 10.1108/TG-04-2021-0069

Andelina, W., & Santoso, A. (2021). Measuring quality determinants of financial statements. *Journal of Business and Management Review*, 2(12), 884–893. DOI: 10.47153/jbmr212.2082021

Arisandi, D., & Khudri, T. M. Y. (2021). *Analysis and design of data governance at the Financial Services Authority. InFestasi, 17(1).* InPres., DOI: 10.21107/infestasi.v17i1.10515

Arzberger, P., Schroeder, P., Beaulieu, A., Bowker, G., Casey, K., Laaksonen, L., Moorman, D., Uhlir, P., & Wouters, P. (2004). Promoting access to public research data for scientific, economic, and social development. *Data Science Journal, 3*, 135–152. DOI: 10.2481/dsj.3.135

Badgujar, P. (2023). The role of data catalogs in driving organizational insights and efficiency. *Journal of Artificial Intelligence & Cloud Computing*, 2(4), 1. DOI: 10.47363/JAICC/2022(1)263

Bao, Y., Lyu, C., Wu, X., & Lian, J. (2022). Optimal decision-making in Chinese cross-border mergers and acquisitions: A perspective of overbidding. *Complexity, 2022*(1). DOI: 10.1155/2022/8298451

Bisht, D., Singh, R., Gehlot, A., Akram, S. V., Singh, A., Montero, E. C., Priyadarshi, N., & Twala, B. (2022). Imperative role of integrating digitalization in the firms finance: A technological perspective. *Electronics (Basel), 11*(19), 3252. DOI: 10.3390/electronics11193252

Calzada, I. (2024). Democratic erosion of data-opolies: Decentralized Web3 technological paradigm shift amidst AI disruption. *Big Data and Cognitive Computing, 8*(3), 26. DOI: 10.3390/bdcc8030026

Carlsson-Wall, M., Goretzki, L., Hofstedt, J., Kraus, K., & Nilsson, C.-J. (2022). Exploring the implications of cloud-based enterprise resource planning systems for public sector management accountants. *Financial Accountability & Management, 38*(2), 177–201. DOI: 10.1111/faam.12300

Chang, V., Valverde, R., Ramachandran, M., & Li, C.-S. (2020). Toward Business Integrity Modeling and analysis framework for risk measurement and analysis. *Applied Sciences (Basel, Switzerland), 10*(9), 3145. DOI: 10.3390/app10093145

Charles, V., Emrouznejad, A., & Gherman, T. (2023). A critical analysis of the integration of blockchain and artificial intelligence for supply chain. *Annals of Operations Research, 327*(1), 1–41. DOI: 10.1007/s10479-023-05169-w

Chauke, T. A., & Ngoepe, M. (2025). Integrating facets of information technology governance at a professional council in South Africa. *Global Knowledge, Memory and Communication, 74*(11), 101–120. DOI: 10.1108/GKMC-08-2023-0270

Committee of Sponsoring Organizations of the Treadway Commission (COSO). (2013). *Internal Control—Integrated Framework.* COSO.

Cosmulese, C. G. (2021). Theoretical perspectives of corporate governance. *European Journal of Accounting. Finance & Business, 9*(1). Advance online publication. DOI: 10.4316/EJAFB.2021.912

Dagar, R., Mahajan, D. S., & Vashisht, D. R. (2024). Enhancing data security in cloud computing using blockchain. *Irish Interdisciplinary Journal of Science & Research, 08*(01), 66–79. DOI: 10.46759/IIJSR.2024.8107

Dolhopolov, A., Castelltort, A., & Laurent, A. (2024). Implementing federated governance in Data Mesh architecture. *Future Internet, 16*(4), 115. DOI: 10.3390/fi16040115

Elragal, A., & Hassanien, H. E.-D. (2019). Augmenting advanced analytics into enterprise systems: A focus on post-implementation activities. *Systems, 7*(2), 31. DOI: 10.3390/systems7020031

Faboyede, O. S., Ogunniyi, O. R., Atanda, O., Adesina, K., & Ben-Caleb, E. (2022). Financial misappropriations, internal control, and Pentecostal Churches in Nigeria. *Research Journal of Business and Economic Management, 5*(2), 23–31. DOI: 10.31248/RJBEM2022.075

Georgiou, I., Sapuric, S., Lois, P., & Thrassou, A. (2024). Blockchain for accounting and auditing—accounting and auditing for cryptocurrencies: A systematic literature review and future research directions. *Journal of Risk and Financial Management, 17*(7), 276. DOI: 10.3390/jrfm17070276

Group, W. B. (2022). *2022 investment policy and regulatory review - India.* World Bank., DOI: 10.1596/38526

Guo, H., & Polak, P. (2024). Finance centralization—Research on enterprise intelligence. *Humanities & Social Sciences Communications*, *11*(1), 1536. Advance online publication. DOI: 10.1057/s41599-024-04098-8

Harvey, F. (2003). Developing geographic information infrastructures for local government: The role of trust. *The Canadian Geographer. Géographe Canadien*, *47*(1), 28–36. DOI: 10.1111/1541-0064.02e10

Henninger, A., & Mashatan, A. (2021). Distributed interoperable records: The key to better supply chain management. *Computers*, *10*(7), 89. DOI: 10.3390/computers10070089

Hustad, E., Sørheller, V. U., Jørgensen, E. H., & Vassilakopoulou, P. (2021). Moving enterprise resource planning (ERP) systems to the cloud: The challenge of infrastructural embeddedness. *International Journal of Information Systems and Project Management*, *8*(1), 5–20. DOI: 10.12821/ijispm080101

Imane, L., Noureddine, M., Driss, S., & Hanane, L. (2023). Towards blockchain-integrated enterprise resource planning: A pre-implementation guide. *Computers*, *13*(1), 11. DOI: 10.3390/computers13010011

Jayeola, O., Sidek, S., Azmawani, , Anuar, , & Jimin, H. (2020). Contextual factors and strategic consequences of cloud enterprise resource planning (ERP) adoption in Malaysian manufacturing SMEs: A conceptual framework. *International Journal of Economics and Business Administration*, *VIII*(3), 176–201. DOI: 10.35808/ijeba/495

Jensen, M. C., & Meckling, W. H. (1976). Theory of the firm: Managerial behavior, agency costs and ownership structure. *Journal of Financial Economics*, *3*(4), 305–360. DOI: 10.1016/0304-405X(76)90026-X

Jiang, S. (2021). Research on big data audit based on financial sharing service model using fuzzy AHP. *Journal of Intelligent & Fuzzy Systems*, *40*(4), 8237–8246. DOI: 10.3233/JIFS-189646

Jim, C. K., & Chang, H.-C. (2018). The current state of data governance in higher education. *Proceedings of the Association for Information Science and Technology*, *55*(1), 198–206. DOI: 10.1002/pra2.2018.14505501022

Khatri, V., & Brown, C. V. (2010). Designing data governance. *Communications of the ACM*, *53*(1), 148–152. DOI: 10.1145/1629175.1629210

Kitsantas, T. (2022). Exploring Blockchain Technology and Enterprise Resource Planning system: Business and technical aspects, current problems, and future perspectives. *Sustainability (Basel), 14*(13), 7633. DOI: 10.3390/su14137633

Kwon, Y., Lee, J.-D., Owens, J., & Bank, A. D. (2023). Managing fintech risks. In *ADB Briefs*. Asian Development Bank., DOI: 10.22617/BRF230170-2

Li, G., & Guo, B. (2024). Construction of enterprise financial compliance management system in the context of digital taxation. *International Business & Economics Studies, 6*(2), 200. DOI: 10.22158/ibes.v6n2p200

Liu, D.-E. (2024). The refined management of medical finance combined with information technology construction. *Expert Systems: International Journal of Knowledge Engineering and Neural Networks, 41*(6), e13151. Advance online publication. DOI: 10.1111/exsy.13151

Majstorovic, V., Stojadinovic, S., Lalic, B., & Marjanovic, U. (2020). ERP in Industry 4.0 Context. In *IFIP Advances in Information and Communication Technology* (pp. 287–294). Springer International Publishing. DOI: 10.1007/978-3-030-57993-7_33

Makhmudov, S., Ravikumar, R. N., Satheesh Kumar, A., Aarthi, S., Rakhimova, S., & Kanimozhi, N. (2026). AI-powered risk analytics in ESG-focused FinTech systems. In *Strategic Frameworks for Managing Risk in FinTech Ecosystems* (pp. 95–126). IGI Global Scientific Publishing., DOI: 10.4018/979-8-3373-2980-2.ch004

Mamadiyarov, Z., Ravikumar, R. N., Aarthi, S., Padma, E., & Umarbek, J. (2026). Computational risk management in ESG-driven FinTech ecosystems. In *Strategic Frameworks for Managing Risk in FinTech Ecosystems* (pp. 35–66). IGI Global Scientific Publishing., DOI: 10.4018/979-8-3373-2980-2.ch002

Manion, M. F., & Porth, S. J. (2025). Introduction to the Special Issue: Economic Challenges Facing Pastoral Leaders. *Review of Religious Research, 67*(2), 303–308. DOI: 10.1177/0034673X251340656

Marfuah, M., Istiqomah, E. N., Ayuntari, C. G., & Prasetyo, P. P. (2023). Determinants of quality of the financial statements of Gunung Kidul Regency Government. *Journal of Contemporary Accounting*, 12–27. DOI: 10.20885/jca.vol5.iss1.art2

McKeen, J. D., & Smith, H. A. (2007). Developments in practice XXIV: Information management: The nexus of business and IT. *Communications of the Association for Information Systems, 19*. Advance online publication. DOI: 10.17705/1CAIS.01903

Mohammed, I. K., & Trzcielinski, S. (2022). The interconnections between ICT, Industry 4.0 and agile manufacturing. *Management and Production Engineering Review*. https://doi.org/DOI: 10.24425/mper.2021.139998

Mohasseb, A. M. A. (2024). The impact of big data predictive analytics on firm performance: The role of cloud ERP and business intelligence integration. , *5*(1), 917–947. DOI: 10.21608/cfdj.2024.329290

Mohd Fariz, N., Farizal Mohammed, N., Syifa Zulkepli, N., & Kamaluddin, A. (2020). Accounting conservatism and financial performance: Accountability of shariah compliant companies in Malaysia. *Humanities and Social Sciences Letters*, *8*(3), 280–297. DOI: 10.18488/journal.73.2020.83.280.297

Mohd Zain, F. A., Muhamad, S. F., Abdullah, H., Sheikh Ahmad Tajuddin, S. A. F., & Wan Abdullah, W. A. (2024). Integrating environmental, social and governance (ESG) principles with Maqasid al-Shariah: A blueprint for sustainable takaful operations. *International Journal of Islamic and Middle Eastern Finance and Management*, *17*(3), 461–484. DOI: 10.1108/IMEFM-11-2023-0422

Mokrani, F., & Abaoub, E. (2024). The governance of companies: A theoretical analysis "evidence from the Tunisian banking.". *International Journal For Multidisciplinary Research*, *6*(1), 13075. Advance online publication. DOI: 10.36948/ijfmr.2024.v06i01.13075

Mrima, R., & Ronald, M. (2022). Assessment of internal control practices on financial performance of state corporations in Kenya. *International Journal of Finance and Accounting*, *7*(4), 35–54. DOI: 10.47604/ijfa.1675

Mushtaq, S., Mohsin, M., & Mushtaq, M. M. (2025). A systematic literature review on the implementation and challenges of Zero Trust Architecture across domains. *Sensors (Basel)*, *25*(19), 6118. DOI: 10.3390/s25196118

Rachmat, D. F., Mulyadi, D., Abdullah, S., Putrianti, S. D., & Nurliawati, R. (2024). Analysis of the governance of one data Indonesia (SDI) at the communication and information office of sukabumi city. In *Advances in Social Science, Education and Humanities Research* (pp. 42–60). Atlantis Press SARL. DOI: 10.2991/978-2-38476-104-3_6

Ravikumar, R. N., Aarthi, S., & Mamadiyarov, Z. (2026). Building the foundations of augmented organizations through AI empowerment. In *Advances in Computational Intelligence and Robotics* (pp. 101–130). IGI Global Scientific Publishing. DOI: 10.4018/979-8-3373-8607-2.ch006

Roth, C. J., Lannum, L. M., & Joseph, C. L. (2016). Enterprise imaging governance: HIMSS-SIIM collaborative white paper. *Journal of Digital Imaging*, *29*(5), 539–546. DOI: 10.1007/s10278-016-9883-z

Saeed, S., Altamimi, S. A., Alkayyal, N. A., Alshehri, E., & Alabbad, D. A. (2023). Digital transformation and cybersecurity challenges for businesses resilience: Issues and recommendations. *Sensors (Basel)*, *23*(15), 6666. DOI: 10.3390/s23156666

Saxena, R., Gayathri, E., & Surya Kumari, L. (2023). Semantic analysis of blockchain intelligence with proposed agenda for future issues. *International Journal of System Assurance Engineering and Management*, *14*(S1), 34–54. DOI: 10.1007/s13198-023-01862-y

Singhania, M., Bhan, I., & Seth, S. (2025). Digitalisation and firm-level ESG performance and disclosures: A scientometric review and research agenda. *International Journal of Finance & Economics*, *30*(4), 4212–4236. DOI: 10.1002/ijfe.3118

Smith, J. A. (2024). Accounting and information systems. In *Research Handbook on Accounting and Information Systems* (pp. 2–17). Edward Elgar Publishing., DOI: 10.4337/9781802200621.00008

Stepanovic, S., Marmier, A., & Mettler, T. (2025). Open research data integration in universities: How data stewards adapt global policies to local contexts. *Journal of the Association for Information Science and Technology*, *76*(13), 1754–1767. DOI: 10.1002/asi.70034

Stoica, R., & Stefan, V. (2018). The role of computerized solutions in consolidating financial results from the European and Anglo-Saxon accounting systems. *Valahian Journal of Economic Sciences*, *9*(2), 83–94. DOI: 10.2478/vjes-2018-0020

Wulandari, S. A. (2020). Data governance maturity level at the National Archives of the Republic of Indonesia. *Jurnal Penelitian Pos Dan Informatika*, *10*(1), 27–40. DOI: 10.17933/jppi.v10i1.306

Yang, L., Li, J., Elisa, N., Prickett, T., & Chao, F. (2019). Towards Big data Governance in Cybersecurity. *Data-Enabled Discovery and Applications*, *3*(1), 10. Advance online publication. DOI: 10.1007/s41688-019-0034-9

Zhang, Y. (2025). Governance strategies for paper and electronic documents in a dual-track archives system. *Information Resources Management Journal*, *38*(1), 1–19. DOI: 10.4018/IRMJ.390238

KEY TERMS AND DEFINITIONS

Automated Controls: Technology-enabled mechanisms such as validation rules, access controls, approval workflows, audit trails, and real-time monitoring used to enforce financial and governance requirements.

Cloud Finance Systems: Cloud-based financial platforms that support scalable, real-time, and cross-platform processing of accounting, procurement, reporting, and related financial activities.

Data Governance: The policies, standards, roles, and processes used to manage data quality, ownership, security, consistency, and compliance throughout its lifecycle.

Data Stewardship: The assigned responsibility for maintaining data quality, accuracy, consistency, and proper management according to established governance policies.

Enterprise Resource Planning (ERP): An integrated enterprise system that connects financial information with organizational functions such as accounting, operations, risk management, supply chain, and human resources.

Financial Control Systems: Policies, procedures, and technological mechanisms used to monitor financial activities, detect anomalies, enforce controls, and support reliable financial reporting.

Financial Information Flow: The movement of financial data through stages of generation, processing, integration, storage, analysis, reporting, and decision-making across digital enterprise systems.

Strategic Decision-Making: The use of reliable, timely, and integrated financial information to support organizational planning, risk assessment, resource allocation, and long-term objectives.

Chapter 5
Financial Reporting Processes in Complex Enterprise Environments

Kuldeep Agnihotri
ISBA Group of Institutes, India

Syed Kumail Sajjad
http://orcid.org/0000-0002-5437-6148
IILM University, India

V. Smitha
http://orcid.org/0000-0003-2082-7710
DC School of Management and Technology, India

R. Klothungasuryapndi
http://orcid.org/0009-0004-9493-6172
Nandha Engineering College, India

Suresh Talamala
http://orcid.org/0000-0001-9026-6459
Aditya University, India

B. Amarnath Reddy
http://orcid.org/0009-0002-9540-0586
Vignana Jyothi Institute of Management, India

M. Menaga
http://orcid.org/0009-0001-5728-5268
Paavai College of Engineering, India

ABSTRACT

Accounting models, consolidation techniques, internal controls, compliance systems, and sophisticated financial analytics are all part of the financial reporting procedures that this chapter examines in complex business contexts. Integrated reporting frameworks, digital financial governance systems, generally accepted accounting principles (GAAP), and international financial reporting standards (IFRS) are all put to the test. Topics covered in this chapter include financial management systems hosted on the cloud, fraud detection, automated reconciliation, and forecasting powered by AI. We take a close look at the difficulties associated with data integration, complicated regulations, cybersecurity, financial crime, and lack of transparency in

DOI: 10.4018/979-8-3373-9230-1.ch005

2027, IGI Global Scientific Publishing. Copying or distributing in print or electronic forms without written permission of IGI Global Scientific Publishing is prohibited. Use of this chapter to rative artificial intelligence (AI) technologies is expressly prohibited. The publisher reserves all rights to license its use for generative AI training and machine learning model development.

reporting. New topics covered include intelligent financial ecosystems, ESG reporting, blockchain-based accounting, and real-time reporting. Organisations benefit from improved operational efficiency, compliance with regulations, transparency, and strategic financial management when their financial reporting systems are efficient.

1. INTRODUCTION

The rising frequency of legislative changes across different jurisdictions has driven significant innovation in the field of corporate accounting in the past several years. While traditional approaches to evaluating the effects of regulations have largely focused on audit findings, financial reporting quality, and compliance metrics, they have often disregarded the significant organisational shifts that occur as accounting systems adapt to different legal frameworks (Hanifah et al., 2024). Rather than viewing regulatory impact as a simple stimulus-response mechanism, this study sheds light on it as a complicated adaptive process, closing a knowledge gap. We argue that when regulations change, it has a domino effect on accounting information systems, altering not just formal procedures but also accounting departments' cognitive frameworks, communication patterns, and innovation trajectories.

Theoretical Framework

Financial reporting in modern enterprises should be understood as an integrated socio-technical process involving regulatory requirements, enterprise resource planning (ERP) systems, artificial intelligence (AI), organisational governance, and decision-making. ERP systems provide an integrated infrastructure for collecting, storing, and processing financial and operational information across organisational functions, while AI technologies extend these capabilities through automation, predictive analysis, fraud detection, risk assessment, and intelligent decision support. From this perspective, regulatory requirements influence accounting and reporting processes, ERP systems facilitate the integration and standardisation of enterprise data, and AI transforms integrated data into analytical information that can improve the accuracy, timeliness, transparency, and usefulness of financial reporting. The effectiveness of this integrated process is further influenced by data quality, internal controls, management support, employee competence, organisational readiness, and cybersecurity. Therefore, the chapter conceptualises technology-enabled financial reporting as a continuous process in which regulatory requirements and organisational conditions influence ERP-enabled data integration, AI-enabled processing, financial reporting quality, and ultimately managerial and stakeholder decision-making. This perspective provides a theoretical connection among the major themes discussed in the chapter rather than treating financial reporting, ERP, AI, and enterprise systems as independent areas.

Contribution

This chapter contributes to the existing literature by developing an integrated perspective that connects financial reporting, ERP systems, artificial intelligence, organisational governance, and regulatory requirements within a common enterprise framework. Rather than examining these domains independently, the chapter explains how ERP systems can provide the integrated data and process infrastructure required for financial reporting, while AI technologies can enhance automation, analytical capabilities, fraud detection, risk assessment, and decision support. The chapter further identifies organisational and institutional factors, including management commitment, employee competence, data quality, internal controls, regulatory knowledge, and organisational readiness, that determine whether these technologies can effectively improve reporting outcomes. This integrated perspective extends existing discussions of financial reporting quality and ERP and AI adoption by emphasising the relationships among technological infrastructure, intelligent processing, reporting quality, and organisational decision-making. The chapter therefore provides a conceptual foundation for future empirical research examining the measurable effects of AI and ERP integration on financial reporting accuracy, timeliness, transparency, compliance, and organisational performance.

2. FUNDAMENTALS OF FINANCIAL REPORTING

2.1 Bank Key Assests Accounting Rules

This article provides a high-level overview of the rules that commercial banks and bank holding companies in the US and Europe must follow when dealing with financial instruments, but it doesn't bother to explain how IFRS differs from US GAAP. I zero in on the rules put in place before the crisis began and analyse major changes to the accounting standards as they emerge. Financial instrument accounting rules use a "mixed-attribute" model that incorporates aspects of both historical cost and fair value accounting (Laux, 2012). Financial institutions' trading portfolio assets are the only ones that are directly related to fair value accounting in its purest form. Solely large commercial banks and bank holding companies involved in major proprietary trading or investment banking activities should consider it. Typically, assets that are meant to be traded are those that are traded in markets that are very liquid, meaning that prices may be found through orderly transactions.

Banks' investment and cash flow loans are tested for impairment at their historical cost, which is the sum of the principal amount outstanding and an adjustment for amortisation. When the creditor can't possibly collect all of the money that's due, the loan is considered impaired under FAS 114. The discounted loan amount is equal to the present value of the expected cash flows in the future. Lending money is the most important thing that banks have (Dichev, 2017). Additionally, the fair values of loans must be disclosed in the notes accompanying the financial statements per FAS 107. There are two ways to classify securities that aren't for trading: "held to maturity" and "available for sale." Many commercial banks and bank holding companies have a large amount of available-for-sale (AFS) securities on their balance sheets. A separate component of shareholders' equity called "accumulated other comprehensive income" reflects unrealised gains and losses that are thought to be temporary swings in fair values.

This component is not included in the income statement. However, if these changes are seen as long-term, the asset needs to be valued at fair market value, and the income statement will reflect the loss that follows. When a bank has the intention and means to hold onto debt securities until their maturity date, we say that they are held to maturity. If held-to-maturity (HTM) securities are determined to be non-temporarily impaired, they are written down to fair value and reported on the balance sheet at historical cost (adjusted for amortisation) (Pinto & Morais, 2019). In addition, the "fair value option" allows financial institutions to record the value of non-trading assets and other financial products as they would be sold. The goal is to reduce the impact of inconsistent asset and liability valuations on accounting inconsistencies and earnings volatility. Securities that a bank chooses to treat as trading assets are those for which the fair value option is available. However, under the fair value option, banks usually revealed a tiny fraction of their non-trading securities.

2.2 Historical Cost Accounting and Fair Value Accounting

Unadulterated fair-value accounting comprises recording assets and liabilities on the balance sheet at their fair value and acknowledging changes in fair value as profits and losses on the income statement. When assets are exchanged, their fair value is determined by using market prices from liquid markets, which are considered Level 1 inputs. When Level 1 inputs are not available, models are used to determine the fair value (Amaefule, Leonard I., 2018). The second level of inputs that models must use are observable prices for similar assets and other relevant market data. Level 3 inputs, which include model assumptions, are used when observable inputs are not available. In contrast, assets are recorded at their cost as at a certain point in time using historical cost accounting. It is common for the fair value to match the historical cost when an asset is first acquired. Thus, amortisations and impairments are the only sources of asset value drops that are compensated for in historical expenses; increases are not taken into account.

The individual asset at issue determines the impairment test that applies, as does the degree to which the book value of the asset is diminished and the magnitude of the loss that is recognised in the income statement (Budrionytė & Gaižauskas, 2018). The level might vary from just considering losses that have already occurred (incurred-loss model) to taking into account losses equal to the difference between the asset's historical cost and market value (the "lower of cost and market value" method) when the market value falls below the historical cost. The inclusion of supplemental information in the notes that accompany financial statements is a requirement of financial reporting (Ciocan, 2022). Assets that are reported at historical cost or the opposite may be required to have fair value information published.

3. COMPLEX ENTERPRISE ENVIRONMENTS

Complexity management is a hot topic in cybernetics, and it covers all the bases: the system's structure, management, behaviour, control, and more. This leads to questions about the best ways to manage, control, modify, design, or partially affect systems in order to bring about emergent adaptive behaviour. Complex systems present a special challenge in that no job description permits the use of a flawless prediction model; as a result, decisions must be based on incomplete data. Theories, techniques, or frameworks that enable self-regulatory behaviour, whether intentional or emergent, are necessary due to the complex structure of systems (Kandjani et al., 2013). Whatever means are used to achieve this control, it must be seen by an outsider as "partial control" that manages to achieve a predetermined set of desired system features (such availability, viability, sustainability, etc.).

No matter how complicated the system is at that level, every controller can only see the system via a flawed model and use this to guide their control decisions. The controller's (manager's) "perceived complexity" of the system is reflected in the model's complexity. Excessive abstraction and general systems principles of 'wholeness,' according to Check land's warning, can make it difficult for theories, frameworks, and models to deal with real-world issues (Lapalme et al., 2016). Despite the fact that there is often no guidance regarding the limits of their applicability, there are theories, frameworks, and models that are extremely specific and context-dependent, sacrificing generalisability and abstraction. A medium ground, with several levels of abstraction suited to different objectives, is the best degree of generality. None of the scientific fields can achieve the goal of General Systems Theory on its own.

Utilising fundamental ideas from the Generalised Enterprise Reference Architecture and Methodology (GERAM) framework, we have developed a model that clarifies how systems and their surroundings have evolved together (Wang et al., 2025). It is crucial to provide a modelling framework that shows this spectrum from the most general to the most specialised, since enterprise architecture frameworks like GERAM acknowledge that the optimal amount of generality depends on the problem domain. A) GERAM lays out GEMCs, which are basically ontological theories; b) GERAM lays out PEMs, which are reference models; and c) GERAM lays out EMs, which are particular enterprise models. Enterprise models (EMs) reflect particular business entities, PEMs encompass qualities shared by categories of enterprise entities inside or across several industries, and GEMCs outline and formalise the most basic principles of business modelling.

Maintaining a "optimal degree of generality" is essential for EA Cybernetics to provide the field and its practitioners with the "appropriate level of abstraction" needed to accomplish their goals. Thus, if we have an abstract theory, a particular system, and a real problem, then we should be able to find a way to solve or understand the problem within the time and resources we have (Zhang et al., 2017). Due to its dynamic nature, enterprise architecture necessitates a structure for theorising, assessing, and producing new knowledge. For each dynamic field, Anderton and Checkland developed a model to show how the three stages of theory development—theory testing, issue framing, and theory creation—are interdependent. Theoretical frameworks, models, and approaches in enterprise-related domains can only grow and adapt in response to real-world enterprise issue domains, which we see as the bedrock of any evolving discipline of enterprise architecture.

These will lay the groundwork for ideas that might lead to two types of theories:

a) Significant ideas culled from relevant fields to apply relevant models, theories, and approaches inside the problem areas, and
b) Concepts from methodology pertaining to the specific use of business-related fields within problem areas.

Theorising in this way makes it possible to state challenges in a new way, including ones that are special to certain business domains as well as those that are codified, standardised, and synthesised from EA cybernetics. The unified cybernetic theory of enterprise architecture (EA) can be used to represent the formalised enterprise issue areas that are produced by EA cybernetics, an emerging theory in the field (Soundappan, 2025). These integrated ideas may be employed to build methodologies applicable in EA practice. 'Case records' are created when the results of such a synthesis are tested in the real world (via action, influence, or observation). These recordings can then be used for critique and to help develop better theories, models, procedures, and processes.

In order to improve both individual and group ideas, it is necessary to document the usage of the aforementioned approaches in case files (Lei, Fangyu, 2025). A wide range of disciplines, including management and control, linguistics, cognitive science, systems engineering, ecology, biology, sociology, and artificial intelligence, contribute to the EA field's models, methodologies, and ideas. Cybernetic thinking facilitates the integration and correlation of various disciplines by representing the core of multiple theories through abstract functions, processes, and meta-processes, along with their interrelations, rules, and axioms, which can be articulated in appropriately chosen logics (Viknianska et al., 2021). Methods by which various fields' findings are compiled, combined, standardised, and finally shown as a unified Cybernetic theory of EA.

4. FINANCIAL REPORTING FRAMEWORK

The US Financial Accounting Standards Board (FASB) and the International Accounting Standards Board (IASB) both have conceptual frameworks that they use to inform their choices on financial accounting standards. However, issues related to accounting measurement are not included in the Framework. The Framework does not provide a conceptual definition of accounting measurement, a goal for measurement, or a basis for standard setters to choose from different measurement bases when creating accounting standards (Barth, 2014). Consequently, judgements on standard setting measurements have been inherently ad hoc, relying more on historical precedent and the collective judgement of individual FASB and IASB members, informed by their experience, skill, and intuition, rather than on established measuring ideas. Improvements in measurement-related financial reporting standards, which make up a large part of the boards' work, are impeded by the Framework's lack of measurement-related ideas.

It has also played a role in the mysterious implementation of several indicators that characterise the present-day system of financial reporting. The thorough evolution of measurement ideas for use in financial reporting is outside the scope of this research. A more modest goal is to lay the groundwork for future work on these ideas, with the goals of financial reporting and the characteristics of useful financial data outlined in the Framework serving as primary sources. It is easier to incorporate measuring ideas into a unified and coherent Framework if they are grounded in established concepts within the Framework (Dennis, 2018). The Framework ensures consistency and unity by stating that the goal of financial reporting should be the logical source for all components, including measurement. Financial reporting, according to the Framework, should help present and future investors, lenders, and creditors make informed decisions about how to allocate resources to a company by providing them with useful financial information about the reporting business.

Financial data is more useful when it is comparable, verifiable, up-to-date, and easy to grasp, according to the Framework, which also identifies accuracy and truthfulness as crucial qualitative features. According to the Framework, data used for financial reporting must improve specific qualitative aspects in order for financial reporting to achieve its goal (Kisaku, 2017). The technique for building measurement ideas in this paper considers the fundamental features of the Framework's definitions of assets and liabilities, as these are the subjects of measurement according to the Framework. The underlying economic principles of assets and liabilities provide the basis for these definitions, which suggest that assets (liabilities) stand for existing rights (obligations) connected with future inflows (outflows) of economic benefits.

Before moving on to the future evaluation of individual assets and liabilities, the text begins by assessing three possible measurement bases. Assets and liabilities take center stage because, according to the Framework, these two items are the foundation upon which the value of all other parts of the financial statement's rests. The focus is on subsequent measurements because large discrepancies between them don't appear until after the initial measurement (Sutton, 2015). The discussion assesses how well the fair value metric, modified historical cost, and unaltered historical cost display the qualitative characteristics outlined in the Framework. The term "unmodified historical cost" refers to cost-based amounts that haven't changed since their original assessment, "modified historical cost" to cost-based amounts that have changed because of things like amortisation and impairment, and "fair value" to the price an asset or liability would fetch in a market-based systematic transaction on the measurement date.

Alternative measuring bases may be contemplated, including those previously recognised and utilised, such as current cost, along with potentially unrecognised options. These three are given special attention because of their unique characteristics that help to illustrate the process for developing measurement ideas and because of their widespread usage in financial reporting. This discussion looks at how different measurement bases impact the relevance of financial statement elements by capturing key components of asset and liability definitions (Stolowy & Paugam, 2018). Total assets, total liabilities, net income, and other financial statement components are included in financial reports as cumulative metrics. According to the Framework, equity is defined as the difference between the book values of assets and liabilities. So, it's important to make sure that the sum and differences between measurements of specific assets and liabilities have the characteristics described in the Framework while coming up with measurement ideas.

In addition, changes in the reporting period's asset and liability valuations (apart from changes caused by transactions involving equity holders in their capacity as equity holders) determine the assessments of income and expense. Thus, comprehensive income is the sum of a basic set of changes in the values of specific assets and liabilities (Weygandt et al., 2018). Statements of financial position and comprehensive income provide consumers of financial statements with complementary information, but the Framework does not explain how this works conceptually. To guarantee that the integration of these two statements helps to meet the aim of financial reporting regarding measurement, measurement concepts must clarify the informative connection between them. Fair value measurement, as opposed to modified or unmodified historical cost, is more in line with the current Framework principles, according to the evaluation of individual assets and liabilities.

Fair value encompasses key components of asset and liability definitions and represents the ideal combination of qualitative traits. Assessment results show that unmodified historical cost is consistent with several Framework ideas; nonetheless, justifying a change to historical cost is difficult, particularly in light of the myriad ways in which accounting standards now alter cost. One of the main concerns raised regarding fair value is the extent to which it accurately represents reality. The extent to which fair value displays other qualitative features could be compromised by this error (Breuer et al., 2018). Nonetheless, it remains ambiguous if fair values are more susceptible to inaccuracies than modified historical cost, or even unmodified historical cost in certain situations. Clarifying the aim of the measurement is necessary in order to identify the reference point for the mistake, which is vital for evaluating the extent of the error. Modified historical cost is not always specified, while fair value and unmodified historical cost are. The degree to which a measuring base exhibits qualitative qualities is contingent upon particular circumstances. The analysis shows that adding up the quantities of individual assets and liabilities, whether using adjusted or unadjusted historical cost, is meaningless; it's the same as adding up the amounts reported in different currencies.

The aggregate fair values of non-financial assets do not represent the fair value of the asset group because they do not take into consideration the synergy among the assets, even if fair values can be aggregated meaningfully. To fix this, it would be necessary to disclose separately the difference between total fair values and the value of the group's non-financial assets, which would include the synergies' worth. Still, it's beyond the scope of this research to determine if this disparity is an asset of the company and, therefore, should be detailed in the financial accounts (de Villiers & Sharma, 2020). Financial Statement Presentation (FSP), a cooperative effort between the FASB and the IASB, sought to enhance financial report information by suggesting changes to measurement impacts on comprehensive income. The recommendation to provide data that highlights how different measuring bases affect the amounts reported in financial statements is highly pertinent to the measurement process. It was also asked whether the entity's operational, financing, and investment operations should use various measurement bases since the initiative wanted each financial statement to distinguish between them.

For example, non-financial companies can utilise unaltered or adjusted historical cost for operational purposes, and fair value for investment and finance purposes. The research shows that different asset and liability measurement bases impact comprehensive income data in different ways. An example of comprehensive income would be the result of using fair value measurement (Feng et al., 2015). This income would include not only the expected return on net assets but also the difference between expected and actual cash flows, the effect of changes to expected returns and future cash flows, and initial estimates of cash flows and discount rates that are relevant to the transactions, events, or circumstances of the current period. There are several unanswered questions about the development of measurement concepts for financial reporting, such as how users of financial statements should interpret and interpret the components of comprehensive income, which is derived from fair values.

5. FINANCIAL REPORTING PROGRESS

5.1 Financial Reporting Quality Consequences

A section of the literature review shows how financial disclosure helps companies, especially after a financial crisis, which starts a conversation on how banks could be more transparent. Experts agree that a company's financial accounts show how well it is doing right now. The public relies on a company's financial statements to portray its true financial health. According to (Palea et al., 2017), IFRS made net income cash flow projections more accurate. Risk reduction and its effect on reporting quality have been the subject of debate among researchers. However, there is a lack of evidence to support the claim that adequate financial disclosures can improve the evaluation and performance of companies. Insurance industry investors were generally supportive of IFRS adoption, according to research by (Aladwan & Shatnawi, 2019).

According to research by Nnadi and Soobaroyen net foreign direct investment was negatively impacted by the full adoption of IFRS because of the comparability effect. Banks' stock returns were less negatively affected and less synchronised when Du found that banks were more transparent with their financial statements. Historically, there has been no established causal relationship between financial reporting and stock performance. Similar to what (Uzoma et al., 2016) discovered, banks' improved profitability was not due to their adherence to IFRS financial statement disclosures. Instead, other factors, like recapitalisation and cross-border listing, might have played a role in this success. Some studies have highlighted the potential for a nonlinear relationship between the clarity of information disclosure and financial results. Furthermore, does the institutional and protective setting impact these consequences? Businesses in code-law nations began to react negatively to Armstrong's recommendations, which mirrored shareholder concerns over the implementation of IFRS in such countries. Reporting quality may also improve in regimes with stronger capital markets, less depositor insurance, and less external scrutiny.

5.2 Timeliness and Transparency

A company's audited annual report is considered timely if it is released no later than the date that the fiscal year ends. One of the main goals of financial reporting is to help external users make better decisions. The value of accounting data is contingent upon its being relevant, accurate, comparable, current, and readily understandable. To maintain its monetary worth, information must be easily available. But few academics have stressed the importance of timely reporting in the financial sector. Larger, more volatile banks in a volatile stock market have a different link between stock price and reporting timeliness, according to (Ben Rejeb Attia et al., 2019). Nevertheless, these studies only looked at banks; we couldn't find any that looked at insurance, investments, or other subsets of this industry's businesses. If people want to understand and assess businesses, they need financial reports that are transparent. Researchers have identified regulatory oversight (Costello et al., 2019), financial literacy (Jin et al., 2021), and gender and top management diversity (Janahi et al., 2021) as key influencers on financial institutions' transparency.

5.3 Auditing and Corporate Governance Financial Reporting

Amidst discoveries of unethical or illegal activity and a lack of responsibility, the biggest firms in the financial sector must maintain market confidence. The industry is crucial, competitive, and prominent. Inadequate financial reporting by many banks that failed to accurately reflect their operations and the 2008 financial crisis, which almost caused the banking sector to collapse, have highlighted the increasing necessity for strict corporate governance practices and the arbitrary nature of audited financial statements over the last twenty years (Mahdi Sahi et al., 2022). Corporate governance and accounting standards have been standardised in response to the importance of providing accurate information about an organization's financial and economic health to investors in today's globalised financial markets. This seems to indicate that the trust between financial institutions has been well-preserved inside the arbitrary institutional structure that mandates better corporate governance practices to forestall fraud and mismanagement.

Several studies have shown that audit committees, internal and external audits, and other related practices can improve the accuracy of financial reports (Aanu et al., 2016). However, the board of directors and other alternative monitoring systems have received very little attention in the academic literature. It is widely recognised that audit regulations have varying impacts on the reporting quality of financial institutions, and that these impacts are substantial (Bratten et al., 2019). The quality of financial reporting can be improved, according to researchers, by increasing the number of professionals on the audit committee, extending the duration of the audit firm, involving internal audit, using specific phrasing for the audit committee disclaimer, and paying for audit services. Furthermore, it was argued that having an accounting expert on the audit committee improves the quality of financial reports more than having general financial and supervisory knowledge, which in turn increases the reliability and relevance of financial reporting. Results from the annual audit showed that better communication both internally and externally led to more thorough financial reporting.

The longer an audit firm is engaged, the better the financial reports will be, particularly for more complex banks. Audit firms' investments in client-specific knowledge will be negatively affected by a short tenure, especially in critical situations where this information is required. The effect of IFRS adoption on auditing fees was investigated by several writers. The implementation of IFRS increases the time commitments of auditors and the complexity of certain parts of the standards, as indicated by the increased fees incurred after the transition to the new standards. The 1998 and 2008 financial crises were linked to insufficient governance functions and almost caused the collapse of the financial sector; nevertheless, very little research has focused on the features and committees of boards. Financial statements are considered as a crucial component of accountability, and a lack of understanding of them may greatly hinder the progress of corporate governance. Financial reporting and the public release of financial accounts are cornerstones of good company governance.

Building an informational advantage for a financial organization involves using both public and private sources of information. The data helps the institutions identify areas where they may improve their strategy, management, and board effectiveness, as well as how these areas affect their financial success. A lack of thorough comprehension of the restrictions and limitations of financial statements casts doubt on the accountability of directors and the effectiveness of corporate governance. Argued that the only disclosures that significantly legitimise financial reporting by boosting the notion that they reflect the organization's real situation are those that pertain to corporate governance processes. According to Karajeh's examination of individual monitoring systems, managers' motivations to enhance the quality of financial disclosure processes and bank dividends were influenced by nationality and the presence of women on the board.

5.4 Financial Reporting Quality Determinants

The effect of non-financial aspects of corporate governance has been the main focus of earlier studies on the quality of financial reports. A decline in the accuracy of financial reports can happen if big banks are less vigilant in their supervision of management's opportunistic actions. Financial enterprises tend to have more ambiguous capital structures and more informational gaps than non-financial firms. Managerial competence and governance norms have a significant impact on the quality of financial reporting in banks, according to empirical study. Skilled bank managers are less likely to manipulate profits for personal gain.

Also, when comparing affected banks to unaffected ones, it was found that internal control requirements made worries about loan loss provisions, cash-flow predictability, and earnings persistence worse, while reducing concerns about accounting conservatism and benchmark-beating performance. However, not all studies found a link between companies' levels of financial transparency and metrics like growth and profitability (Kumar et al., 2025). More effective political, extralegal, and judicial institutions were said to be associated with higher earnings quality across all five indices examined at the macroeconomic level. Moreover, countries with stronger institutions reported slightly lower loan loss provisions. In their explanation of the differences in international reporting, Amidu and Issahaku postulated that the goal of the banking sector in diversifying its revenue streams to include interest and non-interest income, as well as the adoption of IFRS and its interaction with globalisation, might explain why banks in emerging economies show better profit quality.

5.5 Online Financial Reporting

To keep the capital markets apprised of a company's financial situation and performance, financial disclosure and transparency are cornerstones of good corporate governance. To disseminate information to decision-makers, many companies around the world rely on online financial disclosure. When it comes to trading stocks and other financial instruments, one kind of voluntary disclosure is the sharing of financial information through online platforms (Adugna & Kumar, 2021). In recent times, the internet has grown rapidly and gained widespread popularity. This advancement significantly impacts communication methods. Online financial disclosure is a new kind of voluntary disclosure that businesses have started using because paper-based disclosure techniques are expensive and have limits.

While some researchers have looked at what causes financial institutions to report online and what it means for consumers, their results have been mixed. For example, (Bin-Ghanem & Ariff, 2016) state that there is a correlation between online financial transparency and corporate success, but they reach different results. There is little correlation between the breadth and depth of online reporting and stock price movements. Researchers found that performance measures were associated with Islamic banks' levels of online financial openness. The contradictory results make one wonder if various types of financial institutions are subject to varied consequences of internet reporting.

Figure 1. Online Financial Reporting Quality

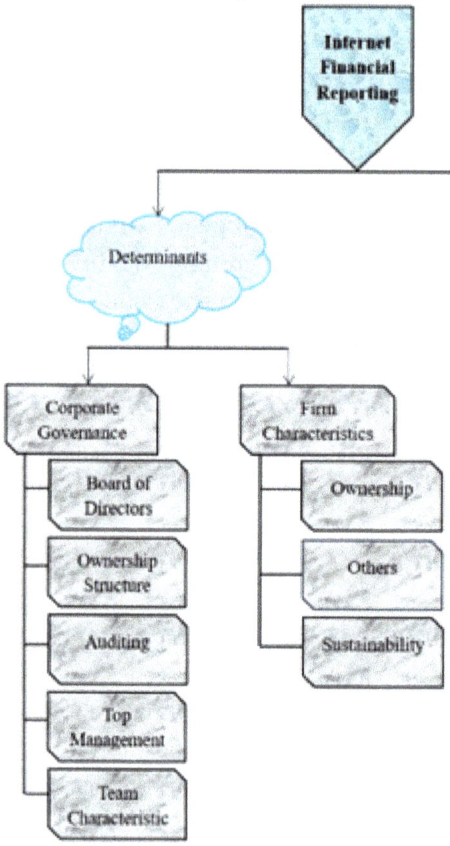

Company attributes such as size, profitability, ownership structure, liquidity, and leverage are shown in Figure 1 as drivers of online financial reporting practices. Future studies should investigate several facets of online disclosure that have been disregarded by earlier academics. One such area of focus is the uniformity of financial reporting conducted online. Businesses must comply with the disclosure obligation by making available sufficiently standardised information about their operations so that users, including creditors, current and future shareholders, and others, can make meaningful comparisons of key facts.

6. LITERATURE SYNTHESIS

The existing literature can be synthesised into four interconnected research streams: financial reporting quality, ERP-enabled organisational integration, AI-based financial automation, and governance and regulatory control. Research on financial reporting primarily emphasises relevance, accuracy, comparability, timeliness, transparency, auditing, and corporate governance, whereas ERP research focuses on integrating organisational functions, standardising business processes, improving information accessibility, and supporting strategic and operational decisions. AI-related studies increasingly examine automated data entry, reconciliation, financial statement preparation, fraud detection, risk assessment, and auditing. However, these research streams are frequently examined separately, creating a fragmented understanding of how financial information moves from enterprise transactions to intelligent reporting and decision support. The literature also demonstrates that technological benefits depend on organisational and institutional conditions, including management support, employee training, data availability, internal controls, and regulatory knowledge. Consequently, an integrated perspective is required to explain how ERP infrastructure and AI capabilities can collectively influence financial reporting quality while maintaining governance, compliance, and organisational accountability.

7. ENTERPRISE RESOURCE PLANNING (ERP) SYSTEMS

Integrating TQM (Total Quality Management) with Business Process there has been a shift in emphasis toward the use of IT in core company functions, and re-engineering (BPR) is a major factor in this shift. With ERP being considered as an essential technology for BPR, many scholars have drawn attention to the links between the two (Al-mashari, 2003). To help modern businesses achieve their long-term goals, ERP systems are increasingly recognised as a useful tool for connecting different departments inside a company to the databases and information systems that make up that company.

Figure 2. ERP Research Taxonomy

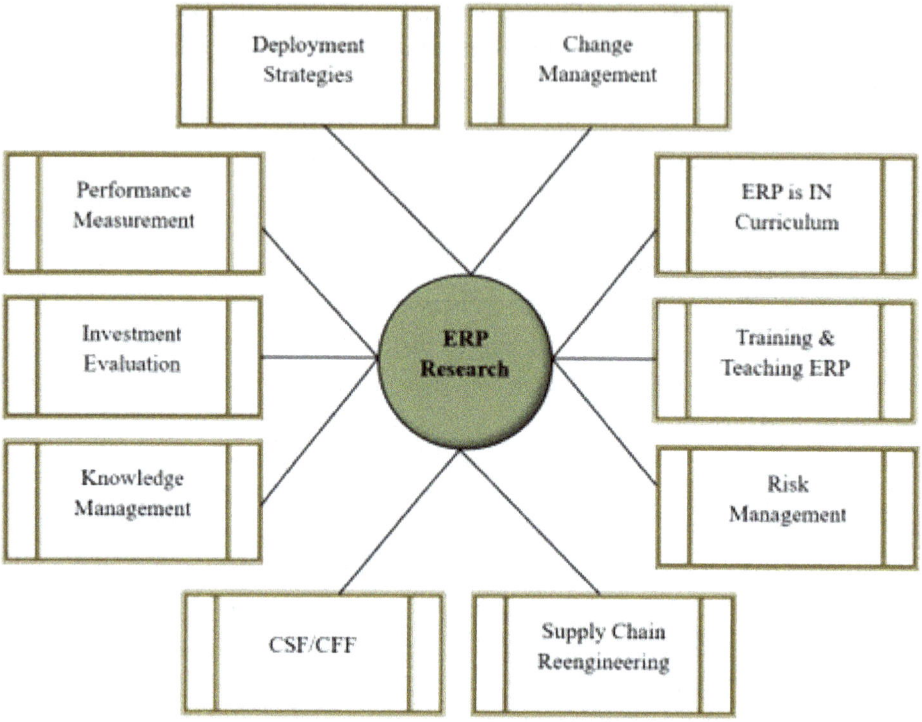

Ensuring flexibility is a significant barrier to ERP implementation. Companies must consistently identify methods to integrate newly acquired business functionalities into their data processing systems as swiftly as possible (Bahssas et al., 2015). ERP solutions are considered flexible if they can be easily changed to accommodate new company models and processes. Because of its effectiveness in standardising company processes and systems and their adaptability to best practices, ERP systems are a major draw for many companies looking to use them. Figure 1 shows the main areas of ERP study based on a thorough review of the current literature on ERP.

In order to integrate different systems, make information easily accessible across the company, and make well-informed decisions regarding both strategic and operational issues, organisations consider ERP-enabled standardisation vital (Ullah et al., 2017). Although there are benefits to ERP, standardisation is not without its downsides. Many experts in the field warn that standardisation efforts could lead to a loss of adaptability, an essential quality for companies to have in the face of rapidly changing business processes and information technology systems.

An in-depth analysis of business and industry needs should guide the ERP solution selection process, which must strike a balance between rigidity and adaptability. In order to have a well-rounded implementation plan, other important factors must be considered. There must be a significant investment of time and energy into the business and technology sides of an organization in order to implement an ERP system (Katuu, 2020). The key to a smooth ERP rollout is thorough organisational planning. The subsequent list created by Rao delineates the principal aspects that must be taken into account throughout the preparatory phase of ERP implementation:

- Infrastructure resource planning entails ensuring that sufficient infrastructure is prepared in a manner that it becomes dependable in a timely manner, before to and after implementation.
- Local area network—providing ERP and other application network functionality.
- Servers set up sufficient server and network infrastructure, even when training and modelling.
- PCs—releasing brand-new PCs with cutting-edge specs that should be more than enough for the majority of ERP systems.
- Training facilities - creating a suitable training center to function as a competency hub.
- Human resource planning—with an emphasis on creating a cooperative atmosphere where team size is cross-functional.
- Education about ERP—All employees should receive ERP training on the best practices for both successful and unsuccessful ERP implementations.
- The commitment to deploy the appropriate personnel for the ERP project is acknowledged as challenging yet essential, necessitating that the most qualified individuals dedicate themselves entirely to the initiative.
- Ready and able to view an existing location as a potential Greenfield site.
- Effectively functioning manual systems requires conducting an audit to assess the current state and identify appropriate corrective measures.
- Selecting between a centralised and a decentralised implementation process.

The key elements for a successful ERP implementation, according to Gupta, are the following: getting buy-in from upper management, creating cross-functional task forces to integrate project management with business units, determining what hardware is needed, deploying in stages rather than all at once, starting early on user training and support, optimising decision-making to speed up implementation, and being patient, because ERP implementation is a long process (Aboabdo et al., 2019). Cissna notes that in order to lessen the impact of resistance to change caused by ERP installation, factors including support from upper management, the right people being assigned to implementation teams, and active participation from field staff are essential. Gupta delineates certain prevalent issues related to ERP adoption.

Resistance to change is a part of this, as is the unwillingness of some workers to learn new processes or take on more responsibility. Unexpected costs stemming from new regulations that emerge after freezing is another concern. Another problem is that end-users aren't properly trained to operate and maintain the system, even when it's up and running. Case studies and empirical investigations of ERP deployment in connection to specific phases of implementation may form the focus of future research in this area (Martins & Belfo, 2023). It would be interesting to look at how different companies have adopted ERP systems using a critical factor analysis. The effects of ERP on HR and IT systems, alignment of strategies, knowledge management, application service providers, organisational learning, outsourcing, and competitive advantage are other potential research directions.

8. EMPIRICAL EVIDENCE AND CASE-BASED DISCUSSION

Empirical evidence from the literature demonstrates that the effectiveness of technology-enabled financial reporting depends on both technological capabilities and organisational conditions. ERP implementation studies indicate that integrated enterprise systems can improve information accessibility and support coordination across organisational functions, but successful implementation requires management commitment, appropriate infrastructure, employee training, cross-functional participation, and effective change management. Research on AI-enabled financial reporting further indicates that automated systems can support data entry, reconciliation, financial statement preparation, financial analysis, fraud detection, risk assessment, and auditing, thereby reducing repetitive manual activities and supporting more efficient decision-making. Evidence concerning IFRS implementation also demonstrates that regulatory changes can generate organisational challenges involving accounting knowledge, policy development, managerial support, data collection, IT capabilities, and implementation planning. These findings collectively demonstrate that technology adoption should not be evaluated solely in terms of system deployment; rather, its success depends on the interaction between technological infrastructure, organisational capabilities, regulatory requirements, internal controls, and human decision-making. This evidence supports the conceptual argument of the chapter that integrated ERP and AI capabilities can strengthen financial reporting when they are implemented within an appropriate organisational and governance environment.

9. ARTIFICIAL INTELLIGENCE AND AUTOMATION IN FINANCIAL REPORTING

Experts across fields need to be aware of the major obstacles related to AI use as technology advances rapidly. AI is a subfield of computer science that aims to program computers to do tasks typically associated with human intelligence (Sreseli & Kadagishvili, 2023). Machine learning is the study and practice of programming computers to perform tasks typically associated with human cognition, such as learning, problem solving, perceiving, reasoning, and processing language.

AI encompasses a range of techniques and concepts, including:

Machine Learning: Machine learning is a subfield of AI that aims to develop models and techniques that enable computers to learn and improve their performance via experience, without the need for explicit programming. Data is processed by ML algorithms, which then use this information to make predictions or assessments.

Deep Learning: One branch of ML, known as "deep learning," concentrates on analysing complicated and massive datasets by means of artificial neural networks that contain multiple layers (Farea et al., 2024). An example of a DL model is a DNN, which can learn to accurately recognise images and voices by building hierarchical representations of the data.

Robotics and Automation: Robots and automation would not be possible without AI, which allows them to perceive their environment, make decisions, and carry out physical activities without human intervention. Enabled by AI, robotic systems can adapt to changing circumstances, learn from interactions, and efficiently and accurately carry out complex tasks.

Cognitive Computing: The goal of cognitive computing is to create machines that can think and solve problems in the same way that humans can. To achieve this goal of cognition and decision-making mimicking human abilities, it combines AI techniques with big data processing, NLP, and ML. Accounting and financial reporting are two areas that can benefit from AI, which will be defined and discussed in this section. The best way for professionals to use AI is for them to understand the potential benefits and drawbacks of the technology so they can make educated judgements.

Current Applications of AI in Financial Reporting and Accounting

Among the many sectors that have been revolutionised by AI is the accounting and financial reporting industry. Improvements in process optimisation, accuracy, and decision-making capacity have emerged from the widespread use of AI technology. There is a wide range of current applications of AI in financial reporting and accounting, which offers significant benefits in terms of accuracy, efficiency, and strategic insights. Several significant applications encompass:

Automated Reconciliation and Data Entry: Accounting software can be automatically populated by AI-driven systems that retrieve financial data from many sources, such as bank statements, invoices, and receipts. This reduces the need for human data entry, which in turn reduces the likelihood of mistakes and increases accuracy while saving time.

Financial Statement Preparation and Analysis: Automating data collection, classification, and report generation are three ways in which AI improves financial statement preparation (Ashraf, 2025). It reduces the time required for financial reporting, increases accuracy, and ensures compliance with accounting rules. Financial ratios, liquidity, profitability, and other key performance indicators can be better understood with the use of AI's thorough financial analysis.

Fraud Detection and Risk Assessment: By analysing data from suppliers, financial transactions, and other relevant sources, AI systems can detect patterns that could indicate fraudulent activity. To aid in the detection and prevention of financial crime, these systems can spot transactions that seem suspicious, unusual, or out of the ordinary.

Risk Management and Auditing: Financial risks can be assessed by AI-powered systems by analysing past data, current market movements, and factors that influence risk (Olakunle Babatunde Alao et al., 2024). They provide auditors with high-tech tools to optimise the audit process, identify potential issues, and analyse risks. By boosting internal control systems, AI can make risk management procedures more precise and effective.

10. CHALLENGES IN FINANCIAL REPORTING

Among the most pressing issues is the lack of proper training on IFRS, which leads to following the lead of other reporting entities. Other problems include a lack of buy-in from upper management, confusion about the wider business effects of IFRS adoption, and difficulties in gathering the necessary data for preliminary IFRS financial statements. The absence of knowledge and experience regarding IFRS was the sole issue addressed by all responders. This issue was raised by seven respondents again, and five people cited it as the worst problem with IFRS (Weaver & Woods, 2015). Eleven respondents brought up the difficulty of developing accounting policies as a major barrier, with four citing this problem as a top priority. The two problems are related because developing accounting rules that are in line with IFRS is complicated due to the assumed lack of understanding and experience with IFRS. Thirteen incidents were attributed to a lack of managerial help, twelve to a failure to anticipate wider business consequences, and two to a lack of prioritisation.

Five respondents cited difficulties in data collecting on six occasions, with three identifying it as a significant worry. Although five additional issues were noted, none of them were deemed to be of substantial concern by the respondents. System and IT capabilities, fees and expenditures, inadequate preliminary planning, reliance on specialists, and the application of certain IFRS requirements were among the highlighted concerns. It is worth mentioning that while a few interviewees mentioned the challenges of following specific IFRS requirements, this did not emerge as a major obstacle to implementation. Since there is a lot of written about how complicated IFRS financial reporting and disclosure requirements are, this came as a bit of a surprise (Yadav et al., 2025). Respondents' difficulties are similar to those mentioned by Jermakowicz and Gornik-Tomaszewski. Our findings supplement theirs by drawing attention to previously unrecognised obstacles, such as poor data capture and a lack of managerial backing, in addition to the previously identified priorities. Next, we'll compare our results to those of Jermakowicz and Gornik-Tomaszewski (2006); but, before that, we'll take a closer look at each individual obstacle.

11. FUTURE RESEARCH SUGGESTIONS

First and foremost, we think it's important to learn more about why developed economies have so many transparency and reporting laws. The need and benefits of regulation are questioned by conventional economic theory and a large body of literature, especially when market failure is severe. When economies and financial markets are doing well, however, strict regulation of corporate reporting and disclosure is commonplace. Is the success of these markets a result of or in opposition to regulation? The seeming gap between traditional economics and the actual application of regulations can be bridged if we take the time to understand this issue (Leuz & Wysocki, 2011). An intriguing avenue for future study in this regard could be to determine whether rules and regulations help by "stabilising expectations" in the financial markets.

In light of this, it would be fascinating to explore how much rules and regulations help by "stabilising expectations" in the financial markets, especially in situations where information is limited, contracts are poor, and market participants display limited rationality. For instance, reporting rules can help with market coordination by providing a standardised, "coarse" method that everyone can understand, which is used in many contracts and transactions and is known by information providers and consumers alike. Standardised financial reporting and disclosure practices in many developed nations seem to be an inadequate and "coarse" answer (Manavadaria et al., 2025). Asset bubbles, in which the market value of a company's shares suddenly increases or decreases dramatically relative to its true worth, are another potential source of market instability that financial reporting and disclosure rules could help to alleviate.

A major misallocation of capital is one way in which financial bubbles damage economies. Consequently, during times of technological or financial innovation, which often coincide with financial bubbles, regulations requiring reporting and disclosure can do two things: (i) reduce the possibility of bubbles caused by information asymmetry among market participants, and (ii) force companies to talk about what really matters, like their verifiable current cash flows, profits, net assets, and ownership claims, rather than their hopes for the future. To put it simply, the present crop of market players facing supposedly "novel" market conditions can benefit from the lessons (and wounds) from the past when it comes to reporting standards and disclosure regulations, which are purportedly out of date. At this time, it is not known how much reporting and disclosure rules help prevent asset bubbles and economic disasters. If it does, it may elucidate why regulation frequently ensues after financial crises.

12. CONCLUSION

Complex corporate environments call for technology-driven, intelligent systems that can handle real-time analytics, regulatory compliance, and large-scale financial operations. By improving automation, openness, precision, and decision-making efficacy, cutting-edge technologies including cloud computing, blockchain, enterprise resource planning systems, artificial intelligence, and robotic process automation are reshaping financial reporting. Modern financial reporting frameworks are making strides towards autonomous, regulatory complexities, and sustainable financial ecosystems, intelligent, despite challenges related to cybersecurity, data aggregation, and fraud reduction. Flexible, secure, and data-driven FMS are the foundation of future corporate financial reporting. These systems will boost organisational resilience and strategic expansion.

REFERENCES

Aanu, O. S., Samuel, F. A., Ajayi, A., & Folashade, O. (2016). Examining the quality of financial reporting in the banking sector in Nigeria: Does audit committee accounting expertise matter? *Journal of Internet Banking and Commerce*, *21*(3).

Aboabdo, S., Aldhoiena, A., & Al-Amrib, H. (2019). Implementing Enterprise Resource Planning ERP System in a Large Construction Company in KSA. *Procedia Computer Science*, *164*, 463–470. DOI: 10.1016/j.procs.2019.12.207

Adugna, B. M., & Kumar, B. (2021). Determinants of internet financial reporting: In the case of Ethiopian insurance and banking sector companies. *Innovations*, *66*(66), 760–778.

Al-mashari, M. (2003). Enterprise resource planning (ERP) systems: A research agenda. *Industrial Management & Data Systems*, *103*(1), 22–27. DOI: 10.1108/02635570310456869

Aladwan, M., & Shatnawi, Y. (2019). The association between accounting disclosures and stock market price: An empirical study on Jordanian commercial banks. *International Journal of Managerial and Financial Accounting*, *11*(1), 73–92. DOI: 10.1504/IJMFA.2019.097831

Olakunle Babatunde Alao, Oritsematosan Faith Dudu, Enoch O. Alonge, & Chukwuka Emmanuel Eze. (2024). Automation in financial reporting: A conceptual framework for efficiency and accuracy in U.S. corporations. *Global Journal of Advanced Research and Reviews*, *2*(2), 040–050. DOI: 10.58175/gjarr.2024.2.2.0057

Amaefule, L. I.. (2018). Fair Value Measurement versus Historical Cost Accounting: A Comparative Effect on Firms' Performance in Nigeria. *Research Journal of Finance and Accounting*, *9*(10), 165–175.

Ashraf, M. (2025). Does automation improve financial reporting? Evidence from internal controls. *Review of Accounting Studies*, *30*(1), 436–479. DOI: 10.1007/s11142-024-09822-y

Bahssas, D. M., AlBar, A. M., & Hoque, M. R. (2015). Enterprise Resource Planning (ERP) Systems: Design, Trends and Deployment. *The International Technology Management Review*, *5*(2), 72. DOI: 10.2991/itmr.2015.5.2.2

Barth, M. E. (2014). Measurement in financial reporting: The need for concepts. *Accounting Horizons*, *28*(2), 331–352. DOI: 10.2308/acch-50689

Ben Rejeb Attia, M., Lassoued, N., & Sassi, H. (2019). Financial reporting timeliness and the value relevance of earnings: Evidence from banks in the MENA countries. *The International Trade Journal, 33*(3), 277–301. DOI: 10.1080/08853908.2018.1459212

Bin-Ghanem, H. O., & Ariff, A. M. (2016). Internet financial reporting and firm value: Evidence from Gulf Cooperation Council countries. *International Journal of Accounting. Auditing and Performance Evaluation, 12*(3), 237–260. DOI: 10.1504/IJAAPE.2016.077891

Bratten, B., Causholli, M., & Omer, T. C. (2019). Audit Firm Tenure, Bank Complexity, and Financial Reporting Quality. *Contemporary Accounting Research, 36*(1), 295–325. DOI: 10.1111/1911-3846.12427

Breuer, M., Hombach, K., & Müller, M. A. (2018). How does financial reporting regulation affect firms' banking? *Review of Financial Studies, 31*(4), 1265–1297. DOI: 10.1093/rfs/hhx123

Budrionytė, R., & Gaižauskas, L. (2018). Historical cost vs fair value in forest accounting: The case of Lithuania. *Entrepreneurship and Sustainability Issues, 6*(1), 60–76. DOI: 10.9770/jesi.2018.6.1(5)

Ciocan, C. C. (2022). Historical Cost vs Fair Value in Accounting: Consequences for the Quality of Financial Information and the True and Fair View. *CECCAR Business Review, 3*(10), 48–59. DOI: 10.37945/cbr.2022.10.07

Costello, A. M., Granja, J., & Weber, J. (2019). Do Strict Regulators Increase the Transparency of Banks? *Journal of Accounting Research, 57*(3), 603–637. DOI: 10.1111/1475-679X.12255

de Villiers, C., & Sharma, U. (2020). A critical reflection on the future of financial, intellectual capital, sustainability and integrated reporting. *Critical Perspectives on Accounting, 70*, 0–25. DOI: 10.1016/j.cpa.2017.05.003

Dennis, I. (2018). What is a Conceptual Framework for Financial Reporting? *Accounting in Europe, 15*(3), 374–401. DOI: 10.1080/17449480.2018.1496269

Dichev, I. D. (2017). On the conceptual foundations of financial reporting. *Accounting and Business Research, 47*(6), 617–632. DOI: 10.1080/00014788.2017.1299620

Farea, M. M., Alifan, B., & Al-Dubai, M. M. M. (2024). Intelligent Automation in Accounting and Financial. *Journal of Tianjin University Science and Technology*, (June), 463–480. DOI: 10.5281/zenodo.12516114

Feng, M., Li, C., McVay, S. E., & Skaife, H. (2015). Does Ineffective Internal Control over Financial Reporting affect a Firm's Operations? Evidence from Firms' Inventory Management. *The Accounting Review*, *35*(4), 619–626. DOI: 10.2308/accr-50909

Hanifah, Sutanto, E., Siswadi, U., & Murniawan, M. W. (2024). The Influence of Regulatory Changes on Auditing Standards and Practices. *Journal of Multidisciplinary Sustainability Asean*.

Janahi, M., Millo, Y., & Voulgaris, G. (2021). CFO gender and financial reporting transparency in banks. *European Journal of Finance*, *27*(3), 199–221. DOI: 10.1080/1351847X.2020.1801481

Jin, J., Kanagaretnam, K., Liu, Y. I., & Cheng, M. (2021). Does Citizens' Financial Literacy Relate to Bank Financial Reporting Transparency? *European Accounting Review*, *30*(5), 887–912. DOI: 10.1080/09638180.2021.1965897

Kandjani, H., Bernus, P., & Nielsen, S. (2013). Enterprise Architecture cybernetics and the edge of chaos: Sustaining enterprises as complex systems in complex business environments. *Proceedings of the Annual Hawaii International Conference on System Sciences*, 3858–3867. DOI: 10.1109/HICSS.2013.199

Katuu, S. (2020). Enterprise Resource Planning: Past, Present, and Future. *New Review of Information Networking*, *25*(1), 37–46. DOI: 10.1080/13614576.2020.1742770

Kisaku, J. M. (2017). Impact of Financial Reporting Frameworks on the Quality of Not-for-Profit Financial Reports. *Walden University*, 1–106.

Kumar, P., Rani, P., Rajesh, T. S., Deebika, R., Harina, A. S., & Bhoopathy, V. (2025). Prediction of Stock Market Using Machine Learning and Cloud Computing. *Advancements in Cloud-Based Intelligent Informative Engineering*, 253–376. DOI: 10.4018/979-8-3373-0781-7.ch016

Lapalme, J., Gerber, A., Van Der Merwe, A., Zachman, J., De Vries, M., & Hinkelmann, K. (2016). Exploring the future of enterprise architecture: A Zachman perspective. *Computers in Industry*, *79*, 103–113. DOI: 10.1016/j.compind.2015.06.010

Laux, C. (2012). Financial instruments, financial reporting, and financial stability. *Accounting and Business Research*, *42*(3), 239–260. DOI: 10.1080/00014788.2012.681857

Lei, F.. (2025). Spider 2.0: Evaluating language models on real-world enterprise text-to-sql workflows. *International Conference on Learning Representations,* 0.

Leuz, C., & Wysocki, P. D. (2011). Economic Consequences of Financial Reporting and Disclosure Regulation: A Review and Suggestions for Future Research. SSRN *Electronic Journal*. DOI: 10.2139/ssrn.1105398

Mahdi Sahi, A., Sahi, A. M., Abbas, A. F., & Khatib, F. A., S. (. (2022). Financial reporting quality of financial institutions: Literature review. *Cogent Business & Management*, *9*(1). Advance online publication. DOI: 10.1080/23311975.2022.2135210

Manavadaria, M. S., Sharma, R. K., Parasar, A., Chauhan, A., Jeyaprakash, N., Mohaideen, A., & Bhoopathy, V. (2025). Machine learning for fraud detection and financial crimes. *Forensic Intelligence and Deep Learning Solutions in Crime Investigation*, 183–206. DOI: 10.4018/979-8-3693-9405-2.ch010

Martins, E. J., & Belfo, F. P. (2023). Major concerns about Enterprise Resource Planning (ERP) systems: A systematic review of a decade of research (2011-2021). *Procedia Computer Science*, *219*, 378–387. DOI: 10.1016/j.procs.2023.01.303

Palea, Vera, and S. D. S. (2017). Earnings reported under IFRS improve the prediction of future cash flows? Evidence from European banks. *Australian Accounting Review*.

Pinto, I., & Morais, A. I. (2019). What matters in disclosures of key audit matters: Evidence from Europe. *Journal of International Financial Management & Accounting*, *30*(2), 145–162. DOI: 10.1111/jifm.12095

Soundappan, S. J. (2025)... *Next Generation AI Enabled Holistic Cognitive Platform for Secure Cloud Network Intelligence Enterprise Systems and Digital Trust Optimization.*, *8*(5), 11534–11542. DOI: 10.15680/IJCTECE.2025.0805031

Sreseli, N., & Kadagishvili, N. (2023). Use of Artificial Intelligence for Accounting and Financial Reporting Purposes: A Review of the Key Issues. *American International Journal of Business Management*, *6*(8), 72–83. www.aijbm.com

Stolowy, H., & Paugam, L. (2018). The expansion of non-financial reporting: An exploratory study. *Accounting and Business Research*, *48*(5), 525–548. DOI: 10.1080/00014788.2018.1470141

Sutton, D. B. (2015). The objectives of financial reporting: the case for coherence the Conceptual Framework, and standards 2 The objectives of financial reporting: the case for coherence the Conceptual. *Abacus*, •••, 1–41.

Ullah, A., & Baharun, R. Bin, Nor, K. M., Siddique, M., & Bhatti, M. N. (2017). Enterprise Resource Planning (ERP) Systems and ERP Quality Factors: A Literature Review. *Journal of Managerial Sciences*, *11*(3), 297–322.

Uzoma, A. B., Olokoyo, F. O., Babajide, A. A., Folashade, O., & Dorcas, A. (2016). Adoption of international financial reporting standards and its implication on bank performance in Nigeria: A comparative approach. *Journal of Internet Banking and Commerce, 21*(Special Issue 5).

Viknianska, A., Kharynovych-Yavorska, D., Sahaidak, M., Zhavoronok, A., & Filippov, V. (2021). METHODOLOGICAL APPROACH to ECONOMIC ANALYSIS and CONTROL of ENTERPRISES under CONDITIONS of ECONOMIC SYSTEMS TRANSFORMATION. *Naukovyi Visnyk Natsionalnoho Hirnychoho Universytetu, 2021*(4), 150–157. DOI: 10.33271/nvngu/2021-4/150

Wang, X., Li, Z., & Cheng, F. (2025). How Business Environments Affect Enterprise Vitality: A Complex Adaptive Systems Theory Perspective. *Systems, 13*(10), 1–36. DOI: 10.3390/systems13100864

Weaver, L., & Woods, M. (2015). The Challenges Faced by Reporting Entities on Their Transition to International Financial Reporting Standards: A Qualitative Study. *Accounting in Europe*, *12*(2), 197–221. DOI: 10.1080/17449480.2015.1103376

Weygandt, . (2018). *Financial accounting with international financial reporting standards*. John Wiley & Sons.

Yadav, S., Singh, A., Peddapalli, N., Chauhan, A., Ahmed, S. A., & Bhoopathy, V. (2025). *ML Use in Fraud Detection in the Financial Sector*. 427–448. DOI: 10.4018/979-8-3693-8507-4.ch023

Zhang, Y., Ren, S., Liu, Y., & Si, S. (2017). A big data analytics architecture for cleaner manufacturing and maintenance processes of complex products. *Journal of Cleaner Production*, *142*, 626–641. DOI: 10.1016/j.jclepro.2016.07.123

Chapter 6
Integrating AI-Driven Insights Into Financial Dashboards for Real-Time Decision Making in Digital Enterprises

Karthikeyan Shanmugam
http://orcid.org/0000-0003-4276-2663
SASTRA (Deemed to be) University, India

ABSTRACT

Digitalization has made the making of financial plans more constant and driven by data. This chapter studies how the strategic financial planning of digital enterprises increases when big data analytics, real-time dashboards, and AI are integrated. By analysing large amounts of financial and behavioural data, big data enhances the accuracy of forecasts, risk analysis, and the allocation of resources. Interactive dashboards put complicated metrics into actionable visualizations, speeding up managerial decisions. Predictive and prescriptive models are powered by AI to generate future scenarios, suggest the best changes, and are continually updated with live and historical data. The chapter introduces a unified mechanism between analytics, visualization, and AI and financial planning performance. Results indicate that data-centric approaches tremendously enhance organizational agility, governance, and competitive advantage. It offers managerial implications to assist managers in aligning financial planning and corporate strategy in digital settings.

DOI: 10.4018/979-8-3373-9230-1.ch006

© 2027, IGI Global Scientific Publishing. Copying or distributing in print or electronic forms without written permission of IGI Global Scientific Publishing is prohibited. Use of this chapter to
erative artificial intelligence (AI) technologies is expressly prohibited. The publisher reserves all rights to license its use for generative AI training and machine learning model development.

1. INTRODUCTION

The accelerated development of digital companies has altered the traditionally descriptive operation of financial planning into a dynamic and data-driven strategic operation. The use of big-data analytics, real-time dashboards, and artificial intelligence-related insights has turned out to be a crucial component in improving the accuracy of forecasting, capital distribution optimization, and financial risk management in digital markets that can change rapidly in the context of modern organisations. The conventional financial-planning methods, which were historically founded on historical accounting data and periodic reporting, are now proving inadequate for the fast-paced decision-making necessities of digitally connected ecosystems, which are characterised by tremendous data velocity and reliability. Recent studies underline that the impact on the performance of firms and their competitiveness in the context of data-driven decision-making is immense at the level of strategic management processes (T. Davenport & Harris, 2017).

Big-data analytics can help organisations derive actionable information out of large, heterogeneous datasets in finance and operations, and dashboards offer easy-to-apply visualisation front-ends that can support managerial thinking processes and prompt tracking of financial metrics (Eckerson, 2010). The insights provided by AI also enhance financial planning by introducing predictive modelling and optimisation algorithms that aid in the processing of scenario-based decision-making and proactive minimisation of risks (T. H. Davenport & Ronanki, 2018). With the growing presence and utilization of digital enterprises deploying platform-based and data-rich business models, the integration of analytics and AI within financial planning is becoming a necessity to adapt to agile, strategic, and sustainable business models.

The chapter investigates the role of the combination of big-data analytics, dashboards, and AI-driven insights in improving the effectiveness of strategic financial planning in digital companies, featuring an integrated analytical model and the description of major managerial implications.

1.1 Evolution of Digital Financial Planning

Financial planning has evolved significantly over the last two decades due to rapid advancements in digital technologies, data analytics, and intelligent information systems. Traditionally, financial planning was largely dependent on historical accounting records, periodic reports, and manual forecasting techniques. Organisations relied on quarterly or annual financial statements to evaluate their performance and make strategic decisions. While these conventional approaches were effective in relatively stable business environments, they have become insufficient in today's digital economy, where market conditions, customer behaviour, and operational dynamics change continuously.

The emergence of digital enterprises has transformed the financial planning process from a static and descriptive activity into a dynamic and predictive strategic function. Digital enterprises generate vast amounts of data through online transactions, customer interactions, supply-chain activities, enterprise systems, and social media platforms. This continuous flow of structured and unstructured data has created opportunities for organisations to improve financial forecasting, budgeting, investment planning, and risk management through advanced analytical techniques (Grover et al., 2018).

Big data analytics has become one of the most influential technologies in modern financial planning because it allows organisations to process large and complex datasets in real time. Through descriptive analytics, managers can analyse historical financial performance and identify trends in profitability, revenue growth, and cost structures. Predictive analytics further enhances decision-making by forecasting future market behaviour, demand fluctuations, and cash-flow requirements using statistical and machine-learning techniques (Wamba et al., 2017). Prescriptive analytics goes a step further by recommending optimal financial actions such as pricing strategies, resource allocation, and investment decisions.

Another major development is the use of dashboard technologies. Dashboards provide visual and interactive representations of financial data, enabling managers to monitor key performance indicators (KPIs) and organisational objectives in real time. Modern dashboards integrate data from enterprise resource planning (ERP) systems, accounting databases, and analytics platforms to create a unified view of financial performance (Eckerson, 2010). Through charts, trend lines, and heat maps, dashboards simplify complex financial information and improve managerial decision-making.

Further, AI has helped to speed up this change with predictive intelligence and automated decision support. Unlike traditional statistical techniques, AI-powered systems are able to use algorithms that leverage machine learning to uncover patterns in financial data and produce highly accurate forecasts, improving budget planning, credit risk analysis, fraud detection, and scenario planning (T. H. Davenport & Ronanki, 2018). AI also facilitates adaptive financial-planning systems that continuously learn from new data and adapt their strategies as business dynamics evolve. These trends have heightened the need for real-time decision-making: businesses in digital markets need to be agile in response to customer preferences, technology, and economic fluctuations, while financial managers are also relying on more integrated systems that integrate analytics, dashboards, and AI-driven insights to drive strategic agility and a competitive edge.

1.2 Need for AI-Driven Decision Making

The increasing complexity and uncertainty of modern business environments have created a strong need for AI-driven decision-making systems in financial management. Traditional financial planning methods are often limited by their dependence on historical data, manual analysis, and static forecasting models. These approaches may not be capable of processing the enormous volumes of real-time data generated by digital enterprises. As a result, organisations are adopting AI-driven technologies to improve the speed, accuracy, and effectiveness of financial decision-making.

AI-driven decision-making refers to the use of machine learning, predictive analytics, optimisation algorithms, and intelligent automation to support strategic financial activities. AI systems analyse large datasets from multiple internal and external sources to identify relationships, trends, and anomalies that may not be visible through conventional analysis. Such capabilities enable managers to make proactive and data-driven financial decisions rather than relying solely on intuition or historical experience. One of the most important applications of AI in financial decision-making is predictive forecasting. AI models can analyse historical sales patterns, market conditions, customer behaviour, and operational data to generate highly accurate predictions of revenue, cash flow, and demand. This predictive capability allows organisations to prepare dynamic budgets, optimise investments, and reduce uncertainty in strategic planning (Brynjolfsson & McAfee, 2014).

AI-driven systems also improve risk management by identifying financial anomalies and fraud patterns in real time. Machine-learning algorithms can detect unusual transactions, operational inefficiencies, and credit risks more effectively than manual auditing systems. Such predictive risk-analysis capabilities strengthen financial governance and help organisations minimise losses and compliance-related issues (Delen & Demirkan, 2013). Another important advantage of AI-driven decision-making is automation. Intelligent financial systems can automate repetitive and time-consuming tasks such as invoice processing, financial reporting, budget monitoring, and variance analysis. Automation not only improves operational efficiency but also allows financial managers to focus more on strategic planning and value-creation activities.

AI also supports scenario-based decision-making, as it allows organisations to model various business scenarios and assess potential financial impacts, such as the impact of market volatility, inflation, interest-rate movements, or disruption to the supply chain, to help organisations make informed decisions in the face of uncertainty. This responsiveness enables firms to adjust their financial strategies rapidly and maintain a competitive edge in dynamic markets. While all of these advantages are considerable, there are also some challenges to consider when implementing AI financial systems, such as data quality, cybersecurity, ethical concerns, algorithmic bias, and a lack of qualified staff; it is important to have robust governance structures, good data-management practices, and ongoing employee training for success.

1.3 Objectives and Scope of the Chapter

This chapter aims to examine the role of big data analytics, dashboard technologies, and AI-driven insights in improving strategic financial planning and real-time decision-making in digital enterprises. The chapter explores how these technologies collectively transform traditional financial-management practices into intelligent and data-driven systems.

Specifically, the chapter examines the use of big data analytics for financial forecasting, budgeting, and risk management, as well as dashboard systems as visual decision support systems to facilitate the interpretation of the data and improve management cognition, and the role of AI in predictive and prescriptive financial planning using machine-learning algorithms and intelligent optimization. Another goal is to create an integrated conceptual model (which is depicted as a labelled figure and described in text) that links the analytics capability, dashboard visualization, and the AI intelligence applied to strategic financial planning and to question the model's plausibility using documented, real-world industry applications. The literature review is also a critical synthesis that explores the gaps in the existing body of knowledge and demonstrates how the proposed framework fills those gaps, and then the managerial and strategic implications of implementing intelligent financial systems in digital enterprises are discussed.

The chapter's focus is on digital enterprises in data-intensive environments – these include e-commerce businesses, technology companies, digital platforms and financial-service organisations. The focus will be on strategic financial planning and not on day-to-day accounting tasks, and on new developments like real-time analytics, intelligent dashboards and AI-driven financial management. The chapter makes a significant contribution to the existing knowledge base on digital finance both in theory and concept and with practical application for managers, researchers and policy makers who are interested in intelligent financial-planning systems.

2. THEORETICAL FOUNDATIONS OF STRATEGIC FINANCIAL PLANNING

2.1 Data-Driven Decision-Making Theory

Data-driven decision-making (DDDM) has emerged as a foundational paradigm in the digital transformation era, representing a significant shift from intuition-based managerial approaches to evidence-based strategic planning. At its core, DDDM theory posits that organizations can optimize operations, gain competitive advantage, and predict market trends by systematically analyzing large-scale datasets rather than relying on heuristic judgment (Jeyaprabha et al., 2025). The theoretical underpinnings draw from multiple disciplines, statistical inference, organizational behavior, and information systems, converging on the principle that structured analysis of empirical data yields superior decision outcomes.

The theory operates on several key premises. First, the information asymmetry reduction premise holds that organizations equipped with analytical capabilities can reduce uncertainty in strategic choices by extracting signals from noise within massive datasets. The Central Limit Theorem and related statistical foundations allow predictable patterns to emerge from large volumes of seemingly random data, transforming raw information into actionable intelligence. Second, the resource optimization premise suggests that data-driven strategies influence business outcomes depending on contextual factors such as company size, organizational maturity, and revenue capacity. Research examining strategic decision-making in Indian enterprises confirms that the effectiveness of DDDM varies according to the size and age of the company, as well as its income level.

DDDM in management encompasses several functional categories, including cost reduction, operational efficiency enhancement, predictive capabilities, faster insight generation, and improved accuracy of decisions. Strategic decision-making can be applied across management domains based on three critical factors: resource utilization, budget overage control, and return on investment. Furthermore, the role of organizational culture cannot be understated — firms that cultivate a data-driven culture demonstrate stronger integration between analytical capabilities and operational performance. Empirical studies have confirmed that a data-driven culture moderates the relationship between big data analytics capability and organizational integration processes. From a theoretical standpoint, the intellectual capital perspective offers additional explanatory power. Intellectual capital, encompassing human, structural, and relational dimensions, interacts with analytical capabilities to shape financial performance outcomes. Research in the banking sector has demonstrated that high-performance work practices mediate the relationship between intellectual capital and financial performance, with big data analytics serving as a significant moderating variable(Hussain et al., 2024)

2.2 Strategic Financial Planning in Digital Enterprises

Strategic financial planning in the digital enterprise context represents a departure from traditional static budgeting and forecasting models toward dynamic, continuously adaptive frameworks. Digital enterprises operate in environments characterized by rapid market shifts, real-time data flows, and complex stakeholder ecosystems, necessitating financial planning approaches that are equally agile.

The principles of strategic financial management in the information economy revolve around aligning financial resource allocation with long-term organizational objectives while maintaining the flexibility to respond to emergent opportunities and threats. (Gavryushenko, 2021). Traditional financial planning relied predominantly on historical accounting data and periodic reporting cycles. In contrast, digital enterprises leverage real-time analytics to create living financial plans that are continuously updated as new data becomes available.

A layered architecture for strategic financial planning in digital enterprises can be conceptualized across three tiers: the strategic layer, focused on long-term capital market positioning and enterprise valuation; the operational layer, centered on resource planning and financial control across business units; and the tactical layer, oriented toward departmental business execution tracking and support. This hierarchical framework ensures that data flows bidirectionally — strategic imperatives inform tactical execution, while granular operational data feeds upward to refine strategic assumptions.

The integration of financial and business data, often termed "business-finance fusion," is critical for digital enterprises. By constructing analytical architectures built on transactional data foundations, organizations can progress from basic financial reporting through performance management to strategic planning in a layered, progressive manner. This fusion enables financial functions to evolve from retrospective record-keeping to prospective strategic advisory roles.

Big data technologies further enable financial management to shift from descriptive analysis to predictive and prescriptive modalities. Organizations employing AI-enhanced business intelligence systems have observed substantial improvements in financial forecasting accuracy by processing large volumes of both structured and unstructured data. The gains from this capability are sector specific — for banking, for example, big data analytics capability has been found to have a positive effect on financial performance, both directly and indirectly, through an intellectual-capital and work-practice pathway, rather than through a single, generalisable gain number (Hussain et al., 2024) — and recent global survey evidence backs this up at scale: 64 per cent of finance leaders report better financial forecast accuracy after introducing AI, with 71 per cent among banking respondents saying they had a mature data governance programme, compared to 44 per cent of organisations with fragmented data foundations (KPMG International, 2026).

2.3 Conceptual Framework of Analytics and AI Integration

The conceptual framework for integrating analytics and artificial intelligence into strategic financial planning rests on a convergence of advanced computational techniques, including machine learning, natural language processing, and real-time streaming analytics, with established financial management principles. This integration creates what can be characterized as a "financial intelligence ecosystem" where data ingestion, processing, modeling, and decision support operate as an interconnected pipeline.

At the foundation of this framework lies data infrastructure, comprising the tools and platforms necessary for capturing, storing, and processing financial data at scale. (Thanasas & Kampiotis, 2024). Technologies such as Hadoop, Apache Spark, and cloud-based data warehouses provide the computational backbone for handling the volume, velocity, and variety inherent in financial big data. These platforms enable organizations to move beyond the limitations of traditional relational databases and process diverse data types — from structured transaction records to unstructured text in analyst reports and social media sentiment.

The intermediate layer of the framework involves analytical modeling, where machine learning algorithms and AI techniques are applied to financial data for pattern recognition, anomaly detection, and predictive modeling. A big data–driven optimization framework for enterprise financial management demonstrates how merging advanced analytics with real-time data can enhance predictive decision-making, risk control, and computational efficiency. AI-driven models incorporate both supervised learning (for tasks like credit scoring and default prediction) and unsupervised learning (for market segmentation and fraud detection), creating a comprehensive analytical toolkit.

The uppermost layer encompasses decision support and strategic integration, where analytical outputs are translated into actionable strategic recommendations. This requires not only technical sophistication but also robust data governance frameworks. Ethical considerations — including data privacy, security, and regulatory compliance — are central to this layer, ensuring that AI-driven financial strategies maintain trust and institutional legitimacy (Titilope Tosin Adewale et al., 2023). Responsible data handling principles, grounded in frameworks such as respect for persons, beneficence, and justice, must govern the deployment of AI in financial decision-making contexts.

Finally, the framework emphasizes the importance of model parsimony and robustness. Principles of parsimony, such as Occam's Razor, are essential for preventing model overfitting, a critical concern when financial models are trained on large but potentially noisy datasets. Balancing model complexity against data fit ensures that predictive models generalize reliably to new market conditions rather than merely memorizing historical patterns.

Figure 1 presents this framework as a labelled, five-layer diagram. Layer 1 comprises the diverse internal, external, operational, and behavioral data sources that supply the system. This data is loaded, cleaned, and governed in Layer 2 (data infrastructure layer) through cloud warehousing, stream processing, and MLOps pipelines. Layer 3 combines descriptive, predictive, and prescriptive analytics in parallel using the governed data foundation. These analytical outputs are translated into role-specific KPI dashboards, drill-down analytics, natural language queries, and automated alerts in Layer 4 (the dashboard visualisation layer). Layer 5 is the outcome of the strategic financial decisions made – budgeting, capital allocation and risk governance – and the organisational outcomes that arise from them: agility, accuracy of forecasting, competitive edge and improved governance. A continuous feedback loop (right of figure) brings realised outcomes and user interactions back as new input to the data-infrastructure layer to enable the system to learn from its own decisions and not just historical baselines. A cross-cutting band below the framework represents governance, ethics, data-privacy, and regulatory-compliance aspects and obligations (such as under the EU AI Act, SEC disclosure rules, GDPR, etc.) that affect each layer throughout the pipeline and not just at one point. The proposed framework is an explicit, closed-loop, governance-integrated structure that differs from previous approaches that consider analytics, visualisation and AI as separate research lines, and this is further operationalised in Section 6.1 and detailed in industry cases in Section 6.4.

Figure 1. Conceptual Framework

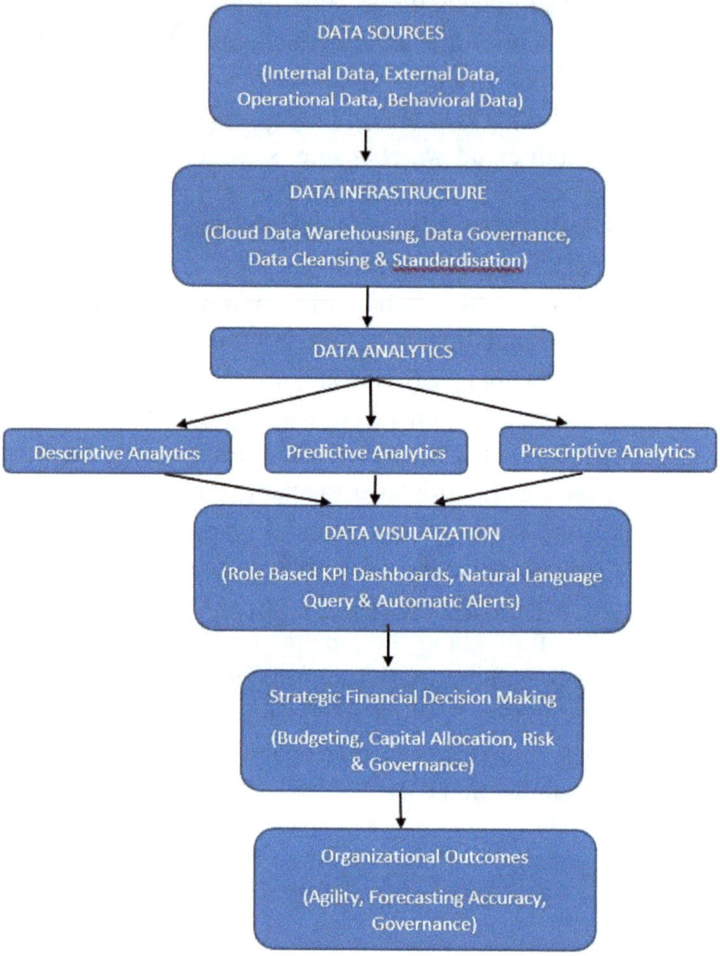

2.4 Critical Synthesis of the Literature and Research Gaps

The flow of literature that supports this chapter is consistent, with some degree of disconnection in the level of integration. The big data analytics capability studies (Wamba et al. 2017; Grover et al. 2018; Raguseo & Vitari, 2018) demonstrate that investment in big data analytics leads to increased firm performance; however, the majority of those studies do not model effects on performance as being mediated by the decision support architecture itself, but rather by some organisational or market-facing variable. Research into business intelligence and dashboarding (Chen, H et. al., 2012; Eckerson, 2010; Sharda et al., 2018) proves the cognitive and organisational utility of visualisation, but mostly they see dashboards as a research entity apart from the AI models they are housing. Research on AI in finance (T. H. Davenport & Ronanki, 2018) confirms that machine learning is predictive and prescriptive, but does not typically tie this back to how these outputs are consumed, visualised and governed by humans. This trend is highlighted in Table 1, which summarises this pattern, based on a representative selection of sources including more recent large sample survey evidence.

Table 1. Synthesis of Literature and Research Gaps

Reference	Study	Technique / Evidence	Key Findings	Gap Addressed by Proposed Framework
Wamba et al. (2017)	Big data analytics & firm performance	Survey / dynamic capabilities lens	Analytics capability has an indirect impact on performance through dynamic capabilities.	Treats analytics separately from dashboards or AI; framework integrates analytics into complete decision journey
Grover et al. (2018)	Strategic value from big data analytics	Conceptual research framework	Value creation relies on orchestration of the resources – not only the volume of data –	Does not indicate any visualisation or AI layers; framework defines instrumentation as explicit layers.
Raguseo & Vitari (2018)	Analytics investment & firm performance	Empirical, mediation analysis	Direct and indirect (market/customer) performance effects of analytics investment	Mediation evidence is descriptive; framework's feedback loop provides a mechanism for sustaining gains.
Hussain et al. (2024)	Big data analytics, work practices & financial performance (banking)	Survey, PLS-SEM, financial performance dimensions	High-performance work practices mediate the intellectual capital–performance relationship, moderated by BDA	The financial performance dimension generalises the human-capital dimension through the governance overlay; BDA is a moderator of the measure, which is also sector-specific (banking)
Gomber et al. (2018)	FinTech innovation and disruption	Conceptual / IS theory synthesis	FinTech is changing financial services with the help of innovative ways	Technology level rather than FP&A decision process; focus shrinks to FP&A decision cycle.

continued on following page

Table 1. Continued

Reference	Study	Technique / Evidence	Key Findings	Gap Addressed by Proposed Framework
KPMG International (2026)	AI adoption in finance functions	Global survey, n = 1,013 finance leaders	AI adoption has almost doubled since 2024, with forecast accuracy gains focused on areas where data governance is more advanced.	Reaffirms the premise of the framework, that the data-infrastructure layer is the glue that holds the value of AI together.
McKinsey & Company (2024)	Generative AI in CFO functions	Global CFO pulse survey	With 71% of respondents saying it has helped boost productivity, and 54% saying it has helped them better use data for decision-making.	The level of adoption is evident; the framework's link to a specific decision support architecture is questionable.

3. BIG DATA ANALYTICS IN FINANCIAL PLANNING

3.1 Descriptive, Predictive, and Prescriptive Analytics

Big data analytics in financial planning operates across three progressively sophisticated tiers: descriptive, predictive, and prescriptive analytics. Each tier builds upon the capabilities of the preceding one, creating a comprehensive analytical continuum that transforms raw financial data into strategic action. Descriptive analytics represents the foundational tier, focused on summarizing historical financial data to answer the question "what happened?" This includes traditional financial reporting, income statements, balance sheets, and cash flow analyses enhanced by big data capabilities that allow for richer, more granular, and more timely summaries. Big data technologies enable organizations to integrate data from multifaceted origins, incorporating not just internal accounting records but also external market data, customer transaction patterns, and macroeconomic indicators (A. K. R. S., 2024). The exponential growth of data has fundamentally revolutionized even this basic analytical function by expanding the breadth and depth of available information.

Predictive analytics moves beyond historical description to forecast future financial states. By leveraging machine learning algorithms and statistical modeling techniques, organizations can anticipate market trends, project revenue trajectories, estimate default probabilities, and model risk scenarios. In one notable approach, graph theory has been applied to big data analytics for default prediction, enabling financial institutions to analyze complex relational structures among borrowers and counterparties that traditional linear models fail to capture (Yıldırım et al., 2021). Predictive modeling in financial contexts encompasses forecasting trends, optimizing resource allocation, and identifying emerging market opportunities before competitors (Titilope Tosin Adewale et al., 2023).

Prescriptive analytics represents the most advanced tier, combining predictive outputs with optimization algorithms to recommend specific courses of action. Rather than merely forecasting what might happen, prescriptive analytics answers "what should we do?" This tier integrates AI-driven decision support with constraint optimization, scenario analysis, and simulation modeling. Advanced tools, including natural language processing and sentiment analysis, contribute to this tier by evaluating market sentiment and consumer behavior, providing a competitive edge in strategic financial decision-making (Titilope Tosin Adewale et al., 2023). Prescriptive frameworks for enterprise financial management merge real-time analytics with optimization algorithms to generate recommendations for budget allocation, investment timing, and risk mitigation strategies.

The progression from descriptive through predictive to prescriptive analytics mirrors the maturation of an organization's analytical capabilities and represents the trajectory that digital enterprises must navigate to fully capitalize on their data assets.

3.2 Risk Management and Financial Forecasting

Risk management and financial forecasting constitute two of the most consequential application domains for big data analytics in financial planning. The ability to identify, quantify, and mitigate financial risks while simultaneously generating accurate forecasts of future financial performance represents a core competitive advantage in volatile market environments.

In the domain of risk management, big data analytics enables organizations to move from reactive risk responses to proactive risk anticipation. AI-driven models and big data analytics have been found to enhance financial stability by enabling more accurate and timely assessment of credit risk, market risk, and operational risk. Traditional risk assessment relied on limited historical datasets and simplistic statistical models; contemporary approaches harness diverse, high-velocity data streams to construct multidimensional risk profiles. Credit risk measurement, for instance, has been transformed by big data approaches that can analyze vast arrays of borrower characteristics, behavioral patterns, and macroeconomic variables simultaneously, though challenges remain in building well-established theoretical frameworks for credit risk measurement in the big data context (Wu, 2022).

Financial forecasting has been similarly revolutionized. Big data analytics allows organizations to process large volumes of structured and unstructured data to refine forecasting accuracy substantially. The incorporation of external data sources — social media sentiment, geopolitical indicators, supply chain signals — into forecasting models enhances their predictive validity beyond what internal financial data alone can provide. Business intelligence tools integrated with big data capabilities enable organizations to predict financial situations and optimize financial costs through more sophisticated modeling approaches (Mishra, 2018).

Real-time analytics plays a particularly critical role in both risk management and forecasting by improving organizational agility and responsiveness to rapidly changing market conditions. The ability to update risk models and forecasts continuously as new data arrives — rather than on periodic reporting cycles — allows enterprises to detect emerging threats and opportunities with minimal latency (Titilope Tosin Adewale et al., 2023). A big data–driven approach to financial analysis and decision support system design demonstrates how real-time data processing capabilities can be architecturally integrated into financial management workflows to support both risk monitoring and dynamic forecasting.

3.3 Benefits and Challenges of Big Data Analytics

The adoption of big data analytics in financial planning yields substantial benefits while simultaneously presenting formidable challenges that organizations must navigate thoughtfully.

Enhanced decision accuracy and speed: Organizations gain the ability to make faster, more evidence-based decisions by extracting valuable insights from large datasets, enabling them to determine strategic plans for risk control, crisis management, and growth management with greater confidence (Yıldırım et al., 2021).

Improved financial performance: Empirical research has demonstrated that investments in big data analytics create measurable business value and positively impact financial performance through both direct effects and indirect pathways mediated by market performance and customer satisfaction (Raguseo & Vitari, 2018).

Competitive advantage: Organizations that successfully deploy analytics capabilities gain an edge through superior market intelligence, more efficient resource allocation, and enhanced fraud detection capabilities (Thanasas & Kampiotis, 2024).

Innovation enablement: The bibliometric literature on big data in finance reveals that analytics is creating new opportunities to advance financial management, financial technology, insurance technology, wealth management technology, and investment strategies (Nobanee, 2021).

Cross-functional integration: Big data analytics facilitates the integration of financial analysis with other business functions, exemplified by the borderless integration of financial management through social media big data analysis, which enables multidimensional performance evaluation across quality, efficiency, cost, and safety dimensions (Tang et al., 2022).

Key challenges are equally significant:

Data quality and integration: The volume, velocity, and variety of big data create substantial challenges for data integration, consistency, and quality assurance. Ensuring that diverse data sources are harmonized into reliable analytical inputs remains a persistent technical hurdle (Thanasas & Kampiotis, 2024; Titilope Tosin Adewale et al., 2023).

Privacy and ethical concerns: Data privacy and security considerations are central to any big data analytics deployment in finance. Organizations must navigate complex regulatory landscapes — including frameworks like GDPR and the EU AI Act (European Parliament and Council of the European Union, 2024), while maintaining the analytical utility of their data assets. The tension between analytical depth and privacy protection requires careful governance frameworks.

Infrastructure and talent requirements: Building robust big data infrastructure demands significant capital investment, and the shortage of skilled data scientists and analysts who also possess financial domain expertise creates a persistent talent gap. Organizations must invest simultaneously in technology platforms and human capital development.

4. DASHBOARD SYSTEMS AS DECISION-SUPPORT TOOLS

Financial dashboards have evolved from static reporting screens into dynamic decision support environments that translate complex data into actionable insights. By bridging raw information and strategic execution, these systems empower finance professionals to make timely, evidence-based decisions (Chen. Y et al., 2024). Historically, financial reporting relied on periodic, manually compiled statements that offered a retrospective view of organizational performance. While adequate for regulatory compliance and historical auditing, such static formats proved increasingly inadequate in fast-moving markets where strategic agility, continuous planning, and rapid resource reallocation are paramount. The emergence of modern business intelligence (BI) architectures, cloud data warehousing, and advanced visualization technologies catalyzed a fundamental paradigm shift, transforming dashboards from passive information displays into active decision-support systems (DSS) that facilitate real-time analysis, scenario testing, and cross-functional strategic alignment (Sharda et al., 2018).

At its core, a decision-support dashboard operates within a structured analytical framework designed to augment human judgment rather than replace it. Drawing from foundational theories of bounded rationality, modern financial dashboards directly address the cognitive constraints that decision-makers face when processing voluminous, multidimensional data streams. Financial executives routinely navigate competing priorities, uncertain market conditions, and incomplete information. By structuring data hierarchically, applying consistent visual encoding, and embedding contextual benchmarks, dashboards reduce cognitive load and direct attention to material deviations, emerging trends, and strategic inflection points. This intentional design enables finance leaders to transition from descriptive reporting—what happened—to diagnostic and predictive analytics—why it happened and what is likely to occur next (T. Davenport & Harris, 2017). Consequently, dashboards function as cognitive scaffolds that accelerate pattern recognition and reduce the likelihood of decision paralysis during periods of economic volatility.

The contextual significance of dashboard systems extends far beyond mere data presentation. In contemporary financial planning, dashboards serve as centralized command centers that consolidate fragmented data streams from enterprise resource planning (ERP) systems, treasury management platforms, market data feeds, and external macroeconomic indicators. This consolidation is critical in organizations where data silos historically delayed insight generation, introduced manual reconciliation errors, and fostered conflicting narratives across departments (Chen, Y et al., 2024). By establishing a single, governed source of truth, dashboards standardize metric definitions, enforce data lineage protocols, and ensure that all stakeholders operate from synchronized information. Consequently, strategic discussions shift from debating data accuracy to evaluating alternative courses of action, significantly compressing the decision-making cycle and improving organizational responsiveness.

Furthermore, the decision-support capacity of financial dashboards is substantially amplified through interactive functionality and embedded analytical workflows. Unlike traditional static reports, modern dashboards enable drill-down analytics, dynamic parameter adjustment, and real-time what-if scenario modeling. Finance professionals can manipulate variables such as discount rates, commodity prices, customer acquisition costs, or supply chain disruptions to observe cascading effects on liquidity, profitability margins, and capital structure. This dynamic simulation capability transforms dashboards into strategic sandboxes where assumptions can be stress-tested before capital commitment. The research also suggests that it drives real results – 64 percent of finance leaders worldwide indicated that they could achieve more accurate forecasts than they did in the prior year, and 71 percent of respondents in the banking sector who had well-developed data foundations said their organization was more likely to use data to make better decisions, according to KPMG (2026) surveying more than 1,000 finance leaders around the world; and McKinsey's (2024) CFO pulse survey showed that 54 percent of finance functions leveraging AI indicated that their data helped them make better decisions. In times of economic flux, with tight budgets set once a year, these abilities are especially useful because they allow for ongoing planning cycles to react to market signals and feedback that comes from operating them.

The organizational impact of dashboard-driven decision support also encompasses cultural and structural transformation. By democratizing access to financial metrics, these systems break down hierarchical information bottlenecks and empower mid-level managers to make data-informed operational decisions without awaiting centralized approvals. This decentralization aligns with agile financial management principles, which emphasize responsiveness, accountability, and cross-functional collaboration. However, the effectiveness of this model depends on robust data literacy programs and clear governance frameworks that prevent misinterpretation of metrics or short-term optimization gaming. Without proper training, contextual guardrails, and ethical usage policies, even the most sophisticated dashboard can produce misleading conclusions or incentivize behaviors that undermine long-term value creation.

Financial markets become increasingly complex, and dashboard solutions are shifting away from being just visualisation tools to being part of a larger analytic architecture. Users can now interact with financial data in a new way, using natural-language queries that generate automated insights, along with prescriptive next steps and risk assessments, that are supported by confidence intervals, rather than having to dig through complex filters. To sum up, the contextual background of financial dashboard systems reflects a fusion of technological progress, cognitive science, and strategic management, and these systems infer ready-to-use, interactive, and structured intelligence from fragmented data, countering the inherent limitations of human decision-making and empowering organisations to make more precise, agile, and foresightful decisions.

4.1 Components and Design of Financial Dashboards

Effective dashboard architecture rests on three foundational pillars: robust data integration, intuitive visualization layers, and responsive interactive controls. Modern financial interface design increasingly applies cognitive load theory to prevent information overload, ensuring that decision-makers can process complex metrics without experiencing analytical fatigue. This is achieved through hierarchical layouts that prioritize strategic indicators, consistent color semantics that denote performance status, and role-based filtering that tailors data exposure to specific user competencies.

Modular components further empower finance professionals to customize their analytical workspace while preserving standardized metric definitions across the organization. Key design principles emphasize contextual drill-down capabilities, which allow users to transition seamlessly from high-level summaries to granular transactional data. Additionally, responsive scaling ensures optimal rendering across desktop and mobile devices, while embedded data annotations provide real-time explanatory context. Collectively, these features enhance analytical precision and significantly reduce interpretation errors during high-stakes financial reviews, where accuracy directly impacts strategic capital allocation.

4.2 Real-Time Monitoring and KPI Visualisation

Real-time monitoring fundamentally transforms financial oversight from retrospective auditing to proactive, forward-looking management. By leveraging continuous data streaming architectures, organizations can simultaneously track both leading indicators, such as pipeline velocity and cash conversion cycles, and lagging metrics like net profit margins and return on equity. Visual representations, including dynamic trend lines, density heat maps, and threshold gauges, facilitate instant status recognition, enabling executives to grasp organizational health at a glance. Automated alerting mechanisms are configured to flag anomalous variances against predefined benchmarks, triggering immediate corrective actions before deviations escalate into material financial risks. This capability is instrumental in supporting agile budgeting frameworks and dynamic resource allocation, particularly in environments characterized by rapid economic shifts.

As traditional monthly reporting cycles increasingly prove insufficient for timely intervention in volatile markets, continuous visibility becomes a competitive necessity rather than a technological luxury. Consequently, finance teams can pivot from historical compliance reporting to strategic value creation, aligning financial performance tracking with real-time operational realities (Kaplan & Norton, 1996). The shift toward live data streams also necessitates rigorous data governance protocols to maintain accuracy and auditability under continuous refresh cycles.

4.3 Dashboard Integration with Enterprise Systems

The operational efficacy of any financial dashboard depends on seamless interoperability with core enterprise platforms, including ERP, CRM, and legacy accounting infrastructure. Through standardised application programming interfaces (APIs) and cloud-native middleware, contemporary dashboards establish a unified, single source of truth that dismantles departmental data silos and eliminates error-prone manual reconciliation (Chen Y et al., 2024).

Beyond passive metric visualization, bidirectional integration empowers users to initiate downstream workflows directly from the dashboard interface, such as approving purchase orders, adjusting forecasting models, or triggering compliance reviews. This embedded intelligence ensures that financial insights are not merely displayed but actively inform operational execution across the enterprise value chain. By reducing decision latency and fostering real-time cross-functional alignment, integrated dashboards transform financial data into a dynamic organizational asset. Furthermore, this interconnected architecture supports scalable analytics, allowing organizations to incorporate external market data and macroeconomic indicators without disrupting core financial reporting pipelines. Ultimately, this structural cohesion bridges the historical gap between financial reporting and day-to-day business execution, enabling enterprises to operate with greater agility and strategic coherence (Chen.Y et al., 2024).

5. ARTIFICIAL INTELLIGENCE IN FINANCIAL PLANNING

The integration of artificial intelligence has fundamentally transformed financial forecasting, risk assessment, and scenario modeling, shifting planning paradigms from deterministic projections to adaptive, data-driven decision-making. Historically, corporate financial planning relied heavily on static spreadsheet architectures and linear extrapolation techniques that assumed stable market conditions and predictable historical continuity. These legacy approaches consistently failed to account for structural economic breaks, exogenous supply shocks, or rapidly evolving consumer behaviors. In contrast, contemporary AI architectures operate as continuous learning ecosystems, dynamically recalibrating baseline projections as new information enters the organizational data pipeline.

By processing both structured financial records and unstructured alternative data at unprecedented scale, AI systems uncover latent patterns and early warning signals that traditional statistical methods frequently overlook. Natural language processing engines now parse earnings call transcripts, regulatory filings, and global news feeds, converting qualitative market sentiment into quantifiable risk indicators. Concurrently, graph-based neural networks map intricate interdependencies across vendor ecosystems, counterparty networks, and logistics corridors, exposing systemic liquidity vulnerabilities long before they crystallize into material financial distress.

This analytical depth enables finance functions to align strategic capital deployment with dynamic market conditions while continuously refining baseline assumptions. Rather than adhering to rigid annual or quarterly budget cycles, AI-enhanced planning platforms facilitate rolling forecasts that automatically adjust to real-time demand fluctuations, commodity price volatility, and shifting interest rate environments. Probabilistic modeling frameworks evaluate thousands of capital allocation pathways simultaneously, optimizing for competing objectives such as revenue growth acceleration, covenant compliance, and cash conversion efficiency. These systems function within closed-loop feedback architectures, where actual operational and financial outcomes are continuously ingested to minimize forecast drift and strengthen long-term predictive accuracy. Bayesian updating mechanisms allow models to weight emerging evidence appropriately, ensuring that projections remain empirically grounded even during periods of macroeconomic turbulence.

Furthermore, AI-driven scenario modeling transcends traditional base-case, best-case, and worst-case frameworks by generating high-resolution probability distributions that explicitly account for tail risks, regulatory realignments, and geopolitical disruptions. This capability proves indispensable in highly volatile market environments, where conventional planning cycles routinely deliver obsolete insights by the time they reach executive review. Consequently, enterprises that institutionalize AI within their financial planning workflows achieve not only superior forecast precision but also sustained strategic agility, elevating the finance function from a historical reporting mechanism to a proactive engine of enterprise value creation.

5.1 Machine Learning and Predictive Modelling

Machine learning algorithms, particularly ensemble methods and temporal neural networks, significantly enhance the accuracy and granularity of revenue, cash flow, and expenditure forecasts. Unlike linear regression models that assume static relationships, these algorithms are trained on extensive historical financial datasets, macroeconomic indicators, and real-time alternative data streams such as consumer sentiment and supply chain telemetry. Through this multi-dimensional training, ML models effectively capture nonlinear relationships, structural breaks, and complex seasonality effects that historically confounded traditional forecasting frameworks (S. Chen et al., 2025).

Predictive modeling further enables dynamic scenario simulation, allowing financial planners to continuously stress-test baseline assumptions against probabilistic outcomes. By generating thousands of Monte Carlo simulations in near real-time, organizations can evaluate the financial impact of supply chain disruptions or demand shocks, thereby adjusting capital allocation strategies with minimal latency. This predictive precision strengthens liquidity management by identifying potential cash shortfalls well before they materialize.

5.2 AI-Based Optimisation and Risk Detection

Beyond forecasting, AI-driven optimization techniques actively refine resource deployment and risk mitigation across the enterprise. Reinforcement learning and stochastic programming algorithms continuously evaluate trade-offs in portfolio construction, working capital management, and debt structuring, identifying optimal financing mixes that minimize cost of capital while maintaining target liquidity buffers.

Concurrently, AI-powered risk detection systems operate as continuous monitoring mechanisms, ingesting high-velocity transactional data, market feeds, and counterparty behavioral signals to identify anomalies, emerging fraud patterns, and latent credit exposures. Unsupervised learning algorithms excel at clustering irregular transaction behaviors, significantly reducing false positive rates while accelerating investigative response times. This proactive detection architecture enables treasury and compliance teams to initiate mitigation protocols before isolated irregularities escalate into material financial losses or regulatory penalties. By embedding these optimization capabilities directly into planning workflows, organizations transition from reactive risk management to anticipatory financial resilience.

5.3 Ethical and Governance Considerations in AI

The rapid deployment of AI in financial planning introduces significant ethical, operational, and regulatory complexities that demand rigorous oversight. Algorithmic bias, model opacity, and stringent data privacy requirements necessitate comprehensive governance frameworks that extend beyond traditional IT controls. To address these challenges, leading organizations are adopting explainable AI (XAI) methodologies that translate complex neural network outputs into interpretable decision pathways, ensuring that financial planners can validate model logic rather than relying on opaque recommendations.

Regular independent model audits, coupled with human-in-the-loop validation protocols, establish critical accountability checkpoints that align automated outputs with institutional risk appetites. These are now increasingly being mandated by new regulatory frameworks such as the European Union's Artificial Intelligence Act, which was adopted in 2024 and obligates high-risk AI systems, including those for creditworthiness assessment, to be transparent to users, tested for bias and audited by the system's creators (European Parliament and Council of the European Union, 2024), and also by securities regulators through new disclosure rules. It is still important to have transparent documentation of the origin, version, and thresholds of the training data to keep institutions trusting and to make sure that AI does not jeopardize financial integrity.

6. INTEGRATION OF BIG DATA, DASHBOARDS, AND AI

The convergence of big data infrastructure, interactive visualization, and artificial intelligence creates a synergistic ecosystem for next-generation financial planning (Davenport, T. H., 2018). Historically, financial analytics operated in fragmented silos, where data collection, analytical modeling, and executive reporting followed sequential, often disconnected workflows. Today, the integration of these three technological pillars enables a unified, dynamic planning environment that transcends traditional reporting boundaries. By harmonizing high-volume data ingestion, algorithmic intelligence, and intuitive user interfaces, organizations can transition from reactive financial management to proactive, insight-driven strategy formulation. This integrated architecture not only accelerates decision velocity but also enhances the accuracy, accessibility, and strategic relevance of financial intelligence across the enterprise.

6.1 Integrated Framework for Intelligent Financial Planning

As shown in Figure 1, an integrated architecture layers data ingestion, AI analytics, and dashboard visualization into a cohesive, end-to-end pipeline. Raw financial and operational data continuously flow into scalable cloud repositories, where automated preprocessing engines normalize, cleanse, and standardize heterogeneous inputs. This data orchestration layer is foundational, as the predictive validity of downstream models is directly contingent upon rigorous data governance, semantic standardization, and lineage tracking across disparate enterprise systems (Chen.Y et al., 2024).

Once structured, AI models process this enriched dataset to generate probabilistic forecasts, liquidity projections, and dynamic risk scores. Machine learning algorithms, particularly gradient-boosted decision trees and temporal neural networks, excel at capturing nonlinear dependencies, structural breaks, and complex seasonality effects that traditional econometric models frequently miss. These analytical outputs are then rendered through role-specific dashboards that translate complex algorithmic results into actionable visual narratives tailored to executives, operational managers, and compliance officers. Grounded in cognitive load theory, modern interfaces employ hierarchical information architecture, contextual drill-down pathways, and consistent semantic color coding to minimize interpretive friction and optimize analytical throughput.

Crucially, this architecture operates as a closed-loop system. As actual financial outcomes materialize and users interact with dashboard interfaces, feedback signals are automatically routed back to the modeling layer through automated MLOps pipelines. This continuous feedback mechanism enables iterative refinement of model parameters, ensuring that predictive algorithms adapt to shifting market dynamics and organizational behaviors rather than relying on static historical baselines (Kreuzberger et al., 2023). Such self-correcting frameworks significantly reduce forecast drift, mitigate model decay, and establish a foundation for perpetual learning within the financial planning function.

6.2 Real-Time Data Processing and Automation

The efficacy of integrated financial systems hinges on their capacity to process information at machine speed. Stream-processing frameworks and event-driven architectures have effectively eliminated traditional batch-processing delays, enabling sub-second data updates and continuous metric recalibration. Technologies such as distributed message brokers and in-memory compute engines facilitate low-latency data ingestion, allowing financial models to ingest market feeds, transactional logs, and operational telemetry as discrete, time-stamped events rather than periodic aggregates. Within this environment, automated workflows are triggered by predefined business events, initiating predictive alerts, reconciling intercompany accounts, and adjusting financial models without manual intervention.

When augmented with robotic process automation (RPA), AI-driven pipelines execute repetitive, rule-based tasks such as invoice validation, variance analysis, and regulatory reporting with exceptional accuracy. This technological convergence, widely recognized as intelligent process automation (IPA), dramatically reduces operational overhead and minimizes human error, allowing finance professionals to redirect their expertise toward strategic scenario planning, capital optimization, and cross-functional collaboration. Real-time automation also ensures that financial models remain up-to-date with real operational data, providing treasury or FP&A teams with real-time visibility into cash positions, working capital cycles, and new liquidity constraints; automates manual reconciliation, speeds up financial close, and creates a tamper-evident audit trail that enables ongoing, real-time compliance readiness and mitigates regulatory friction.

6.3 Strategic Benefits for Digital Enterprises

Organizations that successfully integrate big data infrastructure, AI analytics, and interactive dashboards achieve superior financial agility, reduced operational costs, and enhanced strategic foresight. Real-time intelligence empowers leadership teams to execute rapid market pivots, optimize pricing strategies, and reallocate resources in response to shifting competitive dynamics. This capability aligns closely with dynamic capabilities theory, wherein firms leverage continuous sensing, seizing, and reconfiguring mechanisms to adapt to volatile macroeconomic environments.

AI-augmented dashboards further democratize financial insights, enabling non-financial stakeholders across business units to access standardized, self-service analytics without compromising data governance or analytical rigor. By lowering the technical barrier to entry for complex financial analysis, enterprises foster a data-centric culture where operational decisions are continuously informed by forward-looking financial metrics rather than historical hindsight. By embedding intelligence directly into operational workflows, enterprises transform financial planning from a periodic compliance exercise into a continuous strategic capability. Ultimately, this technological convergence drives sustainable competitive advantage, positioning digital enterprises to navigate economic complexity, regulatory shifts, and macroeconomic volatility with unprecedented precision and organizational resilience(Porter & Heppelmann, 2015). The synergy between scalable data infrastructure, algorithmic foresight, and intuitive visualization thus redefines the strategic mandate of modern finance, elevating it from a retrospective reporting function to a proactive engine of enterprise value creation.

6.4 Illustrative Case Studies:

The conceptual framework outlined in Section 2.3 is abstract in design, and the purpose of this section is to illustrate through three documented, publicly reported industry applications in the form of a table how the layers operate in organisations of different types. The cases are selected from secondary, publicly accessible sources, rather than from independent academic studies, and have been used here as examples of practical plausibility and not as a causal test; this being highlighted as a research gap, further explored in Section 7.3.

Table 2. Summary of documented industry cases

Company Name	Technology / AI - Capability	Financial-Planning Application	Reported Results	Reference
JPMorgan Chase	Contract Intelligence (COiN) — NLP & machine learning document analytics	Automated extraction and risk-flagging of commercial credit agreements; frees up analysts' time for portfolio-level risk and capital decisions	Reduces analysts' time from an estimated 360,000 hours of manual review per year to minutes; materially lower error rates	Ates (2024); DigitalDefynd (2025)
HSBC Holdings	Machine-learning behavioural analytics (MLBA), a partnership with FICO, Ayasdi, EquBot/IBM Watson)	Predictive credit-line projection, transaction-monitoring for fraud/ financial crime, and AI-constructed investment indices feeding advisory dashboards	To simulate 40+ credit-line scenarios for each customer segment, giving enhanced sensitivity in fraud detection and AI-constructed investment indices for personalised financial-planning insights at scale.	Emerj (2022); Klover.ai (2025)
Unilever (with Solvoyo)	AI-driven demand and supply-chain planning platform integrated with ERP/data-warehouse	Automated dashboards with exception-based forecasts and dashboards for planning budgets by business unit and country.	Within a six-month pilot, around 8% improvement in forecast-accuracy-linked predictability, plus a 550-basis-point increase in service levels	Solvoyo (2023)

The cases in the table illustrate the existence in the real world of each of the layers of the proposed framework: governed data infrastructure (Unilever's integrated ERP/ data-warehouse platform), AI-driven analytics on structured and unstructured data (JPMorgan's contract intelligence and HSBC's behavioural models), and dashboard-based decision support that transforms model output into action for credit/risk and planning teams (HSBC's advisory and risk dashboards; Unilever's planning dashboards). The cases also highlight a limitation that is consistent with the evidentiary gap noted in Section 2.4: the outcomes reported are mostly self-reported by the organisation or its technology provider, have not been empirically verified, and do not separate the contribution of the AI or dashboard from additional investments in data infrastructure, process redesign, and staff education. The gap should be filled in the future by empirical research, which should be done in cross-organisational studies in an independent way, as discussed in Section 7.3.

7. MANAGERIAL IMPLICATIONS AND FUTURE TRENDS

7.1 Strategic and Organisational Implications

The integration of big data, interactive dashboards, and artificial intelligence necessitates a fundamental recalibration of managerial practices and organizational architectures. Traditional finance departments, historically structured around periodic reporting cycles and hierarchical approval chains, must evolve into agile, insight-driven centers of excellence. This transformation requires deliberate strategic alignment, where technology adoption is treated not as an isolated IT initiative but as a core business capability that permeates cross-functional decision-making processes. Leaders must redesign organizational workflows to embed real-time analytics directly into operational planning, budgeting, and performance management cycles. Such structural realignment dismantles departmental silos, fostering a culture of collaborative intelligence where financial insights actively inform product development, supply chain optimization, and market expansion strategies. The managerial mandate shifts from retrospective compliance oversight to proactive value orchestration, demanding that executives cultivate data fluency across all leadership tiers rather than confining analytical expertise to specialized FP&A teams.

Talent transformation represents another critical strategic imperative. As automated pipelines assume routine data compilation and variance analysis, finance professionals must upskill in data science literacy, algorithmic interpretation, and strategic scenario modeling. Organizations that invest in continuous learning frameworks, hybrid role architectures, and cross-training programs consistently outperform peers in technology adoption and ROI realization. Simultaneously, the rise of AI-driven forecasting introduces new governance complexities that require robust model risk management protocols. Managers must establish clear accountability matrices that delineate responsibilities between algorithmic outputs and human judgment, ensuring that automated recommendations undergo rigorous validation before influencing capital allocation or strategic pivots. The human-in-the-loop governance model helps reduce overreliance on black-box systems while maintaining institutional accountability, which aligns with survey findings that show that finance workers with more developed governance systems experience significantly fewer errors due to AI (33 percent compared to 6 percent) and that they have a much higher level of confidence in scaling the use of AI (KPMG International, 2026).

The ultimate benefit of this technological convergence for the organisation is strategic agility. It helps enterprises reorganise resources as the market is disrupted, competitive threats arise, or macroeconomic uncertainty exists by creating cycles of institutionalized planning and real-time performance monitoring. This adaptive capacity demands that leaders move away from the traditional budget-performance measurement system and towards metrics that focus on value creation in the future, like customer lifetime value, operating-resilience ratings and innovation-pipeline velocity. Change management is also important, and best practices involve executive buy-in, clear communication of the technology's value, and a series of pilot programmes that gain organisational trust before rolling out enterprise-wide. The strategic and organisational implications of AI-influenced financial planning are so much bigger than operational efficiency, however, and involve a cultural mindset change, in which data-driven foresight, cross-functional collaboration, and ethical governance all play a role in transforming the role of the finance function as a strategic driver of sustainable enterprise growth.

7.2 Emerging Technologies in Financial Intelligence

The path of financial intelligence is gaining momentum that goes beyond the capabilities of AI and dashboards and is driven by new technologies that will deliver more in-depth analytics, more realistic simulations, and more autonomous action. The promise of generative AI is in its ability to go beyond descriptive analytics to creating narrative, modeling communications with stakeholders, and drafting regulatory disclosures with contextual precision – advanced large language models can ingest a range of financial data modalities to generate executive briefings, simulate stakeholder communications, and draft regulatory disclosures without manual model recalibration, while predictive engines, when combined with generative AI, can create what-ifs, enabling planners to explore a multitude of strategic scenarios and synthesize actionable recommendations (Brynjolfsson & McAfee, 2014).

Alongside enterprise digital twins, financial digital twins are becoming another revolutionary simulation environment, reflecting the operations, cash flow, and market exposures of enterprises in real time. Digital twins can be used to continuously simulate and test an organisation's financial planning to withstand economic shocks, allowing for a reduction in the need to use historical backtesting to see the impact and a step up in forward-looking financial resilience, though there is a large amount of work to be done independently assessing the financial-planning value of digital twins at an early stage. The next horizon technology that could transform financial optimisation and risk modelling is quantum computing, which, although still relatively new, holds great promise for problems such as large-scale Monte Carlo simulation, derivative pricing and complex portfolio optimisation, while financial institutions are testing hybrid quantum-classical systems for hedging, credit-risk assessment and multi-asset allocation, making quantum readiness a future strategic approach.

Distributed Ledger Technologies and smart contracts are also reshaping the treasury function and intra-organisational financial processes. These can lower counterparty risk, facilitate cross-border trades, and help increase transparency in multi-party supply-chain financing, while these protocols can also be tied to AI-based monitoring solutions, thereby offering largely self-executing financial flows. The autonomous financial agent takes this one step further, combining reinforcement learning, natural language processing, and robotic process automation with the ability to continuously monitor market conditions, execute a predetermined trading or hedging strategy, negotiate a dynamic pricing contract, and reconcile the financial statements within embedded compliance guards. While full autonomy is limited by regulatory and ethical concerns, human-assisted agent architectures have already demonstrated tangible gains in working-capital optimisation and in cost reduction of operations. Adopting these emerging techs requires careful planning for interoperability, legacy system updates, and ongoing cybersecurity strengthening, and organisations need to be ready to implement 'modular' architectures that allow technology stacking without compromising data integrity and auditing.

7.3 Future Research Directions

While technology continues to develop rapidly, there are still many gaps in the empirical and theoretical understanding of how the use of AI in financial planning affects the outcomes of organisations, decision quality and risk governance, which align closely with the four gaps identified from the comparative synthesis presented in Section 2.4. Future research should validate the proposed five-layer framework by directly testing, with SEMs or configurational approaches, whether the sequential application of data infrastructure, data analytics, data dashboards, and feedback loops is more effective than each component individually. Finally, future research needs to focus more on longitudinal and cross-industry studies that examine how long-term integrated analytics usage impacts the accuracy of forecasting, the efficiency of capital allocation, and strategic agility, particularly beyond the case evidence provided by the vendors in Section 6.4 to case evidence that can be independently audited (S. Chen et al., 2025).

Human-AI interaction gap: Human cognition versus algorithmic decision-making – this requires careful study: Financial planners are increasingly making decisions based on AI-generated recommendations; calibration, trust building, and override behaviour are critical areas of study. Experimental studies that explore the way professionals interpret probabilistic forecasts, how they react to uncertainty in algorithms, and how machine-based knowledge and professional knowledge will be combined in the visualisation layer of the dashboard can shed light on optimal ways to work together between humans and AI in particular. Regarding the governance-embedding gap, research can examine how financial regulators and central banks can facilitate the use of explainable AI techniques and the impact of interpretability tools on model validation, regulatory acceptance, and trust among stakeholders, and can also analyze the differences between regulatory sandboxes that central banks and financial regulators are implementing and how they can stimulate safe innovation without compromising the integrity of financial markets. Research is also required to investigate the role of governance norms, data-privacy regulation, and organisational power structures in the spread of technology adoption for financial planning, as the diffusion of AI-powered financial planning is seen to be quite different between highly regulated sectors and more agile digital enterprises.

This theoretical development must go hand-in-hand with methodological innovation. AI-based financial forecasts are inherently non-linear and multidimensional, which poses challenges for traditional econometric methods to accurately reflect these types of relationships, making it crucial to create hybrid modelling approaches that combine machine-learning predictive capabilities with existing financial theory to validate the output of AI financial models against fundamental economic principles. Collaborative research platforms and open data initiatives could help standardize, validate, and ease the reproducibility of financial AI models, facilitating cross-sector peer validation and benchmarking. Lastly, there is limited research on behavioral finance integration in contexts of AI assistance in planning: The interplay between algorithmic recommendations and cognitive biases, overconfidence and loss aversion, as well as the design of decision support interfaces that actively reduce human errors while maintaining strategic intuition, are relatively unexplored. Scholars can contribute in a way that is directly relevant to the proposed framework by addressing these gaps, both in terms of their empirical relevance and in terms of their capacity to guide technological innovation in a way consistent with organisational resilience, ethical governance and sustainable financial performance.

8. CONCLUSION

The combination of Big Data infrastructure, interactive visualisation, and the power of AI has revolutionised the architecture, the power, and the strategic purpose of financial planning today. What used to be a compliance function based on static spreadsheets and reporting on a regular basis has become a dynamic and predictive enterprise value creation machine. This chapter has proposed these three pillars as sequential layers of a single closed-loop framework (an integrated conceptual framework shown in Figure 1), and, using a comparative synthesis of the literature and three documented industry-based examples, has demonstrated that this integrated perspective not only helps to fill some of the gaps in the previous research, but also provides a plausible practice-based understanding of the way these different layers have been operationalised in organisations like JPMorgan Chase, HSBC and Unilever.

Organisational and managerial change is still the most important factor in the successful integration of technology. Firms that fail to integrate AI and dashboard implementation into their organizational culture, workforce training, and interdepartmental management tend to fall short of their goals, whereas those that do are more likely to succeed. The finance function needs to shift from the old cost-centre reporting to a new strategic architecture that can integrate data-driven foresight, scenario simulation and agile resource allocation, and deliberately invest in hybrid skills, constant upskilling, and human-in-the-loop models that combine algorithmic automation with ethical review and strategic intuition. Regulatory environments are evolving to respond to issues of algorithmic transparency, model risk, data privacy, etc., and organisations need to develop strong audit trails, explainability procedures and compliance guardrails that safeguard institutional trust while allowing innovation to happen.

The future of financial intelligence will be defined by new technologies like financial digital twins, quantum optimisation, autonomous planning agents and generative AI, all of which have the potential to further shrink decision latency, improve simulation fidelity and further push the envelope on predictive accuracy. However, their seamless integration relies on proper planning for interoperability, modernization of legacy systems, and continuous cybersecurity and data governance investments. Academic and practitioner communities need to work together to fill these identified research gaps to ensure that the development of the technology translates into measurable organisational resilience and sustainable value creation: longitudinal performance validation, human-AI cognitive calibration, regulatory impact assessment, and cross-contextual adoption. So, the future of financial planning is not about replacing human judgment with algorithmic automation, but about creating ecosystems of synergy between people and technology, where technology enhances strategic insight, speeds up the examination of scenarios, and provides a concrete basis for decisions. Organisations that are willing to have this integrated mindset and take proper controls to ensure governance and ethical accountability will be best equipped to deal with the complexity of the economy, maximising the opportunities and maintaining the competitive edge over the long-term.

DISCLOSURE OF USE OF AI TOOLS

The authors declare that they have used Grammarly, an AI-powered language and writing assistant, exclusively for grammar checking, editing and correcting English sentences and reworking sentences for clarity and readability. The research ideas, research design, data, analysis, results, interpretation, and conclusions were not generated by Grammarly. The authors are fully responsible for the content, accuracy, originality, and final form of the manuscript.

REFERENCES

A. K. R. S., A. (. (2024). Unveiling the power of big data: Insights into big data analytics, applications, and advancements. *International Journal for Research in Applied Science and Engineering Technology, 12*(6), 2502–2512. DOI: 10.22214/ijraset.2024.63520

Titilope Tosin Adewale, Titilayo Deborah Olorunyomi, & Theodore Narku Odonkor. (2023). Big data-driven financial analysis: A new paradigm for strategic insights and decision-making. International Journal of Frontiers in Science and Technology Research, 4(2), 033–054. DOI: 10.53294/ijfstr.2023.4.2.0060

Ates, E. (2024). JPMorgan's COiN (Contract Intelligence) platform: Using AI in mergers & acquisitions and commercial lending [Case study]. https://www.emreates.co.uk/research-2/jpmorgan's-coin-(contract-intelligence)-platform:-using-ai-in-mergers-&-acquisitions-and-commercial-lending

Brynjolfsson, E., & McAfee, A. (2014). *The second machine age: Work, progress, and prosperity in a time of brilliant technologies*. W. W. Norton & Company.

Chen, H., Chiang, R. H. L., & Storey, V. C. (2012). Business intelligence and analytics: From big data to big impact. *Management Information Systems Quarterly, 36*(4), 1165–1188. DOI: 10.2307/41703503

Chen, S., Ren, S., & Zhang, Q. (2025). Hybrid architectures that combine LLMs and predictive analytics for next-generation financial modeling. *The Journal of Financial Data Science, 6*, 31–43. DOI: 10.6339/25-JDS1161D

Chen, Y., Wang, G.-J., Zhu, Y., Xie, C., & Salah Uddin, G. (2024). Identifying systemic risk drivers of FinTech and traditional financial institutions: Machine learning-based prediction and interpretation. *European Journal of Finance, 30*(18), 2157–2190. DOI: 10.1080/1351847X.2024.2358940

Davenport, T., & Harris, J. (2017). *Competing on analytics: Updated, with a new introduction: The new science of winning*. Harvard Business Review Press.

Davenport, T. H. (2018). *The AI advantage: How to put the artificial intelligence revolution to work*. MIT Press. DOI: 10.7551/mitpress/11781.001.0001

Davenport, T. H., & Ronanki, R. (2018). Artificial intelligence for the real world. *Harvard Business Review, 96*(1), 108–116.

Delen, D., & Demirkan, H. (2013). Data, information and analytics as services. *Decision Support Systems, 55*(1), 359–363. DOI: 10.1016/j.dss.2012.05.044

DigitalDefynd. (2025). 13 ways JP Morgan is using AI: In-depth case study. https://digitaldefynd.com/IQ/jp-morgan-using-ai-case-study/

Eckerson, W. W. (2010). *Performance dashboards: Measuring, monitoring, and managing your business*. John Wiley & Sons.

Emerj. (2022). Artificial intelligence at HSBC – Two use cases. Emerj Artificial Intelligence Research. https://emerj.com/artificial-intelligence-at-hsbc-two-use-cases/

European Parliament and Council of the European Union. (2024). *Regulation (EU) 2024/1689 laying down harmonised rules on artificial intelligence (Artificial Intelligence Act)*. Official Journal of the European Union.

Gavryushenko, A. P. (2021). Principles of strategic financial management and their implementation in the information economy. *Finance and Credit, 27*(12), 2772–2784. DOI: 10.24891/c.27.12.2772

Gomber, P., Kauffman, R. J., Parker, C., & Weber, B. W. (2018). On the fintech revolution: Interpreting the forces of innovation, disruption, and transformation in financial services. *Journal of Management Information Systems, 35*(1), 220–265. DOI: 10.1080/07421222.2018.1440766

Grover, V., Chiang, R. H. L., Liang, T.-P., & Zhang, D. (2018). Creating strategic business value from big data analytics: A research framework. *Journal of Management Information Systems, 35*(2), 388–423. DOI: 10.1080/07421222.2018.1451951

Hussain, A., Nisar, Q. A., Khan, W., Niazi, U. I., & Malik, M. (2024). When and how big data analytics and work practices impact financial performance: An intellectual capital perspective from the banking industry. *Kybernetes, 53*(10), 3271–3293. DOI: 10.1108/K-11-2022-1623

Jeyaprabha, B., Kumar, S. R., Bolla, R. L., Bhatt, A. S., Sera, R. J., & Arora, K. (2025). Data-driven decision making in management: Leveraging big data analytics for strategic planning. 2025 First International Conference on Advances in Computer Science, Electrical, Electronics, and Communication Technologies (CE2CT), 1000–1003. DOI: 10.1109/CE2CT64011.2025.10939548

Kaplan, R. S., & Norton, D. P. (1996). *The balanced scorecard: Translating strategy into action*. Harvard Business School Press.

Klover.ai. (2025). HSBC's AI strategy: Analysis of AI dominance in financial services. https://www.klover.ai/hsbc-ai-strategy-analysis-of-ai-dominance-in-financial-services/

KPMG International. (2026). 2026 global AI in finance: The decision advantage [Survey report]. https://kpmg.com/xx/en/media/press-releases/2026/05/ai-adoption-in-finance-doubles-but-assurance-readiness-determines-who-wins.html

Kreuzberger, D., Kühl, N., & Hirschl, S. (2023). Machine learning operations (MLOps): Overview, definition, and architecture. *IEEE Access : Practical Innovations, Open Solutions, 11*, 31866–31879. DOI: 10.1109/ACCESS.2023.3262138

McKinsey & Company. (2024). CFOs counting on gen AI. https://www.mckinsey.com/featured-insights/week-in-charts/cfos-counting-on-gen-ai

Mishra, S. (2018). Financial management and forecasting using business intelligence and big data analytic tools. *International Journal of Financial Engineering, 5*(2), 1850011. DOI: 10.1142/S2424786318500111

Nobanee, H. (2021). A bibliometric review of big data in finance. *Big Data, 9*(2), 73–78. DOI: 10.1089/big.2021.29044.edi PMID: 33861644

Porter, M. E., & Heppelmann, J. E. (2015). How smart, connected products are transforming companies. *Harvard Business Review, 93*(10), 96–114.

Raguseo, E., & Vitari, C. (2018). Investments in big data analytics and firm performance: An empirical investigation of direct and mediating effects. *International Journal of Production Research, 56*(15), 5206–5221. DOI: 10.1080/00207543.2018.1427900

Sharda, R., Delen, D., & Turban, E. (2018). *Business intelligence, analytics, and data science: A managerial perspective* (4th ed.). Pearson.

Solvoyo. (2023). Unilever: End-to-end autonomous planning & analytics [Case study]. https://solvoyo.com/case-studies/fmcg/fortune-100-global-cpg-end-to-end-autonomous-planning

Tang, J., Li, C., Fu, Y., & Li, C. (2022). The borderless integration of financial management innovation using big data analysis of social media. *Wireless Communications and Mobile Computing, 4711617*(1), 4711617. Advance online publication. DOI: 10.1155/2022/4711617

Thanasas, G. L., & Kampiotis, G. (2024). The role of big data analytics in financial decision-making and strategic accounting. *Technium Business and Management, 10*, 17–33. DOI: 10.47577/business.v10i.11877

Wamba, S. F., Gunasekaran, A., Akter, S., Ren, S. J., Dubey, R., & Childe, S. J. (2017). Big data analytics and firm performance: Effects of dynamic capabilities. *Journal of Business Research, 70*, 356–365. DOI: 10.1016/j.jbusres.2016.08.009

Wu, W. (2022). Credit risk measurement, decision analysis, transformation and upgrading for financial big data. *Complexity*, *8942773*(1), 8942773. Advance online publication. DOI: 10.1155/2022/8942773

Yıldırım, M., Okay, F. Y., & Özdemir, S. (2021). Big data analytics for default prediction using graph theory. *Expert Systems with Applications*, *176*, 114840. DOI: 10.1016/j.eswa.2021.114840

Chapter 7
Managerial and Organizational Determinants of Machine Learning-Enabled Accounting and Management Information Systems Performance

Anusha Palagati
http://orcid.org/0009-0008-7875-5100
Guru Nanak University, India

S. Niranjani
http://orcid.org/0009-0006-8886-4234
Guru Nanak Institute of Technology, India

Ratnamala Bariniki
http://orcid.org/0009-0004-5360-7540
Guru Nanak Institute of Technology, India

Chokkamreddy Prakash
http://orcid.org/0000-0002-3832-3740
Guru Nanak Institutions Technical Campus, India

DOI: 10.4018/979-8-3373-9230-1.ch007

© 2027, IGI Global Scientific Publishing. Copying or distributing in print or electronic forms without written permission of IGI Global Scientific Publishing is prohibited. Use of this chapter to ...erative artificial intelligence (AI) technologies is expressly prohibited. The publisher reserves all rights to license its use for generative AI training and machine learning model development.

ABSTRACT

Machine learning (ML) is transforming the quick digitalization of Accounting and Management Information Systems (AIS/MIS) and is redrawing the financial reporting, internal control, and decision-supports system. The incorporation of these technologies current body of empirical research offered on managerial and organizational issues presented by ML-enabled AIS/MIS is limited. The chapter hypothesizes and empirically tests a model that analyzes the interrelationship between managerial capability, governance controls, the level of maturity in the adoption of the MLS, as well as the effectiveness of decision-support systems as the joint influences on system performance. A total of 524 professionals, the representatives of the manufacturing, banking, and service industries, received the collected data and were studied with the help of the structural equation modeling in SmartPLS and AMOS. The results offer practitioners and scholars actionable advices.

1. INTRODUCTION

1.1 Background Accounting Information Systems (AIS) and Management Information Systems (MIS) in Modern Organisations

Several decades ago, AIS and MIS have been the cornerstones of the organisational planning, control, and decision-making. In their traditional form, AIS focused on the processing of transactions, financial reporting, and compliance, whereas the MIS provided managerial planning in the form of periodic reporting and performance summaries (Maulina & Nazaruddin, 2025; Ndanu, 2025). With the introduction of advanced digital technologies, however, the architecture footprint and the strategic importance of such systems have been changed (Maulina & Nazaruddin, 2025; Ndanu, 2025). In modern AIS/MIS, data at an enterprise-wide scale, real-time analytic functions, and sophisticated calculational procedures, such as artificial intelligence (AI) and machine learning (ML) are integrated. As a result, IRAs no longer serve as a record-keeping tool: they serve as intelligent platforms, which enable predictive forecasting, anomaly detection, risk evaluation and strategy-making (Booker et al., 2024; Kokina and Davenport, 2025). Therefore, AIS/MIS have become central aspects of financial leadership, organisational insourcing, and performance administration in an enormous multitude of industries (Ali and AlSondos, 2025).

1.2 Increasing Managerial Complexity Through Digitalisation, Automation and Regulatory Pressure

Increasing complexity of managerial processes has been fuelled by the unrelenting digitalisation of the accounting and managerial processes. Ability to encroach upon the capabilities of AIS/MIS and the risks that are inherent in it have grow due to automation, AI based analytics, cloud based accounting systems, and built in ERP systems (Barreto et al., 2025; Machucho and Ortiz, 2025). In this regard, now managers have to oversee technologically advanced systems in addition to maintaining accuracy, transparency, ethics and cybersecurity. Concurrently, regulatory requirements in the financial reporting, internal controls, data protection and auditability have increased in severity. Adherence to IFRS, internal governance systems and new AI governance technologies implies the existence of effective custodial instruments and multidisciplinary coordination between the finance departments, IT departments, and top management (Almaqtari, 2024; Eskandarany, 2024). As a result, the management position is being transformed by operational oversight to intelligent information systems strategic governance.

1.3 Problem Statement: Managerial and Organisational Problems in AIS/MIS Effective Overseeing

Even with the advent of technology, many organisations are still struggling with regards to how to well manage and govern AIS/MIS. The existing body of academic work supports the continued existence of managerial challenges, such as the lack of alignment between the business strategy and the capabilities of the systems, undercommitment of managers, technological change resistance, and lack of AI literacy among accounting professionals (Abbas, 2025; Kerr et al., 2025). Besides, the autonomy of ML-based systems also brings the issues concerning control, responsibility, transparency, and ethical decisions. There are often no formalized systems of AI interpretation, automated decision justification and the introduction of intelligent systems into the control systems of managers (Elnakeeb and Elawadly, 2025; Fitriani et al., 2025). These obstacles undermine the power of AIS/MIS and limit the role they can play in the performance of organisations.

1.4 Evolution from Operational Systems to Strategic Intelligence Principles

Over time, AIS and MIS have evolved from operational support tools into strategic intelligence princiles that actively shape organizational competitiveness. Traditionally, these systems were designed to collect, store, and process structured financial and managerial data. Their outputs were largely historical, supporting formality reporting and routine performance monitoring. However, the integration of advanced analytics, cloud computing, and machine learning has altered AIS/MIS into proactive and forward-looking systems.

Modern AIS/MIS now enable predictive, real-time dashboards, automated anomaly detection, and scenario-based simulations. Rather than merely reporting past financial outcomes, these systems assist managers in expect risks, optimizing resource allocation, and enhancing strategic agility. This shift reflects a broader change from descriptive reporting to prescriptive and predictive decision support.

Consequently, AIS/MIS are no longer confined to accounting departments; they are embedded within enterprise-wide strategy elucidation, risk governance, and performance management processes. This transformation enhanced the growing interdependence between technological infrastructure and managerial capability in achieving sustainable organizational performance.

1.5 Research Gap: Scanty Empirical Support between Managerial Challenges and AIS/MIS Effectiveness

Even though the AI-and-accounting literature has grown swiftly, the majority of studies have been conceptual, bibliometric, or systematic reviews with the focus on technological potentials instead of managerial and organisational factors (Barbosa et al., 2025; Sultana et al., 2025). There are limited empirical studies investigating the impact of managerial issues, governance systems, and organisational control on the effectiveness of AIS/MIS, especially in the context of using MLs. Moreover, currently, the mainstream of research focuses on the AIS, MIS, or AI adoption as a separate phenomenon without incorporating the managerial complexity, organisational controls, and decision-support efficacy into one analytical paradigm (Booker et al., 2024; Soluk et al., 2026). The gap prevents theoretical development and practical leadership direction to managers who are to manage the intelligent accounting systems.

1.6 Objectives of the Chapter

The objectives of this chapter are to:

1. Examine the evolution and strategic role of AIS and MIS in contemporary organizations.
2. Identify managerial challenges associated with overseeing AIS/MIS in digital and AI-enabled environments.

3. Analyze organizational control and governance mechanisms relevant to AIS/MIS effectiveness.
4. Explore the role of AIS/MIS as decision-support systems influencing managerial effectiveness.
5. Synthesize prior literature to develop a conceptual foundation for empirical analysis.

1.7 Theoretical Underpinnings of the Research

The three mutually supportive theoretical perspectives that the chapter is rooted in explain the managerial and organisational preconditions of KML-enabled AIS/MIS performance, namely, the Resource-Based View (RBV), Socio-Technical Systems Theory, and the Technology-Organisation-Environment (TOE) frame.

The RBV assumes organisational performance to be based on the ownership of valuable, rare, inimitable, and non-substitutable resource. Managerial ability, which includes technological, strategic and governance acuity, is an important intangible asset that enables organisations to exploit advanced analytics to make high-quality decisions and system output in the ML- enabled AIS/MIS environment.

Socio-Technical Systems Theory focuses more on the dependence between social structures and technological artefacts. ML-enabled AIS / MIS are not entirely technical artefacts, but the effectiveness of such artefacts appears to depend on the interaction between algorithms, judgement of managers, expertise of users, and organisational practices. This view predicts the role of human-ML cooperation, change management, and mistrust in automated decision-support systems.

Last but not least, the TOE model provides a comprehensive perspective to assess the prevalence of ML through the fusion of technological preparedness, organisational control systems, and external forces like regulatory control. All these theoretical backgrounds shape the conceptual framework and the hypothesis in the chapter to provide a sound explanation of the combined impact of managerial, organisational, and technological factors on AIS/MIS performance within an ML-driven environment.

1.8 Structure of the Chapter

The rest of this chapter has been divided in the following manner: Section 2 entails a critical examination of the conceptual and theoretical basis of AIS/MIS, clarification of challenges in management and organizational controls, definition of decision support systems, and considering the integration technology. In section 3, the conceptual framework is presented, and the hypotheses are affirmed. Section 4 describes the methodology of the research. Section 5 describes the results of the empirical. Section 6 also evaluates limitations and describes future research directions, and a final consideration of research implications is provided in Section 7, with implications to practice and policy.

2. CONCEPTUAL BACKGROUND AND LITERATURE REVIEW

2.1 Accounting Information Systems and Management Information Systems

Accounting Information Systems

The AIS and Management Information Systems (MIS) are vital organizational structures that enable the process of taking up, processing, storing, and sharing financial and management information. Along the traditional approaches, AIS was concentrated on transaction processing, financial reporting and compliance, whereas MIS was at the service of managerial planning, control, and performance evaluations. These systems have developed over the years to become integrated systems developed in the enterprise-wide information architecture (Maulina & Nazaruddin, 2025).

The digital transformation has played a major role in the transformations of AIS and MIS through real-time data processing, system integration and advanced analytics. Cloud accounting engines and data-driven architecture have extended the strategic decision-making and financial governance aims and functions of AIS/MIS to enterprise resource planning (ERP) systems (Barreto et al., 2025). Empirical research will always show that a properly developed AIS/MIS will have a beneficial effect on the overall performance of an organization due to their contribution to the accuracy of the information, transparency, and coordination among the functional units (Ali & AlSondos, 2025).

The use of artificial intelligence and machine learning has further made AIS/MIS to be transformed into intelligent systems with a predictive analytics capability, anomaly detection and automated reporting. Machine-learned algorithms enhance the accuracy of the forecasts, and refine the internal controls and risk evaluation, which increases the strategic value of accounting information in organizations (Booker et al., 2024; Kureljusic & Karger, 2024). As a result, AIS/MIS is gradually considered dynamic decision support systems, as opposed to passive reporting systems.

2.2 Managerial Problems of AIS and MIS Management

Regardless of the level of technological advancement, AIS/MIS management and supervision is a challenging undertaking. Strategic alignment is one of the most outstanding problems found in the literature. Companies tend to have integrated high-level information systems without properly fitting them to their overall strategic goal, thus making booked decision making and minimized system use (Machucho & Ortiz, 2025). Misalignment of strategies decreases the usefulness of AIS/MIS and damages the trust of managers in system results.

Quality and reliability of information is also an issue of concern. Although machine-learning models can be processed with great efficiency due to the use of AI and large amounts of data, when the results of the systems are related to a high-stakes financial decision, managers often question their transparency and interpretability (Kerr et al., 2025). According to Booker et al. (2024), such an aspect as the black-box nature of the applications of AI presents a critical problem in terms of the accountability and auditability of a manager.

AIS/MIS oversight is further complicated by the user resistance and skill deficits. Various papers document that accountants, in addition to managers, tend to be technically inexperienced to correctly comprehend AI-generated insights, resulting in opposition or insufficient dependence on automated results (Abbas, 2025; Alruwaili & Mgammal, 2025). These results indicate the significance of training, change management and organization learning that help in successful implementation of AIS/MIS.

Another aspect of managerial challenge is control and compliance complexities. Automation changes the conventional internal control framework, where it is hard to know the logic of the decisions made and where the responsibility lies. Consequently, organizations will have to redesign control systems in order to allow algorithm-driven processes without compromising the accounting standards and the regulation (Elnakeeb & Elawadly, 2025).

Table 1. Managerial Challenges in ML-Enabled AIS/MIS: Prior Empirical Evidence

Author(s), Year	**Context (Industry / Country)**	**Managerial Challenges Identified**	**Methodology**	**Findings**
Booker et al. (2024)	Multi-industry / Global	Lack of managerial interpretability of ML outputs; accountability gaps	Meta-theoretical review	ML enhances prediction accuracy, but managerial oversight mechanisms remain underdeveloped
Abbas (2025)	Management accounting / Global	Skill gaps, resistance to AI-driven decision making	Systematic literature review	Managerial competencies significantly condition the value derived from AI-enabled AIS
Kerr et al. (2025)	Accounting & society / Global	Ethical responsibility, trust in automated decisions	Narrative review	AI adoption shifts managerial roles but raises governance and legitimacy concerns
Eskandarany (2024)	Banking sector / Middle East	Board-level governance and strategic misalignment	Qualitative interviews	Managerial awareness and governance maturity determine ML adoption success
Tenhunen (2025)	Strategic finance / Europe	Change management and cultural resistance	Mixed-methods study	Strategic benefits of AI materialize only with strong managerial leadership
Ali & AlSondos (2025)	SMEs / Emerging economies	Limited managerial commitment and control structures	Survey-based empirical analysis	Management commitment directly improves AIS effectiveness
Sultana et al. (2025)	Developing countries	Weak managerial support and system integration	Systematic literature review	Managerial and organizational factors outweigh technical barriers
Elnakeeb & Elawadly (2025)	Accounting automation / Global	Governance complexity and control redesign	Bibliometric analysis	AI adoption increases need for managerial control innovation

As the comparative evidence discussed in Table 1 can prove, the challenge of management of ML-enabled AIS/MIS is not confined to technical constraints only, but also includes gaps in capacity, the shortage in governance, ethical responsibility and change resistance. In industries and institutional backgrounds, previous research findings are always uniform that the managerial supervision and organization preparedness are influential determinants in evaluating whether the employment of ML leads to better or worse system performance. Notably, the literature indicates common ground on the theme that technological sophistication is not enough; instead, managerial competence and control systems determine the reliability, legitimacy and value of decision of ML-integrated accounting systems. This summary reveals that an integrative framework, which presents managerial issues as antecedents to the adoption of the system and its performance, is necessary.

2.3 Organizational Control and Governance Mechanisms

A foundation of three organizational control and governance mechanisms is part of the costuming the efficacy of Accounting Information Systems (AIS) and Management Information Systems (MIS). System structures Internal control, audit engines, and corporate governance are the structural frameworks underpinning the structural and functional integrity of data, accountability, and regulation assurance. Empirical research points at AI-enabled AIS being capable to strengthen internal controls through constant surveillance and automatic identification of anomalies, although this effect only becomes a reality when it is supported by strong governance frameworks (Rahim and Chishti, 2024).

The matter of regulatory compliance is becoming a central one, especially in the environments under the jurisdiction of International Financial Reporting Standards (IFRS) and the constantly developing body of AI regulating practices. According to Almaqtari (2024), the use of AI initiatives requires effective IT governance systems to achieve the purposes of accounting and auditing. Without defined policies on governance, organisations are facing escalated risks with ethical accountability, data privacy and non-compliance with regulations.

The involvement of top-management turns out to be a vital factor of AIS/MIS success. Empirical research that utilises SMEs, public-sector organisations, and family firms shows that leadership commitment is a key factor in determining the system adoption, control performance, and the quality of decisions (Ali and AlSondos, 2025; Darmawati et al., 2025; Soluk et al., 2026). Financial controllers and high-level accounting practitioners are increasingly playing the role of strategic intermediaries between technical systems and managerial decision maybe.

2.4 Decision Support Role of AIS/MIS and Managerial Effectiveness

AIS and MIS are increasingly being conceptualised as decision-support systems that make managers more effective. Such systems can enable responding to uncertainty and risk more promptly, reliably, and analytically by providing managers with timely, correct, and informative information, owing to the integration of AI and machine learning (Gorka et al., 2025). Real time dashboards and predictive analytics can be used to minimise performance and proactive planning.

However, effectiveness of decisions is not only decided by the capability of the system but also on managerial cognition and behaviour. It has been argued in the research that the trust of AIS/MIS outputs developed by managers is shaped with the perception of reliability, transparency and ethical integrity (Kerr et al., 2025).

Abbas (2025) warns, no amount of diligent judgement should be outsourced to the automated recommendations without risking the quality of decisions.

Empirical evidence shows that organisations achieve high-quality decision results when the outputs of AIS/MIS serves as complementary as opposed to replacing managerial judgements (Tenhunen, 2025). This view highlights the relevance of human machine collaboration in modern accounting world.

The discussed literature thus confirms that the effectiveness of decision support is the crucial mechanism according to which the adoption of machine learning is turned into managerial and organisational performance. Though machine learning enhances the analytical ability of AIS/MIS, the improvement in performance becomes real only when the output of the system is made in time, interpretable and actionable to make managerial decisions. In that regard, implicitly, previous research implies that there is a mediating factor, i.e., decision-support effectiveness, in which case, machine-learning adoption promotes decision quality, which, subsequently, increases the performance of AIS/MIS and managerial effectiveness. However, this is a mediating effect not well empirically tested. To this gap, the current chapter conceptualises decision-support effectiveness as a mediating construct on a central basis of connecting machine-learning adoption with AIS/MIS performance as conceptualised in the conceptual framework of Section 3.

2.5 Technology Integration Challenges in AIS and MIS

The next issue that continues to pose challenges in AIS/MIS implementation is technology integration. Combination of ERP systems, cloud-software to account and AI often result in the lack of interoperability and data fragmentation, especially in organisations that use outdated systems (Fitriani et al., 2025). These problems hinder systematic flow of information and dissipate system performance.

The issue of cybersecurity and privacy of data have escalated in the environment of increased automation and connectivity of systems to one another. Research indicates that AI-based AIS/MIS exposes organisations to a higher cyber threat, meaning that these systems should have improved security measures and be externally monitored on a regular basis (Almaqtari, 2024). These risks may destroy data integrity and organisational trust when they are not addressed.

On the whole, the literature suggests that an interventional approach based on achieving technological capability, organisational preparedness, and effective governance is holistic and essential to successful AIS/MIS integration (Barreto et al., 2025). Failure to pay attention to these dimensions will lead to under-utilisation of advanced accounting technologies.

3. CONCEPTUAL FRAMEWORK AND HYPOTHESES DEVELOPMENT

3.1 Conceptual Model

This chapter has been conceptualised in such a way to explain the impact of managerial and organisational variables in the performance of Accounting Information Systems (AIS) and Management Information Systems (MIS) in an environment that is becoming dominated by machine learning (ML). The model incorporates 5 fundamental constructs and is based on the antecedent literature in the accounting information systems, technology acceptance, organisational control and decision-support theory by building on managerial challenges, organisational control mechanisms, ML adoption and maturity, decision-support effectiveness and AIS/MIS performance.

Managerial issues include constraints in managerial capacity, strategic fit, technological knowledge and change management that is linked to ML-integrated AIS/MIS. In what has been done before, it is argued that managerial competence and commitment would play a significant role in the translation of technological investments into effective system initiatives especially in complicated digital environments.

These organisational control mechanisms include internal controls, audit systems, governance structures and compliance frameworks, which inform the design, monitoring as well as the utilisation of the AIS/MIS. These mechanisms are central in ensuring transparency, accountability and reliability of outputs of the algorithms in ML-enabled systems.

ML adoption and maturity refers to the degree of adaptation to and integration levels of ML technologies into AIS/MIS. This construct measures not only the existence of the ML tools but also measures how sophisticated they are, how well they are accepted by the organisation, and how well the tools support the business processes.

Decision-support effectiveness measures the ability of the AIS/MIS to enable timely provision of accurate, relevant, and actionable information that helps in improving decisions made by managers. This role is likely to be strengthened by ML with the power of predictive analytics and real-time insights and automated recommendations.

Last, the AIS/MIS performance reflects on the overall system effectiveness, which summarises the quality of information, system reliability, user satisfaction and contribution towards the organisational performance.

The given conceptual model assumes that managerial and organisational variables have a direct impact on the results of ML adoption and AIS/MIS, and the effectiveness of decision support serves as a major explanatory variable between the adoption of the ML and the performance of the system. Besides, the organisational culture is placed as a contextual aspect which influences the degree of such relations.

Figure 1. Conceptual Framework for Managerial and Organisational Determinents of ML-enabled AIS/MIS Performance

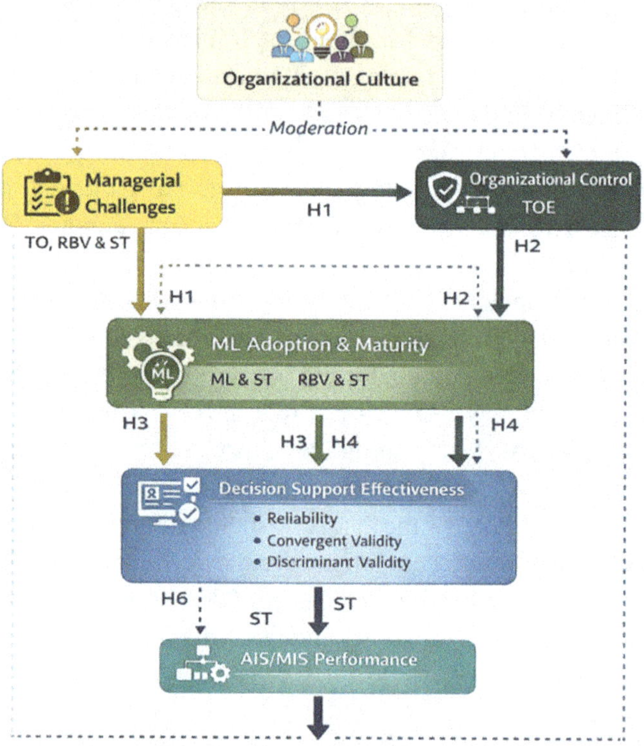

3.2 Hypotheses Development

Managerial Capability and ML-Integrated AIS/MIS Effectiveness

Managerial capability plays a critical role in the management of the complicated information systems. Regarding the application of ML to the AIS/MIS, the managers must now not only be people with extensive knowledge in the accounting field, but also in the domain of analytics, data governance, and algorithmic decision making. Empirical studies support the use of managerial competence and leadership commitment to have a considerable impact on the system utilization and effectiveness, especially in technologically advanced setting.

It is, therefore, postulated that:

H1: Managerial capability has a positive impact on effectiveness of AIS/MIS successful integration with ML.

Mechanisms and Reliability of Systems of Organization Control

The reliability and trustworthiness of the outputs of AIS/MIS would not be possible without the organization control mechanisms. Traditional controls, in the case of ML-based financial systems, need to be modified to deal with algorithmic opacities, integrity, and moral responsibility. Strong governance and audit frameworks make the system more reliable through compliance and openness and constant reviews.

So, the second hypothesis is as follows:

H 2: Organizational control process can effectively contribute to the reliability of ML-based financial systems.

ML Adoption and the Quality of the Decision Support

Machine learning technologies enhance the analysis powers of AIS/MIS by providing predictive modeling, anomaly detection and real-time reporting. Previous research points out that extended use of ML implies a better quality of the decisions of the manager as the manager obtains more confident and relevant financial information.

Accordingly, the research hypothesis is as follows:

H3: The implementation of ML has a positive influence on the quality of the decision support offered by AIS/MIS.

Technology Implementation Problems and AIS/MIS Effectiveness

Although such potential benefits of ML may arise, the performance of AIS/MIS may be compelled to fail because of integration issues, which include system incompatibility, data silos, legacy infrastructure, and cybersecurity risks. This is always recorded in the literature where unresolved integration challenges have a detrimental impact on system performance, customer satisfaction, and data quality.

Following this logic, it is allowed to draw the hypothesis:

H4: The issues of technology integration are a bad thing because they adversely influence the performance of ML-enabled AIS/MIS.

Mediator Effect Decision Support Effectiveness

One important tool whereby the adoption of ML becomes a substance in enhanced managerial and system performance is decision support effectiveness. Although using ML increases the level of analytics, its performance performance is achieved only when managers apply the system outputs to make decisions.

It is, therefore, postulated that:

H5: The quality of decision support mediates the relationship among managerial performance, ML adoption and the quality of managerial decisions.

Moderating Role of Organization Culture

The organizational culture predetermines the perceptions of the managers, their adoption, and use of advanced technologies. A culture that encourages innovation, lifelong learning, and data-driven decision-making would probably enhance the correlation amidst the managerial competency and the effective implementation of ML. On the other hand, this relationship can be undermined by the rigid or risk-averse cultures.

Thus, the hypotheting moderating assumption is as the following:

H6: This organization culture moderates the relationship in the context of managerial challenges and the success of ML adoption in which it enhances the relationship.

4. RESEARCH METHODOLOGY

4.1 Research Design

The research design of this study is a quantitative and cross-sectional research design with the purpose of investigating the managerial and organizational factors of ML-enabled Accounting and Management Information Systems (AIS/MIS). The design is both appropriate to test how the latent constructs are related to each other and allows using structural equation modeling (SEM) in order to understand the direct, mediating, and moderating effects. The chosen methodology was a deductive approach based upon the available literature on the topic of AIS/MIS, management dilemma, control in organizations, and machine-learning adoption.

4.2 Population and Sample

Population: Finance managers, accountants, MIS managers, internal auditors, and data analytics professionals of manufacturing organizations, banks, and service-sector organizations.

Sample Size: 524 respondents that were used through purposive sampling so that subjects could have experience having worked with ML-enabled AIS/MIS systems.

Sample Size Rationale: It has been stated that SEM methods, especially Smart-PLS and AMOS need sufficient sample sizes to obtain stable models. The sample of 524 respondents meets the suggested rule-of-thumb of 1020 cases per parameter under estimation.

Pilot Testing: Pilot Testing- The instrument was piloted along with 30 respondents to determine whether it was clear, relevant, and reliable and had some minor revisions.

Data Collection Mode The data collection mode was online surveys and email-based distribution (augmented by follow-ups to enhance the response rates).

4.3 Data Collection Method

Instrument: A structured questionnaire using a five-point Likert scale (1 = Strongly Disagree to 5 = Strongly Agree).

Table 2. Variables and Measurement

Construct	Measurement Indicators	Source / Adaptation
Managerial Challenges	ML literacy, resistance to change, skill gaps, decision-making capability	Adapted from prior AIS/ML studies
Organizational Control Mechanisms	Internal audit, compliance, risk management, governance	Adapted from COSO / AIS literature
ML Adoption and Maturity	Predictive analytics, automation level, system integration, ML utilization	Based on recent ML-AIS studies
Decision Support Effectiveness	Timeliness, accuracy, predictive insight, managerial satisfaction	Adapted from decision support system literature
AIS/MIS Performance	System reliability, reporting accuracy, decision-making effectiveness, organizational impact	Adapted from AIS performance scales
Organizational Culture (Moderator)	Learning orientation, innovation support, flexibility	Adapted from Denison and Cameron culture scales

The validation of the measurement model will be done through the four steps outlined below:

Reliability: Cronbachs alpha and Composite Reliability (CR) are above 0.70.

Convergent Validity: Average Variance Extracted (AVE) > 0.50.

Discriminant validity: It is ensured using FornellLarcker criterion and HTMT ratio (less than 0.85).

These tests are meant to validate that the model of measurement are appropriate towards structural equation modeling.

4.4 Structural Model and Test of Hypothesis

Software: The analysis of the SEM has been done on SmartPLS 4.0 and cross-validated on AMOS 28.0.

Analysis Steps:

Measurement Model Evaluation: Reliability, convergent and discriminant validity.

Structural Model Evaluation: Path coefficients, significance, t -values (bootstrapping bootstrapping: 5,000 resamples).

Mediation Testing: Effectiveness of Decision Support Mediating the association between AIS/MIS performance and ML adoption.

Moderation Testing: Moderation of organizational culture on the effect of managerial challenges on the adoption of the ML.

Model Fit Indices: SRMR, NFI, and R 2 were analyzed to allow predictive and explanatory power.

4.5 Ethical Considerations

The participation of the respondents was anonymous and voluntary.

Participation in the survey was done through informed consent.

Data storage was done in a safe manner and no research purpose was permitted to be fulfilled.

Besides the usual research ethics, the research will satisfy the principles of data protection and responsible artificial intelligence. Each of the data collection and storage processes were conducted based on GDPR-similar guidelines, such as voluntary participation, informed consent, anonymity, and limited access to data. The research did not entail acquisition of personally identifiable or sensitive financial data. Additionally, the study recognizes ethical issues, which come with machine-learning-based accounting systems, with accountability in the use of AI, accountability, and human accountability. The results are seen as decision-support information and not a prescriptive automatic recommendation, which means that the results of algorithms should not become the sole source of managerial or organizational decisions. This method of approach corresponds with new ethical principles of AI governance in accounting and information systems studies.

4.6 Data Analysis Procedure

Descriptive Statistics: Characteristics of respondents, the level of adopting the ML, and patterns of using the system.

Checks of Reliability and Validity: cronbachs, CR, AVE, discriminant validity.

SEM Analysis:

Direct effects: AIS/MIS performance is a result of managerial concerns, organizational control, and ML usage.

Mediating effect: ML adoption to Decision support to AIS/MIS performance.

Moderating effect: Organization of culture × Managerial challenge 5 Organizational culture x ml adoption.

Interpretation of Findings: In response to hypotheses, prior literature and managerial implications.

Figure 2. Research Design and Data Analysis Flow

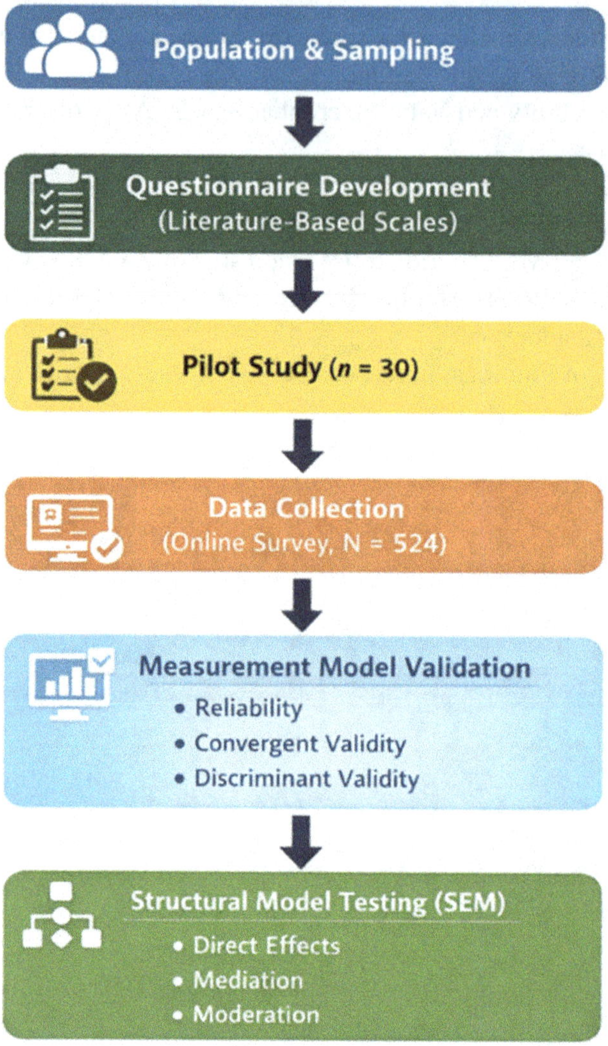

Figure 2 illustrates the overall research design and data analysis process adopted in this study.

The research begins with the identification of the target population and purposive sampling of professionals experienced in ML-enabled AIS/MIS. This is followed by questionnaire development based on established scales, pilot testing to ensure clarity and reliability, and large-scale data collection using online survey methods. The analytical phase involves measurement model validation through reliability and validity assessment, followed by structural model testing using Structural Equation Modeling to evaluate direct, mediating, and moderating relationships.

5. RESULTS AND DISCUSSION

5.1 Respondent and Organizational Profile

The study collected responses from **524 professionals** working in **manufacturing, banking, and service-sector organizations**, all of whom had direct experience with **ML-enabled AIS/MIS**.

Table 3. Demographic Profile of Respondents (N = 524)

Variable	Category	Frequency	Percentage
Gender	Male	312	59.5
	Female	212	40.5
Age	25–34 years	168	32.1
	35–44 years	201	38.4
	45–54 years	155	29.6
Education	Postgraduate	351	67
	Professional Certification	173	33
Designation	Finance/Accounting Managers	219	41.8
	MIS / IT Managers	146	27.9
	Auditors / Analysts	159	30.3

The respondents were highly experienced, with most holding postgraduate degrees or professional certifications. This ensures the reliability of the responses, as participants are directly involved in ML-enabled AIS/MIS management.

ML Adoption Level Across Organizations

Table 4. Level of ML Adoption in AIS/MIS

ML Adoption Level	Frequency	Percentage
Low (Pilot Stage)	128	24.4
Moderate (Partial Implementation)	219	41.8
High (Fully Integrated)	177	33.8

A majority of organizations (75.6%) reported moderate to high ML adoption, indicating substantial experience with intelligent accounting systems, justifying the study's focus on managerial and organizational challenges in ML integration.

5.2 Reliability and Validity Assessment

Table 5. Measurement Model Reliability and Validity

Construct	Cronbach's α	Composite Reliability (CR)	Average Variance Extracted (AVE)
Managerial Challenges	0.86	0.89	0.62
Organizational Control	0.88	0.91	0.65
ML Adoption	0.84	0.87	0.59
Decision Support Effectiveness	0.9	0.92	0.68
AIS/MIS Performance	0.87	0.9	0.64
Organizational Culture (Moderator)	0.85	0.88	0.61

All constructs meet recommended thresholds ($\alpha > 0.70$, CR > 0.70, AVE > 0.50), confirming internal consistency, convergent validity, and reliability. Discriminant validity was confirmed using the Fornell-Larcker criterion and HTMT < 0.85, allowing for SEM analysis.

5.3 Structural Model and Hypothesis Testing

SEM analysis was performed using SmartPLS, with bootstrapping (5000 resamples) to assess the significance of path coefficients.

Table 6. Direct Effects of SEM Analysis

Hypothesis	Path	β	t-value	p-value	Result
H1	Managerial Challenges → AIS/MIS Performance	–0.25	5.81	< .001	Supported
H2	Organizational Control → AIS/MIS Performance	0.29	6.14	< .001	Supported
H3	ML Adoption → Decision Support Effectiveness	0.41	8.12	< .001	Supported
H4	Decision Support Effectiveness → AIS/MIS Performance	0.38	7.95	< .001	Supported
H5	ML Adoption → AIS/MIS Performance	0.21	4.56	< .001	Supported
H6	Managerial Challenges → ML Adoption	–0.27	5.34	< .001	Supported

The negative impact of the managerial issue on the implementation of machine learning and the work of the accounting information system (AIS) and management information system (MIS) critically highlights the critical role of managerial preparedness in technology-based accounting. According to the Resource-Based View, the managerial capability is an intangible resource which is strategic and defines the extent to which organisations introduce successful performance patterns upon investing in technology. Even the most advanced ML technologies cannot help create value when the managers are either not ML-literate, do not strategically align, and are not change-managing to start with. This observation supports the RBV claim that resources in themselves cannot provide competitive advantage unless they are mobilised and managed successfully.

According to the socio-technical systems view, ML-empowered AIS/MIS exist on the border between human judgement and algorithmic intelligence. Managerial issues disrupt this fine balance because they cause a lack of trust, interpretability and the proper utilization of automated insights. As a result, the adoption of ML is often shallow, or they do not use it as much as possible, which restricts its ability to support the quality of decision-making and the work of the entire system. The results thus bring out that the issue of managerial challenge is neither just a hurdle in operations but a key limitation of socio-technical nature that defines the effectiveness of the intelligent accounting systems.

Mediation Analysis

Table 7. Mediating Role of Decision Support Effectiveness

Path	Direct Effect	Indirect Effect	Total Effect	Mediation
ML Adoption → AIS/MIS Performance	0.21**	0.17**	0.38**	Partial Mediation

Decision support quality partially mediates the relationship between ML adoption and AIS/MIS performance, suggesting that ML improves performance primarily through enhanced decision support, though direct effects remain significant.

Moderation Analysis

Table 8. Moderating Effect of Organizational Culture

Interaction	β	t-value	p-value	Interpretation
Managerial Challenges × Organizational Culture → ML Adoption	0.18	2.45	< .05	Supported

The large moderating impact of the organisational culture shows the fact cultural context has a very severe influence on the correlation between managerial issues and the adoption of ML. The culture supporting innovation and learning helps in reducing the resistance to technological complexity through promoting the experimentation, development of the skills, and cooperation between accounting, IT, and management functions. This buffering effect is similar to the Socio-Technical systems Theory which also focuses on the fact that effective use of technology depends on the fit between the social organization and the technical system. According to RBV perspective, organisational culture acts as an enabling meta-resource that raises the usefulness of managerial capabilities and technological resources. When managerial difficulties remain, adaptive and data-driven cultures tend to be in a better position to absorb the ML complexity and convert the analytical findings into actions. These results indicate that culture may decrease the risks of algorithmic opacities and automation anxieties, and may, therefore, support more effective collaboration between humans and ML. Organisational culture, thereupon, becomes a key contextual process that ML-enabled AIS/MIS can actualise to maintain performance increase.

Manageability of managerial challenges negatively affects the adoption of ML but this effect is cushioned by a favourable organisational culture. There is a less difficult approach to integrating ML technologies in organisations that manage to cultivate the environment of learning and promoting innovation.

Figure 3. Final structural model with standardization path coefficients.

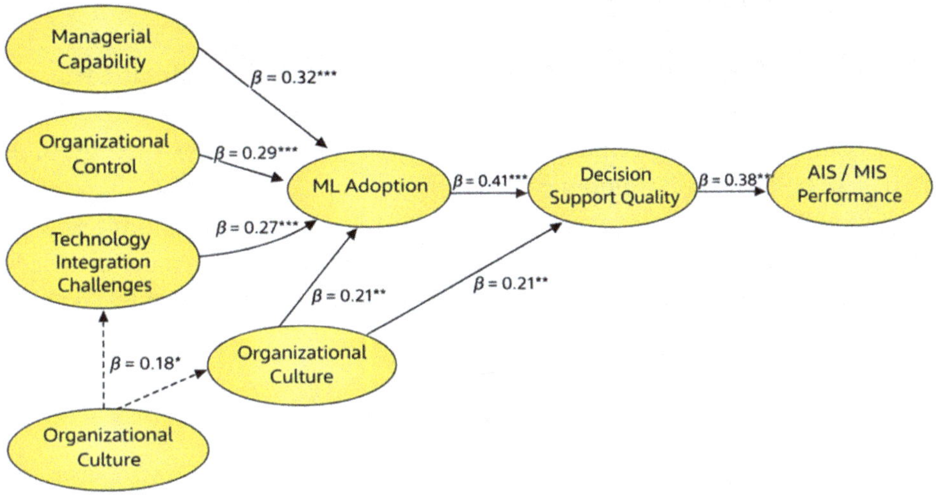

The findings indicate that managerial capability ($\beta = 0.32$, $p < .001$) and organisational control mechanisms ($\beta = 0.29$, $p < .001$) have a strong positive impact on AIS/MIS performance. The challenges of technology integration on the other hand show that it has a significant negative impact ($\beta = -0.27$, $p < .001$). Moreover, the quality of decision-support is greatly improved with the use of ML ($b = 0.41$, $p < .001$) which in its turn positively influences the system performance, which proves the mediation. The modulating effect of organisational culture makes the connection between managerial issues and the success of the MC-ML adoption even stronger, and the socio-technical character of intelligent financial systems is being reinforced.

6. LIMITATIONS AND FUTURE RESEARCH PROJECTIONS

Inasmuch as it has done so, some limitations to the chapter can be identified that can be taken as direction to further studies.

6.1 Limitations of the Methodology and Limitations of the Data.

The research is also based on cross-sectional data which limits capturing dynamic change in the adoption of ML and changes in how managers adapt as time goes by. The self-reported survey data can also cause perceptual bias especially when evaluating the managerial capability and system effectiveness. In addition, the research is largely conducted on perceptions at organisational level but not on objective performance indicators.

6.2 Longitudinal and Mixed-Method research Requirement.

The longitudinal design would be used in future studies to observe the dynamics of ML-based AIS/MIS development and development of managerial competencies and governance systems. Surveys, interviews, and case studies would be prompt, but the mixed-methods method, which incorporates them, would give more knowledge about organisational practices, variables of resistance and situational factors in the adoption of Ml.

6.3 Research Future on explainable AI, blockchain and ML audit.

More in-depth research should be conducted on emerging technologies like explainable artificial intelligence (XAI), accounting systems based on blockchain, and machine learning (ML)-driven auditing software. Studies addressing the effects of XAI to improve trust and transparency in financial decision making processes, or the collective impact of blockchain and ML on the control and assurance processes, would make a welcome addition to AIS/MIS literature.

6.4 Opportunities of Cross-Country Comparative Research.

Other cross-country and cross-industry research might help to determine how regulation settings, cultural conditions, and institution impact the adoption and effectiveness of the ML in the accounting systems. It would be especially helpful to conduct comparative research on the topic of developed and emerging economies to obtain insight into different challenges of adoption and practices related to governance.

7. CONCLUSION

The chapter presents a unified analysis of managerial and organisational dimensions that touch on the performance of machine-learning-assisted accounting information systems and management information systems. The study presents the parameters of managerial capability, organisational control mechanisms, and decision-support quality as crucial to influencing AIS/MIS effectiveness in that way by working with a conceptual framework and empirically testing it. The results highlight the importance of the fact that, technological sophistication is not enough to guarantee successful adoption of ML; managerial skills, management frameworks and organisational culture are critical in converting the potential of ML into rich decision making and performance benefits. The chapter provides practical views to managers and policy makers who need to be able to strike that balance between innovation and control, efficiency and accountability and automation and human judgement.

To conclude, a comprehensive view of integrating technology, management, and governance is the key to the sustainable implementation of machine learning to the AIS/MIS. The organisations, which move ahead and plug managerial issues and institutionalise the institution of formidable control structures is well placed to reap the transformational aspect of ML in the accounting and financial management frontiers.

Furthermore, the chapter emphasizes that successful ML integration within AIS/MIS requires a continuous learning orientation and adaptive governance structures. Organizations must invest in managerial training, cross-functional collaboration, and performance monitoring systems that align technological facility with strategic objectives. Establishing clear accountability frameworks, risk assessment protocols, and ethical AI guidelines ensures that ML-driven insights remain transparent, auditable, and aligned with regulatory expectations. By fostering a culture that combine analytical intelligence with human oversight, firms can enhance resilience, improve decision accuracy, and sustain long-term competitive advantage in an increasingly data-centric financial environment.

7.1 Future Directions

Future research should study longitudinal impacts of ML integration in AIS/MIS to assess sustainability of performance improvements over time. Comparative cross-industry and cross-country studies can provide deeper comprehension into contextual governance and regulatory influences. Further exploration of explainable AI, ethical auditing frameworks, and real-time risk analytics is essential to reinforce transparency and accountability. Researchers may also investigate human–AI collaboration models that optimize managerial judgment alongside automation. Additionally, developing standardized maturity assessment scales for ML adoption in accounting systems would support standard and policy formulation, enabling organizations to strategically align innovation, control systems, and long-term value creation.

REFERENCES

Abbas, K. (2025). Management accounting and artificial intelligence: A comprehensive literature review and recommendations for future research. *The British Accounting Review, 101551*. Advance online publication. DOI: 10.1016/j.bar.2025.101551

Ali, M., & AlSondos, K. (2025). Accounting information systems usage and management commitment toward operational efficiency: Evidence from SMEs. *Economies (Basel), 10*(4), 83. DOI: 10.3390/economies10040083

Almaqtari, F. A. (2024). The Role of IT Governance in the Integration of AI in Accounting and Auditing Operations. *Economies (Basel), 12*(8), 199. DOI: 10.3390/economies12080199

Alruwaili, T. F., & Mgammal, M. H. (2025). The impact of artificial intelligence on accounting practices: An academic perspective. *Humanities & Social Sciences Communications, 12*(1), 104. Advance online publication. DOI: 10.1057/s41599-025-05004-6

Barbosa, S. da C., Leandro, A. C. M. C., Neves, D. O., Vilhena, F. A. D. F., Souza, F. F. S. C., Barros, L. C., Lins, L. da C., de Araujo, P. R., de Oliveira, T. L., & da Silva, E. N. (2025). Accounting and Artificial Intelligence: A Systematic Review of the Literature on the Technological Impacts in the Accounting Field. *Journal of Economics, Business, and Commerce, 2*(2), 150–157. DOI: 10.69739/jebc.v2i2.1083

Barreto, A., Gomes, P., Quesado, P., & O'Sullivan, S. (2025). Advancements in Management Accounting and Digital Technologies: A Systematic Literature Review. Accounting. *Finance & Governance Review, 34*. Advance online publication. DOI: 10.52399/001c.137301

Booker, A., Chiu, V., Groff, N., & Richardson, V. J. (2024). AIS research opportunities utilizing machine learning: From a meta-theory of accounting literature. *International Journal of Accounting Information Systems, 52*, 100661. DOI: 10.1016/j.accinf.2023.100661

Darmawati, D., Jaafar, N. I., Hs, R., Baja, H. K., Purisamya, A. J., Yolanda, A. M. W., Amir, B., & Juanda, M. R. P. (2025). The Role of Artificial Intelligence in Improving the Efficiency and Accuracy of Local Government Financial Reporting: A Systematic Literature Review. *Journal of Risk and Financial Management, 18*(11), 601. DOI: 10.3390/jrfm18110601

Elnakeeb S, Elawadly HSH (2025;), "Automation and artificial intelligence in accounting: a comprehensive bibliometric analysis and future trends". Journal of Financial Reporting and Accounting, Vol. ahead-of-print No. ahead-of-print. https://doi.org/DOI: 10.1108/JFRA-09-2024-0639

Eskandarany, A. (2024). Adoption of artificial intelligence and machine learning in banking systems: A qualitative survey of board of directors. *Frontiers in Artificial Intelligence*, *7*, 1440051. Advance online publication. DOI: 10.3389/frai.2024.1440051 PMID: 39664101

Fitriani, L., Khodra, M. L., & Surendro, K. (2025). A conceptual framework for AI adoption in business architecture with case studies in higher education and government. *Discover Artificial Intelligence*, *5*(1), 409. DOI: 10.1007/s44163-025-00673-3

Górka, E., Baran, D., Wojak, G., Ćwiąkała, M., Zupok, S., Starkowski, D. R., & Okrasa, O. (2025). The impact of artificial intelligence on enterprise decision-making process. arXiv. https://arxiv.org/abs/2512.02048

Kerr, D., Taken Smith, K., Murphy Smith, L., & Xu, T. (2025). A review of AI and its impact on management accounting and society. *Journal of Risk and Financial Management*, *18*(6), 340. DOI: 10.3390/jrfm18060340

. Kokina, J., & Davenport, T. H. (2025). Challenges and opportunities for artificial intelligence in auditing. Journal of Accounting & Technology. https://doi.org/DOI: 10.1016/j.accinf.2025.100734

Kureljusic, M., & Karger, E. (2024). Forecasting in financial accounting with artificial intelligence – A systematic literature review and future research agenda. *Journal of Applied Accounting Research*, *25*(1), 81–104. DOI: 10.1108/JAAR-06-2022-0146

Machucho, R., & Ortiz, D. (2025). The Impacts of Artificial Intelligence on Business Innovation: A Comprehensive Review of Applications, Organizational Challenges, and Ethical Considerations. *Systems*, *13*(4), 264. DOI: 10.3390/systems13040264

Maulina, B. F., & Nazaruddin, I. (2025). System information accounting in business performance: A systematic literature review. *Journal of Accounting and Investment*, *26*(2), 481–499. DOI: 10.18196/jai.v26i2.25146

Ndanu, J. M. (2025). Empirical insights into ICT use and knowledge management in accounting: A PRISMA-guided literature review (2020–2025). *African Journal of Empirical Research*, *6*(4), 266–277. DOI: 10.51867/ajernet.6.4.24

Rahim, R., & Chishti, M. A. "Artificial Intelligence Applications in Accounting and Finance," *2024 ASU International Conference in Emerging Technologies for Sustainability and Intelligent Systems (ICETSIS)*, Manama, Bahrain, 2024, pp. 1782-1786, DOI: 10.1109/ICETSIS61505.2024.10459526

Soluk, J., Miroshnychenko, I., & Nambisan, S. (2026). AI Adoption in Family Firms: A Mixed-Methods Study on the Paradoxical Roles of Passive and Active Family Involvement. *Journal of Product Innovation Management, 43*(1), 125–159. DOI: 10.1111/jpim.12789

. Sultana R, Alam MZ, Hasan N (2025;), "Understanding the emerging success factors gap of accounting information systems in developing countries – a systematic literature review". Journal of Accounting Literature, Vol. ahead-of-print No. ahead-of-print. https://doi.org/DOI: 10.1108/JAL-05-2024-0086

Tenhunen, M.-L. (2025). AI-driven management accounting: A new frontier in strategic finance. *Economics, 14*(4), 87–95. DOI: 10.11648/j.eco.20251404.11

Chapter 8
Harnessing AI-Driven Accounting Information Systems for Enhancing Authenticity, Transparency, and Automation in E-Business Accounting and Auditing

Priyanka Koundal
http://orcid.org/0000-0001-8885-4120
Lovely Professional University, India

Riya Duggal
Lovely Professional University, India

Amrik Singh
http://orcid.org/0000-0003-3598-8787
Lovely Professional University, India

ABSTRACT

The rapid growth of e-business has increased the complexity and volume of accounting data, challenging traditional Accounting Information Systems (AIS) to maintain accuracy, authenticity, and timely reporting. In digital environments, organizations must process large amounts of real-time financial information to support effective decision-making and compliance. This chapter examines the relevance of AIS in

DOI: 10.4018/979-8-3373-9230-1.ch008

© 2027, IGI Global Scientific Publishing. Copying or distributing in print or electronic forms without written permission of IGI Global Scientific Publishing is prohibited. Use of this chapter to
rative artificial intelligence (AI) technologies is expressly prohibited. The publisher reserves all rights to license its use for generative AI training and machine learning model development.

e-business and explains how artificial intelligence (AI) enhances their capabilities through automated processing, real-time analytics, and predictive insights. It also highlights AI's role in transforming auditing through continuous monitoring and automated assurance. Overall, AI-driven AIS strengthen transparency, reliability, and operational efficiency, enabling organizations to build stakeholder trust and support sustainable digital business practices.

1. INTRODUCTION

The transformation of global commerce through digitalization has fundamentally altered the nature of financial transactions, organizational reporting, and regulatory oversight. As businesses increasingly operate within electronic platforms, traditional accounting systems face mounting pressure to process vast volumes of real-time data, ensure data integrity, and deliver transparent financial information to diverse stakeholders(Trigo et al., 2014). In this evolving environment, Accounting Information Systems (AIS) must extend beyond their conventional role of recording and summarizing transactions to become intelligent, adaptive, and analytically capable systems(Koundal et al., 2025a; Md Zillul Karim, 2025). The integration of Artificial Intelligence (AI) into AIS represents a significant advancement that addresses these emerging demands by strengthening authenticity, transparency, and automation within e-business accounting and auditing practices.

Electronic business models generate complex datasets characterized by speed, diversity, and scale. Online transactions may occur across multiple platforms, currencies, and jurisdictions, producing intricate digital trails that require advanced tools for monitoring and verification(Albshaier et al., 2024). Traditional AIS frameworks, which often depend on manual inputs, periodic reconciliations, and rule-based processing, may not be sufficiently equipped to manage such dynamic environments. Artificial intelligence offers a solution by embedding learning algorithms and intelligent automation capabilities into accounting systems, enabling them to process information efficiently, detect anomalies, and support evidence-based decision-making(Qatawneh, 2025). Through these capabilities, AI transforms AIS from passive data repositories into proactive systems capable of enhancing organizational accountability and operational effectiveness.

Authenticity is a central principle in financial reporting, referring to the degree to which accounting data faithfully represent actual economic events. Maintaining authenticity in digital environments is particularly challenging due to the intangible nature of online transactions and the possibility of manipulation or unauthorized alterations. AI-driven accounting systems strengthen authenticity by implementing automated validation mechanisms that cross-verify entries across multiple databases and identify inconsistencies in real time(Qatawneh, 2025). Machine learning algorithms can analyze transaction patterns and detect unusual deviations that may signal errors, fraud, or system malfunctions(Podgorelec et al., 2019). Such continuous monitoring mechanisms significantly reduce reliance on retrospective verification and manual checks, thereby improving the reliability of financial information. The ability of AI systems to learn from historical data further enhances their effectiveness, as they can refine detection models and adapt to evolving transaction behaviors.

Transparency, another essential attribute of effective accounting systems, is closely associated with trust and informed decision-making. Stakeholder including investors, creditors, regulators, and management depend on transparent financial disclosures to evaluate organizational performance and assess risk(Oncioiu et al., 2020). In digital business ecosystems, achieving transparency requires more than the mere presentation of financial statements; it necessitates detailed traceability of transactions and clear documentation of processes. AI-enabled AIS contribute to transparency by generating comprehensive audit trails, maintaining structured logs of system activities, and presenting financial data through intuitive analytical dashboards(Sarferaz, 2025). These features allow users to trace the origin and progression of transactions, thereby fostering confidence in reported figures. Furthermore, AI-driven visualization tools can convert complex financial datasets into meaningful graphical representations, enabling stakeholders to interpret information quickly and accurately.

Automation represents one of the most visible and impactful contributions of AI to accounting systems. Routine accounting tasks, such as invoice processing, ledger posting, expense classification, and bank reconciliation, have historically required substantial manual effort. These activities, while essential, often consume valuable time and increase the risk of human error. AI-based automation technologies, including robotic process automation and intelligent data extraction systems, streamline these tasks by executing them automatically according to predefined logic and learned patterns(Afrin et al., 2024a). As a result, organizations can achieve faster processing speeds, reduced operational costs, and improved accuracy in financial records. Automation also enhances scalability, allowing accounting systems to handle increased transaction volumes without proportional increases in staffing or administrative burden. This shift enables accounting professionals to focus on higher-value activities such as financial analysis, strategic planning, and advisory functions.

The integration of AI into AIS also has profound implications for auditing practices. Conventional auditing approaches frequently rely on sampling methods due to limitations in time and resources, which may restrict the scope of examination. AI technologies enable auditors to analyze complete datasets rather than selected samples, thereby improving the thoroughness and reliability of audit findings(Al-

Omush et al., 2025a). Continuous auditing systems powered by AI can monitor transactions in real time and generate alerts when irregularities or high-risk patterns are detected. This proactive approach allows auditors to address potential issues promptly, reducing the likelihood of material misstatements and enhancing overall audit quality. Additionally, predictive analytics tools can assist auditors in identifying areas of elevated risk, facilitating more targeted and efficient audit planning.

While the advantages of AI-driven AIS are substantial, their implementation presents several challenges that organizations must address. Data security and privacy concerns are particularly significant, as accounting systems handle sensitive financial information that must be protected from unauthorized access or cyber threats. Algorithmic transparency is another critical issue; stakeholders must be able to understand and trust the logic underlying automated decisions(Lepri et al., 2018). Moreover, the adoption of advanced technologies often requires substantial investments in infrastructure, training, and organizational change management. Resistance from employees accustomed to traditional systems may hinder implementation unless adequate support and education are provided. Consequently, successful integration of AI into AIS depends not only on technological capability but also on effective governance frameworks and organizational readiness.

The evolution of AI-enabled accounting systems is reshaping the professional landscape for accountants and auditors. Rather than diminishing the relevance of human expertise, AI is redefining professional roles by shifting emphasis from routine processing to analytical interpretation and strategic advisory functions. Modern accounting professionals must possess interdisciplinary competencies that combine technical accounting knowledge with data analytics, information systems literacy, and critical thinking skills. Educational institutions and professional bodies therefore face the responsibility of updating curricula and training programs to prepare practitioners for technology-driven environments. This transformation underscores the importance of lifelong learning and adaptability within the accounting profession.

From a conceptual standpoint, the adoption of AI within AIS aligns with broader theoretical perspectives on information systems and organizational innovation(Assidi et al., 2025). Technology adoption models suggest that organizations embrace new systems when perceived benefits—such as efficiency gains, accuracy improvements, and enhanced decision support—outweigh associated costs and risks. In the context of e-business, external pressures such as regulatory compliance requirements, stakeholder expectations, and competitive dynamics further motivate the adoption of intelligent accounting technologies. AI-driven AIS thus function as strategic assets that not only improve internal processes but also strengthen an organization's credibility and reputation in the marketplace(Assidi et al., 2025).

In practical applications, businesses engaged in digital commerce must manage diverse transaction types, including electronic payments, subscription-based revenues, digital assets, and platform-mediated sales. Each of these activities generates data requiring accurate classification, measurement, and reporting in accordance with applicable accounting standards. AI-enabled systems facilitate this process by integrating information from multiple sources, applying intelligent classification rules, and generating standardized reports automatically. Such capabilities enhance both efficiency and compliance, ensuring that financial statements reflect current conditions and adhere to regulatory expectations. Moreover, real-time reporting features allow management to monitor performance continuously and respond promptly to emerging trends or risks.

In this chapter, the incorporation of artificial intelligence into accounting information systems represents a transformative development that is redefining how financial information is produced, verified, and communicated in digital business environments. The enhanced authenticity through continuous validation, promoting transparency through detailed and accessible reporting, and enabling automation of routine accounting processes, AI-driven AIS provide a robust foundation for modern e-business accounting and auditing. As organizations increasingly rely on digital platforms for their operations, the importance of intelligent accounting systems will continue to grow. Understanding their capabilities, implications, and challenges is therefore essential for researchers, practitioners, and policymakers seeking to ensure the reliability, efficiency, and integrity of financial information in the contemporary digital economy.

2. ACCOUNTING INFORMATION SYSTEMS IN E-BUSINESS

2.1 Concept and Components of Accounting Information Systems

An Accounting Information System (AIS) refers to a structured mechanism that collects, records, processes, and reports financial data to support decision-making, control, and accountability within an organization(Koundal et al., 2025b). In contemporary digital environments, AIS has evolved from a manual record-keeping framework into a technology-driven system that integrates accounting principles with information technology infrastructure. Its primary objective is to transform raw financial data into meaningful information that is relevant, reliable, timely, and useful for internal management as well as external stakeholders. In the context of e-business, AIS plays a crucial role in managing high-volume electronic transactions, ensuring data accuracy, and facilitating regulatory compliance(Al-Hattami, 2024). When enhanced with artificial intelligence capabilities, AIS becomes more adaptive and analytical, enabling automated data validation, predictive insights, and real-time financial monitoring.

The components of an AIS collectively determine its effectiveness and reliability. The first component is people, which includes accountants, auditors, managers, analysts, and IT professionals who interact with the system and interpret its outputs. The second component is procedures and instructions, referring to standardized methods for data entry, processing, verification, and reporting. These procedures ensure consistency and reduce operational errors. The third component consists of data, representing financial transactions and related information that form the foundation of accounting reports. The fourth component is software, which processes data through programmed algorithms and accounting applications, particularly important in AI-enabled systems that support automation and intelligent analysis. The fifth component is information technology infrastructure, including hardware, servers, networks, and cloud platforms that enable system operation and connectivity. The final component is internal controls and security measures, designed to safeguard data integrity, prevent fraud, and ensure compliance with legal and professional standards.

Together, these components create an integrated system that supports authenticity, transparency, and automation in financial reporting(Al-Hattami et al., 2022). A well-designed AIS not only records transactions but also strengthens organizational governance by providing accurate, timely, and verifiable financial information essential for strategic and operational decision-making.

2.2 Characteristics of E-Business Accounting Data

E-business accounting data differ significantly from traditional accounting information due to their digital nature and dynamic processing environment. One of the primary characteristics is real-time generation and processing, as online transactions occur continuously and must be recorded instantly to maintain accuracy and relevance(Bhimani & Willcocks, 2014). This creates large volumes of financial data that require systems capable of handling high-speed processing without delays.

Another important feature is electronic origin, meaning the data are generated through digital platforms such as online payment systems, enterprise applications, and cloud-based tools. As a result, the data may exist in structured or semi-structured formats and must be integrated from multiple interconnected systems, increasing both their usefulness and complexity. Traceability is also a key characteristic, since digital transactions usually contain detailed logs, timestamps, and user identifiers that enhance auditability and accountability. Additionally, e-business accounting data possess strong analytical value, as they capture detailed transaction-level information that can be used for forecasting, performance evaluation, and risk detection(Enholm et al., 2022). However, these advantages are accompanied by concerns regarding security and integrity, making robust internal controls and cybersecurity measures essential. Overall, these characteristics highlight the need for advanced accounting information systems capable of efficiently managing digital financial data in modern business environments.

2.3 Relevance of AIS in Digital and Platform-Based Business Models

Accounting Information Systems (AIS) play a pivotal role in supporting digital and platform-based business models, where transactions occur electronically, often across multiple users, locations, and currencies. Such business models including e-commerce platforms, digital marketplaces, and subscription-based service generate high volumes of real-time financial data that require accurate recording, classification, and reporting(Rahahle et al., 2024). AIS ensures that these complex transaction flows are processed efficiently while maintaining consistency with accounting standards and regulatory requirements. In platform-based environments, AIS facilitates integration between various operational systems such as payment gateways, inventory modules, and customer databases, thereby enabling seamless data exchange and reducing manual intervention(Shbail et al., 2025). This integration enhances decision-making by providing timely financial insights and performance metrics. Furthermore, AIS strengthens internal controls by monitoring transaction authenticity, detecting irregularities, and maintaining detailed audit trails.

The relevance of AIS is particularly evident in supporting scalability and transparency. As digital businesses expand rapidly, automated accounting systems allow organizations to handle increased transaction volumes without compromising accuracy. Consequently, AIS serves not only as a record-keeping tool but also as a strategic resource that supports financial governance, operational efficiency, and stakeholder confidence in modern digital enterprises.

2.4 Limitations of Traditional AIS in E-Business Environments

Traditional Accounting Information Systems (AIS), originally designed for conventional business structures, often face significant constraints when applied to modern e-business environments(Qatawneh, 2023). One major limitation is their inability to efficiently process real-time, high-volume transactions. Digital businesses generate continuous streams of data, whereas traditional AIS typically operate on periodic processing cycles, leading to delays in recording and reporting financial information. This lag can hinder timely decision-making and reduce the relevance of financial reports.

Another limitation lies in restricted system integration capabilities. E-business models rely on interconnected platforms such as online payment systems, inventory software, customer databases, and cloud applications(Gordijn & Akkermans, 2001). Conventional AIS frequently lack the flexibility to integrate seamlessly with these digital systems, resulting in data silos, duplication, and reconciliation challenges. Additionally, traditional systems often depend heavily on manual inputs and verification procedures, increasing the risk of human error and inefficiency.

Limited analytical and predictive functionality is also a concern. Traditional AIS primarily focus on recording historical transactions rather than analyzing patterns or forecasting trends. In fast-paced digital markets, organizations require advanced analytical insights that conventional systems cannot readily provide. Finally, security vulnerabilities and inadequate control mechanisms may arise because older systems were not designed to address modern cybersecurity threats associated with online transactions. These limitations highlight the need for technologically advanced, intelligent AIS frameworks capable of supporting the speed, complexity, and integration demands of contemporary e-business operations.

3. ARTIFICIAL INTELLIGENCE IN ACCOUNTING INFORMATION SYSTEMS

3.1 Overview of Artificial Intelligence Technologies Relevant to AIS

Artificial Intelligence (AI) encompasses a range of computational technologies that enable systems to perform tasks requiring human-like reasoning, learning, and decision-making. In the context of Accounting Information Systems (AIS), AI functions as an enabling layer that enhances data processing, analytical capability, accuracy, and automation(Assidi et al., 2025). Several AI technologies are particularly relevant to modern AIS environments due to their ability to manage large datasets and support intelligent financial operations.

One of the most significant technologies is machine learning (ML), which allows systems to learn from historical financial data and improve performance without explicit reprogramming(Jordan & Mitchell, 2015). ML algorithms can classify transactions, detect anomalies, predict cash flows, and identify fraud patterns, thereby strengthening both accounting accuracy and audit reliability. Another important technology is natural language processing (NLP), which enables systems to interpret and analyze textual information such as invoices, contracts, and financial statements.

NLP supports automated document processing and facilitates faster extraction of relevant accounting data.

Robotic Process Automation (RPA) is also widely applied in AIS to automate repetitive tasks such as data entry, reconciliation, and report generation(Afrin et al., 2024b). By reducing manual intervention, RPA enhances efficiency and minimizes operational errors. Additionally, expert systems and intelligent decision-support tools assist accountants and auditors by providing rule-based recommendations and analytical insights derived from complex datasets. Together, these AI technologies transform traditional AIS into intelligent systems capable of real-time processing, predictive analysis, and continuous monitoring(Zong & Guan, 2025). Their integration not only improves operational efficiency but also strengthens transparency, reliability, and strategic decision-making in digital accounting environments.

3.2 Integration of AI with Accounting Information Systems

The integration of Artificial Intelligence (AI) with Accounting Information Systems (AIS) represents a significant advancement in modern financial management, particularly within digital business environments(Johri, 2025). AI enhances AIS by embedding intelligent algorithms that automate data processing, validate transactions, and detect irregularities in real time. This integration enables accounting systems to move beyond traditional record-keeping functions toward predictive, analytical, and decision-support roles. Machine learning models can analyze historical financial data to forecast trends, while robotic process automation streamlines routine tasks such as ledger posting, reconciliation, and report generation.

AI-powered AIS also improve accuracy and reliability by minimizing manual errors and ensuring consistent application of accounting rules. Furthermore, the integration strengthens internal controls through continuous monitoring and anomaly detection, which is especially valuable for auditing purposes. By enabling faster processing, improved data quality, and enhanced analytical insights, AI-integrated AIS support organizational efficiency and transparency. Consequently, the convergence of AI and AIS is transforming accounting systems into intelligent platforms capable of meeting the demands of complex, high-volume digital transactions.

3.3 Role of AI in Generating Accurate and Timely Accounting Information

Artificial Intelligence (AI) plays a critical role in enhancing the accuracy and timeliness of accounting information, particularly in digital business environments characterized by high transaction volumes and rapid data flows. Traditional accounting processes often depend on manual data entry, periodic reconciliations, and retrospective verification, which may lead to delays and increased risk of human error. AI-driven systems address these limitations by automating data capture, validation, and processing, ensuring that financial information is recorded correctly and updated in real time.

Machine learning algorithms contribute to accuracy by identifying patterns in historical financial data and detecting anomalies or inconsistencies that may indicate errors or irregularities(Podgorelec et al., 2019). Such automated validation mechanisms strengthen data reliability and reduce the likelihood of misstatements. Additionally, AI-powered tools can integrate information from multiple digital sources, including payment systems and enterprise platforms, thereby minimizing discrepancies caused by fragmented data handling.

Timeliness is significantly improved through intelligent automation, which enables instant transaction recording and rapid report generation. Real-time dashboards and predictive analytics further support decision-making by providing up-to-date financial insights(Popoola & Ibrahim, 2023). Consequently, AI not only enhances the precision of accounting outputs but also ensures that information is available when needed, enabling organizations to respond swiftly to operational and strategic demands in dynamic business environments

3.4 AI-Enabled Real-Time Reporting and Decision Support

Artificial Intelligence (AI) has significantly enhanced the capability of Accounting Information Systems (AIS) to generate real-time reports and support managerial decision-making. In digital business environments, financial data are produced continuously, requiring systems that can process, analyze, and present information instantly. AI-enabled AIS address this need by automating data collection, classification, and analysis, thereby transforming raw transactional data into meaningful financial insights without delay. Real-time reporting ensures that financial statements, performance indicators, and cash flow positions are updated dynamically, allowing managers to monitor organizational performance as events occur rather than relying on periodic summaries(Popoola & Ibrahim, 2023).

AI-driven analytics also strengthen decision support by identifying trends, correlations, and anomalies within financial datasets. Machine learning models can forecast revenue patterns, predict expenses, and evaluate financial risks, providing management with forward-looking insights that enhance strategic planning(Qatawneh, 2023; Yang, 2025). Additionally, interactive dashboards and visualization tools present complex financial information in accessible formats, enabling quicker interpretation and informed responses. The combining automation, predictive analysis, and instant reporting, AI-enabled AIS improve both the speed and quality of financial decision-making. This capability is particularly valuable in competitive and rapidly changing markets, where timely and accurate information serves as a critical determinant of organizational effectiveness and strategic advantage.

4. ROLE OF ARTIFICIAL INTELLIGENCE IN AUDITING OF E-BUSINESS

4.1 Evolution of Auditing in the Digital Economy

Auditing has evolved significantly with the growth of the digital economy and e-business operations. Traditional auditing primarily relied on manual verification, physical documentation, and sampling techniques, which were suitable for conventional business environments with limited transaction volumes(Usul & Alpay, 2024). However, digital business models generate continuous streams of electronic transactions across multiple platforms, making manual and periodic audit approaches insufficient.

In response, auditing practices have shifted toward technology-driven methods that emphasize automation, real-time analysis, and comprehensive data examination. Artificial Intelligence (AI) has played a crucial role in this transformation by enabling auditors to analyze entire datasets, detect anomalies, and identify potential risks quickly and accurately(Zong & Guan, 2025). Unlike traditional methods that focused on historical data, AI-supported auditing allows continuous monitoring of financial activities, improving both efficiency and reliability. This evolution reflects a transition from retrospective verification to proactive assurance, where auditors can detect irregularities as they occur. Consequently, modern auditing in the digital economy increasingly depends on intelligent technologies to ensure transparency, accuracy, and trust in financial reporting.

4.2 AI-Based Audit Techniques and Tools

AI-based audit techniques and tools have transformed contemporary auditing by enhancing efficiency, accuracy, and analytical depth. These technologies enable auditors to examine entire datasets rather than relying on traditional sampling methods, thereby improving the reliability of audit conclusions(Binh, 2025). Machine learning algorithms are widely used to detect anomalies, unusual transaction patterns, and potential fraud indicators by comparing current financial data with historical trends. Such automated analysis strengthens risk assessment and helps auditors focus on high-risk areas.

Natural language processing tools assist in reviewing contracts, invoices, and financial disclosures by extracting relevant information and identifying inconsistencies(Fisher et al., 2016). Similarly, robotic process automation streamlines routine audit procedures such as data extraction, reconciliation, and documentation, reducing manual workload and minimizing errors. Predictive analytics further supports auditors by forecasting financial irregularities and highlighting patterns that may require investigation(Zong & Guan, 2025). Together, these AI-driven techniques enhance audit quality through continuous monitoring, real-time insights, and data-driven evaluation. As a result, auditors can deliver more timely, transparent, and reliable assurance in complex digital business environments.

4.3 Continuous Auditing and Automated Assurance

Continuous auditing and automated assurance represent significant advancements in modern audit practices, driven largely by the integration of intelligent technologies into accounting and financial systems. Unlike traditional auditing, which is conducted periodically and focuses on historical data, continuous auditing involves the real-time or near real-time evaluation of financial transactions and controls. This approach allows auditors to monitor organizational activities continuously, identify irregularities promptly, and respond to potential risks before they escalate into material issues(Al-Omush et al., 2025b). As digital business environments generate large volumes of transactional data, continuous auditing provides a practical and efficient method for maintaining oversight. Automated assurance further strengthens this process by using advanced analytical tools to evaluate financial information without extensive manual intervention. Automated systems can verify data accuracy, test internal controls, and assess compliance with accounting standards through predefined algorithms and intelligent rules. These tools also generate alerts when deviations or unusual patterns are detected, enabling timely investigation and corrective action(Brás et al., 2024).

The combination of continuous auditing and automated assurance enhances audit reliability, transparency, and efficiency. It reduces dependence on manual procedures, improves coverage of financial data, and supports proactive risk management. Consequently, these technology-driven approaches are becoming essential components of auditing in digital and e-business contexts, where speed, complexity, and data volume demand innovative and responsive assurance mechanisms.

4.4 Enhancing Audit Quality, Reliability, and Transparency

Artificial Intelligence (AI) significantly enhances audit quality, reliability, and transparency by strengthening the accuracy and depth of audit procedures. Traditional auditing methods often rely on sampling and manual verification, which may limit coverage and increase the possibility of oversight(Chan & Vasarhelyi, 2018).

AI-driven tools address these limitations by enabling auditors to analyze complete datasets, identify anomalies, and detect irregularities with greater precision. This comprehensive analysis improves the quality of audit evidence and supports more reliable conclusions.

AI also increases reliability through automated validation processes that reduce human error and ensure consistent application of audit rules. Real-time monitoring systems further enhance transparency by maintaining detailed digital audit trails and generating instant alerts when unusual activities occur(Trigo et al., 2014). These features allow auditors and stakeholders to trace transactions and verify financial information easily. The use of AI in auditing strengthens confidence in financial reporting by delivering more accurate, timely, and verifiable audit outcomes, which are essential in complex digital business environments.

5. AUTOMATIZATION OF ACCOUNTING AND AUDITING IN E-BUSINESS

5.1 Concept of Smart Automatization in Accounting and Auditing

Smart automatization in accounting and auditing refers to the use of advanced digital technologies particularly Artificial Intelligence (AI), machine learning, and intelligent process automation to perform financial tasks with minimal human intervention while maintaining accuracy, consistency, and analytical depth(Chan & Vasarhelyi, 2018). Unlike traditional automation, which follows fixed rules and predefined instructions, smart automatization is adaptive and capable of learning from data patterns, past transactions, and system interactions. This enables accounting and auditing systems to not only execute routine processes but also interpret financial information, detect anomalies, and generate insights.

In accounting, smart automatization facilitates tasks such as transaction classification, invoice processing, reconciliation, and financial reporting in real time. In auditing, it supports risk assessment, fraud detection, compliance verification, and continuous monitoring of financial activities. These systems can analyze large datasets quickly, identify irregular patterns, and alert professionals to potential issues requiring investigation. The concept emphasizes collaboration between intelligent systems and professionals rather than replacement of human expertise(Elnakeeb & Elawadly, 2025). By reducing manual workload and operational errors, smart automatization enhances efficiency, reliability, and transparency, allowing accountants and auditors to focus on analytical judgment, strategic evaluation, and decision-making in complex financial environments.

5.2 Impact of Automatization on Operational Efficiency

Automatization has a substantial impact on operational efficiency in accounting and auditing by streamlining processes, reducing manual intervention, and accelerating data handling. Automated systems can perform repetitive tasks such as data entry, reconciliation, invoice processing, and report generation with greater speed and accuracy than manual methods(Chan & Vasarhelyi, 2018). This minimizes human error, lowers processing time, and ensures consistency in financial records. As a result, organizations can manage higher transaction volumes without proportionally increasing labor costs or administrative effort.

In addition, automation improves workflow coordination by integrating different functional systems, enabling seamless data transfer across departments(Milosheski & Karadimce, 2025). Real-time processing allows managers to access up-to-date financial information, supporting faster and more informed decision-making(Koundal et al., 2025c). Automated controls and validation check also enhance compliance and reduce the risk of fraud or discrepancies. Overall, automatization strengthens operational performance by optimizing resource utilization, improving accuracy, and enabling organizations to focus on strategic and analytical activities rather than routine processing tasks.

5.3 Governance, Compliance, and Risk Management Implications

The integration of advanced technologies such as Artificial Intelligence and automation into accounting and auditing systems has significant implications for governance, compliance, and risk management. From a governance perspective, intelligent systems enhance oversight by providing real-time financial insights, detailed audit trails, and transparent reporting mechanisms that support accountability and informed decision-making(Assidi et al., 2025). These capabilities enable management and boards to monitor organizational performance continuously rather than relying solely on periodic reports.

In terms of compliance, automated controls and rule-based algorithms ensure that financial processes consistently adhere to regulatory standards, accounting principles, and internal policies. Such systems can automatically flag deviations, thereby reducing the likelihood of non-compliance and associated penalties. Risk management is also strengthened through predictive analytics and anomaly detection tools that identify potential fraud, operational irregularities, or financial misstatements at an early stage(Ogunsola et al., 2021). However, these technological advancements also introduce new governance considerations, including data privacy, cybersecurity, and algorithmic transparency. Organizations must therefore establish robust control frameworks and ethical guidelines to ensure that technology-driven systems operate reliably, securely, and in alignment with regulatory expectations.

5.4 Value Creation for E-Business Organizations

Advanced accounting and intelligent information systems play a vital role in value creation for e-business organizations by enhancing efficiency, decision quality, and strategic responsiveness. In digital business environments, value is generated not only through revenue growth but also through improved data utilization, cost optimization, and risk reduction(Zhu et al., 2004). Technology-enabled accounting systems support this process by providing accurate, real-time financial information that allows managers to evaluate performance, identify opportunities, and respond quickly to market changes(Zohry & Al-Dhubaibi, 2024).

Automation of routine financial processes reduces administrative costs and processing time, enabling organizations to allocate resources more effectively toward innovation and customer-focused activities. In addition, analytical capabilities embedded in modern systems help businesses forecast trends, assess profitability, and optimize pricing or investment decisions(Yoshikuni et al., 2023). Transparent and reliable financial reporting also strengthens stakeholder confidence, which is essential for sustaining competitive advantage in digital markets.

Thus, intelligent accounting infrastructures function as strategic assets that enhance operational effectiveness, support informed decision-making, and contribute directly to long-term organizational value creation.

6. AUTHENTICITY AND TRANSPARENCY OF ACCOUNTING INFORMATION

6.1 Meaning and Importance of Authenticity in Accounting Data

Authenticity in accounting data refers to the extent to which financial information faithfully represents actual economic transactions and events without distortion, manipulation, or error. Authentic data are accurate, verifiable, complete, and supported by reliable documentation, ensuring that financial records reflect the true financial position and performance of an organization(Vladu et al., 2017). In accounting systems, authenticity is maintained through proper recording procedures, internal controls, audit trails, and validation mechanisms that confirm the legitimacy of each transaction. The importance of authenticity lies in its direct influence on decision-making, accountability, and stakeholder trust(Bayou et al., 2011). Managers rely on genuine financial information to plan operations, allocate resources, and evaluate performance, while investors, creditors, and regulators depend on accurate data to assess risk and compliance. If accounting data lack authenticity, financial reports may be misleading, resulting in poor decisions, legal consequences, and reputational damage(Alexander & Archer, 2003).

In digital and e-business environments, where transactions occur rapidly and electronically, maintaining authenticity becomes even more critical. Robust verification systems and automated validation tools help ensure that accounting data remain reliable, transparent, and trustworthy, thereby strengthening organizational credibility and financial integrity.

6.2 Transparency and Stakeholder Trust in E-Business

Transparency is a fundamental principle in e-business operations, referring to the clear, accurate, and timely disclosure of financial and operational information to stakeholders. In digital business environments, where transactions are conducted electronically and often across multiple platforms, transparency ensures that stakeholders can easily access and verify relevant information regarding organizational performance and financial position(Al-Mutawa et al., 2025; Nicolaou, 2010). Transparent reporting practices reduce information asymmetry between management and stakeholders, thereby fostering confidence in the credibility of financial disclosures.

Stakeholder trust is closely linked to transparency, as investors, customers, creditors, regulators, and business partners rely on reliable information to make informed decisions. When e-business organizations maintain transparent accounting systems, they demonstrate accountability and ethical conduct, which strengthens their reputation and long-term relationships with stakeholders(Al-Mutawa et al., 2025). Conversely, a lack of transparency may raise concerns about data accuracy, financial integrity, or compliance, potentially undermining confidence and affecting organizational sustainability.

Technology-driven accounting systems contribute significantly to transparency by generating detailed audit trails, real-time reports, and standardized financial statements. These features allow stakeholders to trace transactions and verify information efficiently. As a result, transparency supported by robust digital accounting practices becomes a key driver of trust, credibility, and competitive advantage in modern e-business ecosystems.

6.3 Role of AI-Enabled AIS in Ensuring Data Integrity

AI-enabled Accounting Information Systems (AIS) play a crucial role in ensuring data integrity by maintaining the accuracy, consistency, and reliability of financial information throughout its lifecycle. Data integrity is essential for producing trustworthy financial reports and supporting sound managerial and stakeholder decision-making. Traditional systems often rely on manual checks and periodic reconciliations, which may leave room for errors, omissions, or manipulation(Zayed et al., 2024). In contrast, AI-driven AIS incorporate automated validation mechanisms that continuously verify transactions, detect inconsistencies, and flag unusual patterns in real time.

Machine learning algorithms enhance integrity by comparing current data with historical trends to identify anomalies that may indicate inaccuracies or fraudulent activity(Podgorelec et al., 2019). Additionally, intelligent systems maintain detailed digital audit trails, ensuring that every modification or entry can be traced back to its source. Automated controls also enforce standardized accounting rules, reducing the risk of human error and ensuring uniform data processing(Dai & Vasarhelyi, 2017). With integration and continuous monitoring, anomaly detection, and rule-based verification, AI-enabled AIS strengthen financial data integrity and reliability. This capability is particularly valuable in digital business environments, where large volumes of transactions require precise and secure handling to maintain confidence in financial reporting systems.

6.4 Ethical and Data Governance Considerations

The adoption of advanced technologies such as Artificial Intelligence (AI) in accounting and auditing systems introduces important ethical and data governance considerations that organizations must address to ensure responsible and trustworthy use. Ethical concerns primarily relate to the fairness, transparency, and accountability of automated decision-making processes(Schweitzer, 2024). AI systems rely on algorithms and data patterns, and if the underlying data are biased, incomplete, or inaccurate, the resulting outputs may lead to misleading conclusions or discriminatory outcomes. Therefore, organizations must ensure that data inputs are reliable, representative, and ethically sourced.

Data governance is equally critical, as accounting systems handle sensitive financial information that must be protected against unauthorized access, misuse, or breaches. Effective governance frameworks include clearly defined data policies, access controls, encryption measures, and audit mechanisms to safeguard confidentiality and integrity(Munoko et al., 2020). Compliance with legal and regulatory standards is also essential, particularly in digital environments where data may be stored or transmitted across jurisdictions.

Moreover, transparency in algorithmic operations is necessary so that stakeholders can understand how automated decisions are generated. Establishing ethical guidelines, monitoring systems, and accountability structures helps ensure that technology-driven accounting systems operate responsibly. Ultimately, strong ethical and governance practices enhance trust, reliability, and credibility in AI-enabled financial environments.

7. IMPLICATIONS FOR ACCOUNTING PROFESSIONALS AND REGULATORS

7.1 Changing Role of Accountants and Auditors

The integration of advanced technologies such as Artificial Intelligence (AI) into accounting and auditing systems is significantly transforming the roles of accounting professionals and auditors. Traditionally, accountants were primarily responsible for recording transactions, preparing financial statements, and ensuring compliance with accounting standards. However, automation and intelligent systems now perform many routine and repetitive tasks with greater speed and accuracy. As a result, the professional focus is shifting from manual processing toward analytical, interpretative, and strategic functions that require human judgment and expertise.

Modern accountants are increasingly expected to function as data analysts and financial advisors who interpret system-generated insights, evaluate risks, and support managerial decision-making. Similarly, auditors are transitioning from sample-based verification to technology-enabled assurance roles, where they use advanced analytical tools to assess entire datasets, monitor transactions continuously, and identify anomalies. This shift requires professionals to develop interdisciplinary competencies, including data analytics skills, technological literacy, and an understanding of information systems.

For regulators, these developments necessitate the adaptation of standards and oversight frameworks to address emerging technological risks, such as algorithmic transparency, data privacy, and cybersecurity. Consequently, the evolving technological landscape is reshaping the accounting profession into a more strategic, technology-oriented discipline that emphasizes critical thinking, professional judgment, and ethical responsibility.

7.2 Skill Requirements and Professional Judgment in AI-Driven Systems

The adoption of AI-driven systems in accounting and auditing has significantly reshaped the skill requirements expected of professionals in these fields. In addition to traditional accounting knowledge, practitioners must now possess technological competencies, including data analytics, information systems literacy, and an understanding of algorithmic processes. These skills enable professionals to effectively interact with intelligent systems, interpret automated outputs, and evaluate the reliability of system-generated information. As accounting environments become increasingly data-driven, the ability to analyze large datasets and extract meaningful insights has become an essential professional capability.

Despite the advanced capabilities of AI, professional judgment remains a critical component of accounting and auditing practice. AI systems can process data and identify patterns, but they lack contextual understanding, ethical reasoning, and the ability to interpret complex business situations. Accountants and auditors must therefore assess AI-generated results, verify their relevance, and ensure that conclusions align with accounting standards, regulatory requirements, and organizational objectives. This human oversight is vital for preventing overreliance on automated outputs and for maintaining accountability in financial reporting.

Consequently, the modern accounting professional must combine technical expertise with critical thinking, ethical awareness, and decision-making skills. Continuous learning and professional development are essential to remain competent in AI-enabled environments, ensuring that professionals can effectively leverage technology while exercising sound judgment and maintaining the integrity of financial information.

7.3 Implications for Accounting Standards and IFRS

The integration of Artificial Intelligence (AI) into accounting systems has important implications for the development and application of accounting standards, particularly those issued by the International Accounting Standards Board. As financial reporting processes become increasingly automated and data-driven, standard-setting bodies must consider how existing frameworks apply to transactions processed and analyzed by intelligent systems. AI-enabled environments generate complex datasets, real-time valuations, and algorithm-based estimates, which may challenge traditional measurement, recognition, and disclosure principles embedded in current standards.

One key implication involves the need for enhanced guidance on the use of automated judgments and predictive analytics in financial reporting. Standards may need to clarify how organizations should validate AI-generated outputs, ensure reliability of algorithmic estimates, and disclose assumptions embedded within automated processes. Additionally, transparency requirements may expand to include explanations of technological methodologies that influence financial results.

Regulators and standard setters must also address issues related to data integrity, auditability, and comparability of financial statements produced through AI-supported systems. Consequently, the evolution of intelligent accounting technologies is likely to influence future revisions of international accounting standards, encouraging frameworks that accommodate innovation while preserving reliability, consistency, and stakeholder confidence in financial reporting.

7.4 Regulatory Challenges and Policy Recommendations

The increasing adoption of Artificial Intelligence (AI) in accounting and auditing systems presents significant regulatory challenges that policymakers and oversight bodies must address to ensure financial transparency, reliability, and accountability. One major challenge relates to the adequacy of existing regulatory frameworks, which were largely designed for traditional accounting environments and may not fully accommodate automated decision-making, real-time reporting, and algorithm-based financial processes. Regulators must therefore evaluate whether current standards sufficiently address issues such as algorithmic transparency, system validation, and digital audit trails.

Data privacy and cybersecurity risks also pose critical regulatory concerns, as AI-driven accounting systems process vast volumes of sensitive financial information. Inadequate safeguards may expose organizations to data breaches, fraud, or misuse of confidential information. Furthermore, the complexity of AI models can create difficulties in auditing and interpreting system outputs, raising questions about accountability when automated processes produce errors or misleading results.

To address these challenges, policymakers should develop comprehensive guidelines that establish standards for system reliability, data governance, and ethical use of AI in financial reporting. Recommendations include mandating disclosure of automated processes, strengthening digital audit requirements, promoting interdisciplinary training for professionals, and encouraging collaboration between regulators, technology experts, and accounting bodies. Such measures can help ensure that innovation in accounting technologies proceeds in a controlled and trustworthy regulatory environment.

8. FUTURE RESEARCH DIRECTIONS

8.1 Emerging Trends in AI-Driven Accounting and Auditing

Rapid technological advancement is continually reshaping the landscape of accounting and auditing, creating new avenues for scholarly inquiry and professional innovation. One of the most prominent emerging trends is the evolution of predictive and prescriptive analytics within accounting systems. Future research can explore how advanced algorithms move beyond historical analysis to provide forward-looking financial insights and strategic recommendations. Another key trend involves the integration of AI with blockchain and distributed ledger technologies, which has the potential to enhance data reliability, traceability, and auditability in digital transactions.

The expansion of real-time reporting systems also represents a significant research area, particularly in understanding how continuous data processing influences financial decision-making, risk assessment, and regulatory oversight. Additionally, the growing use of intelligent automation raises important questions regarding system governance, ethical considerations, and accountability structures. Scholars may investigate frameworks for evaluating algorithmic transparency, bias mitigation, and validation of automated outputs.

Overall, emerging trends indicate a shift toward highly intelligent, interconnected accounting ecosystems. Future research will play a crucial role in examining how these technologies can be optimized to improve financial reporting quality, strengthen assurance processes, and support sustainable organizational performance in increasingly complex digital environments.

8.2 Research Gaps and Opportunities

Despite rapid advancements in Artificial Intelligence (AI) applications within accounting and auditing, several research gaps remain those present valuable opportunities for further scholarly exploration. One major gap lies in the limited empirical evidence on the long-term effectiveness and reliability of AI-driven accounting systems across diverse organizational contexts. Most existing studies focus on conceptual frameworks or short-term case analyses, leaving a need for longitudinal research that evaluates performance, risk, and cost–benefit outcomes over extended periods.

Another important research opportunity concerns the evaluation of algorithmic transparency and interpretability in financial decision-making. While AI systems can process vast datasets efficiently, understanding how automated conclusions are generated remains a challenge. Future research could develop models for assessing the explainability and auditability of AI outputs in accounting environments. Additionally, there is insufficient comparative research examining how organizations of different sizes, industries, or regulatory settings adopt and benefit from intelligent accounting technologies.

Scholars can also investigate ethical implications, governance structures, and professional skill adaptations associated with AI integration. Addressing these gaps would contribute to more comprehensive theoretical frameworks and practical guidelines, supporting responsible adoption of AI in accounting and auditing.

8.3 Implications for the Fifth Industrial Revolution

The emergence of the Fifth Industrial Revolution (Industry 5.0) emphasizes collaboration between human intelligence and advanced technologies, highlighting a shift from automation-centered production toward human-centric, sustainable, and resilient systems. In the context of accounting and auditing, AI-driven Accounting Information Systems (AIS) are expected to play a pivotal role in supporting this transition. Unlike earlier technological phases that prioritized efficiency alone, the Fifth Industrial Revolution focuses on integrating intelligent technologies with human judgment, creativity, and ethical reasoning. This paradigm aligns closely with modern accounting needs, where automated systems process large volumes of data while professionals provide interpretation, strategic insight, and oversight.

AI-enabled accounting frameworks can enhance sustainability reporting, integrated reporting, and real-time financial transparency—areas increasingly emphasized in Industry 5.0. They also support responsible decision-making by providing predictive analytics that incorporate financial, environmental, and social indicators. However, this transformation requires robust governance structures, interdisciplinary skills, and ethical safeguards to ensure that intelligent systems operate responsibly.

Thus, the implications of the Fifth Industrial Revolution for accounting lie not merely in technological advancement but in the development of collaborative ecosystems where human expertise and intelligent systems work together to create more transparent, resilient, and value-driven financial environments.

9. CONCLUSION

9.1 Key Findings

The analysis presented in this chapter highlights the transformative role of Artificial Intelligence (AI) in reshaping accounting information systems and auditing practices within e-business environments. One of the central findings is that AI-driven systems significantly enhance the authenticity, accuracy, and reliability of financial information by automating data processing, validating transactions, and detecting anomalies in real time. This capability strengthens internal controls and reduces the likelihood of errors or fraudulent activities.

Another key finding is that AI contributes substantially to transparency and stakeholder confidence through detailed audit trails, continuous monitoring, and real-time reporting mechanisms. These features enable organizations to provide timely and verifiable financial information, thereby improving governance and decision-making(Zayed et al., 2024). The study also reveals that automation not only increases operational efficiency but also shifts the role of accounting professionals toward analytical, strategic, and advisory functions(Yigitbasioglu et al., 2023). Furthermore, while AI offers substantial benefits, it introduces challenges related to data governance, regulatory adaptation, and ethical considerations. Overall, the findings indicate that AI-enabled accounting systems are becoming essential for modern organizations seeking to maintain accuracy, compliance, and competitiveness in increasingly complex digital business environments.

9.2 Managerial and Policy Implications

The integration of Artificial Intelligence (AI) into accounting and auditing systems carries significant implications for both managerial practice and public policy. From a managerial perspective, organizations must adopt strategic approaches to technology implementation, ensuring that AI-driven accounting systems are aligned with business objectives, internal controls, and risk management frameworks. Managers should invest in digital infrastructure, staff training, and system monitoring mechanisms to maximize the benefits of intelligent automation while maintaining data accuracy and security. Effective governance structures are also essential to oversee algorithmic decision-making, validate system outputs, and ensure that financial reporting remains transparent and reliable.

From a policy standpoint, regulators and standard-setting bodies must update existing frameworks to address the complexities introduced by AI-enabled financial systems. This includes developing guidelines for algorithmic accountability, data protection, and auditability of automated processes. Policymakers should also encourage collaboration between technology experts, accounting professionals, and regulatory institutions to establish standards that balance innovation with compliance.

Overall, both managerial and policy responses must evolve simultaneously to support responsible adoption of AI in accounting environments. Coordinated efforts can foster technological advancement while safeguarding financial integrity, stakeholder trust, and regulatory effectiveness in digital business ecosystems.

REFERENCES

Afrin, S., Roksana, S., & Akram, R. (2024a). Ai-enhanced robotic process automation: A review of intelligent automation innovations. *IEEE Access*. https://ieeexplore.ieee.org/abstract/document/10781408/

Afrin, S., Roksana, S., & Akram, R. (2024b). Ai-enhanced robotic process automation: A review of intelligent automation innovations. *IEEE Access*. https://ieeexplore.ieee.org/abstract/document/10781408/

Al-Hattami, H. M. (2024). Impact of AIS success on decision-making effectiveness among SMEs in less developed countries. *Information Technology for Development*, *30*(3), 472–492. DOI: 10.1080/02681102.2022.2073325

Al-Hattami, H. M., Abdullah, A. A. H., Kabra, J. D., Alsoufi, M. A., Gaber, M. M., & Shuraim, A. M. (2022). Effect of AIS on planning process effectiveness: A case of SMEs in a less developed nation. *The Bottom Line (New York, N.Y.)*, *35*(2/3), 33–52. DOI: 10.1108/BL-01-2022-0001

Al-Mutawa, H. A., Sowailem, E. K., & Al Mubarak, M. (2025). Business Ethics in E-commerce: Ethical Concerns and Safeguarding Consumer Trust and Loyalty. In Al Mubarak, M. (Ed.), *Sustainable Digital Technology and Ethics in an Ever-Changing Environment* (Vol. 237, pp. 3–20). Springer Nature Switzerland., DOI: 10.1007/978-3-031-86708-8_1

Al-Omush, A., Almasarwah, A., & Al-Wreikat, A. (2025a). Artificial intelligence in financial auditing: Redefining accuracy and transparency in assurance services. *EDPACS*, *70*(6), 1–20. DOI: 10.1080/07366981.2025.2459490

Al-Omush, A., Almasarwah, A., & Al-Wreikat, A. (2025b). Artificial intelligence in financial auditing: Redefining accuracy and transparency in assurance services. *EDPACS*, *70*(6), 1–20. DOI: 10.1080/07366981.2025.2459490

Albshaier, L., Almarri, S., & Hafizur Rahman, M. M. (2024). A review of blockchain's role in E-Commerce transactions: Open challenges, and future research directions. *Computers*, *13*(1), 27. DOI: 10.3390/computers13010027

Alexander, D., & Archer, S. (2003). On economic reality, representational faithfulness and the 'true and fair override.'. *Accounting and Business Research*, *33*(1), 3–17. DOI: 10.1080/00014788.2003.9729628

Assidi, S., Omran, M., Rana, T., & Borgi, H. (2025). The role of AI adoption in transforming the accounting profession: A diffusion of innovations theory approach. *Journal of Accounting & Organizational Change*. https://www.emerald.com/insight/content/doi/10.1108/JAOC-04-2024-0124/full/html

Bayou, M. E., Reinstein, A., & Williams, P. F. (2011). To tell the truth: A discussion of issues concerning truth and ethics in accounting. *Accounting, Organizations and Society*, *36*(2), 109–124. DOI: 10.1016/j.aos.2011.02.001

Bhimani, A., & Willcocks, L. (2014). Digitisation, 'Big Data' and the transformation of accounting information. *Accounting and Business Research*, *44*(4), 469–490. DOI: 10.1080/00014788.2014.910051

Binh, N. T. T. (2025). Transforming auditing in the AI era: A comprehensive review. *Information (Basel)*, *16*(5), 400. DOI: 10.3390/info16050400

Brás, J. C., Pereira, R. F., Fonseca, M., Ribeiro, R., & Bianchi, I. S. (2024). Advances in auditing and business continuity: A study in financial companies. *Journal of Open Innovation*, *10*(2), 100304. DOI: 10.1016/j.joitmc.2024.100304

Chan, D. Y., & Vasarhelyi, M. A. (2018). *Innovation and practice of continuous auditing*. https://www.emerald.com/books/edited-volume/11301/chapter/81123458

Dai, J., & Vasarhelyi, M. A. (2017). Toward blockchain-based accounting and assurance. *Journal of Information Systems*, *31*(3), 5–21. DOI: 10.2308/isys-51804

Elnakeeb, S., & Elawadly, H. S. H. (2025). Automation and artificial intelligence in accounting: A comprehensive bibliometric analysis and future trends. *Journal of Financial Reporting and Accounting*. https://www.emerald.com/jfra/article/doi/10.1108/JFRA-09-2024-0639/1262287

Enholm, I. M., Papagiannidis, E., Mikalef, P., & Krogstie, J. (2022). Artificial Intelligence and Business Value: A Literature Review. *Information Systems Frontiers*, *24*(5), 1709–1734. DOI: 10.1007/s10796-021-10186-w

Fisher, I. E., Garnsey, M. R., & Hughes, M. E. (2016). Natural Language Processing in Accounting, Auditing and Finance: A Synthesis of the Literature with a Roadmap for Future Research. *Intelligent Systems in Accounting, Finance & Management*, *23*(3), 157–214. DOI: 10.1002/isaf.1386

Gordijn, J., & Akkermans, H. (2001). Designing and evaluating e-business models. *IEEE Intelligent Systems*, *16*(04), 11–17. DOI: 10.1109/5254.941353

Johri, A. (2025). Impact of artificial intelligence on the performance and quality of accounting information systems and accuracy of financial data reporting. *Accounting Forum, 49*(5), 1096–1120. DOI: 10.1080/01559982.2025.2451004

Jordan, M. I., & Mitchell, T. M. (2015). Machine learning: Trends, perspectives, and prospects. *Science, 349*(6245), 255–260. DOI: 10.1126/science.aaa8415 PMID: 26185243

Koundal, P., Bhalla, M., & Kailay, M. (2025a). Driving SME management in the digital era: An empirical evidence on the role of accounting information systems in strategic planning, controlling, and coordination activities. *International Journal of Globalisation and Small Business, 15*(2), 135–157. DOI: 10.1504/IJGSB.2025.150129

Koundal, P., Bhalla, M., & Kailay, M. (2025b). Non-financial information as a mediator in the link between accounting information systems and decision-making outcomes in SMEs: A structural equation modelling study. *International Journal of Business and Systems Research, 19*(4), 442–464. DOI: 10.1504/IJBSR.2025.149075

Koundal, P., Bhalla, M., & Kailay, M. (2025c). The Ethical Ledger: A Review of Literature on the Alignment of Accounting Ethics and Blockchain Technology. *Digital Strategy and Governance in Transformative Technologies*, 216–238.

Lepri, B., Oliver, N., Letouzé, E., Pentland, A., & Vinck, P. (2018). Fair, transparent, and accountable algorithmic decision-making processes: The premise, the proposed solutions, and the open challenges. *Philosophy & Technology, 31*(4), 611–627. DOI: 10.1007/s13347-017-0279-x

Md Zillul Karim, M. Z. K. (2025). Accounting Information System Quality and Management Information Systems Integration: A Pathway to Enhanced Financial Risk Management. *Accounting Information System Quality and Management Information Systems Integration: A Pathway to Enhanced Financial Risk Management, 3*(1), 128–142.

Milosheski, F., & Karadimce, A. (2025). Improving operational efficiency with an automated invoicing system. *Financial Engineering, 3*, 221–230. DOI: 10.37394/232032.2025.3.18

Munoko, I., Brown-Liburd, H. L., & Vasarhelyi, M. (2020). The Ethical Implications of Using Artificial Intelligence in Auditing. *Journal of Business Ethics, 167*(2), 209–234. DOI: 10.1007/s10551-019-04407-1

Nicolaou, A. I. (2010). Integrated information systems and transparency in business reporting. *International Journal of Disclosure and Governance, 7*(3), 216–226. DOI: 10.1057/jdg.2009.27

Ogunsola, K. O., Balogun, E. D., & Ogunmokun, A. S. (2021). Enhancing financial integrity through an advanced internal audit risk assessment and governance model. *International Journal of Multidisciplinary Research and Growth Evaluation, 2*(1), 781–790. DOI: 10.54660/.IJMRGE.2021.2.1.781-790

Oncioiu, I., Popescu, D.-M., Aviana, A. E., erban, A., Rotaru, F., Petrescu, M., & Marin-Pantelescu, A. (2020). The role of environmental, social, and governance disclosure in financial transparency. *Sustainability (Basel), 12*(17), 6757. DOI: 10.3390/su12176757

Podgorelec, B., Turkanović, M., & Karakatič, S. (2019). A machine learning-based method for automated blockchain transaction signing including personalized anomaly detection. *Sensors (Basel), 20*(1), 147. DOI: 10.3390/s20010147 PMID: 31881673

Popoola, A. D., & Ibrahim, A. K. (2023). Conceptual Model for Advancing Real-Time Analytics and Financial Transparency in Corporations. *International Journal of Advanced Multidisciplinary Research and Studies, 3.* https://www.multiresearchjournal.com/admin/uploads/archives/archive-1765515403.pdf

Qatawneh, A. M. (2023). Requirements of AIS in building modern operating business environment. *International Journal of Business Information Systems, 44*(3), 422–441. DOI: 10.1504/IJBIS.2023.134957

Qatawneh, A. M. (2025). The role of artificial intelligence in auditing and fraud detection in accounting information systems: Moderating role of natural language processing. *The International Journal of Organizational Analysis, 33*(6), 1391–1409. DOI: 10.1108/IJOA-03-2024-4389

Rahahle, M. Y., Haija, A. A. A., Azzam, M., Anagreh, S., Maabreh, H. M. A., Saatchi, S. G., Sarram, M., Dawood, D. A., Al-Hawary, S. I. S., & Al-Momani, A. (2024). Evaluating the Impact of E-accounting Systems on Firm Performance: A Structural Equation Modeling Approach. In Musleh Al-Sartawi, A. M. A., & Nour, A. I. (Eds.), *Artificial Intelligence and Economic Sustainability in the Era of Industrial Revolution 5.0* (Vol. 528, pp. 1193–1209). Springer Nature Switzerland., DOI: 10.1007/978-3-031-56586-1_87

Sarferaz, S. (2025). Implementing AI into ERP Software. *Communications of the Association for Information Systems, 57*(1), 74. DOI: 10.17705/1CAIS.05758

Schweitzer, B. (2024). Artificial intelligence (AI) ethics in accounting. *Journal of Accounting. Ethics & Public Policy, JAEPP, 25*(1), 67–67.

Shbail, M. O. A., Olimat, N. A., Alshurafat, H., Shbeil, S. A., Baker, M. B., & Jaradat, Z. (2025). Factors influencing cloud AIS adoption: Evidence from Jordan. *International Journal of Business Excellence*, *35*(4), 453–474. DOI: 10.1504/IJBEX.2025.145158

Trigo, A., Belfo, F., & Estébanez, R. P. (2014). Accounting information systems: The challenge of the real-time reporting. *Procedia Technology*, *16*, 118–127. DOI: 10.1016/j.protcy.2014.10.075

Usul, H., & Alpay, M. F. (2024). From Traditional Auditing to Information Technology Auditing: A Paradigm Shift in Practices. *European Journal of Digital Economy Research*, *5*(1), 3–9.

Vladu, A. B., Amat, O., & Cuzdriorean, D. D. (2017). Truthfulness in accounting: How to discriminate accounting manipulators from non-manipulators. *Journal of Business Ethics*, *140*(4), 633–648. DOI: 10.1007/s10551-016-3048-3

Yang, A. (2025). Big data-driven corporate financial forecasting and decision support: A study of CNN-LSTM machine learning models. *Frontiers in Applied Mathematics and Statistics*, *11*, 1566078. DOI: 10.3389/fams.2025.1566078

Yigitbasioglu, O., Green, P., & Cheung, M.-Y. D. (2023). Digital transformation and accountants as advisors. *Accounting, Auditing & Accountability Journal*, *36*(1), 209–237. DOI: 10.1108/AAAJ-02-2019-3894

Yoshikuni, A. C., Dwivedi, R., Dultra-de-Lima, R. G., Parisi, C., & Oyadomari, J. C. T. (2023). Role of Emerging Technologies in Accounting Information Systems for Achieving Strategic Flexibility through Decision-Making Performance: An Exploratory Study Based on North American and South American Firms. *Global Journal of Flexible Systems Managment*, *24*(2), 199–218. DOI: 10.1007/s40171-022-00334-9

Zayed, L. M. M., Nour, M. I., Al Attar, K., Almubaideen, H., & Abdelaziz, G. A. M. (2024). Role of Artificial Intelligence (AI) in Accounting Information Systems in Detecting Fraud. In Musleh Al-Sartawi, A. M. A., & Nour, A. I. (Eds.), *Artificial Intelligence and Economic Sustainability in the Era of Industrial Revolution 5.0* (Vol. 528, pp. 397–409). Springer Nature Switzerland., DOI: 10.1007/978-3-031-56586-1_30

Zhu, K., Kraemer, K. L., & Dedrick, J. (2004). Information Technology Payoff in E-Business Environments: An International Perspective on Value Creation of E-Business in the Financial Services Industry. *Journal of Management Information Systems*, *21*(1), 17–54. DOI: 10.1080/07421222.2004.11045797

Zohry, A. F., & Al-Dhubaibi, A. A. S. (2024). Optimizing business performance through effective accounting information systems: The role of system competence and information quality. *Journal of Risk and Financial Management*, *17*(11), 515. DOI: 10.3390/jrfm17110515

Zong, Z., & Guan, Y. (2025). AI-driven intelligent data analytics and predictive analysis in Industry 4.0: Transforming knowledge, innovation, and efficiency. *Journal of the Knowledge Economy*, *16*(1), 864–903. DOI: 10.1007/s13132-024-02001-z

Chapter 9

Risk Management and Control Systems in Digital Organizations

Mandeep Kour
College of Business Studies, COER University, India

Bhagabat Behera
Ravenshaw University, India

Kuldeep Agnihotri
ISBA Group of Institutes, India

A. Priyadharshini
K.S.R. College of Engineering, India

Ramesh Pettela
http://orcid.org/0000-0002-2661-8779
Aditya University, India

S. Jagadeesha
http://orcid.org/0000-0002-1294-6253
Nitte Meenakshi Institute of Technology, NITTE (Deemed to be) University, India

V. Bhoopathy
http://orcid.org/0000-0003-2175-6328
Sree Rama Engineering College, India

ABSTRACT

This chapter discusses digital organisations' governance models, frameworks, and advanced risk mitigation measures for risk management. Cybersecurity, ERM, fraud detection, digital compliance, and AI-powered predictive risk analytics are covered. This chapter discusses intelligent decision-support platforms, cloud-based monitoring systems, and automation to improve organisational control settings. Its applications in intelligent enterprise, e-commerce, healthcare, banking, and manufacturing are examined. Issues including algorithmic dangers, new cyber threats, difficult rules, data breaches, and ethics are thoroughly investigated. Newer innovations include blockchain-based governance systems, autonomous risk intelligence, zero-trust

DOI: 10.4018/979-8-3373-9230-1.ch009

2027, IGI Global Scientific Publishing. Copying or distributing in print or electronic forms without written permission of IGI Global Scientific Publishing is prohibited. Use of this chapter to rative artificial intelligence (AI) technologies is expressly prohibited. The publisher reserves all rights to license its use for generative AI training and machine learning model development.

architectures, and explainable AI. Integrating resilient digital control systems with sophisticated risk management frameworks improves operational resilience, security, and strategic decision-making.

1. INTRODUCTION

Managing the security and privacy risks in information systems is a complex task that requires everyone in the organization to pitch in(Parween et al., 2026). This includes upper-level management, who set the overall direction and objectives, middle managers, who plan, execute, and oversee projects, and finally, the people who build and maintain the systems that support the organization's goals and operations. Organisational architecture, mission and business planning, Software Development Life Cycle (SDLC) processes, and systems engineering activities vital to those life cycle processes are all touched by risk management in some way or another. Organisational, mission/business process, and information system levels are all included in Figure 1's multi-tiered approach to risk management, which addresses privacy and security concerns(Force, 2017). In order to ensure that risk is handled throughout the company, there is a two-way flow of information known as reporting and communication between the three levels.

Figure 1. Risk Management Approach Across the Organization

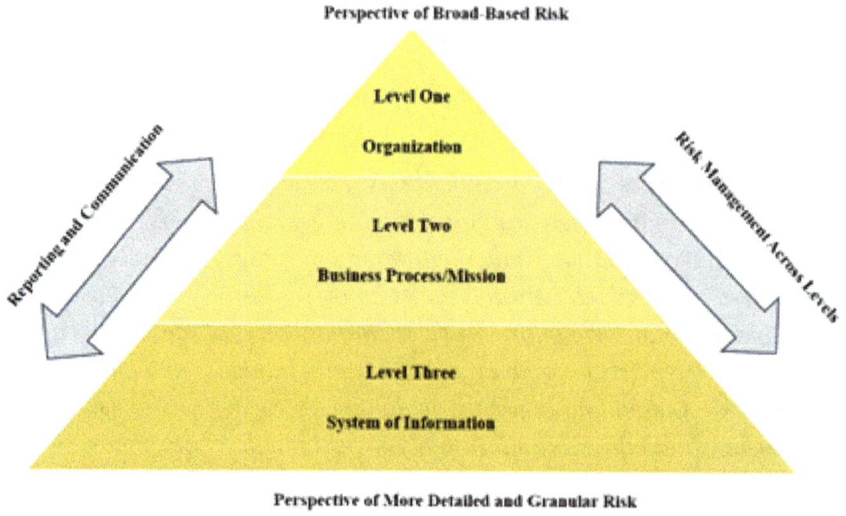

In order to prepare the organization to execute the RMF, it is necessary to complete the tasks at Levels 1 and 2. To be fully prepared, a business must do more than just deal with security and privacy issues that arise from specific technologies; it must also implement essential methods for managing these issues company-wide. It is not possible to make decisions about system-level risk management independently. Decisions of this kind are strongly related to the,

- Objectives or purpose of the organization
- Measures to update parts, infrastructure, and services
- Management and reduction of system complexity through optimisation, consolidation, and standardisation are essential components of enterprise architecture.
- Allocation of resources in a way that ensures the organization can carry out its missions and commercial operations in an efficient, effective, and cost-effective manner.

In order to get the company ready to implement the RMF, it may include,

- Allocating responsibilities for the implementation of risk management processes within an organization.
- Establishing the organization's risk tolerance and creating a strategy for managing risks.
- Identifying the goals, processes, and operations that the information system is intended to support.
- Locating key individuals or organisations that have a vested interest in the data system.
- Identifying and prioritising assets.
- Identifying potential threats to companies' and information systems.
- Realising that others may suffer negative consequences.
- Conducting organisational and systemic risk assessments.
- The identification and prioritisation of security and privacy requirements.
- The process of defining information system and shared control authorisation parameters.
- Information system characterisation using an enterprise architectural framework.
- Information system-appropriate control inheritance is a key component of secure and private architecture.
- Coordinating, recognising, and settling conflicts between privacy and security concerns.
- Information systems, system components, and organisations are given security and privacy mandates.

In contrast to Levels 1 and 2, which include getting the organization ready to adopt RMF, Level 3 is all about risk as it pertains to information systems. This level is impacted by risk decisions made at the organisational and mission/business process levels. Controls at the system level can be selected and implemented based on decisions made at Levels 1 and 2. According to the enterprise architecture, security architecture, privacy architecture, and any customised control baselines or overlays put in place by the business, controls are categorised as common, hybrid, or system-specific controls. Businesses establish a link between controls and the privacy and security requirements they aim to meet.

1.1 Research Gap and Chapter Contribution

Although existing studies have extensively examined enterprise risk management, cybersecurity controls, artificial intelligence and machine learning, cloud computing, and blockchain-based security mechanisms, these technologies are frequently discussed as separate components of digital risk management. This fragmented perspective provides limited understanding of how risk assessment and control mechanisms can be integrated with AI/ML-based analytics, cloud infrastructure, blockchain-enabled trust and data integrity, and organisational resilience within a unified framework. The present chapter addresses this gap by developing an integrated perspective of digital risk management in which risk identification and assessment provide the foundation for control design, AI/ML supports predictive risk analysis and decision-making, cloud computing enables scalable digital infrastructure, and blockchain strengthens transparency, integrity, and distributed trust. The chapter further connects these technological capabilities with organisational governance and resilience, thereby distinguishing its contribution from studies that focus primarily on individual technologies or isolated cybersecurity risks. The chapter contributes a structured conceptual model and a practical implementation perspective that can guide digital organisations in aligning technology adoption, risk controls, governance, and resilience objectives.

2. FUNDAMENTALS OF RISK MANAGEMENT

Modern practise makes heavy use of risk assessment and management. There are a plethora of tried-and-true methods for risk assessment and management that have the backing of authoritative bodies. However, there is still a lack of clarity regarding many basic scientific ideas in the risk assessment and risk management sectors(Aven & Zio, 2014). It is impossible to successfully manage risk in the current climate due to a lack of consensus on basic terminology and principles, inadequate scientific support, and the justification of several definitions and points of view. Efforts to reach a consensus on fundamental issues related to risk assessment and management first emerged in the 1980s and 1990s, especially in the field of nuclear risk. Current risk assessment and risk management approaches have developed via research and practise, revealing new perspectives, definitions, and problems.

Recent years have seen the introduction of new tools, the development of fresh theoretical frameworks, and the entrance of a fresh crop of risk researchers, who may come from a variety of educational backgrounds and bring a wide range of skills to the table. In this changed environment, scientists hardly bring up old, important issues again, and they seldom discuss them in scientific journals or at conferences(Aven, 2024). Novel approaches for tackling particular difficulties or providing insights into particular challenges are the usual focus of community-based research. While these contributions are important for expanding our understanding and solving real-world problems, we must not forget the importance of delving into deeper reflections and publishing them in books that are related to this field. In these books, we must question and develop our perspectives, principles, and concepts in relation to how our knowledge, culture, and technology have changed over time.

On August 3,4, 2012, a workshop was held in Salo, Lake Garda, Italy, inspired by the aforementioned background. Important issues in risk assessment and management were the subject of the session's discussions and debates(Mthiyane et al., 2022). Our presentation in no way claims to have covered every single topic discussed at the workshop. The purpose of this piece is to present the writers' points of view and important points. Many other people who took part in the workshop have also written articles sharing their thoughts. The chapter begins by discussing the concept of "foundations of risk assessment and risk management," covering what it means and how it is interpreted. To discuss the present state of affairs, its challenges, and possible solutions, it is necessary to clarify this idea. Risk "Assessment" includes defining the key ideas, while "Management" is understood to cover a wide range of activities, including governance and the social environment.

2.1 The Concept of Risk Management and Foundation of Risk Assessment

The foundation, in particular, is a source of concern since it provides the basis for risk assessment and management. Problems that are common to many applications are inherent to these foundations. Standard engineering challenges in the fields of nuclear and oil and gas technology can be built and solved using these ideas, but as is often the case when discussing core principles, they may also have broader applications(Guo et al., 2024). Think about model uncertainty: it's important, relevant, and has a big impact on many different kinds of risk assessment and management.

Because most risk assessments rely on models, understanding and interpreting model uncertainty is critically important for the field. The viewpoint taken and insights provided when investigating a methodology or approach to evaluating collision risk in offshore applications, on the other hand, are specific to the problem at hand and may not apply to other risk contexts. Figure 2 shows the illustration of foundation for risk assessment and risk management.

Figure 2. An Illustration of the Foundations for Risk Management and Risk Assessment

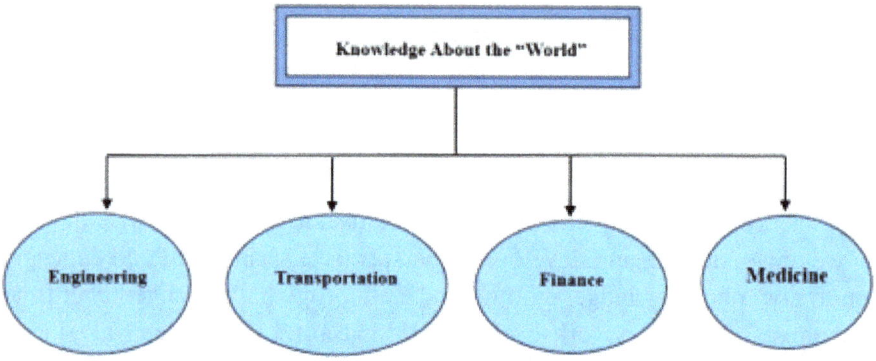

Although studies that focus on a particular application type tend to have a more foundational impact by reflecting on and discussing the concepts used, their meanings, and the framework that was adopted, studies that address more general issues, such as model uncertainty, tend to have more influence(îrcovnicu & Ha egan, 2023). The purpose of the preceding description is to clarify that key concepts like vulnerability, risk, and uncertainty, as well as their interpretation, significance, and management methodologies, as well as communication and governance strategies, are the primary focus of foundational work. Fundamental concepts and the principles and procedures for describing, communicating, conceptualising, and managing them are the primary foci of foundational work, which aims to clarify and explain these ideas(Labaki, 2020). On top of that, you can include in "World" knowledge that's pertinent to these ideas, such human behaviour; however, this is more generally applicable to areas of science outside of risk management and evaluation, like psychology. Although these fields are fundamental to risk management and evaluation, their relevance and reasoning go far beyond these areas.

3. DIGITAL RISK MANAGEMENT FRAMEWORKS

When we talk about digital risk, we're referring to any and all digital upgrades that make risk management easier and more efficient, especially in areas like decision and process automation, digital monitoring and early warning systems, and digitalisation(Ganguly et al., 2017). Optical character recognition, robotic process and interface integration, enhanced analytics, workflow automation, and new data sources are all part of the methodology. In its most basic form, digital risk refers to the coordinated alteration of analytics, IT procedures, data, and the entire organisational structure, which includes culture and talent.

3.1 Three Dimensions of Change: Data, Process, Organization

Financial institutions can reap the benefits of process and decision automation to the fullest extent possible if their systems, procedures, and behaviours are well-aligned with their goals. Priority use cases in the risk environment tend to cluster around tasks like as control, operational risk, compliance, stress testing, and credit underwriting(Anne Ajiri Alex-Omiogbemi et al., 2024). Existing procedures in most banks have developed organically without a well-defined goal in mind, leading to inefficient and even illogical process flows. Before using automation and decision support systems, operational structures need to be modified. To effectively manage digital risks, data, analytics, and information technology architecture are crucial. Digital activities cannot be supported by inefficient and disjointed information technology and data infrastructures.

In order to outline a data strategy for updating risks, create a data vision, enhance data quality, set up complete data governance and metadata, and build a suitable data architecture, there must be clear institutional support(Adekunle et al., 2023). Thanks to developments in cutting-edge technology in a number of important areas, such as cloud computing, big data platforms, AI, ML, and NLP, modern approaches and analytical procedures may now make these goals a reality. To enable rapid digitalisation, new capabilities will be required of the operational and organisational architecture. Risk practitioners should still strive to foster an innovative culture that can withstand challenges, even when risk innovation happens in a very delicate area. The right people need to be in place, and a "Test and learn" attitude of innovation needs to be encouraged. A dynamic regulatory and technological environment necessitates governance frameworks that enable quick reactions. A major difficulty for the digital risk function is effectively managing an innovation culture that is in line with risk tolerance.

3.2 Adapting Digital Transformation to Risk Contexts

The majority of financial institutions are slowly but surely digitising their risk functions using sector-specific modular methodologies(Wilhelmina Afua Addy et al., 2024). Many have undergone radical changes, leading to significant and long-lasting enhancements in productivity and performance. When it comes to risk, it's important to be careful when making changes to test-and-learn pilots that are usually used for digital transformations in other parts of the bank. Due to the inherent low tolerance for flaws and mistakes in risk, stringent controls must be put in place for such pilots. Thorough testing is necessary for solutions to be fully reliable and effective before they are put into production for the digitalisation of Comprehensive Capital Analysis and Review (CCAR) procedures. Banks can make good use of test-and-learn approaches in some risk domains, like commercial credit risk monitoring and early warning systems.

4. RISK ASSESSMENT PROCESS

4.1 Risk Identification

Informally carried out using a variety of approaches depending on the business and project team, risk identification is the first stage of risk management. Looking at similar projects that have already been completed and drawing on past knowledge are the two mainstays of risk detection. During this initial phase, a variety of methods and instruments may be used to identify potential risks to the project. Different types of problems and initiatives call for different approaches, especially when it comes to identifying them(Saeed et al., 2023). Even though it may be difficult to completely eliminate risks and hazards, recognising them allows us to take steps to mitigate or control them. Recognising and assigning hazards' origins before they manifest will make risk management more effective. Ensuring that stakeholders are prepared to handle unexpected challenges that may emerge throughout a project's advancement is the main goal of risk management. With the help of risk management, problems can be foreseen and people can be better prepared to face future obstacles.

Reducing project losses and turning risks into opportunities to generate financial and economic rewards are both achieved through addressing potential threats. Collecting a catalogue of threats that might have a domino effect on the project's development and then developing plans to deal with them is what risk identification is all about. In order to find out what could go wrong with a project, a number of methods are used. For the exercise to be effective, the project team should follow a tried-and-true method. The first step in effective risk management is the accurate identification of risks.

Techniques of Risk Identification

Economic, legal, environmental, political, contractual, planning/scheduling, technical, operational, labour, design, logistics, and stakeholder safety and security are just a few of the hazards that the construction sector encounters.

4.2 Assessment of Risk

The second step in risk management is risk assessment, which involves looking at all the data together to see what could go wrong(Rezvani et al., 2023). Following the discovery of potential dangers to the project, the next step is to rank them according to their potential impact, from low to high. Both quantitative and qualitative evaluations are part of risk assessment.

Assessment of Qualitative Risk

Formal documenting of identified hazards is part of this process. Although not limited to the following, this procedure is formalised with a risk register.

- **Reference and Classification:** Classification helps pinpoint where danger is coming from.
- **Risk Description:** Giving a brief summary of the risk is part of this. For the risk management method to be clear, the description must be separate from similar dangers.
- **Relationship to Other Risks:** The successful execution of risk management relies heavily on the premise that no action in a project can be considered independent of other, related or consequential actions. This premise also applies to hazards.
- **Impact of Potential:** We evaluate risk in connection to quality and cost when we look at the impact on a project. Information may be inadequate to accurately predict the risk's effect on the project if the evaluation takes place too early in the process. Now that we've reached the point where risks are being adequately evaluated, we must ensure that risks with high impacts are given a more thorough evaluation than risks with medium, low, or insignificant impacts. This evaluation will be done using a scale from 1 to 10.
- **Calculation of Risk Factor and Likelihood of Occurrence:** A suitable scale, such as 1–10, where 1 represents low probability and 10 high proba-

bilities, should be used to evaluate the impact (I) and the likelihood of risk occurrence (P). After normalising P and I on a scale of 0-1 by dividing their values by 10, the risk factor for each identified risk is calculated using the formula $RF = P + I - (P * I)$.

- **Mitigation Strategy/ Risk Response:** To lessen the impact of, or completely avoid, the dangers that have been detected, this action is taken. Transferring, avoiding, sharing, and reducing risks are the four most common approaches to risk mitigation. The identified risks are then assigned to the relevant stakeholders based on their level of expertise in risk management.

4.3 Assessment of Quantitative Risk

When the qualitative risk assessment identifies a danger as high, critical, or unmanageable, it is common practice to perform this risk assessment. The goal of this assessment is to find out how much of a buffer to put into the estimate for the known risks so that there will be enough money to cover any extra costs if the risks come to fruition(Shaikh & Siponen, 2023). Extensive analysis is necessary for quantitative approaches. The time and energy put in by the chosen method should be considered when assessing the quality of this analysis. Research must be more extensive for bigger and more complicated undertakings than for simpler ones. Quantitative analysis is to determine how a risk affects a project in terms of scale, cost, quality, time, and scope. Medium and large projects, with their more complex hazards, are better suited to this methodology than smaller ones.

Risk analysis is the process of thoroughly quantifying potential dangers. The possible effects of risks on time, money, and quality are quantified in a quantitative evaluation. There are usually two parts to the estimate: one for the known, with a specific level of assurance, and another for the unknown, with a contingency tolerance. A heuristic approach has traditionally been used to determine the contingencies, which typically range from 5 to 10% of the risk-free baseline estimate. Project risks can be better anticipated and mitigated with the help of a well-thought-out risk management plan. Contingency allowances control risk-related expenses when used correctly. Listed below are the methods that make up quantitative risk assessment.

Monte Carlo Simulation Technique

To assess risks, the Monte Carlo approach employs statistical methods in computer models. This statistical approach uses predetermined parameters to produce data at random, with the goal of producing practical project results(Ogunmokun et al., 2022). By documenting all data and repeatedly simulating all combinations of risk values, we can forecast the full project outcome. The risk forecast is based on the mean, which is determined from all scenarios once the necessary simulations are finished. Recognising that the settings and appropriate distribution used to simulate random data are fundamentally a set of subjective inputs is key.

Modelling Technique: Analysis of Sensitivity

This technique shows how a modification to one or more components or hazards affects the overall system. Decisions in situations with definite ranks, particularly those with marginal rankings, can have their robustness tested using this method(Mohammed Anwar, 2023). It can determine the exact instant in time when changing one parameter affects the final choice. The most common method for conducting sensitivity analysis is to draw a spider diagram that highlights the most important and vulnerable parts of the project. Risks are more likely to affect the objectives if there is a high degree of ambiguity about them.

Decision Tree

When there is a chain of related possible actions and their resulting time and cost consequences, decision tree analysis is often used. This analytical method is commonly used when certain risks have a major impact on the project's time and budget goals(Behie et al., 2023). You can use quantification to strengthen the basis for decision-making when the probabilities and values of likely outcomes are known or estimable. Each decision process's anticipated value EV serves as the foundation of the decision-making framework.

Risk Analysis for Multiple Estimation Techniques

One approach that aims to provide a range of estimates is Multiple Estimating using Risk Analysis (MERA). There are three distinct estimates: the risk-free base estimate, the Average Risk Estimate (ARE), and the Maximum Likely Risk Estimate (MLRE). The risk-free base estimate and the average risk allowance make up ARE, while the maximum risk allowance and ARE are combined to form MLRE. MERA's goal is to find a value that stands for an estimate that has a 50% chance of being correct. It is calculated by multiplying the average allowance by the average likelihood of occurrence; this is called ARE. Just increase the maximum risk allowance by the maximum probability of that risk occurring, and that's the maximum risk allowance(Melnyk et al., 2022). Incorporating this into ARE yields MLRE, which stands for the estimate that is unlikely to be surpassed by more than 90% of the time.

The systematic identification, qualitative assessment, and quantitative evaluation of risk provide the foundation for determining appropriate risk responses. However, in digitally dependent organisations, risk management cannot remain limited to periodic assessment activities; it must be embedded within continuously operating organisational and technological control systems. The transition from risk assessment to digital risk management therefore requires organisations to translate identified risks into measurable controls, monitoring mechanisms, and adaptive response capabilities. This perspective provides the basis for examining how control systems operate within digitally transformed organisations.

4.4 Planning for Risk Response

Appropriate measures will be put in place to mitigate both positive and negative risks as part of the risk response.

5. CONTROL SYSTEMS IN DIGITAL ORGANIZATIONS

Companies, including SMEs, are gradually becoming digitally transformed and organised into a new type of Digital Organization for the future (DOOTF). Within these worldwide digital business ecosystems, the DOOTF will operate, bringing together related business units that share values and goals in order to create value and gain an edge in the fiercely competitive global market. Influenced by the converging digital and global phenomena, DOOTF is service-oriented, as shown in Amazon's growing organisational and economic model(Jari Collin, Kari Hiekkanen, Janne J. Korhonen, Marco Halén, Timo Itälä, 2015). They can take use of value cells, which are interconnected business units, by using business models. Capabilities that are based on value-generating activities form the basis of value cells, which have their own economics.

DOOTFs innovate their services by constantly coordinating with one another to meet the unmet or unspoken demands of the ever-changing markets they service. A widespread value network has emerged as a consequence of the interconnection of the DOOTF ecosystem through information technology. Exemplifying one type of DOOTF is a large multinational firm that is governed by traditional employment-based authority, despite its potential global networked organisational structure. The meta-organization is a type of DOOTF that falls into a broader category. Scholars have described it as “Networks of firms not constrained by authority derived from employment relationships, but distinguished by a system-level objective.” The Linux open-source community and Li & Fung's supply networks are examples of meta-organization.

A more “Actor-oriented” structure is becoming more prevalent in both types of DOOTF. In this model, actors with similar goals but different skillsets can adapt to changing market or institutional conditions by self-organising through shared procedures, collaboration protocols, and infrastructures. In response to or in anticipation of emerging or dormant market demands, these players or value cells dynamically collaborate with one another, either within or across organisations, to co-create value.

5.1 Integrated Digital Risk Management Conceptual Framework

The integrated digital risk management framework proposed in this chapter establishes a relationship among risk management, organisational control systems, AI and machine learning, cloud computing, blockchain, and organisational resilience. The framework begins with systematic risk identification and assessment, through which organisations identify threats, vulnerabilities, likelihood, impact, and risk priorities. The outcomes of risk assessment inform the design and implementation of organisational control systems that establish preventive, detective, corrective, and monitoring mechanisms. AI and ML technologies strengthen these controls by enabling predictive analytics, anomaly detection, automated risk identification, and data-driven decision support. Cloud computing provides scalable infrastructure for data storage, processing, monitoring, and recovery, while simultaneously introducing risks associated with information security, privileged access, regulatory compliance, availability, and provider dependency. Blockchain complements these mechanisms by providing distributed and tamper-resistant records, improving transaction transparency, data integrity, accountability, and trust. The interaction of these components supports organisational resilience by improving the ability of digital organisations to anticipate, withstand, respond to, and recover from operational, technological, security, and compliance-related disruptions. Thus, the framework views digital risk management as a continuous and interconnected process rather than a collection of independent technological controls.

6. AI AND MACHINE LEARNING IN RISK MANAGEMENT

The first thing to do is to define AI and ML, two terms that are not necessarily synonymous. Although there is a somewhat fluid distinction even in research, companies' public relations and fundraising efforts sometimes use the more alluring term "AI," even though they usually mean ML. Machine learning is an essential AI technology that relies on data for learning, but AI covers more ground than just that(Aziz & Dowling, 2018). There needs to be automation in data testing, data identification, and decision-making for an AI system to be considered comprehensive. AI might include methods other than ML, such as logic rules and hard-coded algorithms. ML, on the other hand, usually calls for data scientists to manually identify and evaluate data, as well as use their best judgement when deciding how to apply the generated knowledge. A less technical way of looking at AI is as the intelligence that robots display, with human cognition serving as a backdrop for this intelligence. Artificial super-intelligence, or robots with capabilities similar to or greater than human intellect in a particular domain, is our main focus here in the financial sector.

This more inclusive method has the drawback of not clearly distinguishing between AI and ML. In light of the reality that most claims of AI are actually just ML and that most organisations aren't ready for real AI, this section outlines the basic ML methodologies used in risk management. Following this, and especially in the last chapter, our focus will go to AI as the natural next step from the widespread use of ML methods. Supervised and unsupervised learning are the two main categories of ML. The goal of supervised learning is to determine an output that corresponds to an input. This is similar to the conventional statistical method, which involves looking for a relationship between the dependent variable and a number of independent factors. In unsupervised learning, the goal is to understand the structure of the data by using only the input data.

The methods used in regression ML are quite similar to the ones that have long been used to establish correlations and causes and effects(Abikoye et al., 2024). Credit lending risk assessment using a conventional linear regression model entails a number of independent variables that are hypothesised to influence the dependent variable, which is the likelihood of loan non-repayment. Financial measures including full-time employment, average non-repayment rates, property ownership, and credit history quality are examples of possible independent variables.

ML for regression departs from traditional regression in that it uses methods with a large number of independent variables, some of which can be automatically removed if they don't provide enough explanation(Fritz-Morgenthal et al., 2022). The data scientist has access to a vast assortment of data, making this functionality crucial. Furthermore, it reduces the amount of theoretical work needed to choose suitable independent variables. LASSO regression gets rid of independent variables that don't add much to the model's explanation, while Ridge regression gives less weight to variables that are highly correlated with one another. Both approaches lead to a more streamlined model, which in turn allows the data scientist to narrow down the extensive list of possible explanatory variables to a more manageable subset. In contrast to LASSO and Ridge, which give weights to all variables at zero and then include only those that show explanatory significance, LARS regressions work backwards.

Using LASSO regression and other techniques, the previous researcher developed an automated investment trading advisory system based on stock trend analysis. They show that this method outperforms traditional methods of trading. In their shared goal of reducing the number of variables, Principal Component Analysis (PCA) and Partial Least Squares Regression (PLS) are quite similar. Compared to its alternative, PCA is more common because of its widespread use in classical statistics, which leads to better understanding. A set of prospective criteria for evaluating the likelihood of loan payback, as shown in a PCA example, might include things like having a house, a car, and a sizable savings account; a common factor that could be constructed from these could be called "Asset ownership." Using a practical example provided by (Zhong & Enke, 2017), they use PCA to reduce 60 related economic and financial metrics to a smaller set of components. Then, they use multiple neural network ML techniques to forecast the US S&P 500 index. A common use of PCA in ML is shown here; first, it reduces the number of dimensions, and then, using the PCA components as input, a more advanced ML method is applied.

The risks associated with cloud-based environments demonstrate that digital risk management requires mechanisms that extend beyond infrastructure protection and availability. In particular, organisations require reliable approaches for establishing data integrity, transaction accountability, transparency, and trust across distributed digital ecosystems. Blockchain technology offers complementary capabilities through decentralised record keeping, cryptographic validation, and tamper-resistant transaction histories. Consequently, the following section considers blockchain as an additional technological mechanism for strengthening digital risk controls and reducing selected operational and information-related risks.

7. CLOUD COMPUTING AND DIGITAL RISK CONTROL

Previous research indicates that SMEs can gain access to cloud-based software, services, and infrastructure that would otherwise be out of their reach(Brender & Markov, 2013). As a reason for potentially adopting cloud services, 68.1% of the 70 SMEs surveyed by the European Network and Information Security Agency (ENISA) cited avoiding capital expenditures on hardware, software, IT support, and information security. Cloud computing, on the other hand, presents a number of challenges and dangers(Nutalapati, 2024). Nearly half of the nearly 1800 US-based businesses and IT professionals surveyed by the Information Systems Audit and Control Association see more dangers than benefits in cloud computing. The next parts take a look at the main issues, with an emphasis on how managers see them. Their arrangement is not a reflection of seriousness, but rather it communicates the opinions of experts regarding the main risks of cloud computing and how to mitigate them.

7.1 Information Security

Cloud computing, like any other modern technology, raises serious concerns about data security. Based on their interviews with South African participants, previous studies have identified it as the top threat. According to ENISA, nearly half of the 64 surveyed SMEs expressed privacy concerns, and 43 of those SMEs saw the need to protect sensitive company information as a major obstacle(Drissi et al., 2025). According to the previous researcher, more than three quarters of CIOs voiced security concerns in a survey by the International Data Corporation (IDC). Because of its widespread use on the internet and the massive amounts of data it collects, hackers find it more attractive as a target. Previous study has shown that certain providers lack the tools that Amazon and Microsoft have to prevent and recover from cyberattacks(Oladoyinbo et al., 2023). Cloud defences, on the other hand, rely on provider-side expertise concentration and economies of scale to keep costs down.

Additionally, data stored in multiple data centers inside the cloud reduces the effect of such assaults due to the cloud's decentralised design. Therefore, companies' participation in internet activities is not necessarily bad. Because it is still linked to the internet and thus susceptible to hacking efforts, an in-house IT department is not necessarily more secure than a cloud-based solution, according to the previous researcher(Richard Arogundade, 2023). Before signing up for a service, customers should make sure the provider's security measures meet their needs. When a cloud service incorporates numerous providers, this problem becomes even more severe because the end result is only as safe as the least secure provider.

7.2 Access of Privileged User

The "Physical, logical, and personnel controls" put in place by an organization's internal IT department are rendered ineffective when sensitive data is handled outside of the company's physical location, according to Heiser and other academics(Ganesan, 2024). When customers fail to realise that their data is actually stored in a physical location, the concept of the cloud can become misleading. This exemplifies the danger of an evil insider who could harm the company's reputation and cause consumers to lose money and time. As a result, customers are strongly encouraged to enquire about the processes for hiring and overseeing privileged cloud administrators.

The CSA assesses a number of serious risks in this area, including credential and account hijacking. Hackers can gain access to spy on users, cloud services, change data, and lead them to fake websites if they manage to get their hands on client credentials(Cheng et al., 2022). This might lead to damage to the company's reputation and finances, as well as lay the groundwork for future attacks. Policy is the main emphasis of the repair strategies, which include strong authentication procedures, a thorough grasp of Service Level Agreements (SLAs), and the restriction of shared accounts. It is advised by experts to use the principle of least privilege(Odukoya, 2024). An individual, process, or organization should be granted the fewest privileges and resources needed to do a task in the shortest amount of time possible, according to this idea. Additionally, a person shouldn't have access to a plethora of related functions. Therefore, the question of how to authenticate and manage accounts with the highest level of privileges arises.

7.3 Data Location and Regulatory Compliance

According to the CSA, subcontractors must be held responsible for maintaining adequate data security because the European Economic Area (EEA) contains data protection laws. We have seen similar laws passed in a number of other countries(Vijay Kumar Adari, 2024). In most cases, they state that the onus for ensuring the data's safety and security is on the custodian, not on the data's location but on any third party to whom the data is transferred. In the event that the data is destroyed, lost, or misused, the custodian will be held responsible. Traditional cloud providers, according to the aforementioned researcher, provide customers with visibility into the assessed security measures through external audits and security certifications. If a provider refuses or is unable to conduct such audits or publish the results, they should only be considered for the smallest of tasks.

Concerns about the storage of data in public clouds are connected(Adebola Folorunso et al., 2024). Data kept in high-risk countries, where governments may pass laws allowing access to any data within their borders, or data subject to privacy limitations across multiple jurisdictions make this a major concern. According to the Canadian government, the Patriot Act allows the United States government to access data kept in data centers in the United States.

7.4 Support for Investigation

Previous research has shown that in order for electronic evidence to be discovered in litigation before a trial, a company must know exactly where their data is stored and how they keep it safe. This process is called e-discovery. This assumes, among other things, that the company can physically check storage media for lost files(Malik, 2024). Businesses that use cloud storage have little to no control over the storage and backup processes or media used by the supplier. According to the previous research, there are privacy issues and difficulties in understanding file access and deletion when a single storage device contains data and logs from multiple clients. Also, the data centers where it is stored could change over time.

Even more so, conducting a forensic investigation into an organization's own infrastructure is difficult, time-consuming, and expensive(Enache, 2023). Cloud service providers may be unable or unwilling to help if the company uses their services to process business documents or anticipates the need for an investigation. Lacking proof of previous support and the ability to achieve a contractual agreement, the customer has little chance of receiving future aid with specific investigative actions.

7.5 Disaster Recovery and Availability

Important business processes rely on the availability of cloud services. If your online store uses a cloud-based platform, losing that platform could be disastrous for your company(Ionescu & Diaconita, 2023). Any company planning to move mission-critical tasks to the cloud should work with their provider to create a SLA that guarantees those services will be available when needed, according to the previous study's author. In February 2008, Salesforce.com went down for six hours, and a few days later, Amazon's S3 and EC2 clouds were down as well, according to the previous researcher. Subsequently that year, Amazon's S3 went through yet another 8-hour outage.

Modern events like the protracted April 2011 outage of Amazon's EC2 are also included in the list of comparable situations. In a survey conducted by ENISA, it was found that 28 out of 66 SMEs consider the availability of services and data to be of paramount importance. On the flip side, there are many cases where the service availability beyond what an internal IT staff can handle, especially when it comes to SMEs. Related to this is the subject of disaster recovery. It was ranked second only to information security in terms of essential importance in the interviews conducted by the previous researcher, with 66.7% of the vote. Looking at it from a different angle, ENISA found that 52.8% of SMEs cite the ability to recover from disasters and maintain business continuity as a reason to potentially use cloud computing. Consequently, businesses must gather details about what happens to their data in a disaster and how long it takes to recover.

7.6 Long-Term Viability and Provider Lock-In

According to the previous study, many cloud providers use their own formats for a variety of purposes, including data import/export, APIs, and disaster recovery server images. Concerns about mobility and compatibility will grow in intensity as the number of vendors grows. The possibility of provider failures adds fuel to these concerns(Wen & De Leon, 2024). Therefore, the consequences of the provider's potential bankruptcy or acquisition by another firm are relevant to the topic of long-term viability. The availability of customer data and the ability to move it to another application or cloud provider are dependent on the customer making sure that the SLA covers these scenarios. Online storage services and web application development firm Coghead are among the other examples of failed ventures presented by the earlier researcher.

Clients of Coghead had less than three months to restore all of their data and apps after enterprise software vendor SAP bought out Coghead's intellectual property. There are a number of steps that the previous researcher recommends to lessen the blow of provider failure(Yenugula et al., 2023). Like any other vendor, he says, clients should check a supplier's profitability, sales, customer base, and other important indicators. They have to keep their local storage capacity up to date and deal with the problem of data and app portability again since they have to regularly back up their data and apps on local servers. Customers should find out if the service provider provides technical support in case of data and application migration disasters and create backup strategies accordingly.

8. BLOCKCHAIN FOR RISK MANAGEMENT

The earlier researcher introduced Bitcoin as a decentralised, peer-to-peer currency that did away with middlemen in financial transactions in his seminal work on the core ideas of blockchain(Celestin & Vanitha, 2015). A worldwide team of researchers set out to solve the digital currency double-spending problem by creating a trustless network that uses proof-of-work techniques. To guarantee the security of transaction validation, Nakamoto's methodology used a cryptographic consensus mechanism. Providing a transparent and tamper-resistant system, blockchain might replace traditional trust models, according to the results(Rahman et al., 2024). This fits in with the increasing interest in using blockchain for purposes other than cryptocurrencies, like operational risk management. Since all of Nakamoto's studies were focused on monetary transactions, he failed to fully grasp the potential uses of blockchain technology beyond Bitcoin.

8.1 Trust Mechanism and Blockchain in Non-Financial Sectors

Swan conducted research in the UK in 2014 that looked at blockchain's potential uses outside of cryptocurrencies, with an emphasis on enhancing trust and openness in healthcare and supply chain management, among other areas(Shaytura et al., 2021). Examining potential ways in which decentralised trust models might enhance operational risk management was the primary objective. Swan used a qualitative case study approach to find that blockchain's decentralised structure could reduce risk by reducing dependence on single points of failure. Her research suggested that decentralisation of trust a crucial component of risk management may be possible, suggesting that blockchain applications in operational risk are feasible(Senturk & Baghırov, 2023). However, empirical data on blockchain's tangible effect on operational dangers was lacking in Swan's research, which left a gap for further targeted exploration in operational risk management applications.

8.2 Blockchain for Improved Transparency and Operational Accountability

Previous Canadian studies aimed to delve deeper into blockchain's potential to transform business processes by increasing transparency and accountability, expanding the topic's scope beyond cryptocurrencies(Dzhaparov, 2019). To assess blockchain's impact on supply chain management trust and information asymmetry, their study used a mixed-methods strategy, including interviews and questionnaires. Scientific studies have shown that blockchain technology can help businesses reduce fraud, increase stakeholder accountability, and monitor transactions in real-time, all of which contribute to a lower risk environment. When it comes to operational risk management, where visibility is key for reducing unknown dangers, this openness is highly congruent with what's needed. However, additional research might explore the use of blockchain in regulatory risk management, since Tapscott and Tapscott's study did not thoroughly evaluate how blockchain could handle risks connected to compliance or regulation (Khalifa, 2019).

8.3 Reducing Financial Operational Risks Through Blockchain

Researchers Hufenbach, Maurer, and Welten looked into blockchain's ability to reduce operational risks related to data breaches, fraud, and inefficient transactions in a 2013 study involving Swiss financial institutions(Chung & Caldas, 2022). Their goal was to learn more about how blockchain works as an immutable record that can automate transactions, making them more secure and less susceptible to fraud and human mistake. According to the study, which used quantitative data from operational audits, the immutability of blockchain reduced the possibility of fraud and made transaction audits easier(Etemadi et al., 2021). The study focused on the financial sector and ignored operational risk factors unique to other industries, particularly those with complex logistical needs, even if it was relevant to financial institutions. Because of this void, we can study how blockchain affects different operational frameworks.

8.4 Risk Management Decentralization Using Blockchain

Using case studies of IT companies and banks, researchers in the US compared blockchain's capabilities for decentralising risk control. The objective was to find out whether the decentralised nature of blockchain could reduce reliance on centralised risk management approaches, which are prone to single points of failure(Feng et al., 2021). Their case study results proved that distributed ledger technology improved system resilience, which is critical for effective management of operational risk. Although intriguing, the study mostly ignored potential applications of distributed risk management outside of decentralised banking. Because of this limitation, further study into decentralised operational risk controls is required in other industries, such as healthcare and manufacturing.

9. APPLICATION

In order to evaluate risks and respond to important actions, at least 30% of innovators use technology solutions from the IoT(Gasparian et al., 2021). For example, they use robots to carry out routine activities like data extraction, but AI for more complicated jobs like evaluating databases and controlling monitoring systems. By automating these processes, human resources can be reallocated to tasks that directly contribute to the improvement of the company's efficiency.

- **An Innovative Strategy for Addressing Issues Pertaining to Risk:** A FedEx executive programmed a bot to undertake quarterly quality assessments and generate reports on a variety of economic and financial indicators.
- **Risk of Information Privacy Infractions and Other Critical Risks can be Automated:** For certain businesses, AI makes it easier to gauge the availability of data(Kostova & Zhelev, 2024). As an example, AI is used by Taylor Scott & White Health to analyse medical records' browsing histories. The AI company regularly updates the software that is used, which reduces staff workload and streamlines processes.
- **Embracing Digitalisation could Fuel Quick Growth:** Automation of various risk-related tasks through risk assessment enables quicker digital transformation, which is especially useful for organisations that operate across multiple industries rather than just one(Otoo et al., 2023). The rapid and extensive digitisation has made it easier to handle massive databases. Internal audits can be better allocated resources and operations can be streamlined by the robotization of certain audit areas.

The implementation of an integrated digital risk management strategy requires organisations to translate conceptual principles into structured operational activities. A practical roadmap should begin with the identification and classification of critical assets, processes, data, and stakeholders, followed by systematic assessment of threats, vulnerabilities, likelihood, and potential impact. Organisations should then establish risk priorities and corresponding preventive, detective, and corrective controls. AI and ML capabilities can subsequently be introduced for predictive analytics, anomaly detection, and continuous monitoring, while cloud environments should be governed through appropriate access controls, security requirements, data-location policies, service-level agreements, backup mechanisms, and disaster-recovery procedures. Blockchain should be considered where distributed trust, transaction integrity, traceability, or tamper resistance provides a clear risk-control benefit. Finally, organisations should continuously evaluate control effectiveness through performance indicators, audits, incident analysis, model validation, and feedback mechanisms. The following checklist provides a practical implementation sequence for digital organisations.

10. CONCLUSION

To ensure digital businesses' resilience, security, and sustainability, risk management and control systems are crucial. Organisational risks are getting more complex as businesses rely more on digital infrastructures, AI, cloud computing, and the Internet of Things. Organisations can ensure regulatory compliance and operational continuity by the proactive identification and mitigation of hazards through the use of advanced risk management frameworks, automated control systems, predictive analytics, and cybersecurity technologies. Intelligent, adaptive, and resilient risk management ecosystems are crucial for digital businesses to securely undergo digital transformation, even in the face of persistent challenges related to new privacy concerns, cyber dangers, and technical complexities.

REFERENCES

Abikoye, B. E., Adelusi, W., Umeorah, S. C., Adelaja, A. O., & Agorbia-Atta, C. (2024). Integrating Risk Management in Fintech and Traditional Financial Institutions through AI and Machine Learning. *Journal of Economics. Management and Trade*, *30*(8), 90–102. DOI: 10.9734/jemt/2024/v30i81236

Adari, V. K.Vijay Kumar Adari. (2024). How Cloud Computing is Facilitating Interoperability in Banking and Finance. *International Journal of Scientific Research in Computer Science. Engineering and Information Technology*, *10*(6), 851–859. DOI: 10.32628/CSEIT241061138

Addy, W. A., Ugochukwu, C. E., Oyewole, A. T., Ofodile, O. C., Adeoye, O. B., & Okoye, C. C.Wilhelmina Afua AddyChinonye Esther UgochukwuAdedoyin Tolulope OyewoleOnyeka Chrisanctus OfodileOmotayo Bukola AdeoyeChinwe Chinazo Okoye. (2024). Predictive analytics in credit risk management for banks: A comprehensive review. *GSC Advanced Research and Reviews*, *18*(2), 434–449. DOI: 10.30574/gscarr.2024.18.2.0077

Adekunle, B. I., Damilare Balogun, E., Chukwuma-Eke, E. C., & Ogunsola, K. O. (2023). Developing a Digital Operations Dashboard for Real-Time Financial Compliance Monitoring in Multinational Corporations. *Bolaji Iyanu Adekunle et Al Int. J. Sci. Res. Comput. Sci. Eng. Inf. Technol*, *9*(3), 728–746. http://ijsrcseit.com

Alex-Omiogbemi, A. A., Sule, A. K., Omowole, B. M., & Owoade, S. J.Anne Ajiri Alex-OmiogbemiAumbur Kwaghter SuleBamidele Michael OmowoleSamuel Jesupelumi Owoade. (2024). Conceptual framework for advancing regulatory compliance and risk management in emerging markets through digital innovation. *World Journal of Advanced Research and Reviews*, *24*(3), 1155–1162. DOI: 10.30574/wjarr.2024.24.3.3752

Aven, T. (2024). Risk literacy: Foundational issues and its connection to risk science. *Risk Analysis : An Official Publication of the Society for Risk Analysis*, *44*(5), 1011–1020. DOI: 10.1111/risa.14223 PMID: 37728216

Aven, T., & Zio, E. (2014). Foundational Issues in Risk Assessment and Risk Management. *Risk Analysis : An Official Publication of the Society for Risk Analysis*, *34*(7), 1164–1172. DOI: 10.1111/risa.12132 PMID: 24152111

Aziz, S., & Dowling, M. M. (2018). AI and Machine Learning for Risk Management. SSRN *Electronic Journal*. DOI: 10.2139/ssrn.3201337

Behie, S. W., Pasman, H. J., Khan, F. I., Shell, K., Alarfaj, A., El-Kady, A. H., & Hernandez, M. (2023). Leadership 4.0: The changing landscape of industry management in the smart digital era. *Process Safety and Environmental Protection, 172*(January), 317–328. DOI: 10.1016/j.psep.2023.02.014

Brender, N., & Markov, I. (2013). Risk perception and risk management in cloud computing: Results from a case study of Swiss companies. *International Journal of Information Management, 33*(5), 726–733. DOI: 10.1016/j.ijinfomgt.2013.05.004

Celestin, M., & Vanitha, N. (2015). Blockchain beyond Bitcoin: Revolutionizing operational risk management. *International Journal of Multidisciplinary, I*(I), 725–731. https://www.researchgate.net/profile/Mbonigaba-Celestin/publication/385620336_BLOCKCHAIN_BEYOND_BITCOIN_REVOLUTIONIZING_OPERATIONAL_RISK_MANAGEMENT/links/672cb41677b63d1220e2dd26/BLOCKCHAIN-BEYOND-BITCOIN-REVOLUTIONIZING-OPERATIONAL-RISK-MANAGEMENT.pdf

Cheng, M., Qu, Y., Jiang, C., & Zhao, C. (2022). Is cloud computing the digital solution to the future of banking? *Journal of Financial Stability, 63*(June 2021), 101073. DOI: 10.1016/j.jfs.2022.101073

Chung, I. B., & Caldas, C. (2022). Applicability of Blockchain-Based Implementation for Risk Management in Healthcare Projects. *Blockchain in Healthcare Today, 5*(Special Issue), 1–10. DOI: 10.30953/bhty.v5.191 PMID: 36779025

Jari Collin, Kari Hiekkanen, Janne J. Korhonen, Marco Halén, Timo Itälä, M. H. (2015). *The Impact of Digitalization on Finnish Organizations.*

Drissi, S., Chergui, M., & Khatar, Z. (2025). A Systematic Literature Review on Risk Assessment in Cloud Computing: Recent Research Advancements. *IEEE Access : Practical Innovations, Open Solutions, 13*(April), 76289–76307. DOI: 10.1109/ACCESS.2025.3561123

Dzhaparov, P. (2019). *Application of blockchain and artificial intelligence in bank risk management.*

Enache, G. I. (2023). Logistics Security in the Era of Big Data, Cloud Computing and IoT. *Proceedings of the International Conference on Business Excellence, 17*(1), 188–199. DOI: 10.2478/picbe-2023-0021

Etemadi, N., Borbon-Galvez, Y., Strozzi, F., & Etemadi, T. (2021). Supply chain disruption risk management with blockchain: A dynamic literature review. *Information (Basel), 12*(2), 1–25. DOI: 10.3390/info12020070

Feng, S., Wang, W., Xiong, Z., Niyato, D., Wang, P., & Wang, S. S. (2021). On Cyber Risk Management of Blockchain Networks: A Game Theoretic Approach. *IEEE Transactions on Services Computing, 14*(5), 1492–1504. DOI: 10.1109/TSC.2018.2876846

Folorunso, A., Adewa, A., Babalola, O., & Nwatu, C. E. (2024). A governance framework model for cloud computing: Role of AI, security, compliance, and management. *World Journal of Advanced Research and Reviews, 24*(2), 1969–1982. DOI: 10.30574/wjarr.2024.24.2.3513

Force, J. T. (2017). Risk Management Framework. *Risk Management Framework*, 229–270. DOI: 10.4018/978-1-5225-2503-5.ch007

Fritz-Morgenthal, S., Hein, B., & Papenbrock, J. (2022). Financial Risk Management and Explainable, Trustworthy, Responsible AI. *Frontiers in Artificial Intelligence, 5*(February), 1–14. DOI: 10.3389/frai.2022.779799 PMID: 35295866

Ganesan, P. (2024). Journal of Artificial Intelligence & Cloud Computing Cloud-Based Disaster Recovery : Reducing Risk and Improving Continuity. *Journal of Artificial Intelligence & Cloud Computing., 2024*(February), 1–4. DOI: 10.47363/JAICC/2024(3)E162

Ganguly, S., Harreis, H., Margolis, B., & Rowshankish, K. (2017). Digital risk: Transforming risk management for the 2020s. *McKinsey&Company*, 1–8.

Gasparian, M. S., Kiseleva, I. A., Titov, V. A., & Olenev, L. A. (2021). Simulation and risk management of financial activities in the digital economy era. *Nexo Revista Científica, 34*(04), 1388–1395. DOI: 10.5377/nexo.v34i04.12684

Guo, L., Song, R., Wu, J., Xu, Z., & Zhao, F. (2024). Integrating a machine learning-driven fraud detection system based on a risk management framework. *Applied and Computational Engineering, 87*(1), 80–86. DOI: 10.54254/2755-2721/87/20241541

Ionescu, S. A., & Diaconita, V. (2023). Transforming Financial Decision-Making: The Interplay of AI, Cloud Computing and Advanced Data Management Technologies. *International Journal of Computers, Communications & Control, 18*(6), 1–19. DOI: 10.15837/ijccc.2023.6.5735

Khalifa, E. (2019). Blockchain: Technological Revolution in Business and Administration. *American Journal of Management, 19*(2), 40–46. DOI: 10.33423/ajm.v19i2.2066

Kostova, S., & Zhelev, Z. (2024). Application of Digital Tools Assessing Information Risk in the Control Activity. *Naše Gospodarstvo/Our Economy, 70*(2), 24–31. DOI: 10.2478/ngoe-2024-0009

Labaki, R. (2020). Risk Attitude Determinants and Risk Management in Family Business. *Risk Attitude Determinants and Risk Management in Family Business.*, *7*(3), 285–292.

Melnyk, O., Onyshchenko, S., Pavlova, N., Kravchenko, O., & Borovyk, S. (2022). Integrated Ship Cybersecurity Management as a Part of Maritime Safety and Security System. *IJCSNS International Journal of Computer Science and Network Security*, *22*(3), 135. DOI: 10.22937/IJCSNS.2022.22.3.18

Mohammed Anwar, A. (2023). Elevating Cybersecurity Audits: How AI is Shaping Compliance and Threat Detection. *Elevating Cybersecurity Audits: How AI Is Shaping Compliance and Threat Detection*, 1–9.

Mthiyane, Z. Z. F., van der Poll, H. M., & Tshehla, M. F. (2022). A Framework for Risk Management in Small Medium Enterprises in Developing Countries. *Risks*, *10*(9), 173. Advance online publication. DOI: 10.3390/risks10090173

Nutalapati, P. (2024). A Review on Cloud Computing in Finance-Transforming Financial Services in the Digital Age. *International Research Journal of Engineering & Applied Sciences | Irjeas. Org*, *12*, 35–45.

Odukoya, O. (2024). The Transformative Impact of Cloud Computing on Small and Medium-sized Enterprises (SMEs): A Comprehensive Analysis. *2024 International Conference on Smart Applications, Communications and Networking, SmartNets 2024*. DOI: 10.1109/SmartNets61466.2024.10577703

Ogunmokun, A. S., Balogun, E. D., & Ogunsola, K. O. (2022). A Strategic Fraud Risk Mitigation Framework for Corporate Finance Cost Optimization and Loss Prevention. *International Journal of Multidisciplinary Research and Growth Evaluation.*, *3*(1), 783–790. DOI: 10.54660/.IJMRGE.2022.3.1.783-790

Oladoyinbo, T. O., Adebiyi, O. O., Ugonnia, J. C., Olaniyi, O. O., & Okunleye, O. J. (2023). Evaluating and Establishing Baseline Security Requirements in Cloud Computing: An Enterprise Risk Management Approach. *Asian Journal of Economics. Business and Accounting*, *23*(21), 222–231. DOI: 10.9734/ajeba/2023/v23i211129

Otoo, F. N. K., Kaur, M., & Rather, N. A. (2023). Evaluating the impact of internal control systems on organizational effectiveness. *LBS Journal of Management & Research*, *21*(1), 135–154. DOI: 10.1108/LBSJMR-11-2022-0078

Parween, S., Sanghavi, H., Dubey, N., Prasan, U. D., Bharadwaj, R., Bhoopathy, V., & Reddy, B. A. (2026). Ethics, Bias Mitigation, and Model Risk Management. *Agile AI- Powered Project Management for Modern Delivery Organizations*, 191–215. DOI: 10.4018/979-8-3373-6851-1.ch006

Rahman, M. M., Pokharel, B. P., Sayeed, S. A., Bhowmik, S. K., Kshetri, N., & Eashrak, N. (2024). riskAIchain: AI-Driven IT Infrastructure—Blockchain-Backed Approach for Enhanced Risk Management. *Risks*, *12*(12), 206. Advance online publication. DOI: 10.3390/risks12120206

Rezvani, S. M. H. S., Falcão, M. J., Komljenovic, D., & de Almeida, N. M. (2023). A Systematic Literature Review on Urban Resilience Enabled with Asset and Disaster Risk Management Approaches and GIS-Based Decision Support Tools. *Applied Sciences (Basel, Switzerland)*, *13*(4), 2223. Advance online publication. DOI: 10.3390/app13042223

Richard Arogundade, O. (2023). Strategic Security Risk Management in Cloud Computing: A Comprehensive Examination and Application of the Risk Management Framework. *Iarjset*, *11*(1), 45–55. DOI: 10.17148/IARJSET.2024.11105

Saeed, S., Altamimi, S. A., Alkayyal, N. A., Alshehri, E., & Alabbad, D. A. (2023). Digital Transformation and Cybersecurity Challenges for Businesses Resilience: Issues and Recommendations. *Sensors (Basel)*, *23*(15), 1–20. DOI: 10.3390/s23156666 PMID: 37571451

Senturk, O., & Baghırov, A. (2023). Enhancing Sustainable Development Through Blockchain: A Study on Risk Management and Data Integrity. *Journal of Organizations. Technology and Entrepreneurship*, *1*(2), 110–126. DOI: 10.56578/jote010204

Shaikh, F. A., & Siponen, M. (2023). Information security risk assessments following cybersecurity breaches: The mediating role of top management attention to cybersecurity. *Computers & Security*, *124*, 102974. DOI: 10.1016/j.cose.2022.102974

Shaytura, S. V., Olenev, L. A., Nedelkin, A. A., Minitaeva, A. M., Ordov, K. V., & Feoktistova, V. M. (2021). Blockchain in Technogenic Safety and Risk Management. *International Journal of Emerging Technology and Advanced Engineering*, *11*(12), 72–78. DOI: 10.46338/ijetae1221_08

îrcovnicu, G.-I., & Ha egan, C.-D. (2023). Integration of Artificial Intelligence in the Risk Management Process: An Analysis of Opportunities and Challenges. *Journal of Financial Studies*, *8*(15), 198–214. DOI: 10.55654/JFS.2023.8.15.13

maliWen, H., & De Leon, J. (2024). Research on the Digital Transformation of Financial Management in Small and Medium-sized Enterprises Under the Background of Big Data and Cloud Computing. *Advances in Computer and Communication*, *4*(6), 351–357. DOI: 10.26855/acc.2023.12.002

Yenugula, M., Sahoo, S. K., & Goswami, S. S. (2023). Cloud computing in supply chain management: Exploring the relationship. *Management Science Letters*, *13*(3), 193–210. DOI: 10.5267/j.msl.2023.4.003

Zhong, X., & Enke, D. (2017). Forecasting daily stock market return using dimensionality reduction. *Expert Systems with Applications*, *67*, 126–139. DOI: 10.1016/j.eswa.2016.09.027

Chapter 10
Explainable Machine Learning-Driven Risk Management and Control Systems in Digital Organizations:
Interpreting Credit, Investment, and Financial Decisions

Chokkamreddy Prakash
http://orcid.org/0000-0002-3832-3740
Guru Nanak Institutions Technical Campus, India

Kasireddy Sandeep Reddy
http://orcid.org/0000-0003-4898-5569
Malla Reddy College of Engineering and Technology, India

Afef Amdouni
http://orcid.org/0000-0001-9625-300X
Taibah University, Saudi Arabia

ABSTRACT

The growing adoption of machine learning in digital organizations has enhanced the efficiency of financial risk management and decision-making. However, the opacity of advanced models raises concerns regarding transparency, trust, regulatory compliance, and managerial control. This chapter examines the role of Explainable Machine Learning (XML) in improving the interpretability of credit,

DOI: 10.4018/979-8-3373-9230-1.ch010

2027, IGI Global Scientific Publishing. Copying or distributing in print or electronic forms without written permission of IGI Global Scientific Publishing is prohibited. Use of this chapter to rative artificial intelligence (AI) technologies is expressly prohibited. The publisher reserves all rights to license its use for generative AI training and machine learning model development.

investment, and financial decisions. It develops and empirically tests a conceptual framework linking explainable ML, managerial interpretability, governance, and risk management effectiveness. The findings demonstrate that XML enhances decision transparency, strengthens internal control systems, and supports trust in AI-driven financial environments. The chapter contributes to the literature on explainable AI in financial analytics and offers practical insights for its responsible implementation.

1. INTRODUCTION

The rapid digital transformation of organizations has fundamentally reshaped financial decision-making processes, particularly in areas such as credit risk assessment, investment allocation, and enterprise risk monitoring. With the increasing availability of large-scale data and advanced analytics, digital organizations are progressively adopting machine learning (ML) models to enhance predictive accuracy and operational efficiency in financial risk management (Chen et al., 2024; Martins et al., 2024). These models enable the identification of complex, non-linear risk patterns that are difficult to capture using traditional statistical approaches. Recent research further highlights the expanding role of machine learning in emerging financial domains such as climate finance and sustainable investment, where complex and multidimensional risk structures require advanced analytical approaches (Tian et al., 2025).

Despite these advancements, the increasing reliance on advanced ML models has introduced a critical challenge: the lack of transparency in algorithmic decision-making. Many models operate as opaque "black-box" systems, limiting the ability of managers, regulators, and stakeholders to understand how decisions are generated. This lack of interpretability raises concerns regarding trust, accountability, regulatory compliance, and the effectiveness of internal control systems (Arrieta et al., 2020; Weller, 2019). In financial contexts, where decisions must be both accurate and justifiable, this limitation represents a significant barrier to the effective adoption of AI-driven systems. Moreover, the growing complexity of financial models has amplified concerns related to model risk, as increasingly sophisticated algorithms may introduce new forms of uncertainty and opacity into financial decision-making processes (Cosma et al., 2023).

To address these challenges, Explainable Machine Learning (XML) has emerged as a key research direction. XML encompasses techniques that enhance model interpretability by revealing the contribution of input variables and the logic underlying predictions (Doshi-Velez & Kim, 2017; Biecek & Burzykowski, 2021). In financial applications, explainability plays a critical role in improving transparency, supporting governance, and enabling more informed decision-making (Varshney, 2019).

Empirical evidence suggests that explainable ML techniques—such as SHAP and LIME—enhance transparency in credit risk assessment and strengthen confidence in AI-driven financial decisions (Rafi et al., 2024; Kalra & Mittal, 2024).

However, the existing literature remains fragmented. Prior research has primarily focused on the technical development of explainability methods or their application in isolated financial contexts such as credit scoring and investment analytics (Guidotti et al., 2019; Černevičienė & Kabašinskas, 2024). Limited attention has been given to how explainable ML integrates into broader organizational risk management and control systems. Furthermore, the role of managerial interpretability as a mechanism that translates explainable outputs into effective organizational outcomes remains underexplored. Emerging research also suggests that governance structures play a critical role in shaping how risk-related information is translated into financial outcomes, particularly in contexts involving sustainability and complex financial risks (Barka et al., 2026).

To address this gap, this study develops an integrated framework that examines how explainable machine learning influences risk management effectiveness in digital organizations. The framework proposes that explainable ML affects organizational outcomes both directly and indirectly through managerial interpretability, which serves as a mediating construct linking model explanations to decision-making processes. Figure 1 illustrates the proposed conceptual framework, highlighting the relationships between explainable machine learning, managerial interpretability, and risk management outcomes.

Figure 1. Conceptual Framework of Explainable Machine Learning–Driven Risk Management and Control Systems

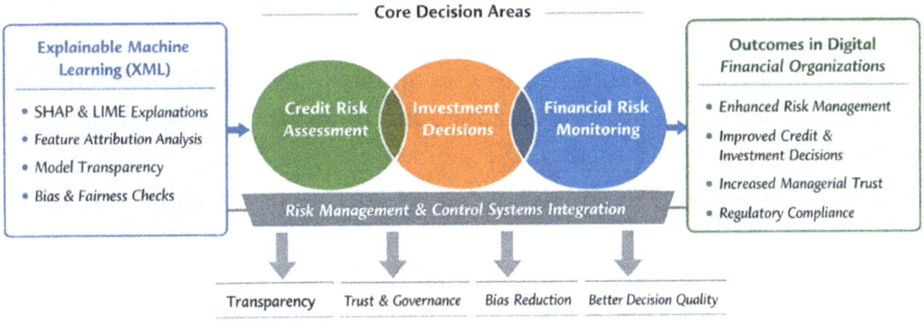

Figure 1 presents the conceptual model in which explainable machine learning (XML) serves as the primary independent construct influencing risk management effectiveness both directly and indirectly through managerial interpretability. The model captures the mediating role of interpretability in translating model explanations into actionable managerial insights. It also reflects the direct impact of XML on key financial decision domains, including credit risk assessment, investment decision-making, and financial risk monitoring, which together contribute to organizational control and governance outcomes.

Accordingly, the study tests the following hypotheses:

H1: Explainable machine learning positively influences risk management effectiveness.

H2: Managerial interpretability mediates the relationship between explainable ML and risk management effectiveness.

H3: Explainable ML improves financial decision quality (credit and investment decisions).

This study makes three main contributions. First, it extends the literature by positioning explainable machine learning as a governance-enabling mechanism rather than merely a technical enhancement. Second, it provides empirical evidence on the mediating role of managerial interpretability in AI-driven financial decision-making. Third, it offers practical insights into how organizations can integrate explainable ML into risk management and control systems.

The remainder of this chapter is structured as follows. Section 2 presents the methodological approach, followed by the empirical results in Section 3. Section 4 discusses the findings and their implications. The final section concludes the chapter and outlines directions for future research.

2. METHODS

2.1 Research Design

This study adopts a hybrid empirical design that integrates machine learning (ML), explainable machine learning (XML), and structural equation modeling (SEM). The research follows a two-stage analytical pipeline. In the first stage, supervised ML models are developed to generate predictive insights related to credit risk, investment decisions, and financial risk monitoring. In the second stage, explainability techniques are applied to extract interpretable outputs, which are then incorporated into a structural framework to examine their effects on managerial interpretability and risk management effectiveness.

2.2 Data and Sample

The empirical analysis is based on a dataset comprising 320 observations covering the period 2019–2024. The dataset integrates multiple data sources, including digital lending records, investment portfolio data, and financial risk indicators. In addition, organizational variables related to managerial interpretability and governance are constructed based on established measurement approaches in the literature. The dataset is cross-sectional, with each observation representing a financial decision instance.

2.3 Unit of Analysis

The unit of analysis is the financial decision instance, defined as an integrated observation that captures credit, investment, and risk-related attributes within a digital organizational context. Multi-level data (credit-level, portfolio-level, and organizational-level variables) are harmonized into a unified analytical structure using normalization and aggregation procedures.

2.4 Variables and Measurement

Explainable Machine Learning (XML) is operationalized through model explanation outputs, including feature importance scores, SHAP values, and local interpretability measures. Managerial interpretability reflects the extent to which decision-makers can understand and utilize model explanations. Risk management effectiveness is measured using indicators related to decision quality, risk monitoring accuracy, and control system performance.

Control variables include macroeconomic conditions, interest rate fluctuations, regulatory constraints, and organizational risk tolerance.

2.5 Machine Learning Models

The study employs multiple supervised learning algorithms, including logistic regression, random forest, gradient boosting (XGBoost), and support vector machines (SVM). The dataset is divided into training and testing sets using an 80:20 split. Model performance is evaluated using k-fold cross-validation to ensure robustness and generalizability.

2.6 Explainable Machine Learning Techniques

To enhance model interpretability, the study applies SHAP (Shapley Additive Explanations) for global and local feature importance, LIME (Local Interpretable Model-Agnostic Explanations) for instance-level explanations, and feature attribution methods to identify key drivers of financial risk.

2.7 Structural Equation Modeling

Structural equation modeling (SEM) is used to test the hypothesized relationships between explainable ML, managerial interpretability, and risk management outcomes. The analysis is conducted using AMOS. Model fit is assessed using standard indices, including chi-square/degrees of freedom (χ^2/df), comparative fit index (CFI), Tucker–Lewis index (TLI), and root mean square error of approximation (RMSEA).

Mediation effects are tested using bootstrapping procedures to estimate indirect effects. The significance of the mediating role of managerial interpretability is evaluated by examining both direct and indirect paths.

2.8 Model Evaluation

Model performance is evaluated using accuracy, precision, recall, F1-score, and area under the ROC curve (AUC). The effectiveness of explainability is assessed through the consistency and usability of model explanations in supporting managerial decision-making.

3. RESULTS

This section presents the empirical findings corresponding to the proposed hypotheses and analytical framework.

3.1 Descriptive Statistics

Descriptive statistics indicate relatively high mean values across the main constructs, including explainable machine learning, managerial interpretability, and risk management effectiveness. The distribution of the variables suggests a generally strong adoption of explainable ML practices within the sampled digital organizations.

Table 1. Descriptive Statistics of Constructs

Construct	Mean	Std. Deviation
Explainable ML Adoption	3.92	0.71
Credit Risk Assessment	3.88	0.74
Investment Decision Quality	3.9	0.72
Financial Risk Monitoring	3.95	0.7

continued on following page

Table 1. Continued

Construct	Mean	Std. Deviation
Risk Management Effectiveness	4.01	0.68
Managerial Interpretability	4.12	0.63

3.2 Model Fit Assessment

The structural equation model demonstrates a satisfactory fit to the data. All model fit indices exceed commonly accepted thresholds, indicating that the proposed model adequately represents the observed relationships. Specifically, χ^2/df values fall within acceptable ranges, while CFI and TLI exceed recommended levels, and RMSEA values indicate a good model fit.

Table 2. Model Fit Indices (AMOS Output)

Fit Index	Recommended Value	Observed Value
χ^2/df	< 3.00	2.36
CFI	≥ 0.90	0.943
TLI	≥ 0.90	0.932
RMSEA	≤ 0.08	0.065

Figure 2 illustrates the estimated structural model, showing standardized path coefficients between the constructs.

Figure 2. Structural Equation Model Results (AMOS Output)

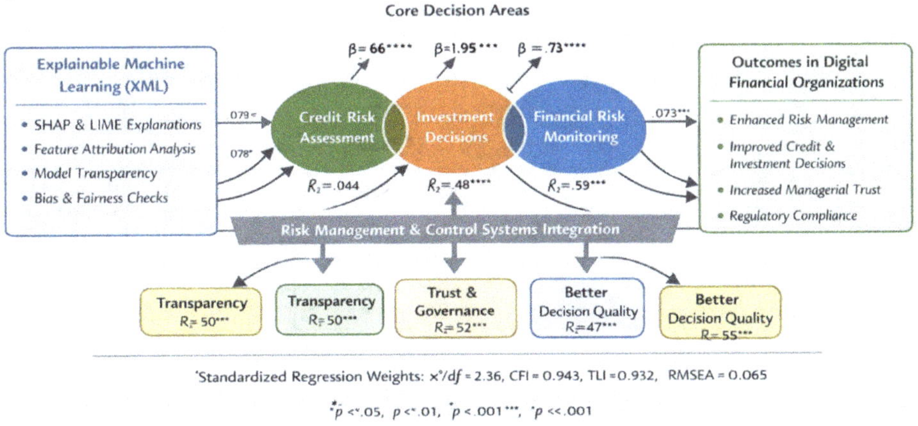

As shown in Figure 2, the standardized path coefficients confirm the hypothesized relationships among explainable ML, managerial interpretability, and risk management effectiveness.

3.3 Hypothesis Testing

The results provide empirical support for all proposed hypotheses. Explainable machine learning has a positive and statistically significant effect on risk management effectiveness. In addition, explainable ML significantly improves financial decision quality, including credit risk assessment and investment decision-making.

The mediation analysis indicates that managerial interpretability has a significant indirect effect on the relationship between explainable ML and risk management effectiveness. The bootstrapping results confirm the presence of partial mediation.

Table 3. Structural Model Results

Hypothesis	Path	Std. β	p-value	Result
H1	XML → Risk Management Effectiveness	0.62	< .001	Supported
H2a	XML → Managerial Interpretability	0.69	< .001	Supported
H2b	Managerial Interpretability → Risk Management	0.56	< .001	Supported
H3	XML → Financial Decision Quality	0.61	< .001	Supported

3.4 Machine Learning Performance

The machine learning models demonstrate high predictive performance across all financial domains examined. Classification metrics—including accuracy, precision, recall, and F1-score—indicate strong model performance. Additionally, AUC values confirm the models' high discriminative capability.

Table 4. Classification Model Performance Metrics

Metric	Credit Risk Model	Investment Risk Model	Financial Risk Monitoring
Accuracy	0.89	0.87	0.91
Precision	0.86	0.84	0.88
Recall	0.83	0.81	0.86
F1-Score	0.84	0.82	0.87
AUC (ROC)	0.92	0.9	0.94

Table 5. Mediation Analysis Results

Path	Indirect Effect	p-value	Mediation Type
XML → Interpretability → Risk Management	0.38	< .001	Partial

3.5 Explainability Evaluation

Explainability techniques produce consistent and stable explanations across different observations. Feature importance analysis and local explanations reveal key drivers of financial risk decisions, indicating that model outputs can be effectively interpreted.

Table 6. Explainability Effectiveness Assessment

Dimension	Mean	Std. Deviation	Interpretation
Stability of Explanations	4.21	0.61	High
Consistency Across Models	4.09	0.64	High
Managerial Interpretability	4.28	0.58	Very High
Usability for Decision-Making	4.34	0.55	Very High
Trust in ML Decisions	4.31	0.57	Very High

**Scale:* 1 = Very Low, 5 = Very High

4. DISCUSSION

The findings provide empirical support for all proposed hypotheses. The findings of this study provide strong empirical evidence that explainable machine learning plays a central role in enhancing financial risk management and control systems in digital organizations. The results indicate that explainability contributes not only to predictive performance but also to the interpretability and usability of model outputs, thereby extending the role of machine learning from a purely technical tool to a decision-enabling and governance-supporting mechanism.

The significant relationship between explainable ML and risk management effectiveness highlights the importance of transparency in algorithmic decision-making. This finding reinforces prior research emphasizing that opacity in AI systems can undermine trust, accountability, and regulatory compliance (Arrieta et al., 2020; Weller, 2019). More importantly, the results suggest that explainability mitigates one of the core limitations of advanced financial analytics—namely, the disconnect between model complexity and managerial understanding.

This insight becomes particularly relevant when viewed through the lens of model risk. As financial models become increasingly complex, they introduce new forms of uncertainty and risk associated with their opacity and interpretability limitations (Cosma et al., 2023). In this context, the findings of this study suggest that explainable machine learning serves not only as a transparency tool but also as a mechanism for reducing model risk by improving traceability, interpretability, and oversight of algorithmic decisions. This finding reinforces the argument that explainability should be considered an integral component of model risk management frameworks rather than a supplementary feature.

The mediation results further highlight the critical role of managerial interpretability as a central mechanism through which explainable ML influences organizational outcomes. This finding supports the argument that technical explanations alone are insufficient unless they are cognitively processed and utilized by decision-makers. In this sense, managerial interpretability functions as a bridging construct that connects algorithmic outputs with actionable decisions, thereby enhancing the effectiveness of risk management systems.

From a governance perspective, the results align with emerging evidence suggesting that governance mechanisms play a crucial role in shaping how risk-related information is translated into financial outcomes (Barka et al., 2026). This implies that explainability and governance should not be treated as separate dimensions, but rather as complementary elements within AI-driven financial systems. Explainable ML enhances governance by enabling auditability and accountability, while governance structures ensure that interpreted insights are effectively embedded into organizational decision processes.

In addition, the positive impact of explainable ML on financial decision quality extends prior research in financial analytics by demonstrating that explainability improves not only model transparency but also the quality of credit and investment decisions. This finding is particularly relevant in emerging financial domains such as climate finance and sustainable investment, where decision-making involves complex, multidimensional risk factors that require both predictive accuracy and interpretability (Tian et al., 2025). In such contexts, explainability enables decision-makers to better understand trade-offs between financial and non-financial risks, thereby improving strategic decision-making.

The study also contributes to the broader literature on AI governance by positioning explainable machine learning as a governance-enabling mechanism rather than merely a technical enhancement. This perspective extends existing research by highlighting that the value of explainability lies not only in improving model outputs but also in facilitating organizational control, regulatory compliance, and strategic alignment.

The findings suggest that organizations should integrate explainable machine learning into their risk management frameworks to enhance transparency, accountability, and decision quality. In particular, managers should prioritize interpretability when adopting AI systems to ensure that model outputs can be effectively understood and utilized. This is especially important in high-stakes financial environments where regulatory scrutiny and risk exposure are significant.

This study is subject to several limitations. First, the dataset is limited in size and scope, which may affect the generalizability of the findings. Second, the integration of multi-level data into a unified analytical framework may introduce measurement challenges. Third, while the study captures key dimensions of explainability, other forms of interpretability and human–AI interaction mechanisms may also influence decision outcomes.

Future research could extend this study by examining the role of explainable machine learning in ESG-driven financial models and climate risk analytics, where the interaction between transparency, governance, and sustainability outcomes remains underexplored (Carè & Weber, 2023). In addition, longitudinal studies could provide deeper insights into how explainability influences organizational learning and decision-making over time.

Further research could also investigate the integration of advanced explainability techniques, such as counterfactual explanations and causal machine learning, to enhance decision quality in complex financial environments. Finally, exploring the behavioral dimensions of interpretability—particularly how different stakeholders perceive and utilize explainable AI—represents a promising avenue for future inquiry.

5. CONCLUSION

This study examined the role of explainable machine learning in enhancing risk management and control systems within digital organizations. By integrating machine learning techniques with explainability methods and structural equation modeling, the study provides empirical evidence that explainable ML improves risk management effectiveness, financial decision quality, and organizational control mechanisms.

The findings demonstrate that explainability addresses a critical limitation of traditional black-box models by enabling transparency, interpretability, and accountability in financial decision-making. More importantly, the results highlight the mediating role of managerial interpretability, showing that the impact of explainable ML on organizational outcomes depends on the ability of decision-makers to understand and utilize model explanations.

From a theoretical perspective, this study contributes to the literature by positioning explainable machine learning as a governance-enabling mechanism rather than merely a technical enhancement. From a practical perspective, it offers a structured approach for integrating explainable ML into risk management frameworks, thereby improving decision transparency and strengthening internal control systems.

Overall, the study suggests that the future effectiveness of AI-driven financial systems will increasingly depend not only on predictive accuracy but also on the ability to ensure transparency, interpretability, and governance of algorithmic decision-making processes.

REFERENCES

Arrieta, A. B., Díaz-Rodríguez, N., Del Ser, J., Bennetot, A., Tabik, S., Barbado, A., García, S., Gil-López, S., Molina, D., Benjamins, R., Chatila, R., & Herrera, F. (2020). Explainable artificial intelligence (XAI): Concepts, taxonomies, opportunities and challenges toward responsible AI. *Information Fusion*, *58*, 82–115. DOI: 10.1016/j.inffus.2019.12.012

Biecek, P., & Burzykowski, T. (2021). *Explanatory model analysis: Explore, explain, and examine predictive models*. CRC Press., DOI: 10.1201/9780429027192

Carè, R., & Weber, O. (2023). The role of ESG in sustainable finance: A review and research agenda. *Business Strategy and the Environment*, *32*(4), 1897–1913. DOI: 10.1002/bse.3210

Černevičienė, J., & Kabašinskas, A. (2024). Explainable artificial intelligence (XAI) in finance: A systematic literature review. *Artificial Intelligence Review*, *57*(8), 216. DOI: 10.1007/s10462-024-10854-8

Chen, J., Li, K., Deng, H., & Wang, S. (2024). Explainable machine learning models for credit risk evaluation. *Expert Systems with Applications*, *238*, 121876. DOI: 10.1016/j.eswa.2023.121876

Cosma, S., Gualandri, E., & Venturelli, V. (2023). Model risk in financial systems: Implications for governance and decision-making. *Finance Research Letters*, *55*, 103867. DOI: 10.1016/j.frl.2023.103867

Doshi-Velez, F., & Kim, B. (2017). Towards a rigorous science of interpretable machine learning. https://doi.org//arXiv.1702.08608DOI: 10.48550

Guidotti, R., Monreale, A., Ruggieri, S., Turini, F., Giannotti, F., & Pedreschi, D. (2019). A survey of methods for explaining black box models. *ACM Computing Surveys*, *51*(5), 1–42. DOI: 10.1145/3236009

Kalra, A., & Mittal, R. (2024). Explainable AI for improved financial decision support in trading. https://doi.org/DOI: 10.1109/ICRITO61523.2024.10522366

Martins, T., de Almeida, A. M., Cardoso, E., & Nunes, L. (2024). Explainable artificial intelligence: A systematic literature review on taxonomies and applications in finance. *IEEE Access : Practical Innovations, Open Solutions*, *12*, 618–629. DOI: 10.1109/ACCESS.2023.3347028

Rafi, M. A., Shaboj, S. M. I., Miah, M. K., Rasul, I., Islam, M. R., & Ahmed, A. (2024). Explainable AI for credit risk assessment: Improving transparency and fairness. *Journal of Economics. Finance and Accounting Studies*, *6*(1), 108–118. DOI: 10.32996/jefas.2024.6.1.11

Varshney, K. R. (2019). Trustworthy machine learning and artificial intelligence. *XRDS*, *25*(3), 26–29. DOI: 10.1145/3313109

Weller, A. (2019). Transparency: Motivations and challenges. In *Explainable AI* (pp. 23–40). Springer. https://doi.org/DOI: 10.1007/978-3-030-28954-6_2

Chapter 11
Financial Data Governance Mechanisms in Open Banking:
Balancing Digital Innovation With Customer Protection

Indra Faisal Rizki Mufid
http://orcid.org/0009-0009-0687-8256
Universitas Sebelas Maret Surakarta, Indonesia

Bayu Tri Cahya
UIN Sunan Kudus, Indonesia

Khalida Kumalasari
http://orcid.org/0009-0009-8433-3825
Universitas Duta Bangsa Surakarta, Indonesia

ABSTRACT

The development of digital technology has changed the way the banking industry operates, particularly through the implementation of the Open Banking concept. In this study, banks no longer stand as closed entities but become part of a financial ecosystem interconnected through Application Programming Interfaces (APIs). This structured data exchange opens opportunities for increased operational efficiency, more responsive financial services, and expanded access to banking services. This study discusses financial data governance in the context of Open Banking by integrating perspectives from information systems, internal control, and banking

DOI: 10.4018/979-8-3373-9230-1.ch011

2027, IGI Global Scientific Publishing. Copying or distributing in print or electronic forms without written permission of IGI Global Scientific Publishing is prohibited. Use of this chapter to
rative artificial intelligence (AI) technologies is expressly prohibited. The publisher reserves all rights to license its use for generative AI training and machine learning model development.

regulations. The discussion focuses on how the role of internal control needs to be adjusted to effectively manage cross-system data flows, and on its implications for the stability and resilience of the banking system in the digital era.

INTRODUCTION

The paradigm of rapidly developing financial technology has enabled traditional financial regulations to face unprecedented challenges. Open banking has emerged as a response to the need for transparency, openness, and innovation in the digital financial sector. For years, customer data has been locked within traditional banking systems, limiting access and utilization to incumbent financial institutions (Dahdal & Zeiler, 2021; Hermawan et al., 2023; Khamitdkhanovich et al., 2025).

In fact, open banking is the integration of technology and regulatory systems that enable customers to securely share their banking information with external service providers via *Application Programming Interfaces* (APIs). This initiative aims to disrupt the dominance of conventional banking, encourage healthy competition, and improve consumer welfare by offering more practical, personalized services. (Babin & Smith, 2022; Kassab et al., 2022) . In this transition to an open system, consumers are no longer passive objects but rightful owners of their data assets, with full autonomy over the distribution of their information. (Blanchard et al., 2026; Dahdal & Zeiler, 2021). Thus, open banking creates opportunities for a more inclusive, efficient, and consumer-oriented financial ecosystem.

The rapid evolution of financial technology has rendered traditional regulations inadequate. Open banking emerged to address requirements for transparency and innovation by breaking the "data lock" held by incumbent institutions. By utilizing Application Programming Interfaces (APIs), customers transition from passive subjects to autonomous owners of their data assets. While initiatives like the EU's PSD2 and Australia's Consumer Data Right (CDR) reflect a commitment to consumer empowerment, they also introduce systemic risks. In Australia, the CDR treats data as "open data capitalism," a strategic asset that requires controlled utilization to prevent market distortion (Jones, 2025). Thus, third-party providers (TPPs) act as critical intermediaries whose governance determines the balance between competition and consumer safety.

Technological developments such as mobile internet, cloud computing, big data, machine learning, artificial intelligence, and *the Internet of Things* (IoT) have created new opportunities and challenges for the banking industry (Hasan et al., 2023; Kapoor et al., 2024; F. Sun, 2021). These innovations not only address technological aspects but also transform the basic structure of the banking industry. Large banks that were previously dominant are now required to adapt to the new ecosystem and emphasize continuous, open cross-sector collaboration. In this ecosystem, consumers are the focus and have greater control over their personal data. This direction of change is reinforced by regulations across various countries, such as the Payment Services Directive 2 (PSD2) in the European Union and the *Consumer Data Right* (CDR) in Australia, which reflect a strong commitment to data protection and consumer empowerment in the digital age.

In this study, it is important to understand open banking regulations across countries, especially as a basis for understanding how Australia implements *the Consumer Data Right* (CDR) system. CDR was born as Australia's first step toward developing the concept of "open data capitalism," which treats consumer data as an asset that can be used safely and under controlled conditions. Similar to the European Union, Australia emphasizes the protection and control of personal data. Open banking regulations there demonstrate a cautious policy response to digital financial developments, while reaffirming the country's ongoing commitment to protecting and empowering consumers in the digital age. Therefore, third-party service providers play an important role in sharing banking data to regulate this concept (Gauci, 2019; Pati & Pratama, 2025). Thus, open banking aims to increase competition and innovation in the financial industry (Ziegler, 2021).

FINANCIAL DATA GOVERNANCE FOR CONSUMER TRUST

Data governance plays a crucial role in preventing third-party misuse of personal data, thereby strengthening consumer trust. Regulations such as *the General Data Protection Regulation* (GDPR) in Europe and the Data Protection Act are key in this context (Bartolacci & Caputo, 2020; Bartolini et al., 2019; Becker et al., 2024; Emili, 2019; Magdolen & Lovecek, 2023). The GDPR introduces several key principles aimed at protecting personal data:

1. Accountability

Organizations must demonstrate compliance with GDPR principles, including legitimacy, fairness, transparency, purpose limitation, data minimization, accuracy, storage limitation, integrity, confidentiality, and data protection. Organizations must not only comply with the rules, but also provide tangible evidence that they have implemented appropriate technical and organizational measures. Accountability in financial data governance is not just about complying with the rules on paper. It is an ethical foundation that requires financial institutions to be truly responsible for every customer data processing operation.

Amid the strict implementation of the GDPR, accountability demands more than mere transparency jargon: organizations must provide concrete evidence that data protection is implemented consistently. This principle has evolved into a risk-mitigation mechanism that protects two things at once: the institution's integrity, ensuring it remains trusted by the public, and customers' digital sovereignty, maintaining their rights to their personal data. With accountability, financial institutions not only avoid regulatory sanctions but also build long-term trust, the primary asset in the digital financial ecosystem.

2. Integrity and Confidentiality

Personal data must be protected from unauthorized or unlawful processing. Entities guarantee that financial data remains accurate, consistent, and is not modified unlawfully. Integrity is fundamental to financial reporting, risk management, and decision-making. It is important to ensure that personal and financial data is accessible only to authorized parties. Confidentiality protects consumers from the misuse of information, identity theft, and privacy violations.

3. Transparency and User Control

The GDPR emphasizes transparent data protection policies and user control over their data. In the context of financial data governance, transparency and user control are not merely additional principles; they are the foundation that determines the quality of the relationship between financial institutions and customers. Regulations such as the GDPR require that every data protection policy be communicated clearly, understandably, and honestly. This includes explanations of how personal data is collected, the purposes for which it is used, and the storage and protection mechanisms that are implemented.

Transparency allows consumers to assess whether data processing is in their best interests, while user control ensures that customers remain the rightful owners of their personal data. This control includes the right to give consent, withdraw permission, and determine the limits of data use. Thus, consumers are no longer passive objects but active actors with full authority over their financial information.

The combination of transparency and user control creates a more ethical and sustainable financial ecosystem. Financial institutions that can present open policies while providing real control to customers will gain stronger public trust. This trust ultimately becomes social capital that encourages widespread adoption of digital services, strengthens institutions' reputations, and ensures the sustainability of financial innovation in the digital economy.

4. Data Protection Officer (DPO)

The appointment of a DPO is one way to ensure compliance and accountability. The appointment of a Data Protection Officer (DPO) is a strategic step that affirms a financial institution's commitment to regulatory compliance while strengthening accountability in the management of personal data. The DPO not only serves as a technical supervisor but also as a guardian of the organization's ethics and integrity, ensuring that all data processing procedures comply with GDPR principles. As a liaison among regulators, institutions, and consumers, the DPO plays a central role in overseeing compliance, providing consultation, and ensuring the effectiveness of data protection mechanisms. Their presence symbolizes the organization's responsibility to go beyond formal compliance by providing tangible evidence that data protection is being implemented consistently.

In the financial sector, the DPO plays an important role in maintaining consumer trust, strengthening institutional integrity, and protecting customer digital sovereignty. Through strict supervision, periodic audits, and privacy risk management, the DPO helps financial institutions build a more transparent, secure, and sustainable ecosystem. Thus, the appointment of a DPO is not merely a regulatory obligation but part of a financial data governance strategy that prioritizes consumer protection while making accountability a competitive advantage in the digital economy.

Digital transformation in the financial sector presents great opportunities through innovations such as fintech, digital banking, and open banking. These innovations promote financial inclusion, accelerate services, and improve efficiency. However, this acceleration also poses new risks: data leaks, consumer exploitation, and legal uncertainty. (Kapoor et al., 2024; Khamitdkhanovich et al., 2025; Shamurailatpam, 2023) . Therefore, balancing innovation with consumer protection has become a strategic agenda in financial data governance.

1. Dimensions of Balance

Innovation in the financial sector, such as the development of technology-based products, open APIs, and data-driven services, offers significant opportunities to improve efficiency and financial inclusion. However, this innovation must go hand in hand with consumer protection that guarantees security, privacy, and control over personal data. Adaptive regulation is key: flexible enough to support technological development, but strict in protecting consumer rights.

2. Mechanisms of Balance

a) *Regulatory Harmonization*: Cross-border regulatory synchronization is necessary to prevent innovation from being hampered by legal fragmentation. This harmonization provides certainty for industry players while protecting consumers in various jurisdictions.
b) *Risk-Based Approach*: Risk-based regulation enables proportional oversight. Services with a significant potential impact on consumers are monitored more closely, while low-risk innovations are given room to grow.
c) *Collaborative Governance*: Collaboration between regulators, financial institutions, and consumers creates a healthy ecosystem. Consumers are not only protected but also involved in decision-making regarding the use of their data.

3. Implications

Transparency in data management practices and strong data protection measures are essential for building consumer trust in digital financial services. This study shows that transparent and ethical data management practices can increase consumer trust (El-Annan & Hassoun, 2024; Prastyanti & Sharma, 2024). Effective data protection laws and transparent practices reduce privacy concerns and increase consumer trust in digital services. Government policy is a very strong foundation for establishing rules across all lines.

BASIC CONCEPTS OF OPEN BANKING

This concept is not just about technological efficiency, but about returning information sovereignty to customers. By breaking down the walls of banking data monopoly, open banking creates space for more personalized and responsive financial services. However, behind the ease of third-party access lies a high demand for accountability to ensure that data exchange remains within the bounds of absolute ethics and security. (de Araluze & Plaza, 2023; Hermawan et al., 2023; Khamitdkhanovich et al., 2025; Stranieri et al., 2021). There are benefits to open banking (Khamitdkhanovich et al., 2025; Oprea, 2024; Premchand & Choudhry, 2018), namely as follows:

1. Increased Competition

Open banking opens up broader competition opportunities within the financial ecosystem. By granting third-party service providers access to banking data based on customer consent, previously high entry barriers are lowered. This encourages the emergence of new business models, accelerates innovation, and challenges the dominance of traditional financial institutions.

2. Enhanced Consumer Services

Open banking enables more personalized, efficient services. Financial data integration enables the development of digital solutions such as electronic wallets, robo-advisors, and financing schemes tailored to individual risk profiles and needs. As a result, the user experience becomes more connected, responsive, and data-driven.

3. Financial Inclusion

Open banking has the potential to expand financial inclusion. By using alternative data and advanced analytics, groups previously underserved by the conventional banking system can gain access to financial services better suited to their circumstances. In this context, open banking serves not only as an instrument of innovation but also as a mechanism for expanding economic participation more evenly.

THE ROLE OF API IN DATA SHARING BETWEEN FINANCIAL INSTITUTIONS

Application Programming Interfaces (APIs) are crucial to facilitating open banking by enabling secure, efficient data sharing between financial institutions and third-party service providers. This integration supports innovation, enhances customer experience, and encourages competition in the financial sector. APIs provide standardized interfaces that facilitate real-time communication between banks and third parties. APIs enable bank customers to share their data with third-party financial institutions and FinTech companies, promoting the adoption of open banking and data portability (Lin et al., 2025). This capability improves the efficiency and security of data sharing, which is essential for modern banking services.

By integrating APIs with *Core Banking Solutions* (CBS), banks can create innovative products tailored to consumer needs, market demand, and regulatory requirements. (Ul Alam et al., 2022). This integration supports the development of digital wallets, robo-advisors, and customized lending solutions. (Khamitdkhanovich et al., 2025). The implementation of *Application Programming Interfaces* (APIs) in the banking sector did not develop naturally. However, it was driven by strict regulations, such as *the European Union's Revised Payment Services Directive (PSD2)*. This regulation requires financial institutions to provide secure data access to authorized third parties, thereby strengthening the competitive climate and encouraging the emergence of financial service innovations. (Hermawan et al., 2023; Khamitdkhanovich et al., 2025) .

However, the obligation to share data also brings new challenges, particularly regarding security risks. APIs are a critical component of system architecture, as any weakness in design or implementation can lead to data leaks and threaten the protection of customer information. (Behbehani et al., 2022; Kumar & Gandhi, 2023; Ul Alam et al., 2022) . Therefore, API security governance must be treated as a strategic priority, not merely a technical requirement or a form of regulatory compliance. With the right approach, APIs can be a catalyst for innovation while maintaining public trust in digital financial systems.

The transition from open banking to open finance marks a further phase in the development of contemporary financial services. This change is not merely an expansion of the scope of technology but a reflection of a more systemic transformation in how financial data and services are managed. This dynamic is driven not only by increasingly sophisticated digital innovations but also by an evolving and increasingly structured regulatory framework governing data governance, consumer protection, and cross-sector financial integration.

Open banking focuses on mechanisms for securely sharing banking data between financial institutions and third-party service providers. The goal is to improve the quality of the customer experience while strengthening competition in the financial industry (Dahdal & Zeiler, 2021; De Pascalis & Brener, 2024; Kassab et al., 2022; Schneider, 2023). Conversely, open finance extends this principle of openness beyond traditional banking to include other sectors, such as insurance, pensions, investments, and other financial products. With a broader scope, open finance aims to build a more comprehensive, integrated, and inclusive financial ecosystem (Khamitdkhanovich et al., 2025; Pereira, 2025; Standaert & Muylle, 2022).

In the public policy framework, (OECD, 2022) emphasizes that the shift towards open finance cannot be understood narrowly as a matter of financial sector innovation, but rather as part of a broader data governance agenda. Regulation serves a strategic function by balancing the need to encourage innovation with the need to protect consumers. At the same time, well-designed policies can foster a more inclusive, accountable, and sustainability-oriented financial ecosystem.

STRATEGIC RISKS AND API GOVERNANCE

Open banking disrupts traditional models but introduces vulnerabilities, including data leakage and authorization abuse. System interconnection increases the attack surface for cyber threats like phishing and malware. First, internal control evolution: Banks must shift from static, periodic transaction checks to real-time and data-flow monitoring. Second, API Vulnerabilities: weaknesses in API design can lead to identity theft and fraudulent transactions. Therefore, implementing robust Data Leakage Prevention (DLP) and AI-driven anomaly detection is a strategic necessity, not just a technical requirement.

FINANCIAL DATA GOVERNANCE MECHANISMS

Financial data management is a critical aspect of modern financial operations, involving the collection, processing, storage, and analysis of financial data to support decision-making and ensure operational efficiency. Financial data governance mechanisms are built on three main principles: transparency, accountability, and security. (Bezzina et al., 2021; Harwood, 2017; Mabillard & Zumofen, 2021). Transparency ensures that the flow of data use and processing is understandable to consumers and regulators, including who accesses the data and for what purposes. Accountability requires financial institutions to be fully responsible for managing customer data, with clear auditing and reporting mechanisms to ensure compliance. Meanwhile, security emphasizes data protection through encryption, access controls, and strict institutional policies to maintain public trust in the digital financial system. Some of the key mechanisms and technologies used in financial data management are (Mou & Xu, 2020; Xu, 2025), including:

1. Big Data and Distributed Systems
   a) Big Data Sharing: The use of distributed file systems and data connection models can simplify data management and improve decision-making processes by integrating collective wisdom and data rationality.
   b) Data Warehousing: Data warehouse technology plays a crucial role in integrating data from various business systems into a central repository, providing comprehensive and real-time data support for decision making.
2. Security and Privacy
   a) Digital Signatures and Encryption: Ensuring the authenticity and security of financial data in open networks through digital signatures and encryption protocols (Lei et al., 2025; Shiraishi, 2021).

b) Data Integrity Management: Using cloud-based ledger databases, database keys, and artificial intelligence (AI) to manage data integrity issues (Lat, 2024).

3. Financial Data Analysis and Fraud Detection

Big Data and Cloud Technologies: Utilizing these technologies for fraud detection, data retrieval, and analysis, ensuring scalability, security, and flexibility (Popovici et al., 2024).

Effective financial data management mechanisms involve a combination of advanced technology, secure data handling practices, and integrated software solutions. These mechanisms not only improve the efficiency and accuracy of financial operations but also ensure the security and integrity of financial data, thereby supporting robust decision-making processes in dynamic market conditions. In practice, financial data management focuses not only on technical aspects but also covers regulatory and ethical dimensions. When data is managed properly, financial institutions can optimize risk management by detecting potential fraud and market instability early. In addition, service quality can be improved by offering more personalized, tailored products to customers' needs. Effective governance also ensures regulatory compliance through audit mechanisms, reporting, and the implementation of strict security standards. Furthermore, the use of advanced analytics and cross-platform integration encourages inclusive digital innovation, making financial data management a strategic pillar for the sustainability and competitiveness of the modern financial industry.

RISKS AND CHALLENGES IN OPEN BANKING

Open banking has emerged as a new paradigm in the financial industry, in which customer data is no longer locked within traditional banking systems. Still, it can be accessed via *Application Programming Interfaces* (APIs) by licensed third parties. This model opens up opportunities for innovation, increases competition, and expands access to financial services. However, behind this potential lie several complex risks and challenges, whether technological, regulatory, or social. The open banking ecosystem is designed to provide better customer choices and experiences by utilizing customer data to offer tailored financial products and services. This enhances the efficiency of money transfers and information sharing between financial institutions and other entities. The open banking ecosystem is built to improve the quality of customer choice and experience through the integrated use of data to deliver more personalized financial products and services, while simplifying and streamlining the process of fund transfers and information exchange between financial institutions and other relevant parties (Kassab et al., 2022; Schneider, 2023). By opening up access to banking data to third-party service providers (TPPs), Open Banking disrupts the traditional banking model by opening up space for new players and accelerating innovation, thereby encouraging the emergence of various technology-based financial services such as digital wallets, robo-advisors, and financing schemes designed according to customer profiles and needs (Kassab et al., 2022; Khamitdkhanovich et al., 2025; Stranieri et al., 2021; Ziegler, 2021).

DATA LEAKAGE AND AUTHORIZATION ABUSE RISKS

Open banking, through its API-based mechanism, enables licensed third parties to access customer data. Although this encourages financial service innovation, it also poses serious risks of data leakage and unauthorized access. These two issues are the focus of regulators, banks, and consumers because they concern trust and the sustainability of the ecosystem. Data leaks involve the accidental or intentional dissemination of sensitive data to unauthorized parties. This can include financial information, personal data, and transaction history. (Shabtai et al., 2012) . The consequences of data breaches are serious, causing direct losses such as regulatory fines, litigation costs, and future lost sales, as well as indirect losses such as reputational damage and customer loss. Data breaches can occur in various ways, including cyber attacks, internal threats, weak security systems, and vulnerabilities in third-party services. The interconnected nature of open banking systems increases the risk of data being accessed or manipulated during transmission. Data breaches can arise from a range of factors, including cyberattacks, internal threats, security system weaknesses, and vulnerabilities in third-party services. In the highly integrated context of Open Banking, the level of interconnection between systems further increases the risk of unauthorized access and data manipulation during transmission (Khanday et al., 2025; Singh et al., 2023). Implementing a robust *Data Leakage Prevention* (DLP) system is essential. This system helps detect and prevent unauthorized access to sensitive data and ensures compliance with security protocols. Additionally, integrating artificial intelligence (AI) for anomaly detection and behavior monitoring can enhance the security of financial systems.

Authorization abuse in open banking can lead to unauthorized access to customer data, potentially resulting in identity theft and fraudulent transactions (Triana & Pangabean, 2021; Zhang et al., 2020). This abuse can occur when application programming interfaces (APIs) are manipulated or when authentication processes are weak. The lack of industry standards and oversight in financial data governance poses serious challenges, as highlighted by various studies. The absence of standardized data governance practices has led to diverse approaches to data management across institutions, resulting in inconsistencies in data quality, security, and implementation.

Financial institutions often face data fragmentation and interoperability issues that can lead to inefficiencies and errors (Amadori et al., 2020; Verma et al., 2025). The rapid digital transformation in the financial services sector has increased vulnerability to sophisticated cyber threats, including phishing, malware, and ransomware (Chatterjee et al., 2023).

Inconsistent regulations and weak cross-sectoral supervision are fundamental obstacles to realizing an inclusive, open financial ecosystem. Regulatory fragmentation not only creates legal loopholes but also triggers systemic failures that undermine public trust, as reflected in the financial scandal in Australia. (Schmulow et al., 2019). The historical experience of the 2007-2009 global financial crisis further confirms that without an integrated supervisory structure, such as the Financial Stability Oversight Council (FSOC) in the United States, systemic risks arising from financial innovation will be difficult to mitigate. (Compton, 2013). Therefore, regulatory accountability is an absolute prerequisite for maintaining stability amid the accelerating digitalization of banking.

REGULATION AND CONSUMER PROTECTION

Financial data regulation and personal data regulation are closely intertwined because both focus on protecting sensitive information held by individuals. Financial data, such as transaction history, credit scores, and investment activities, is considered personal data because it can identify a person's economic condition and is therefore subject to personal data protection laws such as the General Data Protection Regulation (GDPR) (Castellano et al., 2023; Fedorova et al., 2017; Latifzadeh et al., 2021). The GDPR and Financial Data are comprehensive frameworks designed to protect personal data, including financial data, by ensuring that data processing activities are conducted transparently, securely, and in accordance with individual privacy rights. (Fedorova et al., 2017; Gobeo et al., 2018; Latifzadeh et al., 2021). Financial institutions are required to comply with GDPR requirements, which include obtaining explicit consent for data processing, ensuring data minimization, and implementing strong security measures. (Baker, 2017; Fedorova et al., 2017; Gobeo et al., 2018).

The link between financial data regulation and personal data protection regulation is reflected in their shared goal of safeguarding sensitive information. Financial data inherently contains personal information, so its protection is subject to a comprehensive legal framework, such as the General Data Protection Regulation (GDPR), which sets strict standards for financial institutions to ensure data security and privacy. The convergence of these two regulatory regimes underscores the importance of robust compliance strategies and institutions' ability to continuously adapt to regulatory change (Baker, 2017; Castellano et al., 2023; Fedorova et al., 2017; Josyula, 2025; Latifzadeh et al., 2021).

The General Data Protection Regulation (GDPR), which came into effect in 2018 in the European Union, has become a global benchmark in personal data protection, including data related to financial activities. This regulation establishes several fundamental principles that serve as the basis for the collection, processing, and management of data by every entity within its jurisdiction. The GDPR establishes key principles, including lawfulness, fairness, and transparency.

1. Lawfulness

Data processing must be lawful, meaning it must be based on one of the six legal bases listed in Article 6 (1) of the GDPR. This principle is generally well-established and less debated within the EU data protection framework.

2. Fairness

The GDPR emphasizes procedural fairness, ensuring that data processing is carried out in accordance with the rules, including legitimacy and transparency (Häuselmann & Custers, 2024). However, substantive fairness, encompassing elements such as good faith, non-discrimination, and autonomy, is also crucial to effective data protection. Fairness in data processing helps prevent bias and discrimination, promoting ethical decision-making. (Jo & Raj, 2024).

3. Transparency

Transparency requires data controllers to provide data subjects with clear, comprehensive, and easily accessible privacy information 4. This principle is fundamental to the GDPR, ensuring that individuals receive adequate information about how their data is used (Balboni & Francis, 2024; Mesarčík & Hamuľák, 2024).

THE RELATIONSHIP BETWEEN FINANCIAL DATA REGULATION AND PERSONAL DATA REGULATION

The dynamics between conventional banking regulations and personal data protection, such as the GDPR, are now at a crucial crossroads. The crux of the matter lies in a philosophical clash: banking relies on rigid risk control to ensure systemic stability, while the GDPR demands flexibility by placing data sovereignty in individuals' hands. This situation creates a paradox of financial data security. Although not always technically classified as sensitive, financial data is a prime target for financial crimes and highly vulnerable (Baker, 2017). As a result, banking institutions find themselves in a dilemma between fulfilling customers' broad rights to control their data and maintaining strict security protocols. This challenge is further complicated by extensive documentation requirements intended to ensure transparency and accountability, which, in practice, can consume operational resources. Ultimately, the banking industry faces external threats such as cyber risks and fraud, and must also manage internal tensions between detailed legal compliance and the need to maintain efficiency amid accelerating digital transformation (Ceko et al., 2026).

Banking regulations require third parties to access financial data only with consumers' explicit consent, in accordance with data protection principles. This ensures that data sharing is carried out securely and respects consumer privacy. Open banking requires third parties to access financial data only with consumers' explicit consent, in accordance with data protection principles. (OECD, 2022). This ensures that data sharing is done securely and respects consumer privacy. (Ghosh et al., 2024; Usanti, 2022). Effective implementation of open banking requires coordination between various regulatory bodies. For example, in Brazil, the Central Bank and the Administrative Council for Economic Defense (Cade) must work together to manage the Open Financial System and address potential jurisdictional conflicts. (Domingues & Solla, 2024). Similarly, in Indonesia, collaboration between Bank Indonesia and other regulatory bodies is crucial to balance personal data rights and market competition. (Wiwoho et al., 2024). The policy implications of these dynamics call for an integrated data governance framework that aligns financial prudence with privacy protection. Regulations need to be holistic, protecting data throughout its life cycle and harmonizing international standards to maintain public trust in the digital financial system. Amid the innovation opportunities offered by open banking, its success remains dependent on careful data protection management, effective regulatory coordination, strengthened security systems, and consolidated consumer trust.

DIGITAL INNOVATION AND NEW BUSINESS MODELS

Open banking has proven to be a key catalyst in transforming the digital financial ecosystem. This transformation is primarily driven by the secure sharing of customer data between traditional banks and third-party providers via API-based mechanisms, enabling the development of more personalized and innovative financial services. Open banking enables customers to share their financial data with fintech companies, enabling the development of solutions that are more relevant and tailored to the needs of each individual (Garg & Sahu, 2024; Jayesh et al., 2022; Schneider,

2023). The use of data-based technologies such as Artificial Intelligence (AI), Machine Learning (ML), and Big Data analysis further strengthens the system's capacity to generate more personalized and precise recommendations, predictions, and financial services (Khamitdkhanovich et al., 2025).

Open banking promotes increased financial inclusion by enabling fintech companies to provide banking services to previously underserved groups, including low-income communities. This impact is clearly seen in developing countries such as China, where the development of inclusive fintech not only expands financial access but also improves bank performance by enhancing liability structures and lending rates, particularly for national and rural banks. (Liu et al., 2024). Furthermore, the use of virtual platforms in the open banking ecosystem enables financial services to reach vulnerable and marginalized groups in low- and middle-income countries, thereby strengthening the broader financial inclusion agenda. (Kokkinis & Miglionico, 2020) . The use of Application Programming Interfaces (APIs) in the open banking framework enables efficient integration between banks and fintech companies, thereby encouraging the development of innovative financial products such as digital wallets, robo-advisors, and personalized financing.

The implementation of regulations such as the Revised Payment Services Directive (PSD2) in the European Union is also an important foundation, as it ensures secure data exchange while strengthening competition and inclusiveness in the financial ecosystem. (Khamitdkhanovich et al., 2025; Premchand & Choudhry, 2018). The emergence of fintech startups with disruptive technological innovations has challenged the dominance of traditional banks and encouraged adjustments to business models to remain relevant in the competition. (Chambefort, 2025; Nabiyev & Ovenc, 2023; Ovenc & Nabiyev, 2025). The development of digital banking and various fintech solutions has brought about a structural transformation in the financial industry, requiring conventional banks to integrate these technologies into their operational systems and service portfolios as a strategic response to increasingly complex competitive dynamics. (Bhasin & Rajesh, 2021; Karani & Jadhav, 2025; Ramesh, 2019). Banks are proactively building platform-based ecosystems that integrate various financial services and products to deliver a more comprehensive and customer-centric approach. (Evdokimova, 2021; Farrow, 2020; Panova, 2021). In this study, the adoption of open banking platforms enables third parties to obtain controlled access to banking data and services, thereby driving innovation while improving the quality and customer experience. (Farrow, 2020; Pramitasari et al., 2025).

The potential for innovation in data-driven financial products is becoming increasingly prominent as open banking, big data, and advanced analytics technologies develop. Data-driven financial products offer significant opportunities to create more inclusive, efficient, and personalized services. These innovations include service personalization, alternative risk assessment, algorithm-based investing, digital insurance, and cross-platform integration through open banking. However, successful implementation depends on data protection regulations, consumer trust, and the readiness of technological infrastructure. Thus, data is not only a source of information but also the main foundation for the future of digital financial innovation. The impacts of developments in data-driven financial products include:

1. Personalization of Financial Services

Customer transaction data enables financial institutions to develop customized financial products, such as personalized savings plans, algorithm-based investment recommendations, and dynamic pricing for credit products. This is achieved through advanced data analysis techniques, including machine learning and predictive analytics, which help in understanding and anticipating customer needs (Chandra et al., 2025; Jain & Fallon, 2023; Ramlal & Hosein, 2021; Saxena & Muneeb, 2024).

2. Alternative Credit and Risk Assessment

Non-traditional data, such as utility payment history, *e-commerce* transactions, or social media activity, is now used as an alternative in credit assessment. This approach expands financial access for groups that previously had difficulty obtaining credit due to limited banking history. Data-driven analysis enables financial institutions to perform more inclusive and accurate *risk scoring*, thereby supporting financial inclusion while maintaining financial system stability. The use of non-traditional data sources in the digital financial ecosystem has transformed the credit assessment paradigm from a conventional model to a more predictive, inclusive system. By integrating social media activity, telecommunications usage patterns, and utility payment behavior, financial institutions can now mitigate the information asymmetry constraints that have long hindered the unbanked population (Achalapong & Satitsamitpong, 2025; Kazimoto et al., 2024; Yanting & Ali, 2023). However, this transformation is not merely a tool for market expansion; the integration of alternative data serves as a more comprehensive risk management mechanism by providing behavioral variables that are not recorded in traditional credit histories (Achalapong & Satitsamitpong, 2025; Baidoo & Mazzotta, 2025; Mhlanga, 2021; Yanting & Ali, 2023). Through advanced *algorithmic scoring* models, banks can reduce *default* rates while strengthening the overall stability of the financial system. However, the effectiveness of this system depends heavily on algorithmic transparency to ensure that the use of alternative data does not introduce new forms of discrimination but rather serves as a catalyst for inclusive and sustainable economic growth (Achalapong & Satitsamitpong, 2025; Shaji et al., 2022; Y. Sun et al., 2024).

3. Digital Insurance (*InsurTech*)

InsurTech innovations have disrupted conventional insurance models by integrating *real-time* data from the IoT ecosystem and customers' digital footprints. This transformation has enabled a paradigm shift in premium setting: from static, demographic-based segmentation to dynamic pricing models that reflect actual behavior (e.g., *usage-based insurance*). Adjusting premiums based on actual risks, such as driving style or individual health patterns, not only improves the accuracy of risk assessment but also enhances transparency and customer trust through a more objective, personalized pricing mechanism in the digital era. The use *of InsurTech* and *real-time* data can enable telematics in the vehicle insurance sector, a key manifestation of InsurTech's ability to optimize data in real time via IoT. Through the integration of *smartphone* sensors and GPS devices, insurance companies can now record granular driving behavior metrics such as acceleration, braking patterns, and cornering speeds, replacing traditional estimates that rely solely on demographic profiles. This transformation towards a *dynamic pricing* model not only improves the accuracy of individual risk assessment but also creates a fairer and more personalized ecosystem. (Guillén, 2024). By offering lower premiums to disciplined drivers, this technology simultaneously aligns companies' commercial interests with the reinforcement of customer safety behavior on the road.

The use of IoT, AI, and *blockchain* in the InsurTech ecosystem has given rise to a new, more dynamic, behavior-based insurance paradigm. By utilizing real-time data streams, insurance companies can create more personalized and objective premium schemes. The presence of this technology serves a dual purpose: as a catalyst for innovation in product diversification and as an instrument to mitigate moral hazard through greater transparency.

4. Integration with Open banking

The transformation of the financial services sector through open banking enables the exchange of structured data between banking institutions and third-party service providers via *Application Programming Interfaces* (APIs). This integration mechanism creates a competitive financial ecosystem, which catalyzes the emergence of service innovations such as personal financial management, investment consolidation, and cross-platform payment system efficiency (Kassab et al., 2022; Khamitdkhanovich et al., 2025; Nanaeva et al., 2021; Schneider, 2023; Stranieri et al., 2021). The systematic implementation of Open banking reshapes the financial industry landscape by opening up data access, encouraging increased competition, and inviting innovative new players into the ecosystem (Premchand & Choudhry, 2018). This competitive environment forces service providers to create enhanced customer experiences, enabling customers to manage their finances more effectively through flexible, superior financial solutions (Kassab et al., 2022). Macroeconomically, the integration of technology and service efficiency ultimately becomes a strategic instrument for realizing financial inclusion by providing more affordable access to formal services for segments of society that have not been reached by the conventional banking system (underserved) (Babina et al., 2025; Leong & Gardner, 2021). The acceleration of open banking integration fundamentally reconfigures the financial services landscape by catalyzing innovation, intensifying competition, and expanding financial inclusion. However, the sustainability of this paradigm is crucially determined by the rigidity of data governance, the solidity of customer trust, and compliance with an adaptive regulatory framework. The dynamics of this ecosystem are projected to further transform towards Open Finance and Decentralized Finance (DeFi), which will significantly expand its operational scope and socio-economic impact (Khamitdkhanovich et al., 2025; Nanaeva et al., 2021; Torre & Ebardo, 2024).

GLOBAL STRATEGIES IN FINANCIAL DATA GOVERNANCE

The development of financial data governance at the global level shows variations in approaches between countries, reflecting their respective political, economic, and social priorities. A comparison between the United States, the European Union, China, and India shows how data-driven financial innovation is integrated with consumer protection and digital sovereignty.

1. United States

The United States' strategy in data governance focuses on data liberalism, prioritizing economic value creation for the private sector through market-driven innovation and free data flow. However, this highly pro-market approach has led to ambiguity in consumer protection, with a tendency toward laxity on personal data privacy, creating inconsistent standards of individual protection. As a result, the U.S.'s ambition for digital sovereignty, which emphasizes open access to data, often contradicts international trust norms and more restrictive global data protection frameworks (Carr & Llanos, 2021; Oh & Kwon, 2025).

2. European Union

The European Union's data governance strategy adopts an integrative approach that seeks to synergize economic acceleration with comprehensive data protection through regulatory instruments such as the GDPR. This fundamental focus places a rigid emphasis on protecting individual privacy, while still facilitating the use of data as a catalyst for measurable economic growth. Through this strict governance framework, the European Union seeks to strengthen digital sovereignty by ensuring that all data exchanges meet international standards and maintain information security integrity throughout the financial ecosystem (Carr & Llanos, 2021; Mei et al., 2025; Oh & Kwon, 2025).

3. China

China's data governance model represents the absolute integration of digital sovereignty and state authority, where data localization policies and protectionism are aggressively implemented as instruments of national security. This approach transforms data into a strategic national asset that not only functions in optimizing public services but also as a mechanism for social and political control that systematically reduces privacy and individual freedoms for the sake of national governance stability (Carr & Llanos, 2021; Oh & Kwon, 2025).

4. India

India is strategically constructing a data governance framework centered on digital sovereignty, with a strong emphasis on data localization to ensure that domestic control remains aligned with national interests. These efforts are integrated with the development of data protection and privacy regulations to strengthen consumer security in the growing digital ecosystem, although implementation of the framework is currently still in the formalization and refinement stage (Castellano et al., 2023; Chen & Gao, 2022).

The dynamics of global financial data governance are currently fragmented into four main paradigms that reflect divergent political and economic interests: market-based innovation liberalism in the United States, synchronization between privacy rights and economic expansion in the European Union, and centralized state control through the doctrine of data sovereignty in China. In line with this, India is progressively constructing a framework that prioritizes domestic data localization, with these approaches collectively affirming the strategic tension between accelerating financial technology and safeguarding consumer protection and national digital sovereignty.

A transformative paradigm shift, open banking integrates the use of *Application Programming Interfaces* (APIs) to promote efficiency, transparency, and financial inclusion through the development of new services, but this innovation inherently creates a strategic dilemma between digital acceleration and national data protection

(Babin & Smith, 2022; Khamitdkhanovich et al., 2025; Schneider, 2023). Successful implementation depends heavily on the authorities' ability to align these potential economic benefits with critical challenges related to data sovereignty, cybersecurity, and regulatory compliance, ensuring that the transformation of the financial services sector simultaneously protects national interests and consumer privacy.

CONCLUSION

The paradigm shift from physical asset ownership to data governance dominance has reconstructed the operational foundations of modern banking. In the open banking ecosystem, the resilience of financial institutions is determined by the effectiveness of internal controls over real-time data flows, rather than by the rigidity of closed systems. Integration through APIs significantly changes the operational risk profile, so that control failures are not merely technical issues, but threats to the integrity of financial reporting and information transparency.

Financial data governance must be viewed as an instrument of digital sovereignty and competitive advantage, not merely a regulatory compliance burden. Cross-border regulatory harmonization and coordination between regulators, banks, and third parties are prerequisites for maintaining system stability. Ultimately, the success *of* open banking depends on the industry's ability to balance digital innovation with strict auditing standards, so that every innovation remains within the corridor of national financial stability and supports sustainable economic inclusion.

The implementation of open banking has fundamentally disrupted the conventional banking business model, shifting the paradigm from merely controlling physical assets to dominating dynamic data governance. In an ecosystem interconnected through *Application Programming Interfaces* (APIs), the role of internal oversight is no longer adequate if it relies solely on periodic, static transaction checks; instead, internal controls must evolve into responsive, *real-time*, data-flow-based monitoring. Failure to adapt the *internal control* framework to this API architecture not only threatens cybersecurity but also creates systemic risks that could potentially distort the integrity of financial reports and the reliability of *audit trails.* Therefore, system integration through APIs must be viewed as a strategic audit object and a critical point in operational risk mitigation, where the resilience of banks depends heavily on the ability of institutions to ensure the security of data exchange with third parties (TPPs) through encryption mechanisms, double authentication, and the principle *of non-repudiation*.

The transition from physical asset ownership to data governance dominance is the new reality for modern banking. Resilience is no longer defined by closed systems but by the effectiveness of internal controls over real-time API flows.

Regulatory compliance must be viewed as a strategic investment in brand equity. To achieve a sustainable ecosystem, the transition toward Open Finance requires global regulatory harmonization and the integration of AI-based innovation with rigid auditing standards.

Customer trust in this digital era can only be maintained if banks mitigate information asymmetry through algorithmic transparency and adaptive oversight amid divergent global governance strategies. The phenomenon of digital sovereignty in various jurisdictions, such as the GDPR in the European Union and localization policies in China and India, confirms that regulatory compliance should no longer be viewed as a compliance cost, but rather as a strategic investment to build *brand equity* through superior privacy protection. Future competitive advantage will belong to banks that are able to balance AI-based product innovation with rigid consumer protection. Finally, the transition to a broader *Open Finance* ecosystem requires regulatory harmonization and cross-sector collaboration to ensure financial system stability through an ethical and standardized data governance framework. In this context, the appointment of *a Data Protection Officer* (DPO) and the implementation of periodic information technology audits are absolute prerequisites for realizing an inclusive, accountable, and sustainable financial ecosystem for the future of the global banking industry.

REFERENCES

Achalapong, J., & Satitsamitpong, M. (2025). Improving Credit Decisions Through Machine Learning and Alternative Data: Evidence from Nbfis. *ABAC Journal, 45*(4). Advance online publication. DOI: 10.59865/abacj.2025.27

Babin, R., & Smith, D. (2022). Open banking and regulation: Please advise the government. *Journal of Information Technology Teaching Cases, 12*(2), 108–114. DOI: 10.1177/20438869221082316

Baidoo, E., & Mazzotta, S. (2025). On the fringe of credit visibility: The value of alternative data for assessing the credit risk of subprime underbanked consumers. *International Journal of Applied Decision Sciences, 18*(4), 472–492. DOI: 10.1504/IJADS.2025.147286

Baker, L. (2017). The impact of the General Data Protection Regulation on the banking sector: Data subjects' rights, conflicts of laws and Brexit. *Journal of Data Protection and Privacy, 1*(2), 137–145. DOI: 10.69554/EIYO6659

Balboni, P., & Francis, K. (2024). Personal Privacy Policies. In *Computer and Information Security Handbook* (4th ed., Vol. 1-2, pp. 907–916). Elsevier., DOI: 10.1016/B978-0-443-13223-0.00055-2

Bartolacci, F., & Caputo, A. (2020). *Sustainability and financial performance of small and medium sized enterprises: A bibliometric and systematic literature review.* Business Strategy and the., DOI: 10.1002/bse.2434

Bartolini, C., Daoudagh, S., Lenzini, G., & Marchetti, E. (2019). Towards a lawful authorized access: A preliminary GDPR-based authorized access. In van S. M., M. L., & M. L. (Eds.), *ICSOFT 2019 - Proceedings of the 14th International Conference on Software Technologies* (pp. 331–338). SciTePress. DOI: 10.5220/0007978703310338

Becker, R., Chokoshvili, D., Thorogood, A., Dove, E. S., Molnár-Gábor, F., Ziaka, A., Tzortzatou-Nanopoulou, O., & Comandè, G. (2024). Purpose definition as a crucial step for determining the legal basis under the GDPR: Implications for scientific research. *Journal of Law and the Biosciences, 11*(1), lsae001. Advance online publication. DOI: 10.1093/jlb/lsae001

Behbehani, D., Rajarajan, M., Komninos, N., & Al-Begain, K. (2022). Detecting Open Banking API Security Threats Using Bayesian Attack Graphs. *Proceedings - 2022 14th IEEE International Conference on Computational Intelligence and Communication Networks, CICN 2022*, 789–796. DOI: 10.1109/CICN56167.2022.10008365

Bezzina, F., Camilleri, E., & Marmarà, V. (2021). Transparency and Accountability Public Service Reforms. In *Public Administration, Governance and Globalization* (Vol. 22, pp. 91–104). Springer. DOI: 10.1007/978-3-030-74357-4_3

Bhasin, N. K., & Rajesh, A. (2021). Impact of E-Collaboration between Indian Banks and Fintech Companies for Digital Banking and New Emerging Technologies. *International Journal of e-Collaboration, 17*(1), 15–35. DOI: 10.4018/IJeC.2021010102

Blanchard, S. J., Martin, K. D., & Salisbury, L. C. (2026). Consumer financial data exchange: marketing meets digital finance and open banking. *International Journal of Research in Marketing*. https://doi.org/https://doi.org/10.1016/j.ijresmar.2026.01.004

Carr, M., & Llanos, J. T. (2021). Data: Global governance challenges. In *Global Governance Futures* (pp. 286–298). Taylor and Francis. DOI: 10.4324/9781003139836-21

Castellano, G. G., Selga, Ē. K., & Arner, D. W. (2023). The Emergence of Financial Data Governance and the Challenge of Financial Data Sovereignty. In *Data Sovereignty: from the Digital Silk Road to the Return of the State* (pp. 178–210). Oxford University Press., DOI: 10.1093/oso/9780197582794.003.0009

Ceko, E., Komina, B., & Karras, D. (2026). The Importance of GDPR Compliance and a Documentation Framework. In D. K. & S. E. (Eds.), *Communications in Computer and Information Science: Vol. 2670 CCIS* (pp. 310–323). Springer Science and Business Media Deutschland GmbH. DOI: 10.1007/978-3-032-07370-9_23

Chambefort, C. (2025). Alliance with fintech: Are banks opening the Pandor box? In *Encyclopedia of Monetary Policy, Financial Markets and Banking* (p. V4:427-V4:430). Elsevier. DOI: 10.1016/B978-0-44-313776-1.00117-3

Chandra, S., Venkatesh, M., Singh, R., Garg, S., Giri Babu, K., & Katta, S. K. (2025). Personalized Banking Experiences Using AI Leveraging Data Science for Tailored Financial Services. *2025 IEEE 4th World Conference on Applied Intelligence and Computing, AIC 2025*, 833–838. DOI: 10.1109/AIC66080.2025.11211889

Chen, Y., & Gao, Y. (2022). Comparative analysis of digital trade development strategies and governance approaches. *Journal of Digital Economy, 1*(3), 227–238. DOI: 10.1016/j.jdec.2023.02.001

Compton, N. S. (2013). Financial stability oversight council and office of financial research: Elements and assessments. In *Financial Stability Oversight Council and Office of Financial Research: Elements and Assessments*. Nova Science Publishers, Inc. https://www.scopus.com/inward/record.uri?eid=2-s2.0-84936855748&partnerID=40&md5=c888029efb8f14e0ade593e26294a0b8

Dahdal, A. M., & Zeiler, B. (2021). Open Banking and Open Data: Global Context, Innovation, and Consumer Protection. *Banking Law Journal, 138*(7), 385–412. https://www.scopus.com/inward/record.uri?eid=2-s2.0-85123727295&partnerID=40&md5=209f7c14aab48f7821d1553d5ed8bad4

de Araluze, B., & Plaza, C. N. (2023). The Relevance of Initial Trust and Social Influence in the Intention to Use Open Banking-Based Services: An Empirical Study. *SAGE Open, 13*(3), 21582440231187607. Advance online publication. DOI: 10.1177/21582440231187607

Domingues, J. O., & Solla, K. R. (2024). Open Financial System and Cade's competence. *Revista de Defesa da Concorrencia, 12*(2), 104–122. DOI: 10.52896/rdc.v12i2.1137

Emili, A. M. (2019). Data Protection Officer. In *Dictionary of Statuses within EU Law: The Individual Statuses as Pillar of European Union Integration* (pp. 121–126). Springer Science+Business Media. DOI: 10.1007/978-3-030-00554-2_16

Evdokimova, Y. (2021). Financial ecosystems: Analysis and development paths. In Y. A., M. A., & M. O. (Eds.), *IOP Conference Series: Earth and Environmental Science* (Vol. 689, Issue 1). IOP Publishing Ltd. DOI: 10.1088/1755-1315/689/1/012011

Farrow, G. S. D. (2020). Open banking: The rise of the cloud platform. *Journal of Payments Strategy and Systems, 14*(2), 128–146. DOI: 10.69554/TUCN3800

Fedorova, A., Ferrara, M., & Fierro, P. (2017). The General Data Protection Regulation (GDPR): From static to dynamic compliance. *Law and Economics Yearly Review, 6*, 283–302.https://www.scopus.com/inward/record.uri?eid=2-s2.0-85046540701&partnerID=40&md5=0037336eae552068869da0b00b35b760

Gauci, R. (2019). Is Europe a good example of open banking? In *The PAYTECH Book: The Payment Technology Handbook for Investors, Entrepreneurs, and FinTech Visionaries* (pp. 86–87). wiley. DOI: 10.1002/9781119551973.ch25

Ghosh, A., Mukhopadhyay, I., & Chakraborty, S. (2024). Design and Architectural Implementation of Consortium Blockchain Based Framework for Open Banking Customer Consent and Data Handling. *SN Computer Science, 5*(2), 271. Advance online publication. DOI: 10.1007/s42979-023-02593-4

Gobeo, A., Fowler, C., & Buchanan, W. J. (2018). GDPR and Cyber Security for Business Information Systems. In *GDPR and Cyber Security for Business Information Systems*. River Publishers. https://www.scopus.com/inward/record.uri?eid=2-s2.0-85070689188&partnerID=40&md5=9520d22bd3d39a0aeffddb9657d8681f

Guillén, M. (2024). Econometrics of Insurance Based on Telematics Information and Machine Learning. In *Handbook of Insurance* (3rd ed., Vol. I, pp. 401–416). Springer Nature., DOI: 10.1007/978-3-031-69561-2_14

Harwood, W. H. (2017). Secrecy, transparency and government whistleblowing. *Philosophy and Social Criticism*, *43*(2), 164–186. DOI: 10.1177/0191453716677178

Hasan, M., Hoque, A., & Le, T. (2023). Big Data-Driven Banking Operations: Opportunities, Challenges, and Data Security Perspectives. *FinTech*, *2*(3), 484–509. DOI: 10.3390/fintech2030028

Häuselmann, A., & Custers, B. (2024). Substantive fairness in the GDPR: Fairness Elements for Article 5.1a GDPR. *Computer Law & Security Review*, *52*, 105942. Advance online publication. DOI: 10.1016/j.clsr.2024.105942

Hermawan, S., Khoirunisa, Z. A., & Tejomurti, K. (2023). Triangular Insight on Open Banking in Indonesia, Singapore, and Australia. *International Journal of Legal Information*, *51*(3), 197–215. DOI: 10.1017/jli.2024.11

Jain, S., & Fallon, E. (2023). Leveraging Unstructured Data to Improve Customer Engagement and Revenue in Financial Institutions: A Deep Reinforcement Learning Approach to Personalized Transaction Recommendations. In O. M.S., O. M.S., O. M.S., D. F., H. K.-F-., N. P., & G. Y. (Eds.), *Proceedings of the 2023 IEEE International Conference on Computer, Information, and Telecommunication Systems, CITS 2023*. Institute of Electrical and Electronics Engineers Inc. DOI: 10.1109/CITS58301.2023.10188745

Jo, A. A., & Raj, E. D. (2024). Ethical Dimensions in Data-Driven Business: Balancing Fairness, Accountability, Transparency, and Explainability. *2024 15th International Conference on Computing Communication and Networking Technologies, ICCCNT 2024*. DOI: 10.1109/ICCCNT61001.2024.10724314

Jones, S. T. H. (2025). *Consumer Data Right expansion to deliver a better deal for consumers*. https://ministers.treasury.gov.au/ministers/stephen-jones-2022/media-releases/consumer-data-right-expansion-deliver-better-deal

Kapoor, N., Kapoor, T., Sisodiya, D. R., & Sushma, J. (2024). Impact of Fintech: Revolution in Banking and Financial Industry. *2024 IEEE 4th International Conference on ICT in Business Industry and Government, ICTBIG 2024*. DOI: 10.1109/ICTBIG64922.2024.10911635

Karani, G., & Jadhav, B. (2025). How traditional banks adapt to the fintech revolution in banking and finance sector. In *Shaping Cutting-Edge Technologies and Applications for Digital Banking and Financial Services* (pp. 214–225). Taylor and Francis., DOI: 10.4324/9781003501947-13

Kassab, M., Laplante, P., & Voas, J. (2022). Trust Considerations in Open Banking. *IT Professional, 24*(1), 70–73. DOI: 10.1109/MITP.2021.3136015

Khamitdkhanovich, N. A., Senthilkumar, C., Kavitha, V. O., & Ugli, E. R. S. (2025). The evolution of open banking: Transforming financial services with data-driven technologies. In S. J. (Ed.), *AIP Conference Proceedings* (Vol. 3306, Issue 1). American Institute of Physics. DOI: 10.1063/5.0277721

Khanday, M. A., Negi, N., Ahmad, M., Bhat, D. A., & Nakitende, M. G. (2025). AI and Financial Data Leaks: Preventing Corruption and Strengthening Cybersecurity. In *Financial Corruption and Money Laundering in the AI Era* (pp. 219–246). IGI Global. DOI: 10.4018/979-8-3373-0786-2.ch009

Kokkinis, A., & Miglionico, A. (2020). Open banking and libra: A new frontier of financial inclusion for payment systems? *Singapore Journal of Legal Studies, 2020*, 601–629. https://www.scopus.com/inward/record.uri?eid=2-s2.0-85100665733&partnerID=40&md5=4f8878f37edee84094503a891ff93a4c

Kumar, A., & Gandhi, A. (2023). A Study Using OWASP on Secure Open Banking Architecture. *2023 3rd International Conference on Advance Computing and Innovative Technologies in Engineering, ICACITE 2023*, 2062–2067. DOI: 10.1109/ICACITE57410.2023.10182656

Lat, J. S. (2024). Managing Data Integrity for Finance: Discover practical data quality management strategies for finance analysts and data professionals. In *Managing Data Integrity for Finance: Discover practical data quality management strategies for finance analysts and data professionals*. De Gruyter Mouton. https://www.scopus.com/inward/record.uri?eid=2-s2.0-105022525236&partnerID=40&md5=864a2c1174c220561fd795a0e1beda74

Latifzadeh, M., Dorafshan, S. M. M. Q., Mohseni, S., & Abedi, M. (2021). Analysis of the Legal Framework for the Protection of Personal Data in the European Union. *Iranian Journal of Information Processing and Management, 37*(2), 439–472. DOI: 10.52547/jipm.37.2.439

Lei, J., Wei, M., She, Y., & Wang, W. (2025). Research on automatic processing system of financial information in colleges and universities based on NLP-KG fusion algorithm. *Systems and Soft Computing, 7*, 200224. Advance online publication. DOI: 10.1016/j.sasc.2025.200224

Lin, X., Zhang, S. S., & Zachariadis, M. (2025). Open data and API adoption of U.S. banks. *Journal of Financial Intermediation*, *63*, 101162. Advance online publication. DOI: 10.1016/j.jfi.2025.101162

Liu, Z., Li, X., & Li, Z. (2024). Inclusive FinTech, open banking, and bank performance: Evidence from China. *Financial Innovation*, *10*(1), 149. Advance online publication. DOI: 10.1186/s40854-024-00679-3

Mabillard, V., & Zumofen, R. (2021). Transparency and Accountability—The Case of Public Procurement Practices in Switzerland. *Public Works Management & Policy*, *26*(2), 95–114. DOI: 10.1177/1087724X19898699

Magdolen, M., & Lovecek, T. (2023). Legal Aspects of Monitoring and Tracking the Movement of Individuals Using Modern Technologies. *Proceedings - International Carnahan Conference on Security Technology*. DOI: 10.1109/ICCST59048.2023.10726858

Mei, Y., Zeng, J., & Zhan, Y. (2025). U.S.-Europe artificial intelligence regulatory cooperation, divergence, and China's "window of opportunity" for strategic breakthrough. *Bulletin of Chinese Academy of Sciences*, *40*(4), 715–724. DOI: 10.16418/j.issn.1000-3045.20241210001

Mesarčík, M., & Hamuľák, O. (2024). General Data Protection Regulation: Current Challenges and Future Directions. In *Contributions to Political Science: Vol. Part F3080* (pp. 117–133). Springer Science and Business Media Deutschland GmbH. DOI: 10.1007/978-3-031-56045-3_9

Mhlanga, D. (2021). Financial inclusion in emerging economies: The application of machine learning and artificial intelligence in credit risk assessment. *International Journal of Financial Studies*, *9*(3), 39. Advance online publication. DOI: 10.3390/ijfs9030039

Mou, X., & Xu, J. (2020). Analysis and Research on University Financial Decision Based on Distributed Big Data Sharing Mechanism. *Proceedings - 2020 International Conference on Computers, Information Processing and Advanced Education, CIPAE 2020*, 31–34. DOI: 10.1109/CIPAE51077.2020.00016

Nabiyev, A. B., & Ovenc, G. (2023). The symbiotic relationship and collaboration between commercial banks and fintechs in Turkey. *Humanities & Social Sciences Communications*, *10*(1), 932. Advance online publication. DOI: 10.1057/s41599-023-02429-9

Nanaeva, Z., Aysan, A. F., & Shirazi, N. S. (2021). Open banking in Europe: The effect of the Revised Payment Services Directive on Solarisbank and Insha. *Journal of Payments Strategy and Systems, 15*(4), 432–444. https://www.scopus.com/inward/record.uri?eid=2-s2.0-85126287018&partnerID=40&md5=229b07316501cf1b017ec75b2bbb9e7c. DOI: 10.69554/BTQG8491

OECD. (2022). *Shifting from Open banking to Open Finance*. Organisation for Economic Co-operation and Development.

Oh, D.-H., & Kwon, H.-Y. (2025). Diverging Data Strategies of the United States, China, and the EU in the Data Cold War Era. In S. Y.-T., K. M., & R. J. (Eds.), *2025 IEEE/ACIS 23rd International Conference on Software Engineering Research, Management and Applications, SERA 2025 - Proceedings* (pp. 464–471). Institute of Electrical and Electronics Engineers Inc. DOI: 10.1109/SERA65747.2025.11154517

Oprea, I. (2024). Unlocking Financial Innovation: The Synergy of Open Banking and Artificial Intelligence in Banking System. In C. L., I.-F. V., G. G., D. L. R. C. I., & A. J.V. (Eds.), *Springer Proceedings in Business and Economics* (pp. 129–140). Springer Nature. DOI: 10.1007/978-3-031-71329-3_7

Ovenc, G., & Nabiyev, A. B. (2025). Discover how fintech is transforming bank performance: Insights from an emerging economy. *Cogent Economics & Finance, 13*(1), 2477676. Advance online publication. DOI: 10.1080/23322039.2025.2477676

Panova, G. (2021). Digital Platforms and Banks. In *Lecture Notes in Networks and Systems* (Vol. 133, pp. 463–472). Springer., DOI: 10.1007/978-3-030-47458-4_55

Pati, U. K., & Pratama, A. M. (2025). Indonesia's Open Banking Future: Designing Effective Regulatory Approaches. *Jambe Law Journal, 8*(1), 27–60. DOI: 10.22437/home.v8i1.371

Popovici, E.-C., Stalidi, C., Teodoras, D.-A., Suciu, G., & Cosma, I. (2024). De-Fraudify4ALL: Prototyping and Validation of a System for Fraud Detection with Big Data and Cloud Technology. *IEEE International Symposium for Design and Technology of Electronics Packages, SIITME - Conference Proceedings*, 466–470. DOI: 10.1109/SIITME63973.2024.10814887

Pramitasari, T. D., Widaninggar, N., & Rachman, R. (2025). Digital Economy: The Shifting of Traditional to Digital Spending and Saving-Investing Platforms and the Future of Banking Business Model. *WSEAS Transactions on Computer Research, 13*, 542–557. DOI: 10.37394/232018.2025.13.50

Premchand, A., & Choudhry, A. (2018). Open banking and APIs for transformation in banking. In N. S.K., R. J., & R. A.R. (Eds.), *Proceedings of the 2018 International Conference On Communication, Computing and Internet of Things, IC3IoT 2018* (pp. 25–29). Institute of Electrical and Electronics Engineers Inc. DOI: 10.1109/IC3IoT.2018.8668107

Ramesh, L. (2019). Fintech: A new avenue of banks to enhance customer digital experience (DX). *International Journal of Innovative Technology and Exploring Engineering*, *8*(8), 644–648. https://www.scopus.com/inward/record.uri?eid=2-s2.0-85068085893&partnerID=40&md5=b18df8e94cf623eef2f64669c69b707d

Ramlal, K., & Hosein, P. (2021). A Personalized Overdraft Protection Framework. *2021 IEEE 8th International Conference on Data Science and Advanced Analytics, DSAA 2021*. DOI: 10.1109/DSAA53316.2021.9564162

Saxena, A., & Muneeb, S. M. (2024). Transforming financial services through hyper-personalization: The role of artificial intelligence and data analytics in enhancing customer experience. In *AI-Driven Decentralized Finance and the Future of Finance* (pp. 19–48). IGI Global., DOI: 10.4018/979-8-3693-6321-8.ch002

Schmulow, A., Fairweather, K., & Tarrant, J. (2019). Restoring Confidence in Consumer Financial Protection Regulation in Australia: A Sisyphean Task? *Federal Law Review*, *47*(1), 91–120. DOI: 10.1177/0067205X18816240

Schneider, M. (2023). Open Banking and Digital Ecosystems. In *Digital Project Practice for New Work and Industry 4.0* (pp. 169–180). DOI: 10.1201/9781003371397-12

Shabtai, A., Elovici, Y., & Rokach, L. (2012). Data Leakage. In *SpringerBriefs in Computer Science* (Vol. 0, Issue 9781461420521, pp. 5–10). Springer. DOI: 10.1007/978-1-4614-2053-8_2

Shamurailatpam, S. D. D. (2023). Innovations in finance and the future of finance: A critical review. In *Revolutionizing Financial Services and Markets Through FinTech and Blockchain* (pp. 166–182). IGI Global., DOI: 10.4018/978-1-6684-8624-5.ch011

Shiraishi, M. (2021). Customized Database Management based on Digital Signature. In A. N., B. E., L. J.M., & J. Y. (Eds.), *2021 6th International Conference on Fog and Mobile Edge Computing, FMEC 2021*. Institute of Electrical and Electronics Engineers Inc. DOI: 10.1109/FMEC54266.2021.9732564

Singh, V., Raj, M., Gupta, I., & Sayeed, M. A. (2023). Data Leakage Detection and Prevention Using Cloud Computing. In *Sustainable Computing: Transforming Industry 4.0 to Society 5.0* (pp. 159–169). Springer International Publishing. DOI: 10.1007/978-3-031-13577-4_9

Stranieri, A., McInnes, A. N., Hashmi, M., & Sahama, T. (2021). Open Banking and Electronic Health Records. In S. N. & J. V.L. (Eds.), *ACM International Conference Proceeding Series*. Association for Computing Machinery. DOI: 10.1145/3437378.3437397

Sun, F. (2021). Development and Transformation Strategies of Banking Industry under the Background of Fintech. In L. J., W. J., & C. K. (Eds.), *E3S Web of Conferences* (Vol. 253). EDP Sciences. DOI: 10.1051/e3sconf/202125303068

Triana, Y. S., & Pangabean, R. A. M. (2021). Risk Analysis in the Application of Financore Information Systems Using FMEA Method. *Journal of Physics: Conference Series, 1751*(1), 012032. Advance online publication. DOI: 10.1088/1742-6596/1751/1/012032

Ul Alam, M., Azad, M. A. K., & Ali, M. S. (2022). Best Practices to Secure API Implementations in Core Banking System (CBS) in Banks. In P. R. (Ed.), *2022 IEEE 12th Annual Computing and Communication Workshop and Conference, CCWC 2022* (pp. 730–735). Institute of Electrical and Electronics Engineers Inc. DOI: 10.1109/CCWC54503.2022.9720840

Usanti, T. P. (2022). THE PRINCIPLE OF AMANAH IN THE UTILISATION OF CONSUMERS' PERSONAL DATA AND INFORMATION IN OPEN BANKING. *Journal of Central Banking Law and Institutions, 1*(1), 119–140. DOI: 10.21098/jcli.v1i1.2

Wiwoho, J., Pati, U. K., & Pratama, A. M. (2024). Reciprocal Data Portability to Foster Financial Services Competition in the Open Banking System Era. *Yustisia, 13*(2), 134–150. DOI: 10.20961/yustisia.v13i2.75786

Xu, H. (2025). OLAP Technology Financial Statistics Information Platform Based on Big Data Analysis. In X. Z., A. S., L.-G. O., & A. R. N.H. (Eds.), *Lecture Notes in Networks and Systems: Vol. 1351 LNNS* (pp. 283–293). Springer Science and Business Media Deutschland GmbH. DOI: 10.1007/978-3-031-88287-6_27

Yanting, Z., & Ali, M. (2023). Artificial intelligence, digital finance, and financial inclusion: A conceptual framework. In *Financial Inclusion Across Asia: Bringing Opportunities for Businesses* (pp. 77–85). Emerald Group Publishing Ltd. DOI: 10.1108/978-1-83753-304-620231006

Zhang, Q., Zhu, J., & Ding, Q. (2020). OBBC: A Blockchain-Based Data Sharing Scheme for Open Banking. In S. X., J. H., S. Y., Z. J., Z. L., S. X., & L. Z. (Eds.), *Communications in Computer and Information Science: Vol. 1176 CCIS* (pp. 1–16). Springer. DOI: 10.1007/978-981-15-3278-8_1

Ziegler, T. (2021). Implementation of Open Banking Protocols Around the World. In *The Palgrave Handbook of Technological Finance* (pp. 751–782). Springer International Publishing., DOI: 10.1007/978-3-030-65117-6_27

Chapter 12
Digital Risk Management and Financial Control Systems in Public Sector Organizations:
Evidence From Indonesia's E-Government Transformation

Rimi Gusliana Mais
http://orcid.org/0000-0002-2625-0601
Sekolah Tinggi Ilmu Ekonomi Indonesia Jakarta, Indonesia

Erna Lovita
Sekolah Tinggi Ilmu Ekonomi Indonesia Jakarta, Indonesia

Tutty Nuryati
Universitas Bhayangkara Jakarta Raya, Indonesia

Saiful Muchlis
Universitas Islam Negeri (UIN) Alauddin Makassar, Indonesia

ABSTRACT

This chapter examines the growing importance of digital risk management and financial control systems in the context of digital transformation in the public sector. As governments increasingly adopt digital financial management systems to support budgeting, accounting, and financial reporting processes, new risks related to cybersecurity, data integrity, system integration, and governance emerge. The chapter discusses how these risks can affect the reliability, transparency, and accountability

DOI: 10.4018/979-8-3373-9230-1.ch012

2027, IGI Global Scientific Publishing. Copying or distributing in print or electronic forms without written permission of IGI Global Scientific Publishing is prohibited. Use of this chapter to rative artificial intelligence (AI) technologies is expressly prohibited. The publisher reserves all rights to license its use for generative AI training and machine learning model development.

of public financial management. It further explores the role of integrated risk management, internal control systems, and IT governance in mitigating digital financial risks. By presenting a conceptual framework and a digital risk management cycle, the chapter highlights the importance of strengthening institutional capacity and governance mechanisms to ensure secure, reliable, and accountable digital financial systems in public sector organizations.

1. INTRODUCTION: DIGITALIZATION, RISK, AND FINANCIAL CONTROL IN THE PUBLIC SECTOR

Digital transformation has emerged as a vital aspect of modern public sector reform, substantially altering the methods by which governments handle information, provide services, and account for public resources. The incorporation of digital technology in public administration transcends mere technological adoption, involving significant organizational, procedural, and cultural transformations, frequently referred to as a transition to digital era governance (Yang, Gu, & Albitar, 2024). This transformation seeks to enhance efficiency, responsiveness, and openness in governmental operations, especially in financial management tasks that are crucial to public accountability and resource stewardship (OECD, 2026; IMF, 2023).

Nonetheless, the speed and intricacy of digitalization present new dangers and problems that may compromise the integrity of financial information systems if inadequately managed. This encompasses systemic vulnerabilities like cybersecurity threats, data integrity concerns, and integration difficulties across diverse digital platforms (NIST, 2024; OECD, 2024a). In this setting, public sector organizations must enhance their risk management and control structures to guarantee that digital transformation results in improved governance rather than unforeseen repercussions. Effective risk management in a digital context is essential for preserving trust in governmental financial information and protecting public value (Volodina & Grossi, 2024).

This chapter examines the convergence of digital transformation, risk management, and financial oversight within the public sector, focusing specifically on Indonesia's public financial reforms. This chapter analyzes the governance and control of digital financial information systems, emphasizing rising dangers and identifying best practices that promote responsible and transparent public financial management. The discussion is situated within expansive theoretical frameworks that link risk management, internal control, and public sector accountability in the context of digital governance.

1.1 Digital Transformation in Public Sector Organizations

Digital transformation denotes the deliberate incorporation of digital technologies into organizational processes, structures, and practices to enhance performance and provide value to stakeholders. This transition in the public sector is propelled by the necessity for enhanced government efficiency, transparency, and citizen involvement, encompassing comprehensive alterations in administrative culture and governance frameworks, rather than solely focusing on automation (Magnusson, Iqbal, Elm, & Dalipi, 2025). Digital transformation in public administration is recognized as a complex and comprehensive process necessitating cooperation among policy, technology infrastructure, labor capabilities, and regulatory frameworks (OECD, 2026; IMF, 2023).

A key aspect of public sector digital transformation is the extensive implementation of digital financial management systems that automate formerly manual activities associated with budgeting, accounting, reporting, and compliance. These technologies have demonstrated improvements in the timeliness and accuracy of financial reporting, enabling real-time monitoring and decision-making capabilities (International Monetary Fund, 2023). The transformation process varies significantly among countries and institutions, frequently impeded by resource limitations, outdated infrastructure, and deficiencies in digital literacy among civil personnel.

Digital transformation fundamentally alters operational processes and organizational expectations about data governance and service delivery. Governments are progressively anticipated to handle substantial amounts of public data as a valuable asset, facilitating data-driven policymaking and scrutiny, while also exposing public financial systems to emerging vulnerabilities concerning data quality, security, and interoperability.

1.2 Financial Information Risks in Digitally Enabled Governance

The implementation of digital financial information systems presents a unique array of hazards that must be actively mitigated to guarantee the reliability and integrity of public financial data. Digital systems inherently elevate the risk of cybersecurity risks, illicit access, and data breaches, hence eroding stakeholders' confidence in governmental financial information (NIST, 2024; OECD, 2024a). The complexity of linked systems may provide hazards of data inconsistency, inadequate data governance, and operational disruptions in the absence of sufficient controls.

Besides technological concerns, digital transformation may produce institutional and administrative obstacles. Public sector organizations may lack the requisite governance frameworks to synchronize risk mitigation efforts across departments, resulting in fragmented control environments. Likewise, advancing technologies like artificial intelligence and big data analytics, although offering enhanced transparency and efficiency, also introduce novel risk scenarios related to algorithmic bias, unclear decision-making processes, and ethical dilemmas (OECD, 2024a; NIST, 2024).

The AI dimension also requires a governance layer beyond conventional cybersecurity. OECD identifies governance, data, digital infrastructure, skills, investment, procurement, and partnerships as key enablers for trustworthy AI in government, while emphasizing guardrails for transparency, oversight, and risk management. Indonesia has also issued a 2023 ministerial circular on AI ethics for public and private electronic-system providers and, as of 2026, is preparing a national AI roadmap and presidential regulation. For financial-control systems, these developments imply that any future use of AI for anomaly detection, fraud analytics, forecasting, or automated decision support should be subject to explicit accountability, human oversight, data-quality controls, and auditability (OECD, 2024a; Ministry of Communication and Digital Affairs, 2023, 2026).

These hazards highlight the essential requirement for strong control measures that both safeguard digital platforms and conform to wider accountability frameworks. Due to the public sector's obligation to oversee resources for residents, risk management includes not just operational reliability but also the stewardship of public finances and adherence to legal and ethical norms.

1.3 Objectives, Scope, and Contributions of the Research Chapter

This chapter aims to analyze the impact of digital transformation on risk management and financial control systems in public sector organizations, using Indonesia as a documentary case context supported by secondary empirical evidence. This chapter aims to connect theoretical insights with practical implementations by concentrating on digital public finance reforms and their related risks, hence enhancing governance in digitally enabled contexts (OECD, 2026). The chapter's focus includes both conceptual and empirical aspects. It integrates pertinent literature on digital transformation, risk management, and control systems within public administration and accounting. It draws on documented evidence from Indonesia's current digital public finance management projects to demonstrate how risks materialize and are mitigated in practical contexts. This dual emphasis allows the chapter to engage in scholarly discussions on digital governance while providing practical insights for policymakers and practitioners.

Existing digital-government maturity frameworks are useful for assessing broad technological and institutional capabilities, but they do not by themselves explain whether digitalization produces effective financial control. In public financial management, control effectiveness depends on the interaction among digital infrastructure, cybersecurity and resilience, data governance, embedded internal controls, assurance mechanisms, institutional accountability, and organizational capability. This creates a theoretical and practical gap between assessing digital-government maturity and explaining financial-control effectiveness. The chapter addresses this gap by proposing an integrated socio-technical governance framework that connects these dimensions and examines their interaction through traceable documentary evidence from Indonesia. The contribution therefore lies not in establishing a causal effect of digitalization, but in explaining how technological, organizational, assurance, and institutional mechanisms jointly shape the capacity for effective digital financial control.

This chapter specifically contributes by: (1) identifying critical risk factors related to digital financial information systems; (2) analyzing the design of control systems to mitigate these risks; and (3) proposing a framework that incorporates risk management practices into digital transformation strategies within the public sector. This integrated research underscores the significance of risk-aware governance and the function of control mechanisms in preserving public value in the digital era.

1.4 Methodological Approach and Evidence Base

The chapter adopts a qualitative documentary case-analysis design. The purpose is not to estimate a causal effect of digitalization, but to examine how digital risk management and financial control mechanisms operate within Indonesia's public-sector digital transformation and to connect Indonesian evidence with broader international developments. Documentary analysis is appropriate where institutional reports, regulations, implementation records, audit materials, and peer-reviewed studies provide traceable evidence about organizational practices and policy implementation (Bowen, 2009).

The evidence base comprises four source groups: (1) official Indonesian government and regulatory documents, including materials on SAKTI, SIPD, fiscal-information platforms, AI governance, and cybersecurity incidents; (2) oversight and audit-related publications from Indonesian public institutions; (3) international benchmarks and guidance from the OECD, World Bank, IMF, and NIST; and (4) peer-reviewed research examining public financial management, digital transformation, continuous auditing, and digital assurance. Sources were included when they were directly relevant to public-sector financial digitalization, risk/control implications, or governance capability and when the underlying evidence was publicly identifiable and reproducible.

The analysis followed three steps. First, the documents were organized around five analytical domains: digital infrastructure and interoperability; cybersecurity and resilience; data governance and integrity; internal control and continuous assurance; and institutional capacity and accountability. Second, evidence within each domain was compared across Indonesian cases and international benchmarks to identify recurring mechanisms, implementation gaps, and measurable indicators. Third, the findings were synthesized into the integrated framework proposed in Section 9. The analysis therefore treats Indonesia as a contextual and documentary case rather than as a statistically representative sample of public organizations.

The principal empirical anchors are SAKTI as the central-government financial-management case; SIPD and the national fiscal-information architecture as the subnational case; the 2024 PDNS ransomware incident as evidence of systemic cyber-resilience exposure in shared public digital infrastructure; and OECD/World Bank digital-government indicators as comparative benchmarks. These anchors are complemented by peer-reviewed evidence on SAKTI users, regional financial-application integration, and continuous-auditing readiness. This design makes the evidentiary basis, selection logic, and limits of inference explicit.

Table 1. Documentary evidence base and analytical role

Evidence anchor	Source type	Evidence provided	Analytical role
SAKTI	Ministry of Finance / treasury studies	Integrated planning-to-reporting architecture; electronic transactions; rollout indicators	Financial controls, traceability, access and workflow controls
SIPD / fiscal-information architecture	BPK and Ministry of Finance materials	Electronic regional financial information and national consolidation	Interoperability, decentralization and data governance
PDNS ransomware incident (2024)	BSSN/Komdigi public record	Documented disruption of shared public digital infrastructure	Cyber resilience, continuity and concentration risk
OECD DGI / World Bank GTMI	International benchmark datasets	Cross-country maturity indicators	Comparative positioning and maturity gaps
Peer-reviewed Indonesian studies	Journal articles	User-level and organizational evidence on SAKTI, regional systems and continuous auditing	Triangulation and empirical validation

2. DIGITAL GOVERNMENT AS A DIGITAL ENTERPRISE IN THE PUBLIC SECTOR

Digital government has progressively transitioned from a technology-centric reform initiative to a holistic transformation of public sector organizations, establishing them as digital enterprises within the public sector. In this sense, digital government signifies not only the digitization of administrative operations but also the strategic incorporation of digital technologies into fundamental governmental tasks, encompassing financial management, oversight, and governance. This shift redefines the methods by which public sector organizations generate public value, allocate resources, and uphold accountability (Mergel, Edelmann, & Haug, 2019).

Viewing government organizations as digital organizations highlights their dependence on cohesive digital infrastructures to synchronize activities and facilitate decision-making across organizational boundaries. Financial management information systems, enterprise resource planning platforms, and data analytics tools are the foundation of modern digital organizations, facilitating real-time access to financial data and improving managerial supervision (Vial, 2019). Unlike traditional bureaucratic models, digitally enabled public organizations function through interconnected systems that integrate rules, controls, and reporting mechanisms within digital workflows, fundamentally transforming internal control environments.

Nonetheless, digitally enabled public organizations in the public sector markedly differ from those in the private sector. Private digitally enabled public organizations emphasize efficiency, competitiveness, and profitability, whereas public sector digital enterprises are governed by legality, transparency, and public accountability. This differentiation has significant ramifications for financial control systems, which must not only facilitate managerial efficiency but also guarantee adherence to regulatory frameworks and democratic supervision (Grossi, Steccolini, & Reichard, 2019). Consequently, digital government projects impose increased requirements on risk management and control systems to reconcile innovation with the protection of public resources.

The transition to a public sector digital enterprise further exacerbates organizational and institutional complexity. Digital integration enhances dependency across agencies, central and local governments, and external service providers, thus amplifying risk exposure associated with system interoperability, data governance, and cybersecurity (OECD, 2026; OECD/ADB, 2025). Financial information hazards in digital government settings are no longer limited to discrete procedures but can disseminate through interconnected systems, hence magnifying their potential effect on public accountability.

From a governance standpoint, digital government as a public sector digital entity necessitates a reconfiguration of conventional control mechanisms. Ex post controls and periodic audits, although still significant, are progressively supplemented by system-embedded controls, automatic validations, and continuous monitoring instruments. These techniques improve openness and timeliness but necessitate new skills and managerial competencies to analyze and respond to digital financial information (Mergel et al., 2019). In the absence of sufficient organizational capability and governance frameworks, digitally enabled public organizations may provide an illusion of control that conceals fundamental weaknesses.

Viewing digital government as a public sector digital enterprise offers a significant analytical perspective for assessing the interplay among digital transformation, risk management, and financial control systems. It emphasizes the strategic use of financial information systems as governance tools rather than impartial technologies, and it stresses the necessity for cohesive risk management frameworks that match technological advancement with public sector principles. This viewpoint is especially pertinent for nations like Indonesia, where extensive digital public financial reforms are transforming the framework of public sector accounting and control systems (OECD, 2026). The digital transformation of public sector organizations has significantly reshaped the way governments manage financial information. Modern public financial management increasingly relies on integrated digital platforms that connect budgeting, accounting, reporting, and oversight processes across government institutions.

Figure 1. Digital Financial Management Ecosystem in Public Sector Governance

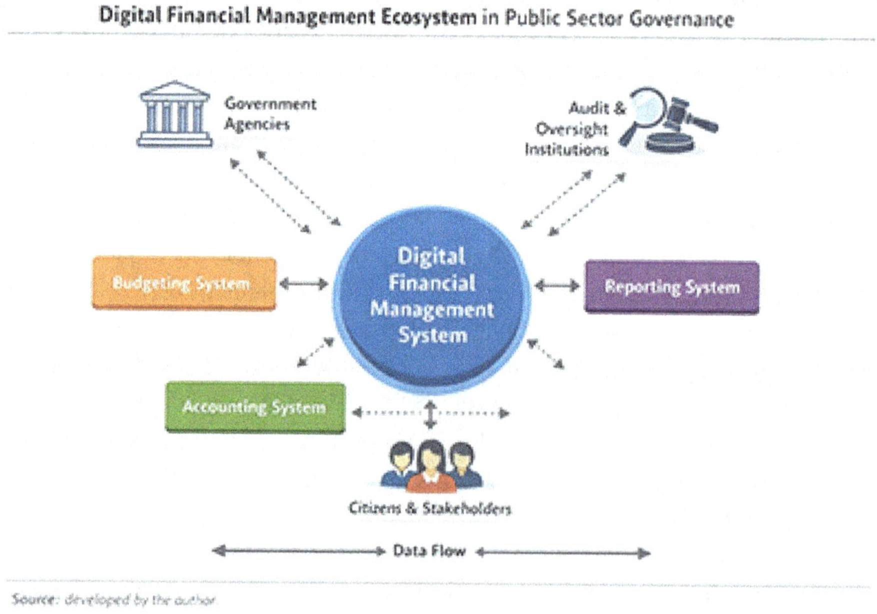

Source: Developed by the author

This figure illustrates the ecosystem of digital financial management in the public sector. The Digital Financial Management System functions as the central platform that integrates key subsystems, including budgeting, accounting, and reporting systems. These subsystems interact with government agencies that generate and manage financial transactions, while audit and oversight institutions ensure accountability and compliance. In addition, citizens and stakeholders represent the broader public who benefit from improved transparency and access to financial information. The interconnected structure demonstrates how data flows across institutional actors and digital platforms to support efficient, transparent, and accountable public financial governance.

2.1 Defining Digital Enterprises within the Public Sector Framework

The notion of a digital enterprise typically denotes firms that strategically utilize digital technologies to unify processes, data, and decision-making along the whole value chain. This concept originated in the commercial sector, but current research increasingly acknowledges its significance for public sector organizations experiencing extensive digital transition. Digital government programs transform public sector entities from mere users of information technology into digital organizations that utilize integrated information systems for resource management, activity coordination, and policy achievement (Mergel, Edelmann, & Haug, 2019).

In the public sector, a digital enterprise is defined by the incorporation of digital platforms into essential administrative operations such as budgeting, accounting, procurement, and reporting. These systems facilitate real-time financial information exchange across organizational borders, therefore transforming internal control mechanisms and managerial responsibility frameworks (Vial, 2019). In contrast to private organizations, public sector digital enterprises function inside intricate institutional frameworks characterized by legal obligations, political supervision, and needs for public accountability.

Viewing government entities as digital enterprises emphasizes the strategic importance of financial information systems as governance instruments rather than simply technical infrastructures. Financial data is an essential organizational asset that facilitates collaboration, performance management, and compliance. This viewpoint corresponds with public sector accounting literature that underscores the significance of control mechanisms in protecting public resources and preserving legitimacy (Grossi, Steccolini, & Reichard, 2019). Thus, digital transformation necessitates a reevaluation of risk management and control systems to guarantee their efficacy inside digitally enabled organizational frameworks.

2.2 E-Government and Digital Financial Management Systems in Indonesia

Indonesia's e-government transformation exemplifies the evolution of public sector entities into digital enterprises. In the last ten years, the Indonesian government has executed a succession of digital public financial management reforms designed to enhance transparency, efficiency, and accountability. Primary activities encompass the implementation of integrated financial management information systems for budgeting, treasury, and accounting operations, aimed at standardizing processes and improving monitoring across central and local governments (International Monetary Fund, 2023).

Digital financial management systems in Indonesia facilitate real-time documentation and reporting of public transactions, minimizing manual involvement and potential for discretionary alteration. These solutions are essential for enhancing internal controls by integrating authorization protocols, audit trails, and compliance verifications into digital workflows (Diamond & Khemani, 2006). Consequently, the management of financial information increasingly depends on system-based controls instead of exclusively on retrospective audits.

Nonetheless, the deployment of digital financial systems also exposes enduring difficulties. System interoperability, disparate technology capabilities among regions, and opposition to organizational transformation persist as threats to effective governance. Furthermore, dependence on centralized digital platforms increases vulnerability to cybersecurity threats and dangers to data integrity, highlighting the necessity for strong governance frameworks (OECD, 2026; OECD/ADB, 2025). These dynamics demonstrate that digitalization, although augmenting control capabilities, concurrently generates new risk profiles that require active management.

2.3 Characteristics of Organizations and Institutions in Public Sector Digitalization

The digitalization of the public sector is significantly influenced by the organizational and institutional attributes that differentiate governmental bodies from private firms. Legal frameworks, regulatory supervision, and political responsibility profoundly affect the design, implementation, and governance of digital systems. Institutional theory posits that public organizations implement digital systems not solely for efficiency improvements but also to adhere to normative standards of transparency and modernity (DiMaggio & Powell).

The capacity of an organization is a crucial factor in the success of digitalization. The efficacy of digital financial control systems is contingent upon managerial capabilities, employee digital literacy, and the congruence of organizational structures with digital workflows. Research indicates that insufficient capacity can undermine control environments, despite the presence of sophisticated digital technologies (Vial, 2019). Moreover, disjointed governance structures within the public sector might hinder inter-agency collaboration, resulting in inconsistent risk management methods.

In Indonesia, these institutional and organizational characteristics are especially prominent due to the decentralized structure of public administration. Although national policies advocate for standardized digital financial systems, local governments demonstrate differing degrees of preparedness and competence. This variance emphasizes the significance of adaptive risk management frameworks that consider institutional variability while upholding fundamental control principles. Comprehending these attributes is crucial for developing financial information management and control systems that are robust, accountable, and congruent with public sector principles in a digital age.

3. RISK MANAGEMENT IN DIGITAL PUBLIC SECTOR ENTITIES

The digital revolution of public sector organizations has profoundly changed the nature, breadth, and complexity of hazards related to financial information management. As governments increasingly depend on integrated digital financial information systems for budgeting, accounting, and reporting, risk management has become a critical element of digital governance. Digital public sector firms encounter interrelated technological, organizational, and institutional risks that, if unaddressed, might jeopardize the reliability, integrity, and validity of financial information, in contrast to traditional risk settings (Volodina & Grossi, 2024).

Risk management in digital public sector organizations transcends technical protections to include managerial and governance aspects. Digital financial systems incorporate regulatory frameworks and decision-making algorithms into automated processes, transferring risk management from human judgment to system architecture, data governance, and interoperability agreements (Vial, 2019). Thus, deficiencies in digital risk management can yield systemic consequences, impacting numerous enterprises and governmental tiers concurrently.

Furthermore, public sector organizations function within legislative and institutional frameworks that enforce stringent accountability standards. Digital hazards consequently have direct repercussions on public trust, fiscal responsibility, and adherence to legislative systems. Risk management transcends a basic technical or operational issue, emerging as a fundamental governance role that fosters openness and accountability in digital government (Grossi et al., 2019). Comprehending the categorization, management, and influence of risks within institutional contexts is crucial for developing effective financial control systems in digitally enabled public sector organizations.

3.1 Classification of Risks in Digital Financial Information Systems

Digital financial information systems subject public sector organizations to a variety of hazards that vary in nature and intensity compared to traditional manual systems. A primary area is technological risk, encompassing cybersecurity threats, system failures, and data breaches. As financial information systems get more interconnected, vulnerabilities in a single component can propagate across platforms, exacerbating possible disruptions to public financial management (NIST, 2024; OECD, 2024a).

A second category is data-related risk, which includes data correctness, completeness, and integrity. Digital systems depend significantly on standardized data inputs and automated processing protocols, rendering them vulnerable to errors due to insufficient data governance or inadequate validation measures. In the public sector, erroneous financial data might compromise budgetary decision-making and diminish accountability mechanisms (OECD, 2026; IMF, 2023).

Organizational and management risks are equally significant in digital financial systems. The dangers arise from inadequate digital competencies, opposition to organizational change, and ambiguous accountability for system monitoring. Poorly defined roles and duties in managing digital systems can lead to control gaps, hence diminishing the efficacy of risk mitigation techniques (Mergel et al., 2019).

Ultimately, institutional and compliance risks emerge from the necessity to synchronize digital systems with legal and regulatory mandates. The digitalization of the public sector frequently surpasses the pace of legislative adaptation, resulting in uncertainty around compliance requirements and auditability. This typology emphasizes that vulnerabilities in digital financial information systems are multifaceted and necessitate comprehensive management strategies. The increasing reliance on digital platforms in public financial management introduces a range of new risks that may affect the reliability, security, and governance of financial information systems. These risks arise from technological vulnerabilities, system integration challenges, and institutional governance issues.

Figure 2. Major Risk Categories in Digital Public Financial Information Systems

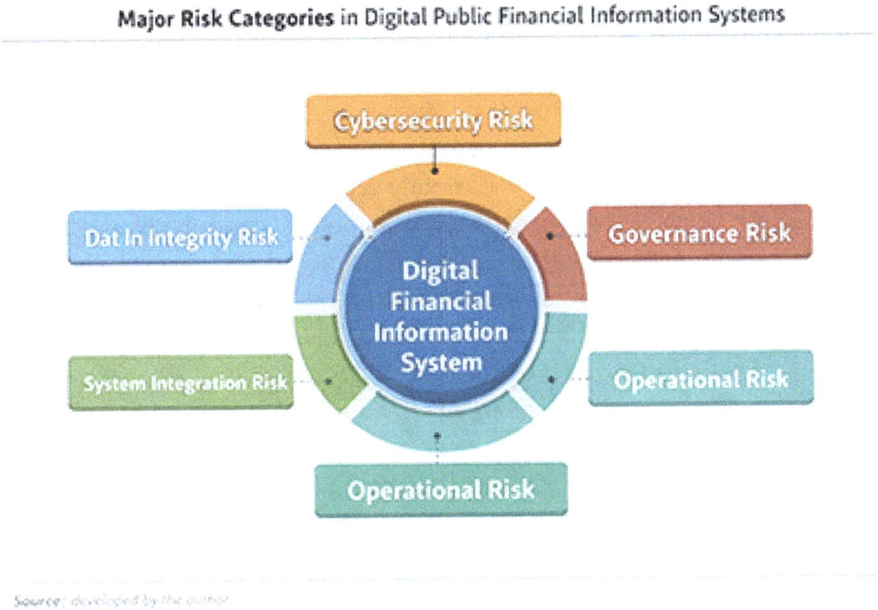

Source: *Developed by the author.*

This figure illustrates the major categories of risks associated with digital public financial information systems. As governments increasingly rely on integrated digital platforms for budgeting, accounting, and reporting, several risk dimensions emerge. These include cybersecurity risk, which relates to potential cyberattacks and unauthorized access; data integrity risk, which concerns the accuracy and reliability of financial information; system integration risk, arising from the interaction between multiple digital platforms; operational risk linked to system failures or human errors; and governance risk related to weaknesses in oversight, policies, and accountability mechanisms. Understanding these interconnected risks is essential for designing effective digital risk management and internal control systems in public sector financial governance.

3.2 Frameworks for Digital Risk Management in Public Organizations

Digital risk management frameworks offer systematic methodologies for discovering, evaluating, and alleviating hazards related to digital financial information systems. In the public sector, prevalent frameworks like COSO Enterprise Risk Management and internal control models have been modified to suit digital environments. These frameworks underscore the incorporation of risk management within organizational strategy and operations, rather than regarding it as an isolated activity (COSO, 2017).

In digital contexts, risk management frameworks increasingly integrate integrated controls, continuous monitoring systems, and data analytics tools. Automated controls facilitate the immediate identification of abnormalities and non-compliance, hence improving the responsiveness of public sector control systems (Diamond & Khemani, 2006). Nonetheless, dependence on automated controls creates additional reliance on the quality of system design and governance.

Public organizations must mix technical solutions with organizational control in effective digital risk management frameworks. This entails the establishment of explicit governance frameworks, delineation of accountability for risk ownership, and facilitation of collaboration among IT, finance, and audit activities. Empirical research indicates that digital risk management is most efficacious when integrated into comprehensive public financial management reforms rather than executed as standalone technology initiatives (IMF, 2023).

3.3 Regulatory and Institutional Impacts on Risk Management Practices

Risk management techniques in digital public sector organizations are significantly influenced by legislative and institutional frameworks. Legal obligations, auditing standards, and public accountability principles shape the perception, prioritization, and management of risks. Institutional theory posits that public organizations frequently implement risk management strategies to attain legitimacy and adhere to external expectations, while enhancing efficiency (DiMaggio & Powell, 1983).

In numerous jurisdictions, regulatory frameworks are outdated compared to technology advancements, resulting in conflicts between innovation and compliance. Digital financial systems may present functionalities inadequately covered by current legislation, heightening uncertainty for managers tasked with risk management. In decentralized systems like Indonesia's, institutional variety exacerbates risk management challenges due to variations in local government capacity and regulatory interpretation (OECD, 2026; OECD/ADB, 2025). These institutional impacts highlight the necessity of adaptive risk management strategies that synchronize digital innovation with regulatory mandates and public sector principles. Effective risk management in digital public sector organizations thus depends not only on technical controls, but also on institutional coherence and governance capacity.

4. FINANCIAL CONTROL MECHANISMS IN A DIGITAL CONTEXT

The digitalization of public sector entities has profoundly altered the architecture and functioning of financial control systems. As financial processes become more integrated into digital platforms, traditional control mechanisms reliant on manual procedures and retrospective verification are being supplemented, and in certain instances replaced, by system-embedded controls and automated monitoring technologies. In a digital world, financial control systems are no longer limited to organizational rules and processes; they are intricately connected to information system architectures and data governance frameworks (Romney & Steinbart, 2021).

In digitally enabled public sector organizations, financial control systems are essential for assuring the dependability, legality, and accountability of financial information. Digital financial management information systems integrate permission protocols, duty segregation, and audit trails directly into transaction processing, thus transforming the control environment. Although these capabilities improve efficiency and transparency, they also create new dependencies on system design, configuration, and governance quality (Vasarhelyi, Kogan, & Tuttle, 2015).

The transition to digital control environments amplifies the significance of cohesive control frameworks that synchronize technological controls with organizational governance. Deficiencies in system setup, data governance, or integration might compromise the efficacy of controls, despite the existence of formal control frameworks. Therefore, comprehending the functioning of internal control systems, their integration with financial information systems, and their capacity to tackle data quality issues is crucial for risk management and ensuring accountability in digital public sector entities.

4.1 Internal Control Mechanisms in Digitally Enabled Organizations

Internal control systems form the basis of financial governance in public sector organizations, ensuring the attainment of operational, reporting, and compliance objectives. In digitally enabled businesses, internal control systems increasingly depend on automated and system-integrated procedures that function continuously rather than intermittently (COSO, 2013). These techniques comprise automatic authorization verifications, system-mandated segregation of responsibilities, and instantaneous exception reporting.

Digital internal controls provide substantial benefits compared to conventional manual controls by minimizing human error, improving consistency, and augmenting the timeliness of control activities. Embedded controls in financial information systems facilitate ongoing monitoring and prompt identification of anomalies, hence aiding proactive risk management (Vasarhelyi et al., 2015). Nonetheless, dependence on automated controls reallocates control risks to system design, access management, and change control procedures.

In the public sector, internal control systems must facilitate accountability to external stakeholders, such as auditors, regulators, and citizens. Digitally enabled controls enhance auditability by producing comprehensive audit trails and consistent reporting outputs, hence reinforcing openness and supervision (Diamond & Khemani, 2006). Simultaneously, insufficient governance over system modifications or user access may diminish control efficacy and render organizations vulnerable to fraud or the misappropriation of public resources. Effective internal control systems in digital environments necessitate a balanced strategy that integrates technology safeguards with organizational oversight, defined accountability mechanisms, and ongoing capacity development.

4.2 Integration of Financial Information Systems and Control Mechanisms

The incorporation of financial information systems is a hallmark of digital public sector entities. Integrated systems connect budgeting, accounting, procurement, treasury, and reporting processes, facilitating uninterrupted financial information exchange among organizational units. This integration augments control capabilities by minimizing data redundancy, enhancing consistency, and facilitating thorough oversight (Granlund & Mouritsen, 2003).

Integrated financial systems incorporate control mechanisms inside business processes, connecting operational operations with financial control goals. Automated workflows ensure adherence to budgetary constraints, permission structures, and regulatory standards, consequently enhancing preventive controls. Moreover, integration facilitates comprehensive cross-functional monitoring and analytics, allowing managers to evaluate financial performance and risks in a holistic manner.

Nonetheless, system integration presents novel control issues. The heightened interconnectedness across systems exacerbates the consequences of control failures, as errors or breaches in one module can disseminate throughout the entire system. In public sector environments, the integration of many agencies and governmental levels affects governance and accountability frameworks (OECD, 2026; OECD/ADB, 2025). To alleviate these risks, integrated financial information systems must be underpinned by strong governance frameworks that delineate control ownership, system duties, and escalation protocols. Effective integration necessitates congruence between technical architecture and institutional governance structures.

Figure 3. Integrated Framework of Digital Risk Management and Financial Control

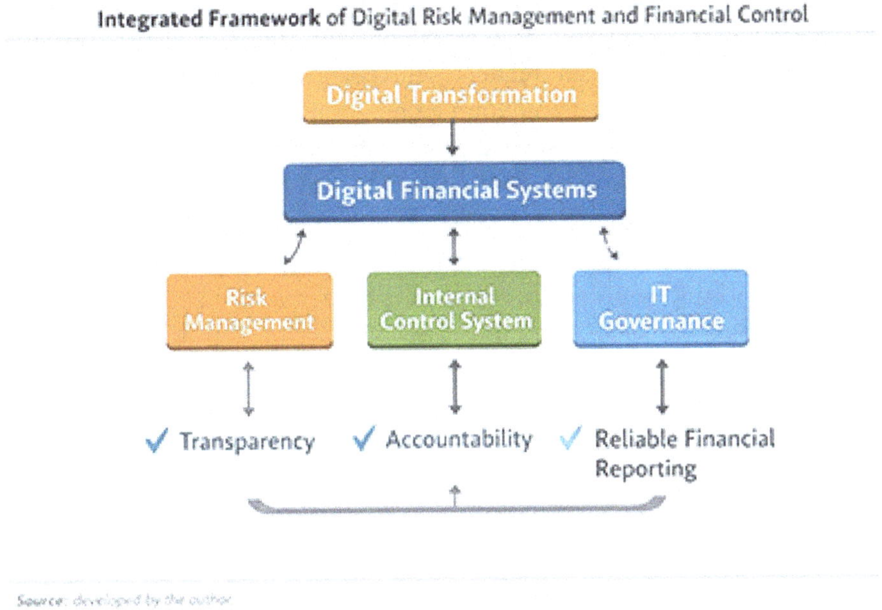

Source: *Developed by the author*

This figure presents an integrated framework illustrating the relationship between digital transformation, digital financial systems, risk management, internal control systems, and IT governance in the public sector. Digital transformation drives the adoption of digital financial systems that support government financial operations. To ensure the reliability and security of these systems, effective risk management, internal control mechanisms, and IT governance must be implemented. The integration of these three components strengthens institutional oversight and enhances the effectiveness of financial management. Ultimately, this integrated framework contributes to improved transparency, stronger accountability, and more reliable financial reporting in public sector organizations.

4.3 Challenges in Data Quality, Reliability, and Control within Digital Accounting Systems

The quality and dependability of data are fundamental to the efficacy of financial control systems in digital contexts. Digital accounting systems depend on standardized data inputs and automated processing protocols, rendering them particularly vulnerable to data errors, discrepancies, and omissions. Subpar data quality can compromise the accuracy of financial reporting, skew managerial decision-making, and diminish accountability mechanisms (Batini, Scannapieco, & Viscusi, 2016). Data quality control difficulties stem from various causes, including deficient data governance policies, weak validation processes, and fragmented data ownership. In interconnected systems, data frequently traverses organizational borders, hence amplifying the complexity of maintaining consistency and accountability. Public sector entities encounter supplementary obstacles stemming from disparate regulatory mandates and differing levels of organizational capability.

Digital accounting systems also raise concerns regarding data reliability over time, particularly in relation to system upgrades, changes in accounting standards, and evolving reporting requirements. In the absence of robust change management and control protocols, such alterations may jeopardize data comparability and auditability (Romney & Steinbart, 2021). Confronting data quality and reliability issues necessitates cohesive control strategies that merge technical solutions, such as automated validation and reconciliation instruments, with organizational initiatives, including explicit data ownership and accountability structures. These steps are crucial for guaranteeing that digital accounting systems facilitate reliable financial information and strong public sector governance.

5. DOCUMENTARY EVIDENCE FROM INDONESIA'S E-GOVERNMENT TRANSFORMATION

Indonesia's e-government transition provides a valuable documentary and empirical context for analyzing the impact of digitalization on risk management and financial control systems within the public sector. In the last twenty years, Indonesia has implemented comprehensive public financial management reforms facilitated by digital technologies, with the objective of enhancing fiscal discipline, transparency, and accountability. These reforms embody wider worldwide movements towards digital governance, significantly influenced by Indonesia's institutional traits, such as decentralization, regulatory intricacy, and varying organizational capabilities across governmental tiers (OECD, 2026; OECD/ADB, 2025).

The digitalization of financial management in Indonesia's public sector has been propelled by the necessity to enhance oversight of public resources and to tackle enduring governance issues. Integrated financial information systems have been implemented to standardize accounting methods, improve real-time monitoring, and mitigate opportunities for fraud and mismanagement. As digital technologies increasingly facilitate financial processes, they concurrently bring novel risks associated with system reliability, data quality, and organizational coordination (Lakat, 2025).

This chapter synthesizes secondary empirical evidence from Indonesia's e-government transformation to demonstrate the practical functioning of digital risk management and financial control systems. This chapter analyzes public sector digital financial reforms, specific organizational examples, and growing implementation issues, illustrating how digitalization transforms control settings and managerial accountability. The Indonesian scenario illustrates that although digital financial systems might greatly improve control potential, their efficacy is ultimately contingent upon governance structures, institutional coherence, and organizational capability.

5.1 Synopsis of Indonesia's Digital Financial Reforms in the Public Sector

The digital financial changes in Indonesia's public sector have developed incrementally, mirroring domestic governance priorities and international best practices in public financial management. Principal activities encompass the creation of integrated financial management information systems intended to facilitate budgeting, treasury operations, accounting, and financial reporting for both central and local governments. These technologies seek to enhance data consistency, minimize manual involvement, and reinforce budgetary control (International Monetary Fund, 2023).

A hallmark of Indonesia's reforms is the focus on standardization and integration. Digital platforms have been implemented to standardize accounting practices and reporting formats, enhancing the consolidation and comparability of financial data. From a governance standpoint, these systems include authorization protocols, budgetary limits, and audit trails into digital operations, thereby augmenting both preventative and investigative controls (Apriyanto, 2025).

Simultaneously, Indonesia's decentralized governance framework presents considerable obstacles to the execution of digital reforms. Local governments exhibit significant disparities in technological capacity, infrastructure preparedness, and human resource proficiency, resulting in inconsistent adoption and exploitation of digital financial systems. The discrepancies impact risk management, as the effectiveness of controls relies on both system design and organizational capacity and compliance culture (OECD, 2026; OECD/ADB, 2025). Indonesia's digital finance reforms exemplify the dual function of e-government projects as tools for modernization and as means to enhance public sector accountability.

The scale of SAKTI implementation is also reflected in the expansion of certified electronic signatures for government payment documents. By August 2024, implementation through Stages I–III C had covered 86 ministries/agencies and 14,238 government work units (Ministry of Finance, 2024). This scale illustrates the extensive institutional reach of system-embedded authorization mechanisms within central-government financial administration. However, implementation scale should not be interpreted as direct evidence of financial-control effectiveness, which also depends on governance, user capability, data integrity, and assurance mechanisms.

At the subnational level, SIPD provides a complementary case of digital integration. BPK describes SIPD as an instrument intended to align central and regional policy and to support integrated electronic regional financial information. More recently, PMK No. 93/2024 established a national fiscal-policy digital platform and a national regional financial-information architecture for data provision, consolidation, and presentation. Together, these developments show that interoperability is not merely a technical issue: it is an institutional mechanism for standardization, consolidation, and accountability across decentralized governments (BPK, 2024; Ministry of Finance, 2024b).

5.2 Risk Management and Financial Control Practices in Selected Public Sector Instances

5.2.1 Comparative Digital-Government Evidence

The Indonesian experience is more informative when positioned against comparable emerging and Southeast Asian systems. OECD/ADB data report 2023 Digital Government Index scores of 0.62 for Singapore, 0.61 for Indonesia, 0.48 for Thailand, and 0.43 for Viet Nam. Indonesia also records a particularly high Digital by Design score (0.96), while weaker results on Open by Default (0.37), Government as a Platform (0.53), Data-driven Public Sector (0.58), and Proactiveness (0.58) indicate that digital infrastructure and strategic design have progressed faster than some dimensions of data openness and proactive government. The comparison supports the chapter's argument that digital maturity should not be equated with control maturity (OECD/ADB, 2025; OECD, 2026).

Table 2. Comparative digital-government indicators in Southeast Asia

Country	OECD DGI (2023)	Digital by Design	Interpretation for the chapter
Singapore	0.62	0.76	High regional benchmark; illustrates mature whole-of-government digital governance
Indonesia	0.61	0.96	Strong digital-by-design foundation, but uneven performance across other dimensions
Thailand	0.48	0.71	Intermediate maturity; useful comparator for regional institutional variation
Viet Nam	0.43	0.72	Lower composite maturity; illustrates different sequencing of digital-government development

Empirical research from Indonesian public sector organizations indicates that digital financial systems have significantly transformed risk management and control processes. In digitally connected organizations, the detection and mitigation of risks increasingly depend on system-based controls, including automated validations, access limits, and exception reporting. These techniques improve the promptness and uniformity of control actions, diminishing dependence on manual supervision (Lakat, 2025).

Nonetheless, documentary and case-based evidence indicates that risk management methods are inconsistent across public organizations. Although central government institutions often demonstrate more developed digital control environments, smaller governments encounter difficulties due to restricted technical proficiency and disjointed governance structures. In many instances, system-based controls exist alongside informal workarounds, diminishing overall control efficacy and heightening residual risk exposure (Mergel et al., 2019).

These instances underscore that digital financial control solutions do not inherently result in enhanced risk management outcomes. Effective methods rely on managerial commitment, well-defined accountability frameworks, and cooperation among finance, IT, and audit units. Digitalization amplifies control capabilities; yet, organizational and institutional variables dictate the actualization of this potential in practice.

A recent North Sulawesi study provides another quantitative anchor. Using questionnaire data from 70 users of regional financial applications, Lakat (2025) explicitly examined perceived usefulness, perceived ease of use, and perceived risk in relation to the effectiveness of digital public financial management. The study therefore provides organization-level evidence that user perceptions and perceived risk are relevant dimensions when evaluating digital financial-management implementation.

5.3 Principal Challenges and Emerging Control Concerns in Digital Implementation

Despite considerable advancements, Indonesia's e-government transformation nevertheless encounters critical hurdles that influence emerging control issues. A primary problem is maintaining data quality and dependability across interconnected systems. Inconsistent data standards, delays in system updates, and discrepancies in user habits might compromise the integrity and comparability of financial information, hence diminishing decision-making and accountability (Batini et al., 2016).

Cybersecurity and system resilience are increasingly significant issues as dependence on centralized digital platforms escalates. Disruptions or breaches can significantly affect public financial management, highlighting the necessity for comprehensive risk mitigation techniques and contingency planning (NIST, 2024; OECD, 2024a). Ultimately, regulatory adaptation continues to be a persistent difficulty. Digital financial activities can advance more rapidly than regulatory frameworks, resulting in ambiguity around compliance and auditability. Resolving these rising control difficulties necessitates ongoing alignment among technological innovation, regulatory advancement, and organizational capacity enhancement. Indonesia's experience highlights that digital transformation is not a singular reform but a continuous process requiring adaptive risk management and control systems.

A concrete illustration of concentration and continuity risk is the June 2024 ransomware attack on Indonesia's Temporary National Data Center (PDNS). BSSN publicly identified ransomware as the cause of the disruption, which affected several public services. Although PDNS is not itself a financial-management application, the incident is analytically relevant because it demonstrates how dependence on shared digital infrastructure can create cross-agency operational exposure. For digital financial systems, the implication is that backup architecture, recovery objectives, incident response, vendor governance, and continuity testing must be treated as components of financial-control resilience rather than as separate IT concerns (BSSN/Komdigi, 2024).

6. DISCOURSE: GOVERNANCE, ACCOUNTABILITY, AND MANAGERIAL CONSEQUENCES

The empirical evidence from Indonesia's e-government transition demonstrates that digitization significantly alters governance, accountability, and managerial practices inside public sector organizations. Digital financial information systems not only automate current activities but also transform control environments, shift duties, and modify the methods of accountability enforcement. As public sector organizations evolve into digitally enabled public organizations, risk management and financial control systems emerge as fundamental governance instruments rather than merely auxiliary administrative tools (Grossi, Steccolini, & Reichard, 2019).

Digitalization exacerbates the dependency between technical infrastructures and organizational governance. Financial control methods are being integrated into information systems, transferring the locus of control from individual agents to system architecture, data governance, and algorithmic regulations. This transition significantly affects public sector accountability, as control failures may result from system configurations rather than human wrongdoing, confounding the attribution of culpability (Volodina & Grossi, 2024).

Moreover, digital government changes contest conventional hierarchical governance frameworks. Integrated financial systems promote horizontal cooperation among agencies and governmental tiers, however they necessitate novel managerial control and inter-organizational collaboration. In the absence of sufficient governance frameworks, digitalization poses the risk of accountability gaps, wherein the duties for managing risks and controls are dispersed beyond organizational borders. This discussion section integrates these dynamics by analyzing the ramifications of digital risk management for accountability, managerial supervision, and performance-driven governance in public sector organizations.

6.1 Digital Risk Management and Accountability in the Public Sector

Digital risk management is essential in influencing public sector responsibility within digitally enabled organizations. Conventional accountability measures in the public sector predominantly depend on formal regulations, retrospective audits, and hierarchical oversight. In digital contexts, accountability increasingly relies on the design and operation of information systems that incorporate control mechanisms and automate compliance procedures (Bovens, Goodin, & Schillemans, 2014).

System-based controls improve transparency by producing real-time financial data and comprehensive audit trails, facilitating ongoing supervision by management, auditors, and external stakeholders. These attributes enhance accountability and diminish chances for discretionary conduct. Simultaneously, digital risk management presents novel accountability difficulties, especially when risks emerge from system failures, data mistakes, or cybersecurity breaches rather than human actions (NIST, 2024; OECD, 2024a).

From an accountability standpoint, successful digital risk management necessitates clear delineation of responsibilities for system design, operation, and control. Public sector entities must explicitly delineate roles and duties across finance, IT, and audit divisions to guarantee effective ownership and management of digital risks. Lack of clarity may lead to fragmented responsibility, hence eroding public trust and confidence in digital government programs (Volodina & Grossi, 2024). Consequently, digital risk management simultaneously augments and complicates responsibility within the public sector. The efficacy is contingent upon governance structures that synchronize technology restrictions with institutional accountability systems and democratic supervision.

Figure 4. Digital Risk Management Cycle in Public Financial Systems

Source: *Developed by the author*

This figure illustrates the digital risk management cycle applied in public financial systems. The process begins with risk identification, where potential threats related to digital financial systems are recognized. This is followed by risk assessment to evaluate the likelihood and impact of identified risks. Based on this assessment, appropriate control mechanisms are designed and implemented to mitigate potential vulnerabilities. Continuous monitoring and auditing ensure that the controls operate effectively and that emerging risks are detected promptly. Finally, the cycle concludes with continuous improvement, where lessons learned from monitoring and evaluation are used to strengthen future risk management practices. This cyclical approach supports adaptive and resilient governance in digitally enabled public financial management.

6.2 Managerial Obstacles in Supervising Digital Financial Control Systems

The shift to digital finance management systems poses considerable managerial issues for public sector officials. Managers are increasingly tasked with supervising intricate, interconnected information systems that function across organizational borders and have advanced control mechanisms. This transition necessitates the acquisition of new skills in digital literacy, data analysis, and risk evaluation, which may be inadequately cultivated in conventional public sector management positions (Mergel, Edelmann, & Haug, 2019).

A significant difficulty pertains to the equilibrium between dependence on automated controls and managerial discretion. Although digital systems improve efficiency and consistency, an overdependence on automation may diminish managerial knowledge of inherent dangers and control deficiencies. Managers must cultivate the ability to critically evaluate system outputs and intervene upon the detection of abnormalities or growing dangers (Vasarhelyi, Kogan, & Tuttle, 2015).

Moreover, digital financial control systems frequently necessitate collaboration among many organizational departments, such as finance, IT, procurement, and internal audit. Disjointed governance frameworks and ambiguous authority delineations can impede effective oversight and undermine risk management protocols. These issues are especially evident in decentralized public sector organizations, where disparities in capacity and institutional frameworks hinder managerial oversight (OECD, 2026; OECD/ADB, 2025).

Resolving these managerial problems necessitates investment in capacity development, interdisciplinary collaboration, and governance structures that facilitate comprehensive monitoring of digital financial control systems.

6.3 Consequences for Governance and Performance Management in Public Entities

The evidence from Indonesia's e-government transformation hold significant implications for governance and performance management inside public sector organizations. Digital financial control systems facilitate prompt and detailed performance statistics, promoting data-driven decision-making and improved performance oversight. When properly administered, these systems enhance the coherence among financial controls, organizational goals, and the generation of public value (OECD, 2026; IMF, 2023).

Nonetheless, achieving these advantages necessitates governance frameworks that incorporate risk management, control systems, and performance management. Digitalization obscures conventional distinctions between control and performance roles, necessitating the alignment of incentives, accountability frameworks, and managerial duties. In the absence of such alignment, digital systems may produce vast amounts of data without yielding enhanced performance results.

From a governance standpoint, public sector entities must embrace adaptive and proactive strategies that see digital transformation as a continuous process rather than a singular reform. This encompasses ongoing assessment of digital risks, regular revision of control structures, and regulatory adjustment to changing technology environments (OECD, 2026; OECD/ADB, 2025). Digital financial control systems have considerable potential to improve governance and performance management inside public sector organizations. Their efficacy, however, relies on the amalgamation of technology innovation with strong governance frameworks, managerial competence, and accountability systems.

7. CONCLUSION AND PROSPECTIVE DIRECTIONS

This chapter has examined digital risk management and financial control systems in public sector organizations undergoing digital transformation, using Indonesia as a documentary case context supported by secondary empirical evidence. The analysis indicates that digitalization changes public financial governance by embedding controls into information systems, increasing interdependence across agencies, and expanding the range of risks associated with cybersecurity, data integrity, interoperability, resilience, and accountability. The Indonesian evidence also shows that digital maturity and control effectiveness should not be treated as equivalent outcomes. Strong digital infrastructure can expand control capability, but governance, assurance, organizational competence, and institutional coordination determine whether that capability is realized.

The evidence indicates that digital financial systems provide significant potential to improve openness, efficiency, and oversight in public sector financial management. This potential depends on strong governance structures, institutional coherence, and managerial competence. Digital transformation presents new vulnerabilities concerning system integration, data quality, and cybersecurity, which, if insufficiently managed, could compromise accountability and public trust (Volodina & Grossi, 2024). This concluding section consolidates the principal findings, delineates the theoretical contributions of the study, and suggests avenues for future research and practice in digital public sector accounting and control.

7.1 Synopsis of Principal Discoveries

The chapter delineates numerous major findings about risk management and financial control systems within digital public sector entities. Initially, digitalization alters financial control environments by transitioning control mechanisms from manual processes to system-integrated and automated controls. These controls improve the timeliness, consistency, and auditability of financial information, hence bolstering public sector accountability (Vasarhelyi, Kogan, & Tuttle, 2015).

The study indicates that hazards in digital financial information systems are multifaceted, involving technological, data-related, organizational, and institutional aspects. Effective risk management necessitates integrated frameworks that synchronize technical safeguards with institutional governance and regulatory mandates (NIST, 2024; OECD, 2024a).

Third, secondary empirical evidence from Indonesia highlights the significance of institutional context in influencing digital risk management results. Decentralization, disparities in organizational capacity, and regulatory intricacy affect the implementation and governance of digital financial systems. Digital changes alone do not provide enhanced governance; their efficacy relies on supplementary investments in capacity development, governance frameworks, and accountability systems (OECD, 2026; OECD/ADB, 2025).

7.2 Theoretical Contributions to the Literature on Financial Information Management and Control

This chapter enhances the literature on financial information management and control systems in several significant ways. Initially, it expands current theories of risk management and internal control by contextualizing them inside digital public sector organizations. The study conceptualizes governments as public sector digitally enabled public organizations, illustrating how digital technologies transform conventional control structures and accountability linkages (Vial, 2019).

The chapter synthesizes lessons from public sector accounting, information systems, and governance literature to offer a comprehensive knowledge of digital financial control systems. This multidisciplinary approach addresses requests for research that integrates managerial, organizational, and technological aspects of digital government (Mergel, Edelmann, & Haug, 2019).

The chapter adds contextual evidence from Indonesia, a significant emerging nation with a multifaceted institutional landscape. This context enhances the primarily Western-focused literature on digital governance and public sector accounting, illustrating the functioning of digital risk management and control systems amid decentralization and institutional variety (OECD, 2026; IMF, 2023).

7.3 Practical Recommendations and Prospective Research Avenues

The findings indicate that public sector organizations ought to implement integrated risk management strategies that incorporate control mechanisms within digital financial systems, while ensuring robust organizational oversight. Policymakers must guarantee that regulatory frameworks adapt alongside technological advancements to mitigate growing digital hazards and uphold auditability and compliance (OECD, 2026; OECD/ADB, 2025).

Managers must prioritize the enhancement of digital competencies, foster cross-functional collaboration, and establish governance frameworks that facilitate effective supervision of digital financial control systems. Prioritizing continuous monitoring, data governance, and cybersecurity resilience is essential to protect public financial information and maintain public trust (NIST, 2024; OECD, 2024a).

Future study may include comparative evaluations of digital risk management techniques across various countries and institutional contexts, in addition to longitudinal studies assessing the evolution of digital control systems over time. Additional examination of the impact of sophisticated technologies, including artificial intelligence and data analytics, on financial control within the public sector constitutes a promising direction for future research (Vasarhelyi et al., 2015). Collectively, these guidelines can enhance comprehension of how digital transformation can be utilized to fortify governance and accountability in public sector entities.

8. IMPLEMENTATION STRATEGY AND COMPETENCY DEVELOPMENT FOR DIGITAL FINANCIAL MANAGEMENT

A consistent lesson from changes in digital public financial management is that the deployment of technology seldom leads to enhanced governance results without a purposeful implementation strategy and systematic capacity development. Perceiving government as a digital enterprise in the public sector suggests that the efficacy of financial control relies on digital competencies, system governance, and organizational learning, rather than only on formal regulations or audit processes (DeLone & McLean, 2003). Implementation roadmaps must consider the "socio-technical" aspects of digital financial controls, as the dependability of outputs relies on the co-evolution of processes, personnel, and technology.

A phased roadmap is highly advised for intricate digital transformations as it mitigates risk exposure and facilitates iterative enhancement of controls. The initial phase primarily emphasizes the standardization of processes and the creation of controls, guaranteeing that financial procedures are re-engineered prior to automation to prevent digitization from merely amplifying existing inefficiencies or control deficiencies. Research in case-based theory development indicates that effective implementation designs clearly define constructs (e.g., control ownership, data governance, access rights) and refine them through empirical validation (Eisenhardt, 1989).

In Indonesian public sector contexts, where decentralization and varying capacities hinder uniform implementation, an initial focus on standardized charts of accounts, expenditure classifications, and control regulations is crucial to prevent inconsistent digital practices that may later incur significant reversal costs. The second stage should emphasize competence development and governance alignment, particularly in digital skills that directly influence the quality of financial control. Digital controls integrate the segregation of roles and permission logic into workflows; nonetheless, these mechanisms may be compromised if users are incompetent, if administrators misconfigure role-based access, or if informal workarounds become widespread.

Consequently, skill building must be structured as an ongoing program rather than a singular training event, incorporating role-specific education (financial, IT, internal audit, program managers) and scenario-based simulations that replicate fraud attempts, data inaccuracies, and system failures. Inductive qualitative rigor approaches methodologically underscore the necessity of transparently linking data (user behavior, control exceptions) to theory (control reliability, governance accountability), which is beneficial for designing learning loops that enhance controls as implementation advances (Gioia, Corley, & Hamilton, 2013).

The third stage should emphasize ongoing improvement and resilience by institutionalizing monitoring, incident management, and change control as enduring functions. Digital government environments are dynamic; accounting regulations vary, reporting obligations change, and cybersecurity threats fluctuate, necessitating ongoing revalidation of controls. Moreover, cyber hazards in digitally enabled financial institutions increasingly impact not only information assets but also citizens and service delivery, hence expanding the risk management scope beyond traditional information security (von Solms & van Niekerk, 2013). A robust roadmap consequently encompasses: (1) governance for system updates and configuration management; (2) regular control testing; (3) incident response protocols; and (4) independent assurance frameworks.

For Indonesia, a pragmatic roadmap must explicitly integrate decentralization realities by employing a federated implementation model: central authorities define core standards and controls, while local governments are provided with implementation toolkits, minimum control baselines, and capability support commensurate with their maturity levels. This method diminishes fragmentation while adhering to local limits, and it corresponds with the notion that digital public organizations necessitate organized decision-making authority and accountability for essential information assets.

8.1 Digital Assurance and Ongoing Auditing in the Public Sector

As financial operations in the public sector become more digitized, assurance approaches reliant primarily on periodic ex post audits are inadequate for controlling rapidly evolving digital risks. Digital financial control systems provide substantial amounts of transaction-level data and system logs, facilitating novel assurance methodologies like continuous auditing and continuous control monitoring. The transition to digital assurance is not merely a technical trend; it signifies a movement in governance that enables oversight to be more timely, detailed, and potentially proactive (Vasarhelyi, Alles, Kuenkaikaew, & Littley, 2012).

Continuous auditing within the public sector can be defined as an assurance methodology that employs automated processes and analytics to evaluate controls and transactions with greater frequency, perhaps in near real-time, compared to conventional audits. This is especially pertinent for public financial systems that manage substantial amounts of spending, procurement activities, and intergovernmental transfers. In these situations, the latency between event occurrence and audit identification constitutes a governance risk; delayed detection may enable control failures to disseminate throughout agencies and governmental tiers. Digital assurance facilitates the prompt detection of abnormalities, such atypical purchase patterns, recurrent split transactions intended to circumvent thresholds, or abuses of access rights.

Nonetheless, the implementation of continuous auditing encounters managerial and institutional obstacles. Initially, it necessitates robust data governance and uniform data access, as analytics-driven assurance is contingent upon the integrity of the foundational data. Secondly, it necessitates organizational structures that delineate ownership of controls and accountability for addressing exceptions. Third, it necessitates that both internal and external auditors cultivate new proficiencies in analytics, system interpretation, and control engineering. Internal audit evidence suggests that acceptance and adoption are influenced by perceived utility, organizational backing, and the capacity to incorporate continuous methodologies into current audit processes (Vasarhelyi et al., 2012). These limits are frequently more evident in the public sector due to audit mandates, procurement regulations, and reporting obligations that introduce further layers of institutional complexity.

In Indonesia, digital assurance possesses significant potential to enhance existing oversight institutions and accountability frameworks. Internal audit functions, such as inspectorates, might establish continuous control monitoring dashboards to identify exceptions for prompt follow-up, whereas supreme audit institutions could employ analytics to enhance risk-based audit planning and focus on high-risk projects. Digital assurance should not be perceived as a substitute for expert judgment; instead, it should be regarded as an enhancement that increases coverage and timeliness while upholding audit standards.

There is also emerging Indonesian evidence on organizational readiness. A study of 32 government internal-audit respondents from BPKP and the Ministry of Finance found that most APIP respondents were ready for continuous auditing, although preparation challenges remained. This evidence supports a cautious interpretation: continuous auditing is feasible, but its effectiveness depends on data access, analytical capability, standardized controls, and auditor readiness rather than on automation alone (Firmansyah et al., 2023).

A significant governance impact is that continuous auditing alters the responsibility paradigm: it transitions businesses from "post-event auditing" to "ongoing control capability." This aligns with the digital enterprise viewpoint, wherein controls are not intermittent but rather integrated and always validated. However, it also prompts ethical and governance inquiries regarding surveillance, data access rights, and the suitable limits of monitoring. A balanced approach necessitates explicit legal frameworks, open governance, and protections to avert the exploitation of analytical tools.

To implement digital assurance, public organizations may adopt a phased strategy: (1) initiate with high-risk processes (procurement, grants, cash management); (2) establish key risk indicators and control objectives; (3) guarantee standardized access to logs and transaction data; (4) enhance auditor and manager competencies; and (5) institutionalize response protocols to ensure that exceptions prompt documented remediation actions. This method facilitates learning cycles whereby control deficiencies recognized through monitoring inform system designs and policy revisions, so enhancing financial governance progressively.

8.2 Data Governance and Information Governance for Digital Financial Integrity

In digital public sector entities, data and information serve as key assets for governance, performance management, and accountability. Thus, the efficacy of financial control increasingly relies on data governance and information governance frameworks that delineate decision rights, norms, duties, and compliance methods for data management. Data governance is crucial as digital financial systems amalgamate various processes and entities, heightening the danger of inconsistent definitions, fragmented ownership, and inadequate validation, which can compromise the dependability of financial reporting and control (Khatri & Brown, 2010; Apriyanto, 2025).

An essential understanding from data governance literature is that governance transcends a mere technical concern of data architecture; it becomes an organizational design challenge that assigns decision-making authority for data assets. Khatri and Brown contend that establishing data governance necessitates the elucidation of essential decisions (e.g., who delineates data standards, who sanctions modifications, who oversees compliance) and the allocation of liability for these decisions (Khatri & Brown, 2010; Apriyanto, 2025).

In public sector financial systems, these decisions encompass: (1) definitions and classifications utilized in budgets and accounting; (2) master data (vendors, programs, organizational units); (3) access rights and role structures; (4) data quality standards and reconciliation protocols; and (5) audit trail retention and integrity mandates.

Information governance enhances this principle by emphasizing the management of information as a valuable tool for decision-making and responsibility, particularly when data is utilized across organizational boundaries. The integrity of digital finance is compromised when several systems read identical transactions divergently, when local units employ inconsistent coding methodologies, or when system modifications are executed without sufficient change management protocols. These challenges are not solely operational; they impact the integrity of performance metrics, the comparability of financial statements, and ultimately the legitimacy of public accountability mechanisms.

From an Indonesian viewpoint, decentralization presents both a justification and a problem for data governance.

The justification is that uniform data definitions and regulatory standards are essential for facilitating consolidated reporting and effective oversight across regions. The challenge lies in the significant disparities across local governments regarding their capabilities, infrastructure, and institutional procedures. A pragmatic governance approach is typically federated: central authorities provide baseline standards, reference data, and interoperability requirements, while local governments oversee implementation within those parameters. This method diminishes fragmentation while facilitating contextual adaptation.

Data governance directly facilitates risk management and cybersecurity within digital financial systems. Ambiguity in data access rights or deficiencies in privilege management heighten the risk of illegal manipulation. Furthermore, cybersecurity in governmental financial systems must be understood comprehensively, since cyber threats can impact service delivery and public trust, in addition to data confidentiality (von Solms & van Niekerk, 2013). Consequently, data governance must incorporate security mandates, including least-privilege access, role-based division of duties, and comprehensive logging and monitoring.

Ultimately, data governance is crucial for attaining quantifiable system success. The DeLone and McLean model asserts that system quality, information quality, and service quality influence usage and net benefits; hence, inadequate data governance may restrict the perceived value of digital financial reforms, even substantial investments (DeLone & McLean, 2003). In conclusion, data governance and information governance are not supplementary elements; they are essential to the administration and control of financial information in digital public sector organizations.

9. FRAMEWORK AND MODEL PROPOSAL FOR DIGITAL RISK MANAGEMENT AND FINANCIAL OVERSIGHT IN PUBLIC SECTOR ENTITIES

This chapter presents an integrated framework for comprehending digital risk management and financial control systems in public sector organizations, based on prior conceptual discourse and secondary empirical evidence from Indonesia's e-government transformation. The framework perceives public sector organizations as digital enterprises where the efficacy of financial control arises from the interplay of digital infrastructures, governance structures, and organizational competencies, rather than from standalone control mechanisms (Tjahyono et al., 2024).

The suggested framework centers on digital financial information infrastructure, encompassing integrated financial management information systems, data architectures, and embedded control functionalities. These infrastructures facilitate automation, real-time reporting, and system-based controls; yet, they also provide novel technological and data-related hazards. In accordance with information systems theory, the quality of infrastructure directly influences the quality of information and the reliability of control (DeLone & McLean, 2003). Inadequate system configuration or insufficient data governance might thus diminish the efficacy of even meticulously established control frameworks.

The digital infrastructure is encircled by a risk management and control layer, which includes internal control systems, enterprise risk management policies, and assurance procedures. This layer in digital settings is defined by embedded system controls, ongoing monitoring, and analytics-driven supervision. Utilizing COSO-based principles, risk management is established as a continuous, integrated process that connects control objectives with corporate strategy and the generation of public value (COSO, 2017). This layer facilitates the connection between technology capabilities and governance results by converting system functionalities into efficient risk mitigation strategies.

The third element of the system is governance and institutional environment, encompassing legal mandates, regulatory frameworks, accountability structures, and intergovernmental connections. Institutional theory posits that public sector organizations implement and influence control methods in reaction to external expectations and legitimacy pressures (DiMaggio & Powell, 1983). In decentralized systems like Indonesia's, institutional diversity profoundly affects the interpretation and enforcement of digital controls among entities.

The paradigm additionally integrates organizational and managerial competencies as a pervasive feature. The efficacy of digital risk management relies on managerial proficiency, digital literacy, and interdepartmental collaboration across finance, IT, and audit divisions. In the absence of these characteristics, digital control systems may devolve into mere symbols rather than effective governance instruments (Mergel, Edelmann, & Haug, 2019). The suggested framework enhances the literature by synthesizing technological, organizational, and institutional aspects into a unified model of digital financial control in the public sector. It provides a basis for subsequent empirical examination and comparative research among nations and governance frameworks.

9.1 Policy Implications Matrix for Digital Financial Governance within the Public Sector

This part provides a policy implications matrix that connects essential aspects of digital risk management and financial control to specific policy and managerial initiatives, translating the analytical findings of this chapter into actionable advice. The matrix aims to assist policymakers, senior public managers, and oversight entities in connecting digital transformation efforts with governance and accountability goals.

The initial dimension of the matrix pertains to digital infrastructure and system architecture. Policies in this domain should emphasize interoperability standards, uniform data definitions, and integrated control needs within financial information systems. Global data indicates that failing to incorporate control objectives early in system design may intensify fragmentation and increase risk exposure during digitalization (Diamond & Khemani, 2006). Policymakers should consequently establish basic control standards, including role-based access, audit trails, and automated validation, for all public sector financial systems.

The second factor emphasizes risk management and assurance techniques. Governments ought to transition from infrequent compliance audits to hybrid assurance approaches that integrate continuous monitoring and analytics-driven risk identification. Digital systems provide detailed transaction data; thus, policy frameworks must facilitate access to standardized data interfaces for internal and external auditors while ensuring data safety and independence (Vasarhelyi et al., 2012). This transition facilitates proactive risk management and improves the promptness of accountability.

The third factor pertains to organizational capacity and human resources. Digital financial governance necessitates the acquisition of new competencies that integrate accounting, information systems, and risk management knowledge. Policies ought to facilitate organized skill enhancement initiatives, role-specific training, and interdisciplinary cooperation. Empirical research demonstrates that managerial capacity is a critical determinant in achieving the governance advantages of digital transformation (Vial, 2019).

The fourth pillar pertains to institutional and regulatory coherence. Regulatory frameworks must adapt alongside technology advancements to delineate obligations, guarantee auditability, and address growing concerns like as cybersecurity and data misuse. In decentralized systems, a federated governance model allows central authorities to establish norms while enabling local governments to maintain flexibility in implementation, thereby balancing consistency with contextual adaptability (OECD, 2026; OECD/ADB, 2025).

The policy implications matrix underscores that good digital financial governance cannot be attained solely through technology. Coordinated policy action is necessary across infrastructure, risk management, human capital, and institutional architecture. By harmonizing these characteristics, public sector organizations can utilize digital transformation to enhance accountability, performance management, and public trust.

9.2 Limitations, Ethical Considerations, and Reproducibility

This chapter is based exclusively on publicly available secondary documentary evidence and does not involve human participants, interviews, experiments, personal data collection, or confidential administrative datasets. Accordingly, the analysis does not claim causal effects or statistical representativeness. Its findings are bounded by the availability, scope, timing, and institutional provenance of the documents reviewed. Official publications may emphasize implementation objectives and institutional achievements differently from independent academic studies, which should be considered when interpreting the evidence.

To strengthen analytical transparency and reproducibility, the chapter identifies the principal evidence categories, source-selection logic, analytical domains, and empirical anchors used in the documentary synthesis. Evidence from Indonesian government institutions is considered alongside international benchmarks and peer-reviewed research to reduce reliance on a single source category. Future research should test the proposed framework using primary organizational data, longitudinal evidence, comparative case designs, and direct measures of financial-control effectiveness across different levels of government.

REFERENCES

Apriyanto, G. (2025). Transformation of public sector behavioral accounting: The critical role of HR in preventing financial fraud through digitalization in Indonesia. *International Journal of Research in Social Science and Humanities*, *6*(9), 199–210. DOI: 10.47505/IJRSS.2025.10.20

Batini, C., Scannapieco, M., & Viscusi, G. (2016). *Data quality management: Models, methods, and applications*. Springer., DOI: 10.1007/978-3-319-24106-7

Bovens, M., Goodin, R. E., & Schillemans, T. (Eds.). (2014). *The Oxford handbook of public accountability*. Oxford University Press. DOI: 10.1093/oxfordhb/9780199641253.001.0001

Bowen, G. A. (2009). Document analysis as a qualitative research method. *Qualitative Research Journal*, *9*(2), 27–40. DOI: 10.3316/QRJ0902027

Committee of Sponsoring Organizations of the Treadway Commission. (2017). *Enterprise risk management: Integrating with strategy and performance*. COSO.

DeLone, W. H., & McLean, E. R. (2003). The DeLone and McLean model of information systems success: A ten-year update. *Journal of Management Information Systems*, *19*(4), 9–30. DOI: 10.1080/07421222.2003.11045748

Diamond, J., & Khemani, P. (2006). Introducing financial management information systems in developing countries. World Bank Policy Research Working Paper No. 3857. DOI: 10.1596/1813-9450-3857

DiMaggio, P. J., & Powell, W. W. (1983). The iron cage revisited: Institutional isomorphism and collective rationality in organizational fields. *American Sociological Review*, *48*(2), 147–160. DOI: 10.2307/2095101

Eisenhardt, K. M. (1989). Building theories from case study research. *Academy of Management Review*, *14*(4), 532–550. DOI: 10.2307/258557

Firmansyah, A., Khairunnisa, D., Gistiani, T. L., & Chaniago, P. R. (2023). The readiness of the Government Internal Supervisory Apparatus (APIP) for continuous auditing implementation. *International Public Sector Accounting Review*, *1*(1). Advance online publication. DOI: 10.31092/ipsar.v1i1.2094

Gioia, D. A., Corley, K. G., & Hamilton, A. L. (2013). Seeking qualitative rigor in inductive research: Notes on the Gioia methodology. *Organizational Research Methods*, *16*(1), 15–31. DOI: 10.1177/1094428112452151

Granlund, M., & Mouritsen, J. (2003). Introduction: Problems and opportunities of IT in management accounting. *European Accounting Review, 12*(1), 77–83. DOI: 10.1080/0963818031000087925

Grossi, G., Steccolini, I., & Reichard, C. (2019). Digital government and public sector accounting: A systematic literature review. *Accounting, Auditing & Accountability Journal, 32*(7), 1883–1906.

International Monetary Fund. (2023). Digital solutions guidelines for public financial management (Technical Notes and Manuals No. 2023/007). DOI: 10.5089/9798400251566.005

Khatri, V., & Brown, C. V. (2010). Designing data governance. *Communications of the ACM, 53*(1), 148–152. DOI: 10.1145/1629175.1629210

Lakat, J. S. (2025). Digital transformation of public financial management: A case study of regional financial application integration in North Sulawesi. *Priviet Social Sciences Journal, 5*(8), 317–337. DOI: 10.55942/pssj.v5i8.552

Mergel, I., Edelmann, N., & Haug, N. (2019). Defining digital transformation: Results from expert interviews. *Government Information Quarterly, 36*(4), 101385. DOI: 10.1016/j.giq.2019.06.002

Ministry of Communication and Digital Affairs, Republic of Indonesia. (2023). Circular Letter No. 9 of 2023 on Artificial Intelligence Ethics.

Ministry of Communication and Digital Affairs, Republic of Indonesia. (2026). Pemerintah bahas Peta Jalan Kecerdasan Artifisial Indonesia 2026–2029 dalam rapat lintas kementerian.

Ministry of Finance, Republic of Indonesia. (2024a). Implementasi tanda tangan elektronik (TTE) SAKTI tahap III C.

Ministry of Finance, Republic of Indonesia. (2024b). Regulation of the Minister of Finance No. 93/PMK.07/2024 on the National Fiscal Policy Synergy Digital Platform.

National Cyber and Crypto Agency (BSSN) & Ministry of Communication and Information Technology, Republic of Indonesia. (2024). BSSN identifies Temporary National Data Center attacked by ransomware.

National Institute of Standards and Technology. (2024). The NIST Cybersecurity Framework (CSF) 2.0 (NIST CSWP 29). DOI: 10.6028/NIST.CSWP.29

OECD. (2024a). Governing with artificial intelligence: Are governments ready? *OECD Artificial Intelligence Papers*, (20). Advance online publication. DOI: 10.1787/dee339a8-en

OECD. (2026). Digital Government Outlook 2026: Indonesia. OECD Publishing. https://doi.org/ OECD/ADB. (2025). Government at a glance: Southeast Asia 2025. OECD Publishing. https://doi.org/DOI: 10.1787/d46c0555-en

Romney, M. B., & Steinbart, P. J. (2021). *Accounting information systems* (15th ed.). Pearson.

Tjahyono, B., Hamsal, M., Rahim, R., & Gunadi, W. (2024). The influence of digital adoption, adaptive leadership and risk management implementation on organizational resilience: An empirical study in the Indonesian banking industry. 2024 International Conference on Science, Engineering and Business for Driving Sustainable Development Goals (SEB4SDG), 1–7. DOI: 10.1109/SEB4SDG60871.2024.10630445

Vasarhelyi, M. A., Alles, M., Kuenkaikaew, S., & Littley, J. (2012). The acceptance and adoption of continuous auditing by internal auditors: A micro analysis. *International Journal of Accounting Information Systems, 13*(3), 267–281. DOI: 10.1016/j.accinf.2012.06.011

Vasarhelyi, M. A., Kogan, A., & Tuttle, B. M. (2015). Big data in accounting: An overview. *Accounting Horizons, 29*(2), 381–396. DOI: 10.2308/acch-51071

Vial, G. (2019). Understanding digital transformation: A review and a research agenda. *The Journal of Strategic Information Systems, 28*(2), 118–144. DOI: 10.1016/j.jsis.2019.01.003

Volodina, T., & Grossi, G. (2024). Digital transformation in public sector auditing: Between hope and fear. *Public Management Review*. Advance online publication. DOI: 10.1080/14719037.2024.2402346

von Solms, R., & van Niekerk, J. (2013). From information security to cybersecurity. *Computers & Security, 38*, 97–102. DOI: 10.1016/j.cose.2013.04.004

World Bank. (2025). *GovTech Maturity Index 2025: Tracking public sector digital transformation worldwide*. World Bank Group.

World Bank. (2025). *GovTech Maturity Index 2025 update: Data and methodology*. World Bank Group.

KEY TERMS AND DEFINITIONS

Continuous Auditing: An assurance approach that uses digital data, automated procedures, and analytical techniques to assess transactions and controls more frequently than conventional periodic auditing.

Cyber Resilience: The capability of an organization and its digital systems to anticipate, withstand, respond to, recover from, and adapt to cybersecurity incidents while maintaining critical public services and financial-control functions.

Data Governance: The allocation of decision rights, responsibilities, standards, and control mechanisms governing the quality, accessibility, security, integrity, and use of organizational data.

Digital Financial Control Systems: Technology-enabled control mechanisms embedded in financial information systems to support authorization, validation, segregation of duties, transaction monitoring, audit trails, compliance, and reliable financial reporting.

Digital Public Financial Management: The application of integrated digital technologies to government budgeting, treasury, accounting, reporting, and oversight processes to improve the management and accountability of public resources.

Digital Risk Management: A systematic process for identifying, assessing, mitigating, monitoring, and responding to risks arising from the use of digital technologies, data, interconnected systems, and digital infrastructures within an organization.

Documentary Case Analysis: A qualitative research approach that systematically examines traceable documentary evidence to understand institutional practices, governance mechanisms, and contextual patterns without claiming causal or statistically representative inference.

Internal Control: An integrated set of governance arrangements, policies, procedures, and system-based mechanisms designed to provide reasonable assurance regarding operational effectiveness, reliable reporting, compliance, and the safeguarding of public resources.

Public Sector Digital Enterprise: A public organization that integrates digital platforms, data, processes, governance mechanisms, and organizational capabilities into its core operations while remaining accountable to legal mandates, public values, and citizens.

SAKTI (Sistem Aplikasi Keuangan Tingkat Instansi): Indonesia's integrated central-government financial management system that supports institutional processes ranging from planning and budgeting to treasury, accounting, and financial reporting.

Chapter 13
From Green Digital Accounting to Financial Sustainability in Developing Economies:
The Role of Green Cumulative Advantage and Digital Transformation Maturity

Masooma Zahara
University of Sargodha, Pakistan

Shamaila Butt
http://orcid.org/0000-0003-1411-9590
Sohar University, Oman

Muhammad Farrukh Shahzad
http://orcid.org/0000-0002-6578-4139
Beijing University of Technology, China

Muhammad Ali Chohan
http://orcid.org/0000-0002-8860-0603
Al Zahra College for Women, Oman

Karima Kahlifa Al-Qartoubi
Sohar University, Oman

DOI: 10.4018/979-8-3373-9230-1.ch013

© 2027, IGI Global Scientific Publishing. Copying or distributing in print or electronic forms without written permission of IGI Global Scientific Publishing is prohibited. Use of this chapter to ...rative artificial intelligence (AI) technologies is expressly prohibited. The publisher reserves all rights to license its use for generative AI training and machine learning model development.

ABSTRACT

Green digital accounting has become a key approach that combines digital technologies with the environment-focused accounting practice. This research study examines how green digital accounting contributes to financial sustainability while exploring the mediating role of digital transformation maturity and the moderating role of green cumulative advantage, which reflects firms' accumulated environmental, digital, and operational efficiencies over time. The survey of the 637 firms were conducted through structured questionnaire. The hypothesized research model was empirically evaluated with the help of the (PLS-SEM) with SmartPLS 4.1, which is most appropriate to examine the mediation and moderation relationships. The findings reveal that green digital accounting has a significant positive impact on financial sustainability. Digital transformation maturity plays a significant mediating role, indicating that green digital accounting is associated with better resource optimization in an organization, reduces operational and compliance costs, and enhances long-term financial stability.

1. INTRODUCTION

In emerging economies, organizations are becoming more dependent on resource, regulatory constraints, and environmental audit (Lu and Nakagawa, 2022). The firms are not only to be financially sustainable, but also to show reasonable environmental responsible behavior even with the escalating costs of energy, climatic challenges, and rules & regulations (Zik-Rullahi and Jide, 2023). Such difficulties are especially acute in environmentally friendly and resource-restricted industries, where the deleterious use of resources and inappropriate accounting systems may upset long-term financial results (Shatila et al., 2024). Consequently, companies in the emerging economies are adopting new strategies that would increase the resilience of the economy and their environmental responsibility (Zhen and Rahman, 2024).

Green digital accounting is one of the strategic organizational practices developed in reflection of these challenges to combine digital technologies (cloud computing, data analytics, automated reporting, etc.) with environmentally oriented accounting principles (Petcu et al., 2024). Incorporating environmental concerns into digital accounting software, companies will become more transparent, track resource use, minimize waste and make decisions based on environmental concerns. In contrast to any previously adopted accounting framework, green digital accounting allows real-time monitoring of the costs and efficiencies of the environment and provides organizations with new opportunities to balance sustainability goals and financial results (Hossain et al., 2024). Despite its increasing relevance, the practical and economic aspects of green digital accounting implementation have not been considered comprehensively, more specifically in developing countries (Alshehadeh et al., 2024).

Based on the concept of green digital accounting, the resource-based view (RBV) helps in conceptualizing digital accounting as a valuable, rare, and strategically embedded organizational competence, which increases competitive advantage by increasing resource use (Nishant et al., 2017). According to this theory, companies that successfully use internal capabilities like digital capabilities and sustainability-oriented systems are in a better place to attain sustainable financial performance (Oduro, 2024). Although previous research has investigated green accounting, digitalization, and sustainability outcomes on their own, there is little empirical literature on the process of converting green digital accounting to financial sustainability through intra-organizational processes (Alshehadeh et al., 2024). Specifically, the mediating and moderating factors that determine this relationship in emerging economies are not fully investigated (Ashfaq et al., 2026).

The digital transformation maturity is a vital factor that defines the extent to which organizations are able to translate digital endeavors into actual performance deliverables (Jie et al., 2025). The better the firm is digitally mature, the more it is in a position to incorporate green digital accounting into its operations, maximize the use of resources, and improve resource efficiency (De Silva et al., 2025). Green cumulative advantage, defined as the long-term accumulation of environmental, digital, and operational efficiencies resulting from sustained green and digital investments (Laradi et al., 2025). Green cumulative advantage is based on a dynamic and path-dependent capability that allows firms to continuously improve their competitive and financial positions, as opposed to the traditional notion of cost reduction effectiveness (Wu et al., 2024). Companies with more advanced GCA have a greater ability to use digital maturity and environmental practices for sustainable and resilient financial results (Li et al., 2024). These constructs are especially important in developing economies where businesses often are constrained by limited resources, institutional issues and growing environmental challenges. Within these settings, green digital accounting contributes to improved resource efficiency, while digital transformation maturity empowers companies to successfully execute digital initiatives and green cumulative advantage contributes to long-term financial stability and sustainable competitiveness.

The study builds an integrated RBV-based framework that connects green digital accounting with financial sustainability via digital transformation maturity and incorporates green cumulative advantage as a boundary condition instead of previous studies, which mainly focused on green accounting, digital transformation or sustainability individually. This integrated mechanism has not been studied in detail and is not well documented in developing countries. Therefore, this research contributes to previous studies by outlining the process and conditions under which the application of green digital accounting can improve financial sustainability.

Moreover, the previous research mainly focused on the direct impact of green accounting or digital transformation on organizational performance. There are very few studies that address both the mediation of the digital transformation maturity and the moderation of the green cumulative advantage in the same RBV framework. The present study combines these mechanisms, providing a more holistic view of the role of green digital accounting in achieving financial sustainability in developing economies.

To fill these gaps, the current research considers the impact of green digital accounting on financial sustainability, and the mediating impact of digital transformation maturity and the moderating effect of green cumulative advantage. Based on the survey data collected by the firms functioning in Pakistan and deployed through the application of PLS-SEM, the present research provides powerful empirical evidence regarding the complex relationships between digital, environmental and financial constructs. The results can be added to the literature on green accounting and sustainability by expanding the RBV to include the context of developing economies and offering a real-world suggestion to managers and policy makers interested in implementing digital and green accounting as a means to achieve financial sustainability in the long term.

2. THEORETICAL SUPPORT & DEVELOPMENT OF HYPOTHESES

2.1. Resource-Based View (RBV) – Supporting Theory

Resource-based view (RBV), originally proposed by Wernerfelt (1984) and further developed by Barney (1991), argues that firms achieve sustainable competitive advantage by possessing valuable, rare, inimitable, and non-substitutable (VRIN) resources and capabilities (Wernerfelt, 1984; Barney, 1991; Uyanık, 2023).Instead of focusing on external market conditions only, RBV reaffirms that internal organizational resources such as technological capabilities, managerial processes, and knowledge-based systems are strategic in nature. Based on sustainability, it became evident that RBV has been increasingly used to articulate how environmentally oriented practices and digital capabilities can be interpreted as strategic resource that can be used to boost firm performance (Dinh and Tran, 2025). In that sense, green digital accounting is an organizational ability of integrating digital infrastructures with environmental accounting practices to allow firms to manage their resources more efficiently, enhance transparency, and support financial and sustainability-related decision-making (Sari et al., 2025). RBV has subsequently been extended through the dynamic capabilities perspective, which emphasizes an organization's ability to integrate, build, and reconfigure internal and external competencies in rapidly changing environments (Teece et al., 1997). This perspective complements the present study because green digital accounting and digital transformation maturity require firms to continuously adapt technological and environmental capabilities to sustain competitive advantage under dynamic business conditions.

Using RBV in this study, as shown in Figure 1, the green digital accounting and maturity of digital transformations are conceptualized as complementary strategic resources that allow firms to translate environmental and digital investments into financial sustainability results (Bindeeba et al., 2025). The companies with greater levels of digital transformation maturity can apply green digital accounting systems to manage resource usage in the best way possible by reducing cost to enhance operational efficiencies (Morea et al., 2025). Moreover, the effectiveness of cost reduction can indicate the capacity of the firm to deploy these internal capabilities to create tangible financial gains and, thus, enhance its long-term financial sustainability. This study expands upon RBV to the developing economy setting by analyzing the mediating and moderating processes through which these resources can operate to reveal how the digitally enabled green accounting practices play the role of a key internal resource to attain sustainable financial performance in the environment of limited resources (Abdelhalim et al., 2023). Furthermore, Green cumulative advantage is introduced as a higher-order capability representing the long-term integration and accumulation of green and digital competencies (Belyamani et al., 2025). Firms with stronger GCA can better convert internal resources into sustainable financial outcomes (Li et al., 2024).

The constructs selected were chosen because they represent complementary organizational capability within the RBV framework. Green digital accounting is the strategic resource, digital transformation maturity is the ability to utilize the resource effectively, and green cumulative advantage is the sum of the strategic advantages that foster long-term financial sustainability. These two mechanisms, in combination, offer a full account of the mechanisms of sustainable financial value creation by firms. In sum, previous research has consistently shown that digital transformation and green accounting are linked to the performance of the organization and sustainability.

The existing literature, however, has focused on one of these relationships at a time, and not much had been done to capture both these relationships in a common RBV framework. Furthermore, there is a lack of evidence on the mechanism of the effect of green digital accounting on financial sustainability when taking digital transformation maturity as the independent variable and the mechanism of the effect of green cumulative advantage on the relationship between digital transformation maturity and green digital accounting. Besides, there is a lack of evidence on how the digital transformation maturity explains the mechanism of the effect of green digital accounting on financial sustainability, and the mechanism of the effect of green cumulative advantage on the relationship between digital transformation maturity and green digital accounting. The current study combines these two views to provide a more complete explanation of financial sustainability in developing economies.

2.2. Green Digital Accounting and Financial Sustainability

Green digital accounting is an integration of digital technologies and environmentally friendly accounting practices, which aims to collect, process and analyze financial and environmental data in a very efficient and timely manner (Petcu et al., 2024). The more accurate data, transparency, and real-time reporting provide organizations with a better basis for aligning environmental goals with financial decision-making, which is known as green digital accounting (Adelakun et al., 2024). This idea is linked to the principles of environmental management accounting (EMA) which focuses on identifying, measuring and managing environmental costs to inform decision-making and sustainability performance of an organization (Gray, 2002; Schaltegger and Burritt, 2000). By integrating these accounting principles with digital technologies, green digital accounting enhances the quality of environmental information, operational transparency, and resource efficiency. The digitalized accounting systems are a strategic way of enhancing financial control and long-term stability in developing economies, where companies tend to experience weaknesses in institutional frameworks, resource shortages, and inefficiencies in the processes (Przychocka and Sikorski, 2024). In the prospect of the RBV, green digital accounting is one of the valuable internal capabilities that facilitate informed decision-making and resource utilization, which make an organization financially sustainable (Al-Taani et al., 2024).

In addition, green digital accounting helps to track better the environmental costs, energy usage, waste minimization, and compliance with regulations, which have a direct financial impact (Napisah et al., 2024). Through a systematic process of identifying expensive and uneconomical processes, companies can implement the requisite corrective measures that boost profitability and minimize the financial risks in the long run. This is especially essential when it comes to organizations operating in developing economies where there are concerns regarding environmental regulations and finance does not provide financial cushions, which makes them sensitive to operational shocks (Al-Nimer, 2024). Therefore, such companies, which can successfully embrace green digital accounting, are in a better place to realize long-term financial performance and resilience (Ao et al., 2023). According to this theoretical and empirical rationale, the hypothesis can be formulated as follows:

H1: Green digital accounting has a significant direct effect on financial sustainability.

2.3. Green Digital Accounting, Digital Transformation Maturity & Financial Sustainability

Green digital accounting is also a crucial aspect of digital transformation maturity as it requires regulation of the organizational processes and the data governance, as well as managerial decision-making processes, which are the key components of the digital systems implementation (Mihu et al., 2023). Going green in digital accounting will also necessitate companies to update their accounting systems, increase digital capacity, and add sustainability indicators to the primary information systems (Napisah et al., 2024; Lodhi et al., 2024). These transformations increase the accuracy, timeliness, and reliability of the environmental and financial information, and, at the same time, enable a digitally empowered organizational culture to propel the entire maturation of digital transformation initiatives (De Silva et al., 2025). In resource-based perspective, green digital accounting can be seen as a driver that enhances the scenario of coordinated development of the technological resources, employee skills and organizational functions in such a way that higher degrees of digital integration and interoperability of the functions across the firms are attained (Nishant et al., 2017; Prasetianingrum and Sonjaya, 2024). These types of integration over time improve the capacity of firms to coordinate digital strategies, sustainability performance goals, and increase the level of digital transformation maturity (Senadjki et al., 2023), which supports to formulate:

H2: Green digital accounting positively influences digital transformation maturity.

Digital transformation maturity, in its turn, has substantial consequences to the financial viability of the firms through its capacity to increase the efficiency, transparency, and ability to plan their financial activities based on the available data (Avira et al., 2023). Mature digital systems are efficient in workflow and minimize the number of mistakes with manual power, are efficient in resource distribution, thus decreasing operational expenses and carry, in addition to more stable and sustainable financial results. This factor is especially severe in less developed economies, in which institutional environments are weak, and there is a scarcity of resources, ensuring that digitally mature firms can withstand the effects of environmental norms, market fluctuations, and funding pressures to be financially much more sustainable. Based on the resource-based view, digital transformation maturity is a strategic, resource-intensive, hard-to-replicate ability that empowers firms to translate technological investment into financial value over time in terms of productivity, better resource management, and sustainability of generating additional value (Vo-Thai and Tran, 2025; Du et al., 2024). Moreover, organizations with a digitally mature level would be closer to incorporating sustainability programs, including green digital accounting, into the core business processes, which would contribute to financial stability (Setyadi et al., 2025). Considering the same, we can formulate the following hypothesis:

H3: Digital transformation maturity positively influences financial sustainability.

Green digital accounting offers technologically supported environment-friendly solutions to cost management, increases resource efficiency, and improves the quality of financial reporting, but its effect on financial sustainability heavily relies on the degree of maturity of digital transformation in the firm (Atukunda et al., 2024). Digital transformation maturity as an important mediating variable enables organizations to successfully integrate green digital accounting into the overall strategy and operational decisions (Alshehadeh et al., 2024; De Silva et al., 2025). Green digital accounting may continue to be a disorganized and underutilized tool until digital maturity is achieved to play a significant role in financial performance in the long term. According to the resource-based perspective, the digital transformation maturity increases the capacity of a firm to utilize green digital accounting as a strategic resource, converting environmental and digital investments into the least resource-intensive operations, high efficiency levels in compliance, and increased financial stability (Belyamani et al., 2025; Al-Taani et al., 2024). Accordingly, digital transformation maturity plays a central mediating role in explaining how green digital accounting contributes to financial sustainability, thereby supporting H4.

H4: Digital transformation maturity mediates the relationship between green digital accounting and financial sustainability.

2.4. The Moderating Role of Green Cumulative Advantage

Green cumulative advantage refers to the long-term accumulation of environmental, digital, and operational efficiencies derived from sustained green and digital investments. It reflects firms' ability to institutionalize learning, optimize processes, and continuously improve environmental and financial performance. From an RBV perspective, GCA represents a dynamic capability that strengthens the value of digital transformation maturity (Belyamani et al., 2025). Firms with high levels of GCA can more effectively transform digital maturity into durable financial benefits, as accumulated efficiencies reinforce strategic resilience and innovation capacity. In contrast, firms with weak cumulative advantages may struggle to sustain financial gains despite digital investments (Alshouha et al., 2025).

Although digital transformation maturity and green cumulative advantage are related, they represent different organizational capabilities. Digital transformation maturity reflects the firm's current capability to integrate digital technologies, processes, and managerial practices. In contrast, green cumulative advantage represents the long-term accumulation of environmental, operational, and digital benefits generated through sustained green investments. Thus, DTM reflects present organizational capability, whereas GCA reflects accumulated strategic advantage developed over time.

While dynamic capabilities emphasize an organization's ability to sense, seize, and reconfigure resources in response to environmental change, green cumulative advantage represents the cumulative outcome of sustained environmental and digital investments that progressively strengthen long-term organizational resilience and financial sustainability. From a strategic management perspective, firms that continuously invest in environmental innovation and resource efficiency are more likely to achieve sustainable competitive advantage while simultaneously improving environmental and financial performance (Porter and van der Linde, 1995; Chen et al., 2025). Unlike green capabilities, which refer to firms' ability to implement environmentally sustainable practices, or green innovation, which emphasizes the development of environmentally friendly products, services, or processes, green cumulative advantage reflects the long-term accumulation of environmental, digital, and operational efficiencies derived from sustained organizational investments. Similarly, unlike green competitive advantage, which focuses on superior market positioning, green cumulative advantage emphasizes the progressive development of strategic organizational resources that strengthen long-term financial sustainability. Therefore, firms with higher levels of green cumulative advantage are expected to convert digital transformation maturity into superior financial sustainability more effectively than firms with lower levels of accumulated green capabilities. Accordingly, the following hypothesis is proposed:

H5: Green cumulative advantage significantly moderates the relationship between digital transformation maturity and financial sustainability.

Figure 1. Conceptual model

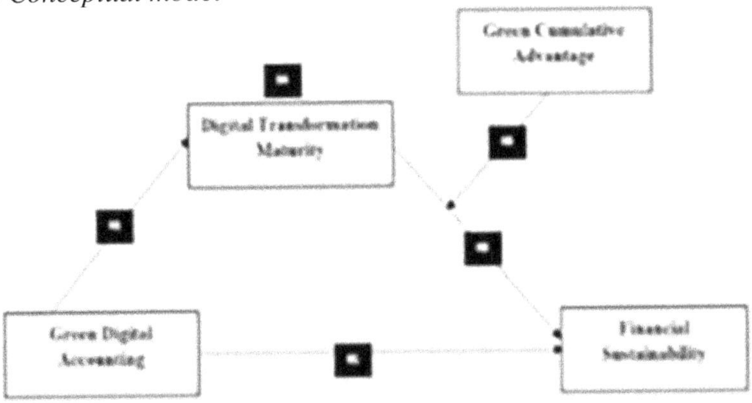

3. RESEARCH METHODOLOGY

3.1. Research Design

The study was a cross-sectional quantitative survey with a research design to test the hypothesis that green digital accounting (GDA) and financial sustainability (FS) are positively correlated and investigate the mediating effect of the digital transformation maturity and the moderating effect of the green cumulative advantage in firms working in Pakistan, specifically in the resource-constrained and environmentally sensitive sphere. Given the cross-sectional nature of the data, this study examines associations among variables rather than establishing causal relationships (Yahya et al., 2022). The above requirements rendered the cross-sectional design effective as this design worked effectively in both perception and technology adoption phenomena in a massive and geographically scattered population at the same time (Maier et al., 2023). The approach according to which the quantitative strategy assisted in the systematic hypothesis testing in accordance to resource-based theory (RBT) and utilized the Partial Least Squares Structural Equation Modeling (PLS-SEM) to assess the association of several latent constructs (Hair et al., 2012). PLS-SEM is a variance-based structural equation modeling technique widely used for analyzing complex research models involving multiple latent constructs, particularly when the research emphasizes prediction, mediation, moderation, and theory development. It is specifically used in studies involving constructs of green digital accounting practices and financial sustainability that best fit this research design as variables that could be measured with the most effective perceptions in an organizational level in the context of developing economies.

3.2. Instruments

The self-administered questionnaire was developed based on an extensive review of prior literature on green accounting, digital transformation, green cumulative advantage, and financial sustainability. Given the absence of fully standardized measurement scales for green digital accounting in developing economy contexts, the measurement items were adapted and contextualized following established scale development procedures (Hinkin, 1998; Hair et al., 2012). Green digital accounting (GDA) was operationalized using a five-item reflective scale adapted from prior research on digital accounting systems, environmental management accounting, and sustainability reporting (Petcu et al., 2024; Napisah et al., 2024; Prasetianingrum and Sonjaya, 2024). The scale measures the degree of use of digital technologies by firms to register, track, and report unstructured environmental and financial data to aid in sustainable decision-making. A five-item reflective scale derived from earlier research on digital maturity, organizational digital capability, and digital integration was used to measure the digital transformation maturity (DTM) (Jie et al., 2025; Senadjki et al., 2023; Przychocka and Sikorski, 2024). The scale indicates the level of integration of digital technologies, competencies, and strategic initiatives in the organizational processes.

The scale development was done in four stages. First, the important construct dimensions were determined relying on the corresponding literature. Second, a set of items was created in preliminary pool in order to model these dimensions. Third, a focus group was used to review the items with academic experts and industry practitioners to improve on content validity. Fourth, pilot study was carried ahead to perfect the wording and structure items. The measurement items were reviewed by subject experts to ensure content validity before pilot testing and final data collection. Green cumulative advantage (GCA) was operationalized using a reflective multi-item scale adapted from prior studies on green capabilities, digital transformation, and sustainable competitive advantage (Belyamani et al., 2025; Li et al., 2024). The financial sustainability (FS) measured was assessed as a five-item reflective scale that was based on Ur Rahman et al. (2020), which defines financial sustainability as the firm in question being able to sustain its financial performance, manage its financial risk and support its growth in the long term. Some small changes in words were made to make it relevant within the context without distorting the original conceptual meaning. Multi-item reflective scales had all constructs measured on a five-point Likert scale that has 1 (strongly disagree) to 5 (strongly agree). The detailed measurement items are presented in Appendix A. The adequacy of the measurement model was further confirmed through reliability and validity assessments.

3.3. Population and Sampling Procedure

The questionnaire was created and conducted with the help of an online data collection system, namely Google Forms, as it allowed effective access to the respondents and the use of a web link and a QR code. The formal and informal business and professional networks were used to reach the target population well. These were companies that operated in environmentally sensitive and resource-constrained industries, professional accounting and finance networks, small and medium enterprise associations, industry organizations, business chambers, and online services that were applicable to organizations in Pakistan. The information was gathered during the period of March to May 2025.

To ensure that the respondents fulfilled the study purpose, the purposive sampling method was adopted, and a criterion-based sampling technique was adopted (Etikan et al., 2016). The inclusion criteria included the fact that the participating firms: (a) were located in Pakistan; (b) were in operation in environmentally sensitive or resource constrained areas; (c) had implemented or were in the process of implementing digital financial systems; (d) included respondents with managerial or decision-making accounting, finance or operations role; and (e) (f) among the small- to medium-sized enterprise category. Data were collected using a structured self-administered questionnaire distributed to managers and professionals working in environmentally sensitive firms in Pakistan. Participation was entirely voluntary, and respondents were selected because of their familiarity with their organizations' digital accounting practices, digital transformation initiatives, and sustainability activities. Before completing the questionnaire, all respondents were informed about the purpose of the study, assured that their responses would remain anonymous and confidential, and informed that participation was voluntary. Completion and submission of the questionnaire were considered to constitute informed consent to participate in the study.

A total of 850 firms were invited to participate in the survey. Of these, 683 questionnaires were returned. After excluding incomplete and inconsistent responses, 637 valid questionnaires were retained for the final analysis. The respondents mainly comprised managers, finance professionals, accountants, and operations managers from environmentally sensitive and resource-constrained firms. Their organizational roles ensured that they possessed sufficient knowledge of digital accounting practices, digital transformation initiatives, and financial sustainability. Prior to data collection, respondents were informed about the objectives of the study and the voluntary nature of their participation. Participation implied informed consent, and respondents could decline or withdraw from the survey at any stage. No personally identifiable information was collected, and all responses were anonymized and analyzed in aggregate to ensure confidentiality and privacy. The study was conducted in accordance with generally accepted ethical principles for survey-based research, including voluntary participation, informed consent, confidentiality, and the protection of participants' anonymity.

G*Power was used to determine the quality of the sample size, and the level of statistical power was set to 0.95 to avoid Type I and Type II errors. The fourth sample of 637 observations met the needed minimum threshold that guaranteed adequate statistical power to test hypotheses. All major constructs were determined by five-point Likert scales. Descriptive statistics revealed that all of the constructs had sufficient variability to employ any inferential statistics, particularly Partial Least Squares Structural Equation Modeling (PLS-SEM), to test hypotheses. Non-response bias was assessed by comparing early and late responses following Armstrong and Overton (1977). No significant differences were observed, indicating that non-response bias was unlikely to affect the findings.

4. RESULTS AND ANALYSIS

Because the data were collected using a single questionnaire, common method bias was assessed using Harman's single-factor test. The first factor explained less than 50% of the total variance, indicating that common method bias was not a serious concern. The results of this research were derived through the usefulness of the Partial Least Squares Structural Equation Modeling (PLS-SEM) with Smart-PLS4.1 to determine the impact of green digital accounting (GDA) on the financial sustainability (FS) of the firms that were working in Pakistan and, in particular, in the resource-constrained and environmentally sensitive industries. The digital transformation maturity serving as a mediating variable and the green cumulative advantage as a moderating variable were also evaluated. The reason why PLS-SEM was chosen is that it is suitable in cases in which the given research is oriented to predictions, it allows complex modeling of research inclusive of mediation and moderation impacts, and it is robust in the circumstances where the data is non-normal.

The findings offer descriptive evidence on how combining green digital accounting practices and digital capabilities can result in an increase in financial sustainability due to efficient use of resources and by developing a green cumulative advantage. The results bring an increased understanding of how digitally empowered green accounting initiatives may assist firms to achieve sustainable financial performance within dynamic and resource-restricted business contexts.

4.1. Measurement Model Assessment

The measurement model was evaluated through the analysis of indicator reliability, internal consistency reliability and convergent validity. All constructs are found to be highly internally consistent, as indicated by the Cronbach's alpha (α) and composite reliability (CR) values, which are greater than the recommended level of 0.70, indicating that measurement scales are reliable (Shahzad et al., 2024). Individual loadings are observed to be high with a majority of the items loading above 0.70 in their respective construct, which illustrates the indication of indicator reliability; Although FS5 exhibited a relatively lower standardized loading (0.530), it was retained because the composite reliability and average variance extracted (AVE) of the financial sustainability construct remained above the recommended thresholds. Furthermore, FS5 captures an important theoretical aspect of financial sustainability, and its retention helps preserve the content validity of the construct. Convergent validity is also established since the AVE of green digital accounting, digital transformation maturity, financial sustainability and green cumulative advantage are all greater than the necessary criterion of 0.50, as this is an indication that each construct contributes more than half of all the indicators (See Table 1).

Overall, these results confirm that the measurement model is reliable and exhibits satisfactory convergent validity, providing a solid foundation for subsequent structural model analysis.

Table 1. Factor analysis of constructs

Constructs	Items	FL	α	CR	AVE
Green Digital Accounting (GDA)			0.923	0.942	0.765
	GDA1	0.881			
	GDA2	0.852			
	GDA3	0.863			
	GDA4	0.909			
	GDA5	0.869			
Digital Transformation Maturity (DTM)			0.922	0.941	0.763
	DTM1	0.891			
	DTM2	0.844			
	DTM3	0.831			
	DTM4	0.890			
	DTM5	0.908			
Financial Sustainability (FS)			0.894	0.926	0.721
	FS1	0.951			
	FS2	0.843			
	FS3	0.886			
	FS4	0.960			
	FS5	0.530			
Green Cumulative Advantage (GCA)			0.887	0.910	0.671
	GCA1	0.769			
	GCA2	0.866			
	GCA3	0.896			
	GCA4	0.807			
	GCA5	0.747			

The discriminant and validity of the constructs are measured using both the Fornell-Larcker criterion and the HTMT. The Fornell-Larcker criterion (square root of the AVE) suggests that each construct has satisfactory discriminant validity regarding other constructs because the square root of its comparisons with other constructs is greater than that of the other constructs. The values of the HTMT also confirm, with no values exceeding the conservative level of 0.85 (Shahzad et al.,

2023). The latter results ensure that the constructs are not empirically similar to each other and that there would be no issue of construct multicollinearity (Table 2). On the whole, the analysis shows that the measurement model meets the requirements of discriminant validity, which can be used with certain reliability as the foundation of the further structural model evaluation (Farrukh Shahzad et al., 2026).

Table 2. Discriminant Validity

Variables	DTM	FS	GCA	GDA
HTMT criterion				
DTM				
FS	0.323			
GCA	0.207	0.082		
GDA	0.294	0.643	0.041	

4.2. Structural Model

The hypothesized relationships in the study were tested by using the bootstrapping method in SmartPLS 4.1 to assess the structural model. The model evaluation showed that the value of R^2, f^2, and Q^2 in the model were within acceptable limits to validate the strength of the proposed framework (Shahzad et al., 2025). The estimates of the coefficients of R^2 indicate that green digital accounting (GDA) and other related constructs explain a significant percentage of the variance of the digital transformation maturity (DTM) and financial sustainability (FS), and this fact demonstrates the explanatory quality of the model. Table 3 shows the hypothesis testing results. The structural model results demonstrate strong empirical support for all proposed relationships.

The direct effects reveal that green digital accounting (GDA) has a substantial and positive influence on financial sustainability (FS) ($\beta = 0.570$, $t = 15.249$, $p < 0.001$), confirming that firms adopting environmentally oriented digital accounting practices are better positioned to achieve long-term financial viability. GDA also exerts a significant positive effect on digital transformation maturity (DTM) ($\beta = 0.278$, $t = 7.488$, $p < 0.001$), indicating that green digital accounting acts as a catalyst for advancing firms' digital capabilities. Furthermore, DTM positively impacts FS ($\beta = 0.162$, $t = 3.432$, $p = 0.001$), suggesting that higher levels of digital transformation maturity enhance firms' ability to sustain financial performance. The mediation analysis shows that DTM partially mediates the relationship between GDA and FS ($\beta = 0.045$, $t = 3.116$, $p = 0.002$), highlighting that GDA contributes to financial sustainability not only directly but also indirectly through strengthening digital transformation maturity. Additionally, the moderation results indicate that green cumulative advantage (GCA) significantly strengthens the relationship between DTM and FS ($\beta = 0.093$, $t = 2.493$, $p = 0.013$), implying that firms with accumulated environmental, digital, and operational efficiencies are better able to convert digital transformation maturity into superior financial sustainability. Overall, the findings validate the proposed structural model and underscore the synergistic role of green digital practices, digital maturity, and cumulative green advantages in driving financial sustainability. The structural model results provide empirical support for the proposed hypotheses. The following discussion interprets these findings in light of the Resource-Based View (RBV) and prior sustainability and digital transformation literature.

Table 3. Hypothesis testing

Hypotheses	Beta (β)	STDV	t-statistic	p-value	Decision
Direct effect					
GDA → FS (H1)	0.570	0.037	15.249	0.000	Supported
GDA → DTM (H2)	0.278	0.037	7.488	0.000	Supported
DTM → FS (H3)	0.162	0.047	3.432	0.001	Supported
Mediation effect					
GDA → DTM → FS (H4)	0.045	0.014	3.116	0.002	Supported
Moderation effect					
GCA x DTM → FS (H5)	0.093	0.037	2.493	0.013	Supported

Note(s): GDA = green digital accounting, DTM = digital transformation maturity, GCA = green cumulative advantage, FS = financial sustainability

5. DISCUSSION

The initial important conclusion of the present study is that green digital accounting (GDA) significantly and positively influences the financial sustainability (FS) of companies operating in the resource-limited and environment-related industries in Pakistan. It implies that the integration of eco-friendly accounting and digital technologies can have a beneficial impact on the work of an organization and its financial sustainability in the future (Kumar et al., 2024). About the resource-based view (RBV), GDA is noted to be a significant, special, and no substitutable factor that can facilitate its utilization of resources, the degree of operational effectiveness, and the strategic decision-making process by companies (Horani et al., 2023). The observation can contribute to the literature since it provides empirical evidence in which a company functions in a developing state, when resource-based difficulties are high, and when environmental pressures are intense (Li et al., 2023).

The second valuable conclusion is that the digital transformation maturity (DTM) is an intermediate between FS and GDA. This means that the benefits of green digital accounting will be determined by the ability of a firm to integrate both practices of digital accounting and the long-term work of organizational processes and the general endeavors of digital transformation (Bocean and Vărzaru, 2023). With the help of an increase in digital maturity, the companies will be able to use the information on green accounting to a greater extent in the process of cost reduction, increase in resource productivity, facilitation of operations, and better financial results (Prasetianingrum and Sonjaya, 2024). The finding is in accordance with the body of literature that highlights the significance of organizational capacities to convert technological usage into real performance assets, claiming that digital maturity is one of the key forces that interrelate technological investment and financial feasibility (Abakpa and Dvouletý, 2025).

The third significant finding establishes the moderating value of the green cumulative advantage (GCA) in the connection between digital transformation maturity and financial sustainability. Those firms that have established robust cumulative environmental, digital and operational strengths will be in a position to achieve long-term financial success when digital transformation projects are converted into long-term financial programs (Bindeeba et al., 2025). It implies that long-term efficiency, organizational learning, and optimization of processes play a critical role in distance-based effectiveness in using technology-facilitated processes to achieve high financial results (Ukko et al., 2019). This observation, in terms of the resource-based view, is an extension of the current theory in that it shows that the dynamic ability to process accumulation of green advantages acts as a strategic contingency that defines how effectively firms can derive permanent value of digital transformation efforts (Setyadi et al., 2025).

Generally, the research has both theoretical and practical implications. Hypothetically, it empirically proves the model that green digital accounting is mediated by the maturity of digital transformation and modulated by green cumulative advantage, which helps in raising financial sustainability in developing economies. In reality, the results of the findings are that companies and policymakers must not merely consider adopting emerging digital accounting tools, but they must put emphasis on the development of the digital capabilities and the process of accruing green cumulative advantage. Through a strategic combination of technology, environmental accounting and industrial practices, as well as constant process optimization, the organizations can institutionalize efficiency gains and convert them into competitive and financial benefits in the long term. This type of integrated approach can help firms to perform in a sustainable manner in terms of finances and remain competitive in resource-constrained markets.

5.1. Theoretical Contributions

First, this study adds value to the resource-based view (RBV) in that it conceptualizes green digital accounting as an organizational resource that is useful, uncommon, and hard to replicate, especially in the developing economy environment. Although the larger part of the previous studies has focused on green accounting or digitalization separately, this research steps forward in terms of theory, by showing that combining digital technologies with place-oriented accounting activities is a unique opportunity, which can improve financial sustainability. The results expand RBV by reducing the conceptual distance between the implementation of green digital resources and sustainable monetary relationships, as environmental practices that rely on technology could be a source of competitive and financial gain over time.

Second, the digital transformation as a meaningful mediating process maturity becomes a promising contribution into the accounting, sustainability, and digital transformation literature. Whereas the existing literature verifies the importance of digital technologies in improving organizational performance, the empirical data regarding the issue of making green digital accounting one of the instruments of financial sustainability is still lacking, which is particularly in developing economies. Necessary to the empirical evidence which is evident in this research study, the adoption of green digital accounting is not always possible in the absence of a sufficiently mature digital infrastructure, strategic alignment, and process integration. By defining the mediating role of digital transformation maturity, this study enables the gap in the digital transformation theory by presenting green digital accounting as an actor that restructures the process of organization and the utilization of resources toward a sustainable financial performance.

Third, the estimation of green cumulative advantage as the moderator is a new theoretical input of the research. The results point to the fact that the sustainability of digitally mature organizations in their financial sustainability initiatives is highly contingent upon their capacity to accumulate and institutionalize long-term environmental, digital, and operational efficiency. Instead of worrying about the immediate cost reduction, companies that have a high green cumulative advantage may make resource utilization, compliance management, and process optimization benefits turn into long-term financial gains. This finding proves that there is a clear parallelism in relation to cost management theory, sustainability studies, and digital transformation literatures, in the sense that efficiency-driven mechanisms are cumulative strategic resources. As a result, the paper validates the position that green cumulative advantage is not a static fact of operation but a dynamic strategic ability that enhances the ultimate motivation of digital change efforts.

Fourth, this research provides a contribution to the entrepreneurship and sustainability literature on the context of developing economies in its empirical validation of a holistic framework, where the concept of green digital accounting, the maturity of digital transformation, and green cumulative advantage are one single model. Unlike the study conducted in the developed economies, the study reveals that firms within the developing countries possess some special constraints, such as the scarcity of resources, policies, and environmental exposure. Green digital accounting would be particularly helpful in such environments, and they are embedded in digitally advanced systems and supported by efficient resource management strategies. The available theoretical foundations were sensitized to the institutional and economic realities of the new markets through this contextualized extension.

Finally, the analysis is applicable to the general sustainability and accounting environment by shedding light on the micro-principles of financial sustainability under the conditions of technology and ecological constraints. The associations among green digital accounting, the state of digital transformation, and the long-term efficiency advantage show that the capabilities at the organization level define long-term financial resilience. The study, by integrating the insights of the RBV, digital transformation, and sustainability accounting, contributes knowledge to the field of theory on how the emergent digital-green practices redefine financial strategy and performance, particularly in the circumstances of accessing resources and in transitioning developing economies. For example, organizations can use green digital accounting systems to monitor real-time energy consumption, carbon emissions, and environmental costs, enabling managers to make more informed sustainability and investment decisions. Such digital tools also support regulatory compliance and improve transparency in sustainability reporting.

5.2. Practical Implications

There would also be certain important practical implications of the research on managers, policymakers, educators and other institutions of the developing economies. The first, the findings provide effective recommendations to the leaders of the organization and accounting professionals, which continue to be targeted at making investments to enhance financial sustainability through involvement in environmentally friendly practices. Companies should position green digital accounting in the heart of their core financial and operational mechanisms instead of discussing it as an implementation tool (compliance or reporting). It is proposed that managers should use digital accounting technologies to enhance the tracking of resource management related to the environmental aspect, the real-time reporting, and the process of decision-making, thus incorporating the idea of sustainability into daily financial management.

Second, the mediating effect of the digital transformation maturity indicates that the impact of digital transformation is attainable only in an organization or institution that invests substantially in digital capabilities over an extended period. The government and the regulatory authorities should prioritize developing digital infrastructure, a common green accounting system and technology-based reporting systems to support the transition of companies to digitized accounting systems. In resource poor environments, digital innovation hubs, shared accounting sites and financial incentives to access green accounting software can overcome the financial and technical hurdles for companies, particularly small and medium-sized businesses, to go digital. However, the adoption of green digital accounting in developing economies is still a challenge due to the poor state of digital infrastructure, financial constraints, lack of technical skills and knowledge, and the lack of uniformity in the support provided by the government. Companies need to tackle these institutional and organizational challenges if they are to maximize the financial and sustainability value of the green digital accounting approach.

Third, the moderating role of green cumulative advantage indicates that digital investments do not automatically translate into financial sustainability unless organizations are able to accumulate, retain, and leverage environmentally oriented benefits over time. This implies that the success of green digital accounting practices is based on the ability of an organization to transform the benefits of operational efficiency into long-term strategic value. Managers are thus advised to foster the development of green cumulative advantage by putting into practice green digital accounting programs based on environmental learning, continuous improvement and sustainability-driven routine. This involves using the finance teams to have systematic data on the environmental performance, monitor the decreasing energy use, waste, and costs associated with compliance, and embedding these gains into both long-term financial planning systems and performance measurement systems. Organizational involvement in digital accounting through sustainability performance measures and cumulative green measures will enhance the conversion of the short-term efficiency benefits into long-term financial benefits.

Fourth, the research results will give valuable information to government agencies, development organization, as well as the donor-funded sustainability program operating in the developing economies. There is a need for these stakeholders to favor specific initiatives that will foster green digital accounting, digital capability and long-term efficiency improvements simultaneously. Much attention must be devoted to those companies that fall within the domain of environmentally sensitive and resource-consuming industries since in such situations, digital accounting tools might become necessary to manage the environmental risks, limit them to the least, and extend financial sustainability in the long run. Such forms of integrated support programs may help the organizations to surmount institutional uncertainty, regulatory stress, and market turbulence as the organizations continue to strive to have sustainable financial performance. This study was carried out in the context of Pakistan, but the framework suggested in this study can also give some insights to other developing countries suffering from the same institutional, regulatory and resource problems. For managers and policymakers in these settings, it might be worth considering implementing integrated green digital accounting practices to increase the digital transformation maturity and improve financial sustainability in the long run. However this proposed framework might not be applicable in every institutional context, and future research is encouraged, to test the model in other countries to explore its generalizability and possible institutional difference.

5.3. Limitation and Future Direction

In spite of its contributions, this study has a number of weaknesses that present research opportunities in the future. To begin with, cross-sectional research design limits causation ability; future research studies may utilize longitudinal or panel research designs to gain deeper insight into the dynamic development of green digital accounting, digital transformation maturity and financial sustainability with time. Second, the sample of the gathered data included the business firms that belong to the resource-constrained and environmentally sensitive industries in Pakistan, which can be a limitation of the generalizability of the results; the comparison of the results with those of other economies, both developing and developed, is recommended to increase the external validity. Third, in this study, self-reported survey data are used, so it is prone to common method bias and perceptual inaccuracy; the prospective studies may utilize objective financial, environmental, and digital measures of performance or mixed-method designs. Alternatively, further research can be carried out to address different theoretical viewpoints such as institutional theory or dynamic capabilities and analyze other conditions of the boundary with regulatory pressure, green innovation capability, or organizational culture to deepen the knowledge of the role that green digital accounting plays in financial sustainability in emerging markets.

REFERENCES

Abakpa, A., & Dvouletý, O. (2025). How does digitalization shape the business financial performance: A systematic review. *Future Business Journal, 11*(1), 235. Advance online publication. DOI: 10.1186/s43093-025-00659-8

Abdelhalim, A. M., Ibrahim, N., & Alomair, M. (2023). The moderating role of digital environmental management accounting in the relationship between eco-efficiency and corporate sustainability. *Sustainability (Basel), 15*(9), 7052. DOI: 10.3390/su15097052

Adelakun, B. O., Antwi, B. O., Ntiakoh, A., & Eziefule, A. O. (2024). Leveraging AI for sustainable accounting: Developing models for environmental impact assessment and reporting. *Finance & Accounting Research Journal, 6*(6), 1017–1048. DOI: 10.51594/farj.v6i6.1234

Al-Nimer, M. (2024). Unpacking the complexity of corporate sustainability: Green innovation's mediating role in risk management and performance. *International Journal of Financial Studies, 12*(3), 78. DOI: 10.3390/ijfs12030078

Al-Taani, A. H. M., Al-Zaqeba, M. A. A., Maabreh, H. M. A., & Jarah, B. A. F. (2024). Exploring the impact of digital accounting and digital zakat on improving business sustainability in the Middle East and Malaysia. *International Journal of Advanced and Applied Sciences, 11*(1), 56–67. DOI: 10.21833/ijaas.2024.01.007

Alshehadeh, A. R., Al-Zaqeba, M. A. A., Elrefae, G. A., AlKhawaja, H. A., & Aljawarneh, N. M. (2024). The effect of digital zakat and accounting on corporate sustainability through financial transparency. *Asian Economic and Financial Review, 14*(3), 228–249. DOI: 10.55493/5002.v14i3.5016

Alshouha, L., Alnaimat, M., Aljaloudi, O., & Al-Mhdawi, M. K. S. (2025). Nexus between ownership structure and fintech in commercial banks: Does female leadership matter? The Jordanian experience *(Preprint). Social Sciences & Humanities Open.* Advance online publication. DOI: 10.2139/ssrn.5358133

Ao, X. Y., Ong, T. S., Aprile, R., & Di Vaio, A. (2023). Environmental uncertainty and digital technologies corporate in shaping corporate green behavior and tax avoidance. *Scientific Reports, 13*(1), 22170. DOI: 10.1038/s41598-023-49687-w PMID: 38092819

Armstrong, J. S., & Overton, T. S. (1977). Estimating nonresponse bias in mail surveys. *JMR, Journal of Marketing Research, 14*(3), 396–402. DOI: 10.1177/002224377701400320

Ashfaq, M., Akhtar, S., Akhlaq, M., Yousaf, A., & Ullah, K. (2026). Integrating digitalization, corporate social responsibility, and human capital for environmental sustainability: The strategic role of green finance in commercial banks. *International Journal of Energy Economics and Policy*, *16*(1), 902–915. DOI: 10.32479/ijeep.22006

Atukunda, G., Musiita, B., Atwiine, J., Atwine, A., & Olyanga, A. M. (2024). Financial innovations and profitability of commercial banks in Uganda. *Journal of Economics and Behavioral Studies*, *16*(2), 32–44. DOI: 10.22610/jebs.v16i2(J).3835

Avira, S., Rofi'ah, R., Setyaningsih, E., & Utami, S. S. (2023). Digital transformation in financial management: Harnessing technology for business success. *INFLUENCE. International Journal of Science Review*, *5*(2), 336–345. DOI: 10.54783/influencejournal.v5i2.161

Barney, J. (1991). Firm resources and sustained competitive advantage. *Journal of Management*, *17*(1), 99–120. DOI: 10.1177/014920639101700108

Belyamani, I., Bani Mfarrej, M. F., Ahmad, S. Z., & Abu Bakar, A. R. (2025). Pathways linking green digital transformation to sustainable development through knowledge sharing and dynamic capabilities. *Discover Sustainability*, *6*(1), 1183. Advance online publication. DOI: 10.1007/s43621-025-02075-y

Bindeeba, D. S., Tukamushaba, E. K., & Bakashaba, R. (2025). How digital capabilities and credit access influence green innovation performance in small and medium enterprises in resource constrained settings. *Discover Sustainability*, *6*(1), 955. Advance online publication. DOI: 10.1007/s43621-025-01916-0

Bocean, C. G., & Vărzaru, A. A. (2023). EU countries' digital transformation, economic performance, and sustainability analysis. *Humanities & Social Sciences Communications*, *10*(1), 875. DOI: 10.1057/s41599-023-02415-1

Chen, A., Wang, S., Mehta, A. M., Asif, M., Xu, S., & Shahzad, M. F. (2025). FinTech adoption for ESG integration through robo advisors, personalization, and perceived trust. *Scientific Reports*, *15*(1), 31125. DOI: 10.1038/s41598-025-17046-6 PMID: 40851039

De Silva, P., Gunarathne, N., & Kumar, S. (2025). Exploring the impact of digital knowledge, integration and performance on sustainable accounting, reporting and assurance. *Meditari Accountancy Research*, *33*(2), 497–552. DOI: 10.1108/MEDAR-02-2024-2383

Dinh, C. T. H., & Tran, N. P. (2025). Artificial intelligence and sustainable performance: Identifying the pivotal role of green intellectual capital and green innovation. *Business Process Management Journal*, •••, 1–22. DOI: 10.1108/BPMJ-12-2024-1165

Du, X., Jiang, K., & Zheng, X. (2024). Reducing asymmetric cost behaviors: Evidence from digital innovation. *Humanities & Social Sciences Communications*, *11*(1), 682. DOI: 10.1057/s41599-024-03179-y

Etikan, I., Musa, S. A., & Alkassim, R. S. (2016). Comparison of convenience sampling and purposive sampling. *American Journal of Theoretical and Applied Statistics*, *5*(1), 1–4. DOI: 10.11648/j.ajtas.20160501.11

Farrukh Shahzad, M., Xu, S., Bilal, A. R., Quratulain, , & Akram, S. (2026). Exploring role of digital literacy and theory of planned behavior in shaping generative AI behavior intentions for educational sustainability. *International Journal of Sustainability in Higher Education*, 1–23. DOI: 10.1108/IJSHE-10-2025-1237

Gray, R. (2002). The social accounting project and accounting organizations and society: Privileging engagement, imaginings, new accountings and pragmatism over critique? *Accounting, Organizations and Society*, *27*(7), 687–708. DOI: 10.1016/S0361-3682(00)00003-9

Hair, J. F., Sarstedt, M., Ringle, C. M., & Mena, J. A. (2012). An assessment of the use of partial least squares structural equation modeling in marketing research. *Journal of the Academy of Marketing Science*, *40*(3), 414–433. DOI: 10.1007/s11747-011-0261-6

Hinkin, T. R. (1998). A brief tutorial on the development of measures for use in survey questionnaires. *Organizational Research Methods*, *1*(1), 104–121. DOI: 10.1177/109442819800100106

Horani, O. M., & Khatibi, A., ALSoud, A. R., Tham, J., Al-Adwan, A. S., & Azam, S. F. (. (2023). Antecedents of business analytics adoption and impacts on banks' performance: The perspective of the TOE framework and resource-based view. *Interdisciplinary Journal of Information, Knowledge, and Management*, *18*, 609–643. DOI: 10.28945/5188

Hossain, R., Ghose, P., Chowdhury, T. M., Hossen, M. D., Hasan, M. N., & Mani, L. (2024). Ownership structures and firm performance: A correlation and regression analysis of financial institutions in Bangladesh. *Pakistan Journal of Life and Social Sciences*, *22*(2), 6278–6295. DOI: 10.57239/PJLSS-2024-22.2.00473

Jie, H., Gooi, L. M., & Lou, Y. (2025). Digital maturity, dynamic capabilities and innovation performance in high-tech SMEs. *International Review of Economics & Finance, 99*, 103971. DOI: 10.1016/j.iref.2025.103971

Kumar, V., Kumar, S., Chatterjee, S., & Mariani, M. (2024). Optimizing the digital transformation capability for enhancing economic sustainability of entrepreneurial venture: The moderating role of entrepreneurial orientation. *IEEE Transactions on Engineering Management, 71*, 1–14. DOI: 10.1109/TEM.2024.3387540

Laradi, S., Elfekair, A., Rehman, H. M., Hanna, D., & Alrawad, M. (2025). Continuance intention of m-Banking adoption: The dynamics of UTAUT3, trust and attitudes. *FIIB Business Review, 23197145251358049*, 23197145251358049. Advance online publication. DOI: 10.1177/23197145251358049

Li, G., Li, X., & Huo, L. (2023). Digital economy, spatial spillover and industrial green innovation efficiency: Empirical evidence from China. *Heliyon, 9*(1), e12875. DOI: 10.1016/j.heliyon.2023.e12875 PMID: 36711307

Li, Z., Rasool, S., Cavus, M. F., & Shahid, W. (2024). Sustaining the future: How green capabilities and digitalization drive sustainability in modern business. *Heliyon, 10*(1).Lu, Z., & Nakagawa, K. (2022). The influence of environmental factors on product innovations in emerging markets: The institutional theory perspective. *International Business Research, 15*(9), 1–15.

Lodhi, R. N., Asif, M., Abdikarimova, A., & Shahzad, M. F. (2024). Impact of innovation and sustainability on green entrepreneurship: A bibliometric exploration. *Environment, Development and Sustainability, 28*(1), 1–26. DOI: 10.1007/s10668-024-05053-y

Maier, C., Thatcher, J. B., Grover, V., & Dwivedi, Y. K. (2023). Cross-sectional research: A critical perspective, use cases, and recommendations for IS research. *International Journal of Information Management, 70*, 102625. DOI: 10.1016/j.ijinfomgt.2023.102625

Mihu, C., Pitic, A. G., & Bayraktar, D. (2023). Drivers of digital transformation and their impact on organizational management. *Studies in Business and Economics, 18*(1), 149–170. DOI: 10.2478/sbe-2023-0009

Morea, D., Iazzolino, G., Giglio, C., Bruni, M. E., Baldissarro, G., & Farinelli, E. (2025). The role of digitalization and ESG on financial performance: An empirical analysis on the energy and utilities sectors. *PLoS One, 20*(2), e0314078. DOI: 10.1371/journal.pone.0314078 PMID: 40014599

Napisah, L. S., Taufikurochman, C., & Harto, B. (2024). The effect of digitalization on the sustainability of accounting practices in the financial industry. *Journal of Social Science and Business Studies*, *2*(4), 268–276. DOI: 10.61487/jssbs.v2i4.100

Nishant, R., Teo, T. S. H., & Goh, M. (2017). Do shareholders value green information technology announcements? *Journal of the Association for Information Systems*, *18*(8), 542–576. DOI: 10.17705/1jais.00466

Oduro, S. (2024). Eco-innovation and SMEs' sustainable performance: A meta-analysis. *European Journal of Innovation Management*, *27*(9), 248–279. DOI: 10.1108/EJIM-11-2023-0961

Petcu, M. A., Sobolevschi-David, M. I., & Curea, S. C. (2024). Integrating digital technologies in sustainability accounting and reporting: Perceptions of professional cloud computing users. *Electronics (Basel)*, *13*(14), 2684. DOI: 10.3390/electronics13142684

Porter, M. E., & van der Linde, C. (1995). Green and competitive: Ending the stalemate. *Harvard Business Review*, *73*(5), 120–134.

Prasetianingrum, S., & Sonjaya, Y. (2024). The evolution of digital accounting and accounting information systems in the modern business landscape. *Advances in Applied Accounting Research*, *2*(1).

Przychocka, I., & Sikorski, M. (2024). Revolutionizing SME management: The digital transformation of financial operations. *European Research Studies*, *27*(2), 78–85. DOI: 10.35808/ersj/3372

Sari, S. I. A. P., Harahap, M. I., & Rahma, T. I. F. (2025). Evaluation of management strategy in increasing the competitiveness of MSMEs at the cooperative and MSME service. *Urwatul Wutsqo*, *14*(3), 1252–1266. Advance online publication. DOI: 10.54437/urwatulwutsqo.v14i3.2592

Schaltegger, S., & Burritt, R. (2000). *Contemporary Environmental Accounting: Issues, Concepts and Practice*. Greenleaf Publishing.

Senadjki, A., Au Yong, H. N., Ganapathy, T., & Ogbeibu, S. (2023). Unlocking the potential: The impact of digital leadership on firms' performance through digital transformation. *Journal of Business and Socio-economic Development*, *4*(2), 161–177. DOI: 10.1108/JBSED-06-2023-0050

Setyadi, A., Pawirosumarto, S., Damaris, A., & Syarif, D. (2025). Integrating green HRM and sustainable operations: The moderating role of digital transformation in the Indonesian energy sector. *Discover Sustainability*, *6*(1), 924. Advance online publication. DOI: 10.1007/s43621-025-01764-y

Shahzad, M. F., Javed, I., & Zahid, I. (2024). The influence of the marketing orientation of textile companies in increasing their competitiveness. In *Industry and innovation: Textile industry* (pp. 95–118). Springer Nature Switzerland.

Shahzad, M. F., Xu, S., An, X., Asif, M., & Javed, I. (2025). Do generative AI technologies play a double-edged sword role in education? Findings from hybrid approach using PLS-SEM and fsQCA. *Education and Information Technologies*, *30*(14), 1–30. DOI: 10.1007/s10639-025-13528-2

Shahzad, M. F., Xu, S., Khan, K. I., & Hasnain, M. F. (2023). Effect of social influence, environmental awareness, and safety affordance on actual use of 5G technologies among Chinese students. *Scientific Reports*, *13*(1), 22442. DOI: 10.1038/s41598-023-50078-4 PMID: 38105309

Shatila, K., Nurzhaubayeva, R., Malishevskaya, N., & Podolskaya, T. (2024). Navigating sustainability: The role of environmental accounting in enhancing business performance. E3S *Web of Conferences*, 479, 09027.

Teece, D. J., Pisano, G., & Shuen, A. (1997). Dynamic capabilities and strategic management. *Strategic Management Journal*, *18*(7), 509–533. DOI: 10.1002/(SICI)1097-0266(199708)18:7<509::AID-SMJ882>3.0.CO;2-Z

Ukko, J., Nasiri, M., Saunila, M., & Rantala, T. (2019). Sustainability strategy as a moderator in the relationship between digital business strategy and financial performance. *Journal of Cleaner Production*, *236*, 117626. DOI: 10.1016/j.jclepro.2019.117626

Ur Rahman, R., Ali Shah, S. M., El-Gohary, H., Abbas, M., Haider Khalil, S., Al Altheeb, S., & Sultan, F. (2020). Social media adoption and financial sustainability: Learned lessons from developing countries. *Sustainability (Basel)*, *12*(24), 10616. DOI: 10.3390/su122410616

Uyanık, M. (2023). Resource-based view in marketing literature. *Journal of Business and Management Studies*, *5*(4), 29–39. DOI: 10.32996/jbms.2023.5.4.4

Vo-Thai, H. C., & Tran, M. L. (2025). Green innovation strategies in Vietnamese enterprises: Leveraging knowledge management and digitalization for sustainable competitiveness. *Journal of Knowledge Management*, *29*(4), 1055–1091. DOI: 10.1108/JKM-06-2024-0642

Wernerfelt, B. (1984). A resource-based view of the firm. *Strategic Management Journal*, *5*(2), 171–180. DOI: 10.1002/smj.4250050207

Wu, S., Cheng, P., & Yang, F. (2024). Study on the impact of digital transformation on green competitive advantage: The role of green innovation and government regulation. *PLoS One*, *19*(8), e0306603. DOI: 10.1371/journal.pone.0306603 PMID: 39088476

Yahya, S., Khan, A., Farooq, M., & Irfan, M. (2022). Integrating green business strategies and green competencies to enhance green innovation: Evidence from manufacturing firms of Pakistan. *Environmental Science and Pollution Research International*, *29*(26), 39500–39514. DOI: 10.1007/s11356-021-18430-1 PMID: 35103945

Zhen, T., & Rahman, M. M. (2024). Greening emerging economies: Enhancing environmental, social, and governance performance through environmental management accounting and green financing. *Sustainability (Basel)*, *16*(11), 4753. DOI: 10.3390/su16114753

Zik-Rullahi, A. A., & Jide, I. (2023). Green accounting: A fundamental pillar of corporate sustainability reporting. *Journal of Accounting and Financial Management*, *9*(8), 59–72. DOI: 10.56201/jafm.v9.no8.2023.pg59.72

Appendix

This list covers the principal reader-facing abbreviations and acronyms used in the chapter narratives, conceptual frameworks, methods, tables, and empirical analyses.

Table 1. List of Abbreviations and Acronyms

Abbreviation	Full Term
AFS	Available-for-Sale
AI	Artificial Intelligence
AIS	Accounting Information Systems
AIS/MIS	Accounting and Management Information Systems
AMOS	IBM SPSS Amos (Analysis of Moment Structures)
API	Application Programming Interface
APIP	Aparat Pengawasan Intern Pemerintah (Government Internal Supervisory Apparatus)
ARE	Average Risk Estimate
AUC	Area Under the Curve
AVE	Average Variance Extracted
BI	Business Intelligence
BPR	Business Process Re-engineering
BSSN	Badan Siber dan Sandi Negara (National Cyber and Crypto Agency, Indonesia)
CBS	Core Banking Solutions
CCAR	Comprehensive Capital Analysis and Review
CDR	Consumer Data Right
CFI	Comparative Fit Index
COSO	Committee of Sponsoring Organizations of the Treadway Commission
CR	Composite Reliability
CSF	Cybersecurity Framework
DDDM	Data-Driven Decision-Making
DFCS	Digital Financial Control Systems
DLP	Data Leakage Prevention

continued on following page

2027, IGI Global Scientific Publishing. Copying or distributing in print or electronic forms without written permission of IGI Global Scientific Publishing is prohibited. Use of this chapter to rative artificial intelligence (AI) technologies is expressly prohibited. The publisher reserves all rights to license its use for generative AI training and machine learning model development.

Table 1. Continued

Abbreviation	Full Term
DMI	Enterprise Digital Maturity Index
DPI	Digital Public Infrastructure
DPO	Data Protection Officer
DSS	Decision-Support Systems
DTM	Digital Transformation Maturity
EA	Enterprise Architecture
EEA	European Economic Area
EMA	Environmental Management Accounting
ENISA	European Union Agency for Cybersecurity
ERM	Enterprise Risk Management
ERP	Enterprise Resource Planning
ESG	Environmental, Social, and Governance
FASB	Financial Accounting Standards Board
FIMCS	Financial Information Management and Control Systems
FIS	Financial Information System
FMIS	Financial Management Information Systems
FS	Financial Sustainability
FSP	Financial Statement Presentation
GAAP	Generally Accepted Accounting Principles
GCA	Green Cumulative Advantage
GDA	Green Digital Accounting
GDPR	General Data Protection Regulation
GERAM	Generalised Enterprise Reference Architecture and Methodology
GST	Goods and Services Tax
HTM	Held-to-Maturity
HTMT	Heterotrait-Monotrait Ratio of Correlations
IASB	International Accounting Standards Board
IFRS	International Financial Reporting Standards
IMF	International Monetary Fund
IPA	Intelligent Process Automation
IT	Information Technology
KYC	Know Your Customer
LASSO	Least Absolute Shrinkage and Selection Operator
LIME	Local Interpretable Model-Agnostic Explanations

continued on following page

Table 1. Continued

Abbreviation	Full Term
MERA	Multiple Estimating using Risk Analysis
MIS	Management Information Systems
ML	Machine Learning
MLRE	Maximum Likely Risk Estimate
MSME	Micro, Small and Medium Enterprises
NFI	Normed Fit Index
NIST	National Institute of Standards and Technology
NLP	Natural Language Processing
OECD	Organisation for Economic Co-operation and Development
PCA	Principal Component Analysis
PDNS	Pusat Data Nasional Sementara (Temporary National Data Center, Indonesia)
PLS	Partial Least Squares
PLS-SEM	Partial Least Squares Structural Equation Modeling
PSD2	Revised Payment Services Directive
RBAC	Role-Based Access Controls
RBI	Reserve Bank of India
RBV	Resource-Based View
RMSEA	Root Mean Square Error of Approximation
ROC	Receiver Operating Characteristic
RPA	Robotic Process Automation
SAKTI	Sistem Aplikasi Keuangan Tingkat Instansi
SDLC	Software Development Life Cycle
SEM	Structural Equation Modeling
SHAP	SHapley Additive exPlanations
SIPD	Sistem Informasi Pemerintahan Daerah
SLA	Service Level Agreement
SOX	Sarbanes-Oxley Act
SPSS	IBM SPSS Statistics
SRMR	Standardized Root Mean Square Residual
SVM	Support Vector Machine
TAM	Technology Acceptance Model
TLI	Tucker-Lewis Index
TOE	Technology-Organization-Environment
UPI	Unified Payments Interface

continued on following page

Table 1. Continued

Abbreviation	Full Term
VRIN	Valuable, Rare, Inimitable, and Non-substitutable
XAI	Explainable Artificial Intelligence
XML	Explainable Machine Learning

Compilation of References

Aanu, O. S., Samuel, F. A., Ajayi, A., & Folashade, O. (2016). Examining the quality of financial reporting in the banking sector in Nigeria: Does audit committee accounting expertise matter? *Journal of Internet Banking and Commerce, 21*(3).

Abakpa, A., & Dvouletý, O. (2025). How does digitalization shape the business financial performance: A systematic review. *Future Business Journal, 11*(1), 235. Advance online publication. DOI: 10.1186/s43093-025-00659-8

Abbas, K. (2025). Management accounting and artificial intelligence: A comprehensive literature review and recommendations for future research. *The British Accounting Review, 101551*. Advance online publication. DOI: 10.1016/j.bar.2025.101551

Abdelhalim, A. M., Ibrahim, N., & Alomair, M. (2023). The moderating role of digital environmental management accounting in the relationship between eco-efficiency and corporate sustainability. *Sustainability (Basel), 15*(9), 7052. DOI: 10.3390/su15097052

Abikoye, B. E., Adelusi, W., Umeorah, S. C., Adelaja, A. O., & Agorbia-Atta, C. (2024). Integrating Risk Management in Fintech and Traditional Financial Institutions through AI and Machine Learning. *Journal of Economics. Management and Trade, 30*(8), 90–102. DOI: 10.9734/jemt/2024/v30i81236

Aboabdo, S., Aldhoiena, A., & Al-Amrib, H. (2019). Implementing Enterprise Resource Planning ERP System in a Large Construction Company in KSA. *Procedia Computer Science, 164*, 463–470. DOI: 10.1016/j.procs.2019.12.207

Abraham, R., Schneider, J., & vom Brocke, J. (2019). Data governance: A conceptual framework, structured review, and research agenda. *International Journal of Information Management, 49*, 424–438. DOI: 10.1016/j.ijinfomgt.2019.07.008

Abu Afifa, M., Saleh, I., & Vo Van, H. (2025). Accounting information quality in the digital era–a perspective from ERP system adoption? *Global Knowledge, Memory and Communication, 74*(5-6), 2022–2046. DOI: 10.1108/GKMC-03-2023-0101

Achalapong, J., & Satitsamitpong, M. (2025). Improving Credit Decisions Through Machine Learning and Alternative Data: Evidence from Nbfis. *ABAC Journal, 45*(4). Advance online publication. DOI: 10.59865/abacj.2025.27

Adari, V. K.Vijay Kumar Adari. (2024). How Cloud Computing is Facilitating Interoperability in Banking and Finance. *International Journal of Scientific Research in Computer Science. Engineering and Information Technology, 10*(6), 851–859. DOI: 10.32628/CSEIT241061138

Addy, W. A., Ugochukwu, C. E., Oyewole, A. T., Ofodile, O. C., Adeoye, O. B., & Okoye, C. C.Wilhelmina Afua AddyChinonye Esther UgochukwuAdedoyin Tolulope OyewoleOnyeka Chrisanctus OfodileOmotayo Bukola AdeoyeChinwe Chinazo Okoye. (2024). Predictive analytics in credit risk management for banks: A comprehensive review. *GSC Advanced Research and Reviews, 18*(2), 434–449. DOI: 10.30574/gscarr.2024.18.2.0077

Adekunle, B. I., Damilare Balogun, E., Chukwuma-Eke, E. C., & Ogunsola, K. O. (2023). Developing a Digital Operations Dashboard for Real-Time Financial Compliance Monitoring in Multinational Corporations. *Bolaji Iyanu Adekunle et Al Int. J. Sci. Res. Comput. Sci. Eng. Inf. Technol, 9*(3), 728–746. http://ijsrcseit.com

Adelakun, B. O., Antwi, B. O., Ntiakoh, A., & Eziefule, A. O. (2024). Leveraging AI for sustainable accounting: Developing models for environmental impact assessment and reporting. *Finance & Accounting Research Journal, 6*(6), 1017–1048. DOI: 10.51594/farj.v6i6.1234

Adepoju, A. H., Austin-Gabriel, B., Eweje, A., & Hamza, O. (2023). A data governance framework for high-impact programs: Reducing redundancy and enhancing data quality at scale. *International Journal of Multidisciplinary Research and Growth Evaluation, 4*(6), 1141–1154. DOI: 10.54660/.IJMRGE.2023.4.6.1141-1154

Adugna, B. M., & Kumar, B. (2021). Determinants of internet financial reporting: In the case of Ethiopian insurance and banking sector companies. *Innovations, 66*(66), 760–778.

Afrin, S., Roksana, S., & Akram, R. (2024a). Ai-enhanced robotic process automation: A review of intelligent automation innovations. *IEEE Access*. https://ieeexplore.ieee.org/abstract/document/10781408/

Afrin, S., Roksana, S., & Akram, R. (2024b). Ai-enhanced robotic process automation: A review of intelligent automation innovations. *IEEE Access*. https://ieeexplore.ieee.org/abstract/document/10781408/

Agostino, D., Saliterer, I., & Steccolini, I. (2022). Digitalization, accounting and accountability: A literature review and reflections on future research in public services. *Financial Accountability & Management, 38*(2), 152–176. DOI: 10.1111/faam.12301

Ahmad, N. R. (2025). Strategic Agility in Crisis: How Pakistani Businesses Adapt Financially to Global Disruptions and Market Shocks. *Center for Management Science Research, 3*(3), 31–39.

Ajayi, O. O., Alozie, C. E., & Abieba, O. A. (2025). Enhancing cybersecurity in energy infrastructure: Strategies for safeguarding critical systems in the digital age. *Trends in Renewable Energy, 11*(2), 201–212. DOI: 10.17737/tre.2025.11.2.00192

Ajayi, R. (2025). Integrating IoT and cloud computing for continuous process optimization in real-time systems. *Int J Res Publ Rev, 6*(1), 2540–2558. DOI: 10.55248/gengpi.6.0125.0441

Ajibade, O. A. (2025). Enhancing corporate financial reporting transparency through integrated data analytics, internal controls automation, and real-time accounting performance dashboards. *Int J Comput Appl Technol Res, 14*(4), 148–166.

Akula, D. K., Mohammed, Y. S., Syed, A., Haque, G. M. M., & Arafat, Y. (2025). The Role of Information Systems in Enhancing Strategic Decision Making: A Review and Future Directions. *Emerging Frontiers Library for The American Journal of Management and Economics Innovations, 7*(8), 80–105. DOI: 10.37547/tajmei/Volume07Issue08-07

Al Maruf, A. (2025). A systematic review of ERP-integrated decision support systems for financial and operational optimization in global retails business. *American Journal of Interdisciplinary Studies, 6*(1), 236–262. DOI: 10.63125/qgbrmf24

Aladwan, M., & Shatnawi, Y. (2019). The association between accounting disclosures and stock market price: An empirical study on Jordanian commercial banks. *International Journal of Managerial and Financial Accounting, 11*(1), 73–92. DOI: 10.1504/IJMFA.2019.097831

Al-Ansi, A. M., Garad, A., & Jaboob, M. (2024). Unraveling the complexities of financial innovation and digital transformation within banking systems. *Multidisciplinary Reviews, 7*(11), 2024265–2024265. DOI: 10.31893/multirev.2024265

Alao, O. B., Dudu, O. F., Alonge, E. O., & Eze, C. E. (2024). Automation in financial reporting: A conceptual framework for efficiency and accuracy in US corporations. *Global Journal of Advanced Research and Reviews, 2*(02), 040-050.

Albshaier, L., Almarri, S., & Hafizur Rahman, M. M. (2024). A review of blockchain's role in E-Commerce transactions: Open challenges, and future research directions. *Computers, 13*(1), 27. DOI: 10.3390/computers13010027

Alexander, D., & Archer, S. (2003). On economic reality, representational faithfulness and the 'true and fair override.'. *Accounting and Business Research, 33*(1), 3–17. DOI: 10.1080/00014788.2003.9729628

Alex-Omiogbemi, A. A., Sule, A. K., Omowole, B. M., & Owoade, S. J.Anne Ajiri Alex-OmiogbemiAumbur Kwaghter SuleBamidele Michael OmowoleSamuel Jesupelumi Owoade. (2024). Conceptual framework for advancing regulatory compliance and risk management in emerging markets through digital innovation. *World Journal of Advanced Research and Reviews, 24*(3), 1155–1162. DOI: 10.30574/wjarr.2024.24.3.3752

Al-Farsi, N., & Lee, B. (2025). Governing Financial Big Data Ecosystems: Data Quality, Statistical Integrity, and Institutional Accountability in Monetary and Financial Statistics. *European Journal of Emerging Data Science and Machine Learning*, *2*(02), 1–6.

Al-Hattami, H. M. (2024). Impact of AIS success on decision-making effectiveness among SMEs in less developed countries. *Information Technology for Development, 30*(3), 472–492. DOI: 10.1080/02681102.2022.2073325

Al-Hattami, H. M., Abdullah, A. A. A. H., Kabra, J. D., Alsoufi, M. A., Gaber, M. M., & Shuraim, A. M. (2022). Effect of AIS on planning process effectiveness: A case of SMEs in a less developed nation. *The Bottom Line (New York, N.Y.), 35*(2/3), 33–52. DOI: 10.1108/BL-01-2022-0001

Ali, M., & AlSondos, K. (2025). Accounting information systems usage and management commitment toward operational efficiency: Evidence from SMEs. *Economies (Basel), 10*(4), 83. DOI: 10.3390/economies10040083

Alles, M. G., Dai, J., & Vasarhelyi, M. A. (2021). Reporting 4.0: Business reporting for the age of mass customization. *Journal of Emerging Technologies in Accounting, 18*(1), 1–15. DOI: 10.2308/jeta-10764

Almaqtari, F. A. (2024). The Role of IT Governance in the Integration of AI in Accounting and Auditing Operations. *Economies (Basel), 12*(8), 199. DOI: 10.3390/economies12080199

Al-mashari, M. (2003). Enterprise resource planning (ERP) systems: A research agenda. *Industrial Management & Data Systems, 103*(1), 22–27. DOI: 10.1108/02635570310456869

Al-Mutawa, H. A., Sowailem, E. K., & Al Mubarak, M. (2025). Business Ethics in E-commerce: Ethical Concerns and Safeguarding Consumer Trust and Loyalty. In Al Mubarak, M. (Ed.), *Sustainable Digital Technology and Ethics in an Ever-Changing Environment* (Vol. 237, pp. 3–20). Springer Nature Switzerland., DOI: 10.1007/978-3-031-86708-8_1

Al-Nimer, M. (2024). Unpacking the complexity of corporate sustainability: Green innovation's mediating role in risk management and performance. *International Journal of Financial Studies*, *12*(3), 78. DOI: 10.3390/ijfs12030078

Al-Omush, A., Almasarwah, A., & Al-Wreikat, A. (2025a). Artificial intelligence in financial auditing: Redefining accuracy and transparency in assurance services. *EDPACS*, *70*(6), 1–20. DOI: 10.1080/07366981.2025.2459490

Alonge, E. O., Dudu, O. F., & Alao, O. B. (2024). The impact of digital transformation on financial reporting and accountability in emerging markets. *International Journal of Science and Technology Research Archive, 7*(2), 025-049.

Alruwaili, T. F., & Mgammal, M. H. (2025). The impact of artificial intelligence on accounting practices: An academic perspective. *Humanities & Social Sciences Communications*, *12*(1), 104. Advance online publication. DOI: 10.1057/s41599-025-05004-6

Alsharari, N. M. (2022). Cloud computing and ERP assimilation in the public sector: Institutional perspectives. *Transforming Government*, *16*(1), 97–109. DOI: 10.1108/TG-04-2021-0069

Alshehadeh, A. R., Al-Zaqeba, M. A. A., Elrefae, G. A., AlKhawaja, H. A., & Aljawarneh, N. M. (2024). The effect of digital zakat and accounting on corporate sustainability through financial transparency. *Asian Economic and Financial Review*, *14*(3), 228–249. DOI: 10.55493/5002.v14i3.5016

Alshouha, L., Alnaimat, M., Aljaloudi, O., & Al-Mhdawi, M. K. S. (2025). Nexus between ownership structure and fintech in commercial banks: Does female leadership matter? The Jordanian experience *(Preprint). Social Sciences & Humanities Open*. Advance online publication. DOI: 10.2139/ssrn.5358133

Al-Taani, A. H. M., Al-Zaqeba, M. A. A., Maabreh, H. M. A., & Jarah, B. A. F. (2024). Exploring the impact of digital accounting and digital zakat on improving business sustainability in the Middle East and Malaysia. *International Journal of Advanced and Applied Sciences*, *11*(1), 56–67. DOI: 10.21833/ijaas.2024.01.007

Amaefule, L. I.. (2018). Fair Value Measurement versus Historical Cost Accounting: A Comparative Effect on Firms' Performance in Nigeria. *Research Journal of Finance and Accounting*, *9*(10), 165–175.

Amdouni, A. (2025a). Artificial intelligence and financial fraud detection: Applications and challenges. In Derbali, A. (Ed.), *Artificial intelligence for financial risk management and analysis* (pp. 271–280). IGI Global Scientific Publishing., DOI: 10.4018/979-8-3373-1200-2.ch013

Andelina, W., & Santoso, A. (2021). Measuring quality determinants of financial statements. *Journal of Business and Management Review*, *2*(12), 884–893. DOI: 10.47153/jbmr212.2082021

Annarelli, A., Battistella, C., Nonino, F., Parida, V., & Pessot, E. (2021). Literature review on digitalization capabilities: Co-citation analysis of antecedents, conceptualization and consequences. *Technological Forecasting and Social Change*, *166*, 120635. DOI: 10.1016/j.techfore.2021.120635

Ao, X. Y., Ong, T. S., Aprile, R., & Di Vaio, A. (2023). Environmental uncertainty and digital technologies corporate in shaping corporate green behavior and tax avoidance. *Scientific Reports*, *13*(1), 22170. DOI: 10.1038/s41598-023-49687-w PMID: 38092819

Apriyanto, G. (2025). Transformation of public sector behavioral accounting: The critical role of HR in preventing financial fraud through digitalization in Indonesia. *International Journal of Research in Social Science and Humanities*, *6*(9), 199–210. DOI: 10.47505/IJRSS.2025.10.20

Arisandi, D., & Khudri, T. M. Y. (2021). *Analysis and design of data governance at the Financial Services Authority. InFestasi, 17(1)*. InPres., DOI: 10.21107/infestasi.v17i1.10515

Armstrong, J. S., & Overton, T. S. (1977). Estimating nonresponse bias in mail surveys. *JMR, Journal of Marketing Research*, *14*(3), 396–402. DOI: 10.1177/002224377701400320

Arner, D. W., Castellano, G. G., & Selga, E. K. (2022). Financial Data Governance. *The Hastings Law Journal*, *74*, 235.

Aro, O. E.Opeyemi E Aro. (2024). Data analytics as a driver of digital transformation in financial institutions. *World J. Adv. Res. Rev.*, *24*(1), 1054–1072. DOI: 10.30574/wjarr.2024.24.1.3124

Arrieta, A. B., Díaz-Rodríguez, N., Del Ser, J., Bennetot, A., Tabik, S., Barbado, A., García, S., Gil-López, S., Molina, D., Benjamins, R., Chatila, R., & Herrera, F. (2020). Explainable artificial intelligence (XAI): Concepts, taxonomies, opportunities and challenges toward responsible AI. *Information Fusion*, *58*, 82–115. DOI: 10.1016/j.inffus.2019.12.012

Arzberger, P., Schroeder, P., Beaulieu, A., Bowker, G., Casey, K., Laaksonen, L., Moorman, D., Uhlir, P., & Wouters, P. (2004). Promoting access to public research data for scientific, economic, and social development. *Data Science Journal*, *3*, 135–152. DOI: 10.2481/dsj.3.135

Ashfaq, M., Akhtar, S., Akhlaq, M., Yousaf, A., & Ullah, K. (2026). Integrating digitalization, corporate social responsibility, and human capital for environmental sustainability: The strategic role of green finance in commercial banks. *International Journal of Energy Economics and Policy*, *16*(1), 902–915. DOI: 10.32479/ijeep.22006

Ashraf, M. (2025). Does automation improve financial reporting? Evidence from internal controls. *Review of Accounting Studies*, *30*(1), 436–479. DOI: 10.1007/s11142-024-09822-y

Assidi, S., Omran, M., Rana, T., & Borgi, H. (2025). The role of AI adoption in transforming the accounting profession: A diffusion of innovations theory approach. *Journal of Accounting & Organizational Change*. https://www.emerald.com/insight/content/doi/10.1108/JAOC-04-2024-0124/full/html

Ates, E. (2024). JPMorgan's COiN (Contract Intelligence) platform: Using AI in mergers & acquisitions and commercial lending [Case study]. https://www.emreates.co.uk/research-2/jpmorgan's-coin-(contract-intelligence)-platform:-using-ai-in-mergers-&-acquisitions-and-commercial-lending

Atukunda, G., Musiita, B., Atwiine, J., Atwine, A., & Olyanga, A. M. (2024). Financial innovations and profitability of commercial banks in Uganda. *Journal of Economics and Behavioral Studies*, *16*(2), 32–44. DOI: 10.22610/jebs.v16i2(J).3835

Aven, T. (2024). Risk literacy: Foundational issues and its connection to risk science. *Risk Analysis : An Official Publication of the Society for Risk Analysis*, *44*(5), 1011–1020. DOI: 10.1111/risa.14223 PMID: 37728216

Aven, T., & Zio, E. (2014). Foundational Issues in Risk Assessment and Risk Management. *Risk Analysis : An Official Publication of the Society for Risk Analysis*, *34*(7), 1164–1172. DOI: 10.1111/risa.12132 PMID: 24152111

Avira, S., Setyaningsih, E., & Utami, S. S. (2023). Digital transformation in financial management: Harnessing technology for business success. *Influence: International Journal of Science Review, 5*(2), 336–345. DOI: 10.54783/influencejournal.v5i2.161

Azevedo, R. R. D., Lino, A. F., Carrara, L. G. C., Aquino, A. C. B. D., & Cardoso, R. L. (2025). Interoperability of financial management systems in local governments and opportunities for digital transformation. *Revista de Administração Pública, 59*(2), e2024–e0249. DOI: 10.1590/0034-761220240249x

Aziz, S., & Dowling, M. M. (2018). AI and Machine Learning for Risk Management. SSRN *Electronic Journal*. DOI: 10.2139/ssrn.3201337

Babin, R., & Smith, D. (2022). Open banking and regulation: Please advise the government. *Journal of Information Technology Teaching Cases, 12*(2), 108–114. DOI: 10.1177/20438869221082316

Badgujar, P. (2023). The role of data catalogs in driving organizational insights and efficiency. *Journal of Artificial Intelligence & Cloud Computing, 2*(4), 1. DOI: 10.47363/JAICC/2022(1)263

Bahssas, D. M., AlBar, A. M., & Hoque, M. R. (2015). Enterprise Resource Planning (ERP) Systems: Design, Trends and Deployment. *The International Technology Management Review, 5*(2), 72. DOI: 10.2991/itmr.2015.5.2.2

Baidoo, E., & Mazzotta, S. (2025). On the fringe of credit visibility: The value of alternative data for assessing the credit risk of subprime underbanked consumers. *International Journal of Applied Decision Sciences, 18*(4), 472–492. DOI: 10.1504/IJADS.2025.147286

Baker, L. (2017). The impact of the General Data Protection Regulation on the banking sector: Data subjects' rights, conflicts of laws and Brexit. *Journal of Data Protection and Privacy, 1*(2), 137–145. DOI: 10.69554/EIYO6659

Balboni, P., & Francis, K. (2024). Personal Privacy Policies. In *Computer and Information Security Handbook* (4th ed., Vol. 1-2, pp. 907–916). Elsevier., DOI: 10.1016/B978-0-443-13223-0.00055-2

Bao, Y., Lyu, C., Wu, X., & Lian, J. (2022). Optimal decision-making in Chinese cross-border mergers and acquisitions: A perspective of overbidding. *Complexity, 2022*(1). DOI: 10.1155/2022/8298451

Barbosa, S. da C., Leandro, A. C. M. C., Neves, D. O., Vilhena, F. A. D. F., Souza, F. F. S. C., Barros, L. C., Lins, L. da C., de Araujo, P. R., de Oliveira, T. L., & da Silva, E. N. (2025). Accounting and Artificial Intelligence: A Systematic Review of the Literature on the Technological Impacts in the Accounting Field. *Journal of Economics, Business, and Commerce*, *2*(2), 150–157. DOI: 10.69739/jebc.v2i2.1083

Barney, J. (1991). Firm resources and sustained competitive advantage. *Journal of Management*, *17*(1), 99–120. DOI: 10.1177/014920639101700108

Barreto, A., Gomes, P., Quesado, P., & O'Sullivan, S. (2025). Advancements in Management Accounting and Digital Technologies: A Systematic Literature Review. Accounting. *Finance & Governance Review*, *34*. Advance online publication. DOI: 10.52399/001c.137301

Barth, M. E. (2014). Measurement in financial reporting: The need for concepts. *Accounting Horizons*, *28*(2), 331–352. DOI: 10.2308/acch-50689

Bartolacci, F., & Caputo, A. (2020). *Sustainability and financial performance of small and medium sized enterprises: A bibliometric and systematic literature review*. Business Strategy and the., DOI: 10.1002/bse.2434

Bartolini, C., Daoudagh, S., Lenzini, G., & Marchetti, E. (2019). Towards a lawful authorized access: A preliminary GDPR-based authorized access. In van S. M., M. L., & M. L. (Eds.), *ICSOFT 2019 - Proceedings of the 14th International Conference on Software Technologies* (pp. 331–338). SciTePress. DOI: 10.5220/0007978703310338

Basiru, J. O., Ejiofor, C. L., Onukwulu, E. C., & Attah, R. (2023). Enhancing financial reporting systems: A conceptual framework for integrating data analytics in business decision-making. *IRE Journals,[online]*, *7*(4), 587-606.

Batini, C., Scannapieco, M., & Viscusi, G. (2016). *Data quality management: Models, methods, and applications*. Springer., DOI: 10.1007/978-3-319-24106-7

Bayou, M. E., Reinstein, A., & Williams, P. F. (2011). To tell the truth: A discussion of issues concerning truth and ethics in accounting. *Accounting, Organizations and Society*, *36*(2), 109–124. DOI: 10.1016/j.aos.2011.02.001

Becker, R., Chokoshvili, D., Thorogood, A., Dove, E. S., Molnár-Gábor, F., Ziaka, A., Tzortzatou-Nanopoulou, O., & Comandè, G. (2024). Purpose definition as a crucial step for determining the legal basis under the GDPR: Implications for scientific research. *Journal of Law and the Biosciences*, *11*(1), lsae001. Advance online publication. DOI: 10.1093/jlb/lsae001

Behbehani, D., Rajarajan, M., Komninos, N., & Al-Begain, K. (2022). Detecting Open Banking API Security Threats Using Bayesian Attack Graphs. *Proceedings - 2022 14th IEEE International Conference on Computational Intelligence and Communication Networks, CICN 2022*, 789–796. DOI: 10.1109/CICN56167.2022.10008365

Behie, S. W., Pasman, H. J., Khan, F. I., Shell, K., Alarfaj, A., El-Kady, A. H., & Hernandez, M. (2023). Leadership 4.0: The changing landscape of industry management in the smart digital era. *Process Safety and Environmental Protection, 172*(January), 317–328. DOI: 10.1016/j.psep.2023.02.014

Belyamani, I., Bani Mfarrej, M. F., Ahmad, S. Z., & Abu Bakar, A. R. (2025). Pathways linking green digital transformation to sustainable development through knowledge sharing and dynamic capabilities. *Discover Sustainability, 6*(1), 1183. Advance online publication. DOI: 10.1007/s43621-025-02075-y

Ben Rejeb Attia, M., Lassoued, N., & Sassi, H. (2019). Financial reporting timeliness and the value relevance of earnings: Evidence from banks in the MENA countries. *The International Trade Journal, 33*(3), 277–301. DOI: 10.1080/08853908.2018.1459212

Bezzina, F., Camilleri, E., & Marmarà, V. (2021). Transparency and Accountability Public Service Reforms. In *Public Administration, Governance and Globalization* (Vol. 22, pp. 91–104). Springer. DOI: 10.1007/978-3-030-74357-4_3

Bhasin, N. K., & Rajesh, A. (2021). Impact of E-Collaboration between Indian Banks and Fintech Companies for Digital Banking and New Emerging Technologies. *International Journal of e-Collaboration, 17*(1), 15–35. DOI: 10.4018/IJeC.2021010102

Bhimani, A., & Willcocks, L. (2014). Digitisation, 'Big Data' and the transformation of accounting information. *Accounting and Business Research, 44*(4), 469–490. DOI: 10.1080/00014788.2014.910051

Biagi, V., & Russo, A. (2022). Data model design to support data-driven IT governance implementation. *Technologies, 10*(5), 106. DOI: 10.3390/technologies10050106

Biecek, P., & Burzykowski, T. (2021). *Explanatory model analysis: Explore, explain, and examine predictive models*. CRC Press., DOI: 10.1201/9780429027192

Bindeeba, D. S., Tukamushaba, E. K., & Bakashaba, R. (2025). How digital capabilities and credit access influence green innovation performance in small and medium enterprises in resource constrained settings. *Discover Sustainability, 6*(1), 955. Advance online publication. DOI: 10.1007/s43621-025-01916-0

Bin-Ghanem, H. O., & Ariff, A. M. (2016). Internet financial reporting and firm value: Evidence from Gulf Cooperation Council countries. *International Journal of Accounting. Auditing and Performance Evaluation, 12*(3), 237–260. DOI: 10.1504/IJAAPE.2016.077891

Binh, N. T. T. (2025). Transforming auditing in the AI era: A comprehensive review. *Information (Basel), 16*(5), 400. DOI: 10.3390/info16050400

Bisht, D., Singh, R., Gehlot, A., Akram, S. V., Singh, A., Montero, E. C., Priyadarshi, N., & Twala, B. (2022). Imperative role of integrating digitalization in the firms finance: A technological perspective. *Electronics (Basel), 11*(19), 3252. DOI: 10.3390/electronics11193252

Blanchard, S. J., Martin, K. D., & Salisbury, L. C. (2026). Consumer financial data exchange: marketing meets digital finance and open banking. *International Journal of Research in Marketing*. https://doi.org/https://doi.org/10.1016/j.ijresmar.2026.01.004

Bocean, C. G., & Vărzaru, A. A. (2023). EU countries' digital transformation, economic performance, and sustainability analysis. *Humanities & Social Sciences Communications, 10*(1), 875. DOI: 10.1057/s41599-023-02415-1

Bondac, G. T., Stanescu, S. G., Ionescu, C. A., Duica, A., & Uzlău, M. C. (2026). Decision-Making in Complex Systems Using AI-Based Decision Support: The Role of Trust, Transparency, and Data Quality. *Electronics (Basel), 15*(2), 372. DOI: 10.3390/electronics15020372

Booker, A., Chiu, V., Groff, N., & Richardson, V. J. (2024). AIS research opportunities utilizing machine learning: From a meta-theory of accounting literature. *International Journal of Accounting Information Systems, 52*, 100661. DOI: 10.1016/j.accinf.2023.100661

Bovens, M., Goodin, R. E., & Schillemans, T. (Eds.). (2014). *The Oxford handbook of public accountability*. Oxford University Press. DOI: 10.1093/oxfordhb/9780199641253.001.0001

Bowen, G. A. (2009). Document analysis as a qualitative research method. *Qualitative Research Journal, 9*(2), 27–40. DOI: 10.3316/QRJ0902027

Brahmandam, B. A. (2025). Cloud Migration and Hybrid Infrastructure in Financial Institutions. *International Journal of Computer Science and Engineering Technology, 9*(1), 42–46.

Brás, J. C., Pereira, R. F., Fonseca, M., Ribeiro, R., & Bianchi, I. S. (2024). Advances in auditing and business continuity: A study in financial companies. *Journal of Open Innovation, 10*(2), 100304. DOI: 10.1016/j.joitmc.2024.100304

Bratten, B., Causholli, M., & Omer, T. C. (2019). Audit Firm Tenure, Bank Complexity, and Financial Reporting Quality. *Contemporary Accounting Research, 36*(1), 295–325. DOI: 10.1111/1911-3846.12427

Brender, N., & Markov, I. (2013). Risk perception and risk management in cloud computing: Results from a case study of Swiss companies. *International Journal of Information Management, 33*(5), 726–733. DOI: 10.1016/j.ijinfomgt.2013.05.004

Breuer, M., Hombach, K., & Müller, M. A. (2018). How does financial reporting regulation affect firms' banking? *Review of Financial Studies, 31*(4), 1265–1297. DOI: 10.1093/rfs/hhx123

Brynjolfsson, E., & McAfee, A. (2014). *The second machine age: Work, progress, and prosperity in a time of brilliant technologies*. W. W. Norton & Company.

Brynjolfsson, E., & McElheran, K. (2016). The rapid adoption of data-driven decision-making. *The American Economic Review, 106*(5), 133–139. DOI: 10.1257/aer.p20161016

Budrionytė, R., & Gaižauskas, L. (2018). Historical cost vs fair value in forest accounting: The case of Lithuania. *Entrepreneurship and Sustainability Issues, 6*(1), 60–76. DOI: 10.9770/jesi.2018.6.1(5)

Calzada, I. (2024). Democratic erosion of data-opolies: Decentralized Web3 technological paradigm shift amidst AI disruption. *Big Data and Cognitive Computing, 8*(3), 26. DOI: 10.3390/bdcc8030026

Carè, R., & Weber, O. (2023). The role of ESG in sustainable finance: A review and research agenda. *Business Strategy and the Environment, 32*(4), 1897–1913. DOI: 10.1002/bse.3210

Carlsson-Wall, M., Goretzki, L., Hofstedt, J., Kraus, K., & Nilsson, C.-J. (2022). Exploring the implications of cloud-based enterprise resource planning systems for public sector management accountants. *Financial Accountability & Management, 38*(2), 177–201. DOI: 10.1111/faam.12300

Carr, M., & Llanos, J. T. (2021). Data: Global governance challenges. In *Global Governance Futures* (pp. 286–298). Taylor and Francis. DOI: 10.4324/9781003139836-21

Carvalho, A. M., Soares, S., Montenegro, J., & Conceição, L. (2025). Data Quality: Revisiting dimensions towards new framework development. *Procedia Computer Science, 253*, 247–256. DOI: 10.1016/j.procs.2025.01.088

Castellano, G. G., Selga, Ē. K., & Arner, D. W. (2023). The Emergence of Financial Data Governance and the Challenge of Financial Data Sovereignty. In *Data Sovereignty: from the Digital Silk Road to the Return of the State* (pp. 178–210). Oxford University Press., DOI: 10.1093/oso/9780197582794.003.0009

Ceko, E., Komina, B., & Karras, D. (2026). The Importance of GDPR Compliance and a Documentation Framework. In D. K. & S. E. (Eds.), *Communications in Computer and Information Science: Vol. 2670 CCIS* (pp. 310–323). Springer Science and Business Media Deutschland GmbH. DOI: 10.1007/978-3-032-07370-9_23

Celestin, M., & Vanitha, N. (2015). Blockchain beyond Bitcoin: Revolutionizing operational risk management. *International Journal of Multidisciplinary*, *I*(I), 725–731. https://www.researchgate.net/profile/Mbonigaba-Celestin/publication/385620336_BLOCKCHAIN_BEYOND_BITCOIN_REVOLUTIONIZING_OPERATIONAL_RISK_MANAGEMENT/links/672cb41677b63d1220e2dd26/BLOCKCHAIN-BEYOND-BITCOIN-REVOLUTIONIZING-OPERATIONAL-RISK-MANAGEMENT.pdf

Černevičienė, J., & Kabašinskas, A. (2024). Explainable artificial intelligence (XAI) in finance: A systematic literature review. *Artificial Intelligence Review*, *57*(8), 216. DOI: 10.1007/s10462-024-10854-8

Challoumis, C. (2024, October). The evolution of financial systems-AI'S role in reshaping money management. In *XVI International Scientific Conference* (pp. 128-151).

Chambefort, C. (2025). Alliance with fintech: Are banks opening the Pandor box? In *Encyclopedia of Monetary Policy, Financial Markets and Banking* (p. V4:427-V4:430). Elsevier. DOI: 10.1016/B978-0-44-313776-1.00117-3

Chan, D. Y., & Vasarhelyi, M. A. (2018). *Innovation and practice of continuous auditing*. https://www.emerald.com/books/edited-volume/11301/chapter/81123458

Chandra, S., Venkatesh, M., Singh, R., Garg, S., Giri Babu, K., & Katta, S. K. (2025). Personalized Banking Experiences Using AI Leveraging Data Science for Tailored Financial Services. *2025 IEEE 4th World Conference on Applied Intelligence and Computing, AIC 2025*, 833–838. DOI: 10.1109/AIC66080.2025.11211889

Chang, V., Valverde, R., Ramachandran, M., & Li, C.-S. (2020). Toward Business Integrity Modeling and analysis framework for risk measurement and analysis. *Applied Sciences (Basel, Switzerland)*, *10*(9), 3145. DOI: 10.3390/app10093145

Charles, V., Emrouznejad, A., & Gherman, T. (2023). A critical analysis of the integration of blockchain and artificial intelligence for supply chain. *Annals of Operations Research, 327*(1), 1–41. DOI: 10.1007/s10479-023-05169-w

Chauke, T. A., & Ngoepe, M. (2025). Integrating facets of information technology governance at a professional council in South Africa. *Global Knowledge, Memory and Communication*, *74*(11), 101–120. DOI: 10.1108/GKMC-08-2023-0270

Chen, A., Wang, S., Mehta, A. M., Asif, M., Xu, S., & Shahzad, M. F. (2025). FinTech adoption for ESG integration through robo advisors, personalization, and perceived trust. *Scientific Reports, 15*(1), 31125. DOI: 10.1038/s41598-025-17046-6 PMID: 40851039

Cheng, M., Qu, Y., Jiang, C., & Zhao, C. (2022). Is cloud computing the digital solution to the future of banking? *Journal of Financial Stability, 63*(June 2021), 101073. DOI: 10.1016/j.jfs.2022.101073

Chen, H., Chiang, R. H. L., & Storey, V. C. (2012). Business intelligence and analytics: From big data to big impact. *Management Information Systems Quarterly, 36*(4), 1165–1188. DOI: 10.2307/41703503

Chen, J., Li, K., Deng, H., & Wang, S. (2024). Explainable machine learning models for credit risk evaluation. *Expert Systems with Applications*, *238*, 121876. DOI: 10.1016/j.eswa.2023.121876

Chen, S., Ren, S., & Zhang, Q. (2025). Hybrid architectures that combine LLMs and predictive analytics for next-generation financial modeling. *The Journal of Financial Data Science*, *6*, 31–43. DOI: 10.6339/25-JDS1161D

Chen, Y., & Gao, Y. (2022). Comparative analysis of digital trade development strategies and governance approaches. *Journal of Digital Economy*, *1*(3), 227–238. DOI: 10.1016/j.jdec.2023.02.001

Chen, Y., Hao, S., & Li, A. (2022). Do governmental, technological and organizational factors influence the performance of financial management systems? *Kybernetes*, *51*(3), 1127–1150. DOI: 10.1108/K-11-2020-0808

Chen, Y., Wang, G.-J., Zhu, Y., Xie, C., & Salah Uddin, G. (2024). Identifying systemic risk drivers of FinTech and traditional financial institutions: Machine learning-based prediction and interpretation. *European Journal of Finance*, *30*(18), 2157–2190. DOI: 10.1080/1351847X.2024.2358940

Choowan, P., & Daovisan, H. (2025). Artificial Intelligence in Data Governance for Financial Decision-Making: A Systematic Review. *Big Data and Cognitive Computing*, *10*(1), 8. DOI: 10.3390/bdcc10010008

Chung, I. B., & Caldas, C. (2022). Applicability of Blockchain-Based Implementation for Risk Management in Healthcare Projects. *Blockchain in Healthcare Today, 5*(Special Issue), 1–10. DOI: 10.30953/bhty.v5.191 PMID: 36779025

Ciocan, C. C. (2022). Historical Cost vs Fair Value in Accounting: Consequences for the Quality of Financial Information and the True and Fair View. *CECCAR Business Review, 3*(10), 48–59. DOI: 10.37945/cbr.2022.10.07

Committee of Sponsoring Organizations of the Treadway Commission (COSO). (2013). *Internal Control—Integrated Framework*. COSO.

Committee of Sponsoring Organizations of the Treadway Commission. (2017). *Enterprise risk management: Integrating with strategy and performance*. COSO.

Compton, N. S. (2013). Financial stability oversight council and office of financial research: Elements and assessments. In *Financial Stability Oversight Council and Office of Financial Research: Elements and Assessments*. Nova Science Publishers, Inc. https://www.scopus.com/inward/record.uri?eid=2-s2.0-84936855748&partnerID=40&md5=c888029efb8f14e0ade593e26294a0b8

Cosma, S., Gualandri, E., & Venturelli, V. (2023). Model risk in financial systems: Implications for governance and decision-making. *Finance Research Letters, 55*, 103867. DOI: 10.1016/j.frl.2023.103867

Cosmulese, C. G. (2021). Theoretical perspectives of corporate governance. *European Journal of Accounting. Finance & Business, 9*(1). Advance online publication. DOI: 10.4316/EJAFB.2021.912

Costello, A. M., Granja, J., & Weber, J. (2019). Do Strict Regulators Increase the Transparency of Banks? *Journal of Accounting Research, 57*(3), 603–637. DOI: 10.1111/1475-679X.12255

Dagar, R., Mahajan, D. S., & Vashisht, D. R. (2024). Enhancing data security in cloud computing using blockchain. *Irish Interdisciplinary Journal of Science & Research, 08*(01), 66–79. DOI: 10.46759/IIJSR.2024.8107

Dahdal, A. M., & Zeiler, B. (2021). Open Banking and Open Data: Global Context, Innovation, and Consumer Protection. *Banking Law Journal, 138*(7), 385–412. https://www.scopus.com/inward/record.uri?eid=2-s2.0-85123727295&partnerID=40&md5=209f7c14aab48f7821d1553d5ed8bad4

Dai, J., & Vasarhelyi, M. A. (2017). Toward blockchain-based accounting and assurance. *Journal of Information Systems, 31*(3), 5–21. DOI: 10.2308/isys-51804

Darmawati, D., Jaafar, N. I., Hs, R., Baja, H. K., Purisamya, A. J., Yolanda, A. M. W., Amir, B., & Juanda, M. R. P. (2025). The Role of Artificial Intelligence in Improving the Efficiency and Accuracy of Local Government Financial Reporting: A Systematic Literature Review. *Journal of Risk and Financial Management, 18*(11), 601. DOI: 10.3390/jrfm18110601

Davenport, T. H. (2018). *The AI advantage: How to put the artificial intelligence revolution to work.* MIT Press. DOI: 10.7551/mitpress/11781.001.0001

Davenport, T. H., & Ronanki, R. (2018). Artificial intelligence for the real world. *Harvard Business Review, 96*(1), 108–116.

Davenport, T., & Harris, J. (2017). *Competing on analytics: Updated, with a new introduction: The new science of winning*. Harvard Business Review Press.

de Araluze, B., & Plaza, C. N. (2023). The Relevance of Initial Trust and Social Influence in the Intention to Use Open Banking-Based Services: An Empirical Study. *SAGE Open, 13*(3), 21582440231187607. Advance online publication. DOI: 10.1177/21582440231187607

De Silva, P., Gunarathne, N., & Kumar, S. (2025). Exploring the impact of digital knowledge, integration and performance on sustainable accounting, reporting and assurance. *Meditari Accountancy Research, 33*(2), 497–552. DOI: 10.1108/MEDAR-02-2024-2383

de Villiers, C., & Sharma, U. (2020). A critical reflection on the future of financial, intellectual capital, sustainability and integrated reporting. *Critical Perspectives on Accounting, 70*, 0–25. DOI: 10.1016/j.cpa.2017.05.003

Debbadi, R. K., & Boateng, O. (2025). Developing intelligent automation workflows in Microsoft Power Automate by embedding deep learning algorithms for real-time process adaptation. *Int J Sci Res Arch, 14*(2), 802–820. DOI: 10.30574/ijsra.2025.14.2.0449

Delen, D., & Demirkan, H. (2013). Data, information and analytics as services. *Decision Support Systems, 55*(1), 359–363. DOI: 10.1016/j.dss.2012.05.044

DeLone, W. H., & McLean, E. R. (2003). The DeLone and McLean model of information systems success: A ten-year update. *Journal of Management Information Systems, 19*(4), 9–30. DOI: 10.1080/07421222.2003.11045748

Dennis, I. (2018). What is a Conceptual Framework for Financial Reporting? *Accounting in Europe, 15*(3), 374–401. DOI: 10.1080/17449480.2018.1496269

Diamond, J., & Khemani, P. (2006). Introducing financial management information systems in developing countries. World Bank Policy Research Working Paper No. 3857. DOI: 10.1596/1813-9450-3857

Dichev, I. D. (2017). On the conceptual foundations of financial reporting. *Accounting and Business Research*, *47*(6), 617–632. DOI: 10.1080/00014788.2017.1299620

DigitalDefynd. (2025). 13 ways JP Morgan is using AI: In-depth case study. https://digitaldefynd.com/IQ/jp-morgan-using-ai-case-study/

DiMaggio, P. J., & Powell, W. W. (1983). The iron cage revisited: Institutional isomorphism and collective rationality in organizational fields. *American Sociological Review*, *48*(2), 147–160. DOI: 10.2307/2095101

Dinh, C. T. H., & Tran, N. P. (2025). Artificial intelligence and sustainable performance: Identifying the pivotal role of green intellectual capital and green innovation. *Business Process Management Journal*, •••, 1–22. DOI: 10.1108/BPMJ-12-2024-1165

Dolhopolov, A., Castelltort, A., & Laurent, A. (2024). Implementing federated governance in Data Mesh architecture. *Future Internet*, *16*(4), 115. DOI: 10.3390/fi16040115

Domingues, J. O., & Solla, K. R. (2024). Open Financial System and Cade's competence. *Revista de Defesa da Concorrencia*, *12*(2), 104–122. DOI: 10.52896/rdc.v12i2.1137

Doshi-Velez, F., & Kim, B. (2017). Towards a rigorous science of interpretable machine learning. https://doi.org//arXiv.1702.08608DOI: 10.48550

Douglas, B. D., Ewell, P. J., & Brauer, M. (2023). Data quality in online human-subjects research: Comparisons between MTurk, Prolific, CloudResearch, Qualtrics, and SONA. *PLoS One*, *18*(3), e0279720. DOI: 10.1371/journal.pone.0279720

Drissi, S., Chergui, M., & Khatar, Z. (2025). A Systematic Literature Review on Risk Assessment in Cloud Computing: Recent Research Advancements. *IEEE Access : Practical Innovations, Open Solutions*, *13*(April), 76289–76307. DOI: 10.1109/ACCESS.2025.3561123

Du, X., Jiang, K., & Zheng, X. (2024). Reducing asymmetric cost behaviors: Evidence from digital innovation. *Humanities & Social Sciences Communications*, *11*(1), 682. DOI: 10.1057/s41599-024-03179-y

Dzhaparov, P. (2019). *Application of blockchain and artificial intelligence in bank risk management.*

Eckerson, W. W. (2010). *Performance dashboards: Measuring, monitoring, and managing your business*. John Wiley & Sons.

Ehrlinger, L., & Wöß, W. (2022). A survey of data quality measurement and monitoring tools. *Frontiers in Big Data, 5*, 850611. DOI: 10.3389/fdata.2022.850611

Eisenhardt, K. M. (1989). Building theories from case study research. *Academy of Management Review, 14*(4), 532–550. DOI: 10.2307/258557

Ekasari, K., Eltivia, N., Pratama, B. B., & Azizah, N. (2022). Improving the quality of business processes with Financial information systems. *International Journal of Informatics, Economics. Management Science, 1*(2), 125–135.

Elnakeeb S, Elawadly HSH (2025;), "Automation and artificial intelligence in accounting: a comprehensive bibliometric analysis and future trends". Journal of Financial Reporting and Accounting, Vol. ahead-of-print No. ahead-of-print. https://doi.org/DOI: 10.1108/JFRA-09-2024-0639

Elnakeeb, S., & Elawadly, H. S. H. (2025). Automation and artificial intelligence in accounting: A comprehensive bibliometric analysis and future trends. *Journal of Financial Reporting and Accounting*. https://www.emerald.com/jfra/article/doi/10.1108/JFRA-09-2024-0639/1262287

Elragal, A., & Hassanien, H. E.-D. (2019). Augmenting advanced analytics into enterprise systems: A focus on post-implementation activities. *Systems, 7*(2), 31. DOI: 10.3390/systems7020031

Emerj. (2022). Artificial intelligence at HSBC – Two use cases. Emerj Artificial Intelligence Research. https://emerj.com/artificial-intelligence-at-hsbc-two-use-cases/

Emili, A. M. (2019). Data Protection Officer. In *Dictionary of Statuses within EU Law: The Individual Statuses as Pillar of European Union Integration* (pp. 121–126). Springer Science+Business Media. DOI: 10.1007/978-3-030-00554-2_16

Enache, G. I. (2023). Logistics Security in the Era of Big Data, Cloud Computing and IoT. *Proceedings of the International Conference on Business Excellence, 17*(1), 188–199. DOI: 10.2478/picbe-2023-0021

Enholm, I. M., Papagiannidis, E., Mikalef, P., & Krogstie, J. (2022). Artificial Intelligence and Business Value: A Literature Review. *Information Systems Frontiers, 24*(5), 1709–1734. DOI: 10.1007/s10796-021-10186-w

Eskandarany, A. (2024). Adoption of artificial intelligence and machine learning in banking systems: A qualitative survey of board of directors. *Frontiers in Artificial Intelligence*, *7*, 1440051. Advance online publication. DOI: 10.3389/frai.2024.1440051 PMID: 39664101

Etemadi, N., Borbon-Galvez, Y., Strozzi, F., & Etemadi, T. (2021). Supply chain disruption risk management with blockchain: A dynamic literature review. *Information (Basel)*, *12*(2), 1–25. DOI: 10.3390/info12020070

Etikan, I., Musa, S. A., & Alkassim, R. S. (2016). Comparison of convenience sampling and purposive sampling. *American Journal of Theoretical and Applied Statistics*, *5*(1), 1–4. DOI: 10.11648/j.ajtas.20160501.11

European Parliament and Council of the European Union. (2024). *Regulation (EU) 2024/1689 laying down harmonised rules on artificial intelligence (Artificial Intelligence Act)*. Official Journal of the European Union.

Evdokimova, Y. (2021). Financial ecosystems: Analysis and development paths. In Y. A., M. A., & M. O. (Eds.), *IOP Conference Series: Earth and Environmental Science* (Vol. 689, Issue 1). IOP Publishing Ltd. DOI: 10.1088/1755-1315/689/1/012011

Faboyede, O. S., Ogunniyi, O. R., Atanda, O., Adesina, K., & Ben-Caleb, E. (2022). Financial misappropriations, internal control, and Pentecostal Churches in Nigeria. *Research Journal of Business and Economic Management*, *5*(2), 23–31. DOI: 10.31248/RJBEM2022.075

Faccia, A., Cavaliere, L. P. L., Petratos, P., & Mosteanu, N. R. (2022, August). Unstructured over structured, big data analytics and applications in accounting and management. In *Proceedings of the 2022 6th International Conference on Cloud and Big Data Computing* (pp. 37-41). DOI: 10.1145/3555962.3555969

Farea, M. M., Alifan, B., & Al-Dubai, M. M. M. (2024). Intelligent Automation in Accounting and Financial. *Journal of Tianjin University Science and Technology*, (June), 463–480. DOI: 10.5281/zenodo.12516114

Farrow, G. S. D. (2020). Open banking: The rise of the cloud platform. *Journal of Payments Strategy and Systems*, *14*(2), 128–146. DOI: 10.69554/TUCN3800

Farrukh Shahzad, M., Xu, S., Bilal, A. R., Quratulain, , & Akram, S. (2026). Exploring role of digital literacy and theory of planned behavior in shaping generative AI behavior intentions for educational sustainability. *International Journal of Sustainability in Higher Education*, 1–23. DOI: 10.1108/IJSHE-10-2025-1237

Fedorova, A., Ferrara, M., & Fierro, P. (2017). The General Data Protection Regulation (GDPR): From static to dynamic compliance. *Law and Economics Yearly Review, 6*, 283–302.https://www.scopus.com/inward/record.uri?eid=2-s2.0-85046540701&partnerID=40&md5=0037336eae552068869da0b00b35b760

Fedyk, A., Hodson, J., Khimich, N., & Fedyk, T. (2022). Is artificial intelligence improving the audit process? *Review of Accounting Studies, 27*(3), 938–985. DOI: 10.1007/s11142-022-09697-x

Feng, M., Li, C., McVay, S. E., & Skaife, H. (2015). Does Ineffective Internal Control over Financial Reporting affect a Firm's Operations? Evidence from Firms' Inventory Management. *The Accounting Review, 35*(4), 619–626. DOI: 10.2308/accr-50909

Feng, S., Wang, W., Xiong, Z., Niyato, D., Wang, P., & Wang, S. S. (2021). On Cyber Risk Management of Blockchain Networks: A Game Theoretic Approach. *IEEE Transactions on Services Computing, 14*(5), 1492–1504. DOI: 10.1109/TSC.2018.2876846

Firmansyah, A., Khairunnisa, D., Gistiani, T. L., & Chaniago, P. R. (2023). The readiness of the Government Internal Supervisory Apparatus (APIP) for continuous auditing implementation. *International Public Sector Accounting Review, 1*(1). Advance online publication. DOI: 10.31092/ipsar.v1i1.2094

Fisher, I. E., Garnsey, M. R., & Hughes, M. E. (2016). Natural Language Processing in Accounting, Auditing and Finance: A Synthesis of the Literature with a Roadmap for Future Research. *Intelligent Systems in Accounting, Finance & Management, 23*(3), 157–214. DOI: 10.1002/isaf.1386

Fitriani, L., Khodra, M. L., & Surendro, K. (2025). A conceptual framework for AI adoption in business architecture with case studies in higher education and government. *Discover Artificial Intelligence, 5*(1), 409. DOI: 10.1007/s44163-025-00673-3

Folorunso, A., Adewa, A., Babalola, O., & Nwatu, C. E. (2024). A governance framework model for cloud computing: Role of AI, security, compliance, and management. *World Journal of Advanced Research and Reviews, 24*(2), 1969–1982. DOI: 10.30574/wjarr.2024.24.2.3513

Force, J. T. (2017). Risk Management Framework. *Risk Management Framework*, 229–270. DOI: 10.4018/978-1-5225-2503-5.ch007

Fritz-Morgenthal, S., Hein, B., & Papenbrock, J. (2022). Financial Risk Management and Explainable, Trustworthy, Responsible AI. *Frontiers in Artificial Intelligence, 5*(February), 1–14. DOI: 10.3389/frai.2022.779799 PMID: 35295866

Galbraith, J. R. (1974). Organization design: An information processing view. *Interfaces, 4*(3), 28–36. DOI: 10.1287/inte.4.3.28

Ganesan, P. (2024). Journal of Artificial Intelligence & Cloud Computing Cloud-Based Disaster Recovery : Reducing Risk and Improving Continuity. *Journal of Artificial Intelligence & Cloud Computing., 2024*(February), 1–4. DOI: 10.47363/JAICC/2024(3)E162

Ganguly, S., Harreis, H., Margolis, B., & Rowshankish, K. (2017). Digital risk: Transforming risk management for the 2020s. *McKinsey&Company*, 1–8.

Gao, X. (2023). Digital transformation in finance and its role in promoting financial transparency. *Global Finance Journal, 58*, 100903. DOI: 10.1016/j.gfj.2023.100903

Garad, A., Riyadh, H. A., Al-Ansi, A. M., & Beshr, B. A. H. (2024). Unlocking financial innovation through strategic investments in information management: A systematic review. *Discover Sustainability, 5*(1), 381. DOI: 10.1007/s43621-024-00542-6

Gasparian, M. S., Kiseleva, I. A., Titov, V. A., & Olenev, L. A. (2021). Simulation and risk management of financial activities in the digital economy era. *Nexo Revista Científica, 34*(04), 1388–1395. DOI: 10.5377/nexo.v34i04.12684

Gauci, R. (2019). Is Europe a good example of open banking? In *The PAYTECH Book: The Payment Technology Handbook for Investors, Entrepreneurs, and FinTech Visionaries* (pp. 86–87). wiley. DOI: 10.1002/9781119551973.ch25

Gaurav, A., & Ambar, M. T. (2025). Cloud-Based Accounting Systems and Financial Reporting Efficiency: A Comparative Review. [IJARMT]. *International Journal of Advanced Research and Multidisciplinary Trends, 2*(1), 882–893.

Gavryushenko, A. P. (2021). Principles of strategic financial management and their implementation in the information economy. *Finance and Credit, 27*(12), 2772–2784. DOI: 10.24891/c.27.12.2772

Genotiva, K. (2025). Enhancing Financial Visibility: A Proposal to Implement Power BI for Group Accounting Analysis and Reporting.

Georgiou, I., Sapuric, S., Lois, P., & Thrassou, A. (2024). Blockchain for accounting and auditing—accounting and auditing for cryptocurrencies: A systematic literature review and future research directions. *Journal of Risk and Financial Management, 17*(7), 276. DOI: 10.3390/jrfm17070276

Ger, P. P. (2025). Enabling Agile Finance Through ERP Modernization: A Comprehensive Analysis of Cloud-Based Enterprise Resource Planning Transformation. *Journal of Computer Science and Technology Studies*, *7*(6), 430–435.

Gholami, A., Khanmohamadi, M. H., Vakilifard, H., & Ranjbar, M. (2025). Presenting the Management Accounting Model in the Digital Era. *Management Strategies and Engineering Sciences*, *7*(4), 71–80. DOI: 10.61838/msesj.7.4.8

Ghosh, A., Mukhopadhyay, I., & Chakraborty, S. (2024). Design and Architectural Implementation of Consortium Blockchain Based Framework for Open Banking Customer Consent and Data Handling. *SN Computer Science*, *5*(2), 271. Advance online publication. DOI: 10.1007/s42979-023-02593-4

Gioia, D. A., Corley, K. G., & Hamilton, A. L. (2013). Seeking qualitative rigor in inductive research: Notes on the Gioia methodology. *Organizational Research Methods*, *16*(1), 15–31. DOI: 10.1177/1094428112452151

Gobeo, A., Fowler, C., & Buchanan, W. J. (2018). GDPR and Cyber Security for Business Information Systems. In *GDPR and Cyber Security for Business Information Systems*. River Publishers. https://www.scopus.com/inward/record.uri?eid=2-s2.0-85070689188&partnerID=40&md5=9520d22bd3d39a0aeffddb9657d8681f

Gomber, P., Kauffman, R. J., Parker, C., & Weber, B. W. (2018). On the fintech revolution: Interpreting the forces of innovation, disruption, and transformation in financial services. *Journal of Management Information Systems*, *35*(1), 220–265. DOI: 10.1080/07421222.2018.1440766

Gordijn, J., & Akkermans, H. (2001). Designing and evaluating e-business models. *IEEE Intelligent Systems*, *16*(04), 11–17. DOI: 10.1109/5254.941353

Górka, E., Baran, D., Wojak, G., Ćwiąkała, M., Zupok, S., Starkowski, D. R., & Okrasa, O. (2025). The impact of artificial intelligence on enterprise decision-making process. arXiv. https://arxiv.org/abs/2512.02048

Götz, F., Buck, C., Rosemann, M., & Meckl, R. (2022). Digital business ecosystems: a comparison of different industries. In *Handbook on digital business ecosystems* (pp. 530–548). Edward Elgar Publishing. DOI: 10.4337/9781839107191.00043

Granlund, M. (2011). Extending AIS research to management accounting and control issues: A research note. *International Journal of Accounting Information Systems*, *12*(1), 3–19. DOI: 10.1016/j.accinf.2010.11.001

Granlund, M., & Mouritsen, J. (2003). Introduction: Problems and opportunities of IT in management accounting. *European Accounting Review*, *12*(1), 77–83. DOI: 10.1080/0963818031000087925

Gray, R. (2002). The social accounting project and accounting organizations and society: Privileging engagement, imaginings, new accountings and pragmatism over critique? *Accounting, Organizations and Society*, *27*(7), 687–708. DOI: 10.1016/S0361-3682(00)00003-9

Grossi, G., Steccolini, I., & Reichard, C. (2019). Digital government and public sector accounting: A systematic literature review. *Accounting, Auditing & Accountability Journal*, *32*(7), 1883–1906.

Group, W. B. (2022). *2022 investment policy and regulatory review - India*. World Bank., DOI: 10.1596/38526

Grover, V., Chiang, R. H. L., Liang, T.-P., & Zhang, D. (2018). Creating strategic business value from big data analytics: A research framework. *Journal of Management Information Systems*, *35*(2), 388–423. DOI: 10.1080/07421222.2018.1451951

Guidotti, R., Monreale, A., Ruggieri, S., Turini, F., Giannotti, F., & Pedreschi, D. (2019). A survey of methods for explaining black box models. *ACM Computing Surveys*, *51*(5), 1–42. DOI: 10.1145/3236009

Guillén, M. (2024). Econometrics of Insurance Based on Telematics Information and Machine Learning. In *Handbook of Insurance* (3rd ed., Vol. I, pp. 401–416). Springer Nature., DOI: 10.1007/978-3-031-69561-2_14

Gunasilan, U. (2024). Digital transformation technologies reshaping financial reporting, transparency, and accountability in public sector organizations. *Accountancy Business and the Public Interest*, *40*, 106–113.

Guo, H., & Polak, P. (2024). Finance centralization—Research on enterprise intelligence. *Humanities & Social Sciences Communications*, *11*(1), 1536. Advance online publication. DOI: 10.1057/s41599-024-04098-8

Guo, L., Song, R., Wu, J., Xu, Z., & Zhao, F. (2024). Integrating a machine learning-driven fraud detection system based on a risk management framework. *Applied and Computational Engineering*, *87*(1), 80–86. DOI: 10.54254/2755-2721/87/20241541

Hair, J. F., Sarstedt, M., Ringle, C. M., & Mena, J. A. (2012). An assessment of the use of partial least squares structural equation modeling in marketing research. *Journal of the Academy of Marketing Science*, *40*(3), 414–433. DOI: 10.1007/s11747-011-0261-6

Halimuzzaman, M., Sharma, J., Karim, M. R., Hossain, M. R., Azad, M. A. K., & Alam, M. M. (2024). Enhancement of Organizational Accounting Information Systems and Financial Control through Enterprise Resource Planning. In *Synergy of AI and Fintech in the Digital Gig Economy* (pp. 315–331). CRC Press. DOI: 10.1201/9781032720104-20

Hanifah, Sutanto, E., Siswadi, U., & Murniawan, M. W. (2024). The Influence of Regulatory Changes on Auditing Standards and Practices. *Journal of Multidisciplinary Sustainability Asean.*

Harvey, F. (2003). Developing geographic information infrastructures for local government: The role of trust. *The Canadian Geographer. Géographe Canadien, 47*(1), 28–36. DOI: 10.1111/1541-0064.02e10

Harwood, W. H. (2017). Secrecy, transparency and government whistleblowing. *Philosophy and Social Criticism, 43*(2), 164–186. DOI: 10.1177/0191453716677178

Hasan, M., Hoque, A., & Le, T. (2023). Big Data-Driven Banking Operations: Opportunities, Challenges, and Data Security Perspectives. *FinTech, 2*(3), 484–509. DOI: 10.3390/fintech2030028

Häuselmann, A., & Custers, B. (2024). Substantive fairness in the GDPR: Fairness Elements for Article 5.1a GDPR. *Computer Law & Security Review, 52*, 105942. Advance online publication. DOI: 10.1016/j.clsr.2024.105942

Henninger, A., & Mashatan, A. (2021). Distributed interoperable records: The key to better supply chain management. *Computers, 10*(7), 89. DOI: 10.3390/computers10070089

Hermawan, S., Khoirunisa, Z. A., & Tejomurti, K. (2023). Triangular Insight on Open Banking in Indonesia, Singapore, and Australia. *International Journal of Legal Information, 51*(3), 197–215. DOI: 10.1017/jli.2024.11

Hinkin, T. R. (1998). A brief tutorial on the development of measures for use in survey questionnaires. *Organizational Research Methods, 1*(1), 104–121. DOI: 10.1177/109442819800100106

Horani, O. M., & Khatibi, A., ALSoud, A. R., Tham, J., Al-Adwan, A. S., & Azam, S. F. (. (2023). Antecedents of business analytics adoption and impacts on banks' performance: The perspective of the TOE framework and resource-based view. *Interdisciplinary Journal of Information, Knowledge, and Management, 18*, 609–643. DOI: 10.28945/5188

Hossain, R., Ghose, P., Chowdhury, T. M., Hossen, M. D., Hasan, M. N., & Mani, L. (2024). Ownership structures and firm performance: A correlation and regression analysis of financial institutions in Bangladesh. *Pakistan Journal of Life and Social Sciences, 22*(2), 6278–6295. DOI: 10.57239/PJLSS-2024-22.2.00473

Hosseinzadeh, E., Afkanpour, M., Momeni, M., & Tabesh, H. (2025). Data quality assessment in healthcare, dimensions, methods and tools: A systematic review. *BMC Medical Informatics and Decision Making, 25*(1), 296. DOI: 10.1186/s12911-025-03136-y

Hossen, M. (2025). Integrating Accounting Information Systems and Enterprise Risk Management for Real-Time Financial Risk Monitoring. *International Journal of Accounting Innovation, 1*(3), 241–254.

Huang, C., & Yin, X. (2023). The Impact of Digital Transformation on Enterprise Accounting. *European Online Journal of Natural and Social Sciences, 12*(4), pp-418.

Hussain, A., Nisar, Q. A., Khan, W., Niazi, U. I., & Malik, M. (2024). When and how big data analytics and work practices impact financial performance: An intellectual capital perspective from the banking industry. *Kybernetes, 53*(10), 3271–3293. DOI: 10.1108/K-11-2022-1623

Hustad, E., Sørheller, V. U., Jørgensen, E. H., & Vassilakopoulou, P. (2021). Moving enterprise resource planning (ERP) systems to the cloud: The challenge of infrastructural embeddedness. *International Journal of Information Systems and Project Management, 8*(1), 5–20. DOI: 10.12821/ijispm080101

Imane, L., Noureddine, M., Driss, S., & Hanane, L. (2023). Towards blockchain-integrated enterprise resource planning: A pre-implementation guide. *Computers, 13*(1), 11. DOI: 10.3390/computers13010011

International Monetary Fund. (2023). Digital solutions guidelines for public financial management (Technical Notes and Manuals No. 2023/007). DOI: 10.5089/9798400251566.005

Ionescu, S. A., & Diaconita, V. (2023). Transforming financial decision-making: The interplay of AI, cloud computing and advanced data management technologies. *International Journal of Computers, Communications & Control, 18*(6). Advance online publication. DOI: 10.15837/ijccc.2023.6.5735

Ionescu, S. A., Diaconita, V., & Radu, A. O. (2025). Engineering Sustainable Data Architectures for Modern Financial Institutions. *Electronics (Basel), 14*(8), 1650. DOI: 10.3390/electronics14081650

Issah, O., Baah, S. A., & Asare, C. A. (2025). Digital Technology and Financial Institutions' Sustainability: The Mediating and Moderating Effect of Staff Competency and Training Programs. *African Journal of Procurement, Logistics &. Supply Chain Management*, *8*(3), 65–89.

Jain, S., & Fallon, E. (2023). Leveraging Unstructured Data to Improve Customer Engagement and Revenue in Financial Institutions: A Deep Reinforcement Learning Approach to Personalized Transaction Recommendations. In O. M.S., O. M.S., O. M.S., D. F., H. K.-F-., N. P., & G. Y. (Eds.), *Proceedings of the 2023 IEEE International Conference on Computer, Information, and Telecommunication Systems, CITS 2023*. Institute of Electrical and Electronics Engineers Inc. DOI: 10.1109/CITS58301.2023.10188745

Jain, V., & Kulkarni, P. A. (2023). Integrating AI techniques for enhanced financial forecasting and budgeting strategies. *International Journal of Economics and Management Studies*, *10*(09), 9–15. DOI: 10.14445/23939125/IJEMS-V10I9P102

Janahi, M., Millo, Y., & Voulgaris, G. (2021). CFO gender and financial reporting transparency in banks. *European Journal of Finance*, *27*(3), 199–221. DOI: 10.1080/1351847X.2020.1801481

Jari Collin, Kari Hiekkanen, Janne J. Korhonen, Marco Halén, Timo Itälä, M. H. (2015). *The Impact of Digitalization on Finnish Organizations.*

Jayeola, O., Sidek, S., Azmawani, , Anuar, , & Jimin, H. (2020). Contextual factors and strategic consequences of cloud enterprise resource planning (ERP) adoption in Malaysian manufacturing SMEs: A conceptual framework. *International Journal of Economics and Business Administration*, *VIII*(3), 176–201. DOI: 10.35808/ijeba/495

Jensen, M. C., & Meckling, W. H. (1976). Theory of the firm: Managerial behavior, agency costs and ownership structure. *Journal of Financial Economics*, *3*(4), 305–360. DOI: 10.1016/0304-405X(76)90026-X

Jeyaprabha, B., Kumar, S. R., Bolla, R. L., Bhatt, A. S., Sera, R. J., & Arora, K. (2025). Data-driven decision making in management: Leveraging big data analytics for strategic planning. 2025 First International Conference on Advances in Computer Science, Electrical, Electronics, and Communication Technologies (CE2CT), 1000–1003. DOI: 10.1109/CE2CT64011.2025.10939548

Jiang, J. (2024). A study on the digital transformation trends in financial management for small and micro enterprises. *International Journal of Global Economics and Management*, *3*(1), 355–363. DOI: 10.62051/IJGEM.v3n1.42

Jiang, S. (2021). Research on big data audit based on financial sharing service model using fuzzy AHP. *Journal of Intelligent & Fuzzy Systems, 40*(4), 8237–8246. DOI: 10.3233/JIFS-189646

Jie, H., Gooi, L. M., & Lou, Y. (2025). Digital maturity, dynamic capabilities and innovation performance in high-tech SMEs. *International Review of Economics & Finance, 99*, 103971. DOI: 10.1016/j.iref.2025.103971

Jim, C. K., & Chang, H.-C. (2018). The current state of data governance in higher education. *Proceedings of the Association for Information Science and Technology, 55*(1), 198–206. DOI: 10.1002/pra2.2018.14505501022

Jin, J., Kanagaretnam, K., Liu, Y. I., & Cheng, M. (2021). Does Citizens' Financial Literacy Relate to Bank Financial Reporting Transparency? *European Accounting Review, 30*(5), 887–912. DOI: 10.1080/09638180.2021.1965897

Jo, A. A., & Raj, E. D. (2024). Ethical Dimensions in Data-Driven Business: Balancing Fairness, Accountability, Transparency, and Explainability. *2024 15th International Conference on Computing Communication and Networking Technologies, ICCCNT 2024*. DOI: 10.1109/ICCCNT61001.2024.10724314

Johri, A. (2025). Impact of artificial intelligence on the performance and quality of accounting information systems and accuracy of financial data reporting. *Accounting Forum, 49*(5), 1096–1120. DOI: 10.1080/01559982.2025.2451004

Jones, S. T. H. (2025). *Consumer Data Right expansion to deliver a better deal for consumers*. https://ministers.treasury.gov.au/ministers/stephen-jones-2022/media-releases/consumer-data-right-expansion-deliver-better-deal

Jordan, M. I., & Mitchell, T. M. (2015). Machine learning: Trends, perspectives, and prospects. *Science, 349*(6245), 255–260. DOI: 10.1126/science.aaa8415 PMID: 26185243

Kafi, M. A., & Akter, N. (2023). Securing financial information in the digital realm: Case studies in cybersecurity for accounting data protection. *American Journal of Trade and Policy, 10*(1), 15–26. DOI: 10.18034/ajtp.v10i1.659

Kalra, A., & Mittal, R. (2024). Explainable AI for improved financial decision support in trading. https://doi.org/DOI: 10.1109/ICRITO61523.2024.10522366

Kandjani, H., Bernus, P., & Nielsen, S. (2013). Enterprise Architecture cybernetics and the edge of chaos: Sustaining enterprises as complex systems in complex business environments. *Proceedings of the Annual Hawaii International Conference on System Sciences*, 3858–3867. DOI: 10.1109/HICSS.2013.199

Kaplan, R. S., & Norton, D. P. (1996). *The balanced scorecard: Translating strategy into action*. Harvard Business School Press.

Kapoor, N., Kapoor, T., Sisodiya, D. R., & Sushma, J. (2024). Impact of Fintech: Revolution in Banking and Financial Industry. *2024 IEEE 4th International Conference on ICT in Business Industry and Government, ICTBIG 2024*. DOI: 10.1109/ICTBIG64922.2024.10911635

Karani, G., & Jadhav, B. (2025). How traditional banks adapt to the fintech revolution in banking and finance sector. In *Shaping Cutting-Edge Technologies and Applications for Digital Banking and Financial Services* (pp. 214–225). Taylor and Francis., DOI: 10.4324/9781003501947-13

Karkošková, S. (2023). Data governance model to enhance data quality in financial institutions. *Information Systems Management, 40*(1), 90–110. DOI: 10.1080/10580530.2022.2042628

Kashchena, N., & Nesterenko, I. (2022). *Digitalization of the innovative development management information service of the enterprise. Mechanisms for ensuring innovative development of entrepreneurship. Monograph*. Teadmus OÜ.

Kassab, M., Laplante, P., & Voas, J. (2022). Trust Considerations in Open Banking. *IT Professional, 24*(1), 70–73. DOI: 10.1109/MITP.2021.3136015

Katari, A., & Ankam, M. (2022). Data governance in multi-cloud environments for financial services: Challenges and solutions. [IJMCER]. *Educational Research, 4*(1), 339–353.

Katuri, D. R. K. (2025). Streamlining Procure-to-Pay Processes in Large-Scale Companies with ERP Finance Systems. *European Journal of Computer Science and Information Technology, 13*(38), 174–190. DOI: 10.37745/ejcsit.2013/vol13n38174190

Katuu, S. (2020). Enterprise Resource Planning: Past, Present, and Future. *New Review of Information Networking, 25*(1), 37–46. DOI: 10.1080/13614576.2020.1742770

Kerr, D., Taken Smith, K., Murphy Smith, L., & Xu, T. (2025). A review of AI and its impact on management accounting and society. *Journal of Risk and Financial Management, 18*(6), 340. DOI: 10.3390/jrfm18060340

Khalifa, E. (2019). Blockchain: Technological Revolution in Business and Administration. *American Journal of Management, 19*(2), 40–46. DOI: 10.33423/ajm.v19i2.2066

Khamitdkhanovich, N. A., Senthilkumar, C., Kavitha, V. O., & Ugli, E. R. S. (2025). The evolution of open banking: Transforming financial services with data-driven technologies. In S. J. (Ed.), *AIP Conference Proceedings* (Vol. 3306, Issue 1). American Institute of Physics. DOI: 10.1063/5.0277721

Khanday, M. A., Negi, N., Ahmad, M., Bhat, D. A., & Nakitende, M. G. (2025). AI and Financial Data Leaks: Preventing Corruption and Strengthening Cybersecurity. In *Financial Corruption and Money Laundering in the AI Era* (pp. 219–246). IGI Global. DOI: 10.4018/979-8-3373-0786-2.ch009

Khatri, V., & Brown, C. V. (2010). Designing data governance. *Communications of the ACM*, *53*(1), 148–152. DOI: 10.1145/1629175.1629210

Khojasteh, Y., Mousavi Jahan Abadi, S. M., & Ng, C. (2026). Enabling supply chain transformation with cutting-edge digital tools. In *Emerging Technologies in Supply Chains: Towards Digital Transformation* (pp. 3–47). Springer Nature Switzerland. DOI: 10.1007/978-3-032-01218-0_1

Khong, I., Yusuf, N. A., Nuriman, A., & Yadila, A. B. (2023). Exploring the impact of data quality on decision-making processes in information intensive organizations. *APTISI Transactions on Management*, *7*(3), 253–260. DOI: 10.33050/atm.v7i3.2138

Kisaku, J. M. (2017). Impact of Financial Reporting Frameworks on the Quality of Not-for-Profit Financial Reports. *Walden University*, 1–106.

Kitsantas, T. (2022). Exploring Blockchain Technology and Enterprise Resource Planning system: Business and technical aspects, current problems, and future perspectives. *Sustainability (Basel)*, *14*(13), 7633. DOI: 10.3390/su14137633

Klover.ai. (2025). HSBC's AI strategy: Analysis of AI dominance in financial services. https://www.klover.ai/hsbc-ai-strategy-analysis-of-ai-dominance-in-financial-services/

Kokkinis, A., & Miglionico, A. (2020). Open banking and libra: A new frontier of financial inclusion for payment systems? *Singapore Journal of Legal Studies*, *2020*, 601–629. https://www.scopus.com/inward/record.uri?eid=2-s2.0-85100665733&partnerID=40&md5=4f8878f37edee84094503a891ff93a4c

Kostova, S., & Zhelev, Z. (2024). Application of Digital Tools Assessing Information Risk in the Control Activity. *Naše Gospodarstvo/Our Economy, 70*(2), 24–31. DOI: 10.2478/ngoe-2024-0009

Kothandapani, H. P. (2022). Optimizing financial data governance for improved risk management and regulatory reporting in data lakes. *International Journal of Applied Machine Learning and Computational Intelligence*, *12*(4), 41–63.

Koundal, P., Bhalla, M., & Kailay, M. (2025c). The Ethical Ledger: A Review of Literature on the Alignment of Accounting Ethics and Blockchain Technology. *Digital Strategy and Governance in Transformative Technologies*, 216–238.

Koundal, P., Bhalla, M., & Kailay, M. (2025a). Driving SME management in the digital era: An empirical evidence on the role of accounting information systems in strategic planning, controlling, and coordination activities. *International Journal of Globalisation and Small Business*, *15*(2), 135–157. DOI: 10.1504/IJGSB.2025.150129

Koundal, P., Bhalla, M., & Kailay, M. (2025b). Non-financial information as a mediator in the link between accounting information systems and decision-making outcomes in SMEs: A structural equation modelling study. *International Journal of Business and Systems Research*, *19*(4), 442–464. DOI: 10.1504/IJBSR.2025.149075

KPMG International. (2026). 2026 global AI in finance: The decision advantage [Survey report]. https://kpmg.com/xx/en/media/press-releases/2026/05/ai-adoption-in-finance-doubles-but-assurance-readiness-determines-who-wins.html

Kreuzberger, D., Kühl, N., & Hirschl, S. (2023). Machine learning operations (MLOps): Overview, definition, and architecture. *IEEE Access : Practical Innovations, Open Solutions*, *11*, 31866–31879. DOI: 10.1109/ACCESS.2023.3262138

Kumar, A., & Gandhi, A. (2023). A Study Using OWASP on Secure Open Banking Architecture. *2023 3rd International Conference on Advance Computing and Innovative Technologies in Engineering, ICACITE 2023*, 2062–2067. DOI: 10.1109/ICACITE57410.2023.10182656

Kumar, P., Rani, P., Rajesh, T. S., Deebika, R., Harina, A. S., & Bhoopathy, V. (2025). Prediction of Stock Market Using Machine Learning and Cloud Computing. *Advancements in Cloud-Based Intelligent Informative Engineering*, 253–376. DOI: 10.4018/979-8-3373-0781-7.ch016

Kumar, V., Kumar, S., Chatterjee, S., & Mariani, M. (2024). Optimizing the digital transformation capability for enhancing economic sustainability of entrepreneurial venture: The moderating role of entrepreneurial orientation. *IEEE Transactions on Engineering Management*, *71*, 1–14. DOI: 10.1109/TEM.2024.3387540

Kureljusic, M., & Karger, E. (2024). Forecasting in financial accounting with artificial intelligence – A systematic literature review and future research agenda. *Journal of Applied Accounting Research*, *25*(1), 81–104. DOI: 10.1108/JAAR-06-2022-0146

Kusumaningtyas, F., & Santoso, B. (2025). Data Entry Contribution to Efficient Corporate Administration-A Case Study of DEF Limited Company. [IJEEFA]. *International Journals of Energy Economics and Financial Analysis*, *1*(2), 20–26.

Kwon, Y., Lee, J.-D., Owens, J., & Bank, A. D. (2023). Managing fintech risks. In *ADB Briefs*. Asian Development Bank., DOI: 10.22617/BRF230170-2

Labaki, R. (2020). Risk Attitude Determinants and Risk Management in Family Business. *Risk Attitude Determinants and Risk Management in Family Business.*, *7*(3), 285–292.

Lakat, J. S. (2025). Digital transformation of public financial management: A case study of regional financial application integration in North Sulawesi. *Priviet Social Sciences Journal*, *5*(8), 317–337. DOI: 10.55942/pssj.v5i8.552

Lapalme, J., Gerber, A., Van Der Merwe, A., Zachman, J., De Vries, M., & Hinkelmann, K. (2016). Exploring the future of enterprise architecture: A Zachman perspective. *Computers in Industry*, *79*, 103–113. DOI: 10.1016/j.compind.2015.06.010

Laradi, S., Elfekair, A., Rehman, H. M., Hanna, D., & Alrawad, M. (2025). Continuance intention of m-Banking adoption: The dynamics of UTAUT3, trust and attitudes. *FIIB Business Review*, *23197145251358049*, 23197145251358049. Advance online publication. DOI: 10.1177/23197145251358049

Lat, J. S. (2024). Managing Data Integrity for Finance: Discover practical data quality management strategies for finance analysts and data professionals. In *Managing Data Integrity for Finance: Discover practical data quality management strategies for finance analysts and data professionals*. De Gruyter Mouton. https://www.scopus.com/inward/record.uri?eid=2-s2.0-105022525236&partnerID=40&md5=864a2c1174c220561fd795a0e1beda74

Latifzadeh, M., Dorafshan, S. M. M. Q., Mohseni, S., & Abedi, M. (2021). Analysis of the Legal Framework for the Protection of Personal Data in the European Union. *Iranian Journal of Information Processing and Management*, *37*(2), 439–472. DOI: 10.52547/jipm.37.2.439

Laux, C. (2012). Financial instruments, financial reporting, and financial stability. *Accounting and Business Research*, *42*(3), 239–260. DOI: 10.1080/00014788.2012.681857

Lei, F.. (2025). Spider 2.0: Evaluating language models on real-world enterprise text-to-sql workflows. *International Conference on Learning Representations,* 0.

Lei, J., Wei, M., She, Y., & Wang, W. (2025). Research on automatic processing system of financial information in colleges and universities based on NLP-KG fusion algorithm. *Systems and Soft Computing*, *7*, 200224. Advance online publication. DOI: 10.1016/j.sasc.2025.200224

Lepri, B., Oliver, N., Letouzé, E., Pentland, A., & Vinck, P. (2018). Fair, transparent, and accountable algorithmic decision-making processes: The premise, the proposed solutions, and the open challenges. *Philosophy & Technology, 31*(4), 611–627. DOI: 10.1007/s13347-017-0279-x

Leuz, C., & Wysocki, P. D. (2011). Economic Consequences of Financial Reporting and Disclosure Regulation: A Review and Suggestions for Future Research. SSRN *Electronic Journal*. DOI: 10.2139/ssrn.1105398

Li, G., & Guo, B. (2024). Construction of enterprise financial compliance management system in the context of digital taxation. *International Business & Economics Studies*, *6*(2), 200. DOI: 10.22158/ibes.v6n2p200

Li, G., Li, X., & Huo, L. (2023). Digital economy, spatial spillover and industrial green innovation efficiency: Empirical evidence from China. *Heliyon*, *9*(1), e12875. DOI: 10.1016/j.heliyon.2023.e12875 PMID: 36711307

Limba, F. B., Sapulette, S. G., & Talla, A. (2025). The Role Of Cloud-Based Accounting Systems In Enhancing Financial Information Quality. *International Journal of Finance & Economics*, *2*(3), 895–913.

Lim, W. M., Kumar, S., Pandey, N., Verma, D., & Kumar, D. (2023). Evolution and trends in consumer behaviour: Insights from Journal of Consumer Behaviour. *Journal of Consumer Behaviour*, *22*(1), 217–232. DOI: 10.1002/cb.2118

Lindström, C. W. J., Maleki Vishkaei, B., & De Giovanni, P. (2024). Subscription-based business models in the context of tech firms: Theory and applications. *International Journal of Industrial Engineering and Operations Management*, *6*(3), 256–274. DOI: 10.1108/IJIEOM-06-2023-0054

Lin, X., Zhang, S. S., & Zachariadis, M. (2025). Open data and API adoption of U.S. banks. *Journal of Financial Intermediation*, *63*, 101162. Advance online publication. DOI: 10.1016/j.jfi.2025.101162

Liu, D.-E. (2024). The refined management of medical finance combined with information technology construction. *Expert Systems: International Journal of Knowledge Engineering and Neural Networks*, *41*(6), e13151. Advance online publication. DOI: 10.1111/exsy.13151

Liu, Z., Li, X., & Li, Z. (2024). Inclusive FinTech, open banking, and bank performance: Evidence from China. *Financial Innovation*, *10*(1), 149. Advance online publication. DOI: 10.1186/s40854-024-00679-3

Livanis, E., Doumpos, M., & Zopounidis, C. (2023). Financial analysis and management of cyber risk. In *Handbook of Research on Artificial Intelligence, Innovation and Entrepreneurship* (pp. 255-271). Edward Elgar Publishing. DOI: 10.4337/9781839106750.00027

Li, Z., Rasool, S., Cavus, M. F., & Shahid, W. (2024). Sustaining the future: How green capabilities and digitalization drive sustainability in modern business. *Heliyon, 10*(1).Lu, Z., & Nakagawa, K. (2022). The influence of environmental factors on product innovations in emerging markets: The institutional theory perspective. *International Business Research, 15*(9), 1–15.

Lodhi, R. N., Asif, M., Abdikarimova, A., & Shahzad, M. F. (2024). Impact of innovation and sustainability on green entrepreneurship: A bibliometric exploration. *Environment, Development and Sustainability, 28*(1), 1–26. DOI: 10.1007/s10668-024-05053-y

Mabillard, V., & Zumofen, R. (2021). Transparency and Accountability—The Case of Public Procurement Practices in Switzerland. *Public Works Management & Policy, 26*(2), 95–114. DOI: 10.1177/1087724X19898699

Machucho, R., & Ortiz, D. (2025). The Impacts of Artificial Intelligence on Business Innovation: A Comprehensive Review of Applications, Organizational Challenges, and Ethical Considerations. *Systems, 13*(4), 264. DOI: 10.3390/systems13040264

Maddipudi, S. (2025). RISE with SAP: Modernize Your Legacy ERP with an AI-Enabled Cloud ERP to Thrive in the Cloud. *IJSAT-International Journal on Science and Technology, 16*(1).

Magdolen, M., & Lovecek, T. (2023). Legal Aspects of Monitoring and Tracking the Movement of Individuals Using Modern Technologies. *Proceedings - International Carnahan Conference on Security Technology*. DOI: 10.1109/ICCST59048.2023.10726858

Magli, F., & Amaduzzi, A. (2025). News in Financial Measures. In *Innovations in Corporate Reporting: The Effects of Digital Innovation, Sustainability, and AI* (pp. 45–127). Springer Nature Switzerland. DOI: 10.1007/978-3-031-80404-5_5

Mahdi Sahi, A., Sahi, A. M., Abbas, A. F., & Khatib, F. A., S. (. (2022). Financial reporting quality of financial institutions: Literature review. *Cogent Business & Management, 9*(1). Advance online publication. DOI: 10.1080/23311975.2022.2135210

Mahmud, D., & Ikbal, M. Z. (2024). Power BI and data analytics in financial reporting: A review of real-time dashboarding and predictive business intelligence tools. *International Journal of Scientific Interdisciplinary Research, 5*(2), 125–157. DOI: 10.63125/yg9zxt61

Maier, C., Thatcher, J. B., Grover, V., & Dwivedi, Y. K. (2023). Cross-sectional research: A critical perspective, use cases, and recommendations for IS research. *International Journal of Information Management, 70*, 102625. DOI: 10.1016/j.ijinfomgt.2023.102625

Majstorovic, V., Stojadinovic, S., Lalic, B., & Marjanovic, U. (2020). ERP in Industry 4.0 Context. In *IFIP Advances in Information and Communication Technology* (pp. 287–294). Springer International Publishing. DOI: 10.1007/978-3-030-57993-7_33

Makhmudov, S., Ravikumar, R. N., Satheesh Kumar, A., Aarthi, S., Rakhimova, S., & Kanimozhi, N. (2026). AI-powered risk analytics in ESG-focused FinTech systems. In *Strategic Frameworks for Managing Risk in FinTech Ecosystems* (pp. 95–126). IGI Global Scientific Publishing., DOI: 10.4018/979-8-3373-2980-2.ch004

maliWen, H., & De Leon, J. (2024). Research on the Digital Transformation of Financial Management in Small and Medium-sized Enterprises Under the Background of Big Data and Cloud Computing. *Advances in Computer and Communication, 4*(6), 351–357. DOI: 10.26855/acc.2023.12.002

Manavadaria, M. S., Sharma, R. K., Parasar, A., Chauhan, A., Jeyaprakash, N., Mohaideen, A., & Bhoopathy, V. (2025). Machine learning for fraud detection and financial crimes. *Forensic Intelligence and Deep Learning Solutions in Crime Investigation*, 183–206. DOI: 10.4018/979-8-3693-9405-2.ch010

Manion, M. F., & Porth, S. J. (2025). Introduction to the Special Issue: Economic Challenges Facing Pastoral Leaders. *Review of Religious Research, 67*(2), 303–308. DOI: 10.1177/0034673X251340656

Marcucci, S., Alarcón, N. G., Verhulst, S. G., & Wüllhorst, E. (2023). Informing the global data future: Benchmarking data governance frameworks. *Data & Policy, 5*, e30. DOI: 10.1017/dap.2023.24

Marfuah, M., Istiqomah, E. N., Ayuntari, C. G., & Prasetyo, P. P. (2023). Determinants of quality of the financial statements of Gunung Kidul Regency Government. *Journal of Contemporary Accounting*, 12–27. DOI: 10.20885/jca.vol5.iss1.art2

Martins, E. J., & Belfo, F. P. (2023). Major concerns about Enterprise Resource Planning (ERP) systems: A systematic review of a decade of research (2011-2021). *Procedia Computer Science, 219*, 378–387. DOI: 10.1016/j.procs.2023.01.303

Martins, T., de Almeida, A. M., Cardoso, E., & Nunes, L. (2024). Explainable artificial intelligence: A systematic literature review on taxonomies and applications in finance. *IEEE Access : Practical Innovations, Open Solutions, 12*, 618–629. DOI: 10.1109/ACCESS.2023.3347028

Maulina, B. F., & Nazaruddin, I. (2025). System information accounting in business performance: A systematic literature review. *Journal of Accounting and Investment, 26*(2), 481–499. DOI: 10.18196/jai.v26i2.25146

McKeen, J. D., & Smith, H. A. (2007). Developments in practice XXIV: Information management: The nexus of business and IT. *Communications of the Association for Information Systems, 19*. Advance online publication. DOI: 10.17705/1CAIS.01903

McKinsey & Company. (2024). CFOs counting on gen AI. https://www.mckinsey.com/featured-insights/week-in-charts/cfos-counting-on-gen-ai

McNulty, D., Miglionico, A., & Milne, A. (2023). Data access technologies and the 'New Governance'techniques of financial regulation. *Journal of Financial Regulation, 9*(2), 225–248. DOI: 10.1093/jfr/fjad008

Md Zillul Karim, M. Z. K. (2025). Accounting Information System Quality and Management Information Systems Integration: A Pathway to Enhanced Financial Risk Management. *Accounting Information System Quality and Management Information Systems Integration: A Pathway to Enhanced Financial Risk Management, 3*(1), 128–142.

Mei, Y., Zeng, J., & Zhan, Y. (2025). U.S.-Europe artificial intelligence regulatory cooperation, divergence, and China's "window of opportunity" for strategic breakthrough. *Bulletin of Chinese Academy of Sciences, 40*(4), 715–724. DOI: 10.16418/j.issn.1000-3045.20241210001

Melnyk, O., Onyshchenko, S., Pavlova, N., Kravchenko, O., & Borovyk, S. (2022). Integrated Ship Cybersecurity Management as a Part of Maritime Safety and Security System. *IJCSNS International Journal of Computer Science and Network Security, 22*(3), 135. DOI: 10.22937/IJCSNS.2022.22.3.18

Mergel, I., Edelmann, N., & Haug, N. (2019). Defining digital transformation: Results from expert interviews. *Government Information Quarterly, 36*(4), 101385. DOI: 10.1016/j.giq.2019.06.002

Mesarčík, M., & Hamuľák, O. (2024). General Data Protection Regulation: Current Challenges and Future Directions. In *Contributions to Political Science: Vol. Part F3080* (pp. 117–133). Springer Science and Business Media Deutschland GmbH. DOI: 10.1007/978-3-031-56045-3_9

Mhaskey, S. V. (2024). Integration of artificial intelligence (AI) in enterprise resource planning (ERP) systems: Opportunities, challenges, and implications. *International Journal of Computer Engineering in Research Trends, 11*(12), 1–9. DOI: 10.22362/ijcert/2024/v11/i12/v11i1201

Mhlanga, D. (2021). Financial inclusion in emerging economies: The application of machine learning and artificial intelligence in credit risk assessment. *International Journal of Financial Studies, 9*(3), 39. Advance online publication. DOI: 10.3390/ijfs9030039

Miaoquan, X., Yu, K. W., Xuewen, L., Yi, W., Jun, Y., & Loang, O. K. (2023). The impact of digital transformation on financial reporting and analysis in the accounting industry. *The International Journal of Accounting, 8*(50), 324–336.

Mihu, C., Pitic, A. G., & Bayraktar, D. (2023). Drivers of digital transformation and their impact on organizational management. *Studies in Business and Economics, 18*(1), 149–170. DOI: 10.2478/sbe-2023-0009

Miller, R., Chan, S. H. M., Whelan, H., & Gregório, J. (2025). A comparison of data quality frameworks: A review. *Big Data and Cognitive Computing, 9*(4), 93. DOI: 10.3390/bdcc9040093

Milosheski, F., & Karadimce, A. (2025). Improving operational efficiency with an automated invoicing system. *Financial Engineering, 3*, 221–230. DOI: 10.37394/232032.2025.3.18

Minarni, E. (2025). Impact of Digital Payment Systems on Financial Inclusion and Small Business Growth in Developing Economies. *International Journal of Innovation and Thinking, 2*(1), 1–12. DOI: 10.71364/ijit.v2i1.6

Ministry of Communication and Digital Affairs, Republic of Indonesia. (2023). Circular Letter No. 9 of 2023 on Artificial Intelligence Ethics.

Ministry of Communication and Digital Affairs, Republic of Indonesia. (2026). Pemerintah bahas Peta Jalan Kecerdasan Artifisial Indonesia 2026–2029 dalam rapat lintas kementerian.

Ministry of Finance, Republic of Indonesia. (2024a). Implementasi tanda tangan elektronik (TTE) SAKTI tahap III C.

Ministry of Finance, Republic of Indonesia. (2024b). Regulation of the Minister of Finance No. 93/PMK.07/2024 on the National Fiscal Policy Synergy Digital Platform.

Mishra, S. (2018). Financial management and forecasting using business intelligence and big data analytic tools. *International Journal of Financial Engineering*, *5*(2), 1850011. DOI: 10.1142/S2424786318500111

Mohammed Anwar, A. (2023). Elevating Cybersecurity Audits: How AI is Shaping Compliance and Threat Detection. *Elevating Cybersecurity Audits: How AI Is Shaping Compliance and Threat Detection*, 1–9.

Mohammed, I. K., & Trzcielinski, S. (2022). The interconnections between ICT, Industry 4.0 and agile manufacturing. *Management and Production Engineering Review*. https://doi.org/DOI: 10.24425/mper.2021.139998

Mohasseb, A. M. A. (2024). The impact of big data predictive analytics on firm performance: The role of cloud ERP and business intelligence integration. , *5*(1), 917–947. DOI: 10.21608/cfdj.2024.329290

Mohd Fariz, N., Farizal Mohammed, N., Syifa Zulkepli, N., & Kamaluddin, A. (2020). Accounting conservatism and financial performance: Accountability of shariah compliant companies in Malaysia. *Humanities and Social Sciences Letters*, *8*(3), 280–297. DOI: 10.18488/journal.73.2020.83.280.297

Mohd Zain, F. A., Muhamad, S. F., Abdullah, H., Sheikh Ahmad Tajuddin, S. A. F., & Wan Abdullah, W. A. (2024). Integrating environmental, social and governance (ESG) principles with Maqasid al-Shariah: A blueprint for sustainable takaful operations. *International Journal of Islamic and Middle Eastern Finance and Management*, *17*(3), 461–484. DOI: 10.1108/IMEFM-11-2023-0422

Mokrani, F., & Abaoub, E. (2024). The governance of companies: A theoretical analysis "evidence from the Tunisian banking.". *International Journal For Multidisciplinary Research*, *6*(1), 13075. Advance online publication. DOI: 10.36948/ijfmr.2024.v06i01.13075

Morea, D., Iazzolino, G., Giglio, C., Bruni, M. E., Baldissarro, G., & Farinelli, E. (2025). The role of digitalization and ESG on financial performance: An empirical analysis on the energy and utilities sectors. *PLoS One*, *20*(2), e0314078. DOI: 10.1371/journal.pone.0314078 PMID: 40014599

Mou, X., & Xu, J. (2020). Analysis and Research on University Financial Decision Based on Distributed Big Data Sharing Mechanism. *Proceedings - 2020 International Conference on Computers, Information Processing and Advanced Education, CIPAE 2020*, 31–34. DOI: 10.1109/CIPAE51077.2020.00016

Mrima, R., & Ronald, M. (2022). Assessment of internal control practices on financial performance of state corporations in Kenya. *International Journal of Finance and Accounting*, *7*(4), 35–54. DOI: 10.47604/ijfa.1675

Mthiyane, Z. Z. F., van der Poll, H. M., & Tshehla, M. F. (2022). A Framework for Risk Management in Small Medium Enterprises in Developing Countries. *Risks*, *10*(9), 173. Advance online publication. DOI: 10.3390/risks10090173

Munoko, I., Brown-Liburd, H. L., & Vasarhelyi, M. (2020). The Ethical Implications of Using Artificial Intelligence in Auditing. *Journal of Business Ethics*, *167*(2), 209–234. DOI: 10.1007/s10551-019-04407-1

Mushtaq, S., Mohsin, M., & Mushtaq, M. M. (2025). A systematic literature review on the implementation and challenges of Zero Trust Architecture across domains. *Sensors (Basel)*, *25*(19), 6118. DOI: 10.3390/s25196118

Nabiyev, A. B., & Ovenc, G. (2023). The symbiotic relationship and collaboration between commercial banks and fintechs in Turkey. *Humanities & Social Sciences Communications*, *10*(1), 932. Advance online publication. DOI: 10.1057/s41599-023-02429-9

Naguib, H. M., Kassem, H. M., & Naem, A. E. H. M. A. (2024). The impact of IT governance and data governance on financial and non-financial performance. *Future Business Journal*, *10*(1), 15. DOI: 10.1186/s43093-024-00300-0

Nanaeva, Z., Aysan, A. F., & Shirazi, N. S. (2021). Open banking in Europe: The effect of the Revised Payment Services Directive on Solarisbank and Insha. *Journal of Payments Strategy and Systems*, *15*(4), 432–444. https://www.scopus.com/inward/record.uri?eid=2-s2.0-85126287018&partnerID=40&md5=229b07316501cf1b017ec75b2bbb9e7c. DOI: 10.69554/BTQG8491

Napisah, L. S., Taufikurochman, C., & Harto, B. (2024). The effect of digitalization on the sustainability of accounting practices in the financial industry. *Journal of Social Science and Business Studies*, *2*(4), 268–276. DOI: 10.61487/jssbs.v2i4.100

National Cyber and Crypto Agency (BSSN) & Ministry of Communication and Information Technology, Republic of Indonesia. (2024). BSSN identifies Temporary National Data Center attacked by ransomware.

Ndanu, J. M. (2025). Empirical insights into ICT use and knowledge management in accounting: A PRISMA-guided literature review (2020–2025). *African Journal of Empirical Research*, *6*(4), 266–277. DOI: 10.51867/ajernet.6.4.24

Nicolaou, A. I. (2010). Integrated information systems and transparency in business reporting. *International Journal of Disclosure and Governance*, *7*(3), 216–226. DOI: 10.1057/jdg.2009.27

Nishant, R., Teo, T. S. H., & Goh, M. (2017). Do shareholders value green information technology announcements? *Journal of the Association for Information Systems*, *18*(8), 542–576. DOI: 10.17705/1jais.00466

Nobanee, H. (2021). A bibliometric review of big data in finance. *Big Data*, *9*(2), 73–78. DOI: 10.1089/big.2021.29044.edi PMID: 33861644

Nofel, M., Marzouk, M., Elbardan, H., Saleh, R., & Mogahed, A. (2024). From sensors to standardized financial reports: A proposed automated accounting system integrating IoT, Blockchain, and XBRL. *Journal of Risk and Financial Management*, *17*(10), 445. DOI: 10.3390/jrfm17100445

Nookala, G. (2024). Adaptive data governance frameworks for data-driven digital transformations. *Journal of Computational Innovation*, *4*(1).

Noviyanti, A. P. (2025). The Evolution of Accounting Information Systems: Recent Trends and Future Directions. *Accounting Research Journal*, *1*(1), 24–38.

Nutalapati, P. (2024). A Review on Cloud Computing in Finance-Transforming Financial Services in the Digital Age. *International Research Journal of Engineering & Applied Sciences| Irjeas. org*, *12*(3), 35-45.

Nutalapati, P. (2024). A Review on Cloud Computing in Finance-Transforming Financial Services in the Digital Age. *International Research Journal of Engineering & Applied Sciences | Irjeas. Org*, *12*, 35–45.

Odukoya, O. (2024). The Transformative Impact of Cloud Computing on Small and Medium-sized Enterprises (SMEs): A Comprehensive Analysis. *2024 International Conference on Smart Applications, Communications and Networking, SmartNets 2024*. DOI: 10.1109/SmartNets61466.2024.10577703

Odunaike, A. (2025). Integrating real-time financial data streams to enhance dynamic risk modeling and portfolio decision accuracy. *Int J Comput Appl Technol Res*, *14*(08), 1–16.

Odunayo, J., Akintoye, R. I., Aguguom, T. A., Sanyaolu, A. W., Omobowale, A., & Osunusi, K. A. (2023). Digital disruption of accounting information and quality of financial reporting of listed money deposit banks in Nigeria. *International Journal of Applied Economics. Finance and Accounting*, *17*(2), 337–352.

Oduro, S. (2024). Eco-innovation and SMEs' sustainable performance: A meta-analysis. *European Journal of Innovation Management, 27*(9), 248–279. DOI: 10.1108/EJIM-11-2023-0961

OECD. (2022). *Shifting from Open banking to Open Finance*. Organisation for Economic Co-operation and Development.

OECD. (2024a). Governing with artificial intelligence: Are governments ready? *OECD Artificial Intelligence Papers*, (20). Advance online publication. DOI: 10.1787/dee339a8-en

OECD. (2026). Digital Government Outlook 2026: Indonesia. OECD Publishing. https://doi.org/ OECD/ADB. (2025). Government at a glance: Southeast Asia 2025. OECD Publishing. https://doi.org/DOI: 10.1787/d46c0555-en

Ogunmokun, A. S., Balogun, E. D., & Ogunsola, K. O. (2022). A Strategic Fraud Risk Mitigation Framework for Corporate Finance Cost Optimization and Loss Prevention. *International Journal of Multidisciplinary Research and Growth Evaluation., 3*(1), 783–790. DOI: 10.54660/.IJMRGE.2022.3.1.783-790

Ogunsola, K. O., Balogun, E. D., & Ogunmokun, A. S. (2021). Enhancing financial integrity through an advanced internal audit risk assessment and governance model. *International Journal of Multidisciplinary Research and Growth Evaluation, 2*(1), 781–790. DOI: 10.54660/.IJMRGE.2021.2.1.781-790

Oh, D.-H., & Kwon, H.-Y. (2025). Diverging Data Strategies of the United States, China, and the EU in the Data Cold War Era. In S. Y.-T., K. M., & R. J. (Eds.), *2025 IEEE/ACIS 23rd International Conference on Software Engineering Research, Management and Applications, SERA 2025 - Proceedings* (pp. 464–471). Institute of Electrical and Electronics Engineers Inc. DOI: 10.1109/SERA65747.2025.11154517

Oladoyinbo, T. O., Adebiyi, O. O., Ugonnia, J. C., Olaniyi, O. O., & Okunleye, O. J. (2023). Evaluating and Establishing Baseline Security Requirements in Cloud Computing: An Enterprise Risk Management Approach. *Asian Journal of Economics. Business and Accounting, 23*(21), 222–231. DOI: 10.9734/ajeba/2023/v23i211129

Olajide, J. O., Otokiti, B. O., Nwani, S., Ogunmokun, A. S., Adekunle, B. I., & Fiemotongha, J. E. (2024). A regulatory compliance model for financial reporting across global supply chain functions. *International Journal of Scientific Research in Science and Technology, 11*(4), 619–635. DOI: 10.32628/IJSRST241151217

Olakunle Babatunde Alao, Oritsematosan Faith Dudu, Enoch O. Alonge, & Chukwuka Emmanuel Eze. (2024). Automation in financial reporting: A conceptual framework for efficiency and accuracy in U.S. corporations. *Global Journal of Advanced Research and Reviews, 2*(2), 040–050. DOI: 10.58175/gjarr.2024.2.2.0057

Oluoha, O. M., Odeshina, A., Reis, O., Okpeke, F., Attipoe, V., & Orieno, O. H. (2025). Designing advanced digital solutions for privileged access management and continuous compliance monitoring. *World Scientific News, 203*, 256–301.

Ombai, P., Kiflemariam, A., & Odollo, L. (2024). Financial and Non-Financial Information on Strategy Management Process; A Systematic Literature Review. *Journal of Strategy and Management, 8*(1), 33–64.

Oncioiu, I., Popescu, D.-M., Aviana, A. E., erban, A., Rotaru, F., Petrescu, M., & Marin-Pantelescu, A. (2020). The role of environmental, social, and governance disclosure in financial transparency. *Sustainability (Basel), 12*(17), 6757. DOI: 10.3390/su12176757

Oprea, I. (2024). Unlocking Financial Innovation: The Synergy of Open Banking and Artificial Intelligence in Banking System. In C. L., I.-F. V., G. G., D. L. R. C. I., & A. J.V. (Eds.), *Springer Proceedings in Business and Economics* (pp. 129–140). Springer Nature. DOI: 10.1007/978-3-031-71329-3_7

Orlikowski, W. J. (1992). The duality of technology: Rethinking the concept of technology in organizations. *Organization Science, 3*(3), 398–427. DOI: 10.1287/orsc.3.3.398

Otley, D. (1999). Performance management: A framework for management control systems research. *Management Accounting Research, 10*(4), 363–382. DOI: 10.1006/mare.1999.0115

Otoo, F. N. K., Kaur, M., & Rather, N. A. (2023). Evaluating the impact of internal control systems on organizational effectiveness. *LBS Journal of Management & Research, 21*(1), 135–154. DOI: 10.1108/LBSJMR-11-2022-0078

Ovenc, G., & Nabiyev, A. B. (2025). Discover how fintech is transforming bank performance: Insights from an emerging economy. *Cogent Economics & Finance, 13*(1), 2477676. Advance online publication. DOI: 10.1080/23322039.2025.2477676

Palea, Vera, and S. D. S. (2017). Earnings reported under IFRS improve the prediction of future cash flows? Evidence from European banks. *Australian Accounting Review.*

Panova, G. (2021). Digital Platforms and Banks. In *Lecture Notes in Networks and Systems* (Vol. 133, pp. 463–472). Springer., DOI: 10.1007/978-3-030-47458-4_55

Papagiannidis, E., Enholm, I. M., Dremel, C., Mikalef, P., & Krogstie, J. (2023). Toward AI governance: Identifying best practices and potential barriers and outcomes. *Information Systems Frontiers*, *25*(1), 123–141. DOI: 10.1007/s10796-022-10251-y

Papiorek, K. L., & Hiebl, M. R. (2024). Information systems quality in management accounting and management control effectiveness. *Journal of Accounting & Organizational Change*, *20*(3), 433–458. DOI: 10.1108/JAOC-09-2022-0148

Parween, S., Sanghavi, H., Dubey, N., Prasan, U. D., Bharadwaj, R., Bhoopathy, V., & Reddy, B. A. (2026). Ethics, Bias Mitigation, and Model Risk Management. *Agile AI- Powered Project Management for Modern Delivery Organizations*, 191–215. DOI: 10.4018/979-8-3373-6851-1.ch006

Pascoe, C., Quinn, S., & Scarfone, K. (2024). *The NIST cybersecurity framework (CSF) 2.0* (NIST CSWP 29). National Institute of Standards and Technology. DOI: 10.6028/NIST.CSWP.29

Pasumarthi, A., & Joyce, S. (2025). Leveraging SAP's Business Technology Platform (BTP) for Enterprise Digital Transformation: Innovations, Impacts, and Strategic Outcomes. *International Journal of Computer Technology and Electronics Communication*, *8*(3), 10720–10732. DOI: 10.15680/IJCTECE.2025.0803008

Pati, U. K., & Pratama, A. M. (2025). Indonesia's Open Banking Future: Designing Effective Regulatory Approaches. *Jambe Law Journal*, *8*(1), 27–60. DOI: 10.22437/home.v8i1.371

Paul, R. (2023). AI integration in e-commerce business models: Case studies on Amazon FBA, Airbnb, and Turo operations. *AIRBNB, AND TURO OPERATIONS (May 05, 2023).*

Pazouki, S., Jamshidi, M. B., Jalali, M., & Tafreshi, A. (2025). The integration of big data in Fintech: review of enhancing financial services through advanced technologies. *World Journal of Advanced Research and Reviews, 25*(1).

Petcu, M. A., Sobolevschi-David, M. I., & Curea, S. C. (2024). Integrating digital technologies in sustainability accounting and reporting: Perceptions of professional cloud computing users. *Electronics (Basel)*, *13*(14), 2684. DOI: 10.3390/electronics13142684

Pillai, P. (2025). Cloud vs. On-Premise Data Warehousing: A Strategic Analysis for Financial Institutions. *Journal of Computer Science and Technology Studies*, *7*(3), 503–513. DOI: 10.32996/jcsts.2025.7.3.57

Pinto, I., & Morais, A. I. (2019). What matters in disclosures of key audit matters: Evidence from Europe. *Journal of International Financial Management & Accounting, 30*(2), 145–162. DOI: 10.1111/jifm.12095

Podgorelec, B., Turkanović, M., & Karakatič, S. (2019). A machine learning-based method for automated blockchain transaction signing including personalized anomaly detection. *Sensors (Basel), 20*(1), 147. DOI: 10.3390/s20010147 PMID: 31881673

Popoola, A. D., & Ibrahim, A. K. (2023). Conceptual Model for Advancing Real-Time Analytics and Financial Transparency in Corporations. *International Journal of Advanced Multidisciplinary Research and Studies, 3*. https://www.multiresearchjournal.com/admin/uploads/archives/archive-1765515403.pdf

Popovici, E.-C., Stalidi, C., Teodoras, D.-A., Suciu, G., & Cosma, I. (2024). De-Fraudify4ALL: Prototyping and Validation of a System for Fraud Detection with Big Data and Cloud Technology. *IEEE International Symposium for Design and Technology of Electronics Packages, SIITME - Conference Proceedings*, 466–470. DOI: 10.1109/SIITME63973.2024.10814887

Porter, M. E., & Heppelmann, J. E. (2015). How smart, connected products are transforming companies. *Harvard Business Review, 93*(10), 96–114.

Porter, M. E., & van der Linde, C. (1995). Green and competitive: Ending the stalemate. *Harvard Business Review, 73*(5), 120–134.

Pourkhodabakhsh, N., & Khajeh, E. (2026). Strategic Management Consultancy in the Age of Industry 5.0: Leveraging the Gig Economy for Business Transformation. In *Smart and Sustainable Gig Economy in the Industrial 5.0 Era* (pp. 303-335). CRC Press.

Pramitasari, T. D., Widaninggar, N., & Rachman, R. (2025). Digital Economy: The Shifting of Traditional to Digital Spending and Saving-Investing Platforms and the Future of Banking Business Model. *WSEAS Transactions on Computer Research, 13*, 542–557. DOI: 10.37394/232018.2025.13.50

Prasetianingrum, S., & Sonjaya, Y. (2024). The evolution of digital accounting and accounting information systems in the modern business landscape. *Advances in Applied Accounting Research, 2*(1).

Prasetianingrum, S., & Sonjaya, Y. (2024). The evolution of digital accounting and accounting information systems in the modern business landscape. *Advances in Applied Accounting Research, 2*(1), 39–53. DOI: 10.60079/aaar.v2i1.165

Premchand, A., & Choudhry, A. (2018). Open banking and APIs for transformation in banking. In N. S.K., R. J., & R. A.R. (Eds.), *Proceedings of the 2018 International Conference On Communication, Computing and Internet of Things, IC3IoT 2018* (pp. 25–29). Institute of Electrical and Electronics Engineers Inc. DOI: 10.1109/IC3IoT.2018.8668107

Prokopenko, O., Koldovskiy, A., Khalilova, M., Orazbayeva, A., & Machado, J. (2024). Development of blockchain technology in financial accounting. *Computation (Basel, Switzerland)*, *12*(12), 250. DOI: 10.3390/computation12120250

Przychocka, I., & Sikorski, M. (2024). Revolutionizing SME management: The digital transformation of financial operations. *European Research Studies*, *27*(2), 78–85. DOI: 10.35808/ersj/3372

Putra, H., Qatrunnada, R., Rahmadoni, J., & Khairati, F. (2025). Enhancing Organizational Control Through Business Intelligence: Monitoring and Automated Alerts. *Electronic Journal of Education. Social Economics and Technology*, *6*(1), 112–120.

Qatawneh, A. M. (2023). Requirements of AIS in building modern operating business environment. *International Journal of Business Information Systems*, *44*(3), 422–441. DOI: 10.1504/IJBIS.2023.134957

Qatawneh, A. M. (2025). The role of artificial intelligence in auditing and fraud detection in accounting information systems: Moderating role of natural language processing. *The International Journal of Organizational Analysis*, *33*(6), 1391–1409. DOI: 10.1108/IJOA-03-2024-4389

Quattrone, P. (2016). Management accounting goes digital: Will the move make it wiser? *Management Accounting Research*, *31*, 118–122. DOI: 10.1016/j.mar.2016.01.003

Rachmad, Y. E., Bakri, A. A., Irdiana, S., Waromi, J., & Sinlae, A. A. J. (2024). Analysis of the influence of financial information systems, internal control systems, and information technology on quality of financial reports. *Jurnal Informasi Dan Teknologi*, *6*(1), 266–271. DOI: 10.60083/jidt.v6i1.513

Rachmat, D. F., Mulyadi, D., Abdullah, S., Putrianti, S. D., & Nurliawati, R. (2024). Analysis of the governance of one data Indonesia (SDI) at the communication and information office of sukabumi city. In *Advances in Social Science, Education and Humanities Research* (pp. 42–60). Atlantis Press SARL. DOI: 10.2991/978-2-38476-104-3_6

Rafi, M. A., Shaboj, S. M. I., Miah, M. K., Rasul, I., Islam, M. R., & Ahmed, A. (2024). Explainable AI for credit risk assessment: Improving transparency and fairness. *Journal of Economics. Finance and Accounting Studies*, *6*(1), 108–118. DOI: 10.32996/jefas.2024.6.1.11

Raguseo, E., & Vitari, C. (2018). Investments in big data analytics and firm performance: An empirical investigation of direct and mediating effects. *International Journal of Production Research*, *56*(15), 5206–5221. DOI: 10.1080/00207543.2018.1427900

Rahim, R., & Chishti, M. A. "Artificial Intelligence Applications in Accounting and Finance," *2024 ASU International Conference in Emerging Technologies for Sustainability and Intelligent Systems (ICETSIS)*, Manama, Bahrain, 2024, pp. 1782-1786, DOI: 10.1109/ICETSIS61505.2024.10459526

Rahman, M. A., Alam, M. S., & Mrida, M. S. H. (2025). How interactive dashboards improve managerial decision-making in operations management. *American Journal of Advanced Technology and Engineering Solutions*, *1*(01), 122–146. DOI: 10.63125/cqm5jk84

Rahman, M. M., Pokharel, B. P., Sayeed, S. A., Bhowmik, S. K., Kshetri, N., & Eashrak, N. (2024). riskAIchain: AI-Driven IT Infrastructure—Blockchain-Backed Approach for Enhanced Risk Management. *Risks*, *12*(12), 206. Advance online publication. DOI: 10.3390/risks12120206

Raisch, S., & Krakowski, S. (2021). Artificial intelligence and management: The automation–augmentation paradox. *Academy of Management Review*, *46*(1), 192–210. DOI: 10.5465/amr.2018.0072

Ramesh, L. (2019). Fintech: A new avenue of banks to enhance customer digital experience (DX). *International Journal of Innovative Technology and Exploring Engineering*, *8*(8), 644–648. https://www.scopus.com/inward/record.uri?eid=2-s2.0-85068085893&partnerID=40&md5=b18df8e94cf623eef2f64669c69b707d

Ramlal, K., & Hosein, P. (2021). A Personalized Overdraft Protection Framework. *2021 IEEE 8th International Conference on Data Science and Advanced Analytics, DSAA 2021*. DOI: 10.1109/DSAA53316.2021.9564162

Ravikumar, R. N., Aarthi, S., & Mamadiyarov, Z. (2026). Building the foundations of augmented organizations through AI empowerment. In *Advances in Computational Intelligence and Robotics* (pp. 101–130). IGI Global Scientific Publishing. DOI: 10.4018/979-8-3373-8607-2.ch006

Reinhardt, L. (2026). A Holistic Framework for Operational Resilience: Error Budgeting Strategies in Financial Site Reliability Engineering. *Academic Reseach Library for International Journal of Economics Finance & Management Science, 11*(01), 61–66.

Remané, G., Schneider, S., & Hanelt, A. (2022). Digital business model types: Understanding their mechanisms as recipes to commercialise digital technologies. *International Journal of Innovation Management, 26*(03), 2240019. DOI: 10.1142/S1363919622400199

Rezvani, S. M. H. S., Falcão, M. J., Komljenovic, D., & de Almeida, N. M. (2023). A Systematic Literature Review on Urban Resilience Enabled with Asset and Disaster Risk Management Approaches and GIS-Based Decision Support Tools. *Applied Sciences (Basel, Switzerland), 13*(4), 2223. Advance online publication. DOI: 10.3390/app13042223

Richard Arogundade, O. (2023). Strategic Security Risk Management in Cloud Computing: A Comprehensive Examination and Application of the Risk Management Framework. *Iarjset, 11*(1), 45–55. DOI: 10.17148/IARJSET.2024.11105

Ridzuan, F., & Zainon, W. M. N. W. (2024). A review on data quality dimensions for big data. *Procedia Computer Science, 234*, 341–348. DOI: 10.1016/j.procs.2024.03.008

Rieg, R. (2026). Exploring the determinants and performance effects of digital dashboard use by management accountants. *Journal of Management Control, 37*(1), 75–110. DOI: 10.1007/s00187-025-00400-0

Roehl, J. M., & Harland, D. J. (2022). Imposter participants: Overcoming methodological challenges related to balancing participant privacy with data quality when using online recruitment and data collection. *The Qualitative Report, 27*(11), 2469–2485. DOI: 10.46743/2160-3715/2022.5475

Roffia, P., & Dabić, M. (2024). The role of management control and integrated information systems for the resilience of SMEs. *Review of Managerial Science, 18*(5), 1353–1375. DOI: 10.1007/s11846-023-00657-6

Romney, M. B., & Steinbart, P. J. (2021). *Accounting information systems* (15th ed.). Pearson.

Roth, C. J., Lannum, L. M., & Joseph, C. L. (2016). Enterprise imaging governance: HIMSS-SIIM collaborative white paper. *Journal of Digital Imaging, 29*(5), 539–546. DOI: 10.1007/s10278-016-9883-z

Saeed, S., Altamimi, S. A., Alkayyal, N. A., Alshehri, E., & Alabbad, D. A. (2023). Digital transformation and cybersecurity challenges for businesses resilience: Issues and recommendations. *Sensors (Basel)*, *23*(15), 6666. DOI: 10.3390/s23156666

Sarferaz, S. (2025). Implementing AI into ERP Software. *Communications of the Association for Information Systems*, *57*(1), 74. DOI: 10.17705/1CAIS.05758

Sari, S. I. A. P., Harahap, M. I., & Rahma, T. I. F. (2025). Evaluation of management strategy in increasing the competitiveness of MSMEs at the cooperative and MSME service. *Urwatul Wutsqo*, *14*(3), 1252–1266. Advance online publication. DOI: 10.54437/urwatulwutsqo.v14i3.2592

Saxena, A., & Muneeb, S. M. (2024). Transforming financial services through hyperpersonalization: The role of artificial intelligence and data analytics in enhancing customer experience. In *AI-Driven Decentralized Finance and the Future of Finance* (pp. 19–48). IGI Global., DOI: 10.4018/979-8-3693-6321-8.ch002

Saxena, R., Gayathri, E., & Surya Kumari, L. (2023). Semantic analysis of blockchain intelligence with proposed agenda for future issues. *International Journal of System Assurance Engineering and Management*, *14*(S1), 34–54. DOI: 10.1007/s13198-023-01862-y

Schaltegger, S., & Burritt, R. (2000). *Contemporary Environmental Accounting: Issues, Concepts and Practice*. Greenleaf Publishing.

Schiavi, G. S., Behr, A., & Marcolin, C. B. (2024). Institutional theory in accounting information systems research: Shedding light on digital transformation and institutional change. *International Journal of Accounting Information Systems*, *52*, 100662. DOI: 10.1016/j.accinf.2023.100662

Schmulow, A., Fairweather, K., & Tarrant, J. (2019). Restoring Confidence in Consumer Financial Protection Regulation in Australia: A Sisyphean Task? *Federal Law Review*, *47*(1), 91–120. DOI: 10.1177/0067205X18816240

Schneider, M. (2023). Open Banking and Digital Ecosystems. In *Digital Project Practice for New Work and Industry 4.0* (pp. 169–180). DOI: 10.1201/9781003371397-12

Schrader, P., Heidelbach, J., Ungern-Sternberg, R., Groß, E., & Bauernhansl, T. (2025). Organizing Digital Innovations. *Journal of Open Innovation*, *11*(3), 100615. DOI: 10.1016/j.joitmc.2025.100615

Schweitzer, B. (2024). Artificial intelligence (AI) ethics in accounting. *Journal of Accounting. Ethics & Public Policy, JAEPP*, *25*(1), 67–67.

Senadjki, A., Au Yong, H. N., Ganapathy, T., & Ogbeibu, S. (2023). Unlocking the potential: The impact of digital leadership on firms' performance through digital transformation. *Journal of Business and Socio-economic Development*, *4*(2), 161–177. DOI: 10.1108/JBSED-06-2023-0050

Senturk, O., & Baghırov, A. (2023). Enhancing Sustainable Development Through Blockchain: A Study on Risk Management and Data Integrity. *Journal of Organizations. Technology and Entrepreneurship*, *1*(2), 110–126. DOI: 10.56578/jote010204

Serra, F., Peralta, V., Marotta, A., & Marcel, P. (2024). Use of context in data quality management: A systematic literature review. *ACM Journal of Data and Information Quality*, *16*(3), 1–41. DOI: 10.1145/3672082

Setyadi, A., Pawirosumarto, S., Damaris, A., & Syarif, D. (2025). Integrating green HRM and sustainable operations: The moderating role of digital transformation in the Indonesian energy sector. *Discover Sustainability*, *6*(1), 924. Advance online publication. DOI: 10.1007/s43621-025-01764-y

Shabtai, A., Elovici, Y., & Rokach, L. (2012). Data Leakage. In *SpringerBriefs in Computer Science* (Vol. 0, Issue 9781461420521, pp. 5–10). Springer. DOI: 10.1007/978-1-4614-2053-8_2

Shafa, H., & Islam, A. (2025). Impact of data privacy and cybersecurity in accounting information systems on financial transparency. *International Journal of Scientific Interdisciplinary Research*, *6*(1), 254–292. DOI: 10.63125/xs0xt970

Shahzad, M. F., Javed, I., & Zahid, I. (2024). The influence of the marketing orientation of textile companies in increasing their competitiveness. In *Industry and innovation: Textile industry* (pp. 95–118). Springer Nature Switzerland.

Shahzad, M. F., Xu, S., An, X., Asif, M., & Javed, I. (2025). Do generative AI technologies play a double-edged sword role in education? Findings from hybrid approach using PLS-SEM and fsQCA. *Education and Information Technologies*, *30*(14), 1–30. DOI: 10.1007/s10639-025-13528-2

Shahzad, M. F., Xu, S., Khan, K. I., & Hasnain, M. F. (2023). Effect of social influence, environmental awareness, and safety affordance on actual use of 5G technologies among Chinese students. *Scientific Reports*, *13*(1), 22442. DOI: 10.1038/s41598-023-50078-4 PMID: 38105309

Shaikh, F. A., & Siponen, M. (2023). Information security risk assessments following cybersecurity breaches: The mediating role of top management attention to cybersecurity. *Computers & Security*, *124*, 102974. DOI: 10.1016/j.cose.2022.102974

Shamurailatpam, S. D. D. (2023). Innovations in finance and the future of finance: A critical review. In *Revolutionizing Financial Services and Markets Through FinTech and Blockchain* (pp. 166–182). IGI Global., DOI: 10.4018/978-1-6684-8624-5.ch011

Sharairi, J. A., Saatchi, S. G., Rahahle, M. Y., Maabreh, H. M. A., Sarram, M., Anagreh, S., & Al-Hawary, S. I. S. (2024). How big data governance meets financial decision-making: evidence from banking sector in emerging economies. In *Artificial Intelligence and Economic Sustainability in the Era of Industrial Revolution 5.0* (pp. 1295–1311). Springer Nature Switzerland. DOI: 10.1007/978-3-031-56586-1_94

Sharda, R., Delen, D., & Turban, E. (2018). *Business intelligence, analytics, and data science: A managerial perspective* (4th ed.). Pearson.

Sharma, R., & Sharma, C. (2025). *The evolution of finance and controlling: SAP and intelligent systems*. World Journal of Advanced Research and Reviews.

Shatila, K., Nurzhaubayeva, R., Malishevskaya, N., & Podolskaya, T. (2024). Navigating sustainability: The role of environmental accounting in enhancing business performance. E3S *Web of Conferences*, 479, 09027.

Shaytura, S. V., Olenev, L. A., Nedelkin, A. A., Minitaeva, A. M., Ordov, K. V., & Feoktistova, V. M. (2021). Blockchain in Technogenic Safety and Risk Management. *International Journal of Emerging Technology and Advanced Engineering*, *11*(12), 72–78. DOI: 10.46338/ijetae1221_08

Shbail, M. O. A., Olimat, N. A., Alshurafat, H., Shbeil, S. A., Baker, M. B., & Jaradat, Z. (2025). Factors influencing cloud AIS adoption: Evidence from Jordan. *International Journal of Business Excellence*, *35*(4), 453–474. DOI: 10.1504/IJBEX.2025.145158

Shinkevich, A. I., Kudryavtseva, S. S., & Samarina, V. P. (2023). Ecosystems as an Innovative Tool for the Development of the Financial Sector in the Digital Economy. *Journal of Risk and Financial Management*, *16*(2), 72. DOI: 10.3390/jrfm16020072

Shiraishi, M. (2021). Customized Database Management based on Digital Signature. In A. N., B. E., L. J.M., & J. Y. (Eds.), *2021 6th International Conference on Fog and Mobile Edge Computing, FMEC 2021*. Institute of Electrical and Electronics Engineers Inc. DOI: 10.1109/FMEC54266.2021.9732564

Simons, R. (1995). *Levers of control: How managers use innovative control systems to drive strategic renewal*. Harvard Business School Press.

Singh, V., Raj, M., Gupta, I., & Sayeed, M. A. (2023). Data Leakage Detection and Prevention Using Cloud Computing. In *Sustainable Computing: Transforming Industry 4.0 to Society 5.0* (pp. 159–169). Springer International Publishing. DOI: 10.1007/978-3-031-13577-4_9

Singhania, M., Bhan, I., & Seth, S. (2025). Digitalisation and firm-level ESG performance and disclosures: A scientometric review and research agenda. *International Journal of Finance & Economics*, *30*(4), 4212–4236. DOI: 10.1002/ijfe.3118

Singh, N., Vishnani, S., Khandelwal, V., Sahoo, S., & Kumar, S. (2024). A systematic review of paradoxes linked with digital transformation of business. *Journal of Enterprise Information Management*, *37*(4), 1348–1373. DOI: 10.1108/JEIM-07-2023-0397

Smith, J. A. (2024). Accounting and information systems. In *Research Handbook on Accounting and Information Systems* (pp. 2–17). Edward Elgar Publishing., DOI: 10.4337/9781802200621.00008

Solano, M. C., & Cruz, J. C. (2024). Integrating analytics in enterprise systems: A systematic literature review of impacts and innovations. *Administrative Sciences*, *14*(7), 138. DOI: 10.3390/admsci14070138

Solihah, R. (2026). The Dynamics of Information Asymmetry in Corporate Financial Decision-Making in the Digital Era. *Riwayat: Educational Journal of History and Humanities*, *9*(1), 86–96. DOI: 10.24815/riwayat.v9i1.112

Soluk, J., Miroshnychenko, I., & Nambisan, S. (2026). AI Adoption in Family Firms: A Mixed-Methods Study on the Paradoxical Roles of Passive and Active Family Involvement. *Journal of Product Innovation Management*, *43*(1), 125–159. DOI: 10.1111/jpim.12789

Solvoyo. (2023). Unilever: End-to-end autonomous planning & analytics [Case study]. https://solvoyo.com/case-studies/fmcg/fortune-100-global-cpg-end-to-end-autonomous-planning

Song, H., Lu, Y., & Yang, Z. (2025). Digital Transformation of Enterprises and Accounting Information Quality: A Resource Dependence Theory Perspective. *Emerging Markets Finance & Trade*, •••, 1–17.

Sonjaya, Y., & Prasetianingrum, S. (2024). Harnessing the Power of Digitalization and Accounting Information Systems for Enhanced Efficiency and Accuracy. *Advances: Jurnal Ekonomi & Bisnis*, *2*(3), 121–135.

Soundappan, S. J. (2025).. . *Next Generation AI Enabled Holistic Cognitive Platform for Secure Cloud Network Intelligence Enterprise Systems and Digital Trust Optimization.*, *8*(5), 11534–11542. DOI: 10.15680/IJCTECE.2025.0805031

Sreseli, N., & Kadagishvili, N. (2023). Use of Artificial Intelligence for Accounting and Financial Reporting Purposes: A Review of the Key Issues. *American International Journal of Business Management*, *6*(8), 72–83. www.aijbm.com

Stepanovic, S., Marmier, A., & Mettler, T. (2025). Open research data integration in universities: How data stewards adapt global policies to local contexts. *Journal of the Association for Information Science and Technology*, *76*(13), 1754–1767. DOI: 10.1002/asi.70034

Stoica, R., & Stefan, V. (2018). The role of computerized solutions in consolidating financial results from the European and Anglo-Saxon accounting systems. *Valahian Journal of Economic Sciences*, *9*(2), 83–94. DOI: 10.2478/vjes-2018-0020

Stolowy, H., & Paugam, L. (2018). The expansion of non-financial reporting: An exploratory study. *Accounting and Business Research*, *48*(5), 525–548. DOI: 10.1080/00014788.2018.1470141

Stranieri, A., McInnes, A. N., Hashmi, M., & Sahama, T. (2021). Open Banking and Electronic Health Records. In S. N. & J. V.L. (Eds.), *ACM International Conference Proceeding Series*. Association for Computing Machinery. DOI: 10.1145/3437378.3437397

Subramanyam, S. V. (2025). Cloud-based enterprise systems: Bridging scalability and security in healthcare and finance. *IJSAT-International Journal on Science and Technology, 16*(1).

Sun, F. (2021). Development and Transformation Strategies of Banking Industry under the Background of Fintech. In L. J., W. J., & C. K. (Eds.), *E3S Web of Conferences* (Vol. 253). EDP Sciences. DOI: 10.1051/e3sconf/202125303068

Sutton, D. B. (2015). The objectives of financial reporting: the case for coherence the Conceptual Framework, and standards 2 The objectives of financial reporting: the case for coherence the Conceptual. *Abacus*, •••, 1–41.

Šuvakov, P., & Sekicki, V. (2025). Contemporary Trends in the Standardization of Accounting and Auditing at the International Level. *Journal of Agronomy, Technology and Engineering Management*, *8*(1), 1411–1428. DOI: 10.55817/YNPH2883

Tabassi, E. (2023). *Artificial intelligence risk management framework (AI RMF 1.0)* (NIST AI 100-1). National Institute of Standards and Technology. DOI: 10.6028/NIST.AI.100-1

Tang, J., Li, C., Fu, Y., & Li, C. (2022). The borderless integration of financial management innovation using big data analysis of social media. *Wireless Communications and Mobile Computing*, *4711617*(1), 4711617. Advance online publication. DOI: 10.1155/2022/4711617

Teece, D. J., Pisano, G., & Shuen, A. (1997). Dynamic capabilities and strategic management. *Strategic Management Journal*, *18*(7), 509–533. DOI: 10.1002/(SICI)1097-0266(199708)18:7<509::AID-SMJ882>3.0.CO;2-Z

Tenhunen, M.-L. (2025). AI-driven management accounting: A new frontier in strategic finance. *Economics*, *14*(4), 87–95. DOI: 10.11648/j.eco.20251404.11

Thanasas, G. L., & Kampiotis, G. (2024). The role of big data analytics in financial decision-making and strategic accounting. *Technium Business and Management*, *10*, 17–33. DOI: 10.47577/business.v10i.11877

Theodorakopoulos, L., Thanasas, G., & Halkiopoulos, C. (2024). Implications of big data in accounting: Challenges and opportunities. *Emerging Science Journal*, *8*(3), 1201–1214. DOI: 10.28991/ESJ-2024-08-03-024

Thomas, A. (2024). Digitally transforming the organization through knowledge management: A socio-technical system (STS) perspective. *European Journal of Innovation Management*, *27*(9), 437–460. DOI: 10.1108/EJIM-02-2024-0114

îrcovnicu, G.-I., & Ha egan, C.-D. (2023). Integration of Artificial Intelligence in the Risk Management Process: An Analysis of Opportunities and Challenges. *Journal of Financial Studies*, *8*(15), 198–214. DOI: 10.55654/JFS.2023.8.15.13

Titilope Tosin Adewale, Titilayo Deborah Olorunyomi, & Theodore Narku Odonkor. (2023). Big data-driven financial analysis: A new paradigm for strategic insights and decision-making. International Journal of Frontiers in Science and Technology Research, 4(2), 033–054. DOI: 10.53294/ijfstr.2023.4.2.0060

Tjahyono, B., Hamsal, M., Rahim, R., & Gunadi, W. (2024). The influence of digital adoption, adaptive leadership and risk management implementation on organizational resilience: An empirical study in the Indonesian banking industry. 2024 International Conference on Science, Engineering and Business for Driving Sustainable Development Goals (SEB4SDG), 1–7. DOI: 10.1109/SEB4SDG60871.2024.10630445

Tomar, M., & Periyasamy, V. (2023). The role of reference data in financial data analysis: Challenges and opportunities. *Journal of Knowledge Learning and Science Technology ISSN: 2959-6386 (online), 1*(1), 90-99.

Triana, Y. S., & Pangabean, R. A. M. (2021). Risk Analysis in the Application of Financore Information Systems Using FMEA Method. *Journal of Physics: Conference Series, 1751*(1), 012032. Advance online publication. DOI: 10.1088/1742-6596/1751/1/012032

Trigo, A., Belfo, F., & Estébanez, R. P. (2014). Accounting information systems: The challenge of the real-time reporting. *Procedia Technology, 16*, 118–127. DOI: 10.1016/j.protcy.2014.10.075

Udoh, O. R. (2024). Enhancing Internal Audit Efficiency For Effective Risk Management and Corporate Governance Frameworks. *International Journal of Research Publication and Reviews, 5*(12), 3646–3659. DOI: 10.55248/gengpi.5.1224.250122

Ukko, J., Nasiri, M., Saunila, M., & Rantala, T. (2019). Sustainability strategy as a moderator in the relationship between digital business strategy and financial performance. *Journal of Cleaner Production, 236*, 117626. DOI: 10.1016/j.jclepro.2019.117626

Ul Alam, M., Azad, M. A. K., & Ali, M. S. (2022). Best Practices to Secure API Implementations in Core Banking System (CBS) in Banks. In P. R. (Ed.), *2022 IEEE 12th Annual Computing and Communication Workshop and Conference, CCWC 2022* (pp. 730–735). Institute of Electrical and Electronics Engineers Inc. DOI: 10.1109/CCWC54503.2022.9720840

Ullah, A., & Baharun, R. Bin, Nor, K. M., Siddique, M., & Bhatti, M. N. (2017). Enterprise Resource Planning (ERP) Systems and ERP Quality Factors: A Literature Review. *Journal of Managerial Sciences, 11*(3), 297–322.

Ur Rahman, R., Ali Shah, S. M., El-Gohary, H., Abbas, M., Haider Khalil, S., Al Altheeb, S., & Sultan, F. (2020). Social media adoption and financial sustainability: Learned lessons from developing countries. *Sustainability (Basel), 12*(24), 10616. DOI: 10.3390/su122410616

Usanti, T. P. (2022). THE PRINCIPLE OF AMANAH IN THE UTILISATION OF CONSUMERS' PERSONAL DATA AND INFORMATION IN OPEN BANKING. *Journal of Central Banking Law and Institutions, 1*(1), 119–140. DOI: 10.21098/jcli.v1i1.2

Usul, H., & Alpay, M. F. (2024). From Traditional Auditing to Information Technology Auditing: A Paradigm Shift in Practices. *European Journal of Digital Economy Research, 5*(1), 3–9.

Uyanık, M. (2023). Resource-based view in marketing literature. *Journal of Business and Management Studies, 5*(4), 29–39. DOI: 10.32996/jbms.2023.5.4.4

Uzoma, A. B., Olokoyo, F. O., Babajide, A. A., Folashade, O., & Dorcas, A. (2016). Adoption of international financial reporting standards and its implication on bank performance in Nigeria: A comparative approach. *Journal of Internet Banking and Commerce, 21*(Special Issue 5).

Varshney, K. R. (2019). Trustworthy machine learning and artificial intelligence. *XRDS, 25*(3), 26–29. DOI: 10.1145/3313109

Vasarhelyi, M. A., Alles, M., Kuenkaikaew, S., & Littley, J. (2012). The acceptance and adoption of continuous auditing by internal auditors: A micro analysis. *International Journal of Accounting Information Systems, 13*(3), 267–281. DOI: 10.1016/j.accinf.2012.06.011

Vasarhelyi, M. A., Kogan, A., & Tuttle, B. M. (2015). Big data in accounting: An overview. *Accounting Horizons, 29*(2), 381–396. DOI: 10.2308/acch-51071

Vial, G. (2019). Understanding digital transformation: A review and a research agenda. *The Journal of Strategic Information Systems, 28*(2), 118–144. DOI: 10.1016/j.jsis.2019.01.003

Viknianska, A., Kharynovych-Yavorska, D., Sahaidak, M., Zhavoronok, A., & Filippov, V. (2021). METHODOLOGICAL APPROACH to ECONOMIC ANALYSIS and CONTROL of ENTERPRISES under CONDITIONS of ECONOMIC SYSTEMS TRANSFORMATION. *Naukovyi Visnyk Natsionalnoho Hirnychoho Universytetu, 2021*(4), 150–157. DOI: 10.33271/nvngu/2021-4/150

Vladu, A. B., Amat, O., & Cuzdriorean, D. D. (2017). Truthfulness in accounting: How to discriminate accounting manipulators from non-manipulators. *Journal of Business Ethics, 140*(4), 633–648. DOI: 10.1007/s10551-016-3048-3

Volodina, T., & Grossi, G. (2024). Digital transformation in public sector auditing: Between hope and fear. *Public Management Review*. Advance online publication. DOI: 10.1080/14719037.2024.2402346

von Solms, R., & van Niekerk, J. (2013). From information security to cybersecurity. *Computers & Security, 38*, 97–102. DOI: 10.1016/j.cose.2013.04.004

Vo-Thai, H. C., & Tran, M. L. (2025). Green innovation strategies in Vietnamese enterprises: Leveraging knowledge management and digitalization for sustainable competitiveness. *Journal of Knowledge Management, 29*(4), 1055–1091. DOI: 10.1108/JKM-06-2024-0642

Vummadi, J. R., & Hajarath, K. C. (2025). *Resilient Horizons: Strategic Planning for Advanced Supply Chain and Logistics Management*. IPR Journals and Book Publishers.

Wamba, S. F., Gunasekaran, A., Akter, S., Ren, S. J., Dubey, R., & Childe, S. J. (2017). Big data analytics and firm performance: Effects of dynamic capabilities. *Journal of Business Research, 70*, 356–365. DOI: 10.1016/j.jbusres.2016.08.009

Wang, J., Liu, Y., Li, P., Lin, Z., Sindakis, S., & Aggarwal, S. (2024). Overview ofdata quality: Examining the dimensions, antecedents, and impacts of data quality. *Journal of the Knowledge Economy, 15*(1), 1159–1178. DOI: 10.1007/s13132-022-01096-6

Wang, N., & Leem, S. G. (2026). *Modernizing Data Quality: Evolving Dimensions for Unstructured Text Data in Big Data*. AI and Ethical Contexts.

Wang, X., Li, Z., & Cheng, F. (2025). How Business Environments Affect Enterprise Vitality: A Complex Adaptive Systems Theory Perspective. *Systems, 13*(10), 1–36. DOI: 10.3390/systems13100864

Weaver, L., & Woods, M. (2015). The Challenges Faced by Reporting Entities on Their Transition to International Financial Reporting Standards: A Qualitative Study. *Accounting in Europe, 12*(2), 197–221. DOI: 10.1080/17449480.2015.1103376

Weller, A. (2019). Transparency: Motivations and challenges. In *Explainable AI* (pp. 23–40). Springer. https://doi.org/DOI: 10.1007/978-3-030-28954-6_2

Wernerfelt, B. (1984). A resource-based view of the firm. *Strategic Management Journal, 5*(2), 171–180. DOI: 10.1002/smj.4250050207

Weygandt, . (2018). *Financial accounting with international financial reporting standards*. John Wiley & Sons.

Wijesooriya, C., & Basnayake, R. (2024). Digital transformation in redefining the role of the finance and audit professional of the future. In *Digital Transformation in Accounting and Auditing: Navigating Technological Advances for the Future* (pp. 61–104). Springer International Publishing. DOI: 10.1007/978-3-031-46209-2_3

Wiwoho, J., Pati, U. K., & Pratama, A. M. (2024). Reciprocal Data Portability to Foster Financial Services Competition in the Open Banking System Era. *Yustisia, 13*(2), 134–150. DOI: 10.20961/yustisia.v13i2.75786

World Bank. (2025). *GovTech Maturity Index 2025 update: Data and methodology*. World Bank Group.

World Bank. (2025). *GovTech Maturity Index 2025: Tracking public sector digital transformation worldwide*. World Bank Group.

Wulandari, S. A. (2020). Data governance maturity level at the National Archives of the Republic of Indonesia. *Jurnal Penelitian Pos Dan Informatika, 10*(1), 27–40. DOI: 10.17933/jppi.v10i1.306

Wulandari, S. S., & Maulana, K. (2023). Enhancing operational efficiency and financial reporting through Oracle NetSuite ERP implementation: A case study in a logistics company. *International Research Journal of Science, Technology, Education, and Management*, *3*(3), 103–121.

Wu, S., Cheng, P., & Yang, F. (2024). Study on the impact of digital transformation on green competitive advantage: The role of green innovation and government regulation. *PLoS One*, *19*(8), e0306603. DOI: 10.1371/journal.pone.0306603 PMID: 39088476

Wu, W. (2022). Credit risk measurement, decision analysis, transformation and upgrading for financial big data. *Complexity*, *8942773*(1), 8942773. Advance online publication. DOI: 10.1155/2022/8942773

Xu, H. (2025). OLAP Technology Financial Statistics Information Platform Based on Big Data Analysis. In X. Z., A. S., L.-G. O., & A. R. N.H. (Eds.), *Lecture Notes in Networks and Systems: Vol. 1351 LNNS* (pp. 283–293). Springer Science and Business Media Deutschland GmbH. DOI: 10.1007/978-3-031-88287-6_27

Yadav, S., Singh, A., Peddapalli, N., Chauhan, A., Ahmed, S. A., & Bhoopathy, V. (2025). *ML Use in Fraud Detection in the Financial Sector*. 427–448. DOI: 10.4018/979-8-3693-8507-4.ch023

Yahaya, O. A. (2026). Does board gender diversity affect financial reporting quality in Nigeria. *Journal of Accounting and Finance Research*, *21*(1), 716–769.

Yahya, S., Khan, A., Farooq, M., & Irfan, M. (2022). Integrating green business strategies and green competencies to enhance green innovation: Evidence from manufacturing firms of Pakistan. *Environmental Science and Pollution Research International*, *29*(26), 39500–39514. DOI: 10.1007/s11356-021-18430-1 PMID: 35103945

Yang, H., Liu, X. Y., & Wang, C. D. (2023). Fingpt: Open-source financial large language models. *arXiv preprint arXiv:2306.06031*. DOI: 10.2139/ssrn.4489826

Yang, A. (2025). Big data-driven corporate financial forecasting and decision support: A study of CNN-LSTM machine learning models. *Frontiers in Applied Mathematics and Statistics*, *11*, 1566078. DOI: 10.3389/fams.2025.1566078

Yang, L., Li, J., Elisa, N., Prickett, T., & Chao, F. (2019). Towards Big data Governance in Cybersecurity. *Data-Enabled Discovery and Applications*, *3*(1), 10. Advance online publication. DOI: 10.1007/s41688-019-0034-9

Yanting, Z., & Ali, M. (2023). Artificial intelligence, digital finance, and financial inclusion: A conceptual framework. In *Financial Inclusion Across Asia: Bringing Opportunities for Businesses* (pp. 77–85). Emerald Group Publishing Ltd. DOI: 10.1108/978-1-83753-304-620231006

Yenugula, M., Sahoo, S. K., & Goswami, S. S. (2023). Cloud computing in supply chain management: Exploring the relationship. *Management Science Letters, 13*(3), 193–210. DOI: 10.5267/j.msl.2023.4.003

Yigitbasioglu, O., Green, P., & Cheung, M.-Y. D. (2023). Digital transformation and accountants as advisors. *Accounting, Auditing & Accountability Journal, 36*(1), 209–237. DOI: 10.1108/AAAJ-02-2019-3894

Yıldırım, M., Okay, F. Y., & Özdemir, S. (2021). Big data analytics for default prediction using graph theory. *Expert Systems with Applications, 176*, 114840. DOI: 10.1016/j.eswa.2021.114840

Yoshikuni, A. C., Dwivedi, R., Dultra-de-Lima, R. G., Parisi, C., & Oyadomari, J. C. T. (2023). Role of Emerging Technologies in Accounting Information Systems for Achieving Strategic Flexibility through Decision-Making Performance: An Exploratory Study Based on North American and South American Firms. *Global Journal of Flexible Systems Managment, 24*(2), 199–218. DOI: 10.1007/s40171-022-00334-9

Yuliantini, Y., Saribanon, E., Olfebri, O., Rahmawati, A., & Yulihapsari, I. U. (2024). Digital Marketing and the Presentation of Corporate Financial Statements: An Analysis of the Literature on Transformation and Impact. *Atestasi: Jurnal Ilmiah Akuntansi, 7*(2), 1072–1090. DOI: 10.57178/atestasi.v7i2.912

Yuniarto, A. A., & Siregar, I. W. (2025). From Manual to Digital: Modernizing the Sales Recording System for Growth at MSME Rumah Abon. *Journal of Scientific Insights, 2*(5), 510–525. DOI: 10.69930/jsi.v2i5.537

Yu, Y., Chen, H., & Xu, N. (2025). Data governance, financial environmental regulation, and enterprise digital transformation. *Finance Research Letters*, 109274.

Zamil, M. H., & Faruq, M. O. (2022). Cybersecurity And Data Integrity in Financial Systems: A Review of Risk Mitigation and Compliance Models. *International Journal of Scientific Interdisciplinary Research, 1*(01), 27–61. DOI: 10.63125/azwznv07

Zareen, M., Hamdan, A., & Binsaddig, R. (2024). The Impact of Robotic Process Automation (RPA) on Accounting Profession. In *Business Development via AI and Digitalization* (Vol. 1, pp. 191–199). Springer Nature Switzerland. DOI: 10.1007/978-3-031-62102-4_16

Zhang, Q., Zhu, J., & Ding, Q. (2020). OBBC: A Blockchain-Based Data Sharing Scheme for Open Banking. In S. X., J. H., S. Y., Z. J., Z. L., S. X., & L. Z. (Eds.), *Communications in Computer and Information Science: Vol. 1176 CCIS* (pp. 1–16). Springer. DOI: 10.1007/978-981-15-3278-8_1

Zhang, J., Xue, R., & Li, H. (2024). Artificial intelligence–enabled financial decision support systems: Implications for governance and control. *Journal of Information Systems, 38*(1), 35–52.

Zhang, Y. (2025). Governance strategies for paper and electronic documents in a dual-track archives system. *Information Resources Management Journal, 38*(1), 1–19. DOI: 10.4018/IRMJ.390238

Zhang, Y., Ren, S., Liu, Y., & Si, S. (2017). A big data analytics architecture for cleaner manufacturing and maintenance processes of complex products. *Journal of Cleaner Production, 142*, 626–641. DOI: 10.1016/j.jclepro.2016.07.123

Zhen, T., & Rahman, M. M. (2024). Greening emerging economies: Enhancing environmental, social, and governance performance through environmental management accounting and green financing. *Sustainability (Basel), 16*(11), 4753. DOI: 10.3390/su16114753

Zhong, X., & Enke, D. (2017). Forecasting daily stock market return using dimensionality reduction. *Expert Systems with Applications, 67*, 126–139. DOI: 10.1016/j.eswa.2016.09.027

Zhu, K., Kraemer, K. L., & Dedrick, J. (2004). Information Technology Payoff in E-Business Environments: An International Perspective on Value Creation of E-Business in the Financial Services Industry. *Journal of Management Information Systems, 21*(1), 17–54. DOI: 10.1080/07421222.2004.11045797

Ziegler, T. (2021). Implementation of Open Banking Protocols Around the World. In *The Palgrave Handbook of Technological Finance* (pp. 751–782). Springer International Publishing., DOI: 10.1007/978-3-030-65117-6_27

Zik-Rullahi, A. A., & Jide, I. (2023). Green accounting: A fundamental pillar of corporate sustainability reporting. *Journal of Accounting and Financial Management, 9*(8), 59–72. DOI: 10.56201/jafm.v9.no8.2023.pg59.72

Zohry, A. F., & Al-Dhubaibi, A. A. S. (2024). Optimizing business performance through effective accounting information systems: The role of system competence and information quality. *Journal of Risk and Financial Management, 17*(11), 515. DOI: 10.3390/jrfm17110515

Zong, Z., & Guan, Y. (2025). AI-driven intelligent data analytics and predictive analysis in Industry 4.0: Transforming knowledge, innovation, and efficiency. *Journal of the Knowledge Economy*, *16*(1), 864–903. DOI: 10.1007/s13132-024-02001-z

About the Contributors

Afef Amdouni is an Assistant Professor of Finance in the Department of Finance, College of Business Administration, Taibah University, Medina, Saudi Arabia. Her research interests focus on financial markets, artificial intelligence applications in finance, behavioral finance, and financial risk modeling. Prior to joining Taibah University, she was affiliated with the Faculty of Economic Sciences and Management at the University of Tunis El Manar, Tunisia. Dr. Amdouni earned her Ph.D. in Finance from the same institution, where she also completed her Master's and Bachelor's degrees. She is actively engaged in academic publishing and peer review activities and has held leadership roles in coordinating editorial initiatives related to interdisciplinary research at the intersection of finance and artificial intelligence.

***

Kuldeep Agnihotri, Director/Principal at ISBA Group of Institutes, Indore (Madhya Pradesh), is an expert in Accounting, Finance, Corporate Law, and Taxation with over 20 years of experience, including 18 years in academia and 2 years in industry. He holds a Ph.D. in Commerce from Devi Ahilya Vishwavidyalaya, along with an MBA in Finance and Marketing, M.Com in Accounting, B.Ed, and COA from ICWAI Kolkata. With more than 71 publications in reputed national and international journals (UGC Care, Scopus, ABDC), he has also authored 16 textbooks, edited 14 books, and published 32 Indian patents along with UK–British patent grant and 4 copyrights. A registered Ph.D. supervisor at Devi Ahilya Vishwavidyalaya, he guides several research scholars. He actively participates in national and international conferences, workshops, and FDPs, including those from IIT Mumbai. He is a member of Academic Councils, Boards of Studies, and editorial boards of various institutions. His contributions have earned him prestigious awards from RFI, WFST California (USA), and other academic bodies. Despite his extensive administrative and research commitments, he remains dedicated to teaching, which he considers his true passion.

Akmal Allakuliev is affiliated with Kimyo International University in Tashkent, Tashkent, Uzbekistan. He is an academic professional engaged in teaching, research, and scholarly activities that contribute to the advancement of higher education. Through his academic role, he supports student learning, intellectual development, and the promotion of research-oriented education. His work reflects a commitment to academic excellence, critical thinking, and the practical application of knowledge in contemporary educational settings. He is dedicated to fostering an environment that encourages innovation, analytical reasoning, and continuous professional growth among students. His academic interests may include interdisciplinary research, higher education development, and the integration of modern knowledge frameworks into teaching and learning practices. As a faculty member, Dr. Akmal Allakuliev contributes to the institutional mission of Kimyo International University by strengthening quality education and supporting scholarly engagement. His professional profile reflects dedication to meaningful teaching, academic service, and the broader development of higher education in Uzbekistan.

Karima Al-Qartoubi is a Lecturer in the Faculty of Business at Sohar University, Sultanate of Oman. She is actively engaged in teaching, research, and academic service, contributing to the development of business education aligned with both regional and global standards. Her academic interests lie in the areas of business management, finance, and sustainability. She has contributed to scholarly research focusing on contemporary issues such as sustainable financial practices and the integration of green technologies in business operations. In her teaching role, Ms. Karima is dedicated to fostering student-centered learning, equipping students with analytical, managerial, and decision-making skills required in today's dynamic business environment. She supports the Faculty's mission of bridging theory and practice through applied learning, industry engagement, and research-informed teaching.

Ismailov Azizbek is affiliated with the Faculty of Economics at Alfraganus University, Tashkent, Uzbekistan. He is an academic professional engaged in teaching, research, and scholarly activities in the field of economics. His work supports the development of students' understanding of economic principles, analytical reasoning, and contemporary issues affecting national and global economies. He is committed to promoting academic excellence through effective teaching and a research-informed approach to higher education. His academic interests may include economic development, business studies, finance, policy analysis, and sustainable economic practices. Through his role at Alfraganus University, he contributes to building a strong learning environment that encourages critical thinking, practical insight, and intellectual growth among students. He also supports the broader advancement of economics education by fostering awareness of real-world economic challenges and opportunities. His contribution reflects dedication to quality education, professional development, and meaningful academic service in the field of economics.

Amarnath B is working as an Assistant Professor, Department of FINANCE & MARKETING, VIGNANA JYOTHI INSTITUTE OF MANAGEMENT (VJIM) A Premium Business School, Hyderabad, Telangana, India. In his 16 years of teaching and research experience, he has served in an array of designations as Assistant Professor, Associate Professor and HOD of MBA Department, Head, Entrepreneurship Development Cell, President to Institution Innovation Council (IIC) and National Institutional Startup Policy (NISP) under MHRD Innovation Cell, also Mentor to various innovations under Innovation Cell, MHRD Has authored 6 Text Books, published 31 patents, 82 National & International Paper Publications, presented papers in 34 International Conferences, Participated in more than 62 FDPs, 91 Webinars, Workshops, Refresher courses and has 24 Coursera Certifications, Won 6 International Awards, life time member in 6 International associations. Reviewer&Editor for 12 International Journals Has presented many Guest lectures and was Resource person for Workshops & Refresher Courses in several Universities, Engineering Colleges and Business Schools on a variety of topics.

Mandeep Bansal is a distinguished academician and finance professional with a Ph.D. in Finance. She holds multiple qualifications, including CFA, MS (Finance), MBA, and DBF, reflecting her strong foundation in financial management and analysis. Currently, she is associated with COER University, Roorkee, Uttarakhand, where she contributes to teaching, research, and academic development. Dr. Mandeep Kour's areas of expertise include financial statistics, investment analysis, and corporate finance. She has published and presented several research papers in reputed journals and conferences. With her extensive experience in academia and industry, she brings practical insights into statistical applications for management. Her analytical approach and commitment to excellence make this book a valuable resource for students and professionals alike.

Ratnamala Bariniki is working as Assistant Professor in Department Computer Science and Engineering at Guru Nanak Institute of Technology, Hyderabad. She completed her Masters of computer Applications (MCA) with Distinction from Andhra University in 2007 and M. Tech CST (Computer Networks) with Distinction from Andhra University, Visakhapatnam, in 2011. She has 10+ years of teaching experience. She has publishednational journals, she attended 05 FDPs, 02 National level workshops.She was Ratified from JNTUKKakinada. She has guided various B.Tech and MCA Projects. Her research interest on Network security, Cryptography and various interdisciplinary areas

Bhagabat Behera has done his post-graduation in Commerce from Utkal University, Bhubaneswar, Odisha and NET (UGC) qualified in 1998. He has completed his Ph.D from F.M University, Balasore and MBA from Indira Gandhi National Open University (IGNOU), New Delhi. Prof. Behera started his teaching career in the year of 1999 in Bhadrak Autonomous College, Bhadrak and consequently in D.D University and V.Deb University, Jeypore, Odisha. Since the year 2013 he is working in the Department of Commerce Ravenshaw University, Cuttack and presently serving as a Professor of Commerce as well as Head of the Department of Commerce. For last 27 year he has been teaching accounting and Finance. His Broad area of research is accounting and Finance, focused on financial reporting and analysis, Earning management, Sustainable development and Ethical Business Practice. He has successfully supervised 07 Ph.D research scholars and 10 M.Phill. scholars. Published two text books and 08 reference books completed one research project s and published 32 research papers in national and international journals of repute. He has presented more than 60 research papers in national and international seminars. He has discharged various administrative responsibilities efeeectively and efficiently. He has also been life member of many academic associations like Indian accounting Association, Indian Commerce Association and Odisha Commerce Association and also member of many academic bodies in other universities and colleges in Odisha.

Shamaila Butt is a highly accomplished professional with a robust academic background and diverse experience. Having earned her Ph.D. in Management specializing in Finance from Universiti Teknologi Malaysia (UTM) in 2020, she demonstrates a commitment to continuous learning. Her extensive educational foundation equips her with strong theoretical knowledge and analytical skills. In her academic journey, Dr. Butt has showcased notable research prowess with a focus on financial complexities, evident in publications such as the "Hybrid model of exchange rate determinants in Malaysia." Transitioning from academia to leadership, she served as the Head of Department of Commerce at the University of Sialkot, Pakistan, showcasing strong organizational acumen. She worked as post doctoral researcher and Director of Research and Innovation at Guangdong CAS Cogniser, Information Technology, Guangzhou, Guangdong, China. Currently, she is working as an Assistant Professor at Faculty of Business, Sohar University, Sohar, Oman.

Muhammad Ali Chohan earned his PhD from Universiti Teknologi Malaysia (UTM), Malaysia, where his doctoral research focused on "Sectorial Analysis on Dividend Policy Across Non-Financial Pakistani Listed Firms." Throughout his academic career, he has collaborated with distinguished scholars, including Prof. Dr. Nur Naha and Prof. Dr. Suresh Ramakrishnan, contributing to initiatives aligned with Malaysia's Higher Education Action Plan. Dr. Chohan has served as a Postdoctoral Researcher and Director at CAS, Cogniser Information Technology, where his research centers on enterprise risk management using deep learning. He is committed to strengthening academia-industry collaboration through a holistic and interdisciplinary approach. He recently completed his tenure as a Global Alumni Research Fellow and is currently serving as a Postdoctoral Researcher at Asia Pacific University (APU), Malaysia, continuing his research in artificial intelligence, risk management, and digital transformation.

R Klothungasuryapandi is an Assistant Professor in the Department of Computer Science and Engineering (Cyber Security) at Nandha Engineering College, Erode. He has a strong academic background and a keen interest in cybersecurity. He is actively involved in research and development, focusing on areas such as data privacy and ethical hacking. Through his teaching and research efforts, he plays a key role in preparing students to address modern technological and cybersecurity challenges.

Erna Lovita is a lecturer at Sekolah Tinggi Ilmu Ekonomi Indonesia Jakarta, Indonesia. She holds a Doctoral Degree in Accounting and has been actively involved in higher education since 1996. Her teaching areas include financial accounting, accounting information systems, financial management, international accounting, corporate governance, and research methodology. Her research interests focus on accounting information systems, financial management, internal control, and accounting practices in small and medium enterprises (SMEs). She is also actively engaged in sustainability reporting and assurance practices. Dr. Lovita holds several professional certifications, including Certified Accountant (CA), Certified Sustainability Reporting Specialist (CSRS), and Certified Sustainability Reporting Assurer (CSRA). Her publications cover topics such as accounting information systems, internal control, organizational culture, and financial management practices, contributing to the development of accounting research and practice, particularly in the context of SMEs and organizational governance.

Rimi Mais is a lecturer at the Sekolah Tinggi Ilmu Ekonomi Indonesia Jakarta, Indonesia, and also serves as the head of the research and community service division. She holds a Doctorate in Accounting from Brawijaya University, Malang.

Her research interests include Islamic Accounting, Public Sector Accounting, CSR, and Sustainability Reporting. Rimi is also a certified specialist in sustainability reporting (Certified Sustainability Reporting Specialist (CSRS) and Certified Sustainability Reporting Assuror (CSRA). Her recent publications also discuss Sustainability Accounting, Public Sector Accounting, and CSR, and contribute to the academic community.

Menaga Mani is an Assistant Professor in the Department of Master of Computer Applications at Paavai College of Engineering. She is currently pursuing a part-time Ph.D. at Anna University, focusing on advanced research in the field of Computer Science.She completed her Master of Computer Applications (M.C.A.) from Vivekanandha College of Engineering, Tiruchengode, and her Master of Engineering (M.E.) in Computer Science and Engineering from Gnanamani College of Engineering, Namakkal. With a strong academic background and dedication to teaching, she has been actively involved in mentoring undergraduate and postgraduate students. Her research interests include emerging areas in computer science such as artificial intelligence, machine learning, data analytics, and cloud computing. She has published research papers in IEEE conferences and other reputed academic forums, contributing to the advancement of knowledge in her domain. She continues to engage in academic and research activities, aiming to develop innovative solutions and contribute to the academic community through quality teaching and scholarly work.

Saiful Muchlis is a senior lecturer in accounting at the Faculty of Economics and Business, Universitas Islam Negeri (UIN) Alauddin Makassar, Indonesia. He earned his Doctoral degree in Accounting from Universitas Sebelas Maret (UNS) Surakarta. His academic background also includes a Master of Science in Accounting and a Professional Accounting degree from Universitas Brawijaya, Malang. His teaching and research interests include public sector accounting, sharia accounting, financial control systems, accounting information systems, and digital governance in public financial management. In addition to his academic role, he holds several professional certifications, including Chartered Accountant (CA) and Certified Government Risk Management (CGRM). Dr. Saiful Muchlis has published various scholarly works in the fields of accounting, governance, and Islamic finance.

Tutty Nuryati, SE., M.Ak., is a full-time lecturer at the Faculty of Economics and Business, Bhayangkara University, Jakarta Raya. She earned a Master of Accounting and a Doctorate in Accounting from Padjadjaran University, Bandung. Her publications include numerous reputable national and international journals related to public sector accounting. Her membership in the Indonesian Tax

Consultants Association (ITA) since 2017 demonstrates her commitment to the world of tax consulting. Furthermore, Dr. Tutty Nuryati is also an active member of several educational organizations, demonstrating her dedication to contributing to the development of education in Indonesia.

Anusha Palagati is working as Assistant Professor at Guru Nanak university, Hyderabad. Currently she is pursuing Ph.D. in Anna University, Chennai. She holds an M.Tech in Computer Science and Engineering with Distinction from Geethanjali Institute of Science and Technology, Nellore (2015).She has 9+ years of teaching experience. She has made significant contributions to research, publishing two SCI papers, two Scopus-indexed papers, and ten papers in various international journals. Additionally, she has presented five papers at IEEE International Conferences indexed in Scopus. She has actively engaged in professional development, attending 30 Faculty Development Programs (FDPs) and 15 webinars on emerging technologies. She has authored the textbooks "Essence of Artificial Intelligence" and "Research Methodology and Intellectual Property Rights" and has filed and published 12 Indian patents. She has also completed five certification courses through NPTEL. Her research interests include Machine Learning, Cloud Computing, Artificial Intelligence, and interdisciplinary areas. She has been ratified by JNTU Hyderabad for her academic credentials and contributions.

Ramesh Pettela is presently working as an Associate Professor of English at Aditya University, Surampalem, Andhra Pradesh, India. He was awarded a Ph.D. in English from Acharya Nagarjuna University, Guntur, A.P., in 2016. He has 27 years of full-time teaching experience across IIITs, universities and autonomous institutions as a Professor and Head of the Department. A prolific academic, Dr. Ramesh has published extensively in reputed journals including Scopus, SCI and UGC and has presented numerous papers at national and international forums. He has successfully submitted research projects exceeding 45 lakhs funded by agencies such as ICSSR and AICTE and holds a patent for his research work. Beyond the classroom, he is a certified communication and soft skills trainer with global credentials from APSCHE, JNTU-A, EFLU, Cambridge University (UK) and ETS (USA), and is an approved trainer for GRE, IELTS, TOEFL and CRT programs. He has served as a resource person at national level conferences and seminars. He is an active member of professional bodies including ELTAI and MISTE and contributes to curriculum development as a Board of Studies member for several autonomous institutions. He is also the author of the insightful books English for Educators: Easy Methods and Techniques and ELT and Theories of Knowledge, reflecting his passion for empowering learners through effective language training.

Chokkamreddy Prakash MBA., M. Com., DTS., Ph.D., is working as an Assistant Professor, at School of Management Studies, Guru Nanak Institutions Technical Campus, Ibrahimpatnam, R.R. Dist., Telangana. He had pursued Ph.D in Andhra University, Andhra Pradesh. He did his MBA from Anna University and M. Com, University of Madras, Tamilnadu. He had completed Diploma in Tourism Studies (DTS) from IGNOU. He is holding 19 years of teaching experience in various reputed colleges. 3 years he worked as Head of the department (HOD) for MBA department. He is a Review member for 4 peer review journals (ABCD index, ASTESJ, IJCS, IJRAR). He had published 23 patents and 53 research papers in various national and international journals like Peer review, Referred Journal, ABDC and Scopus Journals. He had attended 12 national and international conferences. He had also published 4 Text books titled "Project Management for Beginners" and "Research Methodology and Statistical Analysis" and also published 9 chapter books Sopus Indexed. His areas of interest are Finance, Marketing Management, Research Methodology and Project Management.

A. Priyadharshini obtained her Bachelor's degree in Computer Science and Engineering at Ganamani College of Technology and Masters's Degree in Computer Science and Engineering at Kongunadu college of Engineering and Technology. She has a Teaching experience of about 4 years. She is currently working as an Assistant Professor in the department of Computer Science and Engineering (Cyber Security) at K.S.R. College of Engineering. She has published 2 papers in the reputed International Journals and 3 papers in the reputed National Journals. She authored 3 Indian patent. Her areas of interest are Artificial Intelligence, Machine Learning, Cryptography and Network Security.

Ravikumar R. N. is currently a Postdoctoral researcher at Universiti Malaysia Perlis, Malaysia. Also, working as an Assistant Professor (Sr. Grade) in the Department of Computer Science and Engineering at Jain (Deemed-to-be University), Bangalore, Karnataka. He has 13+ years of national and international teaching experience. He completed his PhD at Amity University, Rajasthan, M.E at VMRF Deemed University, B.E at Anna University, Chennai. He also holds a MiniMBA certificate from Swiss eLearning Institute, Switzerland. He has published numerous research articles in Scopus, SCI journals, Book chapters, and Conference papers. Also, he hold several patents and authored books. His specialization is ML, DL, Federated Learning, Recommendation Systems, and Optimization Techniques.

Aarthi S is a dedicated Assistant Professor in Computer Science with over six years of teaching experience. She is currently pursuing her Ph.D. at Marwadi University, Gujarat, and holds an M.Phil. and MCA from Bharathiar University,

Tamil Nadu. Throughout her academic career, Aarthi has specialized in programming languages such as C++, Java, and C, and contributed to research in recommender systems and AI-related data privacy. She has published journal articles, contributed to book chapters, and actively participated in technical workshops. Known for her student mentorship and engagement in academic events, Aarthi remains committed to fostering innovation and excellence in computer science education.

Jagadeesha S is an Associate Professor in the Department of Mathematics at Nitte Meenakshi Institute of Technology, Bengaluru, with over 20 years of teaching, and 8 years of research experience. He obtained his Ph.D. from Visvesvaraya Technological University and has expertise in Applied Mathematics, Fluid Dynamics, Optimization Techniques, and Computational Modeling. He has authored and co-authored more than 30 research publications in reputed journals, conference proceedings, and book chapters, and has presented research papers at several national and international conferences. His teaching methodology emphasizes analytical thinking, problem-solving skills, and interdisciplinary learning. His research interests include transport phenomena, porous media flow, stochastic processes, artificial intelligence applications, and data-driven analytical modeling. He actively contributes to faculty development programs, workshops, and collaborative research initiatives. His current academic interests focus on risk management, computational intelligence, and optimization techniques in digital and engineering systems.

Niranjani S is working as an Assistant Professor at Guru Nanak Institute of Technology. She completed her M.E. from Anna University in 2014. She has 5.6 years of teaching experience and 2 years of industry experience as a Java Developer. She has published one journal article and presented at two international conferences. She has guided various B.Tech student projects and has experience working on real-time projects. Her research interests include Networks, IoT, Artificial Intelligence, and interdisciplinary areas

Syed Kumail Sajjad obtained his Ph.D. in Economics from Aligarh Muslim University, Aligarh. His key research interests and expertise include International Trade, Macroeconomics, Sustainability, and Finance. He also completed both his Bachelor's and Master's degrees in Economics from the Department of Economics at Aligarh Muslim University. Demonstrating strong academic merit, he successfully qualified the NTA NET in Economics. Dr. Sajjad pursued his early education at Lucknow Public School, Lucknow, Uttar Pradesh.

Kasireddy Sandeep Reddy, MBA, MA, M.Phil, PhD, is working as Associate Professor, at Department of Business Management, Malla Reddy College of Engineering & Technology, Dhulapally, Secunderabad, Telangana. He is having more than 11 years of teaching and 9 years of Industrial Experience. He had published 8 Patents and 15 Research Papers in National & International Journals and presented 5 Research Papers in National and International Conferences. He had also published 4 text books titled Project Management for Beginners, Introduction to Management Science, Research Methodology and Statistical Analysis and Entrepreneurs Thinking and Design for Startups. He had also published 4 book chapters in well reputed books. He had reviewed a book titled "Recent Advances in Commerce and Management" as Co-Editor. His areas of interest include HRM, Marketing Management, Research Methodology and Project Management and Data Analytics.

Muhammad Farrukh Shahzad is a distinguished researcher affiliated with the College of Economics and Management at Beijing University of Technology, specializing in technology adoption, human-computer interaction, innovation, and sustainability. He has published extensively in high-impact, peer-reviewed journals indexed in ABS, ABCD, SCI, SSCI, and EI, in addition to contributing book chapters with reputable publishers and presenting papers at leading international conferences. He has garnered prestigious accolades such as the Scientific Innovation Awards (2024, 2025) and the First Contribution Award (2025). He was also honored with the Best Author Award by well-known Publishers in the first quarter of 2025. He has been selected for the "Perceive China - Academic Star" award, which recognizes his exceptional academic achievements during his studies in China, highlighting his distinction among students across the country. This prestigious honor, nominated by the China Scholarship Council (CSC), is a testament to his outstanding contributions to the field. His research has been recognized by the Chinese Academy of Sciences (CAS), and many of his papers have been classified as top category (Zone 1) in the past years. He actively serves as a peer reviewer for leading management and economics journals. Proficient in both qualitative and quantitative research methods, he utilizes software such as SPSS, SmartPLS, NVivo, AMOS, STATA, VOSviewer, Biblioshiny, and R. His work makes a substantial contribution to advancing global academic discourse in management and economics.

Karthikeyan Shanmugam is an accomplished academic and professional with a strong background in Management. He holds a Ph.D. in Management from SASTRA Deemed to be University (May 2024) and an MBA in Marketing & Finance (2005). With nearly two decades of combined experience, including nearly 10 years in academia and 4.5 years in industry, he has a diverse skill set. Dr. Karthikeyan has served as an Assistant Professor at SASTRA Deemed University and held roles as a Head of the Department, Examcell Coordinator. His expertise spans financial services, business economics, and securities market operations. He has also contributed to various academic initiatives, by publishing research articles in peer reviewed journals indexed in Scopus, Web of Science, ABCD etc..

Amrik Singh is working as Professor and HOD in the School of Hotel Management and Tourism at Lovely Professional University, Punjab, India. He obtained his Ph.D. degree in Hotel Management from Kurukshetra University, Haryana, India. He has published 115 Scopus-indexed publications. He has published 12 patents, and 01 patent has been granted in the inter-disciplinary domain. Dr. Amrik Singh participated and acted as a resource person in various national and international conferences, seminars, research workshops, and industry talks. He has published 20 books with IGI Global Publication, Emerald Publication, Bentham Publication, Nova Publication etc., on trending areas such as Food waste, Artificial Intelligence, Mountain Tourism, Virtual tourism, Healthcare Tourism, Guest behavior in tourism and hospitality. His area of research interest are Accommodation management, sustainability, Green practices, Human Resource Management in Hospitality, Artificial Intelligence, AR VR in hospitality, Hotel pricing, Employee Disability, Work life balance, women empowerment etc. He is currently guiding 8 Ph.D. scholars, and 5 Ph.D. scholars have been awarded Ph.D.

V Smitha embodies the modern academic leader—intellectually rigorous, pedagogically innovative, and genuinely committed to transformative education. With a Ph.D. in Management specializing in employee engagement, she brings evidence-based expertise to Human Resource Management education. Her research spans contemporary challenges: AI integration in HR, remote work dynamics, and intellectual capital measurement. Published in Scopus, ABDC C & peer-reviewed journals and with patent applications under examination, her work bridges academic knowledge and organizational reality.As Associate Professor and Head of HR Management at DCSMAT, she designs curricula that prepare graduates for complexity. Her teaching methodology—certified by Harvard Business Publishing and advanced by IIM training—creates dynamic learning environments where theory becomes practice. Dr. Smitha represents education at its highest calling: developing capable, thoughtful leaders who advance both organizations and society.

Suresh Talamala is an enthusiastic faculty member of Data Analytics and Research Methodology. As a faculty he has 18 years of teaching experience, currently working as an Assistant Professor, School of Business, Aditya University, Surampalem, Kakinada. He completed his B.B.M. in 2005 and M.B.A. (HRM & Marketing) in 2008 and began his career as an Assistant Professor. He pursued additional qualifications including B.A. (Mathematics & Statistics), M. Com., PGDHRM, and M.A. (English). He earned his Ph.D. from Andhra University in

2019 on "Stress management among medical consultants". He qualified UGC-NET twice (2012) and cleared AP SET in Commerce (2016) and Management (2012), and completed 8 NPTEL courses. His research papers published in Scopus and ABDC journals. He teaches Operations Research, Probability & Statistics, Business Research Methods, and Accounting for Managers. He has authored 5 books and 3 book chapter. He has actively participated in several seminars, conferences, workshops, and FDPs, aiming to apply academic research to real-world business challenges. His lectures are considered to be practical lessons for the students of the management studies. He taught various management and analytics papers over the years to graduate and post graduate level students.

Annaev Umidjon is associated with the Department of Natural Sciences at Termez University of Economics and Service, Termez, Uzbekistan. He is an academic dedicated to teaching, research, and the advancement of scientific knowledge in the field of natural sciences. His work supports the development of students' analytical thinking, scientific understanding, and practical awareness of core concepts related to the natural world. Through his academic role, he contributes to strengthening interdisciplinary learning and fostering a research-oriented educational environment. His interests may include scientific education, environmental understanding, applied natural science, and the promotion of knowledge that connects theory with real-world applications. He is committed to encouraging students to engage in critical inquiry, problem-solving, and evidence-based learning practices. As a faculty member, Dr. Annaev Umidjon contributes to the academic mission of Termez University of Economics and Service by supporting quality education, intellectual growth, and the broader advancement of natural sciences in higher education.

Dadaboev Umidjon is associated with Tashkent State University of Economics, Tashkent, Uzbekistan. He is an academic professional committed to higher education, research, and scholarly development in the field of economics and related disciplines. His work contributes to strengthening students' knowledge of economic systems, contemporary market trends, and analytical approaches to problem-solving in academic and professional contexts. He is dedicated to fostering an engaging learning environment that supports intellectual growth, critical thinking, and practical understanding. His academic interests may include economic development, business and management studies, public policy, finance, and sustainable growth strategies. Through teaching and academic involvement, he helps students connect theoretical knowledge with real-world economic applications. As a faculty member, Dr. Dadaboev Umidjon contributes to the advancement of quality education and research culture within the university. His professional role reflects commitment to academic excellence, student development, and the broader progress of economics education in Uzbekistan.

Bhoopathy V is a Professor at Sree Rama Engineering College. He holds a Ph.D. in Information and Communication Engineering from Anna University and has over 16 years of academic experience. Specializing in wireless sensor networks and IoT, he has published numerous research papers and holds several international patents. Dr. Bhoopathy is a recipient of prestigious awards for his contributions to education and research. His commitment to academia continues to drive innovation and excellence in the field of computer science.

Masooma Zahara is a dedicated academic professional and currently serves as a Career Development Officer at the University of Sargodha, where she plays a pivotal role in enhancing students' employability and professional growth.With nearly thirteen years of professional experience at the University of Sargodha, Ms. Zahara has served in multiple capacities, including roles in hostel management and career development, demonstrating strong administrative, leadership, and organizational skills.As a Career Development Officer, she actively contributes to designing and implementing skill development programs, career counseling sessions, and professional training workshops aimed at bridging the gap between academia and industry. She is particularly involved in initiatives that focus on soft skills, digital literacy, and career readiness, helping students prepare for evolving job market demands. Ms. Zahara is also engaged in national and international academic and professional collaborations. She has contributed to initiatives that promote youth development, innovation, and global engagement, including participation in international academic visits and expert forums.

Index

E

F

G

I

M

www.ingramcontent.com/pod-product-compliance
Lightning Source LLC
LaVergne TN
LVHW062029101126
852251LV00005B/54